Real Gross Domestic Product in Chain-Weighted Dollars, 1919–1998 (1992 = 100)*

Year	GDP	Personal Consumption Expenditures Total	Gross Private Domestic Investment Total	Net Exports			Government Purchases					Percent Change from Prior Year GDP
				Net	Exports	Imports	Total	Federal			State and Local	
								Total	National Defense	Non-Defense		
1929	942	636	174	2.2	41.3	39.1	129	25.1	—	—	104.0	—
1930	858	596	122	−.3	34.2	34.5	139	28.0	—	—	111.9	−8.9
1931	792	574	100	−2.6	28.3	31.0	143	28.6	—	—	115.5	−7.7
1932	687	537	28	−2.8	22.5	25.2	138	27.4	—	—	108.5	−13.3
1933	673	513	30	−3.4	22.8	26.3	135	35.4	—	—	101.2	−2.1
1934	725	551	47	−1.1	25.6	26.8	150	45.9	—	—	94.5	7.7
1935	781	559	78	−8.3	27.3	35.7	156	46.1	—	—	113.1	7.7
1936	892	612	103	−5.8	29.0	34.9	182	72.8	—	—	109.1	14.2
1937	930	636	120	−2.2	36.6	38.8	174	67.4	—	—	112.9	4.3
1938	893	621	78	4.8	35.2	30.4	186	71.5	—	—	114.9	−4.0
1939	964	675	95	5.3	37.5	32.2	200	97.6	17.4	56.0	124.9	7.9
1940	1,039	687	139	9.4	43.1	33.5	207	87.4	45.0	54.5	119.9	7.8
1941	1,227	721	171	3.2	44.8	41.6	331	215.6	169.0	40.5	114.9	18.2
1942	1,473	721	93	−12.7	30.2	42.9	678	564.9	484.2	28.2	107.2	20.0
1943	1,766	742	61	−37.2	25.6	57.8	995	895.9	781.8	17.9	99.4	19.9
1944	1,915	769	67	−33.3	28.4	72.9	1,113	1,014.3	882.0	21.3	96.0	8.4
1945	1,838	819	94	−27.4	37.6	65.0	951	852.1	748.1	12.7	99.2	−4.0
1946	1,459	893	212	30.4	76.5	46.1	310	201.2	166.1	29.4	109.7	−20.8
1947	1,436	898	228	48.1	90.7	42.6	251	127.0	97.7	33.6	124.0	−1.5
1948	1,491	932	263	19.0	69.6	50.6	276	144.9	94.6	50.2	131.1	3.8
1949	1,497	953	214	19.8	68.7	48.7	308	160.3	105.6	54.7	147.4	.4
1950	1,627	1,002	296	3.7	60.8	57.0	326	167.0	125.1	41.9	159.3	8.7
1951	1,787	1,014	296	12.7	73.8	61.0	455	294.0	257.5	36.5	161.4	8.8
1952	1,863	1,059	323	2.6	71.5	68.7	536	372.3	326.5	45.8	164.0	4.3
1953	1,933	1,012	275	−8.1	79.7	76.4	561	389.6	329.6	60.0	172.2	3.7
1954	1,919	1,132	268	−2.6	71.3	73.9	521	335.7	288.7	47.0	174.3	−.7
1955	2,028	1,200	326	−6.0	77.7	83.6	506	307.9	267.8	40.4	198.4	5.6
1956	2,068	1,231	323	−1.4	89.5	89.7	509	303.7	266.3	37.4	205.5	2.0
1957	2,108	1,268	306	−2.1	97.5	95.7	533	316.7	279.6	37.0	217.0	1.8
1958	2,097	1,287	283	−19.3	84.5	78.6	546	312.0	265.2	46.8	234.0	−.5
1959	2,210	1,394	271	−34.8	71.9	106.6	618	360.5	307.6	58.8	256.8	5.5
1960	2,262	1,432	270	−21.3	86.8	108.1	617	349.4	301.3	54.1	267.2	2.2
1961	2,314	1,461	267	−19.1	88.3	107.3	647	363.0	313.8	55.5	283.8	2.1
1962	2,454	1,533	302	−26.5	93.0	119.5	686	393.2	332.4	66.8	292.1	6.0
1963	2,559	1,596	321	−22.7	100.0	122.7	701	391.8	324.0	72.9	309.7	4.3
1964	2,708	1,692	348	−15.9	113.3	129.2	715	385.2	309.9	79.2	330.9	5.8
1965	2,881	1,799	397	−27.4	115.6	143.0	737	385.2	303.8	84.6	353.2	6.4
1966	3,069	1,902	430	−40.9	123.4	164.2	804	429.1	348.2	85.7	375.9	6.4
1967	3,147	1,958	411	−50.1	126.1	176.2	865	471.7	393.5	84.7	394.2	2.6
1968	3,293	2,070	433	−67.2	135.3	202.5	892	476.3	400.9	82.5	416.5	4.7
1969	3,393	2,147	458	−71.3	142.7	214.0	887	459.9	381.6	84.3	428.0	3.0
1970	3,397	2,197	426	−65.0	158.1	223.1	866	427.2	349.0	83.0	440.0	.0
1971	3,510	2,279	474	−75.8	159.2	235.0	851	397.0	313.7	86.3	454.4	3.3
1972	3,702	2,415	531	−88.9	172.0	261.0	854	390.2	300.3	91.1	464.5	5.4
1973	3,916	2,532	595	−63.0	209.6	272.6	848	371.1	281.2	91.5	478.5	5.7
1974	3,891	2,514	546	−35.6	229.8	265.3	862	368.8	273.5	96.4	495.6	−.4
1975	3,873	2,570	446	−7.2	228.2	235.4	876	367.9	269.7	99.1	510.0	−.6
1976	4,082	2,714	537	−39.9	241.6	281.5	876	364.3	264.7	100.4	514.3	5.6
1977	4,273	2,829	622	−64.2	247.4	311.6	884	370.1	266.4	104.3	516.4	4.9
1978	4,503	2,951	693	−65.6	273.1	338.6	910	377.7	266.7	111.4	534.7	5.0
1979	4,630	3,020	709	−45.3	299.0	344.3	924	383.3	271.0	112.7	543.5	2.5
1980	4,615	3,009	628	10.1	331.4	321.3	941	399.3	280.7	119.0	543.6	−.3
1981	4,720	3,046	686	5.6	335.3	329.7	947	415.9	296.0	120.4	532.8	2.5
1982	4,620	3,081	587	−14.1	311.4	325.5	960	429.1	316.5	113.3	531.4	−2.1
1983	4,803	3,240	642	−63.3	303.3	366.6	987	452.3	334.6	118.5	534.9	4.0
1984	5,140	3,407	833	−127.3	328.4	455.7	1,018	463.4	348.1	115.9	555.0	7.0
1985	5,323	3,566	823	−147.9	337.3	485.2	1,080	495.1	374.1	121.8	584.7	3.6
1986	5,487	3,708	811	−163.9	362.2	526.1	1,135	518.0	393.4	125.2	616.9	3.1
1987	5,649	3,822	821	−156.2	402.0	558.2	1,164	534.9	409.2	125.3	631.8	2.9
1988	5,865	3,972	828	−114.4	465.8	580.2	1,180	524.9	405.5	119.1	656.6	3.8
1989	6,062	4,064	863	−82.7	520.2	603.0	1,213	531.9	401.6	130.1	682.6	3.4
1990	6,136	4,132	815	−61.9	564.4	626.3	1,250	541.4	401.5	140.5	708.6	1.2
1991	6,079	4,105	738	−22.3	599.9	622.2	1,258	539.0	397.5	142.0	718.7	−.9
1992	6,244	4,219	790	−29.5	639.4	669.0	1,263	528.8	375.8	152.2	735.8	2.7
1993	6,389	4,343	863	−70.2	658.2	728.4	1,252	505.1	354.4	151.2	746.4	2.3
1994	6,610	4,486	975	−104.6	712.4	817.0	1,252	486.3	336.9	149.5	765.7	3.5
1995	6,761	4,605	996	−96.5	792.6	889.0	1,254	470.4	323.5	146.9	783.9	2.3
1996	6,994	4,752	1,084	−111.2	860.0	971.2	1,268	465.2	319.1	146.2	802.7	3.4
1997	7,269	4,913	1,206	−136.1	970.0	1,106.1	1,285	458.0	308.9	148.6	827.1	3.9
1998	7,552	5,152	1,332	−238.3	985.0	1,223.3	1,297	453.3	300.4	152.1	844.1	3.9

*Years 1929–1958 approximated with constant 1992 prices.

The Macro Economy Today

The Macro Economy Today

BRADLEY R. SCHILLER
The American University

EIGHTH EDITION

Irwin McGraw-Hill

Boston   Burr Ridge, IL   Dubuque, IA   Madison, WI
New York   San Francisco   St. Louis
Bangkok   Bogotá   Caracas   Lisbon   London   Madrid   Mexico City
Milan   New Delhi   Seoul   Singapore   Sydney   Taipei   Toronto

McGraw-Hill Higher Education

A Division of The **McGraw-Hill** *Companies*

The Macro Economy Today

This book is printed on acid-free paper.

1 2 3 4 5 6 7 8 9 0   WCK   WCK   0 9 8 7 6 5 4 3 2 1 0

ISBN 0-07-366277-1
ISBN 0-07-366279-8 (Wall Street Journal edition)

Editorial director: Mike Junior
Publisher: Gary Burke
Executive editor: Paul Shensa
Development editors: Marilea Fried; Miller Murray
Marketing manager: Nelson Black
Project manager: Eva Strock
Production supervisor: Rich DeVitto
Supplements coordinators: Louis Swaim, Florence Fong, Becky Szura
Designer: Amanda Kavanagh
Cover designer: Amanda Kavanagh
Compositor: York Graphic Services, Inc.
Typeface: Times New Roman
Printer: World Color Book Services

Library of Congress Cataloging-in-Publication Data
Schiller, Bradley R., 1943–
   [Economy today. Selections]
   The macro economy today / Bradley R. Schiller.—8th ed.
     p.   cm.
   Together with The micro economy today comprises a 2 vol. ed. of:
The economy today. 8th ed.
   Inclues index.
   ISBN 0-07-366277-1 (alk. paper)
   1. Macroeconomics. I. Title.
HB172.5.S3425 1999
399—dc21   99-16175
                              CIP

Bradley R. Schiller has over three decades of experience teaching introductory economics at The American University, the University of California (Berkeley and Santa Cruz), and the University of Maryland. He has given guest lectures at nearly 100 colleges ranging from Fresno, California, to Istanbul, Turkey. Dr. Schiller's unique technique contribution to teaching is his ability to relate basic principles to current socioeconomic problems, institutions, and public policy decisions. This perspective is evident throughout *The Macro Economy Today.*

Dr. Schiller derives this policy focus from his extensive experience as a Washington consultant. He has been a consultant to most major federal agencies, many congressional committees, and political candidates. In addition, he has evaluated scores of government programs and helped design others. His studies of discrimination, training programs, tax reform, pensions, welfare, Social Security, and lifetime wage patterns have appeared in both professional journals and popular media. Dr. Schiller is also a frequent commentator on economic policy for television, radio, and newspapers.

Dr. Schiller received his Ph.D. from Harvard in 1969. His B.A. degree, with great distinction, was completed at the University of California (Berkeley) in 1965. He is now a professor of economics in the School of Public Affairs at The American University.

Everyone has high expectations for the twenty-first century. Many people expect the emerging information highway, built of fiber-optic cables and satellite transmitters, to transform the way we communicate, travel, work, and play. Educators foresee virtual classrooms and electronic books replacing college campuses and paper books. Remote access, video conferencing, and distant learning may eventually eliminate the need for classroom interactions, office hours, and even bathing. Everyone wants to jump on the Cyber Express before it leaves the station.

As we embark on a new millennium, however, we should assess not just the *medium* of education but also the *message*. What do we want economics students to learn in the twenty-first century? Is there a twenty-first century paradigm that will make twentieth-century principles as obsolete as analog television (scheduled for extinction in 2006; see Chapter 8)? Or will we discover, as has the burgeoning cable industry, that *content* doesn't evolve as fast as transmission technology? Are any of the economic principles Adam Smith first enunciated back in 1776 relevant in the twenty-first century? Do the lessons of the Great Depression still offer any insights for averting macro failures in the new millennium? Has e-commerce obliterated or reinforced the foundations of competitive markets?

The structural revolutions occurring around the world reflect the continuing search for core principles. Nations are shedding ideology in favor of pragmatism. Countries that once looked to central planners to choose the mix of output, production methods, and distribution of income are placing their bets on freer markets and spreading capitalism. In China, the old collective farms now have de facto property rights. Since 1978, the share of farm output sold on the open market has jumped from 8 percent to over 80 percent. In Russia, more than 70 percent of GDP is now generated in the private sector. In Cuba, after a 40-year hiatus, Fidel Castro not only reinstated Christmas, he is now embracing foreign investments and permitting limited entrepreneurship (see WORLD VIEW in Chapter 22). Despite some backsliding toward "recentralization" in China, Russia, and Cuba, the commitment to greater reliance on the market mechanism is irreversible. Thus economic principles, not ideology, are driving most of the world into the twenty-first century.

The increased commitment to economics is also evident on college campuses. As the accompanying IN THE NEWS reports, enrollments in economics classes are surging. There is both a cyclical component and a long-term trend to this surge. As Yale professor Merton Peck observed in the article, "Now that the Cold War is over, economic issues have become the central core of policy debates." The "hot" issue is no longer whether capitalism or communism is more "just," but which mix of market signals and government directives will best promote growth, reduce poverty, and protect the environment.

CENTRAL FOCUS

Policy Focus

The practical and policy applications of economic principles have always been the central focus of *The Macro Economy Today*. This book has never discussed widgets or Robinson Crusoe fables. Instead, *The Macro Economy Today* lives up to its title by identifying and analyzing the salient policy issues that concern Main Street, Wall Street, Capitol Hill, and other world capitals. These issues range from the dilemma of budget surpluses to policy responses to external shocks like the 1997–1998 Asian crises and the 1999 Brazilian devaluation. Every chapter directly links basic economic principles to headline-capturing issues, enlivening student interest and enhancing the retention of learning.

Economics Enjoys A Bull Run at Colleges

Once Perplexing Subject Is a Top Major for Students

NEW YORK—The dismal science is in vogue again on campus.

After years of trailing history, English and biology as the top undergraduate major, economics is enjoying a surge in popularity with college students, especially at the nation's most elite institutions.

Reasons Behind Trend Why so much interest in a discipline that has been known to induce bouts of nausea in befuddled undergraduates? According to academics, interest in economics as a major has traditionally risen and fallen with the health of the finance industry, the major employer of economics graduates. And with a booming stock market leaving investment bankers, stock pickers and securities analysts among the highest paid professionals in the nation, some college students are hoping to use economics as an entry to Wall Street. . . .

But the swelling ranks of economics majors also reflects more subtle trends, including a sharp reduction in the age at which economics is first introduced to students, stronger mathematical skills among college freshman and heightened interest among all Americans in economic ideas and their impact on everything from wage rates to the price of an airline ticket. . . .

To students of past generations, the ascent of economics up the ivory tower may come as something of a shock. Decades ago, left-leaning scholars held the moral high ground, and the study of markets, commerce and currencies was regarded by many as a less noble, less meaningful pursuit than deconstructing paradigms of power such as race, class or gender.

But for the class of 2002, the Cold War is nothing more than a quickly retreating childhood memory, the questions of military conflict over ideological differences practically moot. If not liberal capitalism, then what? "Now that the Cold War is over, economic issues have become the central core of policy debates," said Yales's Prof. Peck. . . .

"Economics, as it is taught at Yale, is not an ideological subject," he said. "We don't talk about whether capitalists are greedy but rather about the benefits of, say, a fixed exchange rate."

—Tristan Mabry

Analysis: The resurgent interest in economics reflects both cyclical factors and longer-term structural changes. Worldwide, people are looking to the market mechanism for better economic performance.

The Three Core Issues

To emphasize the universal elements in these many policy debates, the three core issues of WHAT, HOW, and FOR WHOM are identified at the very outset of the book and serve as an organizing framework. Chapter 2 gives students a graphic overview of how these issues have been resolved in the United States and other countries. In all subsequent chapters, salient policy issues are explicitly discussed within the WHAT, HOW, and FOR WHOM context.

This emphasis on the three core issues is very different from approaches that emphasize a finite set of core principles or topical applications, approaches which are subjective and necessarily incomplete. More importantly, any list of topical applications is ultimately a collection of variants of the three core issues that command universal acceptance. It's more important that students recognize core content than memorize any particular list of applications.

Who Decides—Markets or Government?

This book also emphasizes the importance of the decision mechanisms we use to resolve the core issues. This is the "markets vs. government" debate. Should we let Adam Smith's "invisible hand" steer the economy, or should the government intervene to alter market outcomes? Do fiscal and monetary policy interventions stabilize the economy, as Keynes promised, or destabilize it, as critics assert? Should nations intervene to "protect" their currencies, or should they let the financial markets alone set international exchange rates? Rather than answering these questions, *The Macro Economy Today* emphasizes the importance of decision mechanisms for our economic welfare. Right up front in Chapter 1, the potential for *market* failure as well as *government* failure is recognized. No panacea is offered, just a scientific way of thinking about how markets work and why we so often depend on them yet at other times reject them.

User-Friendly Pedagogy

As important as the core issues and decision mechanisms are, they won't impress students unless they're taught in a user-friendly and productive way, which is why pedagogy has always been a central concern of this text. In fact, the one adjective invariably used to describe *The Macro Economy Today* is "readability." Professors often express a bit of shock when they realize that students actually enjoy reading the book. (Well, not as much as a steamy novel, but a whole lot better than most textbooks they've had to plow through.) The writing style is lively and issue-focused. Unlike any other textbook on the market, every boxed feature, every graph, and every cartoon is explained and analyzed. Because every feature is also referenced in the text, students actually learn the material rather than skipping over it.

Graphs are *completely* labeled, colorful, and positioned on background grids. Because students often enter the principles course as graph phobics, most graphs are accompanied by synchronized tabular data. Key terms are defined in the margin when they first appear and redefined as necessary in subsequent chapters. Web site references are directly tied to the book's content, not hung on like ornaments. End-of-chapter discussion questions use tables, graphs, and boxed news stories from the text, reinforcing key concepts.

As in previous editions, the back of the book includes built-in numerical and graphing problem sets that build on features in each chapter. Grids for drawing graphs are also provided. Each entire problem set is detachable and includes answer boxes that facilitate grading.

NEW TO THIS EDITION

Besides the more explicit definition and more thorough integration of core issues, this eighth edition includes substantial changes.

Cyber Features

One of the most visible changes in this edition is a new array of cyber features.

In-Margin URLs. A mini Web site directory is provided in each chapter's marginal Cyber Notes. These URLs aren't random picks; they were selected because they let students extend and update adjacent in-text discussions.

- **URLs for Highlighted Material** Internet addresses are also provided for the IN THE NEWS and WORLD VIEW features. Professors and students can use these URLs to pursue policy issues in more depth.
- **Internet Problems** The end of each chapter includes two Web Activities that send students to the Internet for data or issues to use in real-world applications of key concepts.
- **Web-Based Exercises** Although not physically within the text, but directly tied to it, a new Web site offers additional exercises and applications. This cybertutor is available only on the Web and supplements the paperback Study Guide and the CD-based DiscoverEcon tutorial.

Financial Markets

Chapter 17 in *The Macro Economy Today* emphasizes the *economic* rather than the institutional role of financial markets, a topic rarely found in competing texts. The stock and bond markets are viewed as arbiters of risk and mechanisms of resource allocation. The mechanisms of present value discounting are also covered. The chapter starts with the financing of Columbus' New World expedition and ends with a look at to-day's venture capitalists. This chapter from *The Macro Economy Today* can be shrink-wrapped with *The Micro Economy Today* at no extra charge for professors who want to cover financial markets in their macro discussion.

Extensively Revised

Complete revisions and new developments in technology and policy greatly transform the other chapters.

Budget Surpluses. Remember when the number one political and economic issue was the budget deficit? Do you recall how close Congress came in 1998 to passing a constitutional amendment that would have required annually balanced budgets? Now everyone in Washington, D.C., is fighting over the use of budget *surpluses.* Chapter 12 has been retitled and refocused to reflect this dramatic change in budget realities. President Clinton's 1999 proposal for "saving Social Security first" is highlighted.

Globalization of Markets. The growing impacts of cybercommerce can't be ignored; we now have to rethink concepts of market structure and entry barriers. Cyberretailing extends the virtual mall beyond national boundaries, broadening the market boundaries and altering the dynamics of macro adjustment. The trend toward a unified global market is also being accelerated by global (WTO) and regional (NAFTA, EU) pacts that reduce trade barriers, as well as the new euro currency. Chapter 18 (Global Macro) and Chapter 20 (International Trade) emphasize these phenomena.

Short-Run-Macro Instability. Revamped Chapter 10, "Self-Adjustment or Instability?", focuses on the Keynesian explanation for short-run instability by placing the Keynesian theory into the aggregate demand/supply framework. Unlike other texts, *The Macro Economy Today* illustrates the multiplier explicitly with AD shifts (see pages 200 and 203 for examples). By using these explicit AD shifts and an upward-sloping AS curve throughout, there's no need to create a strawman of zero inflation and then tear it apart.

Growth Theory. This eighth edition emphasizes more sharply the distinction between short-run instability and long-run growth, beginning with the start of the macro section (Chapter 8). Chapter 17, "Growth and Productivity: Long-Run Possibilities," now focuses more on the slowdown in growth rates that has occurred during the past two decades. The "new growth" theory is appraised, and the importance of the institutional context of an economy is discussed.

More Applications

Real-world applications rather than fanciful illustrations have long been a differentiating feature of *The Macro Economy Today.* This edition extends that model with scores of new domestic and global applications. Chapter 1 sets the tone by linking North Korea's food shortage to its massive military expenditures, a modern-day guns versus butter trade-off. The broader question of decision mechanisms is illustrated via the 1999 Heritage "freedom" rankings of the world's nations, Cuba's nascent small business sector, and the Microsoft antitrust case. But that's just for starters; later chapters cover everything from the recent creation of the euro currency to the use of the federal budget surplus to "save" Social Security. These real-world applications are within the body of the text itself, in highlighted IN THE NEWS and WORLD VIEW features, in discussion questions, and in the end-of-book problem sets. A special section of the Test Bank provides questions on the boxed applications.

PROVEN FEATURES FROM PRIOR EDITIONS

The Macro Economy Today offers full-chapter coverage of many topics that some texts omit completely and no other text offers in their entirety. These distinctive chapters include the following.

Distinctive Chapters

Profile of the Economy. Most students are woefully ignorant of the dimensions of the U.S. economy, so we professors have an obligation to teach some of the underlying facts of economic life as well as theory. Chapter 2 fulfills this responsibility with a descriptive overview of major economic outcomes, organized around the core issues of WHAT, HOW, and FOR WHOM. Numerous global comparisons highlight the unique features of the U.S. economy.

Global Macro. Chapter 18 is an overview of how global markets interact and constrain domestic macro policy. For professors who want to offer more global perspectives in macro but don't have time to cover the trade and finance chapters, this is a nice, well-contained option. Examples and extended discussions of the Asian crisis, the influence of the IMF and group of seven, and an assessment of the euro will help students develop a sense of macro global linkages.

Theory and Reality. Sometime in the macro course students inevitably wonder why the instructors aren't making the nation's policy decisions since they seem to have all the answers. There's a credibility gap between you and the theory you're presenting. Chapter 19 bridges that gap by discussing the real-world constraints that prevent "perfect" economic policy, from mundane measurement problems to political constraints. This chapter provides both a capstone summary of macro theory and a real sense of its earthly limitations.

Balanced Macro. This isn't a point-of-view text. Keynes hasn't been forgotten, nor have the monetarists or supply-siders. Both old growth theory and new growth theory get heard in this edition, reflecting my belief that students need to be exposed to a variety of perspectives if they're to understand the range and intensity of ongoing debates. One of my most cherished compliments is the question, "Which theory do you believe, Professor Schiller?" I'm not pushing any point of view, just core principles that will help students and instructors sort things out for themselves.

As noted earlier, The Macro Economy Today teaches real-world economics. As the core issues are woven into the narrative, they are enhanced and supported by authentic examples.

Great Applications

IN THE NEWS. These boxed applications focus on domestic hard news events that illustrate key concepts. All the features are annotated and explicitly referenced in the text.

Favorites in macro include the plight of displaced workers (page 120), the rising cost of tuition (page 125), the cell phone bias in CPI (page 136), the 1997 "Kiddie tax credit" (page 215), and the "Misery Index" (page 318).

WORLD VIEWS. The WORLD VIEWS add a global dimension to the real-world applications. Chapter 1 sets the tone with three WORLD VIEWs covering North Korea's guns versus butter trade-off (page 10), the Heritage Foundation's Index of Economic

Freedom (page 14), and Cuba's small business sector (page 16). Later favorites include the Asian crisis (pages 160, 200, 353), Russia's cashless economy (page 253), and the 1998 supply-side devastation of Hurricane Mitch (page 319). As do the IN THE NEWS boxes, all WORLD VIEWS include explanatory captions and are discussed within the body of the text.

 The Economy Tomorrow. Every chapter ends with an Economy Tomorrow capsule that challenges students to assess the implications of core economic ideas. Chapter 1 considers the wisdom of both macro (Federal Reserve rate setting) and micro (Microsoft antitrust suit) intervention. Chapter 2 challenges the student to decide whether the market or the government can best resolve the residue of problems in our otherwise prosperous economy. Chapter 5's proposed "Index of Social Health" challenges the smugness of national-income accounts. Chapter 12 examines the "generational accounting" implicit in the national debt. Chapter 17 confronts students with the $100,000 wager Julian Simon offered in 1996 that *every* dimension of human well-being will improve in the next decade. In the international section, Chapter 20 assesses how and why the global market is becoming more integrated, and Chapter 21 considers the limitations of future currency bailouts.

www.mhhe.com/ economics/schiller

The Macro Economy Today's Web site has been expanded to include even more features that both instructors and students will find engaging and instructive. An Online Learning Center is set up in an easily accessible chapter-by-chapter format. Each chapter in the Learning Center includes a self-quiz with instant grading, a set of Frequently Asked Questions, a chapter summary and the key terms and definitions from the text, and PowerPoint slides.

The Learning Center also includes links to chapter-related articles in the popular online press, the text's Web Activities, and WWWebEcon/, Web-based collaborative projects relevant to each chapter and/or section in the text. Two questions per chapter make use of the EconGraph kit, a tool that lets a student create a graph online and e-mail it to the instructor.

Inside the Beltway includes links to Web sites that complement the text's policy orientation. The Email the Author section enables students to contact me electronically. We'll also use the Web site to post periodic News Flashes and a compendium of links to online economics news sources. In addition to all the above features, the password-protected Instructor's area of the Web site includes the Instructor's Resource Manual and information on McGraw-Hill Economics-related software and supplementary material.

Be sure to consult the Web site frequently for new URLs and policy updates.

NEW AND IMPROVED SUPPLEMENTS

Instructor Aids

Test Bank. Linda Wilson (University of Texas at Arlington) and Tom Anderson (Montgomery College, Maryland) expanded and completely updated the Test Bank. Materials released as a supplementary test bank to the last edition are included, and over one-third of the questions are completely new. All questions are coded by complexity and correlate to the text. The computerized Test Bank is available in Brownstone's Diploma 97, sophisticated test-making software that ensures maximum flexibility in test development, including the reconfiguration of graphing exercises. Both the print and computerized Test Banks will be offered in micro and macro versions, each of which contains overs 3000 questions.

PowerPoint Presentations. Anthony Zambelli of Cuyamaca College created new presentation slides for the eighth edition. Developed using Microsoft PowerPoint software, these slides are a step-by-step review of the key points in each of the book's 22 chapters. They are equally useful to the student at home or in the computer lab.

Overhead Transparencies. Approximately 200 of the *The Economy's Today*'s key tables and graphs have been reproduced as full-color overhead transparency acetates.

Instructor's Resource Manual. Kevin Klein of Illinois College revised the Instructor's Resource Manual. It offers a capsule summary and outline of each chapter, "lecture launchers" to stimulate class discussion, and media exercises to extend the analysis. New features include a section that details common misconceptions students hold regarding the material in a particular chapter, Internet exercises, and a ready-to-use quiz of 15 multiple-choice and true/false questions. The IRM also includes answers to all the text discussion questions and problems.

Issue Modules. For instructors who want to expand beyond the book's contents, we also offer chapter-length (20–30 pages) modules on topics of special interest. The modules look like text chapters but are individually bound and can be made available at no cost to students if ordered in conjunction with the book. Modules currently available include

- Welfare: Too Much or Too Little?
- Social Security: The Economics of an Aging Population
- Budget Deficits: Outcomes, Process, Theory
- Financial Markets: The Links to Economics Questions
- The California Economy Today
- Poverty in America
- The Economics of Discrimination
- Social Justice in the Political Economy
- The Texas Economy Today

These modules can be ordered shrink-wrapped with the text or can be incorporated into a bound custom-designed book. Ask your local McGraw-Hill sales representative for details.

News Flashes. As up-to-date as *The Macro Economy Today* is, it can't foretell the future. As the future becomes the present, however, the author writes 2-page News Flashes describing major economic events and relating them to specific text references. These items provide good lecture material and can be copied for student use. Adopters of *The Macro Economy Today* have the option of receiving News Flashes via fax or mail. They're also available on the Schiller Web site. Four to six News Flashes are sent to adopters each year.

Student Aids

At the instructor's discretion, students may directly use the Issue Modules and News Flashes described above. In addition, the following supplements can facilitate learning.

Study Guide. Linda Wilson and Tom Anderson, the same authors who produced our test banks, revised the Study Guide, which offers extensive self-study exercises with succinct explanations of key points. Each chapter contains Quick Review, Learning Objectives, Using Key Terms, True or False and Multiple Choice questions, Problems and Applications, Common Errors, and Answers. Approximately half the content in each chapter is new. The Study Guide is available in macro and micro splits as well as in the full-text version.

Student Software. The DiscoverEcon software, developed by Gerald Nelson of the University of Illinois at Urbana–Champaign, is an exciting complement to the text, featuring new learning opportunities for the students and easy integration into existing courses for the instructor. The software is like an interactive text: Software chapters parallel text chapters, and software pages include a page reference in the text. Opportunities for active learning abound. All chapters contain a multiple-choice quiz, essay questions with online links, and match-the-terms exercises. Most chapters have numerous opportunities for playing with key concepts presented in the text. Interactive graphs, animated charts, and live tables let you and your students explore ideas, experiment with alternatives, and test your knowledge. Links to the glossary and text references clarify key concepts, and Web-based exercises give students a direct link to the site in question. Exercises are graded immediately, and the results can be submitted to the instructor either on paper or electronically. The software comes on a single CD that can be installed on and run over a network.

ACKNOWLEDGMENTS

Once again I am indebted to the many people who cajoled, motivated, and helped me to develop another edition of *The Macro Economy Today.* I am especially grateful to my collaborators on the package of supplementary aids. Linda Wilson, Tom Anderson, Anthony Zambelli, Gerald Nelson, and Kevin Klein all developed supplements that facilitate both teaching and learning. Diane Keenan and Mark Maier wrote the end-of-chapter Web activities and created the content for WWWebEcon/. I am also indebted to the many instructors who took the time to review and critique the seventh edition or draft versions of this eighth edition. The reviewers include:

Steve Abid
Grand Rapids Community College
Peter Barth
University of Connecticut
Suzanne Boyles
California State University, Fresno
Lawrence Daellenbach
University of Wisconsin, LaCrosse
Diane Flaherty
University of Massachusetts, Amherst
Roger Frantz
San Diego State University
Linda Ghent
East Carolina State University
Barry Harwoth
University of Louisville
Dave Hickman
Frederick Community College
Diane Keenan
Cerritos College
Jennifer Long
Keene State University

Carol McDonough
University of Massachusetts, Lowell
Stephen McGary
Ricks College
Frank Murtaugh
Norwich University
Melinda Nish
Salt Lake Community College
Jeffrey Rous
University of North Texas
Dawn Saunders
University of Vermont
Ted Scheinman
Mount Hood Community College
David Sisk
San Francisco State University
Frederica Shockley
California State University, Chico
Mike Walsh
Kellogg Community College
Ken Woodward
Saddleback College

This eighth edition also benefitted from the efforts of the first-rate team at Irwin/McGraw-Hill. Paul Shensa, the executive editor, and I have worked well together for 20 years, prodding each other to go the extra mile. The development editors, Marilea Fried and Miller Murray; the project manager, Eva Strock; the production supervisor, Pam Auguspurger, all kept this eighth edition on track. Amanda Kavangh deserves mention for her attractive design. To all these individual I offer my heartfelt appreciation.

Finally, I'd like to thank all the professors and students who are going to use *The Macro Economy Today* as an introduction to economic principles. I'd welcome any responses (even bad ones) you'd like to pass on for future editions.

Bradley R. Schiller

CONTENTS IN BRIEF

ECONOMICS ON THE WORLDWIDE WEB *

*Web addresses change often. Consult our Web site (www.mhhe.com/economics) for timely updates.

QuoteCom Data Service www.quote.com

Statistics Canada www.statcan.ca

Canadian Economics Association (CEA) economics.ca

AmchamNet—American Chamber of Commerce—Brazil www.amcham.com.br

Bank of Hawaii Economic Research Center www.boh.com/econ

Australian Bureau of Statistics www.statistics.gov.au

New Zealand Treasury www.treasury.govt.nz

InTechTra's Hong Kong Stocks Reports www.asiawind.com/pub/hksr

Turkish Economics Pages www.siue.edu/~itanris/econtr.html

Israel Central Bureau of Statistics www.cbs.gov.il/engindex.htm

Finnish Society for Economic Research www.hkkk.fi/~fecons

The Research Institute of the Finnish Economy (ETLA) www.etla.fi

Eurostat europa.eu.int/eurostat.html

European Economic Association www.hec.unil.ch/prague/eea/premier.htm

Euro Internet fgr.wu-wien.ac.at/nentwich/euroint2.htm

Carolina Population Center (UNC—Chapel Hill) www.cpc.unc.edu

Central European Regional Research Organization (CERRO) gopher://olymp.wu-wien.ac.at:70/11/.cerro.ind

German Federal Statistical Office www.statistik-bund.de/e_home.htm

REESweb: Russian and East European Studies—Business, Economics, and Law Resources www.pitt.edu/~cjp/rees.html

Paul Krugman http://web.mit.edu/Krugman

Nicolas Economides' The Economics of Networks http://raven.stern.nyu.edu/networks

Hal R. Varian's The Information Economy http://sims.berkeley.edu/resources/infoecon

Brad DeLong's Economic Book Reviews http://econ161.berkeley.edu

Jokes About Economists and Economists www.etla.fi/pkm/JokEc

The Economist www.economist.com

The Wall Street Journal www.wsj.com

The Financial Times www.ft.com

The Brookings Institute www.brookings.org

Forbes Magazine www.forbes.com

"Win Ben Stein's Money" www.comcentral.com/bstein

Association for Evolutionary Economics www.cba.unl.edu/additional/ecafee.html

Job Openings for Economists www.eco.utexas.edu/joe

Barter Is Frugal http://frugalliving.miningco.com/msubbar.htm?pid~2714&cob~home

Merrill Lynch www.merrilllynch.com

Morgan Stanley www.ms.com/gef.html

Vanderbilt University Antitrust Policy www.Antitrust.org

Microsoft www.microsoft.com

U.S. Department of Justice www.usdoj.gov

AFL-CIO www.aflcio.org

NAFTAnet Services www.nafta.net

The China Council for the Promotion of International Trade (CCPIT) www.ccpit.org

U.S. Census Bureau, Foreign Trade Division www.census.gov/ftp/pub/foreign-trade/www

Organization for Economic Co-operation and Development www.oecd.org

Nouriel Roubini www.stern.nyu.edu/~nroubini/asia/AsiaHomepage.html

Economics:
The Core Issues

W ill the "21st Century Economy" be as exciting as people imagine? Will information technology, biotechnology, and space technology really revolutionize the way we live, the way we learn, how we work, and how we communicate? Will virtual books and classrooms make paper books and college campuses obsolete? Will biotechnology end world hunger, extend our lives, and even let us custom design our offspring? Will the colonization of space literally open up a whole new universe of production and consumption possibilities?

At the beginning of the millenium, imaginations broaden and hopes soar. At the beginning of the nineteenth century, futurists dreamed that someone would discover how to grow more grain on an acre of land, thereby averting worldwide famine. At the beginning of the twentieth century, futurists were dreaming about ways to increase industrial output fast enough to bring material prosperity to the average worker. Shortly thereafter, Henry Ford showed the world how this could be done with specialized workers arrayed along a mechanized assembly line. Now, on the brink of the twenty-first century, one of the most urgent technological needs is how to squeeze more electronic circuits onto a silicon wafer. As the electronic density of the information superhighway increases, the more places the highway can take us.

Although technology has changed radically over the centuries, the human motivation underlying the quest for new discoveries has had a common core. Throughout history, people have always sought ways of producing more output from whatever resources they had. To a large extent, the quest for more output has been driven by necessity. The world's population keeps growing, but the amount of land doesn't. That's why the English economist Thomas Malthus predicted in 1798 that the world would run out of food long before the nineteenth century ended. He didn't know that a few years later someone would invent the iron plow (1808), the reaper (1826), or the milking machine (1878). And Malthus had no conception of what biotechnology's "green revolution" might become, which is why predictions of future Doomsdays and other technological limits often end up so wrong and even ludicrous (see WORLD VIEW).

Although we've managed to increase food output faster than the population has grown, we can't be complacent. The United Nations predicts that the world's population, now at 6 billion, will increase by another billion every 10 years. Even if we find ways for food output to keep pace, we can't be satisfied. Our future goals are much more ambitious. We want an ever higher standard of living, not

Cloudy Days in Tomorrowland

We'd like to think all *our* predictions will prove right. But the highways of history are littered with wrong calls, false insights and bad guesses. Here's a sampler of 20th-century futurology that flopped.

I confess that in 1901, I said to my brother Orville that man would not fly for fifty years . . . Ever since, I have distrusted myself and avoided all predictions.
—WILBUR WRIGHT, *U.S. aviation pioneer, 1908*

I must confess that my imagination . . . refuses to see any sort of submarine doing anything but suffocating its crew and floundering at sea.
—H. G. WELLS, *British novelist, 1901*

Airplanes are interesting toys but of no military value.
—MARSHAL FERDINAND FOCH
*French military strategist and
future World War I commander, 1911*

The horse is here to stay, but the automobile is only a novelty—a fad.
—*A president of the Michigan Savings Bank advising* HORACE RACKHAM *(Henry Ford's lawyer) not to invest in the Ford Motor Co., 1903. Rackham ignored the advice, bought $5,000 worth of stock and sold it several years later for $12.5 million.*

Radio has no future.
—LORD KELVIN, *Scottish mathematician and physicist, former president of the Royal Society, 1897*

Everything that can be invented has been invented.
—CHARLES H. DUELL, *U.S. commissioner of patents, 1899*

Who the hell wants to hear actors talk?
—HARRY M. WARNER, *Warner Brothers, 1927*

There is no reason for any individual to have a computer in their home.
—KENNETH OLSEN, *president and founder of Digital Equipment Corp., 1977*

[Man will never reach the moon] regardless of all future scientific advances.
—DR. LEE DE FOREST, *inventor of the Audion tube and a father of radio, Feb. 25, 1967*

We don't like their sound. Groups of guitars are on the way out.
—DECCA RECORDS *rejecting the Beatles, 1962*

What use could this company make of an electrical toy?
—*Western Union president* WILLIAM ORTON, *rejecting Alexander Graham Bell's offer to sell his struggling telephone company to Western Union for $100,000*

Computers in the future may . . . perhaps only weigh 1.5 tons.
—POPULAR MECHANICS, *forecasting the development of computer technology, 1949*

Stocks have reached what looks like a permanently high plateau.
—IRVING FISHER, *professor of economics, Yale University, Oct. 17, 1929*

[Television] won't be able to hold on to any market it captures after the first six months. People will soon get tired of staring at a plywood box every night.
—DARRYL F. ZANUCK, *head of 20th Century-Fox, 1946*

Newsweek, Jan. 27, 1997, p. 86. Reprinted by permission.
www.newsweek.com

Analysis: No one predicts the future well. But the economic choices we make today about the use of scarce resources will determine the kind of future we have.

just enough food on the table. No matter how fast our incomes grow, we always want more. The living standards earlier generations dreamed of we now take for granted. Today's luxuries—high-definition television, satellite phones, DVX-enhanced digital video—will most likely be viewed as necessities in a few years, but only if we keep squeezing more and more output out of available resources.

Ironically, some people fear we will do exactly that—and end up destroying the environment in the process. They foresee a Doomsday in which greenhouse gases generated by ever-rising production levels will overheat the earth, melt the solar icecaps, flood coastal areas, and destroy crops.

No one really knows how the twenty-first century will unfold. But one thing is certain: The future will be shaped in large part by the choices we make along the way. If we build more factories and cyber networks today, we'll be able to produce more output tomorrow. If we install more pollution controls in cars, power plants, and factories today, we'll have cleaner air tomorrow.

The science of economics helps us frame these choices. In a nutshell, **economics** is the study of how people use scarce resources. How do you decide how much time to spend studying? How does Amazon.com decide how many workers to hire? How does Chrysler decide whether to use its factories to produce sports utility vehicles or sedans? What share of a nation's resources should be devoted to development of cyber networks, the delivery of healthcare services, or pollution control? In every instance alternative ways of using scarce labor, land, and building resources are available, and we have to choose one use over another.

economics: The study of how best to allocate scarce resources among competing uses

In this first chapter we explore the nature of scarcity and the kinds of choices it forces us to make. As we'll see, **three core issues must be resolved:**

- **WHAT to produce with our limited resources.**
- **HOW to produce the goods and services we select.**
- **FOR WHOM goods and services are produced;** that is, who should get them.

We also have to decide who should answer these questions. Should the marketplace decide what gets produced and how and for whom? Or should the government dictate output choices, regulate production processes, and redistribute incomes? Should Microsoft decide what gets included in a computer's operating system, or should the government make that decision? Should interest rates be set by private banks alone, or should the government try to control interest rates? The battle over *who* should answer the core questions is often as contentious as the questions themselves.

THE ECONOMY IS US

To learn how the economy works, let's start with a simple truth: *The economy is us.* "The economy" is simply an abstraction referring to the sum of all our individual production and consumption activities. What we collectively produce is what the economy produces; what we collectively consume is what the economy consumes. In this sense, the concept of "the economy" is no more difficult than the concept of "the family." If someone tells you that the Jones family has an annual income of $22,000, you know that the reference is to the collective earnings of all the Joneses. Likewise, when someone reports that the nation's income is approaching $9 trillion per year—as it now is—we should recognize that the reference is to the grand total of our individual incomes. If we work fewer hours or get paid less, both family income *and* national income decline. The "meaningless statistics" (see cartoon on the following page) often cited in the news are just a summary of our collective market behavior.

The same relationship between individual behavior and aggregate behavior applies to specific outputs. If we as individuals insist on driving cars rather than taking public transportation, the economy will produce millions of cars each year and consume vast quantities of oil. In a slightly different way, the economy produces billions of dollars of military hardware to satisfy our desire for national defense. In each case, the output of the economy reflects the collective behavior of the 270 million individuals who participate in the economy.

We may not always be happy with the output of the economy. But we can't ignore the link between individual action and collective outcomes. If the highways are clogged and the air is polluted as a consequence of our transportation choices, we can't blame someone else. If we're disturbed by the size of our military arsenal, we must still accept responsibility for our choices (or nonchoices, if we failed to vote). In either case, we continue to have the option of reallocating our resources. We can create a different outcome the next day, month, or year.

Drawing by Dana Fradon; © 1977 The New Yorker Magazine, Inc.

"Meaningless statistics were up one-point-five per cent this month over last month."

Analysis: Many people think of economics as dull statistics. But economics is really about human behavior—how people decide to use scarce resources and how those decisions affect market outcomes.

SCARCITY: THE CORE PROBLEM

Although we can change economic outcomes, we can't have everything we want. If you go to the mall with $20 in your pocket, you can only buy so much. The money in your pocket sets a *limit* to your spending.

The output of the entire economy is also limited. The limits in this case are set not by money but by the resources available for producing goods and services. Everyone wants more housing, new schools, better transit systems, and a new car; but even a country as rich as the United States can't produce everything people want. So, like every other nation, we have to grapple with the core problem of **scarcity**—the fact that there aren't enough resources available to satisfy all our desires.

> **scarcity:** The fact that available resources are insufficient to satisfy all desired uses thereof.

Factors of Production

> **factors of production:** Resource inputs used to produce goods and services, such as land, labor, capital, and entrepreneurship.

The resources used to produce goods and services are called **factors of production.** *The four basic factors of production are:*

- *Land*
- *Labor*
- *Capital*
- *Entrepreneurship*

These are the *inputs* needed to produce desired *outputs.* To produce this textbook, for example, we needed paper, printing presses, a building, and lots of labor. We also needed people with good ideas who could put it together. To produce the education you're getting in this class, we need not only a textbook but a classroom, a teacher, and a blackboard as well. Without factors of production, we simply can't produce anything.

Land. The first factor of production, land, refers not just to the ground but to all natural resources. Crude oil, water, air, and minerals are all included in our concept of "land."

Labor. Labor too has several dimensions. It's not simply a question of how many bodies there are; when we speak of labor as a factor of production, we refer to the skills and abilities to produce goods and services. Hence both the quantity and the quality of human resources are included in the "labor" factor.

> **capital:** Final goods produced for use in the production of other goods, e.g., equipment, structures.

Capital. The third factor of production is capital. In economics the term **capital** refers to final goods produced for use in further production. The residents of fishing villages in southern Thailand, for example, braid huge fishing nets. The sole purpose of these nets is to catch more fish. The nets themselves become a factor of production in obtaining the final goods (fish) that people desire. Thus they're regarded as *capital.* Blast furnaces used to make steel and desks used to equip offices are, similarly, capital inputs.

Entrepreneurship. The more land, labor, and capital available, the greater the amount of potential output. A farmer with 10,000 acres, 12 employees, and 6 tractors can grow more crops than a farmer with half those resources. But there's no guarantee that he will. The farmer with fewer resources may have better ideas about what to plant, when to irrigate, or how to harvest the crops. ***It's not just a matter of what resources you have but also of how well you use them.*** This is where the fourth factor of production—**entrepreneurship**—comes in. The entrepreneur is the person who sees the opportunity for new or better products and brings together the resources needed for producing them. If it weren't for entrepreneurs, Thai fishermen would still be using sticks to catch fish. Without entrepreneurship, farmers would still be milking their cows by hand. If someone hadn't thought of a way to produce digital video players, you never would have had a chance to use one.

entrepreneurship: The assembling of resources to produce new or improved products and technologies.

The role of entrepreneurs in economic progress is a key issue in the market versus government debate. The Austrian economist Joseph Schumpeter argued that free markets unleash the "animal spirits" of entrepreneurs, propelling innovation, technology, and growth. Critics of communism assert that centrally planned economies were doomed to failure because they don't offer the opportunities and incentives for entrepreneurship that free markets do. As the accompanying WORLD VIEW illustrates, this concern prompted China to experiment with "enterprise zones" and other market-oriented reforms. The entrepreneurship that surfaced helped make China one of the world's fastest growing economies in the 1990s.

WORLD VIEW

Free Enterprise Blooms in Wenzhou, China, Out of the Party's Sight

City of Entrepreneurs May Be a Model for Reviving the Country's Economy

WENZHOU, China—Communist leaders in Beijing are wringing their hands over how to revive rotting Soviet-style state factories. But while they agonize over how best to blend central planning and free markets into a "socialist commodity economy" the entrepreneurial folk of Wenzhou don't waste any time in theory. They just do it.

Isolated along the seacoast near Taiwan, and long paid little heed by the central government, Wenzhou has become one of China's thriving hubs of private enterprise. . . .

The typical Wenzhou living room doubles as either a factory or shop. Family members and employees paid by piecework often toil past midnight, cobbling shoes, sewing together clothes, or providing haircuts, laundry and other services. Profits get plowed into bigger stores, fancier restaurants, more-efficient factories or other businesses. . . .

Planners Stayed Away Isolation has been a blessing for Wenzhou (pronounced one-joe), which has a population of 6.5 million including surrounding rural areas. Until the airport opened in 1990, Beijing bureaucrats coming here had to ride a rusty overnight ferry from Shanghai, 200 miles to the north, or endure a long auto journey along rutted, winding roads.

As a result, Stalinist central planners mostly stayed away as Mao worked in the 1950s and 1960s to squeeze capitalism out of China. . . .

"We've always had to depend on ourselves," says Xu Shunsheng, head of the city's Private Business Management Department. He thinks the rest of China should do likewise. "A few years from now, when you look back and ask why is the Chinese economy so alive, it will be because of private enterprise," he says.

—James McGregor

The Wall Street Journal, Aug. 13, 1992, p. 1. Reprinted by permission of *The Wall Street Journal,* ©1992 Dow Jones & Company, Inc. All Rights Reserved Worldwide. www.wsj.com

Analysis: Although central planners still direct much of China's economy, the Chinese government has been experimenting with market-driven economies. The goal is to encourage entrepreneurs to increase output and efficiency.

Limits to Output

No matter how an economy is organized, there's a limit to how fast it can grow. The most evident limit is the amount of resources available for producing goods and services. These resource limits imply that we can't produce everything we want. Again, this is the core problem of scarcity—the fact that available resources are insufficient to satisfy all desired uses thereof.

Scarcity—the imbalance between our desires and available resources—forces us to make economic choices. When you've got only $20 in your pocket, the necessity for choice is obvious. Even $20 million might not buy everything you want. There are lots of different ways of spending money, and choices have to be made.

Your economics class also represents a decision about the use of scarce resources. The building space used for your economics class can't be used to show movies at the same time. Your professor can't lecture (produce education) and repair motorcycles simultaneously. Someone has made a decision about how these scarce resources (capital, labor) will be used.

Guns vs. Butter

One of the persistent choices about resource use entails defense spending. The U.S. government spends more than $250 billion a year on national defense. That's a lot of money. From an economic view, those defense expenditures also represent an enormous claim on scarce resources. The 1.4 million men and women serving in the armed forces aren't available to build schools, program computers, or teach economics. Similarly, the land, labor, capital, and entrepreneurship devoted to producing military hardware aren't available for producing civilian goods. This is the "guns versus butter" dilemma that all nations confront.

Since the end of the Cold War in 1989, the United States has chosen to produce far fewer "guns." The defense budget has declined from a high of 6.3 percent of total output in 1986 to only 3.3 percent in 1999. The armed forces have been cut by 500,000 men and women. These defense cutbacks freed up scarce resources that now produce more civilian goods ("butter"). This is referred to as the "peace dividend" from military downsizing.

CYBER NOTE

To see how the share of output allocated to national defense has changed in recent decades, visit the Congressional Budget Office Web Site at www.cbo.gov and search for "discretionary outlays."

Opportunity Costs

opportunity cost: The most desired goods or services that are forgone in order to obtain something else.

The peace dividend illustrates the significance of scarcity. *Every time we choose to use scarce resources in one way we give up the opportunity to use them in other ways.* If we build more weapons systems, we give up the opportunity to produce more civilian goods. The forgone civilian goods represent the **opportunity cost** of military output. The opportunity cost of any activity is the most desired goods or services forgone in order to make resources available for that activity. *Opportunity cost is what is*

"There's no such thing as a free lunch."

Analysis: All goods and services have an opportunity cost. Even the resources used to produce a "free lunch" could have been used to produce something else.

given up in order to get something else. Even a so-called free lunch has an opportunity cost (see cartoon). The resources used to produce the lunch could have been used for something else.

Think about the cost of reading this book. That cost is not measured in dollars and cents. The true (economic) cost is, instead, measured in terms of some alternative activity. What would you like to be doing right now? The more time you spend reading this book, the less time you have available for that alternative use of your time. The opportunity cost of reading this text is the best alternative use of your scarce time. If you are missing your favorite TV show, we'd say that show is the opportunity cost of reading this book. It is what you gave up to do this assignment. Hopefully, the benefits you get from studying will outweigh that cost. Otherwise this wouldn't be the best way to use your scarce time.

PRODUCTION POSSIBILITIES

The opportunity costs implied by our every choice can be illustrated easily. Suppose the choice is between producing tennis shoes and assembling televisions. To keep things simple, assume that labor (workers) is the only factor of production needed to produce either good. Although other factors of production (land, machinery) are also needed in actual production, ignoring them for the moment does no harm. Let us assume further that we have a total of only 10 workers available per day to produce shoes or televisions. Our initial problem is to determine the limits of output. How many shoes or televisions can be produced in a day with available resources?

Before going any further, notice how opportunity costs will affect the answer. If we employ all 10 workers in the production of shoes, then no labor will be available to assemble televisions. In this case, forgone televisions would become the opportunity cost of a decision to use all our resources in shoe production.

We still don't know how many shoes could be produced with 10 workers or exactly how many televisions would be forgone by such a decision. To get these answers, we must know a little more about the production processes involved—specifically, how many workers are required to stitch shoes or assemble televisions.

Table 1.1 summarizes the hypothetical choices, or **production possibilities,** that we confront in this case. Row A of the table shows the consequences of a decision to produce shoes only. With 10 workers available and a labor requirement of 2 workers per shoe, we can stitch a maximum of five shoes per day. By so doing, however, we use all available resources, leaving nothing for TV assembly. If we want televisions, we have to cut back on shoe production; this is the essential choice we must make.

The remainder of Table 1.1 describes the full range of production choices. By cutting back shoe production from five to four shoes per day (row B), we reduce labor use from 10 workers to 8. That leaves 2 workers available for other uses.

If we employ these remaining 2 workers to assemble televisions, we can build two televisions a day. We would then end up with four shoes and two televisions per day. What's the opportunity cost of these two televisions? It's the one additional shoe (the fifth shoe) that we could have stitched but didn't.

As we proceed down the rows of Table 1.1, the nature of opportunity costs becomes apparent. Each additional television built implies the loss (opportunity cost) of shoe output. Likewise, every shoe stitched implies the loss of some TV output.

These trade-offs between TV assembly and shoe production are illustrated in the production possibilities curve of Figure 1.1. **Each point on the production possibilities curve depicts an alternative mix of output** that could be produced. In this case, each point represents a different combination of televisions and shoes that we could produce in a single day using all available resources (labor in this case).

Notice in particular how points *A* through *F* in Figure 1.1 represent the choices described in each row of Table 1.1. At point *A,* we're producing five shoes per day and

The Production Possibilities Curve

production possibilities: The alternative combinations of final goods and services that could be produced in a given time period with all available resources and technology.

TABLE 1.1
Production Possibilities Schedule

As long as resources are limited, their use entails an opportunity cost. In this case, resources (labor) used to stitch shoes can't be used for TV assembly at the same time. Hence, the forgone tele- visions are the opportunity cost of additional shoes. If all our re- sources were used to produce shoes (row A), no televisions could be assembled.

		Shoe Production				TV Assembly		
	Total Available Labor	Output of Shoes per Day	× Labor Needed per Shoe	= Total Labor Required for Shoes	Labor Not Used for Shoes	Potential Output of TVs per Day		Increase in TV Output
A	10	5	2	10	0	0		
B	10	4	2	8	2	2.0	>	2.0
C	10	3	2	6	4	3.0	>	1.0
D	10	2	2	4	6	3.8	>	0.8
E	10	1	2	2	8	4.5	>	0.7
F	10	0	2	0	10	5.0	>	0.5

no televisions. As we move down the curve from point *A* to point *B,* shoe production drops from five to four shoes per day while TV assembly increases from zero to two. In other words, we're giving up one shoe to get two televisions assembled. The op- portunity cost of those televisions is one shoe that is given up. A production possibil- ities curve, then, is simply a graphic summary of production possibilities, as described in Table 1.1. It illustrates the alternative goods and services we could produce and the implied opportunity costs of each choice. In other words, **the production possibilities curve illustrates two essential principles:**

FIGURE 1.1
A Production Possibilities Curve

A production possibilities curve de- scribes the various combinations of fi- nal goods or services that could be produced in a given time period with available resources and technology. It represents a "menu" of output choices an economy confronts. Point *B* indi- cates that we could produce a *combi- nation* of four shoes and two televi- sions per day. By giving up one more shoe, we could assemble a third tele- vision, and thus move to point *C.* Points *A, D, E,* and *F,* illustrate still other output combinations that could be produced. This curve is a graphic il- lustration of the production possibili- ties schedule in Table 1.1.

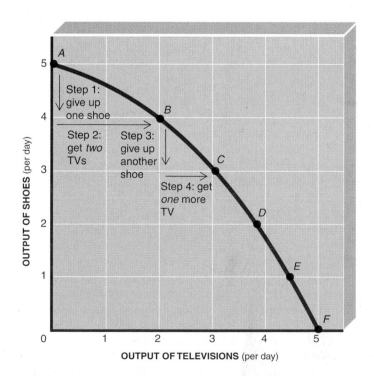

- **Scarce resources.** There's a limit to the amount we can produce in a given time period with available resources and technology.
- **Opportunity costs.** We can obtain additional quantities of any desired good only by reducing the potential production of another good.

The shape of the production possibilities curve reflects another limitation on our choices. Notice how opportunity costs increase as we move along the production possibilities curve. When we cut shoe output from five shoes to four (step 1, Figure 1.1), we get two televisions (step 2). When we cut shoe production further, however (step 3), we get only one television per shoe given up (step 4). The opportunity cost of TV assembly is increasing. This process of increasing opportunity cost continues. By the time we give up the last shoe (row *F*), TV output increases by only 0.5: We get only half a television for the last shoe given up. These increases in opportunity cost are reflected in the outward bend of the production possibilities curve.

Why do opportunity costs increase? Mostly because it's difficult to move resources from one industry to another. It's easy to transform shoes to televisions on a blackboard. In the real world, however, resources don't adapt so easily. Workers who stitch shoes may not have the skills for TV assembly. As we continue to transfer labor from one industry to the other, we start getting fewer televisions for every shoe we give up.

The difficulties entailed in transferring labor skills, capital, and entrepreneurship from one industry to another are so universal that we often speak of the *"law"* of *increasing opportunity cost.* This law says that we must give up ever-increasing quantities of other goods and services in order to get more of a particular good. The law isn't based solely on the limited versatility of individual workers. The *mix* of factor inputs makes a difference as well, because shoe stitching requires less capital than TV assembly. In a pinch, shoes could be stitched almost completely by hand, whereas TV assembly requires more sophisticated machinery. As we move labor from shoe stitching to TV assembly, available capital may restrict our output capabilities.

The kind of opportunity costs that arise in shoe production or TV assembly take on even greater significance in the broader decisions nations make about WHAT to produce. Consider, for example, North Korea's decision to maintain a large military. North Korea is a relatively small country: Its population of 24 million ranks fortieth in the world. Yet North Korea maintains the fourth largest army in the world. To do so, it must allocate nearly 25 percent of all its resources to feeding, clothing, and equipping its military forces. As a consequence, there aren't enough resources available to produce food. Without adequate machinery, seeds, fertilizer, or irrigation, Korea's farmers can't produce enough food to feed the population (see WORLD VIEW). As Figure 1.2 illustrates, the opportunity cost of "guns" in Korea is a lot of needed "butter."

Increasing Opportunity Costs

The Cost of North Korea's Military

CYBER NOTE

The International Institute for Strategic Studies compiles data and publishes studies on national military forces (www.isn.ethz.ch/iiss). To determine what percentage of total population is in the armed forces in different nations, the Central Intelligence Agency may be more convenient (www.odci.gov/cia/publications/factbook).

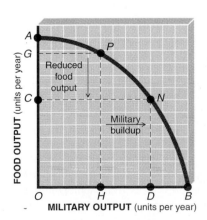

FIGURE 1.2
The Cost of an Army

North Korea devotes one-fourth of its output to the military. The opportunity cost of this decision is reduced output of food. As the military expands from *OH* to *OD*, food output drops from *OG* to *OC*.

WORLD VIEW

North Korea Says It Is Running Out of Food

TOKYO, March 3 (Tuesday)—North Korea issued its most dire assessment yet of its food shortages on Monday, saying that a hungry population already living on starvation rations could run out of food in as little as two weeks.

The official state news agency reported that daily rations for most people had already been cut to seven ounces a day, far below what is generally considered necessary for survival. It said that even if that ration is cut in half, "the stock will run out in mid-March."

Because of North Korea's secretive nature, it is virtually impossible to know whether its statements about the shortages are accurate. If true, millions of people could be at immediate risk of famine and starvation.

—Kevin Sullivan
The Washington Post, Mar. 2, 1998.

North Korea Expanding Missile Programs

Despite international pressure to curtail its missile program, North Korea is building at least two new launch facilities for the medium-range Taepo Dong 1 and has stepped up production of short-range missiles, according to U.S. intelligence and diplomatic sources.

The projects, and a conclusion by U.S. intelligence agencies that North Korea intends to test-fire a second missile capable of striking Japan, are inflaming regional tensions, U.S. officials and Korea experts said.

—Dana Priest and Thomas W. Lippman
The Washington Post, Nov. 20, 1998, p. 1.

Analysis: North Korea's inability to feed itself is partly due to maintaining its large army: Resources used for the military aren't available for producing food.

During World War II, the United States confronted a similar trade-off. In 1944, nearly 40 percent of all U.S. output was devoted to the military. Civilian goods were so scarce that they had to be rationed. Staples like butter, sugar, and gasoline were doled out in small quantities. Even golf balls were rationed. In North Korea, golf balls would be a luxury even without a military buildup. As the share of output devoted to the military has increased, even basic food production has become more difficult.

Efficiency

efficiency: Maximum output of a good from the resources used in production.

Increasing opportunity costs aren't a sign of inefficiency. The production possibilities curve in Figures 1.1 and 1.2 are based on the assumption of maximum efficiency. The curve represents the *greatest* combinations of output we can produce if we not only use all available resources but also use them well. **Efficiency** means "getting the most from what you've got"—that is, using factors of production in the most productive way. As we move from point to point along the production possibilities curve in Figures 1.1 and 1.2 we're seeing the *most* output we can get from various labor (resource) allocations. Opportunity costs increase because resources aren't perfectly transferable, not because we use them inefficiently.

Inefficiency

There's no guarantee, of course, that we'll always use resources efficiently. *A production possibilities curve shows* **potential** *output, not necessarily* **actual** *output.* If we're inefficient, actual output will be less than that potential. This happens. In the real world, workers sometimes loaf on the job. Or they call in sick and go to a baseball game instead of working. Managers don't always give the clearest directions or stay in touch with advancing technology. Even students sometimes fail to put forth their best effort on homework assignments. This kind of slippage can prevent us from achieving maximum production. When that happens, we end up *inside* the production possibilities curve rather than *on* it.

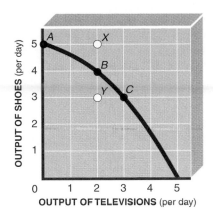

FIGURE 1.3
Points Inside and Outside the Curve

Points outside the production possibilities curve (point *X*) are unattainable with available resources and technology. Points inside the curve (point *Y*) represent the incomplete use of available resources. Only points on the production possibilities curve (*A, B, C*) represent maximum use of our production capabilities.

Point *Y* in Figure 1.3 illustrates the consequences of inefficient production. At point *Y*, we're producing only three shoes and two televisions. This is less than our potential. We could assemble a third television without cutting back shoe production (point *C*). Or we could get an extra shoe without sacrificing any TV output (point *B*). Instead, we're producing *inside* the production possibilities curve at point *Y*. Such inefficiencies plagued centrally planned economies. Government-run factories guaranteed everyone a job regardless of how much output they produced. They became bloated bureaucracies; as much as 40 percent of the workers were superfluous. When communism collapsed, many of these factories were "privatized," that is, sold to private investors. The privatized companies were able to fire thousands of workers and *increase* output. Governments in Europe and Latin America have also sold off many of their state-owned enterprises in the hopes of increasing efficiency and reaching the production possibilities curve.

Countries may also end up inside their production possibilities curve if all available resources aren't used. In 1992, for example, as many as 10 million Americans were looking for work each week, but no one hired them. As a result, we were stuck *inside* the production possibilities curve, producing less output than we could have. A basic challenge for policymakers is to eliminate unemployment and keep the economy on its production possibilities curve. In 1999, the United States was much closer to this goal.

Figure 1.3 also illustrates an output mix that everyone would welcome. Point *X* lies *outside* the production possibilities curve. It suggests that we could get *more* goods than we're capable of producing! Unfortunately, point *X* is only a mirage: All output combinations that lie outside the production possibilities curve are unattainable with available resources and technology.

Things change, however. Over time, population increases and we get more labor. If we continue building factories and machinery, the stock of available capital will also increase. The *quality* of labor and capital will also increase if we train workers and pursue new technologies. Entrepreneurs may discover new products or better ways of producing old ones. All these changes will increase potential output. This is illustrated in Figure 1.4 by the outward *shift* of the production possibilities curve. Before the appearance of new resources or better technology, our production possibilities were limited by the curve PP_1. **With more resources or better technology, our production possibilities increase.** This greater capacity to produce is represented by curve PP_2. This outward shift of the production possibilities curve is the essence of **economic growth.** With economic growth, countries can have more guns *and* more butter. Without economic growth, living standards decline as the population grows. This is the problem that plagues some of the world's poorest nations, where population increases but output often doesn't.

Unemployment

Economic Growth

economic growth: An increase in output (real GDP); an expansion of production possibilities.

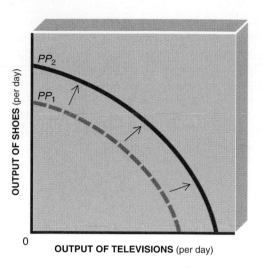

FIGURE 1.4
Growth: Increasing Production Possibilities

A production possibilities curve is based on *available* resources and technology. If more resources or better technology becomes available, production possibilities will increase. This economic growth is illustrated by the *shift* from PP_1 to PP_2.

BASIC DECISIONS

Production possibilities define the output choices that a nation confronts. From these choices every nation must make some basic decisions. As we noted at the beginning of this chapter, the three core economic questions are:

- **WHAT to produce**
- **HOW to produce**
- **FOR WHOM to produce**

WHAT

There are millions of points along a production possibilities curve, and each one represents a specific mix of output. We can choose only *one* of these points at any time. The point we choose determines what mix of output gets produced. That choice determines how many guns are produced, and how much butter.

The production possibilities curve doesn't tell us which mix of output is best; it just lays out a menu of available choices. It's up to us to pick out the one and only mix of output that will be produced at a given time. This WHAT decision is a basic decision every nation must make.

HOW

Decisions must also be made about HOW to produce. Should we generate electricity by burning coal, smashing atoms, or transforming solar power? Should we harvest ancient forests even if that destroys endangered owls or other animal species? Should we dump municipal and industrial waste into nearby rivers, or should we dispose of it in some other way? There are lots of different ways of producing goods and services, and someone has to make a decision about which production methods to use. The HOW decision is a question not just of efficiency but of social values as well.

FOR WHOM

After we've decided what to produce and how, we must address a third basic question: FOR WHOM? Who is going to get the output produced? Should everyone get an equal share? Should everyone wear the same clothes and drive identical cars? Should some people get to enjoy seven-course banquets while others forage in garbage cans for food scraps? How should the goods and services an economy produces be distributed? Are we satisfied with the way output is now distributed?

THE MECHANISMS OF CHOICE

Answers to the questions of WHAT, HOW, and FOR WHOM largely define an economy. But who formulates the answers? Who actually decides which goods are produced, what technologies are used, or how incomes are distributed?

Adam Smith had an answer back in 1776. In his classic work *The Wealth of Nations,* Smith said the "invisible hand" determines what gets produced, how, and for whom. The invisible hand he referred to wasn't a creature from a science fiction movie but, instead, a characterization of the way markets work.

Consider the decision about how many cars to produce in the United States. Who decides to produce over 6 million cars a year? There's no "auto czar" who dictates production. Not even General Motors can make such a decision. Instead, the *market* decides how many cars to produce. Millions of individuals signal their desire to have a car by visiting showrooms and buying cars. Their purchases flash a green light to producers, who see the potential to earn more profits. To do so, they'll increase auto output. If consumers stop buying cars, profits will disappear. Producers will respond by reducing output, laying off workers, and even closing factories. These interactions between consumers and producers determine how many cars are produced.

Notice how the invisible hand moves us along the production possibilities curve. If consumers demand more cars, the mix of output will include more cars and less of other goods. If auto production is scaled back, the displaced autoworkers will end up producing other goods and services, which will change the mix of output in the opposite direction.

Adam Smith's invisible hand is now called the **market mechanism.** Notice that it doesn't require any direct contact between consumers and producers. Communication is indirect, transmitted by market prices and sales. Indeed, *the essential feature of the market mechanism is the price signal.* If you want something and have sufficient income, you can buy it. If enough people do the same thing, the total sales of that product will rise, and perhaps its price will as well. Producers, seeing sales and prices rise, will want to exploit this profit potential. To do so, they'll attempt to acquire a larger share of available resources and use it to produce the goods we desire. That's how the "invisible hand" works.

The market mechanism can also answer the HOW question. To maximize their profits, producers will seek to use the lowest-cost method of producing a good. By observing prices in the marketplace, they can identify the cheapest method and adopt it.

The market mechanism can also resolve the FOR WHOM question. A market distributes goods to the highest bidder. Individuals who are willing and able to pay the most for a good tend to get it in a pure market economy.

Adam Smith was so impressed with the ability of the market mechanism to answer the basic WHAT, HOW, and FOR WHOM questions that he urged government to "leave it alone" (**laissez faire**). In his view the price signals and responses of the marketplace were likely to do a better job of allocating resources than any government could.

The laissez-faire policy Adam Smith favored has always had its share of critics. Karl Marx emphasized how free markets tend to concentrate wealth and power in the hands of the few, at the expense of the many. As he saw it, unfettered markets permit the capitalists (those who own the machinery and factories) to enrich themselves while the proletariat (the workers) toil long hours for subsistence wages. Marx argued that the government not only had to intervene but had to own all the means of production—the factories, the machinery, the land—in order to avoid savage inequalities. In *Das Kapital* (1867) and the *Communist Manifesto* (1848), he laid the foundation for a communist state in which the government would be the master of economic outcomes.

The British economist John Maynard Keynes seemed to offer a less drastic solution. The market, he conceded, was pretty efficient in organizing production and building better mousetraps. However, individual producers and workers had no control over the broader economy. The cumulative actions of so many economic agents could easily tip the economy in the wrong direction. A completely unregulated market might veer off in one direction and then another as producers all rushed to increase output at the same time or throttled back production in a herdlike manner. The government, Keynes reasoned, could act like a pressure gauge, letting off excess steam or building it up as the economy needed. With the government maintaining overall balance in the economy, the

The Invisible Hand of a Market Economy

market mechanism: The use of market prices and sales to signal desired outputs (or resource allocations).

laissez faire: The doctrine of "leave it alone," of nonintervention by government in the market mechanism.

Government Intervention and Command Economies

CYBER NOTE

For more information on Smith, Malthus, Keynes, and Marx, visit the Federal Reserve Bank of San Francisco at www.frbsf.org/econedu and click on "great economists" under "Publications and Resources."

market could live up to its performance expectations. While assuring a stable, full-employment environment, the government might also be able to redress excessive inequalities. In Keynes' view, government should play an active but not all-inclusive role in managing the economy.

Continuing Debates

These historical views shed perspective on today's political debates. The core of most debates is some variation of the WHAT, HOW, or FOR WHOM questions. Much of the debate is how these questions should be answered. Conservatives favor Adam Smith's laissez-faire approach, while liberals tend to think government intervention is likely to improve the answers. Conservatives resist workplace regulation, affirmative action, and minimum wages because such interventions might impair market efficiency. Liberals argue that such interventions temper the excesses of the market and promote both equity and efficiency.

The debate over how best to manage the economy is not unique to the United States. Countries around the world confront the same choice, between reliance on the market and reliance on the government. Few countries have ever relied exclusively on either one or the other to manage their economy. Even the former Soviet Union, where the government owned all the means of production and central planners dictated how they were to be used, made limited use of free markets. In Cuba the government still manages the economy's resources but encourages farmers' markets and some private trade and investment. In Chile, the market has a much larger role in deciding what is produced, how it is produced, and who gets the resulting output.

The WORLD VIEW below categorizes nations by the extent of their market reliance. Singapore scores high on this "Index of Economic Freedom" because its tax rates are relatively low, the public sector is comparatively small, and there are few restrictions on private investment or trade. By contrast, North Korea scores extremely low because

CYBER NOTE

To learn how the Heritage Foundation defines economic freedom, visit their Website at www.heritage.org.

WORLD VIEW

Index of Economic Freedom

Singapore ranks number 1 among the world's nations in economic freedom. It achieves that status with low tax rates, free-trade policies, minimal government regulation, and secure property rights. These and other economic indicators place Singapore at the top of the Heritage Foundation's 1999 country rankings by the degree of "economic freedom." The "most free" and the "least free" (repressed) economies on the list of 161 countries are:

Greatest Economic Freedom	Least Economic Freedom
Singapore	North Korea
Hong Kong	Cuba
Bahrain	Laos
New Zealand	Libya
Switzerland	Iraq
United States	Somalia
Ireland	Bosnia
Luxembourg	Iran
Taiwan	Congo
	Vietnam

Source: Heritage Foundation, *1999 Index of Economic Freedom,* Washington, D.C., 1999.
www.heritage.org

Analysis: All nations must decide whether to rely on market signals or government directives to determine economic outcomes. Nations that rely the least on government intervention score highest on this Index of Economic Freedom.

the government owns all property, directly allocates resources, sets wages, and limits trade. The country scores are a composite of 10 indicators of government intervention in the marketplace.

The rankings shown in the WORLD VIEW are neither definitive nor stable. In 1989, Russia began a massive transformation from a state-controlled economy to a more market-oriented economy. In the past 10 years China has also greatly expanded the role of private markets. Cuba is moving in the same direction in fits and starts. Hong Kong, on the other hand, has become a bit less free since the 1997 Chinese takeover. And both China and Russia are now "recentralizing" some economic activity.

In the United States, the changes have been less dramatic. The most notable shift was President Franklin Roosevelt's New Deal, which greatly expanded the government's role in the economy. In more recent times, the tug-of-war between laissez faire and government intervention has been much less decisive. Although President Reagan often said that "government *is* the problem," he hardly made a dent in government growth during the 8 years of his presidency. Likewise, President Clinton's very different conviction that the government can *fix* problems, not cause them, had only minor effects on the size and scope of government activity. The intensity of electoral debates reflects the desire of both sides for more decisive change.

A Mixed Economy

Adam Smith's invisible hand and the visible hand of central planning represent two very different ways of making basic economic decisions. As we've observed, no nation relies completely on either mechanism. Instead, ***most economies use a combination of market signals and government directives to select economic outcomes.*** The resulting compromises are called **mixed economies.**

mixed economy: An economy that uses both market signals and government directives to allocate goods and resources.

The reluctance of countries around the world to rely exclusively on either market signals or government directives is due to the recognition that both mechanisms can and do fail on occasion. As we've seen, market signals are capable of answering the three core questions of WHAT, HOW, and FOR WHOM. But the answers may not be the best possible ones.

Market Failure

If the market signals don't give the best possible answers, we say that the market mechanism has *failed.* Specifically, **market failure** means that the invisible hand has failed to achieve the best possible outcomes. If the market fails, we end up with the wrong (*sub*optimal) mix of output, too much unemployment, polluted air, or an inequitable distribution of income.

market failure: An imperfection in the market mechanism that prevents optimal outcomes.

In a market-driven economy, for example, producers will select production methods based on cost. Cost-driven production decisions, however, may lead a factory to spew pollution into the environment rather than to use cleaner but more expensive methods of production. The resulting pollution may be so bad that society ends up worse off as a result of the extra production. In such a case we may need government intervention to force better answers to the WHAT and HOW questions.

We could also let the market decide who gets to consume cigarettes. Anyone who had enough money to buy a pack of cigarettes would then be entitled to smoke. What if, however, children aren't experienced enough to balance the risks of smoking against the pleasures? What if nonsmokers are harmed by second-hand smoke? In this case as well, the market's answer to the FOR WHOM question might not be optimal.

Government Failure

Government intervention may move us closer to our economic goals. If so, the resulting mix of market signals and government directives would be an improvement over a purely market-driven economy. But government intervention may fail as well. **Government failure** occurs when government intervention fails to improve market outcomes or actually makes them worse.

government failure: Government intervention that fails to improve economic outcomes.

The collapse of communism revealed how badly government directives can fail. But government failure also occurs in less spectacular ways. For example, the government may intervene to force an industry to clean up its pollution. The government's directives may impose such high costs that the industry closes factories and lays off workers. Some cutbacks in output might be appropriate, but they could also prove excessive.

WORLD VIEW

Against All Odds, Cuban Small Business Finds a Way

HAVANA—This is the only country in Latin America where the state employs three in four workers; the only one where government agencies plot the nationwide distribution of food; the only one without a convertible currency.

It's a place where, "to resolve the problem of shoes," the president of the "Blas Roca" farm cooperative had to perform a small economic planning feat just to set up a cobbler's shop to service his 300 workers. One is tempted to believe the U.S. State Department's view that Cuba has "resisted any credible effort to adopt market-based policies" since the Soviet bloc vanished.

But it's not that simple. A series of limited economic reforms since 1993 have injected doses of capitalism throughout the Cuban economy.

Microenterprise is now legal. Today over 150,000 Cubans work in an incipient entrepreneurial sector—mainly small restaurants, lunch stands, and service businesses. . . . The entrepreneurs have brought commerce back to Cuban streets, and they have some tangible economic freedom, along with some handicaps that have made the pace of change erratic. . . .

Soviet-style state planning is dying. The Economy and Planning Ministry has seen its workforce reduced by two thirds since 1990. "Everything is changed, except for the building," Vice Minister Alfonso Casanova says in an interview. Where his predecessors once decided the precise amount of each raw material to be allocated to each state enterprise, Mr. Casanova spends his time slashing subsidies. He is interested in financial results, which he monitors online in his office.

— Philip Peters

Analysis: If the government distributes income without regard to work effort, people may not give their best effort. Market-based incomes increase inequality but also motivate higher productivity.

The government might also mandate pollution control technologies that are too expensive or even obsolete. None of this has to happen, but it might. If it does, government failure will have worsened economic outcomes.

The government might also fail if it interferes with the market's answer to the FOR WHOM question. For 30 years, socialist Cuba distributed goods by government directive, not market performance. Incomes were more equal, but uniformly low. To increase output and living standards, Cuba has turned to market incentives (see WORLD VIEW). As workers respond to these incentives, everyone may become better off—even while inequality increases.

Excessive taxes and transfer payments can also worsen economic outcomes. If the government raises taxes on the rich to pay welfare benefits for the poor, neither the rich nor the poor may see much purpose in working. In that case, the attempt to give everybody a "fair" share of the pie might end up shrinking the size of the pie. If that happened, society could end up worse off.

Seeking Balance

None of these failures has to occur, but they might. The challenge for society is to minimize failures by selecting the appropriate balance of market signals and government directives. This isn't an easy task. It requires that we know how markets work and why they sometimes fail. We also need to know what policy options the government has and how and when they might work.

WHAT ECONOMICS IS ALL ABOUT

Understanding how economies function is the basic purpose of studying economics. We seek to know how an economy is organized, how it behaves, and how successfully it achieves its basic objectives. Then, if we're lucky, we can discover better ways of attaining those same objectives.

Economists don't formulate an economy's objectives. Instead, they focus on the *means* available for achieving given *goals.* In 1978, for example, the U.S. Congress identified "full employment" as a major economic goal. Congress then directed future presidents (and their economic advisers) to formulate policies that would enable us to achieve full employment. The economist's job is to help design policies that will best achieve this and other economic goals.

The study of economics is typically divided into two parts: macroeconomics and microeconomics. Macroeconomics focuses on the behavior of an entire economy—the "big picture." In macroeconomics we worry about such national goals as full employment, control of inflation, and economic growth, without worrying about the well-being or behavior of specific individuals or groups. The essential concern of **macroeconomics** is to understand and improve the performance of the economy as a whole.

macroeconomics: The study of aggregate economic behavior, of the economy as a whole.
microeconomics: The study of individual behavior in the economy, of the components of the larger economy.

   Microeconomics is concerned with the details of this "big picture." In microeconomics we focus on the individuals, firms, and government agencies that actually compose the larger economy. Our interest here is in the behavior of individual economic actors. What are their goals? How can they best achieve these goals with their limited resources? How will they respond to various incentives and opportunities?

   A primary concern of macroeconomics, for example, is to determine the impact of aggregate consumer spending on total output, employment, and prices. Very little attention is devoted to the actual content of consumer spending or its determinants. Microeconomics, on the other hand, focuses on the specific expenditure decisions of individual consumers and the forces (tastes, prices, incomes) that influence those decisions.

   The distinction between macro- and microeconomics is a matter of convenience. In reality, macroeconomic outcomes depend on micro behavior, and micro behavior is affected by macro outcomes. One can't fully understand how an economy works until one understands how all the participants behave and why they behave as they do. But just as you can drive a car without knowing how its engine is constructed, you can observe how an economy runs without completely disassembling it. In macroeconomics we observe that the car goes faster when the accelerator is depressed and that it slows when the brake is applied. That's all we need to know in most situations. At times, however, the car breaks down. When it does, we have to know something more about how the pedals work. This leads us into micro studies. How does each part work? Which ones can or should be fixed?

   Our interest in microeconomics is motivated by more than our need to understand how the larger economy works. The "parts" of the economic engine are people. To the extent that we care about the welfare of individuals in society, we have a fundamental interest in microeconomic behavior and outcomes. In this regard, we examine how individual consumers and business firms seek to achieve specific goals in the marketplace. The goals aren't always related to output. Gary Becker won the 1992 Nobel Prize in economics for demonstrating how economic principles also affect decisions to marry, to have children, or to engage in criminal activities.

The distinction between macroeconomics and microeconomics is one of many simplifications we make in studying economic behavior. The economy is much too vast and complex to describe and explain in one course (or one lifetime). Accordingly, we focus on basic relationships, ignoring annoying detail. In so doing, we isolate basic principles of economic behavior and then use those principles to predict economic events and develop economic policies. This means that we formulate theories, or *models,* of economic behavior and then use those theories to evaluate and design economic policy.

   Our model of consumer behavior assumes, for example, that people buy less of a good when its price rises. In reality, however, people *may* buy *more* of a good at increased prices, especially if those high prices create a certain snob appeal or if prices are expected to increase still further. In predicting consumer responses to price increases, we typically ignore such possibilities by *assuming* that the price of the good

ceteris paribus: The assumption of nothing else changing.

in question is the *only* thing that changes. This assumption of "other things remaining equal" (unchanged) (in Latin, ***ceteris paribus***) allows us to make straightforward predictions. If instead we described consumer responses to increased prices in any and all circumstances (allowing everything to change at once), every prediction would be accompanied by a book full of exceptions and qualifications. We'd look more like lawyers than economists.

Although the assumption of *ceteris paribus* makes it easier to formulate economic theory and policy, it also increases the risk of error. If other things do change in significant ways, our predictions (and policies) may fail. But, like weather forecasters, we continue to make predictions, knowing that occasional failure is inevitable. In so doing, we're motivated by the conviction that it's better to be approximately right than to be dead wrong.

Politics. Politicians can't afford to be quite so complacent about economic predictions. Policy decisions must be made every day. And a politician's continued survival may depend on being more than approximately right. George Bush's loss in the 1992 election resulted in part from his repeated predictions that the economy was "turning around." When this optimistic forecast proved wrong, voters lost faith in President Bush's ability to direct the economy.

Even if the future were known, economic policy couldn't rely completely on economic theory. Inevitably, political choices must be made. The choice of more guns or more butter, for example, isn't an economic decision. Rather it's a sociopolitical decision based in part on economic trade-offs (opportunity costs). The "need" for more guns or more butter must be expressed politically—ends versus means again. Political forces are a necessary ingredient in economic policy decisions. That's not to say that all "political" decisions are right. It does suggest, however, that economic policies don't always conform to economic theory.

Imperfect Knowledge. One last word of warning before you read further. Economics claims to be a science, in pursuit of basic truths. We want to understand and explain how the economy works without getting tangled up in subjective value judgments. This may be an impossible task. First, it's not clear where the truth lies. For more than 200 years economists have been arguing about what makes the economy tick. None of the competing theories has performed spectacularly well. Indeed, few economists have successfully predicted major economic events with any consistency. Even annual forecasts of inflation, unemployment, and output are regularly in error. Worse still, never-ending arguments about what caused a major economic event continue long after it occurs. In fact, economists are still arguing over the primary causes of the Great Depression of the 1930s!

In part, this enduring controversy reflects diverse sociopolitical views on the appropriate role of government. Some people think a big public sector is undesirable, even if it improves economic performance. But the controversy has even deeper roots. Major gaps in our understanding of the economy persist. We know how much of the economy works, but not all of it. We're adept at identifying all the forces at work, but not always successful in gauging their relative importance. In point of fact, we may *never* find an absolute truth, because the inner workings of the economy change over time. When economic behavior changes, our theories must be adapted.

In view of all these debates and uncertainties, don't expect to learn everything there is to know about the economy today in this text or course. Our goals are more modest. We want to develop a reasonable perspective on economic behavior, an understanding of basic principles. With this foundation, you should acquire a better view of how the economy works. Daily news reports on economic events should make more sense. Congressional debates on tax and budget policies should take on more meaning. You may even develop some insights that you can apply toward running a business or planning a career, or—if Gary Becker is right—developing a lasting marriage.

CYBER NOTE

Comparative data on the percentage of goods and services the various national governments provide is available from the Penn World Tables at www.acadia.chass.utoronto.ca/pwt.

THE ECONOMY TOMORROW

When asked what they wish for, contestants at beauty contests often reply that they want "world peace," "a cure for AIDS," or the "elimination of poverty." Who could object to these goals? The serious question is how we'll achieve them, with or without the contestants' help.

The same can be said for our economic goals. Everyone wants full employment, low inflation, and a chicken in every pot. But how are we going to attain these goals? Should we rely on Adam Smith's invisible hand to lead us into the glow of the economy tomorrow? Or should the government intervene to be sure we get to the right destination? The decision to intervene or not arises repeatedly, at both the micro and macro levels of the economy.

To Intervene or Not?

The 1998 antitrust suit against Microsoft brought the issue to the forefront of microeconomics. Microsoft has long proclaimed itself the world's premier innovator. So the company was appalled in 1998 when the U.S. Department of Justice accused Microsoft of suppressing innovation and harming consumers. A key issue was whether Microsoft could "bundle" its Internet browser with its Windows operating system. Microsoft asserted that by adding applications features to its operating system, it was offering a superior product. Essentially, Microsoft adopted a version of Adam Smith's argument as its central defense. Microsoft claimed that the *market,* not the *government,* should decide what computer products are produced and by whom. If Microsoft produced inferior products or charged excessive prices, the *market* would punish it with declining sales and profits. Since millions of consumers evidently were willing to buy Microsoft's products, the government should just "leave it alone."

Micro Intervention: The Microsoft Antitrust Case

For updates on the Microsoft case, see www.antitrust.org.

The Justice Department rejected that argument. It conceded that Microsoft produced a lot of good products. But it argued that Microsoft's near monopoly on operating systems gave it too much power to decide WHAT is produced. Even *better* products and prices would be available if more firms were able to compete. Government intervention was needed, the department claimed, to stop Microsoft from destroying potential competitors and restricting choices about WHAT to produce.

The question of whether to intervene or not also arises at the macro level. Consider the level of interest rates as an example. Changes in interest rates affect how much consumers end up paying for big-ticket items such as cars and houses that are financed with loans. High interest rates also raise the cost of your credit card balances and any student loans you might take out. For corporations, the interest rate may be a critical factor in deciding whether to invest in a new factory.

Macro Intervention: Fed Intervention

The market is perfectly capable of determining the rate of interest. But the market's decision may not be consistent with our macro goals. If interest rates are too high, consumer and investor spending may decline, leaving output unsold and workers unemployed. If rates are too low, market participants may go on a spending spree that overheats the economy and causes inflation. Either outcome would represent macro failure.

For more on the Fed's intervention, see www.bog.frb.fed.us.

To avert macro failure, the government regulates credit conditions. Specifically, the Federal Reserve (the central bank) tries to keep interest rates at the right level by regulating bank behavior. This gives the Fed enormous influence on macro outcomes. Ideally, the Fed would always use its regulatory power to improve macro performance. The Fed too fails on occasion, however. Recognizing this, each intervention decision has to be made carefully.

In these and all other cases the issue is always the same: Will government intervention *improve* economic outcomes or *worsen* them? As we observed earlier, both the market and the government may *fail* to move the economy in the right direction. Given these possibilities, the question of whether to intervene or not will be as pressing an issue in the economy tomorrow as it is in the economy today.

No Easy Answers

SUMMARY

- Scarcity is a basic fact of economic life. Factors of production (land, labor, capital, entrepreneurship) are scarce in relation to our desires for goods and services.
- All economic activity entails opportunity costs. Factors of production (resources) used to produce one output cannot simultaneously be used to produce something else. When we choose to produce one thing, we forsake the opportunity to produce some other good or service.
- A production possibilities curve illustrates the limits to production and the opportunity costs associated with different output combinations. It shows the alternative combinations of final goods and services that could be produced in a given period if all available resources and technology were used efficiently.
- The bent shape of the production possibilities curve reflects the law of increasing opportunity costs. This law states that increasing quantities of any good can be obtained only by sacrificing ever-increasing quantities of other goods.
- Inefficient or incomplete use of resources will fail to attain production possibilities. Additional resources or better technologies will expand them. This is the essence of economic growth.

- Every country must decide WHAT to produce, HOW to produce, and FOR WHOM to produce with its limited resources.
- The choices of WHAT, HOW, and FOR WHOM can be made by the market mechanism or by government directives. Most nations are mixed economies, using a combination of these two choice mechanisms.
- Market failure exists when market signals generate suboptimal outcomes. Government failure occurs when government intervention worsens economic outcomes. The challenge for economic theory and policy is to find the mix of market signals and government directives that best fulfills our social and economic goals.
- The study of economics focuses on the broad question of resource allocation. Macroeconomics is concerned with allocating the resources of an entire economy to achieve aggregate economic goals (e.g., full employment). Microeconomics focuses on the behavior and goals of individual market participants.

Key Terms

economics	production possibilities	market failure
scarcity	efficiency	government failure
factors of production	economic growth	macroeconomics
capital	market mechanism	microeconomics
entrepreneurship	laissez faire	*ceteris paribus*
opportunity cost	mixed economy	

Questions for Discussion

1. What opportunity costs did you incur in reading this chapter? If you read four more chapters of this book today, would your opportunity cost (per chapter) increase? Explain.
2. How much time could you spend on homework in a day? How much do you spend? How do you decide?
3. What's the real cost of the food in the free lunch cartoon?
4. Should the government build more shelters for the homeless? Where will it get the resources to do so?
5. How large a "peace dividend" should we create? How should that decision be made?
6. Markets reward individuals according to their output; communism rewards people according to their needs. How might these different systems affect work effort?
7. Why might efficiency increase when a company is "privatized," that is, converted from government ownership to private ownership? Could efficiency decrease?
8. How does government intervention affect college admissions? Who would go to college in a completely private (market) college system?
9. Will the Cuban economy benefit from entrepreneurship and material incentives? (See WORLD VIEW page 16.)
10. Web Activity What is your opportunity cost for attending college? First, estimate your annual college-related expenses, including tuition, books and supplies, and room and board if applicable. Since the major opportunity cost for most college students is forgone earnings, you'll need to find the median annual earnings for

your age group at www.census.gov under "Income." Add that figure to your estimated expenses to find your total opportunity cost for a year of college. Then, to reassure yourself that it's worth it, visit http://nces.ed.gov/pubs/digest97/d970005.html#income.

11. Web Activity Do economists have a sense of humor? Check it out at "Jokes About Economists and Economics" at http://netec.wustl.edu/JokEc.html.

Problems for Chapter 1 appear at the back of the book.

A P P E N D I X

USING GRAPHS

Economists like to draw graphs. In fact, we didn't even make it through the first chapter without a few graphs. This appendix looks more closely at the way graphs are drawn and used. The basic purpose of a graph is to illustrate a relationship between two *variables*. Consider, for example, the relationship between grades and studying. In general, we expect that additional hours of study time will lead to higher grades. Hence we should be able to see a distinct relationship between hours of study time and grade-point average.

Suppose that we actually surveyed all the students taking this course with regard to their study time and grade-point averages. The resulting information can be compiled in a table such as Table A.1.

According to the table, students who don't study at all can expect an F in this course. To get a C, the average student apparently spends 8 hours a week studying. All those who study 16 hours a week end up with an A in the course.

These relationships between grades and studying can also be illustrated on a graph. Indeed, the whole purpose of a graph is to summarize numerical relationships.

We begin to construct a graph by drawing horizontal and vertical boundaries, as in Figure A.1. These boundaries are called the *axes* of the graph. On the vertical axis (often called the Y axis) we measure one of the variables; the other variable is measured on the horizontal axis (the X axis).

In this case, we shall measure the grade-point average on the vertical axis. We start at the *origin* (the intersection of the two axes) and count upward, letting the distance between horizontal lines represent half (0.5) a grade point. Each horizontal line is numbered, up to the maximum grade-point average of 4.0.

The number of hours each week spent doing homework is measured on the horizontal axis. We begin at the origin again, and count to the right. The *scale* (numbering) proceeds in increments of 1 hour, up to 20 hours per week.

Study Time (hours per week)	Grade-Point Average
16	4.0 (A)
14	3.5 (B+)
12	3.0 (B)
10	2.5 (C+)
8	2.0 (C)
6	1.5 (D+)
4	1.0 (D)
2	0.5 (F+)
0	0.0 (F)

TABLE A.1
Hypothetical Relationship of Grades to Study Time

FIGURE A.1

The Relationship of Grades to Study Time

The upward (positive) slope of the curve indicates that additional studying is associated with higher grades. The average student (2.0, or C grade) studies 8 hours per week. This is indicated by point *M* on the graph.

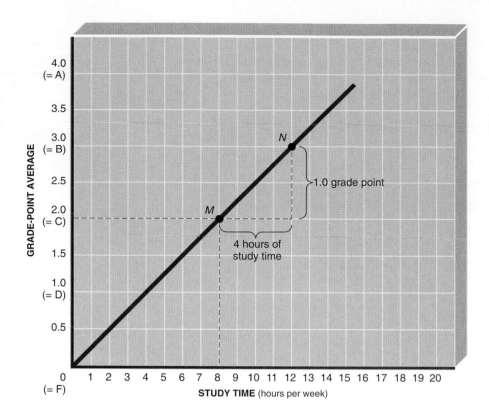

When both axes have been labeled and measured, we can begin illustrating the relationship between study time and grades. Consider the typical student who does 8 hours of homework per week and has a 2.0 (C) grade-point average. We illustrate this relationship by first locating 8 hours on the horizontal axis. We then move up from that point a distance of 2.0 grade points, to point *M*. Point *M* tells us that 8 hours of study time per week is typically associated with a 2.0 grade-point average.

The rest of the information in Table A.1 is drawn (or *plotted*) on the graph the same way. To illustrate the average grade for people who study 12 hours per week, we move upward from the number 12 on the horizontal axis until we reach the height of 3.0 on the vertical axis. At that intersection, we draw another point (point *N*).

Once we've plotted the various points describing the relationship of study time to grades, we may connect them with a line or curve. This line (curve) is our summary. In this case, the line slopes upward to the right—that is, it has a *positive* slope. This slope indicates that more hours of study time are associated with *higher* grades. Were higher grades associated with *less* study time, the curve in Figure A.1 would have a *negative* slope (downward from left to right).

Slopes

The upward slope of Figure A.1 tells us that higher grades are associated with increased amounts of study time. That same curve also tells us *by how much* grades tend to rise with study time. According to point *M* in Figure A.1, the average student studies 8 hours per week and earns a C (2.0 grade-point average). To earn a B (3.0 average), students apparently need to study an average of 12 hours per week (point *N*). Hence an increase of 4 hours of study time per week is associated with a 1-point increase in grade-point average. This relationship between *changes* in study time and *changes* in grade-point average is expressed by the steepness, or *slope,* of the graph.

The slope of any graph is calculated as

$$\text{Slope} = \frac{\text{vertical distance between two points}}{\text{horizontal distance between two points}}$$

In our example, the vertical distance between *M* and *N* represents a change in grade-point average. The horizontal distance between these two points represents the change in study time. Hence the slope of the graph between points *M* and *N* is equal to

$$\text{Slope} = \frac{3.0 \text{ grade} - 2.0 \text{ grade}}{12 \text{ hours} - 8 \text{ hours}} = \frac{1 \text{ grade point}}{4 \text{ hours}}$$

In other words, a 4-hour increase in study time (from 8 to 12 hours) is associated with a 1-point increase in grade-point average (see Figure A.1).

The relationship between grades and studying illustrated in Figure A.1 isn't inevitable. It's simply a graphical illustration of student experiences, as revealed in our hypothetical survey. The relationship between study time and grades could be quite different.

Suppose that the university decided to raise grading standards, making it more difficult to achieve every grade other than an F. To achieve a C, a student now would need to study 12 hours per week, not just 8 (as in Figure A.1). Whereas students could previously expect to get a B by studying 12 hours per week, now they'd have to study 16 hours to get that grade.

Figure A.2 illustrates the new grading standards. Notice that the new curve lies to the right of the earlier curve. We say that the curve has *shifted* to reflect a change in the relationship between study time and grades. Point *R* indicates that 12 hours of study time now "produces" a C, not a B (point *N* on the old curve). Students who now study

Shifts

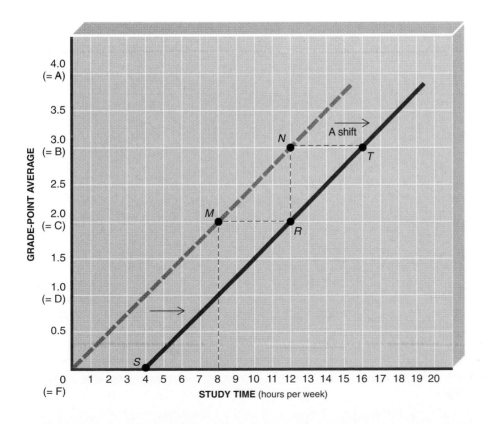

FIGURE A.2
A Shift

When a relationship between two variables changes, the entire curve *shifts*. In this case a tougher grading policy alters the relationship between study time and grades. To get a C, one must now study 12 hours per week (point *R*), not just 8 hours (point *M*).

only 4 hours per week (point *S*) will fail. Under the old grading policy, they could have at least gotten a D. ***When a curve shifts, the underlying relationship between the two variables has changed.***

A shift may also change the slope of the curve. In Figure A.2, the new grading curve is parallel to the old one; it therefore has the same slope. Under either the new grading policy or the old one, a 4-hour increase in study time leads to a 1-point increase in grades. Therefore, the slope of both curves in Figure A.2 is

$$\text{Slope} = \frac{\text{vertical change}}{\text{horizontal change}} = \frac{1}{4}$$

This too may change, however. Figure A.3 illustrates such a possibility. In this case, zero study time still results in an F. But now the payoff for additional studying is reduced. Now it takes 6 hours of study time to get a D (1.0 grade point), not 4 hours as before. Likewise, another 4 hours of study time (to a total of 10) raises the grade by only two-thirds of a point. It takes 6 hours to raise the grade a full point. The slope of the new line is therefore

$$\text{Slope} = \frac{\text{vertical change}}{\text{horizontal change}} = \frac{1}{6}$$

The new curve in Figure A.3 has a smaller slope than the original curve and so lies below it. What all this means is that it now takes a greater effort to *improve* your grade.

Linear vs. Nonlinear Curves

In Figures A.1–A.3 the relationship between grades and studying is represented by a straight line—that is, a *linear curve*. A distinguishing feature of linear curves is that they have the same (constant) slope throughout. In Figure A.1, it appears that *every* 4-hour increase in study time is associated with a 1-point increase in average grades. In Figure A.3, it appears that every 6-hour increase in study time leads to a 1-point increase in grades. But the relationship between studying and grades may not be linear.

FIGURE A.3
A Change in Slope

When a curve shifts, it may change its slope as well. In this case, a new grading policy makes each higher grade more difficult to reach. To raise a C to a B, for example, one must study 6 additional hours (compare points *J* and *K*). Earlier it took only 4 hours to move the grade scale up a full point. The slope of the line has declined from 0.25 (= 1 ÷ 4) to 0.17 (= 1 ÷ 6).

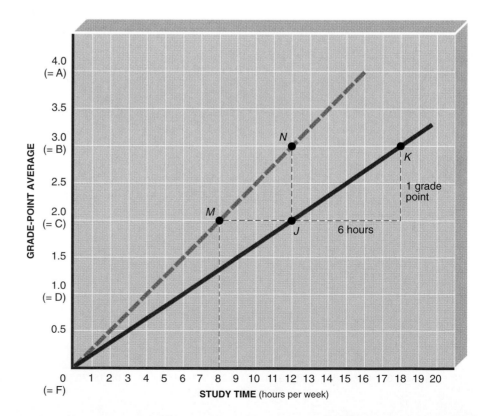

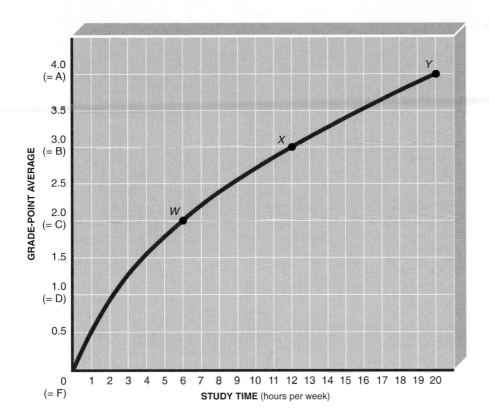

FIGURE A.4
A Nonlinear Relationship

Straight lines have a constant slope, implying a constant relationship between the two variables. But the relationship (and slope) may vary. In this case, it takes 6 extra hours of study to raise a C (point *W*) to a B (point *X*) but 8 extra hours to raise a B to an A (point *Y*). The slope decreases as we move up the curve.

Higher grades may be more difficult to attain. You may be able to raise a C to a B by studying 4 hours more per week. But it may be harder to raise a B to an A. According to Figure A.4, it takes an additional 8 hours of studying to raise a B to an A. Thus the relationship between study time and grades is *nonlinear* in Figure A.4; the slope of the curve changes as study time increases. In this case, the slope decreases as study time increases. Grades continue to improve, but not so fast, as more and more time is devoted to homework. You may know the feeling.

Figure A.4 doesn't by itself guarantee that your grade-point average will rise if you study 4 more hours per week. In fact, the graph drawn in Figure A.4 doesn't prove that additional study ever results in higher grades. The graph is only a summary of empirical observations. It says nothing about cause and effect. It could be that students who study a lot are smarter to begin with. If so, then less able students might not get higher grades if they studied harder. In other words, the *cause* of higher grades is debatable. At best, the empirical relationship summarized in the graph may be used to support a particular theory (e.g., that it pays to study more). Graphs, like tables, charts, and other statistical media, rarely tell their own story; rather, they must be *interpreted* in terms of some underlying theory or expectation.

Causation

2

The U.S. Economy: A Global View

All nations must deal with the central economic questions of WHAT to produce, HOW to produce, and FOR WHOM to produce it. However, the nations of the world approach these issues with vastly different production possibilities. China, Canada, the United States, and Brazil each covers more than *3 million* acres of land. They have far greater production possibilities than Dominica, Tonga, Malta, or Lichtenstein, each of which has less than 500 acres of land. The population of China totals over 1 billion people, 5 times that of the United States, and 25,000 times the population of Greenland. Obviously, these nations confront very different output choices.

In addition to varying production possibilities, the nations of the world use different mechanisms for deciding WHAT, HOW, and FOR WHOM to produce. Belarus, Romania, North Korea, and Cuba still rely heavily on central planning. As we observed in Chapter 1, however, most nations use a mix of market mechanisms and government interventions. This mix varies greatly across nations.

With different production possibilities and mechanisms of choice, economic outcomes also vary widely across nations. This chapter assesses how the U.S. economy stacks up. Specifically,

- WHAT goods and services does the United States produce?
- HOW is that output produced?
- FOR WHOM is the output produced?

In each case, we want to see not only how the United States has answered these questions but also how America's answers compare with those of other nations.

WHAT AMERICA PRODUCES

The United States has less than 5 percent of the world's population and 12 percent of the world's arable land, yet it produces more than 20 percent of the world's output.

GDP Comparisons

The WORLD VIEW shows how total U.S. production compares with other nations. These comparisons are based on the total market value of all the goods and services a nation produces—what we call **gross domestic product (GDP).**

In 1997, the U.S. economy produced about $8 trillion worth of output. The second largest economy, China, produced only half that much. Japan came in third, with about 40 percent of U.S. output. Cuba, by contrast, produced only $1.6

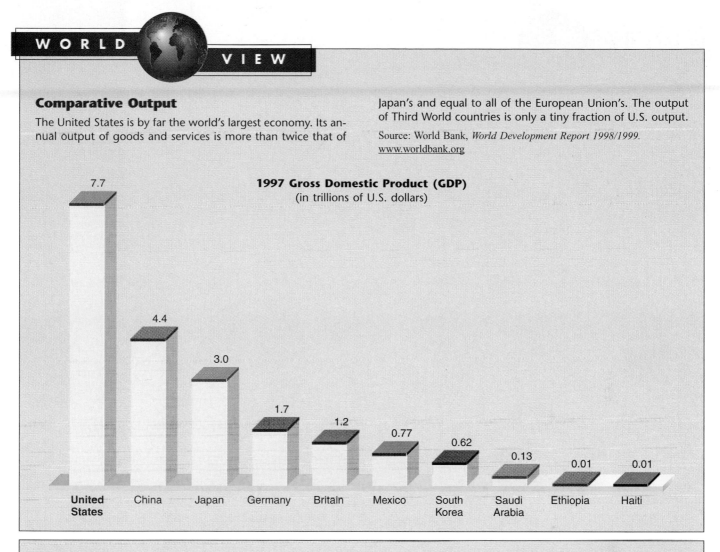

Comparative Output

The United States is by far the world's largest economy. Its annual output of goods and services is more than twice that of Japan's and equal to all of the European Union's. The output of Third World countries is only a tiny fraction of U.S. output.

Source: World Bank, *World Development Report 1998/1999.* www.worldbank.org

1997 Gross Domestic Product (GDP)
(in trillions of U.S. dollars)

United States	China	Japan	Germany	Britain	Mexico	South Korea	Saudi Arabia	Ethiopia	Haiti
7.7	4.4	3.0	1.7	1.2	0.77	0.62	0.13	0.01	0.01

Analysis: The market value of output (GDP) is a basic measure of an economy's size. The U.S. economy is far larger than any other and accounts for nearly one-fourth of the entire world's output.

billion of output, less than the state of South Dakota. Russia, which was once regarded as a superpower, produced only $618 billion, about as much as New York state. The entire 15-member European Union produces less than the United States.

Per Capita GDP. What makes the U.S. share of world output so noteworthy is that with only 5 percent of the world's population, the United States produces far more output *per person* than other countries do. This measure of economic performance is called **per capita GDP.** Per capita GDP is simply total output divided by total population. Per capita GDP tells us how much output is potentially available to the average person. It doesn't tell us how much any specific person gets. ***Per capita GDP is an indicator of how much output the average person would get if all output were divided up evenly among the population.***

In 1997 per capita GDP in the United States was nearly $29,000—more than four times as much as the average in the rest of the world. The following WORLD VIEW provides a global perspective on just how "rich" America is, as measured by the per capita production of goods and services. Some of the country-specific comparisons are

gross domestic product (GDP): The total market value of all final goods and services produced within a nation's borders in a given time period.

per capita GDP: The dollar value of GDP divided by total population; average GDP.

CYBER NOTE

Data on the output of different nations are available from the Central Intelligence Agency at www.odci.gov/cia/publications/factbook.

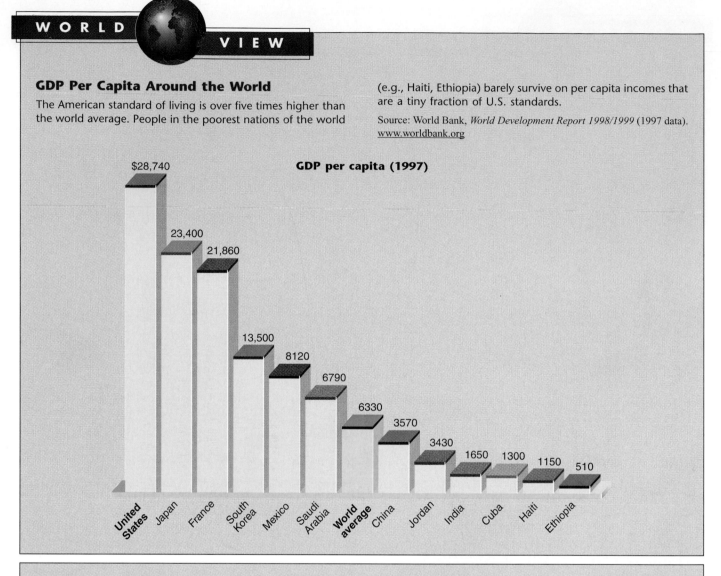

GDP Per Capita Around the World

The American standard of living is over five times higher than the world average. People in the poorest nations of the world (e.g., Haiti, Ethiopia) barely survive on per capita incomes that are a tiny fraction of U.S. standards.

Source: World Bank, *World Development Report 1998/1999* (1997 data). www.worldbank.org

GDP per capita (1997)

Country	GDP per capita
United States	$28,740
Japan	23,400
France	21,860
South Korea	13,500
Mexico	8120
Saudi Arabia	6790
World average	6330
China	3570
Jordan	3430
India	1650
Cuba	1300
Haiti	1150
Ethiopia	510

Analysis: Per capita GDP is a measure of average living standards. Americans have access to far more goods and services than people in other nations do.

startling. China, which has the world's second largest GDP, also contains one-fifth of the world's population. Hence China has a relatively low per capita income. In Ethiopia and Haiti per capita incomes are even lower, at less than $1,200 per year: That's less than $4 per day.

economic growth: An increase in output (real GDP); an expansion of production possibilities.

GDP Growth: The U.S. standard of living today is also much higher than that of earlier generations. During the Great Depression of the 1930s, per capita GDP in the United States was less than a fifth of today's level. Since then, output has increased virtually every year, leading to ever-higher living standards. This track record of **economic growth** is illustrated in Figure 2.1. On average, U.S. output has grown by 3 percent a year while our population has increased by only 1 percent a year. With output growth exceeding population growth, average living standards keep rising. Just a 2-point difference between output and population growth rates implies that per capita GDP will double again in 35 years. If that happens, the next generation will have twice as much output per year as we now enjoy.

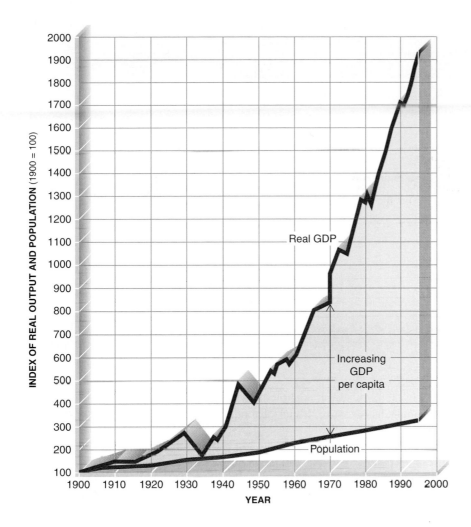

FIGURE 2.1
U.S. Output and Population Growth Since 1900

Over time, the growth of output in the United States has greatly exceeded population growth. As a consequence, GDP per capita has grown tremendously. GDP per capita was five times higher in 1998 than in 1900.

Source: U.S. Department of Labor.

Poor Nations. One reason so much of the world remains poor is that output doesn't always grow as fast as the population. Notice in Table 2.1 the recent experience of Venezuela. Over an 8-year period its output grew by only 1.9 percent a year, while its population grew by 2.2 percent. Hence per capita GDP *declined* with the passage of time. In Haiti—one of the world's poorest nations—per capita GDP declined even faster.

All nations produce two types of output, *goods* (such as cars, HDTVs, potatoes) and *services* (like this economics course, your dentist's work, or a professional baseball game). A century ago, about two-thirds of U.S. output consisted of farm goods (37 percent), manufactured goods (22 percent), and mining (9 percent). Since then, over 25 *million* people have left the farms and sought jobs in other sectors. As a result, today's mix of output is reversed: **Nearly 75 percent of U.S. output consists of services, not goods.** According to the U.S. Bureau of Labor Statistics, that trend is increasing. Over 98 percent of future job growth will be in service-producing industries such as health care, engineering, education, social services, and accounting. This trend will accelerate the change in the mix of output that has been under way for a long time (see Figure 2.2 on the next page).

The *relative* decline in goods production (manufacturing, farming) doesn't mean that we're producing *fewer* goods today than in earlier decades. Quite the contrary. While some industries such as iron and steel have shrunk, others, such as chemicals, publishing, and telecommunications equipment, have grown tremendously. The result is that manufacturing output has increased fourfold since 1950. The same kind of thing

The Mix of Output

TABLE 2.1
Growth Rates in Selected Countries, 1990–1997

Most countries continue to experience economic growth. But the relationship between GDP growth and population growth is very different in rich and poor countries. The populations of rich countries are growing very slowly, and gains in per capita GDP are easily achieved. In the poorest countries, population is still increasing rapidly, making it difficult to raise living standards. Notice how per capita incomes are *declining* in many poor countries (such as Kenya, Venezuela, and Haiti).

	Average Growth Rate (1980–1997) of		
	GDP	Population	Per Capita GDP
High-income countries			
United States	2.5	1.0	1.5
Japan	1.4	0.3	1.1
Canda	2.1	1.2	0.9
France	1.3	0.5	0.8
Low-income countries			
China	11.9	1.1	10.8
India	5.9	1.8	4.1
Haiti	−3.8	2.1	−5.9
Ethiopia	4.5	2.3	−2.2
Kenya	2.0	2.6	−0.6
Venezuela	1.9	2.2	−0.3
Zimbabwe	2.3	2.0	0.3
Nigeria	2.7	2.9	−0.2

Source: World Bank, *World Development Report 1998/1999.*

CYBER NOTE

Data on the mix of output in different nations are compiled in the World Bank's annual World Development Report, available at www.worldbank.org.

Today's Mix of Output

has happened in the farm sector; where output keeps rising even though agriculture's *share* of total output has declined. It's just that output of *services* has increased so much faster.

Development Patterns. The transformation of the United States into a service economy is a reflection of our high incomes. In Ethiopia, where the most urgent concern is still to keep people from starving, over 50 percent of output comes from the farm sector. Poor people don't have enough income to buy dental services, vacations, or even an education, so the mix of output in poor countries is weighted toward goods, not services.

Services have become such a dominant share of the economy's output that we can say that ***America is primarily a service economy and will become increasingly so in the future.*** This generalization doesn't provide much detail, however, about exactly WHAT America produces. What kinds of services are being produced? Which goods?

FIGURE 2.2
The Changing Mix of Output

Two hundred years ago, almost all U.S. output came from farms. Today, 75 percent of output consists of services, not farm or manufactured goods.

Source: U.S. Department of Commerce.

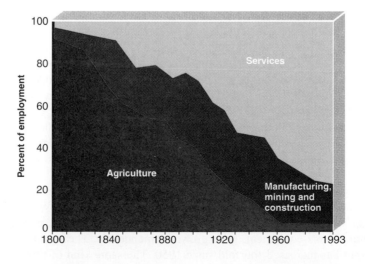

We can develop a clearer picture of our answer to the WHAT question by examining the uses to which our output is put. These uses include the following:

- *Consumption*
- *Investment*
- *Government services*
- *Net exports*

Consumer Goods and Services. Most of America's output consists of consumer goods and services. This output includes everything from breakfast cereals (a good) to movie rentals (a service) and college education (another service)—anything and everything households buy for their own use. As Figure 2.3 illustrates, such consumption goods and services account for over two-thirds of all output.

Investment Goods and Services. Investment goods are a completely different type of output. **Investment** goods are the plant, machinery, equipment, and structures that are produced for the business sector. These investment goods are used to (1) replace worn-out equipment and factories, thus *maintaining* our production possibilities, and (2) increase and improve our stock of capital, thereby *expanding* our production possibilities.

Presently the United States devotes 15 percent of output to investment. The opportunity cost of building more plant and equipment is the extra consumer goods we could have produced instead. There's a payoff, however. New factories, buildings, and machinery allow us to produce *more* of all goods and services in the future.

Poor countries need capital investment desperately. Their incomes are so low, however, that they can't afford to cut back much on consumer goods. When Stalin wanted to make Russia an industrial power, he cut output of consumer goods and forced Russian households to scrape by with meager supplies of food, clothing, and even shelter for decades. Today, most poor nations have to depend on foreign aid and other capital inflows to finance needed investment. Without more investment, they run the risk of continuing stagnation or even a decline of living standards.

Government Services. The third type of output included in GDP is government services. Federal, state, and local governments purchase resources to police the streets, teach classes, write laws, and build highways. The resources the government sector uses

investment: Expenditures on (production of) new plant, equipment, and structures (capital) in a given time period, plus changes in business inventories.

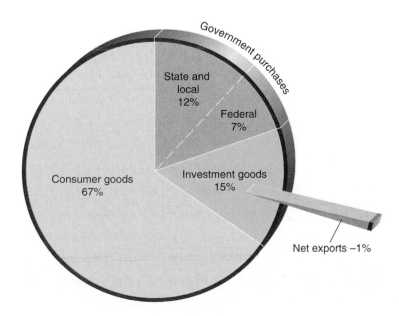

FIGURE 2.3
WHAT America Produces

Two-thirds of America's output consists of consumer goods and services. Investment (such as plant, equipment, buildings) claims about 15 percent of total output. The public sector gets nearly 20 percent. Although we export more than 11 percent of domestic output, we import an even larger share of goods and services; *net* exports are negative.

Source: *Economic Report of the President, 1999.*

income transfers: Payments to individuals for which no current goods or services are exchanged, e.g., Social Security, welfare, unemployment benefits.

for these purposes are unavailable for either consumption or investment. At present, the production of government services absorbs roughly one-fifth of total U.S. output (see Figure 2.3).

Notice the emphasis again on the production of real goods and services. The federal government *spends* over $1.8 trillion every year. Much of that spending, however, is in the form of income transfers, not resource purchases. **Income transfers** are payments to individuals for which no direct service is provided. Social Security benefits, welfare checks, food stamps, and unemployment benefits are all transfer payments. Such transfer payments account for nearly half of all federal spending. This spending is *not* part of our output of goods and services. ***Only that part of federal spending used to acquire resources and produce services is counted in GDP.*** Federal purchases (production) of goods and services account for only 7 percent of total output.

State and local governments are larger providers of public services. What state and local governments lack in size, they make up for in sheer numbers. In addition to the 50 state governments, there are 3000 countries, 18,000 cities, 17,000 townships, 21,000 school districts, and over 20,000 special districts. These are the government entities that build roads; provide schools, police, and firefighters; administer hospitals; and provide social services. The output of all these state and local governments accounts for roughly 12 percent of total GDP.

exports: Goods and services sold to foreign buyers.

imports: Goods and services purchased from international sources.

Net Exports. Finally, we should note that some of the goods and services we produce each year are used abroad rather than at home. In other words, we **export** some of our output to other countries.

International trade isn't a one-way street. While we export some of our own output, we also **import** goods and services from other countries. These imports may be used for consumption (sweaters from New Zealand, Japanese DVDs, travel), investment (German ball bearings, Lloyds of London insurance), or government (French radar screens). Theoretically, imports wouldn't affect the value of GDP since GDP includes only goods and services produced within a nation's borders. In practice, however, estimates of GDP are based on market *purchases,* not surveys of production. As a result, consumption, investment, and government purchases include imports as well as domestically produced goods. To get an accurate reading of *domestic* production, imports must be subtracted out.

net exports: The value of exports minus the value of imports.

Figure 2.4 summarizes America's trade. In 1998 we exported $671 billion worth of goods and another $260 billion of services. These exports amounted to approximately 11 percent of total output. We imported even more goods and services, however, and so ended up with negative **net exports** (a trade deficit).

Comparative Advantage

comparative advantage: The ability of a country to produce a specific good at a lower opportunity cost than its trading partners.

The motivation for this international trade originates in our quest for more output. Most of the goods we import could be produced in the United States. In fact, most imported goods have domestically produced substitutes, for example, cars, computers, and tomatoes. Our decision to import them is not based on our inability to produce them, but on the efficiency of importing them. International trade allows a nation to produce goods in which it has a cost advantage and then trade them for imported goods in which it has a cost disadvantage. This principle of **comparative advantage** entails exporting goods with low opportunity cost and importing goods with high opportunity cost. In other words, international trade allows countries to produce and export what they do best and import goods they don't produce as efficiently.

Although all nations gain from international trade, smaller countries are most in need of specialization. With few resources, a small economy can't produce the whole array of goods and services consumers want. So they need to *specialize*—producing goods they can sell (export) in world markets. Saudi Arabia, for example, exports 40 percent of its total output, mostly in the form of crude oil. It then uses its export earnings to buy desired cars, engineering services, and food that it can't produce efficiently itself.

Exports of goods (in billions)

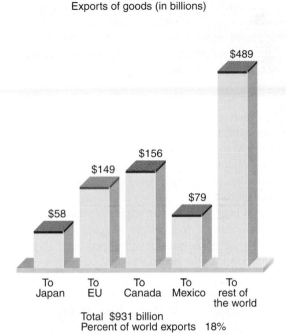

Total $931 billion
Percent of world exports 18%

Imports of goods (in billions)

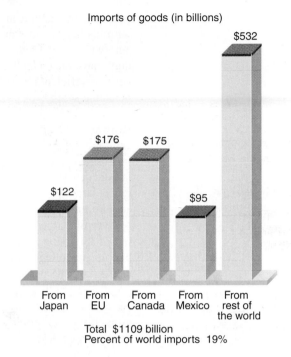

Total $1109 billion
Percent of world imports 19%

FIGURE 2.4
U.S. Exports and Imports

The United States is the world's largest exporter and importer. Over two-thirds of total U.S. trade is with Japan, the European Union, Canada, and Mexico. In 1998, U.S. merchandise (goods) imports exceeded exports by $248 billion. This gap was partially offset by net *service* exports, leaving $169 billion of *net imports* (of goods and services).

HOW AMERICA PRODUCES

All the goods and services included in gross domestic product are produced within the borders of the United States. The production process absorbs not only American-owned **factors of production** but also any foreign-owned land, labor, or capital used to produce goods or services in the United States. A Honda factory in Ohio contributes to America's GDP; a Nike shoe factory in Malaysia doesn't.

One reason the United States is able to produce so much is that it has an abundance of resources. In addition to a labor force of over 135 million people, America also has a huge land area and profuse natural resources. Factors of production alone don't guarantee economic strength, however. China has five times as many people as the United States and equally abundant natural resources. Yet China's annual output is less than half of America's output.

Productivity. In today's economy, the productivity of workers is more important than sheer numbers. **Productivity** refers to the amount of output each worker produces. As a comparison of GDP per capita across nations suggests (see World View, earlier in the chapter), American workers must be among the world's most productive.

Capital Stock. The exceptional productivity of U.S. workers is due in large part to an abundance of capital. America has accumulated a massive stock of capital—over $10 *trillion* worth of machinery, factories, and buildings. As a result of all this prior investment, U.S. production tends to be very **capital-intensive.** The contrast with *labor-*

factors of production: Resource inputs used to produce goods and services, such as land, labor, capital, entrepreneurship.

Factors of Production

productivity: Output per unit of input, such as output per labor-hour.

capital-intensive: Production processes that use a high ratio of capital to labor inputs.

intensive production in poorer countries is striking. A Chinese farmer mostly works with his hands and crude implements, whereas an U.S. farmer works with computers, automated irrigation systems, and mechanized equipment. Russian business managers don't have the computer networks or telecommunications systems that make U.S. business so efficient. In Haiti and Ethiopia, even telephones, indoor plumbing, and dependable sources of power are scarce.

human capital: The knowledge and skills possessed by the workforce.

Human Capital. Indoor plumbing and fiber-optic networks aren't the only kinds of capital a nation can accumulate. **Human capital**—the knowledge and skills workers possess—can also be accumulated. In the Stone Age, one's productive capacity was largely determined by physical strength and endurance. In today's economy, human capital is largely a product of education, training, and experience. Hence, a country can acquire more human capital even without more bodies.

Over time, the United States has invested heavily in human capital. In 1940, only 1 out of 20 young Americans graduated from college; today, over 30 percent of young people are college graduates. High school graduation rates have jumped from 38 percent to over 85 percent in the same time period. In the less developed countries, only 1 out of 3 youth ever *attend* high school, much less graduate (see WORLD VIEW). As a consequence, the United Nations estimates that 1 billion people—a sixth of humanity—will enter the twenty-first century unable to read a book or even write their own names.

The huge output of the United States is thus explained not only by a wealth of resources but by their quality as well. ***The high productivity of the U.S. economy results from using highly educated workers in capital-intensive production processes.***

Factor Mobility. Our continuing ability to produce the goods and the services that consumers demand also depends on our agility in *reallocating* resources from one

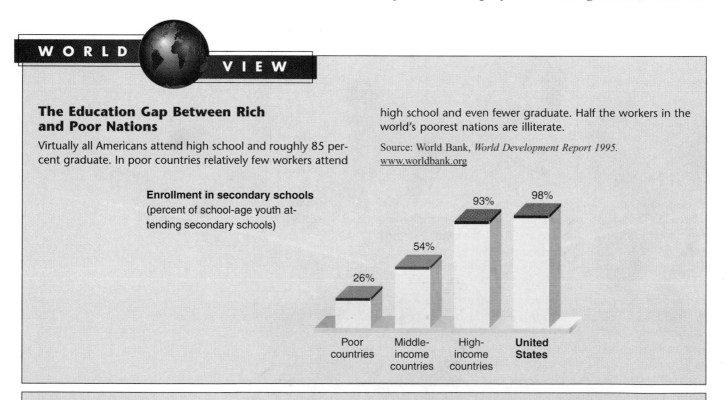

WORLD VIEW

The Education Gap Between Rich and Poor Nations

Virtually all Americans attend high school and roughly 85 percent graduate. In poor countries relatively few workers attend high school and even fewer graduate. Half the workers in the world's poorest nations are illiterate.

Source: World Bank, *World Development Report 1995.*
www.worldbank.org

Enrollment in secondary schools
(percent of school-age youth attending secondary schools)

Poor countries	Middle-income countries	High-income countries	United States
26%	54%	93%	98%

Analysis: The high productivity of the American economy is explained in part by the quality of its labor resources. Workers in poorer, less developed countries get much less education or training.

industry to another. Every year, some industries expand and others contract. Thousands of new firms are created each year and almost as many others disappear. In the process, land, labor, capital, and entrepreneurship move from one industry to another in response to changing demands and technology. In 1975, Federal Express, Compaq Computer, Staples, Oracle, and Amgen didn't even exist. Today these companies employ 200,000 people. These workers came from other firms and industries that weren't growing as fast.

The factors of production released from some industries and acquired by others are organized into productive entities we call *businesses*. A business is an organization that uses the factors of production to produce specific goods or services. Actual production activity takes place in the 20 *million* business firms that participate in the U.S. product markets.

Business Types. Business firms come in all shapes and sizes. A basic distinction is made, however, among three different legal organizations:

- Corporations
- Partnerships
- Proprietorships

The primary distinction among these three business forms lies in their ownership characteristics. A single proprietorship is a firm owned by one individual. A partnership is owned by a small number of individuals. A corporation is typically owned by many individuals—even hundreds of thousands—each of whom owns shares (stock) of the corporation. An important characteristic of corporations is that they, unlike partnerships and proprietorships, have a legal life of their own. Stockholders aren't individually liable for corporate debts or activity. Individuals who own proprietorships and partnerships are not shielded by this "limited liability."

Numbers vs. Size. One consequence of different ownership structures is reflected in the disparate size of proprietorships, partnerships, and corporations. In general, the more people you can get to invest in a firm, the larger the firm's potential size. As a rule, corporations tend to be much larger than the other two forms, partly because their limited-liability feature attracts the financial resources of more individuals. Single proprietorships are typically quite small, because few individuals have vast sources of wealth or credit. The typical proprietorship has less than $10,000 in assets, whereas the average corporation has assets in excess of $1 million. As a result of their size, corporations dominate market transactions, accounting for 90 percent of all business sales (see Figure 2.5 on the next page).

We don't leave the decisions of which goods to produce and how to produce them solely to private businesses. As noted in Chapter 1, America is a "mixed" economy that relies on both market signals and government directives to decide WHAT, HOW, and FOR WHOM. More than 50 federal agencies and thousands of state and local agencies intervene in the market to regulate business behavior.

Providing a Legal Framework. One of the most basic functions of government is to establish and enforce the rules of the game. In some bygone era maybe a person's word was sufficient to guarantee delivery or payment. Businesses today, however, rely more on written contracts. The government gives legitimacy to contracts by establishing the rules for such pacts and by enforcing their provisions. In the absence of contractual rights, few companies would be willing to ship goods without prepayment (in cash). Even the incentive to write textbooks would disappear if government copyright laws didn't forbid unauthorized photocopying. By establishing ownership rights, contract rights, and other rules of the game, the government lays the foundation for market transactions.

Business Organization

Government Regulation

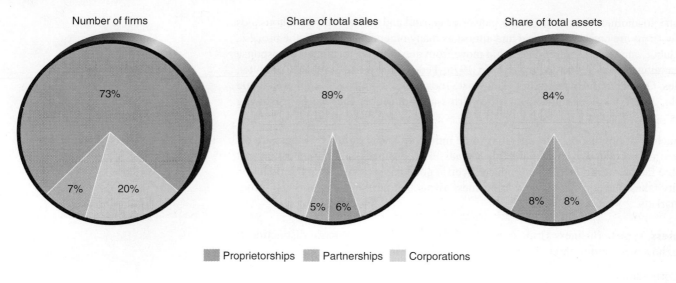

FIGURE 2.5
U.S. Business Firms: Numbers vs. Size

Proprietorships (individually owned companies) are the most common form of U.S. business firm. Corporations are so large, however, that they account for most business sales and assets.

Although only 18 percent of all firms are incorporated, corporations control 90 percent of all sales and 84 percent of all assets.

Source: U.S. Department of Commerce (1997 data).

Protecting the Environment. The government also intervenes in the market to protect the environment. The legal contract system is designed to protect the interests of a buyer and a seller who wish to do business. What if, however, the business they contract for harms third parties? How are the interests of persons who *aren't* party to the contract to be protected?

Numerous examples abound of how unregulated production may harm third parties. Earlier in the century, the steel mills around Pittsburgh blocked out the sun with clouds of sulfurous gases that spewed out of their furnaces. Local residents were harmed every time they inhaled. In the absence of government intervention, such side effects would be common. Decisions on how to produce would be based on costs alone, not on how the environment is affected. However, such **externalities**—spillover costs imposed on the broader community—affect our collective well-being. To reduce the external costs of production, the government limits air, water, and noise pollution and regulates environmental use.

externalities: Costs (or benefits) of a market activity borne by a third party.

Protecting Consumers. The government also uses its power to protect the interests of consumers. One way to do this is to prevent individual business firms from becoming too powerful. In the extreme case, a single firm might have a **monopoly** on the production of a specific good. As the sole producer of that good, a monopolist could dictate the price, the quality, and the quantity of the product. In such a situation, consumers would likely end up with the short end of the stick—paying too much for too little.

monopoly: A firm that produces the entire market supply of a particular good or service.

To protect consumers from monopoly exploitation, the government tries to prevent individual firms from dominating specific markets. Antitrust laws prohibit mergers or acquisitions that would threaten competition. The U.S. Department of Justice and the Federal Trade Commission also regulate pricing practices, advertising claims, and other behavior that might put consumers at an unfair disadvantage in product markets.

Government regulates the safety of many products. Consumers don't have enough expertise to assess the safety of various medicines, for example. If they rely on trial and error to determine drug safety, they might not get a second chance. To avoid this calamity, the government requires rigorous testing of new drugs, food additives, and other products.

Protecting Labor. The government also regulates how our labor resources are used in the production process. In most poor nations, children are forced to start working at very early ages, often for minuscule wages. In the United States, child labor laws and compulsory schooling prevent minor children from being exploited. Government regulations also set standards for workplace safety, minimum wages, fringe benefits, and overtime provisions. After decades of bloody confrontations, the government also established the right of workers to organize and set rules for union-management relations. The introduction of unemployment insurance, Social Security, disability insurance, and guarantees for private pension benefits also protect workers from the vagaries of the marketplace. These social benefits have profoundly affected how much people work, when they retire, and even how long they live.

All these government interventions are designed to change the way resources are used. Such interventions reflect the conviction that the market alone might not select the best possible way of producing goods and services. There's no guarantee, however, that government regulation of HOW goods are produced always makes us better off. Excessive regulation may inhibit production, raise product prices, and limit consumer choices. As noted in Chapter 1, *government* failure might replace *market* failure, leaving us no better off—possibly even worse off. This possibility underscores the importance of striking the right balance between market reliance and government regulation.

Striking a Balance

FOR WHOM AMERICA PRODUCES

As we've seen, America produces a huge quantity of output, using high-quality labor and capital resources, most of which are employed by large corporations. That leaves one basic question unanswered: FOR WHOM is all this output produced?

How many goods and services one gets largely depends on how much income one has to spend. The U.S. economy uses the market mechanism to distribute most goods and services. Those who receive the most income get the most goods. This goes a long way toward explaining why millionaires live in mansions and homeless people seek shelter in abandoned cars. This is the kind of stark inequality that fueled Karl Marx's denunciation of capitalism. Even today, people wonder how some Americans can be so rich while others are so poor.

Table 2.2 summarizes the actual distribution of household incomes in the United States. In this computation, the population is divided into five equally sized quintiles (fifth), ranked by income. Thus, the top **income quintile** includes that fifth of the population with the highest incomes. As Table 2.2 indicates, a household needed at least $71,500 of income to gain entry to the top quintile in 1997. By contrast, households with less than $15,400 of income were at the bottom of the income totem poll. Table 2.2 also

Income Distribution

income quintile: One-fifth of the population, rank-ordered by income (for example, top fifth).

Income Quintile	1997 Income (dollars)	Average Income	Share of Total Income (percent)
Lowest fifth	0–15,400	$ 9,000	3.6
Second fifth	15,400–29,200	$ 22,000	8.8
Third fifth	29,200–46,000	$ 37,000	15.0
Fourth fifth	46,000–71,500	$ 58,000	23.2
Highest fifth	above 71,500	$122,000	49.4

Source: U.S. Department of Commerce, Bureau of the Census (averages rounded to thousands of dollars).

TABLE 2.2
Quintile Distribution of Personal Income

The quintile distribution of income indicates how total income is distributed among income classes. That fifth of our population with the lowest incomes receives less than 4 percent of total income. Households in the highest quintile get nearly half of total income.

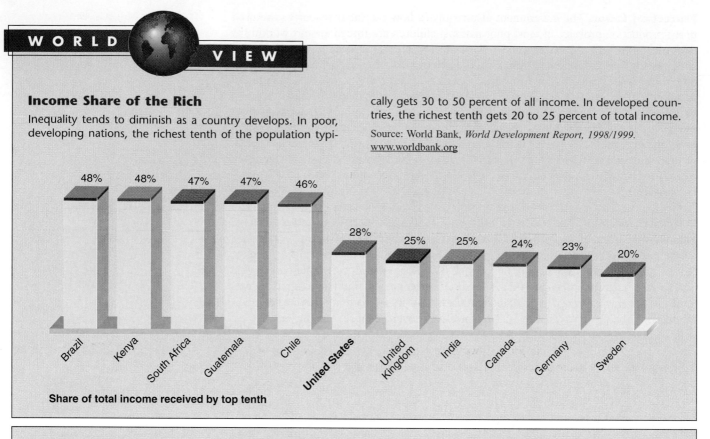

Income Share of the Rich

Inequality tends to diminish as a country develops. In poor, developing nations, the richest tenth of the population typi-cally gets 30 to 50 percent of all income. In developed countries, the richest tenth gets 20 to 25 percent of total income.

Source: World Bank, *World Development Report, 1998/1999.*
www.worldbank.org

Country	Share
Brazil	48%
Kenya	48%
South Africa	47%
Guatemala	47%
Chile	46%
United States	28%
United Kingdom	25%
India	25%
Canada	24%
Germany	23%
Sweden	20%

Share of total income received by top tenth

Analysis: The FOR WHOM question is reflected in the distribution of income. Although the U.S. distribution is very unequal, inequalities loom even larger in most Third World countries.

shows how large a slice of the output pie goes to the rich. **Households in the top quintile end up with nearly half of all household income.** By contrast, people in the bottom quintile get less than 4 percent of all income.

Global Inequality

As unequal as U.S. incomes are, income disparities are actually greater in many other countries. Ironically, income inequalities are often greatest in the poorest countries. In Brazil, Zambia, and Sri Lanka, the richest *tenth* of the population has nearly twice the share of income that the richest 10 percent of Americans have. These and other comparisons of the FOR WHOM resolution are illustrated in the WORLD VIEW above.

Comparisons across countries would manifest even greater inequality. As we saw earlier, Third World GDP per capita is far below U.S. levels. As a consequence, even poor people in the United States receive more goods and services than the average household in most low-income countries.

THE ECONOMY TOMORROW

Levers of Change

Global answers to the basic questions of WHAT, HOW, and FOR WHOM have been shaped by market forces and government intervention. Those answers aren't permanent, however. And the answers haven't always lived up to expectations. People everywhere want changes in the economy of tomorrow—more and better output, a cleaner environment, and less poverty. How will we achieve these goals?

One central concern for the economy tomorrow is how fast incomes will grow. The prosperity that the United States enjoys today is the result of persistent growth in the nation's resources and productivity. In the last decade or so, growth has slowed, however, raising fears of income stagnation. How can we accelerate growth?

Income Stagnation?

Market Signals. Future growth depends on the willingness to allocate scarce resources to investments in human and physical capital. Households in the United States have demanded so many consumer goods and services, however, that relatively few resources have been available for investment. This may change. Aging baby boomers are beginning to worry about retirement and are saving more and spending less. This changed market behavior is sending signals to producers (via lower interest rates and flat consumer sales) that a different mix of output is desired.

Government Directives. If we aren't satisfied with the market's response, we might also try to increase investment and growth with government intervention. Special tax incentives might sweeten the incentives for building new factories or pursuing more research. Subsidized student loans might encourage more human capital investment. The government might also raise taxes (thereby curbing consumption) and use the revenues to improve schools. By changing the market's answer to the WHAT question in these ways, the government might help raise future incomes.

In the quest for faster income growth, we must also pay heed to HOW we produce. Stories about environmental spoilage and habitat destruction are all too familiar. Can we avoid environmental destruction in the economy tomorrow?

Environmental Destruction?

Market Signals. The market itself isn't bent on environmental destruction. On the contrary, advancing technology and rising incomes have made environmental protection both possible and desirable. Few poor countries can afford such luxuries. With increasing affluence, Americans demand not only more pristine environments but also expanded recreational opportunities, which creates market incentives for developing more environmentally sensitive communities. (Would there be so many wild animal parks if consumers weren't willing and able to pay admission?) Rising prices for increasingly scarce resources also create market incentives for conservation, recycling, and new development.

Government Directives. As noted earlier, the market's answers to the HOW question aren't likely to be completely satisfying. Consumers aren't willing to pay voluntarily for auto emissions controls that clean up the air other people breathe. Such controls were available in the market for years, but no one purchased them. The government had to *require* cars to be equipped with smog controls in order to get a better HOW answer. The challenge for tomorrow is to develop a set of government regulations, incentives, and prohibitions that will balance environmental concerns with the continuing quest for material advancement.

How much inequality will we accept in the economy tomorrow? Until now, the FOR WHOM question has been settled quite favorably for the rich. Moreover, it appears that inequalities are widening. What should we do?

Widening Inequality?

Market Signals. The recent surge in inequality is largely due to changing demands for labor. The fastest-growing sectors of the economy have increased the demand for highly educated workers, especially those with advanced technical skills. Rising wages in these fields send a signal to prospective workers that they should stay in school longer and pursue technical training if needed. Rising wages for skilled workers also create a market incentive for employers to offer more training and to reorganize production. Even Michael Jordan's multi-million-dollar paychecks affect human capital decisions. His success motivated thousands of other athletes to work harder, hoping to excel. Likewise, thousands of entrepreneurs are trying to figure out what new toy to create, knowing that consumers reward marketing success with enormous profits. If all incomes were equal, it's unlikely that med students, athletes, entrepreneurs, or the average worker would strive so hard. *Market-driven inequalities are both a reward to productive achievement and an incentive to produce more.* If these market responses emerge, inequalities will diminish.

Government Directives. The market alone may not reduce inequalities quickly or adequately enough, however. The government might have to intervene to break down discriminatory barriers that block access to schools or jobs. Government training subsidies might also give the poor a boost up the economic ladder. The government might also use its tax and transfer policies to force a more even distribution of the nation's income.

The Outlook

The economy tomorrow will look different than the economy today. The mix of output, the methods of production, and the distribution of income change every day. Often the changes occur so slowly that they aren't noticed at first. Like glacier movements, however, the changes can be profound. The farm sector, for example, didn't disappear in a single year. But the exodus of thousands of farmers each year gradually transformed the WHAT, HOW, and FOR WHOM outcomes of the U.S. economy. Those outcomes will continue to change in response to market signals and future decisions about how the government should intervene. The task of economic analysis is to anticipate how the economy will respond to these levers of change.

SUMMARY

- Answers to the core WHAT, HOW, and FOR WHOM questions vary greatly across nations. These differences reflect varying production possibilities, choice mechanisms, and values.
- Gross domestic product (GDP) is the basic measure of how much an economy produces. The United States produces over $8 trillion of output per year, approximately one-fourth of the world's total. The U.S. GDP per capita is five times the world average.
- The high level of U.S. per capita GDP reflects the high productivity of U.S. workers. Abundant capital, education, technology, training, and management all contribute to high productivity.
- Over 75 percent of U.S. output consists of services, including government services. This is a reversal of historical ratios and reflects the relatively high incomes in the United States. Poor nations produce much higher proportions of food and manufactured goods.
- Most of America's output consists of consumer goods and services. Investment goods account for only 15 percent of total output, and government purchases almost 20 percent.

- Proprietorships and partnerships outnumber corporations nearly five to one. Nevertheless, "corporate America" produces nearly 90 percent of total output.
- Incomes are distributed very unequally among households, with households in the highest income class (quintile) receiving over 10 times more income than low-income households. Incomes are even less equally distributed in many poor nations.
- Government intervenes in the economy to improve the market's answers to the WHAT, HOW, and FOR WHOM questions. The risk of government failure spurs debate over the right mix of market reliance and government regulation.
- The mix of output, production methods, and the income distribution continues to change. The WHAT, HOW, and FOR WHOM answers in tomorrow's economy will depend on the interplay of (changing) market signals and (changing) government policy.

Key Terms

gross domestic product (GDP)
per capita GDP
economic growth
investment
income transfers
exports

imports
net exports
comparative advantage
factors of production
productivity
capital intensive

human capital
externalities
monopoly
income quintile

Questions for Discussion

1. Americans already enjoy living standards that far exceed world averages. Do we have enough? Should we even try to produce more?

2. Why is per capita GDP so much higher in the United States than in Mexico?

3. Why do people suggest that the United States needs to devote more output to investment goods? Why not produce just consumption goods?

4. The U.S. farm population has shrunk by over 25 million people since 1900. Where did all the people go? Why did they move?

5. Does the relative decline of manufacturing imply a decline in America's economic strength?

6. How many people are employed by your local or state government? What do they produce? What is the opportunity cost of that output?

7. Why should the government regulate how goods are produced? Can regulation ever be excessive?

8. "Rich" people have over 10 times as much income as "poor" people. Is that fair? How should output be distributed?

9. Do we need more or less government intervention to decide WHAT, HOW, and FOR WHOM? Provide specific examples.

10. Web Activity You can find out which corporations are the world's largest at www.pathfinder.com/fortune/global500/compindex.html. How many of the top 10 are U.S. firms? Compare the latest profits, revenues, assets, and number of employees for two companies. Why might ranking vary for different measures of size?

11. Web Activity The CIA Factbook—www.odci.gov/cia/publications/factbook—provides capsule summaries of country economies. Compare the GDP and GDP/capita for three countries. When would you use GDP to compare these countries? When would you use GDP/capita to compare countries?

Problems for Chapter 2 appear at the back of the book.

3

Supply and Demand

When the Berlin Wall came tumbling down in November 1989, it marked the end of the Cold War and the beginning of the reintegration of Europe. It also provided a quick lesson in the economics of supply and demand. Millions of East Germans flocked to West Berlin to buy goods that weren't available in the East. Electronic toys, radios, cosmetics, tropical fruit, and chocolate were at the top of the shopping list. The East Germans had to pay high prices, but at least they finally had the chance to buy the goods they desired.

West Berliners went on a shopping spree as well. Although fewer goods were available in East Berlin, their prices had been kept low by the East German government, so West Berliners rushed into East Berlin in order to buy boots, sausages, women's lingerie, children's clothes, and Christmas geese. So much merchandise was being carted off to West Berlin that the East German government had to halt sales to the bargain hunters and impose border controls to slow the outflow of available goods.

The cross-border shopping frenzy reflected a basic difference in the way production and prices were established in the two Germanys. West Germany had relied on *decentralized markets* to determine the production and prices of consumer goods: It was a *market economy*. East Germany relied instead on *central planners* to determine which goods to produce and at what prices to sell them: It was a *command economy*. When the Berlin Wall fell, consumers on both sides got a clear view of the differences between market-driven and government-driven economies. People who travel between North and South Korea still see such differences, as do Canadians and the relatively few Americans who visit Cuba. Some goods (e.g., rice, soap, healthcare) look ridiculously cheap in Cuba, while prices of other goods (e.g., cars, televisions) seem prohibitively high.

We can't provide such vivid contrasts between market-driven and government-driven economies in a textbook. We can try, however, to get a clearer view of how markets work. How does the market mechanism decide WHAT to produce, HOW to produce, and FOR WHOM to produce? Specifically:

- What determines the price of a good or service?
- How does the price of a product affect its production or consumption?
- Why do prices and production levels often change?

MARKET PARTICIPANTS

Domestically, over 270 million consumers, about 20 million business firms, and tens of thousands of government agencies participate directly in the U.S. economy. Millions of international buyers and sellers also participate in U.S. markets.

Maximizing Behavior

All these market participants come into the marketplace to satisfy specific goals. Consumers, for example, come with a limited amount of income to spend. Their objective is to buy the most desirable goods and services that their limited budgets will permit. We can't afford *everything* we want, so we must make *choices* about how to spend our scarce dollars. Our goal is to *maximize* the utility (satisfaction) we get from our available incomes.

Businesses also try to maximize in the marketplace. In their case, the quest is for maximum *profits.* Business profits are the difference between sales receipts and total costs. To maximize profits, business firms try to use resources efficiently in producing products that consumers desire.

The public sector also has maximizing goals. The purpose of government is to use available resources to serve public needs. The resources available for this purpose are limited too. Hence local, state, and federal governments must use scarce resources carefully, striving to maximize the general welfare of society. International consumers and producers pursue these same goals when participating in our markets.

Market participants sometimes lose sight of their respective goals. Consumers sometimes buy impulsively and later wish they'd used their income more wisely. Likewise, a producer may take a two-hour lunch, even at the sacrifice of maximum profits. And elected officials sometimes put their personal interests ahead of the public's interest. In all sectors of the economy, however, ***the basic goals of utility maximization, profit maximization, and welfare maximization explain most market activity.***

Specialization and Exchange

The notion that buying and selling goods and services in the market might maximize our well-being originates in two simple observations. First, most of us are incapable of producing everything we desire to consume. Second, even if we *could* produce all our own goods and services, it would still make sense to specialize, producing only one product and trading it for other desired goods and services.

Suppose you were capable of growing your own food, stitching your own clothes, building your own shelter, and even writing your own economics text. Even in this little Utopia, it would still make sense to decide how *best* to expend your limited time and energy and to rely on others to fill in the gaps. If you were *most* proficient at growing food, you would be best off spending your time farming. You could then exchange some of your food output for the clothes, shelter, and books you wanted. In the end, you'd be able to consume *more* goods than if you'd tried to make everything yourself.

Our economic interactions with others are thus necessitated by two constraints:

1. Our absolute inability as individuals to produce all the things we need or desire
2. The limited amount of time, energy, and resources we have for producing those things we could make for ourselves

Together, these constraints lead us to specialize and interact. Most of the interactions that result take place in the market.

THE CIRCULAR FLOW

Figure 3.1 summarizes the kinds of interactions that occur among market participants. Note first that the figure identifies four separate groups of participants. Domestically, the rectangle labeled "Consumers" includes all 270 million consumers in the United States. In the "Business firms" box are grouped all the domestic business enterprises

FIGURE 3.1
The Circular Flow

Business firms supply goods and services to product markets (point **A**) and purchase factors of production in factor markets (**B**). Individual consumers supply factors of production such as their own labor (**C**) and purchase final goods and services (**D**). Federal, state, and local governments acquire resources in factor markets and provide services to both consumers and business (**F**). International participants also take part by supplying imports, purchasing exports (**G**), and buying and selling factors of production (**H**).

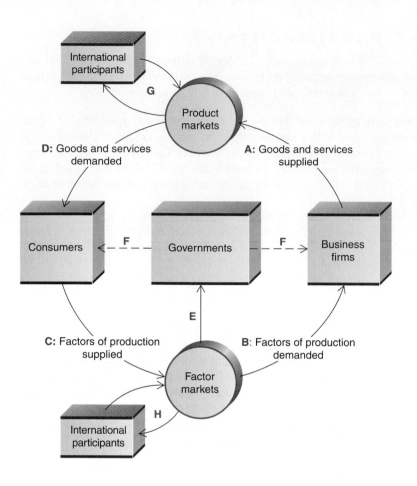

The Two Markets

factor market: Any place where factors of production (e.g., land, labor, capital) are bought and sold.

product market: Any place where finished goods and services (products) are bought and sold.

that buy and sell goods and services. The third participant, "Governments," includes the many separate agencies of the federal government, as well as state and local governments. Figure 3.1 also illustrates the role of global actors.

The easiest way to keep track of all this market activity is to distinguish two basic markets. Figure 3.1 makes this distinction by portraying separate circles for product markets and factor markets. In **factor markets,** factors of production are exchanged. Market participants buy or sell land, labor, or capital that can be used in the production process. When you go looking for work, for example, you're making a factor of production—your labor—available to producers. The producers will hire you—purchase your services in the factor market—if you're offering the skills they need at a price they're willing to pay. The same kind of interaction occurs in factor markets when the government enlists workers into the armed services or when the Japanese buy farmland in Montana.

Interactions within factor markets are only half the story. At the end of a hard day's work, consumers go to the grocery store (or to a virtual store online) to buy desired goods and services—that is, to buy *products.* In this context, consumers again interact with business firms, this time purchasing goods and services those firms have produced. These interactions occur in **product markets.** Foreigners also participate in the product market by supplying goods and services (imports) to the United States and buying some of our output (exports).

The government sector also supplies services. But government services aren't sold in product markets; instead, they're delivered directly to consumers and businesses, usually without any explicit price. This doesn't mean government services are free. There's still an opportunity cost associated with every service the government provides.

Consumers and businesses pay that cost indirectly through taxes, rather than directly through market prices.

In Figure 3.1 the arrow connecting product markets to consumers (point **D**) emphasizes the fact that consumers, by definition, don't supply products. To the extent that individuals produce goods and services, they do so within the government or business sector. For instance, a doctor, a dentist, or an economic consultant functions in two sectors. When selling services in the market, this person is regarded as a "business"; when away from the office, he or she is regarded as a "consumer." This distinction is helpful in emphasizing that *the consumer is the final recipient of all goods and services produced.*

Locating Markets. Although we refer repeatedly to two kinds of markets in this book, it would be a little foolish to go off in search of the product and factor markets. Neither a factor market nor a product market is a single, identifiable structure. The term "market" simply refers to a place or situation where an economic exchange occurs— where a buyer and seller interact. The exchange may take place on the street, in a taxicab, over the phone, by mail, or in cyberspace. In some cases, the market used may in fact be quite distinguishable, as in the case of a retail store, the Chicago Commodity Exchange, or a state employment office. But whatever it looks like, *a market exists wherever and whenever an exchange takes place.*

Figure 3.1 provides a useful summary of market activities, but it neglects one critical element of market interactions: dollars. Each arrow in the figure actually has two dimensions. Consider again the arrow linking consumers and product markets: It's drawn in only one direction because consumers, by definition, don't provide goods and services directly to product markets. But they do provide something: dollars. If you want to obtain something from a product market, you must offer to pay for it (typically, with cash, check, or credit card). Consumers exchange dollars for goods and services in product markets.

The same kinds of exchange occur in factor markets. When you go to work, you exchange a factor of production (your labor) for income, typically a paycheck. Here again, the path connecting consumers to factor markets really goes in two directions: one of real resources, the other of dollars. Consumers receive wages, rent, and interest for the labor, land, and capital they bring to the factor markets. Indeed, nearly *every market transaction involves an exchange of dollars for goods (in product markets) or resources (in factor markets).* Money is thus critical in facilitating market exchanges and the specialization the exchanges permit.

The two sides of each market transaction are called **supply** and **demand.** As noted earlier, we *supply* resources to the market when we look for a job—that is, when we offer our labor in exchange for income. We *demand* goods when we shop in a supermarket—that is, when we're prepared to offer dollars in exchange for something to eat. Business firms may *supply* goods and services in product markets at the same time they're *demanding* factors of production in factor markets. Whether one is on the supply side or the demand side of any particular market transaction depends on the nature of the exchange, not on the people or institutions involved.

DEMAND

Although the concepts of supply and demand help explain what's happening in the marketplace, we aren't yet ready to summarize the countless transactions that occur daily in both factor and product markets. Recall that *every market transaction involves an exchange and thus some elements of both supply and demand.* Then just consider how many exchanges you and several billion other consumers undertake in a single week. To keep track of so much action, we need to summarize the activities of many individuals.

Dollars and Exchange

Supply and Demand

supply: The ability and willingness to sell (produce) specific quantities of a good at alternative prices in a given time period, *ceteris paribus.*

demand: The ability and willingness to buy specific quantities of a good at alternative prices in a given time period, *ceteris paribus.*

Individual Demand

We can begin to understand how market forces work by looking more closely at the behavior of a single market participant. Let's start with Tom, a sophomore at Clearview College. Tom is currently experiencing the torment of writing a paper for his English composition class. To make matters worse, Tom's professor has insisted on typed papers, and Tom can't propel a keyboard with his fingers much better than he can push a pencil with his toes. Even the simplest word processing packages are too complex for him. Under the circumstances, Tom is desperate for a typist.

Although it's apparent that Tom has a strong desire for a typist, his demand for typing services isn't yet evident. ***A demand exists only if someone is willing and able to pay for a good***—that is, exchange dollars for a good or service in the marketplace.

Suppose Tom has some income and is willing to spend some of it to get his English paper typed. Under these assumptions, we can claim that Tom is a participant in the *market* for typing services. He's willing and able to pay.

But *how much* is he willing to pay? Surely Tom isn't prepared to exchange *all* his income for the typing of a single English paper. After all, Tom *could* use his income to buy more desirable goods and services; to give up everything for the typing of just one paper would imply an extremely high **opportunity cost.** There must be *limits* to the amount Tom is willing to pay for any given quantity of typing. These limits will be determined by how much income Tom has to spend and how many other goods and services he must forsake in order to pay for typing services. If the price of typing exceeds these limits, Tom may end up typing all or part of the paper himself.

We assume, then, that when Tom starts looking for a typist, he has in mind some sort of **demand schedule** like the one described in Figure 3.2. According to row *A* of this schedule, Tom is willing and able to buy only 1 page of typing per semester if he must pay $5 per page. At such an outrageous price, he'll have only the first page of his paper typed professionally and will peck out or print the remaining pages himself. That way, the paper will make a good first impression, and Tom won't have to sacrifice so many other goods and services for his paper.

At lower prices, Tom would behave differently. According to Figure 3.2, Tom would want more pages typed if the price of typing were less. We see from row *I* of the demand schedule that Tom is willing to have 20 pages—an entire paper—typed professionally if the price per page is as low as $1.

Notice that the demand schedule doesn't tell us anything about *why* this consumer is willing to pay specific prices for various amounts of typing. Tom's expressed willingness to pay for typing services may reflect a desperate need to finish his paper, a lot of income to spend, or a relatively small desire for other goods and services. All the demand schedule tells us is what the consumer is *willing and able* to buy, for whatever reasons.

Also observe that the demand schedule doesn't tell us how many pages of typing the consumer will *actually* buy. Figure 3.2 simply states that Tom is *willing and able* to pay for 1 page of typing per semester at $5.00 per page, for 2 pages at $4.50 each, and so on. How much typing he purchases will depend on the actual price of typing services in the market. Until we know that price, we can't tell how much typing will be purchased. Hence ***"demand" is an expression of consumer buying intentions—an offer to buy—not a statement of actual purchases.***

The **demand curve** provides a convenient summary of buying intentions; it's a graphical illustration of the demand schedule. The demand curve in Figure 3.2 tells us again that this consumer is willing to pay for only 1 page of professional typing per semester if the price is $5.00 per page (point *A*), for 2 pages if the price is $4.50 (point *B*), for 3 pages at $4.00 a page (point *C*), and so on. Once we know what the market price of typing actually is, a quick look at the demand curve tells us how much typing this consumer will buy.

A common feature of any demand curve is its downward slope. As the price of a good falls, people tend to purchase more of it. In Figure 3.2 the quantity of typing demanded increases (moves rightward along the horizontal axis) as the price per page decreases (moves down the vertical axis). This inverse relationship between price and quantity is so common that we refer to it as the **law of demand.**

opportunity cost: The most desired goods or services that are forgone in order to obtain something else.

demand schedule: A table showing the quantities of a good a consumer is willing and able to buy at alternative prices in a given time period, *ceteris paribus.*

demand curve: A curve describing the quantities of a good a consumer is willing and able to buy at alternative prices in a given time period, *ceteris paribus.*

law of demand: The quantity of a good demanded in a given time period increases as its price falls, *ceteris paribus.*

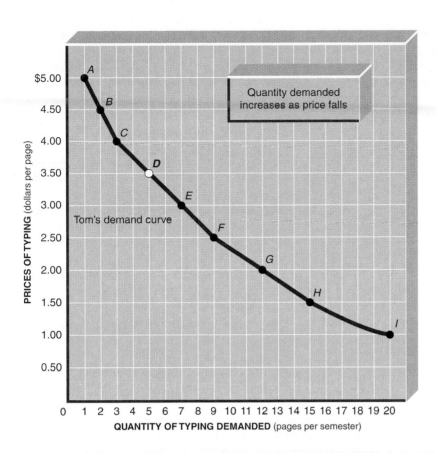

FIGURE 3.2
A Demand Schedule and Curve

A demand schedule indicates the quantities of a good consumers are able and willing to buy at alternative prices (*ceteris paribus*). The demand schedule (*below*) indicates that Tom would buy 5 pages of typing per semester if the price of typing were $3.50 per page (row *D*). If typing were less expensive (rows *E–I*), Tom would purchase a larger quantity.

A demand curve is a graphical illustration of a demand schedule. Each point on the curve refers to a specific quantity that will be demanded at a given price. If, for example, the price of typing were $3.50 per page, this curve tells us the consumer would purchase 5 pages per semester (point *D*). If typing cost $3 per page, 7 pages per semester would be demanded (point *E*). Each point on the curve corresponds to a row in the schedule.

	Tom's Demand Schedule	
	Price of Typing (per page)	Quantity of Typing Demanded (pages per semester)
A	$5.00	1
B	4.50	2
C	4.00	3
D	3.50	5
E	3.00	7
F	2.50	9
G	2.00	12
H	1.50	15
I	1.00	20

The demand curve in Figure 3.2 has only two dimensions: quantity demanded (on the horizontal axis) and price (on the vertical axis). This seems to imply that the amount of typing demanded depends only on the price of typing; but surely this isn't the case. A consumer's willingness and ability to buy a product at various prices depend on a variety of forces. ***Determinants of market demand include***

- ***Tastes*** (desire for this and other goods)
- ***Income*** (of the consumer)
- ***Other goods*** (their availability and price)
- ***Expectations*** (for income, prices, tastes)
- ***Number of buyers***

Tom's "taste" for typing has nothing to do with taste buds. "Taste" is just another word for desire. In this case Tom's taste for typing is clearly acquired from his English

Determinants of Demand

substitute goods: Goods that substitute for each other; when the price of good *x* rises, the demand for good *y* increases, *ceteris paribus.*

complementary goods: Goods frequently consumed in combination; when the price of good *x* rises, the demand for good *y* falls, *ceteris paribus.*

professor, who requires typed papers. If all professors required typed papers, Tom's "taste" for typing would be even greater.

We also noted that Tom's ability to buy typing services is limited by his income. The amount of income available affects the price a consumer is able to pay. If Tom had no income to spend, he wouldn't be a participant in the typing market.

Other goods also affect the demand for typng. Their effect depends on whether they're *substitute* goods or *complementary* goods. A **substitute good** is one that might be purchased instead of typing. In Tom's simple world, pizza is a substitute for typing services. If the price of pizza fell, Tom would buy more pizzas and cut back on his purchases of typing services. When the price of a substitute good falls, the demand for typing declines.

A **complementary good** is one that's typically consumed with, rather than instead of, typing services. If textbook prices or tuition increases, Tom might take fewer classes and demand *less* typing. In this case, a price increase for a complementary good causes the demand for typing to decline.

Expectations also play a role in consumer decisions. If Tom expected to flunk English anyway, he probably wouldn't waste any money getting his paper typed; his demand for typing would disappear. On the other hand, if he expects a typed composition to determine his college fate, he might be more willing to buy typing services.

Ceteris Paribus

ceteris paribus: The assumption of nothing else changing.

If demand is in fact such a multidimensional decision, how can we reduce it to only the two dimensions of price and quantity? In Chapter 1 we first encountered this *ceteris paribus* trick. To simplify their models of the world, economists focus on only one or two forces at a time and *assume* nothing else changes. We know a consumer's tastes, income, other goods, and expectations all affect the decision to buy typing services. But we want to focus on the relationship between quantity demanded and price. That is, we want to know what *independent* influence price has on consumption decisions. To find out, we must isolate that one influence, price, and assume that the determinants of demand remain unchanged.

The *ceteris paribus* assumption is not as farfetched as it may seem. People's tastes, income, and expectations do not change quickly. Also, the prices and availability of other goods don't change all that fast. Hence a change in the *price* of a product may be the only factor that prompts a change in quantity demanded.

The ability to predict consumer responses to a price change is important. What would happen, for example, to enrollment at your school if tuition doubled? Must we guess? Or can we use demand curves to predict how the quantity of applications will change as the price of college goes up? ***Demand curves show us how changes in market prices alter consumer behavior.*** We used the demand curve in Figure 3.2 to predict how the appearance of Tom's English papers would change at different typing prices.

Shifts in Demand

shift in demand: A change in the quantity demanded at any (every) given price.

Although demand curves are useful in predicting consumer responses to market signals, they aren't infallible. The problem is that ***the determinants of demand can and do change.*** When they do, a specific demand curve may become obsolete. A ***demand curve (schedule) is valid only so long as the underlying determinants of demand remain constant.*** If the *ceteris paribus* assumption is violated—if tastes, income, other goods, or expectations change—the ability or willingness to buy will change. When this happens, the demand curve will **shift** to a new position.

Suppose, for example, that Tom won the state lottery. This increase in his income would greatly increase his ability to pay for typing services. Figure 3.3 shows the effect of this windfall on Tom's demand for typing. The old demand curve, D_1, is no longer relevant. Tom's lottery winnings enable him to buy more pages at any price, as illustrated by the new demand curve, D_2. According to this new curve, lucky Tom is now willing and able to buy 12 pages per semester at the price of $3.50 per page (point d_2). This is a large increase in demand; previously (before winning the lottery) he demanded only 5 pages at that price (point d_1).

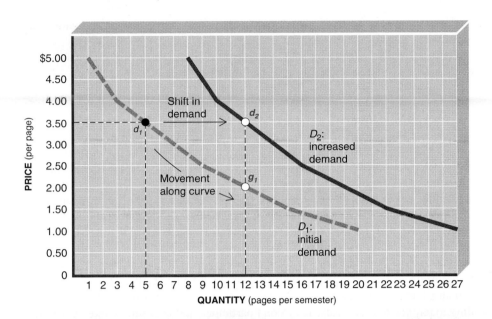

FIGURE 3.3
Shifts vs. Movements

A demand curve shows how a consumer responds to price changes. If the determinants of demand stay constant, the response is a *movement* along the curve to a new quantity demanded. In this case, the quantity demanded increases from 5 (point d_1), to 12 (point g_1), if price falls from $3.50 to $2.00.

If the determinants of demand change, the entire demand curve *shifts*. In this case, an increase in income increases demand. With more income, Tom is willing to buy 12 pages even at the initial price of $3.50 (point d_2).

		Quantity Demanded	
	Price (per page)	Initial Demand	After Increase in Income
A	$5.00	1	8
B	4.50	2	9
C	4.00	3	10
D	3.50	5	12
E	3.00	7	14
F	2.50	9	16
G	2.00	12	19
H	1.50	15	22
I	1.00	20	27

With his higher income, Tom can buy more typing at every price. Thus ***the entire demand curve shifts to the right when income goes up.*** Figure 3.3 illustrates both the old (prelottery) and the new (postlottery) demand curves.

Income is only one of the basic determinants of demand. Changes in any of the other determinants of demand would also cause the demand curve to shift. Tom's taste for typing might increase dramatically, for example, if his parents promised to buy him a new car for passing English composition. In that case, he might be willing to forgo other goods and spend more of his income on typing. ***An increase in taste (desire) also shifts the demand curve to the right.***

Pizza and Politics. A similar demand shift occurs at the White House when a political crisis erupts. On an average day, White House staffers order about $180 of pizzas from the nearby Domino's. When a crisis hits, however, staffers work well into the night and their demand for pizza soars. During the 1998 impeachment hearings, White House staffers ordered more than $1000 of pizza per day!

It's important to distinguish shifts of the demand curve from movements along the demand curve. ***Movements along a demand curve are a response to price changes for that good.*** Such movements assume that determinants of demand are unchanged. By contrast, ***shifts of the demand curve occur when the determinants of demand change.***

Movements vs. Shifts

Market Demand

market demand: The total quantities of a good or service people are willing and able to buy at alternative prices in a given time period; the sum of individual demands.

When tastes, income, other goods, or expectations are altered, the basic relationship between price and quantity demanded is changed (shifts).

For convenience, movements along a demand curve and shifts of the demand curve have their own labels. Specifically, take care to distinguish:

- *Changes in quantity demanded:* movements along a given demand curve, in response to price changes of that good
- *Changes in demand:* shifts of the demand curve due to changes in tastes, income, other goods, or expectations

Tom's behavior in the typing market will change if either the price of typing changes (a movement) or the underlying determinants of his demand for typing are altered (a shift). Notice in Figure 3.3 that he ends up buying 12 pages of typing if either the price of typing falls or his income increases. Demand curves help us predict those market responses.

Whatever we say about demand for typing services on the part of one harassed English major we can also say about every student at Clearview College (or, for that matter, about all consumers). Some students have no need for professional typing and aren't willing to pay for such services: They don't participate in the typing market. Other students want such services but don't have enough income to pay for them: They too are excluded from the typing market. A large number of students, however, not only have a need (or desire) for typing services but also are willing and able to purchase such services.

What we start with in product markets, then, is many individual demand curves. Fortunately, it's possible to combine all the individual demand curves into a single **market demand.** The aggregation process is no more difficult than simple arithmetic. Suppose you'd be willing to buy 1 page of typing per semester at a price of $8.00 per page. George, who is desperate to make his English essays at least *look* good, would buy 2 at that price; and I would buy none, since I only grade papers and don't have to type the grades. What would our combined (market) demand for typing services be at that price? Together we'd be willing to buy a total of 3 pages of typing per semester if the price were $8.00 per page. Our combined willingness to buy—our collective market demand—is nothing more than the sum of our individual demand schedules. The same kind of aggregation can be performed for all consumers, leading to a summary of the total market demand for typing services at Clearview College. This *market demand is determined by the number of potential buyers and their respective tastes, incomes, other goods, and expectations.*

What's nice about the market demand concept is that it permits us to ignore some idiosyncrasies of our friends and neighbors. With thousands of students at Clearview College, the typing market is large. Accordingly, we don't have to consider whether George's roommate will move out if George starts doing his own typing or whether you'll buy more typing if you win the state lottery. The market demand for typing services will be little affected by these great moments in your life. In so large a market, the demand for typing services tends to be more stable and predictable than the demands of the separate individuals who participate in that market.

The Market Demand Curve. Figure 3.4 illustrates a typing services market with four potential participants. Notice the very different demand of the four individuals. Tom has to turn in several papers each semester, has a good income, and is willing to purchase typing services. Column 1 of the schedule in Figure 3.4 shows Tom's demand schedule (this schedule is identical to the one we examined in Figure 3.2). George, as we already noted, is desperate to improve the appearance of his papers and is willing to pay relatively high prices for typing services. His demand schedule is summarized in column 2 under Quantity Demanded. The third consumer in this market is Lisa, who

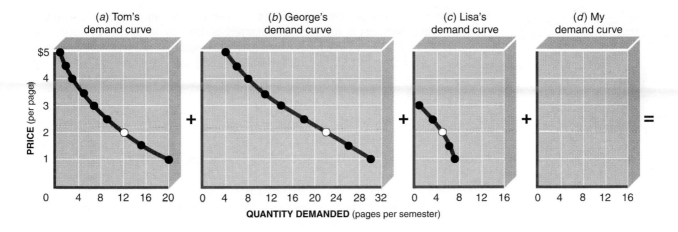

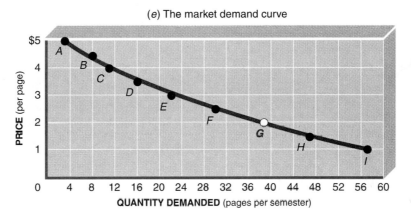

FIGURE 3.4
Construction of the Market Demand Curve

Market demand represents the combined demands of all market participants. To determine the total quantity of typing demanded at any given price, we add the separate demands of the individual consumers. Row *G* of this schedule indicates that a *total* quantity of 39 pages per semester will be demanded at a price of $2.00 per page. This same conclusion is reached by adding the individual demand curves, leading to point *G* on the market demand curve.

	Price (per page)	Tom	+	George	+	Lisa	+	Me	=	Market Demand
A	$5.00	1		4		0		0		5
B	4.50	2		6		0		0		8
C	4.00	3		8		0		0		11
D	3.50	5		11		0		0		16
E	3.00	7		14		1		0		22
F	2.50	9		18		3		0		30
G	2.00	12		22		5		0		39
H	1.50	15		26		6		0		47
I	1.00	20		30		7		0		57

has a very limited budget and can do her own typing if she must; she isn't willing to buy any typing services at higher prices. As prices drop below $3.50 per page, however, her demand schedule indicates that she will get some of her work professionally typed. Finally, there is my demand schedule (column 4 under Quantity Demanded), which confirms that I really don't participate in the local typing market.

The differing personalities and consumption habits of Tom, George, Lisa, and me are expressed in our individual demand schedules and associated curves in Figure 3.4. To determine the *market* demand for typing services from this information, we simply add these four separate demands. The end result of this aggregation is, first, a *market* demand schedule and, second, the resultant *market* demand curve. These market summaries describe the various quantities of typing that Clearview College students are *willing and able* to purchase each semester at various prices.

How much typing will be purchased each semester? Knowing how much typing Tom, George, Lisa, and I are willing to buy at various prices doesn't tell you how much we're actually going to purchase. To determine the actual consumption of typing services, we have to know something about prices and supplies. What's the price of typing in this market, and how is it determined?

SUPPLY

market supply: The total quantities of a good that sellers are willing and able to sell at alternative prices in a given time period, *ceteris paribus*.

To understand how the price of typing services is established, we have to look also at the other side of the market: the supply side. We need to know how many pages of typing people are willing and able to *sell* at various prices, that is, the **market supply.** As on the demand side, the *market supply* depends on the behavior of all the individuals willing and able to supply typing services at some price. Some of those individuals are represented in the accompanying NEWS feature.

Individual Suppliers

As we approach the supply side of the market, we should recognize up front that no one types for the fun of it. Typing entails the use of scarce time. It also requires one to buy or rent word processing equipment. Then there are the minor costs of paper, printer cartridges, and such. All these inputs entail opportunity costs. Anyone who offers typing services will at least want to be compensated for these factor costs.

Technology also affects supply decisions. If the only typing equipment available is an old standard with sticky keys, an individual may be loath to offer typing services. On the other hand, a computer with state-of-the-art word processing software makes the job a lot easier. When more advanced technology is available, individuals will be more willing and able to type.

Potential typists will also consider alternative ways to earn some income. If babysitting jobs are plentiful and well paid, individuals may prefer to babysit rather than type.

IN THE NEWS

Typing Services

PROFESSIONAL TYPING COMPANY. Dissertations, theses, manuscripts. $2/page. Campus pickup. Jane Davis, 840-8854.
PROF. TYPING—$1.50 per page, exp. Zena 589-2419.

TYPING. Computer-scripted dissertations, texts, papers. Perfect. $2 per page. Anita 686-2479.
TYPING. 24-hour service (4 typists) Masters theses, term papers, etc. Professionally typed and corrected. 653-2880.

Analysis: Supply is the offer to sell (produce) goods or services at specific prices. Market supply is the sum of all individual supplier offers.

On the other hand, if other jobs are scarce, more people may feel compelled to offer typing services to get a little extra income.

Expectations also play a role. If you expect word processing jobs to give you an entry into more desirable job settings, you may want to develop typing skills. If you expect to run out of money before the semester ends, you may also be more willing to offer typing services now.

All these considerations—factor costs, technology, expectations—affect the decision to offer typing services, and at what price. In general, we assume that typists will be willing to churn out more typing if the per-page price is high and less if the price is low. In other words, there is a **law of supply** that parallels the law of demand. On the supply side the law says that *larger quantities will be offered for sale at higher prices.* Here again, the laws rest on the *ceteris paribus* assumption: The quantity supplied increases at higher prices *if* the determinants of supply are constant. **Supply curves are upward-sloping to the right,** as in Figure 3.5. Note how the *quantity supplied* jumps from 39 pages (point *d*) to 130 pages (point *h*) when the price of typing doubles (from $2.00 to $4.00 per page).

Figure 3.5 also illustrates how market supply is constructed from the supply decisions of individual sellers. In this case, only three typists are available. Ann is willing to do a lot of typing at low prices, whereas Bob requires at least $2.00 a page. Cory won't touch the keyboard for less than $4.00 a page.

By adding the quantity each typist is willing to offer at every price, we can construct the market supply curve. Notice in Figure 3.5, for example, how the quantity supplied to the market at $4.50 (point *i*) comes from the individual efforts of Ann (93 pages),

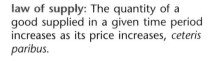

law of supply: The quantity of a good supplied in a given time period increases as its price increases, *ceteris paribus*.

Market Supply

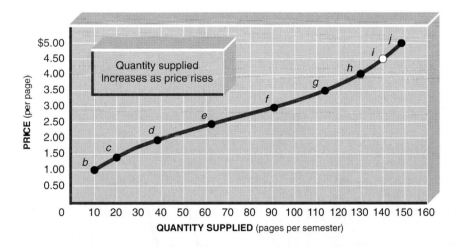

Price	Quantity Supplied By			
(per page)	Ann +	Bob +	Cory =	Market
j $5.00	94	35	19	148
i 4.50	93	33	14	140
h 4.00	90	30	10	130
g 3.50	86	28	0	114
f 3.00	78	12	0	90
e 2.50	53	9	0	62
d 2.00	32	7	0	39
c 1.50	20	0	0	20
b 1.00	10	0	0	10

FIGURE 3.5
Market Supply

The market supply curve indicates the *combined* sales intentions of all market participants. If the price of typing were $4.50 per page (point *i*), the *total* quantity of typing supplied would be 140 pages per semester. This quantity is determined by adding the supply decisions of all individual producers. In this case, Ann supplies 93 pages, Bob supplies 33, and Cory supplies the rest.

Bob (33 pages), and Cory (14 pages). *The market supply curve is just a summary of the supply intentions of all producers.*

Whatever influences the supply decisions of individual producers also affects market supply. *Determinants of market supply include*

- *Factor costs*
- *Technology*
- *Profitability of alternative pursuits*
- *Expectations*
- *Number of sellers*

As we observed, the price of computers and printers (factor costs) and the ease of word processing (technology) affect the supply decision. So too do the availability and pay of other income-earning opportunities. Expectations of future needs may also affect supply behavior. Finally, the number of producers will affect the *market* supply of a product.

None of the points on the market supply curve (Figure 3.5) tells us how much typing is actually being sold on the Clearview campus. *Market supply is an expression of sellers' intentions—an offer to sell—not a statement of actual sales.* My next door neighbor may be willing to sell his 1987 Honda Civic for $8000, but most likely he'll never find a buyer at that price. Nevertheless, his *willingness* to sell his car at that price is part of the *market supply* of used cars.

Shifts of Supply

As with demand, there's nothing sacred about any given set of supply intentions. Supply curves *shift* when the underlying determinants of supply change. Thus we again distinguish

- *Changes in quantity supplied:* movements along a given supply curve
- *Changes in supply:* shifts of the supply curve

IN THE NEWS

News: Analysis

Orange Prices Start to Rise After Calif. Freeze

LOS ANGELES—Consumers will pay dramatically more for fresh oranges, the result of a killer freeze in California that has already doubled wholesale prices....

California supplies about 80% of the nation's eating oranges and lemons. Four days of freezing temperatures in the Central Valley last month caused about $530 million in damage....

A standard 37 1/2-pound box of oranges is selling at wholesale for $20 to $24 depending on size and quality, double the price before the frost, the California Farm Bureau Federation reported.

"Our supply will be severely damaged, so the price of fruit will go up," said Shann Blue of California Citrus Mutual, a growers' group.

—Chris Woodyard

USA Today, Jan. 4, 1999, p. 4A. Copyright 1999, USA TODAY. Reprinted by permission. www.usatoday.com

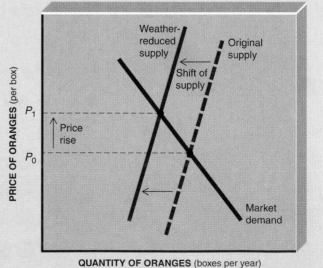

Analysis: The market supply curve *shifts* when a determinant of supply changes. In this case bad weather reduced the available supply of oranges, driving up their price.

Our Latin friend *ceteris paribus* is once again the decisive factor. If the price of typing services is the only variable changing, then we can *track changes in quantity supplied along the supply curve.* But if *ceteris paribus* is violated—if technology, factor costs, the profitability of producing other goods, expectations, or the number of sellers change—then *changes in supply are illustrated by shifts of the supply curve.*

The NEWS box illustrates a leftward shift—a decline in the supply of California oranges. The shift was caused by bad weather that reduced crop yields (effectively raising factor costs per box). Unusually good weather would shift the orange supply rightward, reducing orange prices.

EQUILIBRIUM

The purpose of drawing supply and demand curves is to see how markets answer the basic questions of WHAT, HOW, and FOR WHOM. We're now in a position to see how those questions were answered in the typing services market at Clearview College. We do this in Figure 3.6 by bringing together the market supply and market demand curves. When we put the two curves together, we see that *only one price and quantity are compatible with the existing intentions of both buyers and sellers.* This equilibrium

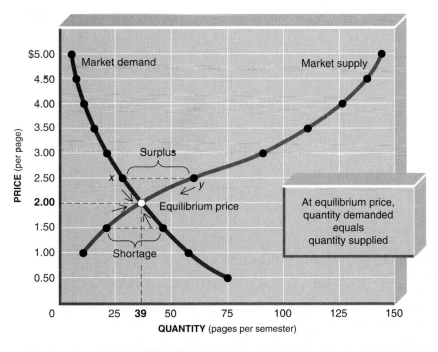

Price (per page)	Quantity Supplied (pages per semester)		Quantity Demanded (pages per semester)
$5.00	148		5
4.50	140		8
4.00	130	market	11
3.50	114	surplus	16
3.00	90		22
2.50	62		30
2.00	39	equilibrium	39
1.50	20	market	47
1.00	10	shortage	57

FIGURE 3.6
Equilibrium Price

Only at equilibrium is the quantity demanded equal to the quantity supplied. In this case, the equilibrium price is $2.00 per page, and 39 pages is the equilibrium quantity. At higher prices, a market surplus exists—the quantity supplied exceeds the quantity demanded. At prices below equilibrium, a market shortage exists.

The intersecton of the demand and supply curves in the graph represents equilibrium price and output in this market.

equilibrium price: The price at which the quantity of a good demanded in a given time period equals the quantity supplied.

Market Clearing

market mechanism: The use of market prices and sales to signal desired outputs (or resource allocations).

Surplus and Shortage

market surplus: The amount by which the quantity supplied exceeds the quantity demanded at a given price; excess supply.

occurs at the intersection of the two curves in Figure 3.6. Once it's established, typing will cost $2.00 per page. At that **equilibrium price,** campus typists will sell a total of 39 pages of typing per semester—the same amount that students wish to buy at that price.

An equilibrium doesn't imply that everyone is happy with the prevailing price or quantity. Notice in Figure 3.6, for example, that some students who want to buy typing services don't get any. These would-be buyers are arrayed along the demand curve *below* the equilibrium. Because the price they're *willing* to pay is less than the equilibrium price, they don't get any typing services.

Likewise, some would-be sellers in the market don't sell as much typing as they might like. These people are arrayed along the supply curve *above* the equilibrium. Because they insist on being paid a price higher than the equilibrium price, they don't actually sell anything.

Although not everyone gets full satisfaction from the market equilibrium, that unique outcome is efficient. The equilibrium price and quantity reflect a compromise between buyers and sellers. No other compromise yields a quantity demanded that's exactly equal to the quantity supplied.

The Invisible Hand. The equilibrium price isn't determined by any single individual. Rather, it's determined by the collective behavior of many buyers and sellers, each acting out his or her own demand or supply schedule. It's this kind of impersonal price determination that gave rise to Adam Smith's characterization of the market mechanism as "the invisible hand." In attempting to explain how the **market mechanism** works, the famed eighteenth-century economist noted a certain feature of market prices. The market behaves as if some unseen force (the invisible hand) were examining each individual's supply or demand schedule and then selecting a price that assured an equilibrium. In practice, of course, the process of price determination isn't so mysterious: It's a simple process of trial and error.

Suppose for the moment that campus typists believed typing could be sold for $2.50 per page rather than the equilibrium price of $2.00 and offered it only at this higher price. From the demand and supply schedules depicted in Figure 3.6 we can foresee the consequences. At $2.50 per page, campus typists would be offering more typing services (point *y*) than Tom, George, and Lisa were willing to buy (point *x*) at that price. A **market surplus** of typing services would exist in the sense that more typing was being offered for sale (supplied) than students cared to purchase at the available price.

As Figure 3.6 indicates, at a price of $2.50 per page, a market surplus of 32 pages per semester exists. Under these circumstances, campus typists would be spending many idle hours at their keyboards waiting for customers to appear. Their waiting will be in vain because the quantity of typing demanded will not increase until the price of typing falls. That is the clear message of the demand curve. As would-be typists get this message, they'll reduce their prices. This is the response the market mechanism signals.

As sellers' asking prices decline, the quantity demanded will increase. This concept is illustrated in Figure 3.6 by the movement along the demand curve from point *x* to lower prices and greater quantity demanded. As we move down the market demand curve, the *desire* for typing doesn't change, but the quantity people are *able and willing to buy* increases. When the price falls to $2.00 per page, the quantity demanded will finally equal the quantity supplied. This is the *equilibrium* illustrated in Figure 3.6.

An Initial Shortage. A very different sequence of events would occur if a market shortage existed. Suppose someone were to spread the word that typing services were available at only $1.50 per page. Tom, George, and Lisa would be standing in line to get their papers typed, but campus typists wouldn't be willing to supply the quantity desired at that price. As Figure 3.6 confirms, at $1.50 per page, the quantity demanded

(47 pages per semester) would greatly exceed the quantity supplied (20 pages per semester). In this situation, we may speak of a **market shortage,** that is, an excess of quantity demanded over quantity supplied. At a price of $1.50 a page, the shortage amounts to 27 pages of typing.

When a market shortage exists, not all consumer demands can be satisfied. Some people who are *willing* to buy typing at the going price ($1.50) won't be able to do so. To assure themselves of sufficient typing, Tom, George, Lisa, or some other consumer may offer to pay a *higher* price, thus initiating a move up the demand curve in Figure 3.6. The higher prices offered will in turn induce other enterprising students to type more, thus ensuring an upward movement along the market supply curve. Thus a higher price tends to evoke a greater quantity supplied, as reflected in the upward-sloping supply curve. Notice, again, that the *desire* to type hasn't changed; only the quantity supplied has responded to a change in price.

market shortage: The amount by which the quantity demanded exceeds the quantity supplied at a given price; excess demand.

Self-Adjusting Prices. What we observe, then, is that *whenever the market price is set above or below the equilibrium price, either a market surplus or a market shortage will emerge.* To overcome a surplus or shortage, buyers and sellers will change their behavior. Typists will have to compete for customers by reducing prices when a market surplus exists. If a shortage exists, buyers will compete for service by offering to pay higher prices. Only at the *equilibrium* price will no further adjustments be required.

Sometimes the market price is slow to adjust, and a disequilibrium persists, as is often the case with tickets to rock concerts, football games, and other events. People initially adjust their behavior by standing in ticket lines for hours, hoping to buy a ticket at the below-equilibrium price (see NEWS). The tickets are typically resold ("scalped"), however, at prices closer to equilibrium.

Business firms can discover equilibrium prices by trial and error. If they find that consumer purchases aren't keeping up with production, they may conclude that their price is above the equilibrium price. They'll have to get rid of their accumulated

---

IN THE NEWS

News: Analysis

For Fans, What's 4 Nights for U2?

After an 80-hour ordeal—four nights stuffed in a car, three days breathing bus exhaust, scarfing Cokes and franks, running blocks for pit stops—the three University of Maryland seniors who camped out at RFK Stadium prevailed. They beat the scalpers to U2 concert tickets.

At 8 A.M. today they would be, if all went as planned, first on line at the RFK box office. By 9 A.M. the 52,000-seat stadium will sell out, predicted a Ticketmaster official.

"It's what you got to do to get good seats," said Crawford Conniff, 22, stretched out near the stadium among traffic island dandelions.

"We have unlimited time," said Mike Collins, 22. "If we had a job making 50 grand, we could pay $150 to scalpers."

Actually, $150 sounds cheap for the $28.50 face-value tickets. Today's ticket sale for the Aug. 15 concert, one of the summer's hottest, is likely to ignite an orgy of profiteering.

When the band played Los Angeles, scalpers scored up to $1,200 a ticket for prime seats. In Washington, as early as Tuesday, ticket brokers had stationed students, unemployed and even homeless people at ticket outlets to snap up hundreds of choice seats.

—Laura Blumenfeld

The Washington Post, Apr. 25, 1992, p. A1. © 1992, The Washington Post. Reprinted with permission. www.washingtonpost.com

---

Analysis: In equilibrium, everyone who is willing and able to pay the equilibrium price gets to see the show. If price is below equilibrium, the quantity demanded exceeds the quantity supplied, so only people willing and able to stand in line for tickets will get them initially.

inventory. To do so they'll have to lower their price (by a Grand End-of-Year Sale, perhaps). In the happy situation where consumer purchases are outpacing production, a firm might conclude that its price was a trifle too low and give it a nudge upward. In any case, the equilibrium price can be established after a few trials in the marketplace.

Changes in Equilibrium

No equilibrium price is permanent. The equilibrium price established in the Clearview College typing market, for example, was the unique outcome of specific demand and

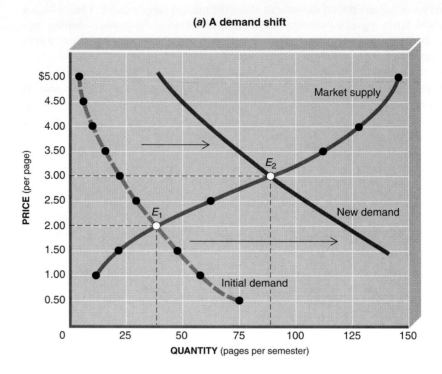

(a) A demand shift

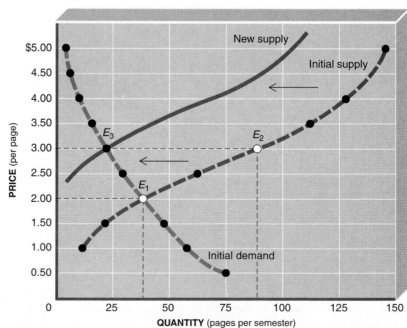

(b) A supply shift

FIGURE 3.7

Changes in Equilibrium

If demand or supply change (shift), market equilibrium will change as well. **Demand shift.** In *(a)*, the rightward shift of the demand curve illustrates an increase in demand. When demand increases, the equilibrium price rises. (from E_1 to E_2).

   Supply shift. In *(b)*, the leftward shift of the supply curve illustrates a decrease in supply. This raises the equilibrium price to E_3.

   Demand and supply curves shift only when their underlying determinants change, i.e., when *ceteris paribus* is violated.

supply schedules. Those schedules themselves were based on our assumption of *ceteris paribus.* We assumed that the "taste" (desire) for typing was given, as were consumers' incomes, the price and availability of other goods, and expectations. Any of these determinants of demand could change. When one does, the demand curve has to be redrawn. Such a shift of the demand curve will lead to a new equilibrium price and quantity. Indeed, *the equilibrium price will change whenever the supply or demand curve shifts.*

A Demand Shift. We can illustrate how equilibrium prices change by taking one last look at the Clearview College typing market. Our original supply and demand curves, together with the resulting equilibrium (point E_1), are depicted in Figure 3.7. Now suppose that the professors at Clearview begin assigning additional papers and homework, all of which must be typed. The increased need (desire) for typing services will affect market demand. Tom, George, and Lisa are suddenly willing to buy more typing at every price than they were before. That is, the *demand* for typing has increased. We can represent this increased demand by a rightward *shift* of the market demand curve, as illustrated in Figure 3.7*a.*

Note that the new demand curve intersects the (unchanged) market supply curve at a new price (point E_2), the equilibrium price is now $3.00 per page. This new equilibrium price will persist until either the demand curve or the supply curve shifts again.

A Supply Shift. Figure 3.7*b* illustrates a *supply* shift. The decrease (leftward shift) in supply might occur if some on-campus typists got sick. Or approaching exams might convince would-be typists they have no time to spare. *Whenever supply decreases (shifts left), price tends to rise,* as in Figure 3.7*b.*

The kinds of price changes we are describing here are quite common. As the baby boomers have aged, they've turned away from low-fat foods and vented their craving for richer foods. As the accompanying NEWS explains, this change in tastes has pushed ice cream prices higher. The same kind of price changes occur in other markets whenever the behavior of buyers or sellers changes. If you want to see how fast equilibrium prices change, watch the prices of stocks or bonds for an hour or two on television, the Internet, or at a brokerage firm. The WORLD VIEW on the next page even shows how a restaurant can use price changes to ensure orders for every item on its menu.

IN THE *News: Analysis* **NEWS**

Changing Ice Cream Tastes Push Up Prices

The price of ice cream is on the rise, and you can blame richer tastes.

Demand for low-fat ice cream, booming for a decade, is inexplicably down 12% this year. Premium ice creams have almost 20% bufferfat, double that of most low-fat versions. The shift to the sinful stuff has created a butterfat shortage, driving up the cost of the ingredient, and therefore the cost of ice cream itself. . . .

Meanwhile, Dreyer's will be raising its prices 10 cents to 30 cents a half gallon in some markets because butterfat prices are at record highs. Dreyer's prices range from $4.39 to $4.79 a half gallon.

Ice cream prices could eventually go up $1 a gallon or more, says Michael Vierra of McConnell's Fine Ice Creams.

—Del Jones

USA Today, June 24, 1998, p. B1. Copyright 1998, USA TODAY. Reprinted with permission. www.usatoday.com

Analysis: When a determinant of demand (e.g., tastes) changes, the demand curve shifts. When this happens, the equilibrium price changes.

Dining on the Downtick

Americans aren't the only consumers who fall for packaging. Since late January, Parisians (not to mention TV crews from around the world) have been drawn to 6 rue Feydeau to try La Connivence, a restaurant with a new gimmick. The name means "collusion," and yes, of course, La Connivence is a block away from the Bourse, the French stock exchange.

What's the gimmick? Just that the restaurant's prices fluctuate according to supply and demand. The more a dish is ordered, the higher its price. A dish that's ignored gets cheaper.

Customers tune in to the day's menu (couched in trading terms) on computer screens. Among a typical day's options: *forte baisse du haddock* ("precipitous drop in haddock"), *vif recul de la côte de boeuf* ("rapid decline in beef ribs"), *la brochette de lotte au plus bas* ("fish kabob hits bottom"). Then comes the major decision—whether to opt for the price that's listed when you order or to gamble that the price will have gone down by the time you finish your meal.

So far, only main dishes are open to speculation, but co-owners Pierre Guette, an ex-professor at a top French business school, and Jean-Paul Trastour, an ex-journalist at *Le Nouvel Observateur,* are adding wine to the risk list.

La Connivence is open for dinner, but the midday "session" (as the owners call it) is the one to catch. That's when the traders of Paris leave the floor to push their luck *à table*. But here, at least, the return on their $15 investment (the average price of a meal) is immediate—and usually good.

—Christina de Liagre

New York, Apr. 7, 1986, p. 30. Copyright © 1986 K-III Magazine Corporation. All rights reserved. Reprinted with the permission of *New York* magazine. www.newyorkmag.com

Analysis: A market surplus signals that price is too high; a market shortage suggests that price is too low. This restaurant adjusts price until the quantity supplied equals the quantity demanded.

MARKET OUTCOMES

Notice how the market mechanism resolves the basic economic questions of WHAT, HOW, and FOR WHOM.

WHAT The WHAT question refers to the amount of typing services to include in society's mix of output. The answer at Clearview College was 39 pages per semester. This decision wasn't reached in a referendum, but instead in the market equilibrium (Figure 3.6). In the same way but on a larger scale, millions of consumers and a handful of auto producers decide to include 6 million or so cars in each year's mix of output. Auto prices and quantities adjust until consumers buy the same quantity that auto manufacturers produce.

HOW The market mechanism also determines HOW goods are produced. Profit-seeking producers will strive to produce typing and automobiles in the most efficient way. They'll use market prices to decide not only WHAT to produce, but also what resources to use in the production process. If new software simplifies word processing—and is priced low enough—typists will use it. Likewise, auto manufacturers will use robots rather than humans on the assembly line if robots reduce costs and increase profits.

FOR WHOM Finally, the "invisible hand" of the market will determine who gets the goods produced. At Clearview College, who got their papers typed? Only those students who were willing and able to pay $2.00 per page for that service. FOR WHOM are all those automobiles produced each year? The answer is the same: those consumers who are willing and able to pay the market price for a new car.

Optimal, Not Perfect Not everyone is happy with these answers, of course. Tom would like to pay only $1.00 a page for his typing. And some of the Clearview students don't have enough income to buy any typing. They think it's unfair that they have to type their own papers while richer students can have someone else do their typing for them. Students who can't afford cars are even less happy with the market's answer to the FOR WHOM question.

Although the outcomes of the marketplace aren't perfect, they're often optimal. Optimal outcomes are the best possible *given* our incomes and scarce resources. In other words, we expect the choices made in the marketplace to be the best possible choices for each participant. Why do we draw such a conclusion? Because Tom and George and everybody in our little Clearview College drama had (and continue to have) absolute freedom to make their own purchase and consumption decisions. And also because we assume that sooner or later they'll make the choices they find most satisfying. The results are thus *optimal* in the sense that everyone has done as well as she or he could, given their income and talents.

THE ECONOMY TOMORROW

The market's ability to achieve the equilibrium price and allocate the equilibrium quantity is evident. Nevertheless, people often are upset with those outcomes. Such discontent may erupt into pleas for the government to intervene. Consumers may insist that government outlaw "price gouging"; producers may insist that "unfair competition" be prohibited. In all such cases, some market participants are convinced that the market has failed and seek government intervention to improve market outcomes. That isn't always the way it works out, however, as rent controls illustrate.

Rent Controls— New York and Moscow

In a market-driven economy, rents are set by the forces of supply and demand. Everyone needs shelter. But the quantity and quality people *demand* in the marketplace depend on incomes, tastes, price and availability of other goods, and expectations. Some people prefer to spend less on rent and more on clothes and cars. Others want more spacious living quarters but can't afford it. All these diverse circumstances are reflected in the market demand curve. As in other markets, we observe that the housing demand curve is downward-sloping: more rental units are demanded at lower rents.

Market Rents

Figure 3.8 also illustrates the market supply curve. If rents are high, builders have more incentive to hire factors of production and build housing units. When rents are high, some homeowners even rent out spare rooms, adding to the quantity of rental housing available. When rents are low, builders seek out more profitable ventures and homeowners use their extra rooms for storage or other activities.

The interaction of market supply and demand establishes a rental equilibrium. In Figure 3.8 the average market-established rent is R_e. At that equilibrium rent, q_e rental units are offered and rented.

Notice that some people who *desire* rental housing don't get it in this market-driven economy. Everyone on the demand curve below the point E wants rental housing and is willing to pay for it. But the price they're willing and able to pay is less than the equilibrium rent.

Where are these would-be renters? Are they living in the streets? Not likely. Most have decided to rent smaller apartments or houses. Others have chosen to share housing with family or roommates. Some have decided to live elsewhere. Very few are homeless. Nevertheless, they would all *like* to have more housing and wish rents were lower.

People on the demand curve *above* point E would also like lower rents. They're getting as much housing as they're willing and able to buy at the equilibrium rent R_e. But they'd *like* to pay less. Included in this group are many poor people who have so little income left after paying their rent that they can't afford enough food, clothes, or other "necessities." Housing costs absorb over one-third of the average family's income and often an even larger chunk of a poor family's income.

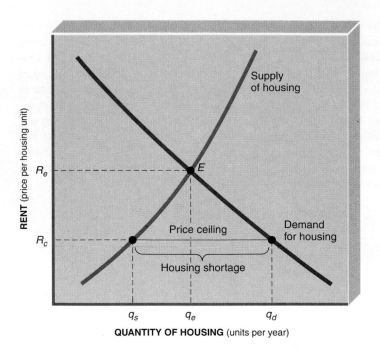

Rent Control

The pervasive desire for lower rents often leads to government intervention. Typically, the plea for intervention is based on the plight of the poor. To make housing *affordable,* it is argued, the government must force landlords to reduce rents. More than 200 local governments—including New York City, Boston, Washington, D.C., and San Francisco—have responded with rent controls of varying severity. In all cases, rent controls are a **price ceiling**—an upper limit imposed on the price of a good or service.

Rent controls have the immediate effect of making housing more affordable. But such controls are *disequilibrium* prices and will change housing decisions in unintended ways.

Consider first the demand side of the market. At the equilibrium rent R_e, only q_e are demanded in Figure 3.8. If rents are forced down to R_c, however, the quantity demanded increases to q_d. More people are now actively looking for rental units than before.

But what about the *supply* of rental units? Will more housing become available to satisfy the increase in quantity demanded? Not according to the law of supply. Instead, the quantity of available rental units actually shrinks when rent controls are imposed. Prior to rent control, q_e units were available; with rent controls, only q_s units are offered. Thus the quantity of rental units *supplied* has decreased at the same time that the quantity *demanded* has increased! This creates the market shortage illustrated in Figure 3.8 by the distance $q_d - q_s$. Thus, *price ceilings have three predictable effects; they*

- *Increase the quantity demanded*
- *Decrease the quantity supplied*
- *Create a market shortage*

You may well wonder where the "lost" housing went. The houses didn't disappear. However, some landlords decided that renting their units was no longer worth the effort. They chose instead to sell the units, convert them to condominums, or even live in them themselves. Other landlords stopped maintaining their buildings, letting the units deteriorate. The rate of new construction slowed too, as builders decided that rent control made new construction less profitable. Slowly but surely the quantity of housing declines from q_e to q_s. Hence *there will be less housing for everyone when rent controls are imposed to make housing more affordable for some.*

Figure 3.8 illustrates another problem. As we saw, the rent ceiling R_c created a housing shortage—a gap between the quantity demanded (q_d) and the quantity supplied

price ceiling: Upper limit imposed on the price of a good.

(q_s). Who will get the increasingly scarce housing? The market would have settled this FOR WHOM question by permitting rents to rise and allocating available units to those consumers willing and able to pay the rent R_e. Now, however, rents can't rise, and we have lots of people clamoring for housing that isn't available. A different method of allocating rental units must be found. Vacant units will go to those who learn of them first, patiently wait on waiting lists, or offer a gratuity to the landlord or renting agent.

In New York City, rent regulation began as an emergency measure during World War II. The goal was to keep housing affordable while shortages of labor and material precluded new construction. After the war ended, however, tenants didn't want to give up their below-market rents. In Manhattan, about 85 percent of residents rent apartments and 69 percent of these units are rent-controlled. As a result, not only the poor get cheap rent. Mia Farrow lives in a 10-room rent-controlled apartment on Central Park West, paying a fraction of market rents. Former mayors Ed Koch and David Dinkins, singer Carly Simon, and hundreds of other celebrities end up benefiting from rent controls designed to make housing affordable for the poor. In the meantime, New York has a perennial housing shortage.

Rent controls have created even greater problems in Russia. The central planners of the former Soviet Union were dedicated to making housing affordable for everyone. To achieve this goal, they fixed rents far below what a market economy would charge. Families in Moscow paid as little as $10 a month for a two-bedroom apartment. Since there weren't enough apartments to go around, a market shortage emerged. As in New York City, people responded to the shortage by selling apartments in the black market or currying favor with housing authorities to get to the top of the waiting list for vacant units.

SUMMARY

- Individual consumers, business firms, government agencies, and foreigners participate in the marketplace by offering to buy or sell goods and services, or factors of production. Participation is motivated by the desire to maximize utility (consumers), profits (business firms), or the general welfare (government agencies) from the limited resources each participant has.

- All interactions in the marketplace involve the exchange of either factors of production or finished products. Although the actual exchanges can occur anywhere, they take place in product markets or factor markets, depending on what is being exchanged.

- People willing and able to buy a particular good at some price are part of the market demand for that product. All those willing and able to sell that good at some price are part of the market supply. Total market demand or supply is the sum of individual demands or supplies.

- Supply and demand curves illustrate how the quantity demanded or supplied changes in response to a change in the price of that good, if nothing else changes (*ceteris paribus*). Demand curves slope downward; supply curves slope upward.

- Determinants of market demand include the number of potential buyers and their respective tastes (desires), incomes, other goods, and expectations. If any of these de-

terminants change, the demand curve shifts. Movements along a demand curve are induced only by a change in the price of that good.

- Determinants of market supply include factor costs, technology, profitability of other goods, expectations, and number of sellers. Supply shifts when these underlying determinants change.

- The quantity of goods or resources actually exchanged in each market depends on the behavior of all buyers and sellers, as summarized in market supply and demand curves. At the point where the two curves intersect, an equilibrium price—the price at which the quantity demanded equals the quantity supplied—is established.

- A distinctive feature of the equilibrium price and quantity is that it's the only price-quantity combination acceptable to buyers and sellers alike. At higher prices, sellers supply more than buyers are willing to purchase (a market surplus); at lower prices, the amount demanded exceeds the quantity supplied (a market shortage). Only the equilibrium price clears the market.

- Price ceilings (such as rent control) are disequilibrium prices imposed on the marketplace. Such price controls create an imbalance between quantities demanded and supplied, resulting in market shortages.

Key Terms

factor market	law of demand	law of supply
product market	substitute goods	equilibrium price
supply	complementary goods	market mechanism
demand	*ceteris paribus*	market surplus
opportunity cost	shift in demand	market shortage
demand schedule	market demand	price ceiling
demand curve	market supply	

Questions for Discussion

1. In our story of Tom, the nontypist confronted with a typing assignment, we emphasized the great urgency of his desire for typing services. Many people would say that Tom had an "absolute need" for typing and therefore was ready to "pay anything" to get his paper typed. If this were true, what shape would his demand curve have? Why isn't this realistic?

2. Illustrate the market situation for the U2 concert (see page 57). Why didn't the concert promoters set an equilibrium price?

3. Which determinants of pizza demand change when the White House is in crisis?

4. Can you explain the practice of scalping tickets for major sporting events in terms of market shortages? How else might tickets be distributed?

5. If rent controls are so counterproductive, why do cities impose them? How else might the housing problems of poor people be solved?

6. Who is harmed by rent controls? Who is helped?

7. What would happen in the apple market if the government set a *minimum* price of $2.00 per apple? What might motivate such a policy?

8. The WORLD VIEW on page 60 describes the use of prices to achieve an equilibrium in the kitchen. What happens to the food at more traditional restaurants?

9. Is there a shortage of on-campus parking at your school? How might the shortage be resolved?

10. Do Internet price information services tend to raise or lower the price consumers pay for a product?

11. Web Activity Go to an auction site, such as E-Bay at www.ebay.com or WebAuction at http://webauction.com. Pick a product and track its "current winning lowest bid" price over 1 day. How does the price change as the time draws nearer to closing time? Draw a supply and demand diagram of the auction.

12. Web Activity The New York Mercantile Exchange at www.nymex.com/chartsdata.html is a market in which buyers and sellers set prices for the promises to deliver various commodities in the future. For one commodity, find the most recent change in price. Use a supply and demand diagram to illustrate a possible explanation for this price change.

Problems for Chapter 3 appear at the back of the book.

The Public Sector

The market has a keen ear for private wants, but a deaf ear for public needs.
—Robert Heilbroner

Markets do work: The interaction of supply and demand in product markets *does* generate goods and services. Likewise, the interaction of supply and demand in labor markets *does* yield jobs, wages, and a distribution of income. As we've observed, the market is capable of determining WHAT goods to produce, HOW, and FOR WHOM.

But are the market's answers good enough? Is the mix of output produced by unregulated markets the best possible mix? Will producers choose the production process that strikes a desirable balance between production and the environment? Will the market-generated distribution of income be fair enough?

We've already seen that the market's answers might not be the best. Monopoly power might constrain the mix of output, raise product prices, and grab too large a share of total income. Such situations call for antitrust action to regulate or dismantle market power. Other circumstances may also prevent the market from offering up the optimal mix of output, method of production, or distribution of income. Whenever that happens, government intervention may be needed to ensure better answers to the WHAT, HOW, and FOR WHOM questions.

This chapter identifies the circumstances under which government intervention is desirable. To this end, we answer the following questions:

- Under what circumstances do markets fail?
- How can government intervention help?
- How much government intervention is desirable?

As we see, there's substantial agreement about how and when markets fail to give us the best WHAT, HOW, and FOR WHOM answers. But there's much less agreement about whether government intervention improves the situation. Indeed, an overwhelming majority of Americans are ambivalent about government intervention. They want the government to "fix" the mix of output, protect the environment, and ensure an adequate level of income for everyone. But voters are equally quick to blame government meddling for many of our economic woes.

MARKET FAILURE

We can visualize the potential for government intervention by focusing on the WHAT question. Our goal here is to produce the best possible mix of output with existing resources. We illustrated this goal earlier with production possibilities curves. Figure 4.1 assumes that of all the possible combinations of output we could produce, the unique combination at point X represents the most desirable one; in other words, it's the **optimal mix of output.**

The market mechanism can help us find this desired mix of output. The **market mechanism** moves resources from one industry to another in response to consumer demands. If we demand more computers—offer to buy more at a given price—more resources (labor) will be allocated to computer manufacturing. Similarly, a fall in demand will encourage producers to stop making computers and offer their services in another industry. *Changes in market prices direct resources from one industry to another,* moving us along the perimeter of the production possibilities curve.

A core economic issue is whether the mix of output selected by the market mechanism is the one most desired by society. If it is, we don't need government intervention to change the mix of output. If it's not, we may need government intervention to guide the invisible hand of the market.

We use the term **market failure** to refer to situations where the market generates less than perfect (suboptimal) outcomes. If the invisible hand of the marketplace produces a mix of output that's different from the one society most desires, then it has failed. *Market failure implies that the forces of supply and demand haven't led us to the best point on the production possibilities curve.* Such a failure is illustrated by point M in Figure 4.1. Point M is assumed to be the mix of output generated by market forces. Notice that the market mix (M) doesn't represent the optimal mix, which is assumed to be at point X. The market in this case *fails;* we get the wrong answer to the WHAT question.

Market failure opens the door for government intervention. If the market can't do the job, we need some form of *nonmarket* force to get the right answers. In terms of Figure 4.1, we need something to change the mix of output—to move us from point M (the market mix of output) to point X (the optimal mix of output). Accordingly, *market failure establishes a basis for government intervention.* We look to the government to push market outcomes closer to the ideal.

Because market failure is the justification for government intervention, we need to know how and when market failure occurs. *The four specific sources of market failure are:*

- *Public goods*
- *Externalities*
- *Market power*
- *Equity*

optimal mix of output: The most desirable combination of output attainable with existing resources, technology, and social values.

market mechanism: The use of market prices and sales to signal desired outputs (or resource allocations)

market failure: An imperfection in the market mechanism that prevents optimal outcomes.

FIGURE 4.1
Market Failure

We can produce any mix of output on the production possibilities curve. Our goal is to produce the optimal (best possible) mix of output, as represented by point X. Market forces, however, might produce another combination, like point M. In that case, the market fails—it produces a suboptimal mix of output.

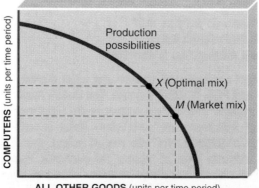

First we examine the nature of these problems and then we see why government intervention is called for in each case.

The market mechanism has the unique capability to signal consumer demands for various goods and services. By offering to pay higher or lower prices for some goods, we express our collective answer to the question of WHAT to produce. However, the market mechanism works efficiently only if the benefits of consuming a particular good or service are available only to the individuals who purchase that product.

Consider doughnuts, for example. When you eat a doughnut, you get the satisfaction from its taste and your fuller stomach—that is, you derive a private benefit. No one else benefits from your consumption of a doughnut: The doughnut you purchase in the market is yours alone to consume; it's a **private good.** Accordingly, your decision to purchase the doughnut will be determined only by your anticipated satisfaction, your income, and your opportunity costs.

Joint Consumption. Most of the goods and services produced in the public sector are different from doughnuts—and not just because doughnuts look, taste, and smell different from nuclear submarines. When you buy a doughnut, you effectively exclude others from consumption of that product. If Dunkin' Donuts sells you a particular pastry, it can't supply the same pastry to someone else. If you devour it, no one else can. In this sense, the transaction and product are completely private.

The same exclusiveness is not characteristic of national defense. If you buy a nuclear submarine to patrol the Pacific Ocean, there's no way you can exclude your neighbors from the protection your submarine provides. Either the submarine deters would-be attackers or it doesn't. In the former case, both you and your neighbors survive happily ever after; in the latter case, we're all blown away together. In that sense, you and your neighbors consume the benefits of nuclear submarine defenses *jointly.* National defense isn't a divisible service. There's no such thing as exclusive consumption here. The consumption of nuclear defenses is a communal feat, no matter who pays for them. Accordingly, national defense is regarded as a **public good** in the sense that *consumption of a public good by one person doesn't preclude consumption of the same good by another person.* By contrast, a doughnut is a private good because if I eat it, no one else can consume it.

The Free-Rider Dilemma. The "communal" nature of public goods creates a dilemma. If you and I will *both* benefit from nuclear defenses, which one of us should buy the nuclear submarine? I'd prefer that *you* buy it, thereby giving me protection at no direct cost. Hence I may profess no desire for nuclear subs, secretly hoping to take a **free ride** on your market purchase. Unfortunately, you too have an incentive to conceal your desire for national defenses. As a consequence, neither one of us may step forward to demand nuclear subs in the marketplace. We'll both end up defenseless.

Flood control is also a public good. No one in the valley wants to be flooded out. But each landowner knows that a flood-control dam will protect *all* the landowners, regardless of who pays. Either the entire valley is protected or no one is. Accordingly, individual farmers and landowners may say they don't *want* a dam and aren't willing to *pay* for it. Everyone is waiting and hoping that someone else will pay for flood control. In other words, everyone wants a *free ride.* Thus, if we leave it to market forces, no one will *demand* flood control and all the property in the valley will be washed away.

The difference between public goods and private goods rest on *technical considerations,* not political philosophy. The central question is whether we have the technical capability to exclude nonpayers. In the case of national defense or flood control, we simply don't have that capability. Even city streets have the characteristics of public goods. Although theoretically we could restrict the use of streets to those who paid to use them, a tollgate on every corner would be exceedingly expensive and impractical. Here again, joint or public consumption appears to be the only feasible alternative.

Public Goods

private good: A good or service whose consumption by one person excludes consumption by others.

public good: A good or service whose consumption by one person does not exclude consumption by others.

free rider: An individual who reaps direct benefits from someone else's purchase (consumption) of a public good.

To the list of public goods we could add the administration of justice (including prisons), the regulation of commerce, and the conduct of foreign relations. These services—which cost tens of *billions* of dollars and employ thousands of workers—provide benefits to everyone, no matter who pays for them. In each instance it's impossible or prohibitively expensive to exclude nonpayers from the services provided.

The free riders associated with public goods upset the customary practice of paying for what you get. If I can get all the streets, defenses, and laws I want without paying for them, I'm not about to complain. I'm perfectly happy to let you pay for the services while we all consume them. Of course, you may feel the same way. Why should you pay for these services if you can consume just as much of them when your neighbors foot the whole bill? It might seem selfish not to pay your share of the cost of providing public goods. But you'd be better off in a material sense if you spent your income on doughnuts, letting others pick up the tab for public services.

Because the familiar link between paying and consuming is broken, public goods can't be peddled in the supermarket. People are reluctant to buy what they can get free, a perfectly rational response for consumers who have limited incomes to spend. Hence *if public goods were marketed like private goods, everyone would wait for someone else to pay.* The end result might be a total lack of public services. This is the kind of dilemma Robert Heilbroner had in mind when he spoke of the market's "deaf ear" (see quote at the beginning of this chapter).

The production possibilities curve in Figure 4.2 illustrates the dilemma created by public goods. Suppose that point *A* represents the optimal mix of private and public goods. It's the mix of goods and services we'd select if everyone's preferences were known and reflected in production decisions. The market mechanism won't lead us to point *A,* however, because the demand for public goods will be hidden. If we rely on the market, nearly everyone will withhold demand for public goods, waiting for a "free ride" to point *A.* As a result, we'll get a smaller quantity of public goods than we really want. The market mechanism will leave us at a mix of output like that at point *B,* with few, if any, public goods. Since point *A* is assumed to be optimal, point *B* must be *suboptimal* (inferior to point *A*). The market fails: We can't rely on the market mechanism to allocate resources to the production of public goods, no matter how much they might be desired.

Note that we're using "public good" in a different way then most people use it. To most people, the term "public good" refers to any good or service the government produces. In economics, however, the meaning is much more restrictive. The term "public good" refers only to those nonexcludable goods and services that must be consumed jointly, both by those who pay for them and by those who don't. Public goods can be produced by either the government or the private sector. Private goods can be produced

FIGURE 4.2
Underproduction of Public Goods

Suppose point *A* represents the optimal mix of output, that is, the mix of private and public goods which maximizes society's welfare. Because consumers won't demand purely public goods in the marketplace, the price mechanism won't allocate so many resources to their production. Instead, the market will tend to produce a mix of output like point *B,* which includes fewer public goods (0*R*) than is optimal (0*S*).

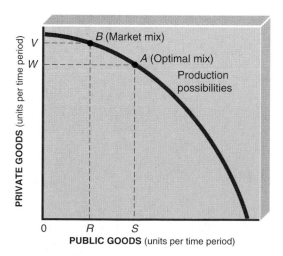

in either sector as well. The problem is that ***the market tends to underproduce public goods and overproduce private goods.*** If we want more public goods, we need a *nonmarket* force—government intervention—to get them. The government will have to force people to pay taxes, then use the tax revenues to pay for the production of defense, flood control, and other public goods.

Externalities

The free-rider problem associated with public goods is one justification for government intervention. It's not the only justification, however. Further grounds for intervention arise from the tendency of costs or benefits of some market activities to "spill over" onto third parties.

Your demand for a good reflects the amount of satisfaction you expect from its consumption. The price you're willing to pay acts as a market signal to producers of your preferences. Often, however, your consumption may affect others. The purchase of cigarettes, for example, expresses a smoker's demand for that good. But others may suffer from that consumption. In this case, smoke literally spills over onto other consumers, causing them discomfort and possibly even ill health (see NEWS). Yet their loss isn't reflected in the market: The harm caused to nonsmokers is *external* to the market price of cigarettes.

The term **externalities** refers to all costs or benefits of a market activity borne by a third party, that is, by someone other than the immediate producer or consumer. ***Whenever externalities are present, the preferences expressed in the marketplace won't be a complete measure of a good's value to society.*** As a consequence, the market will fail to produce the right mix of output. Specifically, ***the market will underproduce goods that yield external benefits and overproduce those which generate external costs.***

Figure 4.3 shows how external costs cause the market to overproduce cigarettes. The market demand curve includes only the wishes of smokers, that is, those who are willing and able to purchase cigarettes. The forces of market demand and supply result in a market equilibrium at E_M in which q_M cigarettes are produced and consumed.

externalities: Costs (or benefits) of a market activity borne by a third party; the difference between the social and private costs (benefits) of a market activity.

IN THE NEWS

The Human Cost of Secondhand Smoke

Estimated U.S. annual morbidity and mortality in nonsmokers from secondhand smoke

DEVELOPMENTAL EFFECTS

Low birthweight	9,700–18,600 cases
Sudden infant death syndrome	1,900–2,700 deaths

RESPIRATORY EFFECTS IN CHILDREN

Middle ear infection	700,000–1.6 million visits to the doctor
Asthma induction	8,000–26,000 new cases
Asthma exacerbation	400,000–1 million children
Bronchitis or pneumonia*	150,000–300,000 cases
	7,500–15,000 hospitalizations
	136–212 deaths

CANCER   3,000 deaths from lung cancer**

CARDIOVASCULAR EFFECTS

Ischemic heart disease	35,000–62,000 deaths

Source: California Environmental Protection Agency   *18 months and younger   **Estimates unavailable for nasal sinus cancer.
The Washington Post, Sept. 29, 1997, p. A3. © 1997, The Washington Post. Reprinted with permission. www.washingtonpost.com

Analysis: The health risks imposed on nonsmokers via "passive smoke" represent external costs. The market price of cigarettes doesn't reflect these costs.

FIGURE 4.3
Externalities

The market responds to consumer demands, not externalities. Smokers demand q_M cigarettes. But external costs on nonsmokers make q_O the optimal level of production. The market overproduces goods with external costs.

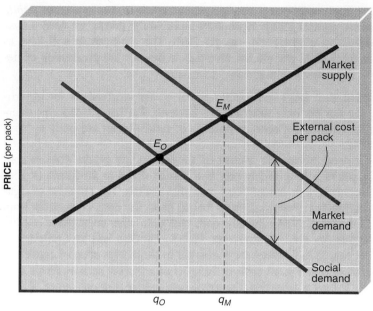

QUANTITY OF CIGARETTES (packs per year)

The well-being of *non*smokers isn't reflected in the market equilibrium at E_M. To take the *non*smoker's interests into account, we must subtract the external costs imposed on *them* from the value that *smokers* put on cigarettes. The "social demand" curve in Figure 4.3 reflects this computation. To find this curve, we simply subtract the amount of external cost from every price on the market demand curve. What the *social* demand curve tells us is how much society would be willing and able to pay for cigarettes if the preferences of both smokers and nonsmokers were taken into account.

The social demand curve in Figure 4.3 creates a new equilibrium at q_O. This is the *optimal* quantity of cigarettes to produce (and consume). Yet the market alone would produce more than that (q_M). Government intervention may be needed to move the mix of output closer to society's optimal point.

The externalities associated with cigarette consumption have prompted many forms of government intervention, including mandatory health warnings on cigarette packaging, bans on advertising, and restrictions on locales where people may smoke. Courts have even determined that child custody decisions may be influenced by the smoking habits of the divorcing parents. All these interventions restrict the ability of individuals to maximize their personal utility in the marketplace. They're motivated by the recognition that the market mechanism responds only to the market demands of smokers and is unable to respond to nonmarketed externalities.

Externalities also exist in production. A power plant that burns high-sulfur coal damages the surrounding environment. Yet the damage inflicted on neighboring people, vegetation, and buildings is external to the cost calculations of the firm. Because the cost of such pollution is not reflected in the price of electricity, the firm will tend to produce more electricity (and pollution) than is socially desirable. To reduce this imbalance, the government has to step in and change market outcomes.

External Benefits. Externalities can also be beneficial. A product may generate external *benefits* rather than external *costs*. Your college is an example. The students who attend your school benefit directly from the education they receive. That's why they (and you) are willing to *pay* for tuition, books, and other services. The students in attendance aren't the only beneficiaries of this educational service, however. The research that a university conducts may yield benefits for a much broader community. The values and knowledge students acquire may also be shared with family, friends, and

Check out the pollution problems in your neighborhood at www.epa.gov/enviro/zipcode_js.html.

coworkers. These benefits would all be *external* to the market transaction between a paying student and the school. Positive externalities also arise from immunizations against infectious diseases.

   If a product yields external benefits, the social demand is greater than the market demand. Society wants *more* of the product than the market mechanism alone will produce. To get that additional output, the government may have to intervene with subsidies or other policies. We conclude then that ***the market fails by***

*   ***Overproducing goods that have external costs***
*   ***Underproducing goods that have external benefits***

   If externalities are present, the market won't produce the optimal mix of output. To get that optimal mix, we need government intervention.

   In the case of both public goods and externalities, the market fails to achieve the optimal mix of output because the price signal is flawed. The price consumers are willing and able to pay for a specific good doesn't reflect all the benefits or cost of producing that good.

   The market may fail, however, even when the price signals are accurate. The *response* to price signals, rather than the signals themselves, may be flashed.

Market Power

Restricted Supply. Market power is often the cause of a flawed response. Suppose there were only one airline company in the world. This single seller of airline travel would be a **monopoly**—that is, the only producer in that industry. As a monopolist, the airline could charge extremely high prices without worrying that travelers would flock to a competing airline. At the same time, the high prices paid by consumers would express the importance of that service to society. Ideally, such prices would act as a signal to producers to build and fly more planes—to change the mix of output. But a monopolist doesn't have to cater to every consumer whim. It can limit airline travel and obstruct our efforts to achieve an optimal mix of output.

   Monopoly is the most severe form of **market power.** More generally, market power refers to any situation in which a single producer or consumer has the ability to alter the market price of a specific product. If the publisher (McGraw-Hill) charges a high price for this book, you'll have to pay the tab. McGraw-Hill has market power because there are relatively few economics textbooks and your professor has required you to use this one. You don't have power in the textbook market because your decision to buy or not won't alter the market price of this text. You're only one of the million students who are taking an introductory economics course this year.

   The market power McGraw-Hill possesses is derived from the copyright on this text. No matter how profitable textbook sales might be, no one else is permitted to produce or sell this particular book. Patents are another common source of market power because they also preclude others from making or selling a specific product. Market power may also result from control of resources, restrictive production agreements, or efficiencies of large-scale production.

   Whatever the source of market power, the direct consequence is that one or more producers attain discretionary power over the market's response to price signals. They may use that discretion to enrich themselves rather than to move the economy toward the optimal mix of output. In this case, the market will again fail to deliver the most desired goods and services.

   The mandate for government intervention in this case is to prevent or dismantle concentrations of market power. That's the basic purpose of **antitrust policy.** Another option is to *regulate* market behavior. This was one of the goals of the 1998 antitrust case against Microsoft. The government was less interested in breaking Microsoft's near monopoly on operating systems than in changing the way Microsoft behaved.

   In some cases, it may be economically efficient to have one large firm supply an entire market. Such a situation arises in **natural monopoly,** where a single firm can achieve economies of scale over the entire range of market output. Utility companies,

monopoly: A firm that produces the entire market supply of a particular good or service.

market power: The ability to alter the market price of a good or a service.

antitrust: Government intervention to alter market structure or prevent abuse of market power.

natural monopoly: An industry in which one firm can achieve economies of scale over the entire range of market supply.

local telephone service, subway systems, and cable all exhibit such scale (size) efficiencies. In these cases, a monopoly *structure* may be economically desirable. The government may have to regulate the *behavior* of a natural monopoly, however, to ensure that consumers get the benefits of that greater efficiency.

Inequity

Public goods, externalities, and market power all cause resource misallocations. Where these phenomena exist, the market mechanism will fail to produce the optimal mix of output.

Beyond the question of WHAT to produce, we're also concerned about FOR WHOM output is to be produced. The market answers this question by distributing a larger share of total output to those with the most income. Although this result may be efficient, it's not necessarily equitable. As we saw in Chapter 2, the market mechanism may enrich some people while leaving others to seek shelter in abandoned cars. If such outcomes violate our vision of equity, we may want the government to change the market-generated distribution of income.

Taxes and Transfers. The tax-and-transfer system is the principal mechanism for redistributing incomes. The idea here is to take some of the income away from those who have "too much" and give it to those whom the market has left with "too little." Taxes are levied to take back some of the income received from the market. Those tax revenues are then redistributed via transfer payments to those deemed needy, such as the poor, the aged, the unemployed. **Transfer payments** are income payments for which no goods or services are exchanged. They're used to bolster the incomes of those for whom the market itself provides too little.

transfer payments: Payments to individuals for which no current goods or services are exchanged, like Social Security, welfare, unemployment benefits.

To some extent, government intervention in the distribution of income can also be explained by the theory of public goods. If the public sector didn't provide help to the aged, the disabled, the unemployed, and the needy, what would they do? Some might find a little extra work, but many would starve, even die. Others would resort to private solicitations or criminal activities to fend off hunger or death. This would mean more homeless people and muggers on the streets. In nearly all cases, the general public would be beset with the consequences of poverty and disability. Because the sight or knowledge of hungry or sick neighbors is something most people seek to avoid, the elimination of poverty creates some satisfaction for a great many people.

But even if the elimination of poverty were a common objective, it could be accomplished by individual action. If I contributed heavily to the needy, then you and I would both be relieved of the burden of the poor. We could both walk the streets with less fear and better consciences. Hence you could benefit from my expenditure, just as was possible in the case of national defense. In this sense, the relief of misery is a *public* good. Were I the only taxpayer to benefit substantially from the reduction of poverty, then charity would be a private affair. As long as income support substantially benefits the public at large, then income redistribution is a *public* good, for which public funding is appropriate. This is the *economic* rationale for public income-redistribution activities. To this rationale one can add such moral arguments as seem appropriate.

Macro Instability

The micro failures of the marketplace imply that we're at the wrong point on the production possibilities curve or inequitably distributing the output produced. There's another basic question we've swept under the rug, however. How do we get to the production possibilities curve in the first place? To reach the curve, we must utilize all available resources and technology. Can we be confident that the invisible hand of the marketplace will use all our resources? Or will some people remain **unemployed**—that is, willing to work but unable to find a job?

unemployment: The inability of labor-force participants to find jobs.

And what about prices? Price signals are a critical feature of the market mechanism. But the validity of those signals depends on some stable measure of value. What good is a doubling of salary when the price of everything you buy doubles as well? Generally, rising prices will enrich people who own property and impoverish people who rent. That's why we strive to avoid **inflation**—a situation in which the *average* price level is increasing.

inflation: An increase in the average level of prices of goods and services.

Historically, the marketplace has been wracked with bouts of both unemployment and inflation. These experiences have prompted calls for government intervention at the macro level. ***The goal of macro intervention is to foster economic growth—to get us on the production possibilities curve (full employment), maintain a stable price level (price stability), and increase our capacity to produce (growth).***

GROWTH OF GOVERNMENT

The potential micro and macro failures of the marketplace provide specific justifications for government intervention. The question then turns to how well the activities of the public sector correspond to these implied mandates.

Until the 1930s the federal government's role was largely limited to national defense (a public good), enforcement of a common legal system (also a public good), and provision of postal service (equity). The Great Depression of the 1930s spawned a new range of government activities, including welfare and Social Security programs (equity), minimum wage laws and workplace standards (regulation), and massive public works (public goods and externalities). In the 1950s the federal government also assumed a greater role in maintaining macroeconomic stability (macro failure), protecting the environment (externalities), and safeguarding the public's health (externalities and equity).

These increasing responsibilities have greatly increased the size of the public sector. In 1902 the federal government employed fewer than 350,000 people and spent a mere $650 *million.* Today the federal government employs 5 million people and spends $1.8 *trillion* a year.

Figure 4.4 summarizes the growth of the public sector since 1930. World War II caused a massive increase in the size of the federal government. Federal purchases of goods and services for the war accounted for over 40 percent of total output during the

Federal Growth

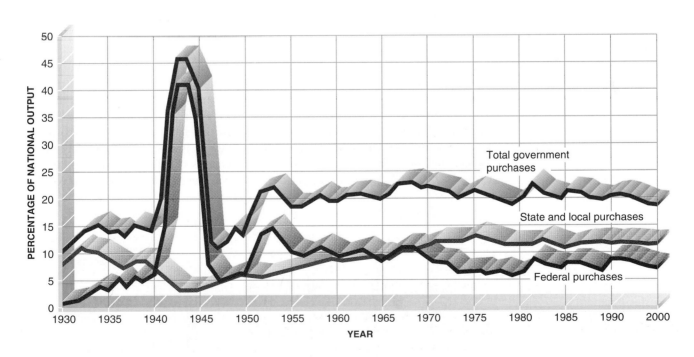

FIGURE 4.4
Government Growth

During World War II the public sector purchased nearly half of total U.S. output. Since the early 1950s the public-sector share of total output has declined to less than 20 percent. Within the public sector, however, there's been a major shift: State and local claims on resources have grown, while the federal share has declined significantly.

Source: *Economic Report of the President, 1999.*

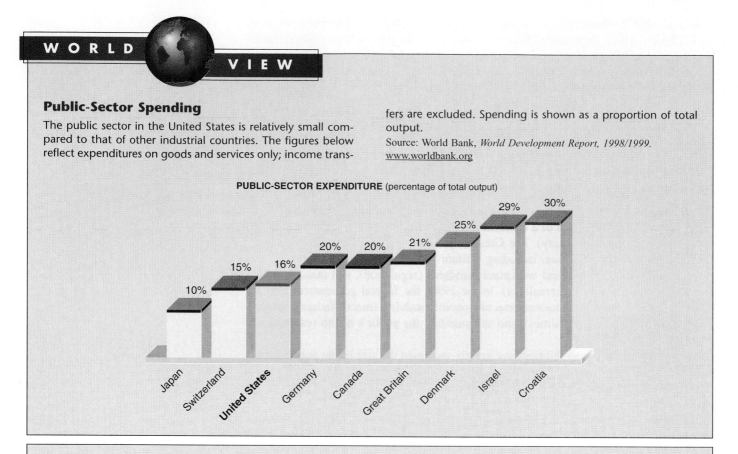

Public-Sector Spending

The public sector in the United States is relatively small compared to that of other industrial countries. The figures below reflect expenditures on goods and services only; income transfers are excluded. Spending is shown as a proportion of total output.

Source: World Bank, *World Development Report, 1998/1999.* www.worldbank.org

PUBLIC-SECTOR EXPENDITURE (percentage of total output)

Japan	Switzerland	United States	Germany	Canada	Great Britain	Denmark	Israel	Croatia
10%	15%	16%	20%	20%	21%	25%	29%	30%

Analysis: The share of total output allocated to government services varies widely across nations. In the United States, the government share of output is relatively low.

year 1943–1944. The federal share of total U.S. output fell abruptly after World War II, rose again during the Korean War, and has declined slightly since them.

The decline in the federal share of total output is somewhat at odds with most people's perception of government growth. This discrepancy is explained by two phenomena. First, people see the *absolute* size of the government growing every year. But we're focusing here on the *relative* size of the public sector. Since the 1950s the public sector has grown more slowly than the private sector, slightly reducing its relative size. As the accompanying WORLD VIEW shows, other countries have significantly larger public sectors.

FIGURE 4.5
Rising Transfer Payments

Transfer payments have absorbed an ever larger share of all federal outlays. Less than half of federal expenditure now entails the purchase of goods and services.

Source: Office of Management and Budget, *Historical Tables, Fiscal Year 1996.*

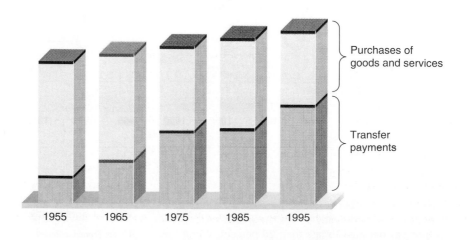

Purchases of goods and services

Transfer payments

1955 1965 1975 1985 1995

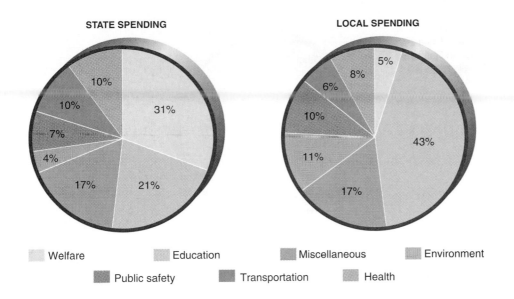

STATE SPENDING

LOCAL SPENDING

Welfare ● Education ● Miscellaneous ● Environment

Public safety ● Transportation ● Health

FIGURE 4.6
State and Local Spending

Spending on education and welfare accounts for half of all state and local expenditure. There are important differences, however, in the content of spending at each level of government.

Source: U.S. Bureau of the Census.

Figure 4.4 depicts spending on goods and services only, not all public expenditure. Specifically not included in Figure 4.4 are government transfer payments. Income transfers redistribute incomes among households but absorb few resources. Since our primary interest is in how resources are being used, we focus on those government activities that absorb available factors of production. The primary effect of income transfers is *distributional*, not *allocative*. As Figure 4.5 indicates, however, ***virtually all recent growth in federal expenditure has come from increased income transfers, not purchases of goods and services.***

State and Local Growth

State and local spending on goods and services has followed a very different path than federal expenditure. Prior to World War II, state and local governments dominated public-sector spending. During the war, however, the share of total output going to state and local governments fell, hitting a low of 3 percent in that period (Figure 4.4).

State and local spending caught up with federal spending in the mid-1960s and has exceeded it ever since. Today more than 80,000 state and local government entities buy much more output than Uncle Sam and employ three times as many people.

Figure 4.6 is an overview of state and local budgets. Education is a huge expenditure at both levels of government. Most direct state spending is on colleges; most local spending is for elementary and secondary education. The fastest-growing areas for state expenditure are prisons (public safety) and welfare. At the local level, sewage and trash services are claiming an increasing share of budgets.

TAXATION

Whatever we may think of any specific government expenditure, we must recognize one basic fact of life: We pay for government spending. In real terms, the cost of government spending can be measured by the private goods and services that are forsaken when the public sector takes command over factors of production. Factors of production used to produce national defense or schools can't be used at the same time to produce private goods or services.

The **opportunity costs** of public spending aren't always apparent. We don't directly hand over factors of production to the government. Instead, we give the government part of our income in the form of taxes. Those dollars are then used to buy factors of production or goods and services in the marketplace. Thus *the primary function of taxes is to transfer command over resources (purchasing power) from the private*

opportunity cost: The most desired goods or services that are forgone in order to obtain something else.

FIGURE 4.7
Federal Taxes

Taxes transfer purchasing power from the private sector to the public sector. The largest federal tax is the individual income tax. The second-largest source of federal revenue is the Social Security tax.

Source: Office of Management and Budget, 1998 data.

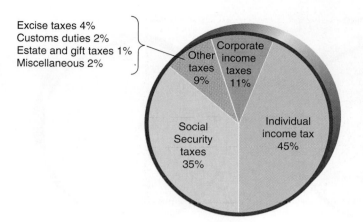

Excise taxes 4%
Customs duties 2%
Estate and gift taxes 1%
Miscellaneous 2%

Other taxes 9%

Corporate income taxes 11%

Individual income tax 45%

Social Security taxes 35%

Federal Taxes

sector to the public sector. Although the government also borrows dollars to finance its purchases, taxes are the primary source of government revenues.

As recently as 1902, much of the revenue the federal government collected came from taxes imposed on alcoholic beverages. The federal government didn't have authority to collect income taxes. As a consequence, *total* federal revenue in 1902 was only $653 million.

Income Taxes. All that has changed. The Sixteenth Amendment to the U.S. Constitution, enacted in 1915, granted the federal government authority to collect income taxes. The government now collects over $800 *billion* in that form alone. Although the federal government still collects taxes on alcoholic beverages, the individual income tax has become the largest single source of government revenue (see Figure 4.7).

progressive tax: A tax system in which tax rates rise as incomes rise.

In theory, the federal income tax is designed to be **progressive**—that is, to take a larger *fraction* of high incomes than of low incomes. In 1998, for example, a single person with less than $7000 of income paid no federal income tax. A person with $7000 to $30,000 was obligated to turn over 15 percent of each additional dollar of income to Uncle Sam. People with between $30,000 and $65,000 income confronted a 28 percent tax rate on their additional income. The marginal tax rate got as high as 39.6 percent for people earning more than $300,000 in income. Thus people with high incomes not only pay more taxes but also pay a larger *fraction* of their income in taxes.

Social Security Taxes. The second major source of federal revenue is the Social Security payroll tax. As noted earlier, people now working transfer part of their earnings to retired workers by making "contributions" to Social Security. There's nothing voluntary about these "contributions"; they take the form of mandatory payroll deductions. In 1998, each worker paid 7.65 percent of his or her wages to Social Security and employers contributed an equal amount.[1] As a consequence, the government collected more than $600 billion.

Corporate Taxes. The federal government taxes the profits of corporations as well as the incomes of consumers. But there are far fewer corporations than consumers, and their profits are small in comparison to total consumer income. In 1998, the federal government collected only $200 billion in corporate income taxes, despite the fact that it imposed a tax rate of 34 percent on corporate profits.

Excise Taxes. The last major source of federal revenue is excise taxes. Like the early taxes on whiskey, excise taxes are sales taxes imposed on specific goods and services.

[1]In 1999, this tax rate was imposed on the first $72,600 of income; the income ceiling increases every year, and the tax rate is increased occasionally as well.

"I can't find anything wrong here, Mr. Truffle . . . you just seem to
have too much left after taxes."

Analysis: Taxes are a financing mechanism that enables the
government to purchase scarce resources. Higher taxes imply less
private-sector purchases.

The federal government taxes not only liquor ($12.50 per gallon) but also gasoline
(18 cents per gallon), cigarettes (24 cents per pack), telephone service (3 percent), and
a variety of other goods and services. Such taxes not only discourage production and
consumption of these goods—by raising their price and thereby reducing the quantity
demanded—they also raise a substantial amount of revenue.

Taxes. State and local governments also levy taxes on consumers and businesses. In
general, cities depend heavily on property taxes, and state governments rely heavily on
sales taxes (see Figure 4.8). Although nearly all states and many cities also impose income taxes, effective tax rates are so low (averaging less than 2 percent of personal income) that income tax revenues are much less than sales and property tax revenues.
   Note one important feature of state and local tax structures. State and local taxes
tend to be **regressive**—that is, they take a larger share of income from the poor than
from the rich. Consider a 4 percent sales tax, for example. It might appear that a uni-
form tax rate like this would affect all consumers equally. But people with lower incomes tend to spend most of their income on goods and services. Thus most of their
income is subject to sales taxes. By contrast, a person with a high income can afford

State and Local Revenues

regressive tax: A tax system in
which tax rates fall as incomes rise.

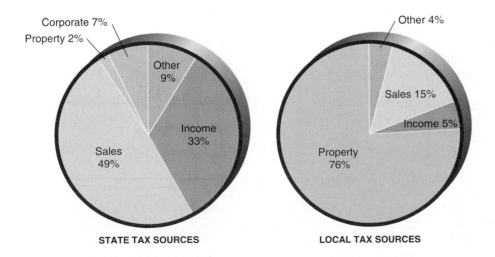

STATE TAX SOURCES   LOCAL TAX SOURCES

FIGURE 4.8
State and Local Tax Sources

State governments get half their tax
revenue from sales taxes. By contrast,
local governments depend heavily on
property taxes.

Source: U.S. Department of Commerce (1997
data).

CYBER NOTE

The U.S. Census Bureau compiles the most comprehensive data on state and local government finances. For details visit www.census.gov/ftp/pub.

categorical grants: Federal grants to state and local governments for specific expenditure purposes.

to save part of his or her income and thereby shelter it from sales taxes. A family that earns $40,000 and spends $30,000 of it on taxable goods and services, for example, pays $1200 in sales taxes when the tax rate is 4 percent. In effect, then, they are handing over 3 percent of their *income* ($1200 ÷ $40,000) to the state. By contrast, the family that makes only $12,000 and spends $11,500 of it for food, clothing, and shelter pays $460 in sales taxes in the same state. Their total tax is smaller, but it represents a much larger *share* (3.8 versus 3.0 percent) of their income.

Local property taxes are also regressive because poorer people devote a larger portion of their incomes to housing costs. Property taxes directly affect housing costs. Hence a larger share of a poor family's income is subject to property taxes. According to the Advisory Council on Intergovernmental Relations, a family earning $50,000 a year devotes only 2.5 percent of its income to property taxes, whereas a family earning $10,000 pays out 4.5 percent of its income in property taxes. State lotteries are also regressive, for the same reason (see NEWS).

Federal Aid. Up until 1986, the federal government gave state and local governments some of its revenues for whatever purposes those entities desired. But such general "revenue sharing" was always small. Most grants to state and local governments are for specific purposes and included in the federal budget under the appropriate category. For example, the federal government spent $22 billion on natural resources and environment in 1998. But one-fifth of this amount was simply given to local communities for the construction of sewage treatment plants. The local governments actually purchased or built these plants; the federal government only provided the necessary revenue. Accordingly, the federal government maintained control over WHAT to produce, but local governments exercised some judgment on HOW to produce it.

This "strings-attached" nature of most federal aid is the distinguishing feature of **categorical grants.** Funds bestowed on state and local governments in the form of categorical grants have to be used for specific purposes. If a city government needs street lighting but federal grants are available only for sewage treatment or job training, the city must choose between one of the latter or do without federal aid. Categorical grants cannot be shifted from one use to another.

In 1998, the federal government gave over $400 billion to state and local governments in the form of categorical grants (including those for employment programs,

IN THE NEWS
News: Analysis

Some Taxing Facts about Lotteries

In 1964 New Hampshire started the first modern state lottery. By 1995, 36 states and the District of Columbia had taken in over $100 billion in state lottery revenues. In 1995 alone, these states collected over $16 billion in lottery revenues. Per capita ticket sales averaged $125, up from $23 in 1975.

The transfer of these revenues to state treasuries is an implicit tax on lottery bettors, and that tax is "decidedly regressive," an NBER study concludes. Furthermore, the implicit tax rate on lottery purchases is higher than the total tax on cigarettes or alcohol according to NBER Research Associate

Charles Clotfelter and Philip Cook. . . .

Clotfelter and Cook observe that since "average lottery expenditures exhibit no consistent relationship to income," the implicit tax on those expenditures (as a percentage of income) generally falls as incomes increase. For example, average yearly lottery expenditures in California in 1986 fell from 1.4 percent of income in the lowest income class (under $10,000) to only 0.1 percent in the $50,000–$60,000 class.

NBER Digest, National Bureau of Economic Research, July 1987 and August 1989. www.nber.org/digest

Analysis: Poor people spend a larger percentage of their income on lottery tickets than do rich people. This makes lotteries a regressive source of government revenue.

Medicaid, schools, and highways). These federal grants accounted for about one-fifth of all state and local revenues.

User Charges. The third major source of state and local revenues consists of **user charges.** The tuition that college students (or their parents) pay for attending a state university or community college is an all-too-familiar user charge. But tuition fees never cover the full costs of maintaining public colleges. Part of the costs of providing higher education are borne by all state taxpayers, whether or not they attend college. Public hospitals and highways are financed the same way, with users paying part of the costs directly and all taxpayers paying the remaining costs through state and local taxes. Hence user charges aren't identical to market prices because they're not intended to cover the full costs of supplying a particular good.

user charge: Fee paid for the use of a public-sector good or service.

GOVERNMENT FAILURE

Some government intervention in the marketplace is clearly desirable. The market mechanism can fail for a variety of reasons, leaving a laissez-faire economy short of its economic goals. But how much government intervention is desirable? Communist nations once thought that complete government control of production, consumption, and distribution decisions was the surest path to utopia. They learned the hard way that not only markets but governments as well can fail.

In this context, **government failure** means that government intervention fails to move us closer to our economic goals. In Figure 4.1, such a failure would mean that government intervention moved us from point *M* to a mix of output still further away from the optimal point *X*. Government failure would also exist if the distribution of income got worse, not better, as a result of government intervention. The government would also fail if the costs of government intervention exceeded the benefits of an improved output mix, cleaner production methods, or a fairer distribution of income.

government failure: Government intervention that fails to improve economic outcomes.

Taxpayers seem to have strong opinions about government failure. When asked whether the government "wastes" their tax dollars or uses them well, the overwhelming majority see waste in government (see NEWS on the next page). Moreover, perceptions of waste have increased along with the size of the public sector. The average taxpayer now believes that state governments waste 29 cents out of each dollar, while the federal government wastes 42 cents out of each tax dollar!

Government "waste" implies that the public sector isn't producing as many services as it could with the sources at its disposal. Such inefficiency implies that we're producing somewhere *inside* our production possibilities curve rather than on it. If the government is wasting resources this way, we can't possibly be producing the optimal mix of output.

Perceptions of Waste

Even if the government weren't wasting resources, it might still be guilty of government failure. As important as efficiency in government may be, it begs the larger question of how many government services we really want. In reality, **the issue of government "waste" encompasses two distinct questions:**

Opportunity Cost

- **Efficiency:** Are we getting as much service as we could from the resources we allocate to government?
- **Opportunity cost:** Are we giving up too many private-sector goods in order to get those services?

If the government is producing goods inefficiently, we end up *inside* the production possibilities curve, with less output than attainable. Even if the government is efficient, however, the *mix* of output may not be optimal. **Everything the government does entails an opportunity cost.** The more police officers or schoolteachers employed by the public sector, the fewer workers available to private producers and consumers.

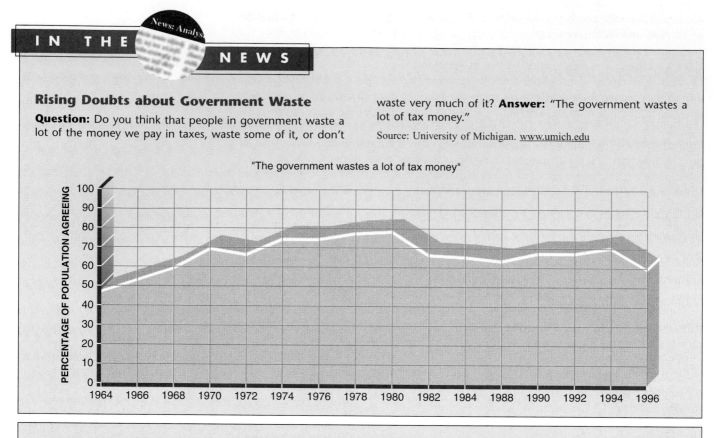

IN THE NEWS

Rising Doubts about Government Waste

Question: Do you think that people in government waste a lot of the money we pay in taxes, waste some of it, or don't waste very much of it? **Answer:** "The government wastes a lot of tax money."

Source: University of Michigan. www.umich.edu

"The government wastes a lot of tax money"

Analysis: Market failure justifies government intervention. If the government wastes resources, however, it too may fail to satisfy our economic goals.

CYBER NOTE

For more public opinion on the role of government, visit the University of Michigan's National Election Studies site at www.umich.edu/nnes/nesguide.

Similarly, the more computers, pencils, and paper consumed by government agencies, the fewer accessible to individuals and private companies.

When assessing government's role in the economy, then, *we must consider not only what governments do, but also what we give up to allow them to do it.* The theory of public goods tells us only what activities are appropriate for government, not the proper *level* of such activity. National defense is clearly a proper function of the public sector. Not so clear, however, is how much government should spend on tanks and aircraft carriers. The same is true of environmental protection or law enforcement.

The concept of opportunity costs puts a new perspective on the whole question of government size. Before we can decide how big is "too big," we must decide what we're willing to give up to support the public sector. A military force of 1.5 million men and women is "too big" from an economic perspective only if we value the forgone private production and consumption more highly than we value the added strength of our defenses. The government has gone "too far" if the highway it builds is less desired than the park and homes it implicitly replaced. In these and all cases, the assessment of bigness must come back to a comparison of what is given up with what is received. The assessment of government failure thus comes back to points on the production possibilities curve. Has the government moved us closer to the optimal mix of output or not?

Cost-Benefit Analysis

This is a tough question to answer in the abstract. We can, however, use the concept of opportunity cost to assess the effectiveness of specific government interventions. From this perspective, *additional public-sector activity is desirable only if the benefits from that activity exceed its opportunity costs.* In other words, we compare the benefits of a public project to the value of the private goods given up to produce it. By performing this calculation repeatedly along the perimeter of the production possibilities curve, we could locate the optimal mix of output—the point at which no further increase in public-sector spending activity is desirable.

This same principle can be used to decide *which* goods to produce within the public sector. A public project is desirable only to the extent that it promises to yield some benefits (or utility). But all public projects involve some costs. Hence a project should be pursued only if it can deliver a satisfactory *ratio* of benefits to costs. Otherwise we wouldn't be making very good use of our limited resources. In general, we'd want to pursue those projects with the highest benefit-cost ratio. They'll maximize the amount of utility we get from the resources we devote to the public sector.

Valuation Problems. Although the principles of benefit-cost analysis are simple enough, they're deceptive. How are we to measure the potential benefits of improved police services, for example? Should we estimate the number of robberies and murders prevented, calculate the worth of each, and add up the benefits? And how are we supposed to calculate the worth of a saved life? By a person's earnings? value of assets? number of friends? And what about the increased sense of security people have when they know the police are patrolling in their neighborhood? Should this be included in the benefit calculation? Some people will attach great value to this service; others will attach little. Whose values should be the standard?

When we're dealing with (private) market goods and services, we can gauge the benefits of production by the amount of money consumers are willing to pay for a particular product. In the case of public goods, however, we must make crude and highly subjective estimates of the benefits yielded by a particular output. Accordingly, cost-benefit analyses are valuable only to the extent that they're based on broadly accepted perceptions of benefits (or costs). In practice, consensus on the value of benefits is hard to reach, and locating the optimal mix of output entails political as well as economic judgments.

The same problems arise in evaluating the government's efforts to redistribute incomes. Government transfer payments now go to retired workers, disabled people, veterans, farmers, sick people, students, pregnant women, unemployed people, poor people, and a long list of other recipients. To pay for all these transfers, the government must raise tax revenues. With so many people paying taxes and receiving transfer payments, the net effects on the distribution of income aren't easy to figure out. Yet we can't determine whether this government intervention is "worth it" until we know how the FOR WHOM answer was changed and what the tax-and-transfer effort cost us. Here again, there's at least a possibility of government failure.

In practice, we rely on political mechanisms, not cost-benefit calculations, to decide what to produce in the public sector and how to redistribute incomes. *Voting mechanisms substitute for the market mechanism in allocating resources to the public sector and deciding how to use them.* Some people have even suggested that the variety and volume of public goods are determined by the most votes, just as the variety and volume of private goods are determined by the most dollars. Thus governments choose that level and mix of output (and related taxation) that seem to command the most votes.

Sometimes the link between the ballot box and output decisions is very clear and direct. State and local governments, for example, are often compelled to get voter approval before building another highway, school, housing project, or sewage plant. *Bond referendums* are direct requests by a government unit for the authority and purchasing power to expand the production of particular public goods. In 1998, for example, governments sought voter approval for over $13 billion of new borrowing to finance public expenditure; 70 percent of those requests were approved.

Although the direct link between bond referendums and spending decisions is important, it's more the exception than the rule. Bond referendums account for less than

Ballot Box Economics

CYBER NOTE

The National Conference of State Legislatures tracks bond referenda and other ballot issues. Visit them at www.ncsl.org to review recent ballots.

1 percent of state and local expenditures. As a consequence, voter control of public spending is much less direct. Although federal agencies must receive authorization from Congress for all expenditures, consumers get a chance to elect new representatives only every 2 years. Much the same is true at state and local levels. Voters may be in a position to dictate the general level and pattern of public expenditures but have little direct influence on everyday output decisions. In this sense, the ballot box is a poor substitute for the market mechanism.

Even if the link between the ballot box and allocation decisions were stronger, the resulting mix of output might not be optimal. A "democratic" vote, for example, might yield a 51 percent majority for approval of new local highways. Should the highways then be built? The answer isn't obvious. After all, a large minority (49 percent) of the voters have stated that they don't want resources used this way. If we proceed to build the highways, we'll make those people worse off. Even the voters who voted for the highways may end up worse off, depending on how the benefits and costs of the highway are distributed and what other opportunities exist. The basic dilemma is really twofold. ***We don't know what the real demand for public goods is, and votes alone don't reflect the intensity of individual demands.*** Moreover, real-world decision making involves so many choices that a stable consensus is impossible.

Public-Choice Theory

In the midst of all this complexity and uncertainty, another factor may be decisive—namely, self-interest. In principle, government officials are supposed to serve the people. It doesn't take long, however, before officials realize that the public is indecisive about what it wants and takes very little interest in government's day-to-day activities. With such latitude, government officials can set their own agendas. Those agendas may give higher priority to personal advancement than to the needs of the public. Agency directors may foster new programs that enlarge their mandate, enhance their visibility, and increase their prestige or income. Members of Congress may likewise pursue legislative favors like tax breaks for supporters more diligently than they pursue the general public interest. In such cases, the probability of attaining the optimal mix of output declines.

The recognition of self-interest raises concerns about the whole question of public-sector decision making. Many citizens would prefer to believe that elected officials selflessly pursue the "public good" rather than narrow, selfish goals. But the "public good" is ill-defined, and the motivations for such public service are uncertain. It's also evident that some public-policy decisions harm rather than help us. In this context, the notion of self-interest as a basic motivation for public policy has a seductive appeal.

public choice: Theory of public-sector behavior emphasizing rational self-interest of decision makers and voters.

The theory of **public choice** emphasizes the role of self-interest in public decision making. Public-choice theory essentially extends the analysis of market behavior to political behavior. Public officials are assumed to have specific personal goals (for example, power, recognition, wealth) that they'll pursue in office. **A central tenet of public-choice theory is that bureaucrats are just as selfish (utility maximizing) as everyone else.**

Public-choice theory provides a neat and simple explanation for public-sector decision making. But critics argue that the theory provides a woefully narrow view of public servants. Some people do selflessly pursue larger, "public" goals, such critics argue, and ideas can overwhelm self-interest. Steven Kelman of Harvard, for example, argues that narrow self-interest can't explain the War on Poverty of the 1960s, the tax revolt of the 1970s, or the deregulation movement of the 1980s. These tidal changes in public policy reflect the power of ideas, not simple self-interest.

Although self-interest can't provide a complete explanation of public decision making, it adds important perspectives on the policy process. James Buchanan of George Mason University (Virginia) won the 1986 Nobel Prize in economics for helping develop this public-choice perspective. It adds a personal dimension to the faceless mechanics of ballot box economics, cost-benefit analysis, and other "objective" mechanisms of public-sector decision making.

THE ECONOMY TOMORROW

Downsizing Government

The Great Depression of the 1930s devastated the world economy. For many people, it was compelling evidence that the market alone couldn't be trusted to answer the WHAT, HOW, and FOR WHOM questions. With unemployment, hunger, and homelessness at record levels, people everywhere turned to government for help. In the United States, Franklin Roosevelt's New Deal envisioned a more activist government, restoring full employment and assuring everyone some minimal level of economic security. In Eastern Europe, the communist party advanced the notion that outright government *control* of the economy was the only sure way to attain economic justice for all.

Confidence in the ability of government to resolve core economic issues continued to increase in the post-World War II era. But doubts about the effectiveness of government intervention began surfacing in the 1960s. Since then, public opinion has become increasingly skeptical about government's ability to fix anything. A 1995 public opinion poll conducted by Harvard University, the Kaiser Foundation, and *The Washington Post* revealed how much the public's faith in government intervention has changed. When people were asked about how much confidence they have in Washington actually solving a problem, 4 percent said "A lot," 35 percent said "Some," 38 percent said "Just a little," and, 23% said, "None at all." A lot of people now suspect government intervention *creates* more problems than it solves.

The increasing skepticism about government intervention has prompted a worldwide downsizing of the public sector. The downsizing has been most dramatic in the former communist nations, like the Soviet Union, where the mechanisms of central planning have been removed. In Europe and Latin America, the downsizing of government has taken the form of privatization of government-owned industries such as railroads, airlines, and telephone service. In the United States, the downsizing has been observed in the shrinking government share of total output (Figure 4.4). Whether this trend continues in the economy tomorrow depends on how well the market alone resolves the core WHAT, HOW, and FOR WHOM questions.

SUMMARY

- Government intervention in the marketplace is justified by a variety of market failures.
- The micro failures of the market originate in public goods, externalities, market power, and an inequitable distribution of income. These flaws deter the market from achieving the optimal mix of output or distribution of income.
- Public goods are those that can't be consumed exclusively; they're jointly consumed regardless of who pays. Because everyone seeks a free ride, no one demands public goods in the marketplace.
- Externalities are costs (or benefits) of a market transaction borne by a third party. Externalities create a divergence between social and private costs, causing suboptimal market outcomes.
- Market power enables a producer to thwart market signals and maintain a suboptimal mix of output. Antitrust policy seeks to prevent or restrict market power. The government may also regulate the behavior of powerful firms.

- The market-generated distribution of income may be unfair. This inequity may prompt the government to intervene with taxes and transfer payments.
- The macro failures of the marketplace are reflected in unemployment and inflation. Government intervention is intended to achieve full employment and price stability.
- The federal government expanded greatly after 1930. More recent growth, however, has been in transfer payments, which now account for over half of federal expenditure.
- State and local governments purchase more output (11 percent of GDP) than the federal government (7 percent) and employ three times as many workers.
- Income and payroll taxes provide most federal revenues. States get most revenue from sales taxes; local governments rely on property taxes.
- Government failure occurs when intervention moves us away from rather than toward the optimal mix of output

(or income). Failure may result from outright waste (operational inefficiency) or from a misallocation of resources. All government activity must be evaluated in terms of its opportunity cost, that is, the *private* goods and services forgone to make resources available to the public sector.

- Allocation decisions within the public sector may be based on benefit-cost analysis or votes. The self-interests of government agents may also affect decisions of when and how to intervene.

Key Terms

optimal mix of output	monopoly	opportunity cost
market mechanism	market power	progressive tax
market failure	antitrust	regressive tax
private good	natural monopoly	categorical grants
public good	transfer payments	user charge
free rider	unemployment	government failure
externalities	inflation	public choice

Questions for Discussion

1. Why should taxpayers subsidize public colleges and universities? What benefits do they receive from someone else's education?

2. If everyone seeks a free ride, what mix of output will be produced in Figure 4.2? Why would anyone voluntarily contribute to the purchase of public goods like flood control?

3. Could local fire departments be privately operated, with their services sold directly to customers? What problems would be involved in such a system?

4. Identify specific government activities that are justified by each source of micro failure.

5. Can you cite examples of government "waste"? Would we be better off if the government were not involved at all in that activity?

6. The government now spends over $400 billion a year on Social Security benefits. Why don't we leave it to individuals to save for their own retirement?

7. No user fees are charged for Washington, D.C.'s public museums and exhibits. Should an entrance fee be levied?

8. Are subway fares progressive or regressive? How about highway tolls?

9. Should the government be downsized? Which functions should be cut back?

10. Web Activity Find out about market power at www. antitrust.org. Choose one recent case to study. What is the source of market power in this case? What are the consequences for the U.S. economy? What is the proposed government intevention?

11. Web Activity Data on state taxes and state expenditures are available at www.census.gov/ftp/pub/govs/www/ stsum97.html. For your own state, find the most important tax and the largest expenditure category. How does your state compare with the total for all states? (See Figures 4.6 and 4.8.)

Problems for Chapter 4 appear at the back of the book.

Major Problems

Macroeconomics focuses on the performance of the entire economy rather than on the behavior of individual participants (a micro concern). The central concern of macroeconomics is the business cycle—recurrent bouts of expansion and contraction of the nation's output. These cycles affect jobs, prices, economic growth, and international trade and financial balances. Chapters 5 through 7 focus on the measurement tools for gauging the nation's macroeconomic health and the problems created by unemployment and inflation.

5

National-Income Accounting

A favorite cliché of policymakers in Washington is that government likes to tackle only those problems it can measure. Politicians need visible results. They want to be able to brag to their constituents about the miles of new highways built, the number of students who graduated, the number of families that left welfare, and the amount by which wages and income increased. To do this, they need to know how large the problems are and be able to track their achievements.

The Great Depression of the 1930s was an object lesson in the need for better measures of economic performance. There were plenty of anecdotes about factories closing, farms failing, and people selling apples on the streets. But nobody knew the dimensions of the nation's economic meltdown until millions of workers had lost their jobs. The need for more timely information about the health of the national economy was evident. From that experience a commitment to **national-income accounting**—the measurement of aggregate economic activity—emerged. During the 1930s the economist Simon Kuznets (who later received a Nobel Prize for his work) and the U.S. Department of Commerce developed an accounting system that gauges the economy's health. That national-accounting system now churns out reams of data that are essential to tracking the economy's performance. They answer such questions as

- How much output is being produced? What is it being used for?
- How much income is being generated in the marketplace?
- What's happening to prices and wages?

It's tempting of course, to ignore all these measurement questions, especially since they tend to be rather dull. But if we avoid measurement problems, we severely limit our ability to understand how the economy works or how well (or poorly) it's performing. We also limit our ability to design policies for improving economic performance.

National-income accounting also provides a useful perspective on the way the economy works. It shows how factor markets relate to product markets, how output relates to income, and how consumer spending and business investment relate to production. It also shows how the flow of taxes and government spending may alter economic outcomes.

MEASURES OF OUTPUT

The array of goods and services we produce is truly massive, including everything from professional baseball to guided-missile systems. All these things are part of our total output; the problem is to find a summary measure.

Itemizing the amount of each good or service produced each year won't solve our measurement problems. The resulting list would be so long that it would be both unwieldy and meaningless. We couldn't even add it up, since it would contain diverse goods measured in a variety of units, for example, packages, pounds, quarts. Nor could we compare one year's output to another's. Suppose that last year we produced 2 billion oranges, 2 million bicycles, and 700 rock concerts, whereas this year we produced 3 billion oranges, 4 million bicycles, and 600 rock concerts. Which year's output was larger? With more of some goods, but less of others, the answer isn't obvious.

To facilitate our accounting chores, we need some mechanism for organizing annual output data into a more manageable summary. The mechanism we use is prices. *Each good and service produced and brought to market has a price. That price serves as a measure of value for calculating total output.* Consider again the problem of determining how much output was produced this year and last. There's no obvious way to answer this question in physical terms alone. But once we know the price of each good, we can calculate the *value* of output produced in a given time period. The total dollar value of final output produced each year is what we refer to as **gross domestic product (GDP).** GDP is simply the sum of all final goods and services produced for the market in a given time period, with each good or service valued at its market price.

Table 5.1 illustrates the use of prices to value total output in two hypothetical years. If oranges were 20 cents each last year and 2 billion oranges were produced, then the *value* of orange production last year was $400 million ($0.20 × 2 billion). In the same

national-income accounting: The measurement of aggregate economic activity, particularly national income and its components.

Gross Domestic Product

gross domestic product (GDP): The total market value of all final goods and services produced within a nation's borders in a given time period.

Output	Amount
A. Last Year's Output	
In physical terms:	
Oranges	2 billion
Bicycles	2 million
Rock concerts	700
Total	?
In monetary terms:	
2 billion oranges @ $0.20 each	$ 400 million
2 million bicycles @ $50 each	100 million
700 rock concerts @ $1 million each	700 million
Total	$1200 million
B. This Year's Output	
In physical terms:	
Oranges	3 billion
Bicycles	4 million
Rock concerts	600
Total	?
In monetary terms:	
3 billion oranges @ $0.20 each	$ 600 million
4 million bicycles @ $50 each	200 million
600 rock concerts @ $1 million each	600 million
Total	$1400 million

TABLE 5.1
The Measurement of Output

It's impossible to add up all output when output is counted in *physical* terms. Accordingly, total output is measured in *monetary* terms, with each good or service valued at its market price. GDP refers to the total market value of all goods and services produced in a given time period. According to the numbers in this table, the total *value* of the oranges, bicycles, and rock concerts produced last year was $1.2 billion.

manner, we can determine that the value of bicycle production was $100 million and the value of rock concerts was $700 million. By adding these figures, we can say that the value of last year's production—last year's GDP—was $1200 million (Table 5.1A).

Now we're in a position to compare one year's output to another's. Table 5.1B shows that the use of prices enables us to say that the *value* of this year's output is $1400 million. Hence *total output* has increased from one year to the next. ***The use of prices to value market output allows us to summarize output activity and to compare the output of one period with that of another.***

GDP vs. GNP. The concept of GDP is of relatively recent use in U.S. national-income accounts. Prior to 1992, most U.S. statistics focused on gross *national* product or G*N*P. Gross *national* product refers to the output produced by American-owned factors of production regardless of where they're located. Gross *domestic* product refers to output produced within America's borders. Thus GNP would include some output from an Apple computer factory in Singapore but exclude some of the output produced by a Honda factory in Ohio. In an increasingly global economy, where factors of production and ownership move easily across international borders, the calculations of GNP became ever more complex. It also became a less dependable measure of the nation's economic health. **GDP is geographically focused, including all output produced within a nation's borders regardless of whose factors of production are used to produce it.** Apple's output in Singapore ends up in Singapore's GDP; the cars produced at Honda's Ohio plant are counted in America's GDP.

International Comparisons. The geographic focus of GDP facilitates international comparisons of economic activity. Is Japan's output as large as that of the United States? How could you tell? Japan produces a different mix of output than we do, making *quantity*-based comparisons difficult. We can compare the *value* of output produced in each country, however. The WORLD VIEW, "Comparative Output" in Chapter 2, shows that the value of America's GDP is nearly 2.5 times larger than Japan's.

GDP per capita: Total GDP divided by total population; average GDP.

GDP per Capita. International comparisons of total output are even more vivid in *per capita terms.* **GDP per capita** relates the total value of annual output to the number of people who share that output; it refers to the average GDP per person. In 1998 America's total GDP of $8.5 trillion was shared by 270 million citizens. Hence our average, or *per capita,* GDP was nearly $31,500. By contrast, the average GDP for the entire world's inhabitants was less than $6500. In these terms, America's position as the richest country in the world clearly stands out.

Statistical comparisons of GDP across nations are abstract and lifeless. They do, however, convey very real differences in the way people live. The accompanying WORLD VIEW examines some everyday realities of living in a poor nation, compared with a rich nation. Disparities in per capita GDP mean that people in low-income countries have little access to telephones, televisions, paved roads, or schools. They also die a lot younger than do people in rich countries.

But even the WORLD VIEW fails to fully convey how tough life is for people at the *bottom* of the income distribution in both poor and rich nations. Per capita GDP is only a statistical phenomenon and shouldn't be interpreted as a measure of what every citizen is getting. In the United States, for example, millions of individuals have access to far more goods and services than our average per capita GDP. Similarly, millions of others must get by with much less. Although per capita GDP in Kuwait is three times larger than that of Brazil's, we can't conclude that the typical citizen of Kuwait is three times as well off as the typical Brazilian. All these figures tell us is that the average Kuwaiti *could have* almost three times as many goods and services each year as the average Brazilian *if* GDP were distributed in the same way in both countries. ***Measures of per capita GDP tell us nothing about the way GDP is actually distributed or used; they're only a statistical average.*** When countries are quite similar in

CYBER NOTE

Global data on per capita incomes and other social indicators are available from the United Nations at www.un.org/depts/unsd/social/inc-eco.htm.

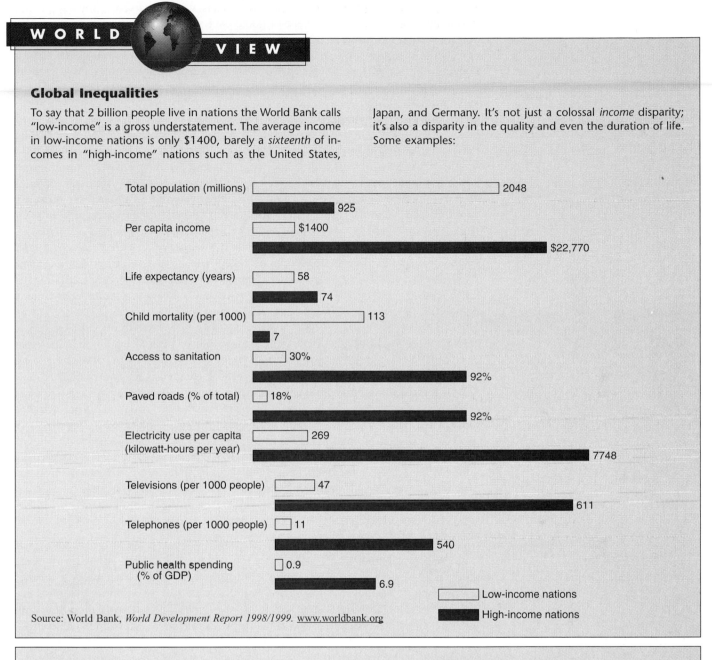

Global Inequalities

To say that 2 billion people live in nations the World Bank calls "low-income" is a gross understatement. The average income in low-income nations is only $1400, barely a *sixteenth* of incomes in "high-income" nations such as the United States, Japan, and Germany. It's not just a colossal *income* disparity; it's also a disparity in the quality and even the duration of life. Some examples:

Source: World Bank, *World Development Report 1998/1999.* www.worldbank.org

Analysis: Hidden behind dry statistical comparisons of per capita GDP lie very tangible and dramatic differences in the way people live. Low GDP per capita reflects a lot of deprivation.

structure, institutions, and income distribution, however—or when historical comparisons are made within a country—per capita GDP can be viewed as a rough-and-ready measure of relative standards of living.

Nonmarket Activities. Although the methods for calculating GDP and per capita GDP are straightforward, they do create a few problems. For one thing, our GDP measures exclude most goods and services that are produced but not sold in the market. This may appear to be a trivial point, but it isn't. Vast quantities of output never reach

Measurement Problems

the market. For example, the homemaker who cleans, washes, gardens, shops, and cooks definitely contributes to the output of goods and services. Because she's not paid a market wage for these services, however, her efforts are excluded from the calculation of GDP. At the same time, we do count the efforts of those workers who sell identical homemaking services in the marketplace. This seeming contradiction is explained by the fact that a homemaker's services aren't sold in the market and therefore carry no explicit, market-determined value.

The exclusion of homemakers' services from the GDP accounts is particularly troublesome when we want to compare living standards over time or between countries. In the United States, for example, women have demonstrated an increasing tendency to hire domestic help and leave the house to find outside employment. As a result, much housework and child care that were previously excluded from GDP statistics (because they were unpaid family help) are now included (because they're done by paid help). In this respect, our historical GDP figures may exaggerate improvements in our standard of living.

Homemaking services aren't the only output excluded. If a friend helps you with your homework, the services never get into the GDP accounts. But if you hire a tutor or engage the services of a term paper-writing agency, the transaction becomes part of GDP. Here again, the problem is simply that we have no way to determine how much output was produced until it enters the market and is purchased.[1]

Unreported Income. The GDP statistics also fail to capture market activities that aren't reported to tax or census authorities. Many people work "off the books," getting paid in unreported cash. This so-called underground economy is motivated by tax avoidance and the need to conceal illegal activities. Although illegal activities capture most of the headlines, tax evasion on income earned in otherwise legal pursuits accounts for most of the underground economy. The Internal Revenue Service estimates that over two-thirds of underground income comes from legitimate wages, salaries, profits, interest, and pensions that simply aren't reported. As the accompanying NEWS indicates, unreported income is particularly common in the service sector. People who mow lawns, clean houses, paint walls, or provide childcare services are apt to get paid in cash that isn't reported. The volume of such mundane transactions greatly exceeds the underground income generated by drug dealers, prostitutes, or gambling.

Value Added

Not every reported market transaction gets included at full value in GDP statistics. If it did, the same output would get counted over and over. The problem here is that the production of goods and services typically involves a series of distinct stages. Consider the production of a bagel, for example. For a bagel to reach Einstein's or some other bagel store, the farmer must grow some wheat, the miller must convert it to flour, and the baker must make bagels with it. Table 5.2 illustrates this chain of production.

Notice that each of the four stages of production depicted in Table 5.2 involves a separate market transaction. The farmer sells to the miller (stage 1), the miller to the baker (stage 2), the baker to the bagel store (stage 3), and finally, the store to the consumer. If we added up the separate value of each market transaction, we'd come to the conclusion that $1.75 of output had been produced. In fact, though, only one bagel has been produced, and it's worth only 75 cents. Hence we should increase GDP—the value of output—only by 75 cents.

To get an accurate measure of GDP we must distinguish between *intermediate* goods and *final* goods. **Intermediate goods** are goods purchased for use as input in further stages of production. Final goods are the goods produced at the end of the production sequence, for use by consumers (or other market participants).

intermediate goods: Goods or services purchased for use as input in the production of final goods or in services.

---

[1] The U.S. Commerce Department does, however, *estimate* the value of some nonmarket activities (e.g., food grown by farmers for their own consumption, the rental value of homeownership) and includes such estimates in GDP calculations.

IN THE NEWS

A Lot Going on Under the Table

- Percentage of households making untaxed or unmeasured "underground" purchases: 83
  Estimated amount of such expenditures on child care annually: $11 billion
  On home improvements: $28 billion
- Estimated unreported income per person in 1992, excluding illegal activities: $2113
  In 1982: $951
- Percentage of unreported income from wages and salaries in 1982: 25
  In 1992: 18
  Percentage from capital gains in 1982: 2.9
  In 1992: 13
- Unreported income as a percentage of GDP: 9
  Estimates taxes lost from unreported income in 1992: $65 billion
  Percentage by which lost taxes could reduce projected 1993 federal deficit: 21

The underground economy—transactions that are untaxed or unaccounted for in GDP—involves more than nannies.

	Estimated Percentage of Services Supplied by the Underground Economy
Lawn maintenance	90
Domestic help	83
Child care	49
Home repair/improvements	34
Laundry/sewing services	25
Appliance repair	17
Car repairs	13
Haircuts/beauty service	8
Catering	8

Data from University of Michigan Institute for Social Research, U.S. Department of Labor.

U.S. News and World Report, Feb. 22, 1993, p. 13. Copyright © Feb. 22, 1993, U.S. News & World Report. Reprinted by permission. www.usnews.com/usnews/home.htm

Analysis: GDP statistics include only the value of reported market transactions. Unreported transactions in the underground economy can't be counted and may therefore distort perceptions of economic activity.

We can compute the value of *final* output in one of two ways. The easiest way would be to count only market transactions entailing final sales (stage 4 in Table 5.2). To do this, however, we'd have to know who purchased each good or service in order to know when we had reached the end of the process. Such a calculation would also exclude any output produced in stages 1, 2, and 3 in Table 5.2 but not yet reflected in stage 4.

Another way to calculate GDP is to count only the **value added** at each stage of production. Consider the miller, for example. He doesn't really contribute $0.28 worth of production to total output, but only $0.16. The other $0.12 reflected in the price of his flour represents the contribution of the farmer who grew the wheat. By the same token,

value added: The increase in the market value of a product that takes place at each stage of the production process.

Stages of Production	Value of Transaction	Value Added
1. Farmer grows wheat, sells it to miller	$0.12	$0.12
2. Miller converts wheat to flour, sells it to baker	0.28	0.16
3. Baker bakes bagel, sells it to bagel store	0.60	0.32
4. Bagel store sells bagel to consumer	0.75	0.15
Total	$1.75	$0.75

TABLE 5.2
Value Added in Various Stages of Production

The value added at each stage of production represents a contribution to total output. Value added equals the market value of a product minus the cost of intermediate goods.

the baker *adds* only $0.32 to the value of output, as part of his output was purchased from the miller. By considering only the value *added* at each stage of production, we eliminate double counting. We don't count twice the *intermediate* goods and services that producers buy from other producers, which are then used as inputs. As Table 5.2 confirms, we can determine that value of final output by summing up the value added at each stage of production. (Note that $0.75 is also the price of a bagel.)

Real vs. Nominal GDP

Although prices are a convenient measure of market value, they can also distort perceptions of real output. Imagine what would happen to our calculations of GDP if all prices were to double from one year to the next. Suppose, for example, that the price of oranges, as shown in Table 5.1, rose from $0.20 to $0.40, the price of bicycles to $100, and the price of rock concerts to $2 million each. How would such price changes after this year's GDP? Obviously, the price increases would double the *value* of final output. Measured GDP would rise from $1400 million to $2800 million.

Such a rise in GDP doesn't reflect an increase in the *quantity* of goods and services available to us. We're still producing the same quantities shown in Table 5.1; only the prices of those goods have changed. Hence **changes in GDP brought about by changes in the price level can give us a distorted view of economic activity.** Surely we wouldn't want to assert that our standard of living had improved just because price increases raised measured GDP from $1400 millions to $2800 million.

To distinguish increases in the quantity of goods and services from increases in their prices, we must construct a measure of GDP that takes into account price-level changes. We do so by distinguishing between *real* GDP and *nominal* GDP. **Nominal GDP** is the value of final output measured in *current* prices, whereas **real GDP** is the value of output measured in *constant* prices. ***To calculate real GDP, we adjust the market value of goods and services for changing prices.***

Note, for example, that in Table 5.1 prices are unchanged as we go from last year to this year. In this case, prices in the marketplace are constant, and interyear comparisons of prices are simple. But if all prices double, the comparison becomes more complicated. If all prices doubled from last year to this year, this year's nominal GDP would rise to $2800 million. But these price increases wouldn't alter the quantity of goods produced. In other words, *real* GDP, valued at constant prices, would remain at $1400 million. Thus ***the distinction between nominal and real GDP is important whenever the price level changes.***

Because the price level changes every year, both real and nominal GDP are regularly reported. Nominal GDP is computed simply by adding the current dollar value of production. Real GDP is computed by making an adjustment for changes in prices from year to year.

Consider the GDP statistics for 1997 and 1998, as displayed in Table 5.3. The first row shows nominal GDP in each year: nominal GDP increased by $388 billion between 1997 and 1998 (row 2). This 4.6 percent increase looks very impressive. However, some of that gain was fueled by higher prices, not increased output. Row 3 indicates that the price level rose by 1.0 percent during that same period.

Row 4 in Table 5.3 adjusts the GDP comparison for the change in prices. We deflate the 1998 nominal GDP by factoring out the 1.0 percent price increase. Simple division is all we need to compute *real* GDP in 1998 as being $8415 billion. Hence *real* GDP increased by only $304 billion in 1998 (row 5), not by the larger inflation-exaggerated amount in row 2.

Notice in Table 5.3 that in 1997 real and nominal GDP are identical because we're using that year as the basis of comparison. We're comparing 1998's performance to that of the 1997 **base period.** Real GDP can be expressed in the prices of a particular year; that year serves as the base for computing price-level and output changes. The general formula for computing real GDP is

nominal GDP: The value of final output produced in a given period, measured in the prices of that period (current prices).
real GDP: The value of final output produced in a given period, adjusted for changing prices.

base period: The time period used for comparative analysis; the basis for indexing, for example, of price changes.

$$\text{Real GDP in year } t = \frac{\text{nominal GDP in year } t}{\text{price index}}$$

	1997	1998
1. Nominal GDP (in billions)	$8111	$8499
2. Change in nominal GDP		+ $388
3. Change in price level, 1997 to 1998		1.0%
4. Real GDP in 1997 dollars	$8111	$8415 $\left(=\dfrac{\$8499}{1.01}\right)$
5. Change in real GDP		+ $304

TABLE 5.3
Computing Real GDP

Real GDP is the inflation-adjusted value of nominal GDP. Between 1997 and 1998, nominal GDP increased by $388 billion (row 2). Some of this gain was due to rising prices (row 3). After adjusting for inflation, real GDP increased only by $304 billion (row 5).

The price index shows how average prices have changed between the base year and year *t*. Between 1997 and 1998 average prices rose 1.0 percent. This price-level change is indexed as 1.01. Thus, real GDP in 1998 is calculated as

$$\frac{\text{Real GDP in 1998}}{\text{(1997 prices)}} = \frac{\$8499 \text{ billion}}{1.01} = \$8415 \text{ billion}$$

This is the figure shown in row 4, Table 5.3.

The distinction between nominal and real GDP becomes critical when more distant years are compared. Between 1933 and 1990, for example, prices rose by 800 percent. Table 5.4 shows how such price-level changes can distort our views of how living standards have changed since the Great Depression.

Figure 5.1 (page 95) shows how nominal and real GDP have changed since 1975. Real GDP is calculated here on the basis of the level of prices prevailing in 1992. (Note that real and nominal GDP are identical in that year.) The dollar value of output produced each year has risen considerably faster than the quantity of output, reflecting persistent increases in the price level—that is, **inflation.**

Notice in particular that continuing inflation tends to obscure the actual *declines* in real output. Real GDP actually declined in 1980, 1982, and 1991, though nominal GDP kept rising. Although the *value* of final output continued to rise in those years, the annual production of goods and services was falling; nominal and real GDP moved in opposite directions.

Chain-Weighted Price Adjustments. Although the distinction between real and nominal GDP is critical in measuring the nation's economic health, the procedure for making inflation adjustments isn't perfect. When we use the prices of a specific year as the base for computing real GDP, we're implicitly "freezing" *relative* prices as well as *average* prices. Over time, however, relative prices can change markedly. Computer prices, for example, have fallen sharply in recent years in both absolute and relative terms. During the same period, unit sales of computers have increased by 20 to 25 percent a year. If we use the higher computer prices of 1992 to compute that sales growth, we'll greatly exaggerate the *value* of today's computer output. If we use today's prices, however, we'll underestimate the value of output in the period since 1992. To resolve this problem, the U.S. Department of Commerce uses a *chain-weighted* price index to compute real GDP. Instead of using the prices of a *single* base year to compute real GDP, **chain-weighted indices use a *moving average* of price levels in consecutive years as an inflation adjustment.** When chain-weighted price adjustments are made, real GDP still refers to the inflation-adjusted value of GDP but isn't expressed in terms of the prices prevailing in any specific base year. All official estimates of real GDP are now based on chain-weighted price indices.

Changes in real GDP from one year to the next tell us how much the economy's output is growing. Some of that growth, however, may come at the expense of future

CYBER NOTE

Find out how much real GDP fell per year during the Great Depression (1929–1940) at www.bea.doc.gov/bea/dn/0898nip3/table1.htm.

inflation: An increase in the average level of prices of goods and services.

CYBER NOTE

If you want to see some great charts on GDP and other economic statistics, visit Dr. Ed Yardeni's Web site at www.yardeni.com.

Net Domestic Product

TABLE 5.4
Real vs. Nominal GDP: An Historical View

Suppose we want to determine how much better off the average American was in 1990, as measured in terms of new goods and services, than people were during the Great Depression. To do this, we'd compare GDP per capita in 1990 with GDP per capita in 1933. The following data make that comparison:

	GDP	Population	Per Capita GDP
1933	$ 56 billion	126 million	$ 444
1990	5600 billion	250 million	22,400

In 1933 the nation's GDP of $56 billion was shared by 126 million Americans, yielding a *per capita* GDP of $444. By contrast, 1990's GDP was roughly 100 times larger, at $5600 billion. This vastly larger GDP was shared by 250 million people, giving us a per capita GDP of $22,400. Hence it would appear that our standard of living in 1990 was 50 times higher than the standard of 1933.

But this increase in *nominal* GDP vastly exaggerates our material well-being. The average price of goods and services—the *price level*—increased by 800 percent between 1933 and 1990. The goods and services you might have bought for $1 in 1933 cost $9 in 1990. In other words, we needed a lot more dollars in 1990 to buy any given combination of real goods and services.

To compare our *real* GDP in 1990 with the real GDP of 1933, we have to adjust for this tremendous jump in prices (inflation). We do so by measuring both years' output in terms of *constant* prices. Since prices went up, on average, ninefold between 1933 and 1990, we simply divide 1990 *nominal* output by nine. The calculation is

$$\text{Real GDP in 1990 (1933 prices)} = \text{nominal 1990 GDP} \times \frac{\text{1933 price level}}{\text{1990 price level}}$$

By arbitrarily setting the level of prices in 1933 at 100 and noting that prices have increased ninefold since then, we can calculate

$$\text{Real GDP in 1990 (1933 prices)} = \$5600 \text{ billion} \times \frac{100}{900}$$
$$= \$622 \text{ billion}$$

With a population of 250 million, this left us with real GDP per capita of $2488 in 1990—as measured in 1933 dollars. This was more than five times the *real* per capita GDP of the depression ($444), but not nearly so great an increase as comparisons of *nominal* GDP suggest.

production possibilities: The alternative combinations of final goods and services that could be produced in a given time period with all available resources and technology.

depreciation: The consumption of capital in the production process; the wearing out of plant and equipment.

net domestic product (NDP): GDP less deprecation.

output. Recall that our **production possibilities** determine how much output we can produce. Those limits are, in turn, established by the availability of factors of production and technology. If we use up some of these resources to produce this year's output, future production possibilities may shrink. ***Next year we won't be able to produce as much output unless we replace factors of production we use this year.***

We routinely use up plant and equipment (capital) in the production process. To maintain our production possibilities, therefore, we have to at least replace what we've used. The value of capital used up in producing goods and services is commonly called **depreciation.**[2] In principle, it's the amount of capital worn out by use in a year or made obsolete by advancing technology. In practice, the amount of capital depreciation is estimated by the U.S. Department of Commerce.

By subtracting depreciation from GDP we get **net domestic product (NDP).** This is the amount of output we could consume without reducing our stock of capital and therewith next year's production possibilities.

---

[2]The terms "depreciation" and "capital consumption allowance" are used interchangeably. The depreciation charges firms commonly make, however, are determined in part by income tax regulations, and thus may not accurately reflect the amount of capital consumed.

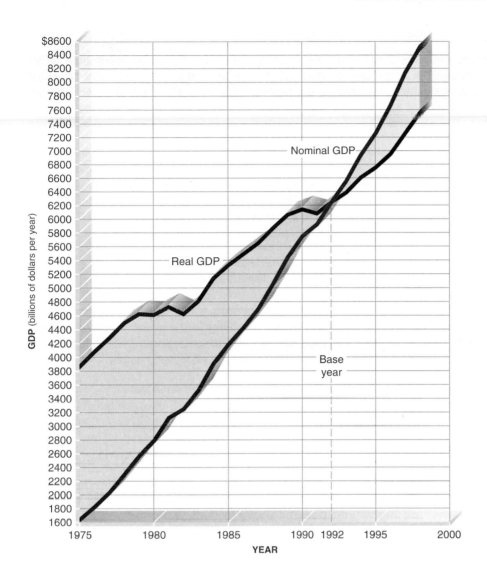

FIGURE 5.1
Changes in GDP: Nominal vs. Real

Increases in *nominal* GDP reflect higher prices as well as more output. Increases in *real* GDP reflect more output only. To measure these real changes, we must value each year's output in terms of common base prices. In this figure the reference year is 1992. Notice that *real* GDP declined in 1980, 1982, and 1991, although *nominal* GDP continued to rise. Nominal GDP rises faster than real GDP as a result of inflation.

Source: *Economic Report of the President, 1999.*

The distinction between GDP and NDP has direct implications for the mix of output. To maintain our production possibilities, we must at least replace the capital we consume. This means that at least some of each year's output must consist of newly produced plant and equipment—that is, **investment** goods. Indeed, our total production of new plant, equipment, and structures—that is, our gross investment—must at least match our depreciation. If we fail to allocate at least that much of our output to investment, our stock of capital and production possibilities will shrink.

The distinction between GDP and NDP is mirrored in a distinction between *gross* investment and *net* investment. **Gross investment** is positive as long as some new plant and equipment are being produced. But ***the stock of capital—the total collection of plant and equipment—won't grow unless gross investment exceeds depreciation.*** That is, the *flow* of new capital must exceed depreciation, or our *stock* of capital will decline. Whenever the rate of gross investment exceeds depreciation, **net investment** is positive.

Notice that net investment can be negative as well; in such situations we're wearing out plant and equipment faster than we're replacing it. When net investment is negative, our capital stock is shrinking. This was the situation during the period 1932–1934 for the U.S. economy. Gross investment fell so sharply (see front endpaper of book) that it wasn't even replacing used-up machinery and structures. As a result, the economy's ability to produce goods and services declined.

investment: Expenditures on (production of) new plant, equipment, and structures (capital) in a given time period, plus changes in business inventories.

gross investment: Total investment expenditure in a given time period.

net investment: Gross investment less depreciation.

THE USES OF OUTPUT

The role of investment in maintaining or expanding our production possibilities helps focus attention on the uses to which GDP is put. It's not just the total value of annual output that matters, but also the use that we make of it. ***The GDP accounts also tell us what mix of output we're selected, that is, society's answer to the core issue of WHAT to produce.***

Consumption

The major uses of total output conform to the four sets of market participants we encountered in Chapter 2, namely, consumers, business firms, government, and foreigners. Those goods and services used by households are called *consumption goods* and range all the way from donuts to online computer services and include all goods and services households purchase in product markets. As we observed in Chapter 2, all this consumer spending claims two-thirds of our annual output (see Figure 2.3).

Investment

Investment goods represent another use of GDP. Investment goods are the plant, machinery, and equipment we produce. Net changes in business inventories and expenditures for residential construction are also counted as investment. To produce any of these investment goods we must use scarce resources that could be used to produce something else. Resources used to produce buildings or machinery can't simultaneously be used to produce television sets or video disks (opportunity costs again). Investment spending claims approximately 15 percent of our total output.

Government Spending

The third major uses of GDP is the *public sector.* Federal, state, and local governments purchase resources to police the streets, teach classes, write laws, and build highways. The resources purchased by the government sector are unavailable for either consumption or investment purposes. At present, government spending claims less than one-fifth of total output.

Net Exports

exports: Goods and services sold to international buyers.

Finally, remember that some of the goods and services we produce each year are used abroad rather than at home. That is, we **export** some of our output to other countries, for whatever use they care to make of it. Thus GDP—the value of output produced—will be larger than the sum of our own consumption, investment, and government purchases to the extent that we succeed in exporting goods and services.

imports: Goods and services purchased from international sources.

We **import** goods and services as well. A flight to London on British Air is an imported service; a Jaguar is an imported good. These goods and services aren't part of America's GDP since they weren't produced within our borders. In principle, these imports never enter the GDP accounts. In practice, however, it's difficult to distinguish imports from domestic-made products, especially when goods include value added from both foreign and domestic producers. Over one-fifth of the 1995 Ford Contour, for example, consisted of parts manufactured in Japan, Mexico, Thailand, Britain, Spain, and Germany; final assembly took place in Kansas City. Should that car be counted as an "American" product or as an import? Rather than try to sort out all these products and parts, the U.S. Commerce Department simply subtracts the value of all imports from the value of total spending. Thus exports are *added* to GDP and *imports* are subtracted.

net exports: The value of exports minus the value of imports.

The difference between the two expenditure flows is called **net exports.**

What we end up with is a simple method for computing GDP. ***The value of GDP can be computed by adding up expenditures of market participants.*** Specifically, we note that

$$GDP = C + I + G + (X - IM)$$

where C = consumption expenditure

I = investment expenditure

G = government expenditure

X = exports

IM = imports

This approach to GDP accounting emphasizes the fact that all the output produced in the economy is claimed by someone. If we know who's buying our output, we know how much was produced and what uses were made of it.

MEASURES OF INCOME

There's another way of looking at GDP. Instead of looking at who's *buying* our output, we can look at who's *being paid* to produce it. Like markets themselves. **GDP accounts have two sides: One side focuses on expenditure (the demand side), the other side focuses on income (the supply side).**

We've already observed (see Figure 3.1) that every market transaction involves an *exchange* of dollars for a good or resource. Moreover, the *value* of each good or resource is measured by the amount of money exchanged for it (its market price). Hence **the total value of market incomes must equal the total value of final output, or GDP.** In other words, one person's expenditure always represents another person's income.

Figure 5.2 illustrates the link between spending on output and incomes. This is a modified version of the circular flow we saw in Chapter 3. The spending that flows into the product market gets funneled into the factor market when resources are employed to produce the goods people want. The expenditure then flows into the hands of business owners, workers, landlords, and other resource owners. With the exception of sales taxes and depreciation, all spending on output becomes income to factors of production.

The equivalence of output and income isn't dependent on any magical qualities possessed by money. Were we to produce only one product—say, wheat—and pay everyone in bushels and pecks, total income would still equal total output. People couldn't receive in income more wheat than we produced. On the other hand, all the wheat produced would go to *someone*. Hence one could say that the production possibilities of the economy define the limits to real income. The amount of income actually generated in any year depends on the production and expenditure decisions of consumers, firms, and government agencies.

Table 5.5 shows the actual flow of output and income in the U.S. economy during 1998. Total output is made up of the familiar components of GDP: consumption, investment, government goods and services, and net exports. The figures on the left side of Table 5.5 indicate that consumers spent $5806 billion, businesses spent $1369 billion on plant and equipment, governments spent $1488 billion, and net imports were $154 billion. Our total output value (GDP) was thus more than $8.5 trillion in 1998.

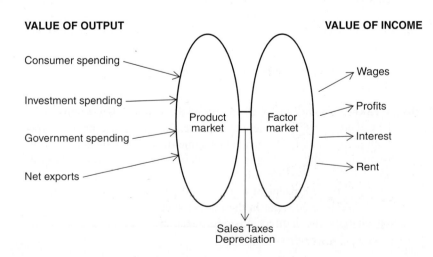

VALUE OF OUTPUT

VALUE OF INCOME

FIGURE 5.2
Output = Income

All the spending that establishes the value of output also determines the value of incomes. With minor exceptions, the market value of incomes must equal the market value of output.

TABLE 5.5
The Equivalence of Expenditure and Income
(in billions of dollars)

The value of total expenditure must equal the value of total income. Why? Because every dollar spent on output becomes a dollar of income for someone.

Expenditure		Income	
Consumer goods and services	$5808	Wages and salaries	$4981
Investment in plant,		Corporate profits	825
equipment, and inventory	1367	Proprietors' income	548
Government goods and		Farm income	29
services	1487	Rents	163
Exports	959	Interest	449
Imports	(1110)	Sales taxes	608
		Depreciation	908
Total value of output	$8511	Total value of income	$8511

Source: U.S. Department of Commerce (1998 data).

The right-hand side of Table 5.5 indicates who received the income generated from these markets transactions. Every dollar spent on goods and services provides income to someone. It may go to a worker (as wage or salary) or to a business firm (as profit and depreciation allowance). It may go to a landlord (as rent), to a lender (as interest), or to government (as sales or property tax). None of the dollars spent on goods and services disappears into thin air.

National Income

Although it may be exciting to know that we collectively received $8.5 trillion of income in 1998, it might be of more interest to know who actually got all that income. After all, in addition to the 270 million pairs of outstretched palms among us, millions of businesses and government agencies were also competing for those dollars and the goods and services they represent. By charting the flow of income through the economy, we can see FOR WHOM our output was produced.

Depreciation. Our annual income flow originated in product-market sales. Purchases of final goods and services create a flow of income to producers and, through them, to factors of production. But a major diversion of sales revenues occurs immediately, as a result of depreciation charges made by businesses. As we noted earlier, some of our capital resources are used up in the process of production. For the most part, these resources are owned by business firms that expect to be compensated for such investments. Accordingly, they regard some of the sales revenue generated in product markets as reimbursement for wear and tear on capital plant and equipment. They therefore subtract *depreciation charges* from gross revenues in calculating their incomes. Depreciation charges reduce GDP to the level of NDP before any income is available to current factors of production. As we saw earlier,

$$\text{NDP} = \text{GDP} - \text{depreciation}$$

Indirect Business Taxes. Another major diversion of the income flow occurs at its point of origin. When goods are sold in the marketplace, their purchase price is typically encumbered with some sort of sales tax. Thus some of the revenue generated in product markets disappears before any factor of production gets a chance to claim it. These *indirect business taxes,* as they're called, aren't considered part of national income because they don't represent payment to factors of production. But they do account for a large part of the income spent in the marketplace.

Once depreciation charges and indirect business taxes are subtracted from GDP, we're left with **national income,** which is the total income earned by factors of production. Thus

$$NI = NDP - \text{indirect business taxes}$$

As Table 5.6 illustrates, our national income in 1998 was $6995 billion, which is more than $1 trillion less than GDP.

National income is the income earned not only by households (consumers) but also by corporations. Theoretically, all the income corporations receive represents income for their owners—the households who hold stock in the corporations. But the flow of income through corporations to stockholders is far from complete. First, corporations may pay taxes on their profits. Accordingly, some of the income received on behalf of a corporation's stockholders goes into the public treasury rather than into private bank accounts. Second, corporate managers typically find some urgent need for cash. As a result, part of the profits are retained by the corporation rather than passed on to the stockholders in the form of dividends. Accordingly, both *corporate taxes* and *retained earnings* must be subtracted from national income before we can determine how much income flows into the hands of consumers.

Still another deduction must be made for *Social Security taxes.* Nearly all people who earn a wage or salary are required by law to pay Social Security "contributions." In 1999 the Social Security tax rate for workers was 7.65 percent of the first $72,600 of earnings received in the year. Workers never see this income because it is withheld by employers and sent directly to the U.S. Treasury. Thus the flow of national income is reduced considerably before it becomes **personal income,** the amount of income received by households before payment of personal taxes.

Not all of our adjustments to national income are negative. Households receive income in the form of transfer payments from the public treasury. More than 45 million people receive monthly Social Security checks, for example, and another 20 million receive some form of public welfare. These income transfers represent income for the people who receive them. People also receive interest payments in excess of those they pay (largely because of interest payments on the government debt). This *net* interest is

national income (NI): Total income earned by current factors of production: GDP less depreciation and indirect business taxes.

Personal Income

personal income (PI): Income received by households before payment of personal taxes.

Income flow	Amount (in billions)
Gross domestic product (GDP)	$8511
Less depreciation	(908)
Net domestic product (NDP)	7603
Less indirect business taxes	(608)
National income (NI)	6995
Less corporate taxes	(240)
Less retained earnings*	(299)
Less Social Security taxes	(768)
Plus transfer payments	1122
Plus net interest	316
Personal income (PI)	7126
Less personal taxes	(1098)
Disposable income (DI)	6028

*Retained earnings are net of inventory valuation changes and depreciation.
Source: U.S. Department of Commerce.

TABLE 5.6
The Flow of Income, 1998

The revenue generated from market transactions passes through many hands. Households end up with disposable income equal to about 70 percent of GDP, after depreciation and taxes are taken out and net interest and transfer payments are added back in. Disposable income is either spent (consumption) or saved by households.

another source of personal income. Accordingly, our calculation of personal income is as follows:

- *national income* (= income earned by factors of production)
  less   corporate taxes
          retained earnings
          Social Security taxes
  plus   transfer payments
          net interest
- *equals **personal income*** (= income received by households)

The total flow of income generated in production is significantly reduced before it gets into the hands of individual households. But we haven't yet reached the end of the reduction process. We have to set something aside for personal income taxes. To be sure we don't forget about our obligations, Uncle Sam and his state and local affiliates usually arrange to have their share taken off the top. Personal income taxes are withheld by the employer, who thus acts as a tax collector. Accordingly, to calculate **disposable income,** which is the amount of income consumers may themselves spend (dispose of), we reduce personal income by the amount of personal taxes:

$$\text{Disposable income} = \text{personal income} - \text{personal taxes}$$

Disposable income is the end of the accounting line. As Table 5.6 shows, households end up with roughly 70 percent of the revenues generated from final market sales (GDP). Once consumers get this disposable income in their hands, they face two choices. They may choose to *spend* their disposable income on consumer goods and services. Or they may choose to *save* it. These are the only two choices in GDP accounting. **Saving,** in this context, simply refers to disposable income that isn't spent on consumption. In the analysis of income and saving flows, we don't care whether savings are hidden under a mattress, deposited in the bank, or otherwise secured. All we want to know is whether disposable income is spent or not. Thus ***all disposable income is, by definition, either consumed or saved; that is,***

$$\text{Disposable income} = \text{consumption} + \text{saving}$$

disposable income (DI): After-tax-income of households; personal income less personal taxes.

CYBER NOTE

For the latest data on GDP and its components visit the Bureau of Economic Analysis at www.bea.doc.gov.

saving: That part of disposable income not spent on current consumption; disposable income less consumption.

THE FLOW OF INCOME

Figure 5.3 summarizes the relationship between expenditure and income. The essential point again is that every dollar spent on goods and services flows into somebody's hands. Thus ***the dollar value of output will always equal the dollar value of income.*** Specifically, total income (GDP) ends up distributed in the following way:

- To *households,* in the form of disposable income
- To *business,* in the form of retained earnings and depreciation allowances
- To *government,* in the form of taxes

Income and Expenditure

The annual flow of income to households, businesses, and government is part of a continuing process. Households rarely stash their disposable income under the mattress; they spend most of it on consumption. This spending adds to GDP in the next round of activity, thereby helping to keep the flow of income moving.

Business firms also have a lot of purchasing power tied up in retained earnings and depreciation charges. This income, too, may be recycled—returned to the circular flow—in the form of business investment.

Even the income that flows into public treasuries finds its way back into the marketplace, as government agencies hire police officers, soldiers, and clerks, or they buy goods and services. Thus ***the flow of income that starts with GDP ultimately returns to the market in the form of new consumption (C), investment (I), and government***

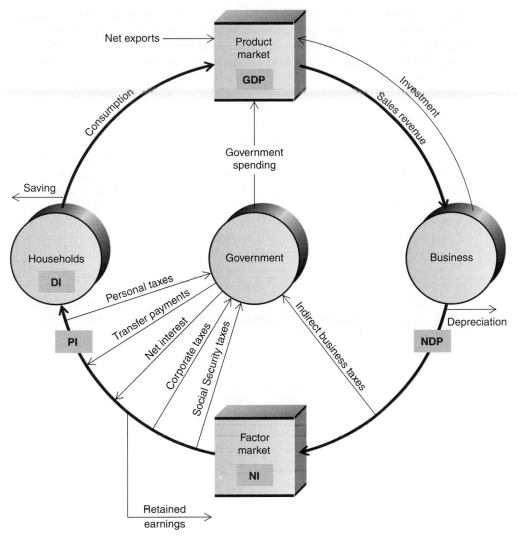

FIGURE 5.3
The Circular Flow of Spending and Income

GDP represents the dollar value of final output sold in the product market. The revenue stream flowing from GDP works its way through NDP, NI, and PI before reaching households in the form of smaller DI. DI is in turn either spent or saved by consumers. This consumption, plus investment, government spending, and net exports, continues the circular flow.

purchases (G). A new GDP arises, and the flow starts all over. In later chapters we examine in detail these *expenditure* flows, with particular emphasis on their ability to keep the economy producing at its full potential.

THE ECONOMY TOMORROW

Money, money, money—it seems that's all we talk about. Why don't we talk about important things like beauty, virtue, or the quality of life? Will the economy of tomorrow be filled with a glut of products but devoid of real meaning? Do the GDP accounts—either the expenditure side or the income side—tell us anything we really want to know about the quality of life? If no, why should we bother to examine them?

The Quality of Life

Intangibles

All the economic measures discussed in this chapter are important indexes of individual and collective welfare; they tell us something about how well people are living. They don't, however, capture the completeness of the way in which we view the world or the totality of what makes our lives satisfying. A clear day, a sense of accomplishment, even a smile can do more for a person's sense of well-being than can favorable movements in the GDP accounts. Or, as John Kenneth Galbraith put it, "In a rational life-style, some people could find contentment working moderately and then sitting by the street—and talking, thinking, drawing, painting, scribbling, or making love in a suitably discreet way. None of these requires an expanding economy."[3]

The emphasis on economic outcomes arises not from ignorance of life's other meanings but from the visibility of the economic outcomes. We all realize that well-being arises from both material and intangible pleasures, but the intangibles tend to be elusive. It's not easy to gauge individual happiness, much less to ascertain the status of our collective satisfaction. We have to rely on measures we can see, touch, and count. As long as the material components of our environment bear some positive relation to our well-being, they at least serve a useful purpose.

In some situations, however, more physical output may actually worsen our collective welfare. If increased automobile production raises congestion and pollution levels, the rise in GDP occasioned by those additional cars is a misleading index of society's welfare. In such a case, the rise in GDP might actually mask a *decrease* in the well-being of the population. We might also wonder whether more casinos, more prisons, more telemarketing, more divorce litigation, and more Prozac—all of which contribute to GDP growth—are really valid measures of our well-being (see cartoon). Exclusive emphasis on measurable output would clearly be a mistake in many cases.

What is true of automobile production might also be true of other outputs. Increased development of urban areas may cause a loss of social welfare if that development occurs at the expense of space, trees, and relative tranquillity. Increased mechanization

[3]Cited in Leonard Silk, *Nixonomics,* 2d ed. (New York: Praeger, 1973), p. 163.

Analysis: GDP includes *everything* produced and sold in the product market, no matter how much each good or service contributes to our social well-being.

IN THE NEWS

America's Declining Social Health

National-income accounts are regularly reported and widely quoted. They do not, however, adequately reflect the nation's *social* performance. To measure more accurately the country's social health, a Fordham University team of social scientists has devised an "Index of Social Health" with sixteen indicators, including infant mortality, drug abuse, health-insurance coverage, and poverty among the aged. According to this index, America's social health deteriorated sharply in the mid-1970s. The index of social health stayed flat in the 1980s and 1990s despite a sustained rise in the nation's economy.

Fordham Institute, *1998 Index of Social Health,* Tarrytown, N.Y.

Analysis: The national-income accounts emphasize material well-being. They are an important, but not complete, gauge of our societal welfare.

---

on the farm may raise agricultural output but isolate and uproot farmers. So, too, increased productivity in factories and offices might contribute to a sense of alienation. These ill effects of increased output needn't occur; but if they do, indexes of output tell us less about social or individual well-being.

Researchers at Fordham University devised an alternative index of well-being. Their Index of Social Health includes a few economic parameters (such as unemployment and weekly earnings) but puts more emphasis on sociological behavior (such as child abuse and teen suicides). They claim that this broader view points to a decline in societal well-being over the past two decades, even though GDP was rising (see NEWS.)

Index of Well-Being

Even if the Index of Social Health is a valid gauge of our collective well-being, we shouldn't conclude that the national-income accounts are useless or irrelevant. These points help underscore the fact that *social welfare* and *economic welfare* aren't synonymous. The GDP accounts tell us whether our economic welfare has increased, as measured by the value of goods and services produced. They don't tell us how highly we value additional goods and services relative to nonmarket phenomena. Nor do they even tell us whether important social costs were incurred in the process of production. These judgments must be made outside the market; they're social decisions.

Finally, note that any given level of GDP can encompass many combinations of output. Choosing WHAT to produce is still a critical question, even after the goal of *maximum* production has been established. The quality of life in the economy tomorrow will depend on what specific mix of goods and services we include in GDP.

CYBER NOTE

The United Nations has constructed a Human Development Index that offers a broader view of social well-being than GDP alone. For details and country rankings, visit www.undp.org.

SUMMARY

- National-income accounting is the measurement of our annual output and income flows. The national-income accounts provide a basis for assessing our economic performance, designing public policy, and understanding how all the parts of the economy interact.

- The most comprehensive measure of our output is gross domestic product (GDP), the total market value of all final goods and services produced within a nation's borders during a given time period.

- In calculating GDP, we include only the value added at each stage of production. This procedure eliminates the possibility of the double counting that would result because business firms buy intermediate goods from other firms and include the associated costs in their selling price. For the most part, only marketed goods and services are included in GDP.

- To distinguish physical changes in output from monetary changes in its value, we compute both nominal and real

GDP. Nominal GDP is the value of output expressed in *current* prices. Real GDP is the value of output expressed in *constant* prices (the prices of some *base* year).

- Each year some of our capital equipment is worn out in the process of production. Hence GDP is larger than the amount of goods and services we could consume without reducing our production possibilities. The amount of capital used up each year is referred to as "depreciation."

- By subtracting depreciation from GDP we derive net domestic product (NDP). The difference between NDP and GDP is also equal to the difference between *gross* investment—the sum of all our current plant and equipment expenditures—and *net* investment—the amount of investment over and above that required to replace worn-out capital.

- All the income generated in market sales (GDP) is received by someone. The sequence of flows involved in this process is

GDP
less depreciation
equals NDP
less indirect business taxes
equals national income (NI)
less corporate taxes,
    retained earnings, and
    Social Security taxes
plus transfer payments and
    net interest
equals personal income (PI)
less personal income taxes
equals disposable income (DI)

- The incomes received by households, business firms, and governments provide the purchasing power required to buy the nation's output. As that purchasing power is spent, further GDP is created and the circular flow continues.

Key Terms

national-income accounting
gross domestic product (GDP)
GDP per capita
intermediate goods
value added
nominal GDP
real GDP
base period

inflation
production possibilities
depreciation
net domestic product (NDP)
investment
gross investment
net investment

exports
imports
net exports
national income (NI)
personal income (PI)
disposable income (DI)
saving

Questions for Discussion

1. The manuscript for this book was typed by a friend. Had I hired a secretary to do the same job, GDP would have been higher, even though the amount of output would have been identical. Why is this? Does this make sense?

2. GDP in 1981 was $2.96 trillion. It grew to $3.07 trillion in 1982, yet the quantity of output actually decreased. How is this possible?

3. If gross investment is not large enough to replace the capital that depreciates in a particular year, is net investment greater or less than zero? What happens to our production possibilities?

4. Can we increase consumption in a given year without cutting back on either investment or government services? Under what conditions?

5. Why is it important to know how much output is being produced? Who uses such information?

6. How might the quality of life be adversely affected by an increase in GDP?

7. Is the Fordham Index of Social Health, discussed in The Economy Tomorrow, a better barometer of well-being than GDP? What are its relative advantages or disadvantages?

8. Web Activity Go on a data hunt at the U.S. Department of Commerce's Bureau of Economic Analysis (www.bea.doc.gov) and find the dollar value of nominal GDP for the most recent quarter available. What was the GDP growth rate for that period? Breaking the number down into its four components—consumer spending, business investment, net exports, government spending—estimate each component's contribution to the overall growth rate.

9. Web Activity The United Nations Human Development Index (www.undp.org) ranks countries by GDP per capita and by "human development" based on health, education, and income. Locate a country whose GDP per capita rank is much higher than its human development rank and another with the opposite circumstance. Use the data provided to explain why each country ranked so differently on the two scales.

Problems for Chapter 5 appear at the back of the book.

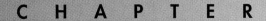
Unemployment

George H. had worked at the paper mill for 18 years. Now he was 37 years old, with a wife and three children. With his base salary of $38,200 and the performance bonus he received nearly every year, he was doing pretty well. He had his own home, two cars, company-paid health insurance for the family, and a growing nest egg in the company's pension plan. The H. family wasn't rich, but it was comfortable and secure.

Or so they thought. Overnight the H. family's comfort was shattered. Without warning, the paper mill was closed in February 1991. George H., along with 2300 fellow workers, was permanently laid off. The weekly paychecks and the company-paid health insurance stopped immediately; the pension nest egg was in doubt. Within a few weeks, George H. was on the street looking for a new job—an experience he hadn't had since high school. The unemployment benefits the state provided didn't come close to paying the mortgage payment, groceries, insurance, and other necessities. And even those benefits soon ran out. The H. family quickly used up its savings, including the $5000 they'd set aside for the children's college education.

George H. stayed unemployed for nearly 2 years. His wife found a part-time waitressing job and his oldest son went to work rather than college. George himself ultimately found a warehousing job that paid only half as much as his previous job.

In the recession of 1990–1991 nearly 2 *million* workers lost their jobs as companies "downsized," "restructured," or simply closed. Not all these displaced workers fared as badly as George H. and his family. But the job loss was a painful experience for every one of those displaced workers. That's the human side of an economic downturn.

The pain of joblessness is not confined to those who lose their jobs. In recessions, students discover that jobs are hard to find in the summer. College graduates also discover that jobs aren't waiting for them. No matter how good their grades were or how nice their résumés look, graduates find they just aren't getting any job offers. Even people with jobs feel some economic pain: their paychecks shrink when hours or wages are scaled back.

In this chapter we take a closer look at the problem of unemployment, focusing on the following questions:

- When is a person "unemployed"?
- What are the costs of unemployment?
- What's an appropriate goal for "full employment"?

As we answer these questions, we'll develop a sense of why full employment is a major goal of macro policy and begin to see some of the obstacles we face in achieving it.

THE LABOR FORCE

To assess the dimensions of our unemployment problems, we first need to decide who wants a job. Millions of people are jobless, yet they're not part of our unemployment problem. Full-time students, young children playing with their toys, and older people living in retirement are all jobless. We don't expect them to be working, so we don't regard them as part of the unemployment problem. We're not concerned that *everybody* be put to work, only with ensuring jobs for all those persons who are ready and willing to work.

To distinguish between those who want a job from those who don't, we separate the entire population into two distinct groups. One group consists of "labor-force participants"; the other group encompasses all "nonparticipants."

labor force: All persons over age 16 who are either working for pay or actively seeking paid employment.

The **labor force** includes everyone age 16 and older who is actually working plus all those who aren't working but are actively seeking employment. Individuals are also counted as employed in a particular week if their failure to work is due to vacation, illness, labor dispute (strike), or bad weather. All such persons are regarded as "with a job but not at work." Also, unpaid family members working in a family enterprise (farming, for example) are counted as employed. *People who are neither employed nor actively seeking work aren't counted as part of the labor force;* they're referred to as "nonparticipants." As Figure 6.1 shows, only half the U.S. population participates in the labor force.

Note that our definition of labor-force participation excludes most household and volunteer activities. A woman who chooses to devote her energies to household responsibilities or to unpaid charity work isn't counted as part of the labor force, no matter how hard she works. Because she's neither in paid employment nor seeking such employment in the marketplace, she's regarded as outside the labor market (a nonparticipant). But if she decides to seek a paid job outside the home and engages in an active job search, we'd say that she's "entering the labor force." Students too are typically

FIGURE 6.1
The Labor Force, 1998

Only half the total U.S. population participates in the civilian labor force. The rest of the population is too young, in school, at home, retired, or otherwise unavailable.

Unemployment statistics count only those participants who aren't currently working but are actively seeking paid employment. Nonparticipants are neither employed nor actively seeking employment.

Source: U.S. Bureau of Labor Statistics.

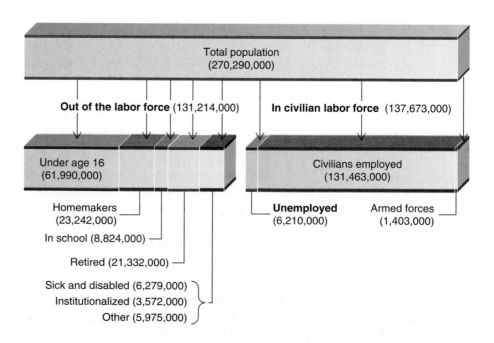

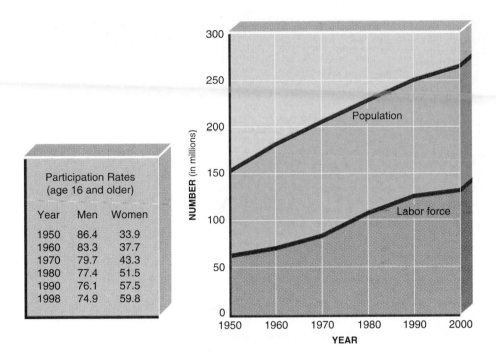

FIGURE 6.2
A Growing Labor Force

The labor force expands as the population increases. A big increase in the participation rate of women has also added to labor-force growth.

Source: *Economic Report of the President, 1999.*

Participation Rates
(age 16 and older)

Year	Men	Women
1950	86.4	33.9
1960	83.3	37.7
1970	79.7	43.3
1980	77.4	51.5
1990	76.1	57.5
1998	74.9	59.8

out of the labor force until they leave school. They "enter" the labor force when they go looking for a job, either during the summer or after graduation. People "exit" the labor force when they go back to school, return to household activities, or retire. These entrants and exits keep changing the size and composition of the labor force.

Since 1950, the U.S. labor force has more than doubled in size. As Figure 6.2 indicates, this labor-force growth has come from two distinct sources: population growth and a rising **labor-force participation rate.** The U.S. population has increased by 80 percent since 1950, but the labor force has increased even more: by 120 percent. The difference is explained by a rising labor-force participation rate. Notice in Figure 6.2, though, that all the increase in labor-force participation results from women increasingly choosing to work. The labor-force participation rate for men has actually declined.

labor-force participation rate: The percentage of the working-age population working or seeking employment.

Continuing growth of the labor force has increased both our capacity to produce and our need to keep creating jobs for people who want to work. As we first saw in Chapter 1, the quantity of goods and services an economy can produce in any time period is limited by two factors:

Production Possibilities

- Availability of factors of production
- Our technological know-how

Figure 6.3 illustrates the limits to our production of any two goods (here called simply "consumption goods" and "investment goods"), given some level of resources and technology. With all our resources devoted to the production of consumption goods, we could produce the amount *B* of such goods in a year. By devoting all our resources and technology to the production of investment goods, we could produce *A* of such goods. In the more likely situation that we chose to produce some of both goods, we could have any combination of goods represented on the **production possibilities** curve.

Institutional Constraints. Although resource availability and technological know-how clearly limit our potential GDP, production has other constraints as well. In particular, the size of the labor force is limited by participation rates and social regulation. Child labor laws, for example, prohibit small children from working, no matter

production possibilities: The alternative combinations of final goods and services that could be produced in a given time period with all available resources and technology.

FIGURE 6.3
Labor-Force Growth

The amount of labor available for work—the *labor force*—is a prime determinant of a nation's production possibilities. As the labor force grows, so does the capacity to produce.

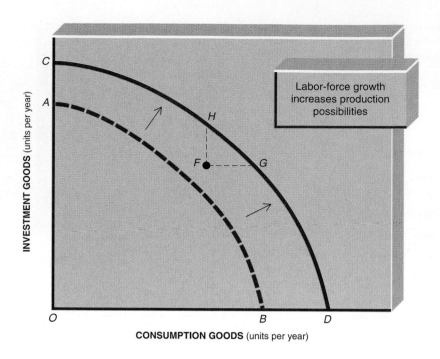

Labor-force growth increases production possibilities

how much they or their parents yearn to contribute to total output. Yet we could produce more output this year if we put all those little bodies to work. In fact, we could produce a little more output this year if you were to put down this book and get a job. To the extent that small children, students, and others are precluded from working, both the size of our labor force (our *available* labor) and our potential output shrink.

Constraints are also imposed on the use of material resources and technology. We won't cut down all the forests this year and build everybody a wooden palace. We've collectively decided to preserve some natural habitat for owls and other endangered species. Therefore, the federal government limits each year's tree harvest on public lands. The federal government also restricts the use of nuclear technology. In both cases, the need for environmental protection constrains the use of resources or technology and limits annual output. These are *institutional* constraints on our productive capacity. Without such constraints, we could produce more output. Our production possibilities in any year therefore depend not only on what resources and technology are available but also on how we choose to restrict their use.

Labor-Force Growth. As the labor force grows, the production possibilities curve shifts outward, as in Figure 6.3. That outward shift illustrates the increased *capacity* to produce goods and services, given available technology and institutional constraints.

Unemployment

An expanding labor force not only increases our capacity to produce but also implies the need to keep creating new jobs. Even in the short run (with given resources and technology), we have to confront the issue of job availability.

We can't reach points beyond the production possibilities curve, but we can easily end up somewhere inside that curve, such as at point *F* in Figure 6.3. At point *F* we're producing fewer consumption goods than we could *and* fewer investment goods. Any point on the curve between points *H* and *G* gives us more of both goods. To get there, however, we have to find a job for everyone who's ready and willing to work. **To reach a point on the production possibilities curve, the labor force must be fully employed.** If we fail to provide jobs for all labor-force participants, we end up with less output and the related problem of **unemployment**.

unemployment: The inability of labor-force participants to find jobs.

Okun's Law. Arthur Okun quantified the relationship between the shortfall in output and unemployment. According to the original formulation of **Okun's Law,** each additional 1 percent of unemployment translated into a loss of 3 percent in real output. More recent estimates of Okun's Law put the ratio at about 1 to 2, largely due to the changing composition of both the labor force (more women and teenagers) and output (more services). Using that 2-to-1 ratio allows us to put a dollar value on the aggregate cost of unemployment. In 1992, high unemployment left us $240 billion short of our production possibilities. This shortfall implied a loss of $920 of goods and services for every American.

Okun's Law: 1 percent more unemployment is estimated to equal 2 percent less output.

MEASURING UNEMPLOYMENT

To determine how many people are actually employed, the U.S. Census Bureau surveys about 60,000 households each month. The Census interviewers first determine whether a person is employed—that is, worked for pay in the previous week (or didn't work due to illness, vacation, bad weather, or a labor strike). If the person isn't employed, he or she is either unemployed or out of the labor force. To make that distinction, the Census interviewers ask whether the person actively looked for work in the preceding 4 weeks. *If a person is both not employed* and *actively seeking a job, he or she is counted as unemployed.* Individuals neither employed nor actively seeking a job are counted as outside the labor force (nonparticipants). The responses to this survey provide the basis for estimating the total number of people who are unemployed across the country.

In 1998 an average of 6.2 million persons were counted as unemployed in any month. As Figure 6.1 suggests, these unemployed individuals accounted for 4.5 percent of our total labor force. Accordingly, the average **unemployment rate** in 1998 was 4.5 percent.

The Unemployment Rate

unemployment rate: The proportion of the labor force that is unemployed.

$$\frac{\text{Unemployment}}{\text{rate}} = \frac{\text{number of unemployed people}}{\text{labor force}}$$

The monthly unemployment figures indicate not only the total amount of unemployment in the economy but also which groups are suffering the greatest unemployment. Typically, teenagers just entering the labor market have the greatest difficulty finding (or keeping) jobs. They have no job experience and relatively few marketable skills. Employers will be reluctant to hire them, especially if they must pay the federal minimum wage of $5.15 an hour. As a consequence, teenage unemployment rates are typically three times higher than adult unemployment rates (see Figure 6.4 next page).

Minority workers also experience above-average unemployment. Notice in Figure 6.4 that black unemployment rates are more than twice as high as white unemployment rates.

Education also affects the chances of being unemployed. If you graduate from college, your chances of being unemployed drop sharply, regardless of gender or race (see Figure 6.4). Advancing technology and a shift to services from manufacturing have put a premium on better-educated workers. Very few people with master's or doctoral degrees stand in unemployment lines.

CYBER NOTE

Data on unemployment by race and gender from 1948 to the present are available from the Bureau of Labor Statistics at www.bls.gov.

Although high school dropouts are more likely to be unemployed than college graduates, they don't *stay* unemployed. In fact, most people who become unemployed remain jobless for a relatively brief period of time. As Table 6.1 indicates, the median spell of unemployment in 1998 was 6.7 weeks. Less than 1 out of 6 unemployed individuals had been jobless for as long as 6 months (27 weeks or longer). People who lose their jobs do find new ones. When the economy is growing, both unemployment rates and the average duration of unemployment decline. Recessions have the opposite effect—raising the costs of unemployment significantly.

The Duration of Unemployment

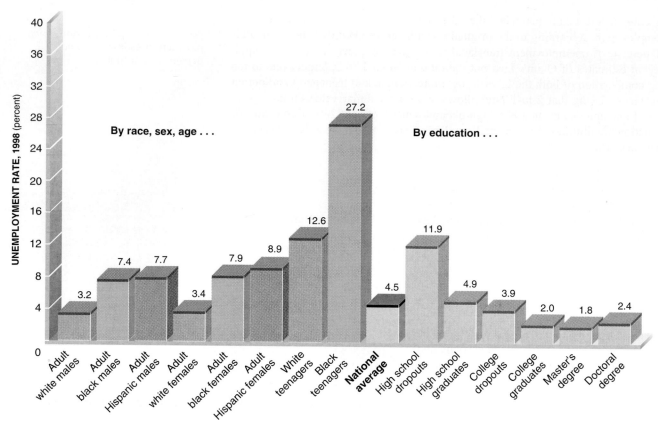

FIGURE 6.4

Unemployment Isn't Experienced Equally by Race, Sex, or Education

Minority groups, teenagers, and less educated individuals experience high rates of unemployment. Teenage unemployment rates are particularly high, especially for black and other minority youth.

Source: U.S. Department of Labor.

Reasons for Unemployment

The reason a person remains unemployed also affects the length of time the person is out of work. A person just entering the labor market might need more time to identify job openings and develop job contacts. By contrast, an autoworker laid off for a temporary plant closing can expect to return to work quickly. Figure 6.5 depicts these and other reasons for unemployment. In 1998 nearly half the unemployed were job losers (laid off or fired), and 1 in 9 were job leavers (quit). The rest were new entrants (primarily teenagers) or reentrants (primarily mothers returning to the workforce). Like the

TABLE 6.1
Duration of Unemployment

The severity of unemployment depends on how long the spell of joblessness lasts. About one-third of unemployed workers return to work quickly, but many others remain unemployed for 6 months or longer.

Duration	Percent of Unemployed
Less than 5 weeks	42.2
5 to 14 weeks	31.4
15 to 26 weeks	12.3
27 weeks or more	14.1

Source: U.S. Bureau of Labor Statistics (1998 data).

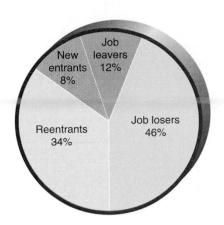

FIGURE 6.5
Reasons for Unemployment

People become unemployed for various reasons. Less than half of the unemployed were job losers in 1998. Just as many were entering or reentering the labor market in search of a job.

duration of unemployment, the reasons for joblessness are very sensitive to economic conditions. In really bad years, most of the unemployed are job losers, and they remain out of work a long time.

Discouraged Workers

Unemployment statistics don't tell the complete story about the human costs of a sluggish economy. When unemployment persists, job seekers become increasingly frustrated in their efforts to secure employment. After repeated rejections, job seekers often get so discouraged that they give up the search and turn to their families, friends, or public welfare for income support. When the Census Bureau interviewer asks whether they're actively seeking employment, such **discouraged workers** are apt to reply no. Yet they'd like to be working, and they'd probably be out looking for work if job prospects were better.

discouraged worker: An individual who isn't actively seeking employment but would look for or accept a job if one were available.

Discouraged workers aren't counted as part of our unemployment problem because they're technically out of the labor force. The Labor Department estimates that in 1998 330,000 individuals fell into this uncounted class of discouraged workers.

Underemployment

Some people can't afford to be discouraged. Many people who become jobless have family responsibilities and bills to pay: They simply can't afford to drop out of the labor force. Instead, they're compelled to take some job—any job—just to keep body and soul together. The resultant job may be part-time or full-time and may pay very little. Nevertheless, any paid employment is sufficient to exclude the person from the count of the unemployed, though not from a condition of **underemployment.**

underemployment: People seeking full-time paid employment who work only part time or are employed at jobs below their capability.

Underemployed workers represent labor resources that aren't being fully utilized. They're part of our unemployment problem, even if they're not officially counted as unemployed. In 1998 more than 3 million workers were underemployed in the U.S. economy.

The Phantom Unemployed

Although discouraged and underemployed workers aren't counted in official unemployment statistics, some of the people who *are* counted probably shouldn't be. Many people report that they're actively seeking a job even when they have little interest in finding employment. To some extent, public policy actually encourages such behavior. For example, some adult welfare recipients are required to look for a job, even though some welfare mothers would prefer to spend all their time raising their children. Their resultant job search is likely to be perfunctory at best, including perhaps only one trip to the state employment office. Similarly, most states require people receiving unemployment benefits to provide evidence that they're looking for a job, even though some recipients may prefer a brief period of joblessness. Here again, reported unemployment may conceal labor-force nonparticipation. More generous benefits in European nations are thought to create similar problems (see the following WORLD VIEW).

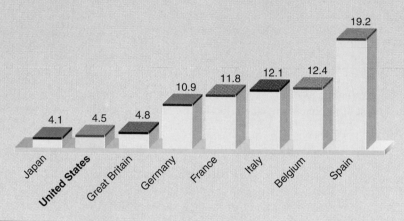

Europe's Unemployment Woes

Years of sluggish economic growth raised unemployment rates in Europe to levels rarely seen in the United States. Generous unemployment benefits cushion the personal losses from job-lessness, but also discourage European workers from accepting new jobs.

Source: International Monetary Fund (1998 data). www.imf.org

Japan 4.1 | United States 4.5 | Great Britain 4.8 | Germany 10.9 | France 11.8 | Italy 12.1 | Belgium 12.4 | Spain 19.2

Analysis: Throughout the 1990s unemployment rates were significantly higher in Europe than in the United States. Analysts blame both sluggish economic growth and high unemployment benefits.

CYBER NOTE

Compare unemployment rates of different countries at http://stats.bls.gov/flshome.htm.

THE HUMAN COSTS

Although our measures of unemployment aren't perfect, they're a reliable index to a serious macro problem. Unemployment statistics tell us that millions of people are jobless. That may be all right for a day or even a week, but if you need income to keep body and soul together, prolonged unemployment can hurt.

The immediate impact of unemployment on individuals is the loss of income associated with working. For workers who've been unemployed for long periods of time, such losses can spell financial disaster. Typically, an unemployed person must rely on a combination of savings, income from other family members, and government unemployment benefits for financial support. After these sources of support are exhausted (see NEWS), public welfare is often the only legal support left.

Not all unemployed people experience such a financial disaster, of course. College students who fail to find summer employment, for example, are unlikely to end up on welfare the following semester. Similarly, teenagers and others looking for part-time employment won't suffer great economic losses from unemployment. Nevertheless, the experience of unemployment—of not being able to find a job when you want one—can still be painful. This sensation isn't easily forgotten, even after one has finally found employment.

It's difficult to measure the full impact of unemployment on individuals. A study for Congress, however, provides some frightening suggestions. The author of the study estimates that a prolonged 1-point increase in the national unemployment rate—say, from 6 percent to 7 percent—leads, on average, to

- 920 suicides
- 648 homicides

IN THE NEWS

Unemployment Benefits Not for Everyone

In 1998, over 8 million people collected unemployment benefits averaging $197 per week. But don't rush to the state unemployment office yet—not all unemployed people are eligible. To qualify for weekly unemployment benefits you must have worked a substantial length of time and earned some minimum amount of wages, both determined by your state. Furthermore, you must have a "good" reason for having lost your last job. Most states will not provide benefits to students (or their professors!) during summer vacations, to professional athletes in the off-season, or to individuals who quit their last jobs.

If you qualify for benefits, the amount of benefits you receive each week will depend on your previous wages. In most states the benefits are equal to about one-half of the previous weekly wage, up to a state-determined maximum. The maximum benefit in 1998 ranged from $180 in Mississippi to a high of $390 in New Jersey.

Unemployment benefits are financed by a tax on employers and can continue for as long as 26 weeks. During periods of high unemployment, the duration of benefit eligibility may be extended another 13 weeks or more.

Analysis: Some of the income lost due to unemployment is replaced by unemployment insurance benefits. Not all unemployed persons are eligible, however, and the duration of benefits is limited.

- 20,240 fatal heart attacks or strokes
- 495 deaths from liver cirrhosis
- 4227 admissions to mental hospitals
- 3340 admissions to state prisons[1]

The NEWS on the next page cites similar consequences. Although all such estimates are subject to serious statistical qualifications, they underscore the notion that prolonged unemployment poses a real danger to many individuals. Like George H., the worker discussed at the beginning of this chapter, many unemployed workers simply can't cope with the resulting stress. Thomas Cottle, a lecturer at Harvard Medical School, stated the case more bluntly: "I'm now convinced that unemployment is *the* killer disease in this country—responsible for wife beating, infertility, and even tooth decay."

German psychiatrists have also observed that unemployment can be hazardous to your health. They estimate that the anxieties and other nervous disorders that accompany 1 year of unemployment can reduce life expectancy by as much as 5 years. In Japan, the suicide rate jumped by 18 percent in 1997 when the economy plunged into recession.

DEFINING FULL EMPLOYMENT

In view of the economic and social losses associated with unemployment, it's not surprising that *full employment* is one of our basic macroeconomic goals. You may be surprised to learn, however, that "full" employment isn't the same thing as "zero" unemployment. There are in fact several reasons for regarding some degree of unemployment as inevitable and even desirable.

Some joblessness is virtually inevitable as long as we continue to grow crops, build houses, or go skiing at certain seasons of the year. At the end of each such "season,"

Seasonal Unemployment

[1]Harvey Brenner, "Estimating the Social Costs of National Economic Policy: Implications for Mental and Physical Health, and Criminal Aggression," study prepared for the Joint Economic Committee, U.S. Congress (Washington, D.C., October 1976).

Recession's Cost: Lives

The economy may be killing us.

A study out today says a poor economy in 30 selected cities is responsible for:

- 6.7% more murders—730 a year.
- 3.1% more deaths from stroke—1,386 annually.
- 5.6% more fatal heart disease—17,654 a year.

Another report blames the recession for 1,170 more suicides in the USA—up 3.9%.

The middle class was hurting before the recession, says University of Utah economist Mary Merva.

"We were already pushed to the limit," says Merva, who co-authored a study of unemployment in 30 big cities with 80 million people from 1976 to 1990.

"This could be the straw that breaks our back."

The study found that a 1 percentage point rise in unemployment meant more crime:

- Violent, up 3.4%.
- Non-violent, up 2.4%.

"Stress can be directed inward, like smoking, drinking or having higher blood pressure," Merva says, "or outward like beating your wife, abusing your child."

Johns Hopkins University economist Harvey Brenner, author of a similar report, says a troubled economy breeds a sick society.

"Health and social well-being of the country is directly affected by the behavior of the economy," he says.

"When national economic decisions are made, health concerns should have a seat at the table."

—Robert Davis

USA Today, Oct. 16, 1992, p. A1. Copyright 1992, USA TODAY. Reprinted with permission. www.usatoday.com

---

Analysis: The cost of unemployment is not measured in lost wages alone. Prolonged unemployment also impairs health, social relationships, and productivity.

---

seasonal unemployment: Unemployment due to seasonal changes in employment or labor supply.

thousands of workers must go searching for new jobs, experiencing some **seasonal unemployment** in the process.

Seasonal fluctuations also arise on the supply side of the labor market. Teenage unemployment rates, for example, rise sharply in the summer as students look for temporary jobs. To avoid such unemployment completely, we'd either have to keep everyone in school or ensure that all students went immediately from the classroom to the workroom. Neither alternative is likely, much less desirable.[2]

Frictional Unemployment

There are other reasons for expecting a certain amount of unemployment. Many workers have sound financial or personal reasons for leaving one job to look for another. In the process of moving from one job to another, a person may well miss a few days or even weeks of work without any serious personal or social consequences. On the contrary, people who spend more time looking for work may find *better* jobs.

The same is true of students first entering the labor market. It's not likely that you'll find a job the moment you leave school. Nor should you necessarily take the first job offered. If you spend some time looking for work, you're more likely to find a job you like. The job-search period gives you an opportunity to find out what kinds of jobs are available, what skills they require, and what they pay. Accordingly, a brief period of job search may benefit labor market entrants and the larger economy. The unemploy-

---

[2]Seasonal variations in employment and labor supply not only create some unemployment in the annual averages but also distort monthly comparisons. Unemployment rates are always higher in February (when farming and housing construction come to a virtual standstill) and June (when a mass of students go looking for summer jobs). The Labor Department adjusts monthly unemployment rates according to this seasonal pattern and reports "seasonally adjusted" unemployment rates for each month. Seasonal adjustments don't alter *annual* averages, however.

ment associated with these kinds of job searches is referred to as **frictional unemployment.**

Three factors distinguish frictional unemployment from other kinds of unemployment. First, enough jobs exist for those who are frictionally unemployed—that is, there's adequate demand for labor. Second, those individuals who are frictionally unemployed have the skills required for available jobs. Third, the period of job search will be relatively short. Under these conditions, frictional unemployment resembles an unconventional game of musical chairs. There are enough chairs of the right size for everyone, and people dance around them for only a brief period of time.

No one knows for sure just how much of our unemployment problem is frictional. Most economists agree, however, that friction alone is responsible for an unemployment rate of 2 to 3 percent. Accordingly, our definition of "full employment" should allow for at least this much unemployment.

frictional unemployment: Brief periods of unemployment experienced by people moving between jobs or into the labor market.

Structural Unemployment

For many job seekers, the period between jobs may drag on for months or even years because they don't have the skills that employers require. Imagine, for example, the predicament of steelworkers. During the 1980s the steel industry contracted as consumers demanded fewer and lighter-weight cars and as construction of highways, bridges, and buildings slowed. In the process, over 300,000 steelworkers lost their jobs. Most of these workers had a decade or more of experience and substantial skill. But the skills they'd perfected were no longer in demand. They couldn't perform the jobs available in computer software, biotechnology, or other expanding industries. Although there were enough job vacancies in the labor market, the steelworkers couldn't fill them: These workers were victims of **structural unemployment.**

The same kind of structural displacement hit the defense industry in the 1990s. Cutbacks in national defense spending forced weapons manufacturers, aerospace firms, and electronics companies to reduce output and lay off thousands of workers. The displaced workers soon discovered that their highly developed skills weren't immediately applicable in nondefense industries.

Teenagers from urban slums also suffer from structural unemployment. Most poor teenagers have an inadequate education, few job-related skills, and little work experience. From their perspective, almost all decent jobs are "out of reach." As a consequence, these teenagers, many of whom are black or from other minority groups, remain unemployed far longer than can be explained by frictional forces.

Structural unemployment violates the second condition for frictional unemployment: that the job seekers can perform the available jobs. Structural unemployment is analogous to a musical chairs game in which there are enough chairs for everyone, but some of them are too small to sit on. It's a more serious concern than frictional unemployment and incompatible with any notion of full employment.

structural unemployment: Unemployment caused by a mismatch between the skills (or location) of job seekers and the requirements (or location) of available jobs.

Cyclical Unemployment

The fourth type of unemployment is **cyclical unemployment**—joblessness that occurs when there aren't simply enough jobs to go around. Cyclical unemployment exists when the number of workers demanded falls short of the number of persons in the labor force. This isn't a case of mobility between jobs (frictional unemployment) or even of job seekers' skills (structural unemployment). Rather, it's simply an inadequate level of demand for goods and services and thus for labor. Cyclical unemployment resembles the most familiar form of musical chairs, in which the number of chairs is always less than the number of players.

The Great Depression is the most striking example of cyclical unemployment. The dramatic increase in unemployment rates that began in 1930 (see Figure 6.6) wasn't due to any increase in "friction" or sudden decline in workers' skills. Instead, the high rates of unemployment that persisted for a *decade* were caused by a sudden decline in the market demand for goods and services. How do we know? Just notice what happened to our unemployment rate when the demand for military goods and services increased in 1941!

cyclical unemployment: Unemployment attributable to a lack of job vacancies, that is, to an inadequate level of aggregate demand.

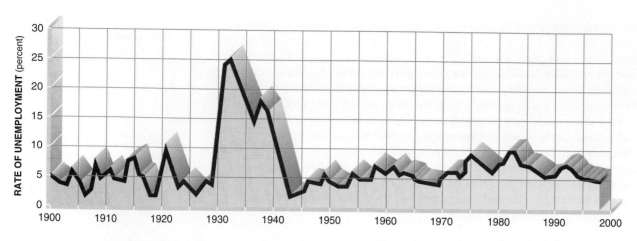

FIGURE 6.6
The Unemployment Record

Unemployment rates reached record heights during the Great Depression. The postwar record is much better than the prewar record, even though "full employment" has been infrequent.

Source: U.S. Department of Labor.

The Full-Employment Goal

In later chapters we examine the causes of cyclical unemployment and explore some potential policy responses. At this point, however, we're just establishing some perspective on the goal of full employment. In the Employment Act of 1946, Congress committed the federal government to pursue a goal of "maximum" employment but didn't specify exactly what that rate was. Presumably, this meant avoiding as much cyclical and structural unemployment as possible while keeping frictional unemployment within reasonable bounds. As guidelines for public policy, these perspectives are admittedly vague.

Inflationary Pressures. The first attempt to define "full employment" more precisely was undertaken in the early 1960s. At that time the Council of Economic Advisers (itself created by the Employment Act of 1946) decided that our proximity to "full employment" could be gauged by watching *prices*. As the economy approached its production possibilities, labor and other resources would become increasingly scarce. As market participants bid for these remaining resources, wages and prices would start to rise. Hence ***rising prices are a signal that employment is nearing capacity.***

After examining the relationship between unemployment and inflation, the Council of Economic Advisers decided to peg full employment at 4 percent unemployment. The unemployment rate could fall below 4 percent. If it did, however, price levels would begin to rise. Thus 4 percent unemployment was regarded as an acceptable compromise of our employment and price goals.

Changes in Structural Unemployment. During the 1970s and early 1980s, this view of our full-employment potential was considered overly optimistic. Unemployment rates stayed far above 4 percent, even when the economy expanded. Moreover, inflation began to accelerate at higher levels of unemployment. Critics suggested that structural barriers to full employment had intensified, necessitating a redefinition of our full-employment goal. These structural barriers included the following:

- ***More youth and women.*** Between 1956 and 1979, the proportion of teenagers in the labor force increased from 6 percent to 9 percent. During the same period, the proportion of adult women in the labor force grew tremendously (see Figure 6.2).

Many of these women were entering the labor force for the first time—or reentering it after long periods of homemaking. These trends increased frictional and structural unemployment.

- *Liberal transfer payments.* Higher benefits and easier rules for unemployment insurance, food stamps, welfare, and Social Security made unemployment less painful. As a result, critics suggested, more people were willing to stay unemployed rather than work.
- *Structural changes in demand.* Changes in consumer demand, technology, and trade shrank the markets in steel, textiles, autos, and other industries. The workers dislocated from these industries couldn't be absorbed fast enough in new high-tech and other service industries.

In view of these factors, the Council of Economic Advisers later raised the level of unemployment thought to be compatible with price stability. In 1983 the Reagan administration concluded that the "inflation-threshold" unemployment rate was between 6 and 7 percent (see cartoon).

Declining Structural Pressures. The structural barriers that intensified inflationary pressures in the 1970s and early 1980s receded in the 1990s. The number of teenagers declined by 3 million between 1981 and 1993. The upsurge in women's participation in the labor force also leveled off. High school and college attendance and graduation rates increased. All these structural changes made it easier to lower unemployment rates without increasing inflation. In 1991 the Bush administration concluded that **full employment** was equivalent to 5.5 percent unemployment. In 1999, the Clinton administration suggested the full-employment threshold might have dropped even further, to 5.3 percent. In reality, the national unemployment rate stayed below even that benchmark for 3 years (Figure 6.6) without any upsurge in inflation.

full employment: The lowest rate of unemployment compatible with price stability; variously estimated at between 4 percent and 6 percent unemployment.

"I don't like six-per-cent unemployment, either. But I can live with it."

Drawing by Lorenz; © 1974 The New Yorker Magazine, Inc. Used by permission.

Analysis: So-called full employment entails a compromise between employment and inflation goals. That compromise doesn't affect everyone equally.

The "Natural" Rate of Unemployment

natural rate of unemployment: Long-term rate of unemployment determined by structural forces in labor and product markets.

The ambiguity about which rate of unemployment might trigger an upsurge in inflation has convinced some analysts to abandon the inflation-based concept of "full" employment. They prefer to specify a "natural" rate of unemployment that doesn't depend on inflation trends. In this view, the natural rate of unemployment consists of frictional and structural components only. It's the rate of unemployment that will prevail in the long run. In the short run, both the unemployment rate and the inflation rate may go up and down. However, the economy will tend to gravitate toward the long-run **natural rate of unemployment.**

Although the natural rate concept avoids specifying a short-term inflation "trigger," it too is subject to debate. As we've seen, the *structural* determinants of unemployment (for example, age and composition of the labor force) change over time. When structural forces change, the level of "natural" unemployment presumably changes as well.

Congressional Targets

CYBER NOTE

To see the Fed's annual Humphrey-Hawkins report to Congress, go to www.bog.frb.fed.us/boarddocs/hh.

Although most economists agree that an unemployment rate of 4 to 6 percent is consistent with either "natural" or "full" employment, Congress has set tougher goals for macro policy. According to the Full Employment and Balanced Growth Act of 1978 (commonly called the Humphrey-Hawkins Act), our national goal is to attain a 4 percent rate of unemployment. The act also requires a goal of 3 percent inflation. There was an escape clause, however. In the event that both goals couldn't be met, the president could set higher, "provisional" definitions of unemployment. Each year, the Council of Economic Advisers dutifully explains why a higher unemployment rate is a more appropriate benchmark for full employment.

CYBER NOTE

To get a more vivid image of the Great Depression than unemployment statistics provide, see the photo collection of the Farm Security Administration at http:/memory .loc.gov/ammem/fsowhome.html.

THE HISTORICAL RECORD

Although there's some ambiguity about the specific definition of full employment, the historical record is clear on our failure to maintain it. Our greatest failure occurred during the Great Depression, when as much as one-fourth of the labor force was unemployed. As Figure 6.6 shows, unemployment rates were extraordinarily high throughout the 1930s.

Unemployment rates fell dramatically during World War II. In 1944 virtually anyone who was ready and willing to work quickly found a job: The civilian unemployment rate hit a rock-bottom 1.2 percent.

Since 1950, the unemployment rate has fluctuated from a low of 2.8 percent during the Korean War (1953) to a high of 10.8 percent during the 1981–1982 recession. From 1982 to 1989 the unemployment rate receded, but it shot up again in the 1990–1991 recession. As many as 10 million workers were unemployed at one time during that recession. Millions more experienced joblessness during the course of that economic downturn. During the last half of the 1990s the unemployment rate fell steadily. As the economy started to slow in 1999, however, the unemployment rate started creeping up again.

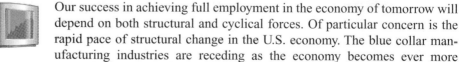

THE ECONOMY TOMORROW

A Growing Skills Gap?

New Jobs

Our success in achieving full employment in the economy of tomorrow will depend on both structural and cyclical forces. Of particular concern is the rapid pace of structural change in the U.S. economy. The blue collar manufacturing industries are receding as the economy becomes ever more service-oriented. The U.S. Bureau of Labor Statistics estimates that **98 percent of all new jobs created in the next decade will be service jobs.** These new service jobs

Industry	Annual Change (percent)
Fastest growing	
Computer services	+7.0
Health services	+5.3
Management and public relations	+4.8
Residential care	+4.8
Recreational services	+3.5
Nursing	+3.2
Stockbrokers	+3.0
Business services	+2.5
Most rapidly declining	
Coal mining	−6.0
Footwear, except rubber and plastic	−4.0
Leather products	−3.6
Tobacco manufacturing	−3.1
Apparel	−3.0
Petroleum refining	−2.3
Household appliances	−2.2
Steel products	−2.0

Source: U.S. Bureau of Labor Statistics.

TABLE 6.2
Projected Employment Changes, 1996–2006

As the economy grows, some industries expand and others contract. These industry shifts will create structural unemployment problems, particularly for workers displaced from declining industries and labor market entrants with little education.

will be highly concentrated in computer hardware and software, legal services, health services, research and testing, and management (see Table 6.2).

The new jobs of the economy tomorrow will require increasing levels of education and skill. Workers with the requisite skills will enjoy high wages and experience little unemployment. Workers without the right skills, however, will find themselves out of step with a fast-changing market. This trend was already evident in the 1980s. The wage gap between college graduates and high school graduates widened, and unemployment differentials increased as well.

The **skills gap** isn't confined to young workers first entering the labor market. Old-line industries are downsizing and restructuring in response to changing markets. In the 1980s, for example, the steel industry shed over 300,000 workers and the auto industry over 400,000 workers. In the next decade still more workers will lose jobs in these and other declining industries (see Table 6.2). The workers dislocated from these and other industries have solid work experience and skill, but *not* the skills required in today's economy. These dislocated workers, like the coal miners of earlier decades, increase structural employment. As revealed in the NEWS on the next page, it took a long time for these dislocated workers to find new jobs. When they did, their wage on the new job was often less than their prior wage. *As the skills gap widens, structural unemployment increases.*

The employment challenge of the economy tomorrow is to reduce the structural unemployment that accompanies economic growth. This will require not only macroeconomic policies that minimize cyclical unemployment but also education and training initiatives that narrow the skills gap.

Old Skills

skills gap: Gap between skills required for emerging jobs and the skills of workers.

IN THE NEWS

What Lies in Store for Displaced Workers?

What do laid-off workers have to fear in today's labor market? For those only a year or two on the job—especially younger workers, the issue may not be a burning one. But for many of those severed from more permanent jobs, it's compelling. That's why the Labor Dept.'s latest survey of displaced long-tenured workers conducted in early 1998 is so revealing.

Looking at the 3.1 million workers who were laid off from full-time permanent jobs (held at least three years) from 1995 through 1997, the survey found that in many respects their fates were comparable to those found in the 1996 survey for workers laid off in 1993 and 1994. Specifically, in each case about 67% of workers were reemployed at full-time jobs, 14% to 16% were working part-time or at home, and 12% to 14% had dropped out of the labor force.

The main difference was that recent earnings declines were far less pronounced. Whereas 55% of reemployed full-timers in the earlier survey experienced pay drops, and 34% of them suffered cuts of more than 20%, the figures in the 1998 survey were 38% and 21%, respectively. And the median period between jobs fell from 8.3 to 5 weeks.

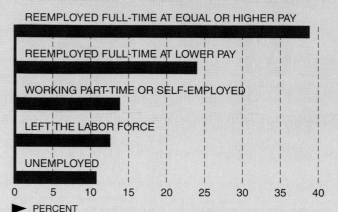

STATUS IN EARLY 1998 OF FULL-TIMERS WHO LOST PERMANENT JOBS IN 1995-1997*

▶ PERCENT

DATA: BUREAU OF LABOR STATISTICS

Reprinted from Dec. 28, 1998, issue of *Business Week* by special permission, copyright © 1998 by the McGraw-Hill Companies. www.businessweek.com

Analysis: Workers who lose their jobs in declining industries are likely to become structurally unemployed. They remain unemployed for long periods and must often accept lower wages on a new job.

SUMMARY

- To understand unemployment, we must distinguish the labor force from the larger population. Only people who are working (employed) or spend some time looking for a job (unemployed) are participants in the labor force. People neither working nor looking for work are outside the labor force.

- The size of the labor force affects production possibilities. As the labor force grows, so does the capacity to produce goods and services.

- Unemployment implies that we're producing inside the production possibilities curve rather than on it.

- The macroeconomic loss imposed by unemployment is reduced output of goods and services. Okun's Law suggests that 1 percentage point in unemployment is equivalent to a 2 percentage point decline in output.

- The human cost of unemployment includes not only financial losses but social, physical, and psychological costs as well.

- Unemployment is distributed unevenly; blacks, teenagers, and the less educated have much higher rates of unemployment. Also hurt are discouraged workers—those who've stopped looking for work at part-time or menial jobs because they can't find full-time jobs equal to their training or potential.

- There are four types of unemployment: seasonal, frictional, structural, and cyclical. Because some seasonal frictional unemployment is inevitable and even desirable, full employment is not defined as zero unemployment. These considerations, plus fear of inflationary consequences, result in full employment being defined as an unemployment rate of 4 to 6 percent.

- The "natural" rate of unemployment is based on frictional and structural forces, without reference to short-term price (inflation) pressures.

- Unemployment rates got as high as 25 percent in the 1930s. Since 1960, the unemployment rate has ranged from 3.4 to 10.8 percent.

- Our ability to achieve full employment in the future depends on our success in closing the skills gap. This necessitates more and better education and training activity.

Key Terms

labor force	unemployment rate	structural unemployment
labor-force participation rate	discouraged worker	cyclical unemployment
production possibilities	underemployment	full employment
unemployment	seasonal unemployment	natural rate of unemployment
Okun's Law	frictional unemployment	skills gap

Questions for Discussion

1. Is it possible for unemployment rates to increase at the same time that the number of employed persons is increasing? How?
2. If more teenagers stay in school longer, what happens to (*a*) production possibilities? (*b*) unemployment rates?
3. What factors might explain (*a*) the rising labor-force participation rate of women, and (*b*) the declining participation of men? (See Figure 6.2 for trends.)
4. Why might job (re)entrants have a harder time finding a job than job losers?
5. If the government guaranteed some income to unemployed persons, how might the unemployment rate be affected? Who should get unemployment benefits? (See NEWS page 113.)
6. Can you identify three institutional constraints on the use of resources (factors of production)? What has motivated these constraints?
7. Why is frictional unemployment deemed desirable?

8. What's the difference between "full" and "natural" employment rates?
9. How did the unemployment rate exceed "full" during the period 1996–1998?
10. Web Activity At the U.S. Bureau of Labor Statistics—www.bls.gov—find the unemployment rate for your own age group, your gender, and your race or ethnicity. Compare each rate with the overall U.S. unemployment rate. Using the types of unemployment described in the text of this chapter, explain why each unemployment rate differs from the overall unemployment rate.
11. Web Activity What are the employment prospects in your chosen profession (or one that you might consider)? Find out at www.bls.gov/oco/ocoiab.htm. Look at the employment outlook. What factors will create jobs (or decrease the number of jobs) in this field?

Problems for Chapter 6 appear at the back of the book.

7

Inflation

By global standards, the United States didn't have much of an inflation problem in the 1990s. The U.S. inflation rate averaged less than 3 percent per year. Few countries achieve such price stability. Japan has a lower inflation rate, but most western European nations experience faster price increases. As the WORLD VIEW indicates, prices rise *much* faster in developing countries. In 1994, prices in Zaire rose an astonishing 23,760 percent; prices *tripled* every month. In 1998, Bulgarian prices nearly *doubled* every month. Seen in this global context, U.S. inflation looks very tame.

Despite our comparatively mild experiences with inflation, fear of rising prices has had a major influence on our economic policy. According to public opinion polls, inflation is always one of America's greatest worries. In response to these fears, every president since Franklin Roosevelt has expressed a determination to keep prices from rising. In 1971 the Nixon administration took drastic action to stop inflation: With prices rising an average of only 3 percent, President Nixon imposed price controls on U.S. producers to keep prices from rising any faster. For 90 days all wages and prices were frozen by law—price increases were prohibited. For 3 more years, wage and price increases were limited by legal rules.

At the beginning of the 1990s the inflation rate in the United States was around 5 percent. Alan Greenspan, the chairman of the Federal Reserve, asserted that 5 percent inflation was "unacceptable" and set a goal of *zero* percent inflation for the 1990s. He acknowledged that the pursuit of the zero-inflation goal might require us to forsake other macro goals (like full employment) but concluded that such a sacrifice was worthwhile. The rate of inflation did drop in 1991 and 1992, but unemployment increased substantially.

This chapter examines the basis for these policy concerns. Why is inflation so feared? If inflation is such a problem, why not stamp it out? To assess these concerns, we ask the following questions:

- What kind of price increases are referred to as "inflation"?
- Who is hurt (or helped) by inflation?
- What is an appropriate goal for "price stability"?

As we'll discover, inflation is a serious problem, but not for the reasons most people cite. We'll also see why deflation—falling prices—isn't as welcome as it might appear.

Worldwide Inflation

In many countries prices rise at rates much higher than those in the United States. In 1998 the inflation rate in Bulgaria was so high that prices nearly doubled every *month*.

In the United States the inflation rate for the entire *year* was only 1.6 percent. What are the implications of such wildly different inflation rates?

Country	Inflation Rate	Country	Inflation Rate
Bulgaria	1082	Sudan	47
Congo	199	Iraq	45
Romania	151	European Union	1.9
Angola	111	Japan	1.7
Turkey	86	United States	1.6
Venezuela	50		

Source: International Monetary Fund, *World Economic Outlook, 1998*. www.imf.org

Analysis: Although inflation is regarded as a major macro problem in the United States, American inflation rates are comparatively low. Many developing countries have extraordinarily fast price increases.

WHAT IS INFLATION?

Most people associate **inflation** with price increases on specific goods and services. The economy isn't necessarily experiencing an inflation, however, every time the price of a cup of coffee goes up. We must be careful to distinguish the phenomenon of inflation from price increases for specific goods. *Inflation is an increase in the average level of prices, not a change in any specific price.*

inflation: An increase in the average level of prices of goods and services.

The Average Price

Suppose you wanted to know the average price of fruit in the supermarket. Surely you wouldn't have much success in seeking out an average fruit—nobody would be quite sure what you had in mind. You might have some success, however, if you sought out the prices of apples, oranges, cherries, and peaches. Knowing the price of each kind of fruit, you could then compute the average price of fruit. The resultant figure wouldn't refer to any particular product but would convey a sense of how much a typical basket of fruit might cost. By repeating these calculations every day, you could then determine whether fruit prices, *on average,* were changing. On occasion, you might even notice that apple prices rose while orange prices fell, leaving the *average* price of fruit unchanged.

The same kinds of calculations are made to measure inflation in the entire economy. We first determine the average price of all output—the average price level—then look for changes in that average. A rise in the average price level is referred to as inflation.

The average price level may fall as well as rise. A decline in average prices—a **deflation**—occurs when price decreases on some goods and services outweigh price increases on all others. This happened in Japan in 1995. Such deflations are rare, however: The United States has not experienced any general deflation since 1940.

deflation: A decrease in the average level of prices of goods and services.

Relative Prices vs. the Price Level

Because inflation and deflation are measured in terms of average price levels, it's possible for individual prices to rise or fall continuously without changing the average price level. We already noted, for example, that the price of apples can rise without increasing the average price of fruit, so long as the price of some other fruit, such as

TABLE 7.1
Prices That Have Fallen

Inflation refers to an increase in the *average* price level. It doesn't mean that *all* prices are rising. In fact, many prices fall, even during periods of general inflation.

Item	Early Price	1998 Price
Long-distance telephone call (3-minute rate, coast to coast)	$ 20.70 (1915)	$0.10
Pocket electronic calculator	200.00 (1972)	5.90
Digital watch	2000.00 (1972)	1.99
Polaroid camera (color)	150.00 (1963)	29.95
Pantyhose	2.16 (1967)	1.29
Ballpoint pen	0.89 (1965)	0.29
Transistor radio	55.00 (1967)	5.99
Videocassette recorder	1500.00 (1977)	89.00
Air fare (New York-Paris)	490.00 (1958)	328.00
Microwave oven	400.00 (1972)	89.00
Contact lenses	275.00 (1972)	39.00
Television (19-inch, color)	469.00 (1980)	199.00
Compact disk player	1000.00 (1985)	69.00

relative price: The price of one good in comparison with the price of other goods.

oranges, falls. In such circumstances, **relative prices** are changing, but not average prices. An increase in the relative price of apples, for example, simply means that apples have become more expensive in comparison with other fruits (or any other goods or services).

Changes in relative prices may occur in a period of stable average prices, or in periods of inflation or deflation. In fact, in an economy as vast as ours—in which literally millions of goods and services are exchanged in the factor and product markets—relative prices are always changing. Indeed, relative price changes are an essential ingredient of the market mechanism. Recall from Chapter 3 what happens when the market price of typing services rises relative to other goods and services. This (relative) price rise alerts typists (producers) to increase their output, cutting back on other production or leisure activities.

A general inflation—an increase in the average price level—doesn't perform this same market function. If all prices rise at the same rate, price increases for specific goods are of little value as market signals. In less extreme cases, when most but not all prices are rising, changes in relative prices do occur but aren't so immediately apparent. Table 7.1 reminds us that some prices do fall even during periods of general inflation.

REDISTRIBUTIVE EFFECTS OF INFLATION

The distinction between relative and average prices helps us determine who's hurt by inflation—and who's helped. Popular opinion notwithstanding, it's simply not true that everyone is worse off when prices rise. *Although inflation makes some people worse off, it makes other people better off.* Some people even get rich when prices rise! The micro consequences of inflation are reflected in redistributions of income and wealth, not general declines in either measure of our economic welfare. These redistributions occur because people buy different combinations of goods and services, own different assets, and sell distinct goods or services (including labor). The impact of inflation on individuals therefore depends on how the prices of the goods and services each person buys or sells actually change.

Price Effects

Price changes are the most familiar of inflation's pains. If you've been paying tuition, you know how the pain feels. Ten years ago, the average in-state tuition at public colleges and universities was $500 per year. Today the average in-state tuition exceeds

$3200 (see the accompanying NEWS). At private universities, tuition has increased eightfold in the past 10 years, to over $14,000. You don't need a whole course in economics to figure out the implications of these tuition hikes. To stay in college, you (or your parents) must forgo increasing amounts of other goods and services. You end up being worse off since you can't buy as many goods and services as you could before tuition went up.

The effect of tuition increases on your economic welfare is reflected in the distinction between nominal income and real income. **Nominal income** is the amount of money you receive in a particular time period; it's measured in current dollars. **Real income,** by contrast, is the purchasing power of that money, as measured by the quantity of goods and services your dollars will buy. If the number of dollars you receive every year is always the same, your *nominal income* doesn't change—but your *real income* will rise or fall with price changes.

nominal income: The amount of money income received in a given time period, measured in current dollars.

real income: Income in constant dollars; nominal income adjusted for inflation.

Suppose your parents agree to give you $6000 a year while you're in school. Out of that $6000 you must pay for your tuition, room and board, books, and everything else. The budget for your first year at school might look like this:

FIRST YEAR'S BUDGET

Nominal income	$6000
Consumption	
Tuition	$3000
Room and board	2000
Books	300
Everything else	700
Total	$6000

After paying for all your essential expenses, you have $700 to spend on clothes, entertainment, or anything else you want. That's not exactly living high, but it's not poverty.

Now suppose tuition increases to $3500 in your second year, while all other prices remain the same. What will happen to your nominal income? Nothing. Unless your parents take pity on you, you'll still be getting $6000 a year. Your nominal income is

IN THE NEWS

Average Tuition Rises 4% in a Year, More Than Twice the Rate of Inflation

Washington—The average cost of college tuition rose roughly 4 per cent this year, a slightly smaller increase than last year's, according to the annual survey by the College Board.

This year's increase is more than twice the rate of inflation as measured by the Consumer Price Index, as was last year's. The C.P.I. rose 1.6 per cent for the 12 months ending in August.

Four-year private institutions raised their prices the most, despite the many news stories in recent years noting how expensive such institutions have become.

- At four-year private colleges, students are paying an average of $14,508, a 5-per-cent increase.
- Four-year public colleges are charging an average of $3,243, up 4 per cent.
- At two-year private colleges, tuition and fees rose 4 per cent, to $7,333.
- At two-year public colleges, tuition is $1,633, a 4-per-cent increase.

—Ben Gose

The Chronicle of Higher Education, Oct. 16, 1998, p. A56.
http://chronicle.com

Analysis: Tuition increases reduce the real income of students. How much you suffer from inflation depends on what happens to the prices of the products you purchase.

unchanged. Your *real* income, however, will suffer. This is evident in the second year's budget:

SECOND YEAR'S BUDGET

Nominal income	$6000
Consumption	
Tuition	$3500
Room and board	2000
Books	300
Everything else	200
Total	$6000

You now have to use more of your income to pay tuition. This means you have less income to spend on other things. You'll have to cut back somewhere. Since room and board and books still cost $2300 per year, there's only one place to cut: the category of "everything else." After tuition increases, you can spend only $200 per year on movies, clothes, pizzas, and dates—not $700, as in the "good old days." This $500 reduction in purchasing power represents a *real* income loss. Even though your *nominal* income is still $6000, you have $500 less of "everything else" in your second year than you had in the first.

Although tuition hikes reduce the real income of students, nonstudents aren't hurt by such price increases. In fact, if tuition *doubled,* nonstudents really wouldn't care. They could continue to buy the same bundle of goods and services they'd been buying all along. Tuition increases reduce the real incomes only of people who go to college.

Two basic lessons about inflation are to be learned from this sad story:

- *Not all prices rise at the same rate during an inflation.* In our example, tuition increased substantially while other prices remained steady. Hence the "average" price increase wasn't representative of any particular good or service. Typically, some prices rise rapidly, others only modestly, and some actually fall.
- *Not everyone suffers equally from inflation.* This follows from our first observation. Those people who consume the goods and services that are rising faster in price bear a greater burden of inflation; their real incomes fall more. Other consumers bear a lesser burden, or even none at all, depending on how fast the prices rise for the goods they enjoy.

Table 7.2 illustrates some of the price changes that occurred in 1995. The average rate of inflation was only 1.6 percent. This was little solace to college students, however, who confronted tuition increases of 3.9 percent. On the other hand, price reductions on gasoline and computers spared consumers of these products from the pain of the average inflation rate.

TABLE 7.2
Price Changes in 1998: Not All Prices Rise at the Same Rate

The average rate of inflation conceals substantial differences in the price changes of specific goods and services. The impact of inflation on individuals depends in part on which goods and services are consumed. People who buy goods whose prices are rising fastest lose more real income. In 1998 smokers were particularly hard-hit by inflation.

Prices That Rose (Percent)		Prices That Fell (Percent)	
Cigarettes	+33.7	Pork chops	− 7.1
Oranges	+18.5	Lettuce	− 8.8
Bananas	+ 9.3	Cellular phone service	− 8.3
Ice cream	+ 7.2	Gasoline	−15.4
Cable TV	+ 6.9	PCs	−35.8
College Tuition	+ 3.9		
Average inflation rate: +1.6%			

Source: U.S. Bureau of Labor Statistics.

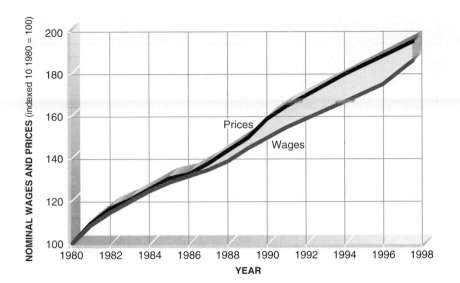

FIGURE 7.1
Nominal Wages and Prices

Inflation implies not only higher prices but higher wages as well. Hence inflation can't make *everyone* worse off. This graph confirms that average wages have risen along with average prices. Average wages rise faster than prices when productivity increases and more slowly when payroll taxes or fringe benefits like health insurance and pensions increase.

Source: *Economic Report of the President, 1999.*

Income Effects

Even if all prices rose at the *same* rate, inflation would still redistribute income. The redistributive effects of inflation originate not only in *expenditure* patterns but also *income* patterns. Keep in mind that there are two sides to every market transaction. ***What looks like a price to a buyer looks like an income to a seller.*** If students all pay higher tuition, the university will take in more income. To the extent that the nominal incomes colleges receive increase faster than average prices, they actually *benefit* from inflation. They end up being able to buy *more* goods and services (including faculty, buildings, and library books) after a period of inflation than they could before. Their real income rises.

On average, people's incomes do keep pace with inflation. Again, this is a direct consequence of the circular flow: What one person pays out someone else takes in. ***If prices are rising, incomes must be rising, too.*** Notice in Figure 7.1 that average wages have pretty much risen in step with prices. From this perspective, it makes no sense to say that "inflation hurts everybody." On *average,* at least, we're no worse off when prices rise, since our (average) incomes increase at the same time.[1]

No one is exactly "average," of course. In reality, some people's incomes rise faster than inflation while others' increase more slowly. Some people have fixed incomes that *don't* go up with inflation. Fixed-income groups include those retired people who depend primarily on private pensions and workers with multiyear contracts that fix wage rates at preinflation levels. Lenders (like banks) that have lent funds at fixed interest rates also suffer real income losses when price levels rise. They continue to receive interest payments fixed in *nominal* dollars that have increasingly less *real* value. All these market participants experience a declining share of real income (and output) in inflationary periods.

Wealth Effects

The same kind of redistribution occurs between those who hold some form of wealth and those who don't. Suppose you deposit $100 in a savings account on Jan. 1, where it earns 5 percent interest. At the end of the year you'll have more nominal wealth ($105) than you started with ($100). But what if all prices have doubled in the meantime? In that case, your $105 will buy you no more at the end of the year than $52.50 would have bought you at the beginning. Inflation in this case reduces the *real* value

---

[1] In fact, average incomes have usually risen even faster than prices because of increasing output per worker. Thus average real incomes have increased significantly over time. In those years when wages didn't keep up with prices, taxes were usually to blame.

TABLE 7.3
The Real Story of Wealth

Households hold their wealth in many different forms. As the value of various assets changes, so does a person's wealth. Between 1987 and 1997, inflation was very good to people who held stocks. By contrast, the real value of oil, farmland, and gold and silver fell.

Asset	Percentage Change in Value, 1987–1997
Stocks	326
Bonds	141
Housing	45
Average price level	41
U.S. farmland	17
Stamps	8
Oil	6
Silver	−12
Gold	−26

of your savings, and you end up worse off than those individuals who spent all their income earlier in the year!

Table 7.3 shows how the value of various assets have changed. Between 1987 and 1997, the average price level increased 41 percent. The average value of stocks and bonds rose much faster than the price level, increasing the *real* value of those assets. House prices rose too, but just a bit more than average prices. Hence the *real* value of housing was nearly constant. Wealth was effectively redistributed from people who owned oil fields, farmland, and gold to people who owned stocks, and real estate.

Redistributions

By altering relative prices, incomes, and the real value of wealth, inflation turns out to be a mechanism for redistributing incomes and wealth. ***The redistributive mechanics of inflation include***

- ***Price effects.*** People who prefer goods and services that are increasing in price least quickly end up with a larger share of real income.
- ***Income effects.*** People whose nominal incomes rise faster than the rate of inflation end up with a larger share of total income.
- ***Wealth effects.*** People who own assets that are increasing in real value end up better off than others.

On the other hand, people whose nominal incomes don't keep pace with inflation end up with smaller shares of total output. The same thing is true of those who enjoy goods that are rising fastest in price or who hold assets that are declining in real value. In this sense, ***inflation acts just like a tax, taking income or wealth from one group and giving it to another.*** But we have no assurance that this particular tax will behave like Robin Hood, taking from the rich and giving to the poor. In reality, inflation often redistributes income in the opposite direction.

Social Tensions

Because of its redistributive effects, inflation also increases social and economic tensions. Tensions—between labor and management, between government and the people, and among consumers—may overwhelm a society and its institutions. As Gardner Ackley of the University of Michigan observed, "A significant real cost of inflation is what it does to morale, to social coherence, and to people's attitudes toward each other." "This society," added Arthur Okun, "is built on implicit and explicit contracts. . . . They are linked to the idea that the dollar means something. If you cannot depend on the value of the dollar, this system is undermined. People will constantly feel they've been fooled and cheated."[2] This is how the middle class felt in Germany in 1923 and in China in 1948, when the value of their savings was wiped out by sudden and unanticipated inflation. A surge in prices also stirred social and political tensions in Russia as it moved from a price-controlled economy to a market-driven economy in the 1990s.

---

[2]Quoted in *Business Week,* May 22, 1978, p. 118.

WORLD VIEW

Tortilla Price Hike Hits Mexico's Poorest

Mexico City—When the Mexican government ended its long-standing subsidy of tortillas on Jan. 1, the result was a five-day crash course in free-market economics and tortilla politics that left a bad taste in everyone's mouth.

For 25 years, the government has subsidized tortilla production and regulated the price of the popular corn-flour pancakes, which are to Mexicans what baguettes are to Parisians or rice is to the Chinese. But falling oil prices and pressure from international lenders have forced the government to cut spending. When the ax fell on tortilla subsidies, prices responded like a basketball released from the bottom of a swimming pool, more than doubling in some places.

The result has been an angry backlash, particularly among impoverished Mexicans who rely on the soft, chewy disks for half their daily diet.

"Tortillas are the most politically sensitive product in the Mexican economy, and that was why they were the last to be liberalized," said political commentator Sergio Sarmiento.

—John Ward Anderson

The Washington Post, Jan. 12, 1999, p. A11. © 1999, The Washington Post. Reprinted with permission, www.washingtonpost.com

Analysis: The redistributive effects of inflation can cause a political backlash. No one wants to pay higher prices.

A similar political backlash occurred in Mexico in 1999 when tortilla prices jumped (see WORLD VIEW).

Despair

It's not too hard to see how unsettling inflation can be. With prices changing all the time, a person's comfortable habits are easily upset. People are compelled to cope with uncertainty. Should they continue to save part of their incomes, even though the real value of savings is falling? Should they be shopping for different goods and services at different stores? How can they boost their income to keep up with inflation? All these worries seem to accumulate quickly when prices start to rise rapidly. Psychotherapists report that "inflation stress" leads to more frequent marital spats, pessimism, diminished self-confidence, and even sexual insecurity. Some people turn to crime as a way of solving the problem.

Money Illusion

Even those people whose nominal incomes "keep up" with inflation often feel oppressed by rising prices. People feel that they *deserve* any increases in wages they receive. When they later discover that their higher (nominal) wages don't buy any additional goods, they feel cheated. They feel worse off, even though they haven't suffered any actual loss of real income. This phenomenon is called **money illusion.** People suffering from money illusion are forever reminding us that they used to pay only $1 to see a movie or $8 for a textbook. What they forget is that nominal incomes were also a lot lower in the "good old days" than they are today.

money illusion: The use of nominal dollars rather than real dollars to gauge changes in one's income or wealth.

MACRO CONSEQUENCES

Although redistributions of income and wealth are the primary consequences of inflation, inflation has *macroeconomic* effects as well. Inflation can alter the rate and mix of output by changing consumption, work, saving, investment, and trade behavior.

Uncertainty

One of the most immediate consequences of inflation is uncertainty. When the average price level is changing significantly in either direction, economic decisions become more difficult. As the cartoon on page 130 suggests, even something as simple as ordering a restaurant meal is more difficult if menu prices are changing. Longer-term decisions are even more difficult. Should you commit yourself to 4 years of college, for example, if you aren't certain that you or your parents will be able to afford the full

From *The Wall Street Journal*—permission, Cartoon Features Syndicate.

"DO I HAVE YOUR ASSURANCE THAT PRICES WILL NOT BE INCREASED BEFORE WE ARE SERVED?"

Analysis: The uncertainty caused by rising prices causes stress and may alter consumption and investment decisions.

CYBER NOTE

To see how much the cost of college or any product will change at different inflation rates, use the CPI inflator provided by the Federal Reserve Bank of Minneapolis at http://woodrow.mpls.frb.fed.us/economy/calc/cpihome.html.

Shortened Time Horizons

hyperinflation: Inflation rate in excess of 200 percent, lasting at least 1 year.

costs? In a period of stable prices you can at least be fairly certain of what a college education will cost over a period of years. But if prices are rising, you can no longer be sure how large the bill will be. Under such circumstances, many individuals may decide not to enter college rather than risk the possibility of being driven out later by rising costs.

Price uncertainties created affect production decisions as well. Imagine a firm that's considering building a new factory. Typically the construction of a factory takes 2 years or more, including planning, site selection, and actual construction. If construction costs change rapidly, the firm may find that it's unable to complete the factory or to operate it profitably. Confronted with this added uncertainty, the firm may decide not to build a new plant.

When market participants become less certain about the future, the economy is likely to suffer in the end. In general, *people shorten their time horizons in the face of inflation uncertainties.* If consumers and producers postpone or cancel their expenditure plans, the demand for goods and services will fall. Eventually our production of goods and services will fall as well, and we'll end up somewhere inside our production possibilities curve, with increased unemployment.

The effect of rising price levels on time horizons was dramatically illustrated when Germany suffered a bout of **hyperinflation** in the early 1920s. As the accompanying WORLD VIEW observes, German prices were doubling every *week* in 1923! Confronted with these skyrocketing prices, German workers couldn't afford to wait until the end of the week to do their shopping. Instead, they were paid twice daily and given brief "shopping breaks" to make their essential purchases. In this case, the rate of expenditure on goods and services actually increased as a result of inflation, but the rate of production fell. The same kind of frenzy occurred in China during 1948 and 1949. The Nationalist Chinese yuan declined precipitously in value, and market participants rushed to spend their incomes as fast as they could. No one saved income or even tried to.

Hyperinflation also crippled the Russian economy during the period 1990–1992. Prices rose by 200 percent in 1991 and by another 1000 percent in 1992. These price increases rendered the Russian ruble nearly worthless. No one wanted to hold rubles or trade for them. Farmers preferred to hold potatoes rather than sell them. Producers of shoes and clothes likewise decided to hold rather than sell their products. The resulting contraction in supply caused a severe decline in Russian output.

Hyperinflation

Inflation and the Weimar Republic

At the beginning of 1921 in Germany, the cost-of-living index was 18 times higher than its 1913 prewar base, while wholesale prices had mushroomed by 4,400%. Neither of these increases are negligible, but inflation and war have always been bedfellows. Normally, however, war ends and inflation recedes. By the end of 1921, it seemed that way; prices rose more modestly. Then, in 1922, inflation erupted.

Zenith of German Hyperinflation Wholesale prices rose fortyfold, an increase nearly as large as during the prior eight years, while retail prices rose even more rapidly. The hyperinflation reached its zenith during 1923. Between May and June 1923, consumer prices more than quadrupled; between July and August, they rose more than 15 times; in the next month, over 25 times; and between September and October, by 10 times the previous month's increase.

The German economy was thoroughly disrupted. Businessmen soon discovered the impossibility of rational economic planning. Profits fell as employees demanded frequent wage adjustments. Workers were often paid daily and sometimes two or three times a day, so that they could buy goods in the morning before the inevitable afternoon price increase. The work ethic suffered; wage earners were both more reluctant to work and less devoted to their jobs. Bankers were on the phone hour after hour, quoting the value of the mark in dollars, as calls continuously came in from merchants who needed the exchange rate to adjust their mark prices.

In an age that preceded the credit card, businessmen traveling around the country found themselves borrowing funds from their customers each stage of the way. The cash they'd allocated for the entire trip barely sufficed to pay the way to the next stop. Speculation began to dominate production.

As a result of the decline in profitability, in the ability to plan ahead, and the concern with speculation rather than production, unemployment rose, increasing by 600% between Sept. 1 and Dec. 15, 1923. And, as the hyperinflation intensified, people found goods unobtainable.

Hyperinflation crushed the middle class. Those thrifty Germans who had placed their savings in corporate or government bonds saw their lifetime efforts come to naught. Debtors sought out creditors to pay them in valueless currency. The debts of German government and industry disappeared. Farmers, too, profited, for, like farmers elsewhere, they were debtors. Nevertheless, the hyperinflation left a traumatic imprint on the German people, a legacy which colors their governmental policy to this day.

—Jonas Prager

Analysis: During inflationary periods, time horizons are shortened as people attempt to spend money before it loses further value. Debtors gain and creditors lose when price levels rise.

Speculation

Inflation threatens not only to reduce the level of economic activity but to change its very nature. If you really expect prices to rise, it makes sense to buy goods and resources now for resale later. If prices rise fast enough, you can make a handsome profit. These are the kinds of thoughts that motivate people to buy houses, precious metals, commodities, and other assets. But such speculation, if carried too far, can detract from the production process. If speculative profits become too easy, few people will engage in production; instead, everyone will be buying and selling existing goods. People may even be encouraged to withhold resources from the production process, hoping to sell them later at higher prices, which is what Russian farmers were doing in 1991 when they withheld potatoes from the market. As such behavior becomes widespread, production declines and unemployment rises.

Bracket Creep

Another reason that savings, investment, and work effort decline when prices rise is that taxes go up, too. Federal income tax rates are *progressive;* that is, tax rates are higher for larger incomes. The intent of these progressive rates is to redistribute income from rich to poor. However, inflation tends to increase *everyone's* income. In the process, people are pushed into higher tax brackets and confront higher tax rates. The process is referred to as **bracket creep.** In recent years bracket creep has been limited by the inflation indexing of personal income tax rates and a reduction in the number of tax brackets. However, Social Security payroll taxes and most state and local taxes aren't indexed.

bracket creep: The movement of taxpayers into higher tax brackets (rates) as nominal incomes grow.

Although the public sector still reaps some gain from inflation, inflation stress tends to create a political backlash. Voters are quick to blame the government for inflation. If the administration doesn't put a stop to inflation, the voters will turn to someone who promises to do so.

Deflation Dangers

CYBER NOTE

Want a "down-under" view of inflation? The Reserve Bank of New Zealand offers insights into the problems of inflation and hyperinflation at www.rbnz.govt.nz/educate/costs.htm.

Ironically, a *falling* price level—a deflation—might not make people happy either. In fact, a falling price level can do the same kind of harm as a rising price level. When prices are falling, people on fixed incomes and long-term contracts gain more *real* income. Lenders win and creditors lose. People who hold cash or bonds win: Homeowners and stamp collectors lose. A deflation simply reverses the kinds of redistributions caused by inflation.

A falling price level also has similar macro consequences. Time horizons get shorter. Businesses are more reluctant to borrow money or to invest. People lose confidence in themselves and public institutions when declining price levels deflate their incomes and assets.

MEASURING INFLATION

In view of the macro and micro consequences of price-level changes, the measurement of inflation serves two purposes: to gauge the average rate of inflation and to identify its principal victims.

Consumer Price Index

Consumer Price Index (CPI): A measure (index) of changes in the average price of consumer goods and services.

The most common measure of inflation is the **Consumer Price Index (CPI).** As its name suggests, the CPI is a mechanism for measuring changes in the average price of consumer goods and services. It's analogous to the fruit price index we discussed earlier. The CPI doesn't refer to the price of any particular good but to the average price of all consumer goods.

By itself, the "average price" of consumer goods isn't a very useful number. But once we know the average price of consumer goods, we can observe whether that average rises—that is, whether inflation is occurring. By observing the extent to which prices increase, we can calculate the **inflation rate.**

inflation rate: The annual percentage rate of increase in the average price level.

We can get a better sense of how inflation is measured by observing how the CPI is constructed. The process begins by identifying a "market basket" of goods and services the typical consumer buys. For this purpose, the Bureau of Labor Statistics surveys a large sample of families every year to determine what goods and services consumers actually buy. Figure 7.2 summarizes the results of the 1993–1995 surveys, which reveal that 39.6 cents out of every consumer dollar is spent on housing (shelter, furnishings, and utilities), 16.3 cents on food, and another 17.6 cents on transportation. Only 6.2 cents of every consumer dollar is spent on recreation.

Within these broad categories of expenditure, the Bureau of Labor Statistics itemizes specific goods and services. The details of the expenditure survey show, for example, that private expenditures for reading and education account for only 2 percent of the typical consumer's budget, less than is spent on alcoholic beverages and tobacco. It also shows that we spend 7 cents out of every dollar on fuel, to drive our cars (3.1 cents) and to heat and cool our houses (3.9 cents).

CYBER NOTE

At the U.S. Bureau of Labor Statistics, www.bls.gov, you can find the CPI for the most recent month and the same month last year.

Once we know what the typical consumer buys, it's relatively easy to calculate the average price of a market basket. The Bureau of Labor Statistics actually goes shopping in 85 cities across the country, recording the prices of the 184 items that make up the typical market basket. Approximately 19,000 stores are visited, and 60,000 landlords, renters, and homeowners are surveyed—every month!

As a result of these massive, ongoing surveys, the Bureau of Labor Statistics can tell us what's happening to consumer prices. Suppose, for example, that the market basket cost $100 last year and that the same basket of goods and services cost $110 this year. On the basis of those two shopping trips, we could conclude that consumer prices had risen by 10 percent in 1 year.

FIGURE 7.2
The Market Basket

To measure changes in average prices, we must first know what goods and services consumers buy. This diagram, based on consumer surveys, shows how the typical urban consumer spends each dollar. Housing, transportation, and food account for over two-thirds of consumer spending.

Source: U.S. Bureau of Labor Statistics (1993–1995 data).

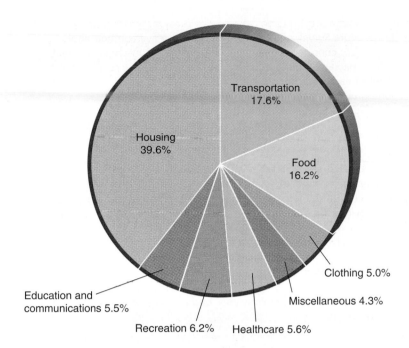

In practice, the CPI is usually expressed in terms of what the market basket cost in a specific **base period.** The price level in the base period is arbitrarily designated as 100. In the case of the CPI, the average price level for the period 1982–1984 is usually used as the base for computing price changes. Hence the price index for that base period is set at 100. In January 1999, the CPI registered 165. In other words, it cost $165 in 1999 to buy the same market baskets that cost only $100 in the base period. Prices had increased by an average of 65 percent over that period. Each month the Bureau of Labor Statistics updates the CPI, telling us how the current cost of that same basket compares to its cost between 1982 and 1984.[3]

Table 7.4 on the next page illustrates how changes in the official CPI are computed. Notice that all price changes don't have the same impact on the inflation rate. Rather, *the effect of a specific price change on the inflation rate depends on the product's relative importance in consumer budgets.*

The relative importance of a product in consumer budgets is reflected in its **item weight,** which refers to the percentage of a typical consumer budget spent on the item. Table 7.4 shows the item weights for college tuition and housing. College tuition may loom very large in your personal budget, but less than 1 percent of *all* consumer expenditure is spent on college tuition. Hence, the item weight for college tuition in the *average* consumer budget is only 0.0085.

Housing costs absorb a far larger share of the typical consumer budget. As Table 7.4 shows, the item weight for housing is 0.396. Accordingly, rent increases have a much larger impact on the CPI than do tuition hikes.

In addition to the familiar Consumer Price Index, there are three Producer Price Indexes (PPIs). The PPIs keep track of average prices received by producers. One index includes crude materials, another covers intermediate goods, and the last covers

base period: The time period used for comparative analysis: the basis for indexing, for example, of price changes.

item weight: The percentage of total expenditure spent on a specific product; used to compute inflation indexes.

Producer Price Indexes

---

[3]Since January 1978, the Bureau of Labor Statistics has actually been computing two CPIs, one for urban wage earners and clerical workers and the second and larger one for all urban consumers (about 80 percent of the population). A third index, which uses rent rather than ownership costs of shelter, was introduced in 1983. The "urban/rental" index is most commonly cited.

TABLE 7.4
Computing Changes in the CPI

The Consumer Expenditure Survey of 1994 revealed that the average household spends 0.85 cent of every consumer dollar on college tuition. Households without college students don't pay any tuition, of course. And your family probably devotes *more* than 0.85 cent of each consumer dollar to tuition. On *average,* however, 0.85 cent is the proportion of each dollar spent on tuition. This figure is the *item weight* of tuition in computing the CPI.

The impact on the CPI of a price change for a specific good is calculated as follows:

Item weight × percentage change in price of item = percentage change in CPI

Suppose that tuition prices suddenly go up 20 percent. What impact will this single price increase have on the CPI? In this case, where tuition is the only price that increases, the impact on the CPI will be only 0.17 percent (0.0085 × 20), as illustrated below. Thus a very large increase in the price of tuition (20%) has a tiny impact (0.17%) on the *average* price level.

Housing, on the other hand, accounts for 39.6 percent of consumer expenditure. Thus is housing prices increase 20 percent, and housing is the only price that increases, the impact on the CPI will be 7.92 percent, as shown below.

The relative importance of an item in consumer budgets—its "item weight"—is a key determinant of its inflationary impact.

Item	Item Weight	3	Price Increase for the Item	5	Impact on the CPI
College tuition	0.0085		20%		0.17%
Housing	0.396		20%		7.92%

finished goods. The three PPIs don't include all producer prices but primarily those in mining, manufacturing, and agriculture. Like the CPI, changes in the PPIs are identified in monthly surveys.

Over long periods of time, the PPIs and the CPI generally reflect the same rate of inflation. In the short run, however, the PPIs usually increase before the CPI, because it takes time for producers' price increases to be reflected in the prices that consumers pay. For this reason, the PPIs are watched closely as a clue to potential changes in consumer prices.

The GDP Deflator

GDP deflator: A price index that refers to all goods and services included in GDP.

The broadest price index is the GDP deflator. The GDP deflator covers all output, including consumer goods, investment goods, and government services. Unlike the CPI and PPIs, the **GDP deflator** isn't based on a fixed "basket" of goods or services. Rather, it allows the contents of the basket to change with people's consumption and investment patterns. The GDP deflator therefore isn't a pure measure of price change. Its value reflects both price changes and market responses to those price changes, as reflected in new expenditure patterns. Hence the GDP deflator typically registers a lower inflation rate than the CPI.

nominal GDP: The value of final output produced in a given period, measured in the prices of that period (current prices).
real GDP: The value of final output produced in a given period, adjusted for changing prices.

Real vs. Nominal GDP. The GDP deflator is used to adjust nominal output values for changing price levels. Recall that **nominal GDP** refers to the *current*-dollar value of output, whereas **real GDP** denotes the *inflation-adjusted* value of output. These two measures of output are connected by the GDP deflator:

$$\text{Real GDP} = \frac{\text{nominal GDP}}{\text{GDP deflator}}$$

The nominal values of GDP were $8.5 trillion in 1998 and $5.7 trillion in 1990. However, the price level rose by 20 percent between those years. Hence, real GDP in 1998 in the base-period prices of 1990 was

$$\frac{\text{1998 real GDP}}{\text{(in 1990 prices)}} = \frac{\text{nominal GDP}}{\text{price deflator}} = \frac{\$8.5 \text{ trillion}}{1.20} = \$7.1 \text{ trillion}$$

Changes in real GDP are a good measure of how output and living standards are changing. Nominal GDP statistics, by contrast, mix up output and price changes.

THE GOAL: PRICE STABILITY

In view of the inequities, anxieties, and real losses caused by inflation, it's not surprising that price stability is a major goal of economic policy. As we observed at the beginning of this chapter, every U.S. president since Franklin Roosevelt has decreed price stability to be a foremost policy goal. Unfortunately, few presidents (or their advisers) have stated exactly what they mean by "price stability." Do they mean *no* change in the average price level? Or is some upward creep in the price index acceptable?

price stability: The absence of significant changes in the average price level; officially defined as a rate of inflation of less than 3 percent.

A Numerical Goal

An explicit numerical goal for **price stability** was established for the first time in the Full Employment and Balanced Growth Act of 1978. According to that act, the goal of economic policy is to hold the rate of inflation under 3 percent.

Unemployment Concerns

Why did Congress choose 3 percent inflation rather than zero inflation as the benchmark for price stability? One reason was concern about unemployment. To keep prices from rising, the government might have to restrain spending in the economy. Such restraint could lead to cutbacks in production and an increase in joblessness. In other words, there might be a trade-off between declining inflation and rising unemployment. From this perspective, a little bit of inflation might be the "price" the economy has to pay to keep unemployment rates from rising.

Recall how the same kind of logic was used to define the goal of full employment. The fear there was that price pressures would increase as the economy approached its production possibilities. This suggested that some unemployment might be the "price" the economy has to pay for price stability. Accordingly, the goal of "full employment" was defined as the lowest rate of unemployment *consistent with stable prices*. The same kind of thinking is apparent here. The amount of inflation regarded as tolerable depends in part on the effect of anti-inflation strategies on unemployment rates. After reviewing our experiences with both unemployment and inflation, Congress concluded that 3 percent inflation was a "safe" target.

Quality Changes

The second argument for setting our price-stability goal above zero inflation relates to our measurement capabilities. The Consumer Price Index isn't a perfect measure of inflation. In essence, the CPI simply monitors the price of specific goods over time. Over time, however, the goods themselves change, too. Old products become better as a result of *quality improvements*. A TV set costs more today than it did in 1955, but today's television also delivers a bigger, clearer picture—and in digital color! Hence increases in the price of TV sets tend to exaggerate the true rate of inflation: Part of the higher price represents more product.

The same is true of automobiles. The best-selling car in 1958 (a Chevrolet Bel Air) had a list price of only $2618. That makes a 1999 Ford Taurus look awfully expensive at $19,225. The quality of today's cars is much better, however. Improvements since 1958 include seat belts, air bags, variable-speed windshield wipers, electronic ignition, rear-window defrosters, radial tires, antilock brakes, emergency flashers, remote-control mirrors, crash-resistant bodies, a doubling of fuel mileage, and a 100-fold decrease in exhaust pollutants. As a result, today's higher car prices also buy cars that are safer, cleaner, and more comfortable.

Ignoring Cell Phones Biases CPI Upward

Cellular telephones have been in commercial operation in the United States for 13 years. Beginning in Chicago in late 1983, and then at the Los Angeles Olympic Games in 1984, cellular telephone usage spread first to the top thirty Metropolitan Statistical Areas (MSAs), then to the other 300 or so MSAs, and finally to rural areas. At year end 1996, there were over 40 million cellular subscribers in the United States. . . .

Yet the cellular telephone will not be included in the calculation of the Consumer Price Index (CPI) until 1998 or 1999. "This neglect of new goods leads to an upward bias in the CPI," NBER Research Associate Jerry Hausman concludes.

The CPI estimates that since 1988, telecommunications prices have increased by 8.5 percent, or 1.02 percent per year. A corrected index that includes cellular service decreased 1.28 percent per year since 1988, Hausman figures. "Thus, the bias in the BLS [Bureau of Labor Statistics] telecommunications services CPI equals approximately 2.3 percentage points per year."

Source: National Bureau of Economic Research, *NBER Digest,* June 1997. www.nber.org/digest

Analysis: Since the CPI tracks prices for a fixed basket of goods, it misses the effects of falling prices on new goods that appear between survey periods.

The U.S. Bureau of Labor Statistics does adjust the CPI for quality changes. Such adjustments inevitably entail subjective judgments, however. Critics are quick to complain that the CPI overstates inflation because quality improvements are undervalued.

The problem of measuring quality improvements is even more difficult in the case of new products. The computers and word processors used today didn't exist when the Census Bureau conducted its 1972–1973 survey of consumer expenditure. The 1982–1984 expenditure survey included those products, but not still newer ones such as the cellular phone. As the accompanying NEWS explains, the omission of cellular phones caused the CPI to overstate the rate of inflation. The consumer expenditure survey of 1993–1995 included cell phones, but not digital cameras, HDTVs, or DVD players—all of which have had declining prices. As a result, there's a significant (though unmeasured) element of error in the CPI insofar as it's intended to gauge changes in the average prices paid by consumers. The goal of 3 percent inflation allows for such errors.

THE HISTORICAL RECORD

In the long view of history, the United States has done a good job of maintaining price stability. On closer inspection, however, our inflation performance is very uneven. Table 7.5 summarizes the long view, with data going back to 1800. The base period for pric-

TABLE 7.5
The Consumer Price Index, Selected Years 1800–1999

Before World War II, the average level of prices rose in some years and fell in others. Since 1945, prices have risen continuously. The Consumer Price Index has more than doubled since 1980.

Year	CPI	Year	CPI	Year	CPI	Year	CPI
1800	17.0	1900	8.3	1940	14.0	1980	82.4
1825	11.3	1915	10.1	1950	24.1	1982–1984	100.0
1850	8.3	1920	20.0	1960	29.6	1990	130.5
1875	11.0	1930	16.7	1970	38.8	1999	165.3

Note: Data from 1915 forward reflect the official all-items Consumer Price Index, which used the pre-1983 measure of shelter costs. Estimated indexes for 1800 through 1900 are drawn from several sources.

Source: U.S. Bureau of Labor Statistics.

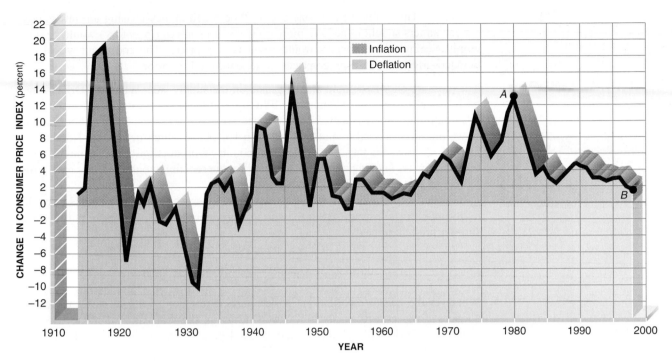

FIGURE 7.3
Annual Inflation Rates

During the 1920s and 1930s, consumer prices fell significantly, causing a general deflation. Since the Great Depression, however, average prices have risen almost every year. But even during this inflationary period, the annual rate of price increase has varied widely. In 1980 the rate of inflation was 13.5 percent (point *A*); in 1998 average prices rose only 1.6 percent (point *B*).

Source: U.S. Bureau of Labor Statistics.

ing the market basket of goods is again 1982–1984. Notice that the same market basket cost only $17 in 1800. Consumer prices increased 500 percent in 183 years. But also observe how frequently the price level *fell* in the 1800s and again in the 1930s. These recurrent deflations held down the long-run inflation rate. Because of these periodic deflations, average prices in 1945 were at the same level as in 1800!

Figure 7.3 provides a closer view of our more recent experience with inflation. In this figure we simply transformed annual changes in the CPI into percentage rates of inflation. The CPI increased from 72.6 to 82.4 during 1980. This 9.8-point jump in the CPI translates into a 13.5 percent rate of inflation (9.8 ÷ 72.6 = 0.135). This inflation rate, represented by point *A* in Figure 7.3, was the highest in a generation. Since then, prices have continued to increase, but at much slower rates.

CAUSES OF INFLATION

The evident variation in year-to-year inflation rates requires explanation. So do the horrifying bouts of hyperinflation that have erupted in other nations at various times. What causes price levels to rise or fall?

In the most general terms, this is an easy question to answer. Recall that all market transactions entail two converging forces, namely, *demand* and *supply*. Accordingly, any explanation of changing price levels must be rooted in one of these two market forces.

Excessive pressure on the demand side of the economy is often the cause of inflation. Suppose the economy was already producing at capacity, but that consumers were willing and able to buy even more goods. With accumulating savings or easy access to credit, consumers could end up trying to buy more output than the economy was

Demand-Pull Inflation

Cost-Push Inflation

CYBER NOTE

For current news stories on inflation, check out the Excite server http://nt.excite.com/15062/31683/page.html.

producing. This would be a classic case of "too much money chasing too few goods." As consumers sought to acquire more goods, store shelves (inventory) would begin to empty. Seeing this, producers would begin raising prices. The end result would be a demand-driven rise in average prices, or demand-pull inflation.

The pressure on prices could also originate on the supply side. When the Organization of Petroleum Exporting Countries (OPEC) abruptly increased oil prices in the mid-1970s, production costs increased in a broad array of industries. To cover these higher costs, producers raised output prices. When Hurricane Mitch devastated Honduras in 1998, it destroyed a huge portion of that country's production capacity, including its farm output. As market participants scurried for the remaining output, prices rose across the board.

Inflationary pressures could also originate in higher wages. If labor unions were able to abruptly push up wage rates, the costs of production would increase, putting pressure on product prices.

PROTECTIVE MECHANISMS

Whatever the *causes* of inflation, market participants don't want to suffer the consequences. Even at a relatively low rate of inflation, the real value of money declines over time. If prices rise by an average of just 4 percent a year, the real value of $1000 drops to $822 in 5 years and to only $676 in 10 years (see Table 7.6). Low rates of inflation don't have the drama of hyperinflation, but they still redistribute real wealth and income.

COLAs

cost-of-living adjustment (COLA): Automatic adjustments of nominal income to the rate of inflation.

Market participants can protect themselves from inflation by *indexing* their nominal incomes, as is done with Social Security benefits, for example. In any year that the rate of inflation exceeds 3 percent, Social Security benefits go up *automatically* by the same percentage as the inflation rate. This **cost-of-living adjustment (COLA)** ensures that nominal benefits keep pace with the rising prices. Because of the COLA, much of the real income of retirees is protected (private pensions typically don't include COLAs).

Landlords often protect their real incomes with COLAs as well, by including in their leases provisions that automatically increase rents by the rate of inflation. COLAs are also common in labor union agreements, government transfer programs (like food stamps), and many other contracts. In every such case *a COLA protects real income from inflation.*

TABLE 7.6
Inflation's Impact, 1999–2009

In the past 20 years the U.S. rate of inflation ranged from a low of 1 percent to a high of 13 percent. Does a range of 12 percentage points really make much difference? One way to find out is to see how a specific sum of money will shrink in real value in a decade.

Here's what would happen to the real value of $1000 from January 1, 1999, to January 1, 2009 at different inflation rates. At 2 percent inflation, $1000 held for 10 years would be worth $820. At 10 percent inflation that same $1000 would buy only $386 worth of goods in the year 2009.

Year	Annual Inflation Rate				
	2 Percent	**4 Percent**	**6 Percent**	**8 Percent**	**10 Percent**
1999	$1000	$1000	$1000	$1000	$1000
2000	980	962	943	926	909
2001	961	925	890	857	826
2002	942	889	840	794	751
2003	924	855	792	735	683
2004	906	822	747	681	621
2005	888	790	705	630	564
2006	871	760	665	584	513
2007	853	731	627	540	467
2008	837	703	592	500	424
2009	820	676	558	463	386

WORLD VIEW

Sky-High Interest Rates South of the Border

Fed up with those measly interest payments the bank pays on your hard-earned savings? Why not move your savings account to Brazil, where banks were paying interest rates in excess of 40 percent on savings accounts in early 1999? That's right, 40 percent! Or you can get up to 25 percent in nearby Mexico.

These sky-high interest rates look tempting, but there's a catch. The inflation rate in Brazil was climbing in 1999 and might exceed 40 percent. So most of the interest payments will be needed just to keep up with rising prices. After inflation, there won't be much left over. What economists call the *real* interest rate—bank interest minus inflation—will be less than 10 percent. That hardly justifies a trip to South America.

Analysis: The appropriate measure of a return on savings is the *real* interest rate. The real rate equals the *nominal* rate minus anticipated inflation.

Cost-of-living adjustments have also become more common in loan agreements. As we noted before, debtors win and creditors lose when the price level rises. Suppose a loan requires interest payments equal to 5 percent of the amount (principal) borrowed. If the rate of inflation jumps to 7 percent, prices will be rising faster than interest is accumulating. Hence the **real interest rate**—the inflation-adjusted rate of interest—will actually be negative. The interest payments made in future years will buy fewer goods than can be bought today.

The real rate of interest is calculated as

$$\text{Real interest rate} = \text{nominal interest rate} - \text{anticipated rate of inflation}$$

In this case, the nominal interest rate is 5 percent and inflation is 7 percent. Hence the *real* rate of interest is *minus* 2 percent. The WORLD VIEW above illustrates how inflation can make even sky-high (nominal) interest rates look pretty mundane.

The distinction between real and nominal interest rates isn't too important if you're lending or borrowing money for just a couple of days. But the distinction is critical for long-term loans like home mortgages. Mortgage loans typically span a period of 25 to 30 years. If the inflation rate stays higher than the nominal interest rate during this period, the lender will end up with less *real* wealth than was initially lent.

To protect against such losses, the banking industry developed a new kind of loan, with adjustable interest rates. An **adjustable-rate mortgage (ARM)** stipulates an interest rate that changes during the term of the loan. A mortgage paying 5 percent interest in a stable (3 percent inflation) price environment may later require 9 percent interest if the inflation rate jumps to 7 percent. Such an adjustment would keep the real rate of interest at 2 percent.

The proliferation of COLAs and ARMs has made the CPI a critical statistic in today's economy. The problem is simple: If the CPI goes up, so do government transfer payments, union wages, and nominal interest rates. Critics charge that the Bureau of Labor Statistics has persistently exaggerated the inflation rate by undervaluing quality improvements, new products, and changes in expenditure patterns. If the CPI overstates inflation by just 1 percentage point, the federal government loses $140 billion per year in increased outlays and reduced tax revenues (see NEWS next page). In 1998 the CPI's market basket of goods and services was overhauled. The new index, based on 1993–1995 expenditure patterns, includes more new products such as cell phones and new adjustments for quality improvements. As products continue to emerge and change, however, the CPI will remain an imperfect but highly useful measure of inflation.

ARMs

real interest rate: The nominal interest rate minus the anticipated inflation rate.

adjustable-rate mortgage (ARM): A mortgage (home loan) that adjusts the nominal interest rate to changing rates of inflation.

The Cost of Mismeasurement

CPI Overstates Inflation, Senate Panel Says

The government's most widely used inflation gauge, the consumer price index, will overstate future inflation by about 1 percentage point every year, according to a panel of five experts appointed by the Senate Finance Committee. . . .

The Congressional Budget Office has calculated that by shaving 1 percentage point off the cost-of-living increases in entitlement programs, the government would save the government about $140 billion a year by 2005. That would cut the projected budget deficit that year by about a third. . . .

In its interim report, the advisory committee estimated that the CPI now overstates the rise in living costs for the average household by somewhere from 0.7 percent to 2.0 percent each year, and has been doing so for at least the past 20 years.

—Steven Pearlstein

The Washington Post, Sept. 15, 1995, p. F2. © 1995, The Washington Post. Reprinted with permission. www.washingtonpost.com

Analysis: Changes in product quality and expenditure patterns may cause inflation to be overestimated. Any overstatement will increase federal outlays and reduce tax revenues because of inflation indexing.

THE ECONOMY TOMORROW

(Reprinted from *The Economist,* Jan. 22, 1992, p. 11. © 1992 The Economist Newspaper Group, Inc. Reprinted with permission.) www.economist.com

The End of Inflation?

The earth spins, the sun shines, prices rise: two generations have grown up believing that inflation is an unalterable fact of life. No wonder. A dollar today is worth only 13 cents in 1945 money; a pound is worth only 6p. Much of the damage was done in the 1970s and early 1980s, and much has improved since then. In the OECD countries inflation is now hovering around its 1960s level of 3–4%. That gives governments the best chance they have had for decades to kill it off and achieve price stability. Sadly, they may fluff it.

Historical Stability

Price stability is not as extraordinary as it sounds. It does not mean that all prices stay the same: some will fall, others rise, but the average price level remains constant. Anyway, inflation, in the sense of continuously rising prices, is historically the exception, not the rule. On the eve of the first world war, prices in Britain were on average no higher than at the time of the fire of London in 1666. . . . During those 250 years, the longest unbroken run of rising prices was six years. Since 1946, by contrast, prices in Britain have risen every year, and the same is true of virtually every other OECD country.

It is easy to say that double-digit inflation is bad, but harder to agree on the ideal rate. Should governments aim for 5%, 3% or 0%? Some claim that the extra benefits of zero inflation are tiny and would be outweighed by the short-term cost—lost output, lost jobs—of pushing inflation lower. A little bit of inflation, they say, acts like a lubricant, helping relative prices and wages to adjust more efficiently, since all wages and most prices are hard to cut in absolute terms. But a little inflation sounds like "a little drink" for an alcoholic. It can too easily accelerate. That is the lesson of the past 40 years—that and the fact that the economies with the lowest inflation have tended to be the ones with the least unemployment. Beyond the short term governments cannot choose to have a bit faster growth in exchange for a bit more inflation. The choice does not exist.

The Virtue of Zero

The rewards of reducing inflation from 5% to 0% may be smaller than those from crunching inflation from 5,000% to 5%, but they are still highly desirable. The best inflation rate is one that least affects the behaviour of companies, investors, shoppers and workers. That means zero, because anything higher interferes with the most fundamental function of prices—their ability to provide information about relative scarcities. If prices in general are rising by 5% a year, the fact that the price of one particular product rises by 8% goes largely unnoticed. Yet that product's relative 3% increase ought to attract the attention of potential new producers, and to encourage buyers to look elsewhere—in short, to set in train the changes that maximize economic efficiency. It would do that if the 3% rise was like a hillock in an otherwise flat landscape; but, in the mountains of generalized inflation, nobody notices a crag. Even with an annual inflation rate of 5%, the general price level doubles every 14 years, obscuring changes in relative prices.

Now imagine a world without inflation. Once it was believable, it would transform the way people behave. Companies would be confident about borrowing long-term money, and lenders confident about providing it. Real interest rates would fall. Firms would invest more because the probable pay-out would be clearer; the same would be true of individuals investing time and money on their education. Governments could budget for infrastructural projects, knowing that their plans would not be derailed by unexpected surges in prices. In general, everyone would think more about the long term because the long term would be easier to see.

SUMMARY

- Inflation is an increase in the average price level. Typically it's measured by changes in a price index such as the Consumer Price Index (CPI).

- At the micro level, inflation redistributes income by altering relative prices, income, and wealth. Because not all prices rise at the same rate and because not all people buy (and sell) the same goods or hold the same assets, inflation doesn't affect everyone equally. Some individuals actually gain from inflation, whereas others suffer a loss of real income or wealth.

- At the macro level, inflation threatens to reduce total output because it increases uncertainties about the future and thereby inhibits consumption and production decisions. Fear of rising prices can also stimulate spending, forcing the government to take restraining action that threatens full employment. Rising prices also encourage speculation and hoarding, which detract from productive activity.

- Fully anticipated inflation reduces the anxieties and real losses associated with rising prices. However, few people can foresee actual price patterns or make all the necessary adjustments in their market activity.

- The U.S. goal of price stability is defined as an inflation rate of less than 3 percent per year. This goal recognizes potential conflicts between zero inflation and full employment as well as the difficulties of measuring quality improvements and new products.

- From 1800 to 1945 prices both rose and fell, leaving the average price level unchanged. Since then, prices have risen nearly every year but at widely different rates.

- Inflation is caused by either excessive demand (demand-pull inflation) or structural changes in supply (cost-push inflation).

- Cost-of-living adjustments (COLAs) and adjustable-rate mortgages (ARMs) help protect real incomes from inflation. Universal indexing, however, wouldn't eliminate inflationary redistributions of income and wealth.

- Worldwide inflation rates have diminished in recent years. Experience with inflation and changing patterns of asset ownership are creating political pressure for greater price stability.

Key Terms

inflation	Consumer Price Index	real GDP
deflation	(CPI)	price stability
relative price	inflation rate	cost-of-living adjustment
nominal income	base period	(COLA)
real income	item weight	real interest rate
money illusion	GDP deflator	adjustable-rate mortgage
hyperinflation	nominal GDP	(ARM)
bracket creep		

Questions for Discussion

1. Why would farmers rather store their output than sell it during periods of hyperinflation? How does this behavior affect prices?

2. In the German hyperinflation of the 1920s, how was production affected? (See the WORLD VIEW on page 131.)

3. Whose real wealth (see Table 7.3) declined in the 1980s? Who else might have lost real income or wealth? Who gained as a result of inflation?

4. Does an increase in the price level automatically lower society's real income? Explain.

5. Would it be advantageous to borrow money if you expected prices to rise? Would you want a fixed-rate loan or one with an adjustable interest rate?

6. Are people worse off when the price level rises as fast as their income? Why do people often feel worse off in such circumstances?

7. Who'd be harmed by a *falling* price level?

8. Could demand-pull inflation occur before an economy was producing at capacity? How?

9. Web Activity How does the inflation rate in your hometown compare with others? Compare the percentage change in the CPI for your area and two others at http://stats.bls.gov/newrelease/cpi.t103.html. How can you account for the differences?

10. Web Activity Have a job and planning to relocate? Check out the estimated cost of living in three different cities at www.homefront.com. What might explain the different costs, and how might they influence your decision to move there?

Problems for Chapter 7 appear at the back of the book.

Cyclical Instability

One of the central concerns of macro-economics is the short-run business cycle—recurrent bouts of expansion and contraction of the nation's output. These cycles affect jobs, prices, economic growth, and international trade and financial balances. Chapters 8 through 10 focus on the nature of the business cycle and the market forces that might affect it.

8

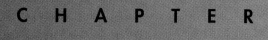

The Business Cycle

n 1929 it looked as though the sun would never set on the U.S. economy. For 8 years in a row, the U.S. economy had been expanding rapidly. During the Roaring Twenties, the typical American family drove its first car, bought its first radio, and went to the movies for the first time. With factories running at capacity, virtually anyone who wanted to work found a job readily.

All systems were "GO," and everyone was optimistic. In his Acceptance Address in November 1928, President-elect Herbert Hoover echoed this optimism by declaring: "We in America today are nearer to the final triumph over poverty than ever before in the history of any land. . . . We shall soon with the help of God be in sight of the day when poverty will be banished from this nation."

The booming stock market seemed to confirm this optimistic outlook. Between 1921 and 1927 the stock market's value more than doubled, adding billions of dollars to the wealth of U.S. households and businesses. The stock market boom accelerated in 1927, causing stock prices to double again in less than 2 years. The roaring stock market made it look easy to get rich in America.

The party ended abruptly on October 24, 1929. On what came to be known as Black Thursday, the stock market crashed. In a few short hours, the market value of U.S. corporations tumbled, in the most frenzied selloff ever seen (see NEWS). The next day President Hoover tried to assure America's stockholders that the economy was "on a sound and prosperous basis." But despite his assurances and the efforts of leading bankers to stem the decline, the stock market continued to plummet. The following Tuesday (October 29) the pace of selling quickened. By the end of the year, more than $40 billion of wealth had vanished in the Great Crash. Rich men became paupers overnight; ordinary families lost their savings, their homes, and even their lives.

The devastation was not confined to Wall Street. The financial flames engulfed the farms, the banks, and industry. Between 1930 and 1935, millions of rural families lost their farms. Automobile production fell from 4.5 million cars in 1929 to only 1.1 million in 1932. So many banks were forced to close that newly elected President Roosevelt had to declare a "bank holiday" in March 1933 to stem the outflow of cash to anxious depositors.

Throughout these years, the ranks of the unemployed continued to swell. In October 1929 only 3 percent of the workforce was unemployed. A year later the total was over 9 percent, and millions of additional workers were getting by on lower wages and shorter hours. But things got worse. By 1933 over one-fourth of the labor force was unable to find work. People slept in the streets, scavenged for food, and sold apples on Wall Street.

IN THE NEWS

Market in Panic as Stocks Are Dumped in 12,894,600 Share Day; Bankers Halt It

Effect Is Felt on the Curb and Throughout Nation—Financial District Goes Wild

The stock markets of the country tottered on the brink of panic yesterday as a prosperous people, gone suddenly hysterical with fear, attempted simultaneously to sell a record-breaking volume of securities for whatever they would bring.

The result was a financial nightmare, comparable to nothing ever before experienced in Wall Street. It rocked the fi-

nancial district to its foundations, hopelessly overwhelmed its mechanical facilities, chilled its blood with terror.

In a society built largely on confidence, with real wealth expressed more or less inaccurately by pieces of paper, the entire fabric of economic stability threatened to come toppling down.

Into the frantic hands of a thousand brokers on the floor of the New York Stock Exchange poured the selling orders of the world. It was sell, sell, sell—hour after desperate hour until 1:30 p.m.

—Laurence Stern

The World, Oct. 25, 1929.

Analysis: Stock markets are a barometer of confidence in the economy. If people have doubts about the economy, they're less willing to hold stocks. The crash of 1929 mirrored and worsened consumer confidence.

The Great Depression seemed to last forever. In 1933 President Roosevelt lamented that one-third of the nation was ill-clothed, ill-housed, and ill-fed. Thousands of unemployed workers marched to the Capitol to demand jobs and aid. In 1938, 9 years after Black Thursday, nearly 20 percent of the workforce was still idle.

The Great Depression shook not only the foundations of the world economy but also the self-confidence of the economics profession. No one had predicted the depression, and few could explain it. The ensuing search for explanations focused on three central questions:

- How stable is a market-driven economy?
- What forces cause instability?
- What, if anything, can the government do to promote steady economic growth?

The basic purpose of **macroeconomics** is to answer these questions—to *explain* how and why economies grow and what causes the recurrent ups and downs of the economy that characterize the **business cycle.** In this chapter we first look at the theoretical model economists use to describe and explain the short-run business cycle. Later, we'll examine theories of long-run growth.

Macroeconomic theories try to explain macro outcomes, but economic policy tries to *control* them. People don't want to be subjected to recurrent periods of unemployment, inflation, slow growth, or high interest rates. They want the business cycle to be eliminated, or at least tempered. And they expect their elected representatives in Washington to take the necessary action.

What can Congress and the President do? What policy tools might they use to promote growth and control the business cycle? Will those tools work? If the tools are adequate, why is the economy still subject to booms and busts?

There's an obvious link between macro theory and macro policy. If business cycles are inevitable, then no policy intervention will work. On the other hand, if macro theory can identify major causes of the business cycle, there's at least some hope of controlling it.

This chapter introduces the major policy options for controlling the short-run business cycle. There's a lot of disagreement about what policies, if any, are likely to stem the tides of the business cycle. The theories do provide some clues, however, about what might work at various times.

macroeconomics: The study of aggregate economic behavior, of the economy as a whole.

business cycle: Alternating periods of economic growth and contraction.

Classical Theory

STABLE OR UNSTABLE?

Prior to the 1930s, macro economists thought there could never be a Great Depression. The economic thinkers of the time asserted that a market-driven economy was inherently stable. There was no need for government intervention in the macro economy.

laissez faire: The doctrine of "leave it alone," of nonintervention by government in the market mechanism.

This **laissez-faire** view of macroeconomics seemed reasonable at the time. During the nineteenth century and the first 30 years of the twentieth, the U.S. economy experienced some bad years in which the nation's output declined and unemployment increased. But most of these episodes were relatively short-lived. The dominant feature of the Industrial Era was growth: an expanding economy, with more output, more jobs, and higher incomes nearly every year.

A Self-Regulating Economy. In this environment, classical economists, as they later became known, propounded an optimistic view of the macro economy. *According to the classical view, the economy "self-adjusts" to deviations from its long-term growth trend.* Producers might occasionally reduce their output and throw people out of work, but these dislocations would cause little damage. If output declined and people lost their jobs, the internal forces of the marketplace would quickly restore prosperity. Economic downturns were viewed as temporary setbacks, not permanent problems.

The cornerstones of classical optimism were flexible prices and flexible wages. If producers couldn't sell all their output at current prices, they had two choices. They could reduce the rate of output and throw some people out of work, or they could reduce the price of their output, thereby stimulating an increase in the quantity demanded. According to the **law of demand,** price reductions cause an increase in unit sales. If prices fall far enough, all the output produced can be sold. Thus flexible prices—prices that would drop when consumer demand slowed—virtually guaranteed that all output could be sold. No one would have to lose a job because of weak consumer demand.

law of demand: The quantity of a good demanded in a given time period increases as its price falls, *ceteris paribus.*

Flexible prices had their counterpart in factor markets. If some workers were temporarily out of work, they'd compete for jobs by offering their services at lower wages. As wage rates declined, producers would find it profitable to hire more workers. Ultimately, flexible wages would ensure that everyone who wanted a job would have a job.

Say's Law: Supply creates its own demand.

These optimistic views of the macro economy were summarized in Say's Law. **Say's Law**—named after the nineteenth-century economist Jean-Baptiste Say—decreed that "supply creates its own demand." Whatever was produced would be sold. All workers who sought employment would be hired. **Unsold goods and unemployed labor could emerge in this classical system, but both would disappear as soon as people had time to adjust prices and wages.** There could be no Great Depression—no protracted macro failure—in this classical view of the world.

Macro Failure. The Great Depression was a stunning blow to classical economists. At the onset of the depression, classical economists assured everyone that the setbacks in production and employment were temporary and would soon vanish. Andrew Mellon, Secretary of the U.S. Treasury, expressed this optimistic view in January 1930, just a few months after the stock market crash. Assessing the prospects for the year ahead, he said: "I see nothing . . . in the present situation that is either menacing or warrants pessimism. . . . I have every confidence that there will be a revival of activity in the spring and that during the coming year the country will make steady progress."[1] Merrill Lynch, one of the nation's largest brokerage houses, was urging that people should buy stocks. But the depression deepened. Indeed, unemployment grew and persisted *despite* falling prices and wages (see Figure 8.1). The classical self-adjustment mechanism simply didn't work.

[1]David A. Shannon, *The Great Depression* (Englewood Cliffs, NJ: Prentice Hall, 1960), p. 4.

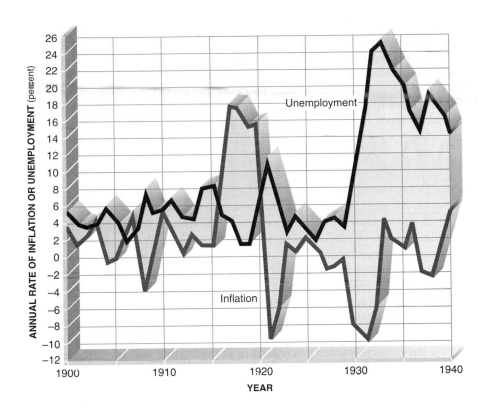

FIGURE 8.1
Inflation and Unemployment,
1900–1940

In the early 1900s, falling price levels (deflation) appeared to limit increases in unemployment. Periods of high unemployment also tended to be brief. These experiences were consistent with Say's Law.

In the 1930s, unemployment rates rose to unprecedented heights and stayed high for a decade. Falling wages and prices did not restore full employment. This macro failure prompted calls for new theories and policies to control the business cycle.

Source: U.S. Bureau of the Census, *The Statistics of the United States*, 1957.

The Keynesian Revolution

The Great Depression effectively destroyed the credibility of classical economic theory. As John Maynard Keynes pointed out in 1935, classical economists

> were apparently unmoved by the lack of correspondence between the results of their theory and the facts of observation:—a discrepancy which the ordinary man has not failed to observe. . . .
>
> The celebrated optimism of [classical] economic theory . . . is . . . to be traced, I think, to their having neglected to take account of the drag on prosperity which can be exercised by an insufficiency of effective demand. For there would obviously be a natural tendency towards the optimum employment of resources in a Society which was functioning after the manner of the classical postulates. It may well be that the classical theory represents the way in which we should like our Economy to behave. But to assume that it actually does so is to assume our difficulties away.[2]

Inherent Instability. Keynes went on to develop an alternative view of the macro economy. Whereas the classical economists viewed the economy as inherently stable, ***Keynes asserted that a market-driven economy is inherently unstable.*** Small disturbances in output, prices, or unemployment were likely to be magnified, not muted, by the invisble hand of the marketplace. The Great Depression was not a unique event, Keynes argued, but a calamity that would recur if we relied on the market mechanism to self-adjust.

Government Intervention. In Keynes' view, the inherent instability of the marketplace required government intervention. When the economy falters, we can't afford to wait for some assumed self-adjustment mechanism but must instead intervene to protect jobs and income. The government can do this by "priming the pump": buying more

[2]John Maynard Keynes, *The General Theory of Employment, Interest and Money* (London: Macmillan, 1936), pp. 33–34.

WORLD VIEW

Global Depression

The Great Depression wasn't confined to the U.S. economy. Most other countries suffered substantial losses of output and employment over a period of many years. Between 1929 and 1932, industrial production around the world fell 37 percent. The United States and Germany suffered the largest losses, while Spain and the Scandinavian countries lost only modest amounts of output.

Some countries escaped the ravages of the Great Depression altogether. The Soviet Union, largely insulated from Western economic structures, was in the midst of Stalin's forced industralization drive during the 1930s. China and Japan were also relatively isolated from world trade and finance and so suffered less damage from the depression.

Country	Decline in Industrial Output
Chile	−22%
France	−31
Germany	−47
Great Britain	−17
Japan	−2
Norway	−7
Spain	−12
United States	−46

Analysis: International trade and financial flows tie nations together. When the U.S. economy tumbled in the 1930s, other nations lost export sales. Such interactions made the Great Depression a worldwide calamity.

recession: A decline in total output (real GDP) for two or more consecutive quarters.

recession to mean a decline in real GDP that continues for at least two successive quarters. As Table 8.1 indicates, there have been 10 recessions since 1944. The most severe postwar recession occurred immediately after World War II ended. Sudden cutbacks in defense production caused GDP to decline sharply in 1945. That postwar recession was relatively brief, however. Pent-up demand for consumer goods and a surge in investment spending helped restore full employment. The Korean War (1950–1953) further increased the demand for goods, accelerating economic growth.

TABLE 8.1
Business Slumps

The U.S. economy has experienced 12 business slumps since 1929. In the post-World War II period, these downturns have been much less severe. The typical recession lasts around 10 months. When will the next recession occur, and how long will it last?

Dates	Duration (months)	Percentage Decline in Real GDP	Peak Unemployment Rate
Aug. '29–Mar. '33	43	53.4%	24.9%
May '37–June '38	13	32.4	20.0
Feb. '45–Oct. '45	8	38.3	4.3
Nov. '48–Oct. '49	11	9.9	7.9
July '53–May '54	10	10.0	6.1
Aug. '57–Apr. '58	8	14.3	7.5
Apr. '60–Feb. '61	10	7.2	7.1
Dec. '69–Nov. '70	11	8.1	6.1
Nov. '73–Mar. '75	16	14.7	9.0
Jan. '80–July '80	6	8.7	7.6
July '81–Nov. '82	16	12.3	10.8
July '90–Feb. '91	8	2.2	6.5
The next one?	?	?	?

The 1980s started with two recessions, the second lasting 16 months (July 1981–November 1982). Despite the onset of a second recession at midyear, the economy's total output actually increased in 1981. But the growth rate was so slow (1.9 percent) that few people noticed any improvement in their standard of living. Indeed, because output was growing more slowly than the labor force, the number of unemployed workers actually increased in 1981. These kinds of experiences are called **growth recessions**—the economy grows, but at a slower rate than the long-run (3 percent) average: Thus *a growth recession occurs when the economy expands too slowly. A recession occurs when real GDP actually contracts.* A depression is an extremely deep and long recession—or when you don't even get socks for Christmas (see the cartoon).

In November 1982 the U.S. economy began an economic expansion that lasted over 7 years. During that period real GDP increased by over $1 trillion, and nearly 20 million new jobs were created. It was the second-longest peacetime expansion in American history. As the expansion continued, however, the *rate* of economic growth diminished. By the end of the decade economic growth had slowed to a crawl and another growth recession occurred.

The 1990s started poorly as a result. The growth recession of 1989 became a full-blown recession in 1990. Beginning in July 1990 real GDP started declining. Although the recession officially ended 8 months later (February 1991), subsequent growth was so slow that unemployment kept increasing. By the end of 1991, the recession had destroyed 2 million jobs and reduced total output by nearly 2 percent.

In 1992, the economy started to grow a bit faster, but unemployment rates stayed high for the entire year. The increase in output was so small that unemployment kept rising to a peak of 7.7 percent in June of that year, which turned out to be the peak unemployment rate during the 1990s expansion. From 1992 through the end of 1998 total output kept increasing. Growth of GDP once again created millions of new jobs. In the summer of 1998 the national unemployment rate fell to 4.3 percent, the lowest in over two decades. By early 1999, the economic expansion had set a longevity record. As the millenium approached, however, the economy was slowing and there was fear that another recession might occur.

The 1980s

growth recession: A period during which real GDP grows, but at a rate below the long-term trend of 3 percent.

The 1990s

ROB ROGERS reprinted by permission of United Features Syndicate, Inc.

Analysis: Recessions occur when total output in the economy declines. In recessions, household income and spending fall.

A MODEL OF THE MACRO ECONOMY

The bumpy growth record of the U.S. economy lends some validity to the notion of a recurring business cycle. Every decade seems to contain at least one boom or bust cycle. But the historical record doesn't really answer our key questions. Are business cycles *inevitable?* Can we do anything to control them? ***Keynes and the classical economists weren't debating whether business cycles occur but whether they're an appropriate target for government intervention.*** That debate continues.

To determine whether and how the government should try to control the business cycle, we first need to understand its origins. What causes the economy to expand or contract? What marketplace forces dampen ("self-adjust") or magnify economic swings?

The bulk of the macro course tries to answer these questions. At this early stage, however, we can take a broad view of how the macro economy works. Figure 8.4 is such a summary view: This very basic macro model simply emphasizes that the performance of the economy depends on a finite set of determinants.

The primary measures of macroeconomic performance are arranged on the right side of Figure 8.4. These basic ***macro outcomes include***

- ***Output:*** total value of goods and services produced
- ***Jobs:*** levels of employment and unemployment
- ***Prices:*** average price of goods and services
- ***Growth:*** year-to-year expansion in production capacity
- ***International balances:*** international value of the dollar; trade and payments balances with other countries

These macro outcomes define our economic welfare; we measure our economic well-being in terms of the value of output produced, number of jobs created, price stability, and rate of economic expansion. We also seek to maintain a certain balance in our international trade and financial relations. The economy's performance is rated by the "scores" on these five macro outcomes.

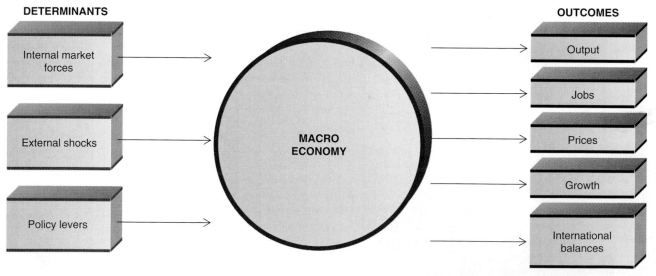

FIGURE 8.4
The Macro Economy

The primary outcomes of the macro economy are output of goods and services, jobs, prices, economic growth, and international balances (trade, currency). These outcomes result from the in-

terplay of internal market forces such as population growth, innovation, and spending patterns; external shocks such as wars, weather, and trade disruptions; and policy levers such as tax and budget decisions.

Figure 8.4 is also an overview of the separate forces that affect macro outcomes. Three very broad forces are depicted; these *determinants of macro performance are*

- *Internal market forces:* population growth, spending behavior, invention and innovation, and the like
- *External shocks:* wars, natural disasters, trade disruptions, and so on
- *Policy levers:* tax policy, government spending, changes in the availability of money, and credit regulation, for example

In the absence of external shocks or government policy, an economy would still function: It would still produce output, create jobs, develop prices, and maybe even grow. The U.S. economy operated with minimal government intervention for much of its history. Even today, many less developed countries operate in relative isolation from government or international events. In these situations, macro outcomes depend exclusively on internal market forces.

The crucial macro controversy is whether such pure, market-driven economies are inherently stable or unstable. Classical economists viewed internal market forces as self-stabilizing and saw no need for the box in Figure 8.4 labeled "Policy levers." Keynes argued that policy levers were both effective and necessary. Without such intervention, Keynes believed, the economy was doomed to bouts of repeated macro failure.

Modern economists hesitate to give policy intervention that great a role. Nearly all economists recognize that policy intervention affects macro outcomes. But there are great arguments about just how effective any policy lever is. Some economists even echo the classical notion that policy intervention may be either ineffective or, worse still, inherently destabilizing.

AGGREGATE DEMAND AND SUPPLY

To determine which views of economic performance are valid, we need to examine the inner workings of the macro economy. All Figure 8.4 tells us is that macro outcomes depend on certain identifiable forces. But the figure doesn't reveal *how* the determinants and outcomes are connected. What's in the mysterious circle labeled "Macro Economy" at the center of Figure 8.4?

When economists peer into the mechanics of the macro economy they see the forces of supply and demand at work. All the macro outcomes depicted in Figure 8.4 are the result of market transactions—an interaction between supply and demand. Hence *any influence on macro outcomes must be transmitted through supply or demand.*

By conceptualizing the inner workings of the macro economy in supply and demand terms, economists have developed a remarkably simple model of how the economy works. To operationalize that model, however, we need to know more about the macro-economic dimensions of supply and demand.

Economists use the term "aggregate demand" to refer to the collective behavior of all buyers in the marketplace. Specifically, **aggregate demand** refers to the various quantities of output that all people, taken together, are willing and able to buy at alternative price levels in a given period. Our view here encompasses the collective demand for *all* goods and services rather than the demand for any single good.

To understand the concept of aggregate demand better, imagine that everyone is paid on the same day. With their incomes in hand, people then enter the product market. The question becomes: How much output will people buy?

To answer this question, we have to know something about prices. If goods and services are cheap, people will be able to buy more with their available income. On the other hand, high prices will limit both the ability and willingness to purchase goods and services. Note that we're talking here about the *average* price level, not the price of any single good.

Aggregate Demand

aggregate demand: The total quantity of output demanded at alternative price levels in a given time period, *ceteris paribus.*

Figure 8.5 illustrates this simple relationship between average prices and real spending. The horizontal axis depicts the various quantities of (real) output that might be purchased. The vertical axis shows various price levels that might exist.

The aggregate demand curve illustrates how the real value of purchases varies with the average level of prices. The downward slope of the aggregate demand curve suggests that with a given (constant) level of income, people will buy more goods and services at lower prices. Among the several reasons why the aggregate demand curve is downward-sloping are the following three.

Real-Balances Effect. The most obvious explanation for the downward slope of the aggregate demand curve is that cheaper prices make dollars more valuable. Suppose you had $1000 in your savings account. How much output could you buy with that savings balance? That depends on the price level. At current prices, you could buy $1000 worth of output. But what if the price level rose? Then your $1000 wouldn't stretch as far. *The real value of money is measured by how many goods and services each dollar will buy.* As the *real* value of your savings declined, your ability to purchase goods and services would decline as well.

Suppose inflation pushes the price level up by 25 percent in a year. What will happen to the real value of your savings balance? At the end of the year, you'll have

$$\begin{array}{r}\text{Real value of savings}\\ \text{at year-end}\end{array} = \dfrac{\text{savings balance}}{\dfrac{\text{price level at year-end}}{\text{price level at year-start}}}$$

$$= \dfrac{\$1000}{\dfrac{125}{100}}$$

$$= \$800$$

In effect, inflation has wiped out a chunk of your purchasing power. At year's end, you can't buy as many goods and services with your savings as you could have at the beginning of the year. The quantity of output you demand will decrease. In Figure 8.5 this would be illustrated by a movement up the aggregate demand curve.

FIGURE 8.5
Aggregate Demand

Aggregate demand refers to the total output demanded at alternative price levels (*ceteris paribus*). The vertical axis here measures the average level of all prices, rather than the price of a single good. Likewise, the horizontal axis refers to the real value of all goods and services, not the quantity of only one product.

The downward slope of the aggregate demand curve is due to the real-balances, foreign-trade, and interest-rate effects.

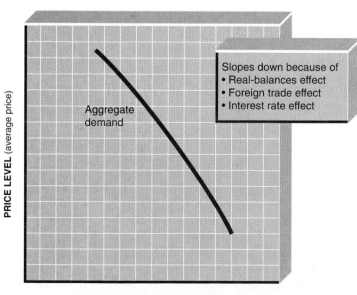

Slopes down because of
• Real-balances effect
• Foreign trade effect
• Interest rate effect

Aggregate demand

PRICE LEVEL (average price)

REAL OUTPUT (quantity per year)

A declining price level (deflation) has the opposite effect. Specifically, lower price levels make you "richer": ***The cash balances you hold in your pocket, in your bank account, or under your pillow are worth more when the price level falls.*** As a result, you can buy more goods, even though your *income* hasn't changed.

Lower price levels increase the purchasing power of other dollar-denominated assets as well. Bonds, for example, tend to rise in value when the price level falls, which increases the real value of bondholdings. This may tempt consumers to use some of their bonds to buy goods and services. With greater real wealth, consumers might also decide to save less and spend more of their current income. In either case, the quantity of goods and services demanded at any given income level will increase. These real-balances effects create an inverse relationship between the price level and the real value of output demanded—that is, a downward-sloping aggregate demand curve.

Foreign Trade Effect. The downward slope of the aggregate demand curve is reinforced by changes in imports and exports. Consumers have the option of buying either domestic or foreign goods. A decisive factor in choosing between them is their relative price. If the average price of U.S.-produced goods is rising, Americans may buy more imported goods and fewer domestically produced products. Conversely, falling price levels in the United States may convince consumers to buy more "Made in the USA" output and fewer imports.

International consumers are also swayed by relative price levels. When our price levels decline, overseas tourists flock to Disney World. Global consumers also buy more U.S. wheat, airplanes, and computers when our price levels decline. Conversely, the quantity of U.S. output demanded by international consumers declines when our price levels rise. These changes in imports and exports contribute to the downward slope of the aggregate demand curve.

Interest Rate Effect. Changes in the price level also affect the amount of money people need to borrow and so tend to affect interest rates. At lower price levels, consumer borrowing needs are smaller. As the demand for loans diminishes, interest rates tend to decline as well. This "cheaper" money stimulates more borrowing and loan-financed purchases. These interest rate effects reinforce the downward slope of the aggregate demand curve, as illustrated in Figure 8.5.

Aggregate Supply

Although lower price levels tend to increase the volume of output demanded, they have the opposite effect on the aggregate quantity supplied. As we observed, our production possibilities are defined by available resources and technology. Within those limits, however, producers must decide how much output they're *willing* to supply. Their supply decisions are influenced by changes in the price level.

Profit Effect. The primary motivation for supplying goods and services is the chance to earn a profit. Producers can earn a profit so long as the prices they receive for their output exceed the costs they pay in production. Hence ***changing price levels will affect the profitability of supplying goods.***

If the price level declines, profits tend to drop. In the short run, producers are saddled with some relatively constant costs like rent, interest payments, negotiated wages, and inputs already contracted for. If output prices fall, producers will be hard-pressed to pay these costs, much less earn a profit. Their response will be to reduce the rate of output.

Higher output prices have the opposite effect. Because many costs are relatively constant in the short run, higher prices for goods and services tend to widen profit margins. As profit margins widen, producers will want to produce and sell more goods. Thus ***we expect the rate of output to increase when the price level rises.*** This expectation is reflected in the upward slope of the aggregate supply curve in Figure 8.6. **Aggregate supply** reflects the various quantities of real output that firms are willing and able to produce at alternative price levels, in a given time period.

aggregate supply: The total quantity of output producers are willing and able to supply at alternative price levels in a given time period, *ceteris paribus.*

FIGURE 8.6
Aggregate Supply

Aggregate supply is the real value of output producers are willing and able to bring to the market at alternative price levels (*ceteris paribus*). The upward slope of the aggregate supply curve reflects both profit effects (the lure of widening profit margins) and cost effects (increasing cost pressures).

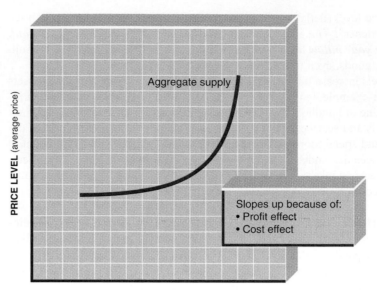

Aggregate supply

PRICE LEVEL (average price)

Slopes up because of:
• Profit effect
• Cost effect

REAL OUTPUT (quantity per year)

Macro Equilibrium

equilibrium (macro): The combination of price level and real output that is compatible with both aggregate demand and aggregate supply.

Cost Effect. The upward slope of the aggregate supply curve is also explained by rising costs. The profit effect depends on some costs remaining constant when the average price level rises. Not all costs will remain constant, however. Producers may have to pay overtime wages, for example, to increase output, even if *base* wages are constant. Tight supplies of other inputs may also unleash cost increases. Such cost pressures tend to multiply as the rate of output increases. As time passes, even costs that initially stayed constant may start creeping upward.

All these cost pressures will make producing output more expensive. Producers will be willing to supply additional output only if prices rise at least as fast as costs.

The upward slope of the aggregate supply curve in Figure 8.6 illustrates this cost effect. Notice how the aggregate supply curve is practically horizontal at low rates of aggregate output and then gets increasingly steeper. At high output levels the aggregate supply curve almost turns straight up. This changing slope reflects the fact that *cost pressures are minimal at low rates of output but intense as the economy approaches capacity.*

When all is said and done, what we end up with here is two rather conventional looking supply and demand curves. But these particular curves have special significance. Instead of describing the behavior of buyers and sellers in a single market (for example, the Clearview College typing market in Chapter 3), *aggregate supply and demand curves summarize the market activity of the whole (macro) economy.* These curves tell us what *total* amount of goods and services will be supplied or demanded at various price levels.

These graphic summaries of buyer and seller behavior provide some important clues about the economy's performance. The most important clue is point E in Figure 8.7, where the aggregate demand and supply curves intersect. This is the only point at which the behavior of buyers and sellers is compatible. We know from the aggregate demand curve that people are willing and able to buy the quantity Q_E when the price level is at P_E. From the aggregate supply curve we know that businesses are prepared to sell quantity Q_E at the price level P_E. Hence buyers and sellers are willing to trade exactly the same quantity (Q_E) at that price level. We call this situation **macro equilibrium**—the unique combination of prices and output compatible with both buyers' and sellers' intentions.

To appreciate the significance of macro equilibrium, suppose that another price or output level existed. Imagine, for example, that prices were higher, at the level P_1 in

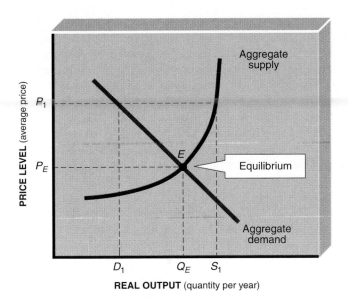

FIGURE 8.7
Macro Equilibrium

The aggregate demand and supply curves intersect at only one point (*E*). At that point, the price level (*P_E*) and output (*Q_E*) combination is compatible with both buyers' and sellers' intentions. The economy will gravitate to those equilibrium price (*P_E*) and output (*Q_E*) levels. At any other price level (e.g., *P_1*), the behavior of buyers and sellers is incompatible.

Figure 8.7. How much output would people want to buy at that price level? How much would business want to produce and sell?

The aggregate demand curve tells us that people would want to buy only the quantity D_1 at the higher price level P_1. In contrast, business firms would want to sell a larger quantity, S_1. This is a *dis*equilibrium situation in which the intentions of buyers and sellers are incompatible. The aggregate quantity supplied (S_1) exceeds the aggregate quantity demanded (D_1). Accordingly, a lot of goods will remain unsold at price level P_1.

To sell these goods, producers will have to reduce their prices. As prices drop, producers will decrease the volume of goods sent to market. At the same time, the quantities that consumers seek will increase. This adjustment process will continue until point E is reached and the quantities demanded and supplied are equal. At that point, the lower price level P_E will prevail.

The same kind of adjustment process would occur if a lower price level first existed. At lower prices, the aggregate quantity demanded would exceed the aggregate quantity supplied. The resulting shortages would permit sellers to raise their prices. As they did so, the aggregate quantity demanded would decrease, and the aggregate quantity supplied would increase. Eventually, we would return to point E, where the aggregate quantities demanded and supplied are equal.

Equilibrium is unique; it's the only price-output combination that is mutually compatible with aggregate supply and demand. In terms of graphs, it's the only place the aggregate supply and demand curves intersect. At point E there's no reason for the level of output or prices to change. The behavior of buyers and sellers is compatible. By contrast, any other level of output or prices creates a disequilibrum that requires market adjustments. All other price and output combinations, therefore, are unstable. They won't last. Eventually, the economy will return to point E.

There are two potential problems with the macro equilibrium depicted in Figure 8.7. The *two potential problems with macro equilibrium are*

Macro Failures

- *Undesirability:* The price-output relationship at equilibrium may not satisfy our macroeconomic goals.
- *Instability:* Even if the designated macro equilibrium is optimal, it may be displaced by macro disturbances.

full-employment GDP: The total market value of final goods and services that could be produced in a given time period at full employment; potential GDP.

inflation: An increase in the average level of prices of goods and services.

Undesirability. The macro equilibrium depicted in Figure 8.7 is simply the intersection of two curves. All we know for sure is that people want to buy the same quantity of output that businesses want to sell at the price level P_E. This quantity (Q_E) may be more or less than our full-employment capacity. This contingency is illustrated in Figure 8.8. The output level Q_F represents our **full-employment GDP** potential. In this case, the equilibrium rate of output (Q_E) falls far short of capacity production. We've failed to achieve our goal of full employment.

Similar problems may arise from the equilibrium price level. Suppose that P^* represents the most desired price level. In Figure 8.8 we see that the equilibrium price level P_E exceeds P^*. If market behavior determines prices, the price level will rise above the desired level. The resulting increase in the average level of prices is what we call **inflation.**

It could be argued, of course, that our apparent macro failures are simply an artifact. We could have drawn the aggregate supply and demand curves to intersect at point F in Figure 8.8. At that intersection we'd be assured of both price stability and full employment. Why didn't we draw them there, instead of intersecting at point E?

On the graph we can draw curves anywhere we want. In the real world, however, *only one set of aggregate supply and demand curves will correctly express buyers' and sellers' behavior.* We must emphasize here that these "correct" curves may *not* intersect at point F, thus denying us price stability or full employment, or both. That is the kind of economic outcome illustrated in Figure 8.8.

Instability. Figure 8.8 is only the beginning of our macro worries. Suppose, just suppose, that the aggregate supply and demand curves actually intersected in the perfect spot. That is, imagine that macro equilibrium yielded the optimal levels of both employment and prices. If this happened, could we settle back and stop fretting about the state of the economy?

Unhappily, even a "perfect" macro equilibrium doesn't ensure a happy ending. The aggregate supply and demand curves aren't permanently locked into their respective positions. They can *shift*—and they will, whenever the behavior of buyers and sellers changes.

FIGURE 8.8
An Undesired Equilibrium

Equilibrium establishes only the level of prices and output that are compatible with both buyers' and sellers' intentions. These outcomes may not satisfy our policy goals. In this case, the equilibrium price level is too high (above P^*) and the equilibrium output rate falls short of full employment (Q_F).

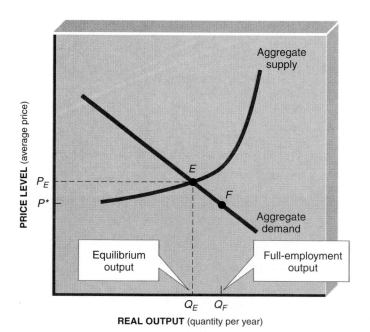

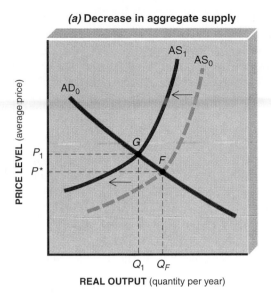

(a) Decrease in aggregate supply

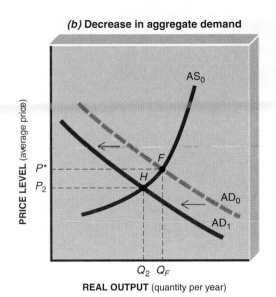

(b) Decrease in aggregate demand

FIGURE 8.9
Macro Disturbances

(a) **Aggregate supply**   A decrease (leftward shift) of the aggregate supply (AS) curve tends to reduce real GDP and raise average prices. When supply shifts from AS_0 to AS_1, the equilibrium moves from F to G. Such a supply shift may result from higher import prices, changes in tax policy, or other events.

(b) **Aggregate demand**   A decrease (leftward shift) in aggregate demand (AD) tends to reduce output and price levels. A fall in demand may be caused by decreased export demand, changes in expectations, taxes, or other events.

Suppose the Organization of Petroleum Exporting Countries (OPEC) increased the price of oil. In 1974 OPEC doubled the world price of oil and managed to raise the price further in 1979 and again in 1980. These oil price hikes directly increased the cost of production in a wide range of U.S. industries, making producers less willing and able to supply goods at prevailing prices. Thus the aggregate supply curve *shifted to the left,* as in Figure 8.9a.

The impact of a leftward supply shift on the economy is evident. Whereas macro equilibrium was originally located at the optimal point F, the new equilibrium is located at point G. At point G, less output is produced and prices are higher. Full employment and price stability have vanished before our eyes.

A shift of the aggregate demand curve could do similar damage. Between 1997 and 1998, the currencies of Thailand, Indonesia, South Korea, and Malaysia collapsed, losing anywhere from 30 to 60 percent of their dollar value. As a consequence, Asian companies and consumers couldn't afford as many goods made in the United States. The quantity of real output (U.S. exports) they demanded at the price level P^* declined, causing the aggregate demand for U.S. output to shift to the left, as illustrated in Figure 8.9b. The leftward shift forced U.S. exporters to cut back production, increasing unemployment. As the WORLD VIEW on the next page relates, the West Coast suffered the most from this external shock.

The situation gets even crazier when the aggregate supply and demand curves shift repeatedly in different directions. A leftward shift of the aggregate demand curve can cause a recession, as the rate of output falls. A later rightward shift of the aggregate demand curve can cause a recovery, with real GDP (and employment) again increasing. Shifts of the aggregate supply curve can cause similar upswings and downswings. Thus *business cycles are likely to result from recurrent shifts of the aggregate supply and demand curves.*

California Feels Asia's Pain

LOS ANGELES—The wave of Asian trade that lifted California to a $1 trillion gross state product last year—the USA's largest—is washing out again.

The ebb tide threatens to erode jobs and profits across the West Coast and casts a pall over the city that Port of Los Angeles Executive Director Larry Keller calls "the capital of the next century." Nowhere in the country is Asia's financial crisis more keenly felt.

Ships arriving from Asia fully loaded are departing 30% to 40% empty, southern California port officials say. Bluechip companies, such as Intel, Microsoft and National Semiconductor—all big exporters to Asia—report reduced foreign sales demand.

Tourism is down, as many of the 1.5 million Japanese and South Koreans who normally visit California each year stay home. And farmers from the citrus groves of Ventura County to the beef and cotton belt of the San Joaquin Valley fear the potential double whammy of lost markets abroad worth hundreds of millions of dollars and depressed prices at home.

Smith Barney economist Kathryn Chin predicts Asia's problems could clip U.S. exports by $46 billion this year, deepening the estimated trade deficit to $193 billion, a record, and trimming gross domestic product by 0.7%. In California and the West, the proportionate damage is far greater. Chin says the Asian storm could slash the Western states' net exports by $14 billion, 1.2% of the region's gross product.

The Economic Policy Institute in Washington, D.C., says lost trade could trim 1 million jobs nationwide, led by 126,681 fewer jobs in California.

—Elliot Blair Smith

USA Today, Feb. 12, 1998, p. 1B © 1998, USA Today. Reprinted with permission. www.usatoday.com

Analysis: A recession in Asia reduces the demand for U.S. exports. During 1997 and 1998, the "Asian flu" hit California particularly hard.

COMPETING THEORIES OF SHORT-RUN INSTABILITY

Figures 8.8 and 8.9 hardly inspire optimism about the macro economy. Figure 8.8 suggests that the odds of the market generating an equilibrium at full employment and price stability are about the same as finding a needle in a haystack. Figure 8.9 suggests that if we're lucky enough to find the needle, we'll probably drop it again. From this perspective, it appears that our worries about the business cycle are well founded.

The classical economists had no such worries. As we saw earlier, they believed that the economy would gravitate toward full employment. Keynes, on the other hand, worried that the macro equilibrium might start out badly and get worse in the absence of government intervention.

The AS/AD model doesn't really settle this controversy. It does, however, provide a convenient framework for comparing these and other theories about how the economy works. Essentially, ***macro controversies focus on the shape of aggregate supply and demand curves and the potential to shift them.*** With the right shape—or the correct shift—any desired equilibrium could be attained. As we'll see, there are differing views as to whether and how this happy outcome might come about. These differing views can be classified as demand-side explanations, supply-side explanations, or some combination of the two.

Demand-Side Theories

Keynesian Theory. Keynesian theory is the most prominent of the demand-side theories. Keynes argued that a deficiency of spending would tend to depress an economy. This deficiency might originate in consumer saving, inadequate business investment, or insufficient government spending. Whatever its origins, the lack of spending would leave goods unsold and production capacity unused. This contingency is illustrated by point E_1 in Figure 8.10a. Notice that the equilibrium at E_1 leaves the economy at Q_1, below its full-employment potential (Q_F). Thus, ***Keynes concluded that inadequate aggregate demand would cause persistently high unemployment.***

Keynes developed his theory during the Great Depression, when the economy seemed to be stuck at a very low level of equilibrium output, far below full-employment GDP. The only way to end the depression, he argued, was for someone to start demanding more goods. He advocated a big hike in government spending to start the economy moving toward full employment. At the time his advice was largely ignored. When the United States mobilized for World War II, however, the sudden surge in government spending shifted the aggregate demand curve sharply to the right, restoring full employment. In times of peace, Keynes also advocated changing government taxes and spending to shift the aggregate demand curve in whatever direction is desired. Chapters 9 through 11 examine the details of Keynes' theory.

Monetary Theories. Another demand-side theory emphasizes the role of money in financing aggregate demand. Money and credit affect the ability and willingness of people to buy goods and services. If credit isn't available or is too expensive, consumers won't be able to buy as many cars, homes, or other expensive products. "Tight" money might also curtail business investment. In these circumstances, aggregate demand might prove to be inadequate, as illustrated in Figure 8.10a. In this case, an increase in the money supply may be required to shift the aggregate demand curve into the desired position.

Both the Keynesian and monetarist theories also regard aggregate demand as a prime suspect for inflationary problems. In Figure 8.10b, the curve AD_2 leads to an equilibrium at E_2. At first blush, that equilibrium looks desirable, as it offers more output (Q_2) than the full-employment threshold (Q_F). Notice, however, what's happening to prices: The price level rises from P_0 to P_2. Hence, ***excessive aggregate demand may cause inflation.***

The more extreme monetary theories attribute all our macro successes and failures to management of the money supply. According to these *monetarist* theories, the economy will tend to stabilize at something like full-employment GDP. Thus only the price level will be affected by changes in the money supply and resulting shifts of aggregate demand. We'll examine the basis for this view in a moment. At this juncture we simply note that **both Keynesian and monetarist theories emphasize the potential of aggregate-demand shifts to alter some macro outcomes.**

Figure 8.11 illustrates an entirely different explanation of the business cycle. Notice that the aggregate *supply* curve is on the move in Figure 8.11. The initial equilibrium is again at point E_0. This time, however, aggregate demand remains stationary, while

Supply-Side Theories

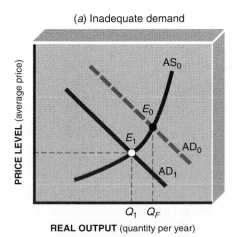

(a) Inadequate demand

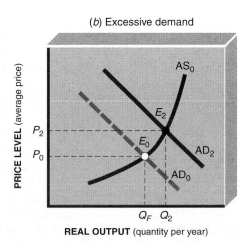

(b) Excessive demand

FIGURE 8.10
Demand-Side Theories

Inadequate demand may cause unemployment. In part (a), the demand AD_1 creates an equilibrium at E_1. The resulting output Q_1 falls short of full employment (Q_F). In part (b), excessive aggregate demand causes inflation. The price level rises from P_0 to P_2 when aggregate demand expands to AD_2. Demand-side theories emphasize how inadequate or excessive AD can cause macro failures.

FIGURE 8.11
Supply-Side Theories

Inadequate supply can keep the economy below its full-employment potential and cause prices to rise as well. AS_1 leads to output Q_3 and increases the price level from P_0 to P_3. Supply-side theories emphasize how AS shifts can worsen or improve macro outcomes.

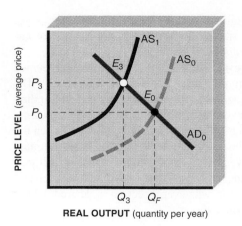

REAL OUTPUT (quantity per year)

The U.S. Bureau of Economic Analysis compiles data on gross domestic product. Using data from their Web site at www.bea.doc.gov, determine the GDP growth rate for each of the last six quarters. What supply or demand shifts might explain recent quarterly fluctuations in real GDP?

aggregate supply shifts. The resulting decline of aggregate supply causes output and employment to decline (to Q_3 from Q_F).

Figure 8.11 tells us that aggregate supply may be responsible for downturns as well. Our failure to achieve full employment may result from the unwillingness of producers to provide more goods at existing prices. That unwillingness may originate in simple greed, in rising costs, in resource shortages, or in government taxes and regulation. Inadequate investment in infrastructure (e.g., roads, sewer systems) or skill training may also limit supply potential. Whatever the cause, if the aggregate supply curve is AS_1 rather than AS_0, full employment will not be achieved with the demand AD_0.

The inadequate supply illustrated in Figure 8.11 causes not only unemployment but inflation as well. At the equilibrium E_3, the price level has risen from P_0 to P_3. Hence, a decrease in aggretate supply can cause multiple macro problems. On the other hand, an increase—a rightward shift—in aggregate supply can move us closer to both our price-stability and full-employment goals. Chapter 16 examines the many ways of inducing such a shift.

Eclectic Explanations

Not everyone blames either the demand size or the supply side exclusively. The various macro theories tell us that both supply and demand can cause us to achieve or miss our policy goals. These theories also demonstrate how various shifts of the aggregate supply and demand curves can achieve any specific output or price level. One could also shift *both* the AS and AD curves to explain unemployment, inflation, or recurring business cycles. Such eclectic explanations of macro failure draw from both sides of the market.

LONG-RUN SELF-ADJUSTMENT

Some economists argue that these various theories of short-run instability aren't only confusing but also pointless. As they see it, what really matters is the *long*-run trend of the economy, not *short*-run fluctuations around those trends. In their view, month-to-month or quarter-to-quarter fluctuations in real output or prices are just statistical "noise." The *long*-term path of output and prices is determined by more fundamental factors.

This emphasis on long-term outcomes is reminiscent of the classical theory: the view that the economy will self-adjust. A decrease in aggregate demand is only a *temporary* problem. Once producers and workers make the required price and wage adjustments, the economy will return to its long-run equilibrium growth path.

The monetarist theory we encountered a moment ago has a similar view of long-run stability. According to the monetarist theory, the supply of goods and services is determined by institutional factors such as the size of the labor force and technology.

These factors determine a "natural" rate of output that's relatively immune to short-run fluctuations in aggregate demand. If this argument is valid, the long-run aggregate supply curve is vertical, not sloped.

Figure 8.12 illustrates the classical/monetarist view of long-run stability. The vertical long-run AS curve is anchored at the "natural" rate of output Q_N. The natural rate Q_N is itself determined by demographics, technology, market structure, and the institutional infrastructure of the economy.

If the long-run AS curve is really vertical, as the classical and monetarist theories assert, some startling conclusions follow. The most startling implication is that **aggregate-demand shifts affect prices but not output in the long run.** Notice in Figure 8.12 how the shift from AD_1 to AD_2 raises the price level but leaves output anchored at Q_N.

What has happened here? Didn't we suggest earlier that an increase in aggregate demand would spur producers to increase output? And aren't rising prices an extra incentive for doing so?

Monetarists concede that *short-run* price increases tend to widen profit margins. This profit effect is an incentive to increase the rate of output. In the *long run,* however, costs are likely to catch up with rising prices. Workers will demand higher wages, landlords will increase rents, and banks will charge higher interest rates as the price level rises. Hence a rising price level has only a *temporary* profit effect on supply behavior. In the *long run,* cost effects will dominate. In the *long run,* a rising price level will be accompanied by rising costs, giving producers no special incentive to supply more output. Accordingly, output will revert to its natural rate Q_N.

Short vs. Long-Run Perspectives

All this may well be true. But as Keynes pointed out, it's also true that "in the long run we are all dead." Whatever the long run may hold, it's in the short run that we must consume, invest, and find a job. However stable and predictable the long run might be, short-run variations in macro outcomes will determine how well we fare in any year. Moreover, *the short-run aggregate supply curve is likely to be upward-sloping,* as shown in our earlier graphs. This implies that both aggregate supply and aggregate demand influence short-run macro outcomes.

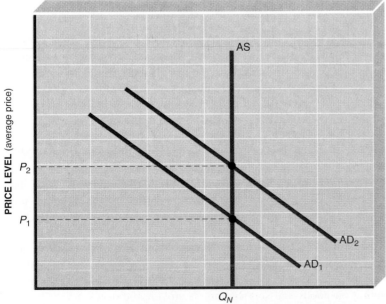

FIGURE 8.12
The "Natural" Rate of Output

Monetarists and neoclassical theorists assert that the level of output is fixed at the "natural" rate Q_N by the size of the labor force, technology, and other institutional factors. As a result, fluctuations in aggregate demand affect the price level, but not real output.

By distinguishing between short-run and long-run aggregate supply curves, competing economic theories achieve a standoff. Theories that highlight the necessity of policy intervention emphasize the importance of short-run macro outcomes. On the other hand, theories that emphasize the "natural" stability of the market point to the predictability of long-run outcomes. Even this fragile truce, however, is easily broken when the questions turn to the duration of the "short" run or the effectiveness of any particular policy option.

THE ECONOMY TOMORROW

Macro Policy Options

The aggregate supply-demand model is a convenient summary of how the macro economy works. The model raises more questions than it answers, however. We could draw the AS and AD curves—or shift them—to "create" any outcome we wanted. The real challenge for macro theory is to determine which curves (or shifts) best represent market reality. We'll spend a lot of time sifting through evidence and looking for the "correct" theory. At the outset of that quest, however, we might consider how the AS/AD model also helps define our macro policy options.

Basic Policy Strategies

The basic choice between market-driven and government-directed behavior underlies all policy options. The aggregate supply-demand (AS/AD) framework adds a new dimension to this dichotomy. We can now identify *three distinct macro policy strategies:*

- *Shift the aggregate demand curve.* Find and use policy tools that stimulate or restrain total spending.
- *Shift the aggregate supply curve.* Find and implement policy levers that reduce the cost of production or otherwise stimulate more output at every price level.
- *Laissez faire.* If we can't identify or control the determinants of aggregate supply or demand, then we shouldn't interfere with the market.

The first two policy options entail government intervention. The third option, laissez faire, relies on market forces to self-adjust.

Specific Policy Options

All these policy strategies have been tried at one time or another.

Classical Approaches. The classical approach to economic policy embraced the laissez-faire perspective. Prior to the Great Depression, most economists were convinced that the economy would self-adjust to full employment. If the initial equilibrium rate of output were too low, the resulting imbalances would alter prices and wages, inducing changes in market behavior. The aggregate supply and demand curves would "naturally" shift, until they reached the intersection where full employment (Q_F) prevails.

Recent versions of the classical theory—dubbed the "new classical economics"—stress not only the market's "natural" ability to self-adjust to *long-run* equilibrium, but also the inability of the government to improve *short-run* market outcomes. New classical economists point to the increasing ability of market participants to anticipate government policies—and to take defensive actions that thwart them.

Fiscal Policy. The Great Depression cast serious doubt on the classical self-adjustment concept. According to Keynes' view, the economy would *not* self-adjust. Rather, it might stagnate until aggregate demand was forcibly shifted. An increase in government spending on goods and services might provide the necessary shift. Or a cut in taxes might be used to stimulate greater consumer and investor spending. These budgetary tools are the hallmark of fiscal policy. Specifically, **fiscal policy** is the use of government tax and spending powers to alter economic outcomes.

Fiscal policy is an integral feature of modern economic policy. Every year the president and Congress debate the budget. They argue about whether the economy needs to be stimulated or restrained. They then argue about the level of spending or taxes required to ensure the desired outcome. This is the heart of fiscal policy.

Monetary Policy. The government budget doesn't get all the action. As suggested earlier, the amount of money in circulation may also affect macro equilibrium. If so, then the policy arsenal must include some levers to control the money supply. These are the province of monetary policy. **Monetary policy** refers to the use of money and credit controls to alter economic outcomes.

The Federal Reserve (the "Fed") has direct control over monetary policy. The Fed is an independent regulatory body, charged with maintaining an "appropriate" supply of money. In practice, the Fed increases or decreases the money supply in accordance with its views of macro equilibrium.

Supply-Side Policy. Fiscal and monetary policies focus on the demand side of the market. Both are motivated by the conviction that appropriate shifts of the aggregate demand curve can bring about desired changes in output or price levels. **Supply-side policies** offer an alternative; they seek to shift the aggregate supply curve.

There are scores of supply-side levers. The most familiar are the tax cuts implemented by the Reagan administration in 1981. These tax cuts were designed to increase *supply,* not just demand (as does traditional fiscal policy). By reducing tax rates on wages and profits, the Reagan tax cuts sought to increase the willingness to supply goods at any given price level. The promise of greater after-tax income was the key incentive for the supply shift. President Clinton also embraced tax incentives but emphasized the long-term importance of infrastructure development and worker training in shifting the aggregate supply curve.

Eclecticism. Few presidents commit themselves entirely to one macroeconomic strategy. Herbert Hoover, for example, was a fervent proponent of laissez faire. But even he was prepared to accelerate public works spending and income transfers to stop the Great Depression. Ironically, Franklin Roosevelt campaigned against these fiscal policies, arguing that such demand-side levers would unbalance the federal deficit. He later became a fervent believer in Keynesian-style fiscal policy.

Ronald Reagan was a champion of supply-side economics. But he also "primed the pump" with a huge increase in defense expenditures, a demand-side policy option. George Bush repeatedly expressed his confidence in the market's ability to self-adjust. But when the recession of 1990–1991 began to cloud his reelection prospects, President Bush pushed for supply-side tax incentives and accelerated government spending. President Clinton emphasized the need for supply-side investments in human and physical capital to promote his "New Direction." He also relied on tax hikes and spending cuts (fiscal policy), however, to achieve his macroeconomic goals.

In part, the eclectic use of policy options reflects a "do-whatever-it-takes-to-win" attitude on the part of politicians. But "politics" isn't the only explanation for the lack of clear-cut policy strategies. No economic theory has proved infallible. As we'll see, different theories provide important insights into how the economy works, but each falls short in explaining one or more of our economic problems. In these circumstances, policymakers are reluctant to put all their economic eggs in one basket. They prefer more "flexible" strategies, using an eclectic mix of classical, fiscal, monetary, and supply-side policies.

fiscal policy: The use of government taxes and spending to alter macroeconomic outcomes.

monetary policy: The use of money and credit controls to influence macroeconomic outcomes.

supply-side policy: The use of tax incentives, (de)regulation, and other mechanisms to increase the ability and willingness to produce goods and services.

SUMMARY

- The long-term growth rate of the U.S. economy is approximately 3 percent a year. But output doesn't increase 3 percent every year. In some years real GDP grows much faster than that; in other years growth is slower. Sometimes total output actually declines.

- These short-run variations in GDP growth are the focus of macroeconomics. Macro theory tries to explain the alternating periods of growth and contraction that characterize the business cycle; macro policy attempts to control the cycle.

- The primary outcomes of the macro economy are output, prices, jobs, and international balances. The outcomes result from the interplay of internal market forces, external shocks, and policy levers.

- All the influences on macro outcomes are transmitted through aggregate supply or aggregate demand. Aggregate supply and demand determine the equilibrium rate of output and prices. The economy will gravitate to that unique combination of output and price levels.

- Macro equilibrium may not be consistent with our nation's employment or price goals. Macro failure occurs when the economy's equilibrium isn't optimal.

- Macro equilibrium may be disturbed by changes in aggregate supply (AS) or aggregate demand (AD). Such changes are illustrated by shifts of the AS and AD curves, and they lead to a new equilibrium.

- Competing economic theories try to explain the shape and shifts of the aggregate supply and demand curves, thereby explaining the business cycle. Specific theories tend to emphasize demand or supply influences.

- In the long run the AS curve tends to be vertical, implying that changes in aggregate demand affect prices but not output. In the short run, however, the AS cruve is sloped, making macro outcomes sensitive to both supply and demand.

- Macro policy options range from laissez faire (the classical approach) to various strategies for shifting either the aggregate demand curve or the aggregate supply curve.

Key Terms

macroeconomics	recession	full-employment GDP
business cycle	growth recession	inflation
laissez faire	aggregate demand	fiscal policy
law of demand	aggregate supply	monetary policy
Say's Law	equilibrium (macro)	supply-side policy
real GDP		

Questions for Discussion

1. If business cycles were really inevitable, what purpose would macro policy serve?

2. What considerations might prompt consumers to demand fewer goods at current prices?

3. If equilibrium is compatible with both buyers' and sellers' intentions, how can it be undesirable?

4. The stock market crash of October 1987 greatly reduced the wealth of the average U.S. household. How might this have affected aggregate demand? Aggregate supply?

5. What exactly did Say mean when he said "supply creates its own demand"?

6. Why might rising prices stimulate short-run production but have no effect on long-run production?

7. What factors might cause consumers to spend more of their income on goods and services, thereby shifting the AD curve rightward?

8. Web Activity Draw two recent business cycles, from peak to trough, using data at www.nber.org/cycles.html. Label two peaks and troughs, and identify the number of months between them. Find the unemployment rate at each trough at www.bls.gov. Which recession was worse? Why?

9. Web Activity Using the data from the Organisation for Economic Co-operation and Development at www.oecd.org, find out which country has experienced the longest recession and which has enjoyed the greatest growth. Using your knowledge of current events, was the first country's recession caused by reductions in aggregate supply, demand, or both? Was the second country's growth caused by increases in aggregate supply, demand, or both?

Problems for Chapter 8 appear at the back of the book.

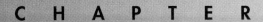

Aggregate Spending

9

Disaster struck much of the world with the Great Depression of the 1930s: In the United States alone, as many as 13 million people were out of work. They were capable people and eager to work. But no one would hire them. As sympathetic as employers might have been, they simply couldn't use any more workers. Consumers weren't buying the goods and services already being produced. Nor was anyone else: Business investment and exports were falling precipitously, and even government spending was declining. Confronted with this reality, employers kept cutting back on production and laying off workers. Not until the outbreak of World War II were enough jobs found for the "army of the unemployed," and most of these "jobs" were in the armed forces.

As noted in Chapter 8, the Great Depression was the springboard for the Keynesian approach to macro policy. John Maynard Keynes concluded that a market-driven economy could fall into a recessionary trap—and not get out. The problem, as he saw it, lay on the *demand* side of product markets. If market participants were unwilling to buy all the output produced, full employment couldn't be achieved. Waiting for some alleged "self-adjustment" was fruitless, Keynes argued. Rather than wait interminably—until, as Keynes put it, we're all "dead"—the government should intervene to boost total spending and get the economy back on track.

In this and the next two chapters we focus on the demand side of the macro economy. We start with the same questions Keynes posed:

- What are the components of aggregate demand?
- What determines the level of spending for each component?
- Will there be enough demand to maintain full employment?

MACRO EQUILIBRIUM

In Chapter 8 we got a bird's-eye view of how macro equilibrium is established. Producers have some notion of how much output they're willing and able to produce at various price levels. Likewise, consumers, businesses, governments, and the rest of the world have some notion of how much output they're willing and able to buy at different price levels. These forces of **aggregate demand** and **aggregate supply** confront each other in the marketplace. Eventually, buyers and sellers discover that only one price level and output combination is acceptable to

aggregate demand: the total quantity of output demanded at alternative price levels in a given time period, *ceteris paribus*.

The Desired Adjustment

aggregate supply: The total quantity of output producers are willing and able to supply at alternative price levels in a given time period, *ceteris paribus*.
equilibrium (macro): The combination of price level and real output that is compatible with both aggregate demand and aggregate supply.

Components of Aggregate Demand

both sides. This is the price-output combination we designate as **(macro) equilibrium.** At equilibrium, the aggregate quantity of goods demanded exactly equals the aggregate quantity supplied. In the absence of macro disturbances, the economy will gravitate toward equilibrium.

Figure 9.1 illustrates again this general view of macro equilibrium. In the figure, aggregate supply (AS) and demand (AD$_1$) establish an equilibrium at E_1. At this equilibrium, the value of real output is Q_E, significantly short of the economy's full-employment potential at Q_F. Accordingly, the economy depicted in Figure 9.1 is saddled with excessive unemployment.

All economists recognize that such a *short-run* macro failure is possible. We also realize that the unemployment problem depicted in Figure 9.1 would disappear if either the AD or AS curve shifted rightward. A central macro debate is over whether the curves *will* shift on their own (self-adjust). If not, the government might have to step in and do some heavy shifting.

The British economist John Maynard Keynes had a distinctive view of this macro failure. Keynes said deficient aggregate demand was likely to be the cause of high unemployment. Hence, the AD$_1$ curve is the culprit in Figure 9.1. Moreover, ***Keynes said a market-driven AD curve might not shift when needed.*** He feared that the AD curve could get stuck at AD$_1$, leaving the economy mired in recession. The market offered no "automatic" self-adjustment, as the classical economists had asserted. To get out of a recession, Keynes argued, the government would have to intervene and shift the AD curve rightward.

To assess the possibilities of such a macro failure, we need to examine the nature of aggregate demand more closely. Who's buying the output of the economy? What factors influence their purchase decisions?

We can best understand the nature of aggregate demand by breaking it down into its various components. ***The four components of aggregate demand are***

- *Consumption (C)*
- *Investment (I)*
- *Government spending (G)*
- *Net exports (X − IM)*

How are spending decisions made in each of these sectors? What factors might *change* the level of spending, thereby *shifting* aggregate demand?

FIGURE 9.1
Escaping a Recession

Aggregate demand (AD) might be insufficient to ensure full employment (Q_F), as illustrated by the intersection of AD$_1$ and the aggregate supply curve. The question is whether and how AD will increase—that is, *shift* rightward—say to AD$_2$. To answer these questions, the components of demand must be examined.

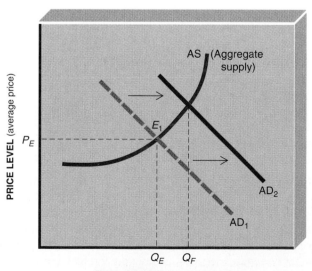

CONSUMPTION

Consider first the largest component of aggregate demand, namely, **consumption.** Consumption refers to expenditures by households (consumers) on final goods and services. As we observed in Chapter 2, *consumer expenditures account for two-thirds of total spending.* Hence, whatever factors alter consumer behavior are sure to have an impact on aggregate demand.

The aggregate demand curve asserts that the *real* value of output demanded depends on the price level. Keynes, however, argued that consumers don't really think in such terms. The typical consumer simply decides how much he or she is going to *spend*. While the price level, interest rates, wealth, and other factors might influence the level of consumer spending, the most decisive influence is available income: We spend what we have. Hence, Keynes argued that we could learn a lot about consumption simply by focusing on the relationship between income and spending.

Figure 9.2 seems to confirm Keynes' view. Year after year, consumer spending has risen in tandem with income. Accordingly, if we know how much income consumers have, we should be able to predict how much they'll spend on consumption.

Disposable income is the key concept here. As noted in Chapter 5, **disposable income** is the amount of income consumers actually take home. This is the share of total income remaining in the hands of households after all taxes have been paid, transfers (for example, Social Security benefits) have been received, and depreciation charges and retained earnings have been subtracted (see Figure 5.2). Disposable income (Y_D) represents the amount of income consumers can actually choose to spend or not spend (save) in a given time period. **By definition, all disposable income is either consumed (spent) or saved (not spent);** that is,

$$\text{Disposable income} = \text{consumption} + \text{saving}$$
$$(Y_D) \qquad\qquad (C) \qquad\qquad (S)$$

consumption: Expenditure by consumers on final goods and services.

Income and Consumption

disposable income: After-tax income of consumers; personal income less personal taxes.

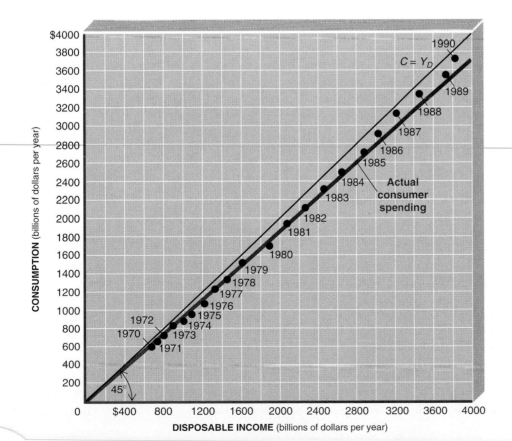

FIGURE 9.2
U.S. Consumption and Income

The points on the graph indicate the actual rates of U.S. disposable income and consumption for the years 1970–1990. By connecting these dots, we can approximate the long-term consumption function. Clearly, consumption rises with income. Indeed, consumers spend almost every extra dollar they receive.

Consumption vs. Saving

saving: That part of disposable income not spent on current consumption; disposable income less consumption.

What interested Keynes is how consumers divide up their disposable income between consumption and **saving.** Two distinct decisions are involved:

- What fraction of *total* disposable income is spent on consumption?
- What fraction of *added* disposable income is spent on consumption?

The first question reflects an interest in overall patterns of consumption; the second question is concerned with consumer responses to *changes* in income. As we'll discover, this distinction is critical.

average propensity to consume (APC): Total consumption in a given period divided by total disposable income.

The proportion of *total* disposable income spent on consumer goods and services is referred to as the **average propensity to consume (APC).** To determine the APC, we simply observe how much consumers spend in a given time period out of that period's disposable income. In 1998, for example, the disposable income of U.S. households amounted to $5865 billion. Out of this amount consumers spent $5806 billion and saved only $59 billion. Accordingly, we may calculate the *average* propensity to consume as

$$\text{APC} = \frac{\text{total consumption}}{\text{total disposable income}} = \frac{C}{Y_D}$$

For 1998 this works out to

$$\text{APC} = \frac{\$5806 \text{ billion}}{\$5865 \text{ billion}} = 0.99$$

In other words, consumers spent, on average, about $0.99 out of every $1.00 received. The remaining penny of every $1.00 was saved.

The Marginal Propensity to Consume

The fact that the average propensity to consume was 0.99 in 1998 doesn't imply that every consumer spent exactly $0.99 out of each $1.00 received. The APC is simply an *average* that summarizes the behavior of millions of consumers. With different incomes, consumers might have spent more or less out of each dollar.

It's particularly important to observe how the choice between consumption and saving is affected by *changes* in income. For this purpose, we use a second measure of consumption behavior, called the *marginal* propensity to consume. The **marginal propensity to consume (MPC)** tells us how much consumer expenditure will *change* in response to changes in disposable income. With the delta symbol, Δ, representing "change in," MPC can be written as

marginal propensity to consume (MPC): The fraction of each additional (marginal) dollar of disposable income spent on consumption; the change in consumption divided by the change in disposable income.

$$\text{MPC} = \frac{\text{change in consumption}}{\text{change in disposable income}} = \frac{\Delta C}{\Delta Y_D}$$

To calculate the marginal propensity to consume, we could ask how consumer spending in 1998 was affected by the *last* dollar of disposable income. That is, how did consumer spending change when disposable income increased from $5,864,999,999 to $5,865,000,000? If consumer spending increased by $0.80 when this last $1.00 was received, we'd calculate the *marginal* propensity to consume as

CYBER NOTE

Go to the U.S. Bureau of Economic Activity (BEA) Web site at www.bea.doc.gov, and determine the rate of disposable income and consumer spending in the most recent two quarters. What was the APC in the most recent quarter? What was the MPC between the two quarters?

$$\text{MPC} = \frac{\Delta C}{\Delta Y_D} = \frac{\$0.80}{\$1.00} = 0.8$$

Notice that the MPC in this particular case (0.8) is lower than the APC (0.99). Suppose we had incorrectly assumed that consumers would always spend $0.99 of every dollar's income. Then we'd have expected the rate of consumer spending to rise by $0.99 as the last dollar was received. In fact, however, the rate of spending increased by only $0.80. In other words, consumers responded to an *increase* in their income differently than past averages implied.

No one would be upset if our failure to distinguish the APC from the MPC led to an error of only $0.19 in forecasts of consumer spending. After all, the rate of con-

MPS = 0.20   MPS = 0.80

FIGURE 9.3
MPC and MPS

The marginal propensity to consume (MPC) tells us what portion of an extra dollar of income will be spent. The remaining portion will be saved. The MPC and MPS help us predict consumer behavior.

sumer spending in the U.S. economy exceeds $6 *trillion* per year! However, policy decisions are rarely calibrated in single dollars; typically, they involve billion-dollar changes in income. When we start playing with those sums—the actual focus of economic policymakers—the distinction between APC and MPC is significant.

Once we know how much of their income consumers will spend, we also know how much they'll save. Remember that all ***disposable income is, by definition, either consumed (spent on consumption) or saved.*** Saving is just whatever income is left over after consumption expenditures. Accordingly, if the MPC is 0.80, then $0.20 of each additional dollar is being saved and $0.80 is being spent (see Figure 9.3). The **marginal propensity to save (MPS)**—the fraction of each additional dollar saved (that is, *not* spent)—is simply

$$MPS = 1 - MPC$$

As Table 9.1 illustrates, if we know how much of their income consumers spend, we also know how much of it they save.

The Marginal Propensity to Save

marginal propensity to save (MPS): The fraction of each additional (marginal) dollar of disposable income not spent on consumption; 1 − MPC.

MPC. The marginal propensity to consume (MPC) is the *change* in consumption that accompanies a *change* in disposable income; that is,

$$MPC = \frac{\Delta C}{\Delta Y_D}$$

APC. We may also be interested in the proportion of *total* disposable income that's spent on consumption. This is referred to as the *average* propensity to consume, and is computed:

$$APC = \frac{C}{Y_D}$$

MPS. The marginal propensity to *save* (MPS) is the fraction of each additional (marginal) dollar of disposable income *not* spent—that is, saved. This is summarized as

$$MPS = \frac{\Delta S}{\Delta Y_D}$$

MPS equals 1 − MPC, since every additional dollar is either spent (consumed) or not spent (saved).

APS. The average *propensity* to save equals $\frac{S}{Y_D}$.

TABLE 9.1
Average and Marginal Propensities

THE CONSUMPTION FUNCTION

The MPC, MPS, APC, and APS are simply statistical measures of observed consumer behavior. What we really want to know is what drives these measures. If we know, then we'd be in a position to *predict* rather than just *observe* consumer behavior.

Autonomous Consumption

Keynes had several ideas about the determinants of consumption. Although he observed that consumer spending and income were highly correlated (Figure 9.2), he knew consumption wasn't *completely* determined by current income. In extreme cases, this is evident. People who have no income in a given period continue to consume goods and services. They finance their purchases by dipping into their savings accounts (past income) or using credit (future income) instead of spending current income. We also observe that people's spending sometimes *changes* even when income doesn't, suggesting that income isn't the *only* determinant of consumption. Other, *non*income determinants of consumption include

- *Expectations:* People who anticipate a pay raise often start spending more even before the extra income is received. Conversely, workers who anticipate being laid off tend to save more and spend less. Hence, *expectations* may alter consumer spending before income itself changes.
- *Wealth:* The amount of wealth an individual owns will affect that person's ability and willingness to consume. A homeowner may take out a home equity loan to buy a new car. In this case, consumer spending is being financed by wealth, not current income. *Changes* in wealth will also *change* consumer behavior. When the stock market rises, stockholders may be better able and willing to buy goods and services.
- *Credit:* The availability of credit allows people to spend more than their current income. On the other hand, the need to repay past debts may limit current consumption. Here again, *changes* in credit availability or cost (interest rates) may alter consumer behavior.
- *Taxes:* Taxes are the link between total and disposable income. If income tax rates go up, disposable income will decline. With less income to spend, consumers won't be able to buy as many goods and services.
- *Price levels:* Rising price levels reduce the real value of money balances and may cause people to curtail spending. (This is the real-balances effect, which also helps explain aggregate demand.)

Income-Dependent Consumption

In recognition of these many determinants of consumption, Keynes distinguished between two kinds of consumer spending: (1) spending *not* influenced by current income, and (2) spending that *is* determined by current income. This simple categorization is summarized as

$$\text{Total consumption} = \frac{\text{autonomous}}{\text{consumption}} + \text{income-dependent consumption}$$

where *autonomous* consumption refers to that consumption spending independent of current income. The level of autonomous spending depends instead on expectations, wealth, credit, taxes, price levels, and other nonincome influences.

These various determinants of consumption are summarized in an equation called the **consumption function,** which is written as

$$C = a + bY_D$$

where C = current consumption
a = autonomous consumption
b = marginal propensity to consume
Y_D = disposable income

consumption function: A mathematical relationship indicating the rate of desired consumer spending at various income levels.

At first blush, the consumption function is just a mathematical summary of consumer behavior. It has important *predictive* power, however: ***The consumption function provides a precise basis for predicting how changes in income (Y_D) will affect consumer spending (C).*** It also shows how changes in *non*income forces will affect consumer spending.

One Consumer's Behavior

To see how the consumption function works, consider the plight of Justin, a college freshman who has no income. How much will Justin spend? Obviously he must spend *something,* otherwise he'll starve to death. At a very low rate of income—in this case, zero—consumer spending depends less on current income than on basic survival needs, past savings, and credit. The *a* in the consumption function expresses this autonomous consumption; let's assume it's $50 per month. Thus we may say that the monthly rate of consumption expenditure in this case is

$$C = \$50 + bY_D$$

Now suppose that Justin finds a job and begins earning $100 per month. Will his spending be affected? The $50 per month he'd been spending provided very few goods and services. Now that he's earning a little income, Justin will want to improve his lifestyle. That is, ***we expect consumption to rise with income.*** The marginal propensity to consume tells us how fast spending will rise.

Suppose Justin responds to the new-found income by increasing his consumption from $50 per month to $125. The *change* in his consumption is therefore $75. Dividing this *change* in his consumption ($75) by the *change* in income ($100) reveals that his marginal propensity to consume is 0.75.

Once we know the level of autonomous consumption ($50 per month) and the marginal propensity to consume (0.75), we can predict consumer behavior with uncanny accuracy. In this case, the consumption function is

$$C = \$50 + 0.75Y_D$$

With these numerical values we can predict exactly how much Justin will spend each month at various income levels. Figure 9.4 summarizes this predictive power.

We're already noted that Justin will spend $125 per month when his income is only $100. This observation is summarized in row *B* of the table in Figure 9.4 and by point *B* on the graph. Notice that his spending exceeds his income by $25 at this point. The other $25 is still being begged, borrowed, or withdrawn from savings. Without peering further into Justin's personal finances, we may simply conclude that he's **dissaving** $25 per month. Dissaving occurs whenever current consumption exceeds current income.

If Justin's income continues to rise, he'll stop dissaving at some point. Perhaps he'll even start saving enough to pay back all the people who have sustained him through these difficult months. Figure 9.4 shows just how and when this will occur.

dissaving: Consumption expenditure in excess of disposable income; a negative saving flow.

The 45 Degree Line. The green line in Figure 9.4, with a 45 degree angle, represents all points where consumption and income are exactly equal ($C = Y_D$). Recall that Justin currently has an income of $100 per month. By moving up from the horizontal axis at $Y_D = \$100$, we see all the consumption possibilities he confronts. Were he to spend exactly $100 on consumption, he'd end up on the 45 degree line at point *G*. But we already know he doesn't stop there. Instead, he proceeds further, to point *B*. At point *B* the consumption function lies above the 45 degree line, so consumption exceeds income; dissaving is occurring.

Observe, however, what happens when his disposable income rises to $200 per month (row *C* in the table in Figure 9.4). The upward slope of the consumption function (see graph) tells us that consumption spending continues to rise with income. In fact, ***the slope of the consumption function equals the marginal propensity to consume.*** In this case, we see that when income increases from $100 to $200, consumption rises

FIGURE 9.4
An Individual's Consumption Function

The rate of consumer spending (C) depends on dispoable income (Y_D). The marginal propensity to consume indicates how much consumption will increase with each added dollar of income. In this case, when disposable income rises from $100 to $200, consumption increases by $75 (from point B to point C). The MPC = 0.75.

The consumption function can be expressed in an equation, a table, or a graph. Point B on the graph, for example, corresponds to row B in the table. Both indicate that this consumer desires to spend $125 per month when his income is $100 per month. The difference between income and consumption equals (dis)saving.

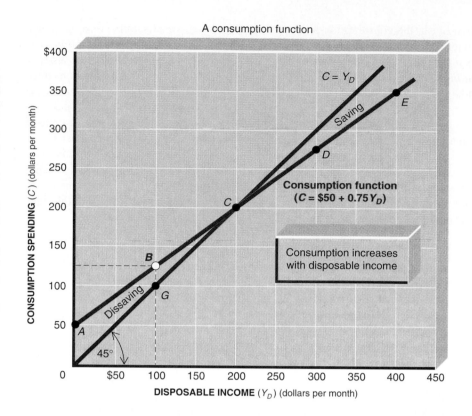

A consumption function

	Disposable Income (Y_D)	Autonomous Consumption	1	Income-Dependent Consumption	5	Total Consumption
			Consumption (C 5 $50 1 0.75$Y_D$)			
A	$ 0	$50		$ 0		$ 50
B	100	50		75		125
C	200	50		150		200
D	300	50		225		275
E	400	50		300		350
F	500	50		375		425

from $125 (point B) to $200 (point C). Thus the *change* in consumption ($75) equals three-fourths of the *change* in income. The MPC is still 0.75.

Point C has further significance. At an income of $200 per month Justin is no longer dissaving but is now breaking even—that is, disposable income equals consumption, so saving equals zero. Notice that point C lies on the 45 degree line, where current consumption equals current income.

What would happen to spending if income increased still further? According to Figure 9.3, Justin will start *saving* once income exceeds $200 per month. To the right of point C, the consumption function always lies below the 45 degree line.

The Aggregate Consumption Function

Repeated studies of consumers suggest that there's nothing remarkable about Justin. The consumption function we've constructed for him can be used to depict all consumers simply by changing the numbers involved. Instead of dealing in hundreds of dollars per month, we now play with trillions of dollars per year. But the basic relationship is the same. That is, we still assume that the rate of consumption spending depends on disposable income. This aggregate relationship was already confirmed in

Figure 9.2., which shows that Americans have a marginal propensity to consume of approximately 0.9: We spend almost every extra dime we get. Also observe in Figure 9.2 how all the data points fall very close to a straight line, indicating that the marginal propensity to consume has been fairly constant for a long time.

Finally, notice in both Figures 9.2 and 9.4 how the 45 degree line is used again. *At all points on the 45 degree line, consumption and disposable income are equal.* Actual consumer spending lies below the 45 degree line, indicating that U.S. families, on average, save at least something.

Although the consumption function is a handy device for predicting consumer behavior, its dimensions may change. Specifically, in the function $C = a + bY_D$, either the value of a or the value of b may change. If either does, the entire consumption function *shifts* to a new position.

Consider first the value for a. We noted earlier that autonomous consumption depends on nonincome determinants like wealth, credit, expectations, taxes, and price levels. If any of these nonincome determinants changes, the value of the a in the consumption function will change as well.

Suppose consumers became more optimistic about the future, for whatever reason, such as a newly elected president, a definitive Middle East peace accord, or another New York Yankee's World Series win. Would their greater optimism prompt more spending? Probably so! Notice what happens to the consumption function when this happens. In Figure 9.5 the consumption function is initially at $C = a_1 + bY_D$. When consumer confidence increases, autonomous consumption rises to a_2. The new consumption function is therefore $C = a_2 + bY_D$. The consumption function has *shifted* upward; more consumption occurs at every rate of income.

Were consumers to become more pessimistic, the consumption function would shift downward rather than upward. In the recession of 1990–1991, for example, consumption spending took a double whammy. The lower incomes that accompanied the recession induced a *leftward movement* along the consumption function, to a lower level of spending and income. Because consumer confidence also fell, consumers were less willing to buy goods and services at any given level of income. Hence *autonomous* consumption declined, and the entire consumption function *shifted* downward. These two distinct effects are illustrated in Figure 9.6 (next page). A similar drop in consumer confidence in 1998 (see NEWS) prompted economists to predict an economic slowdown for 1999–2000.

Shifts of the Consumption Function

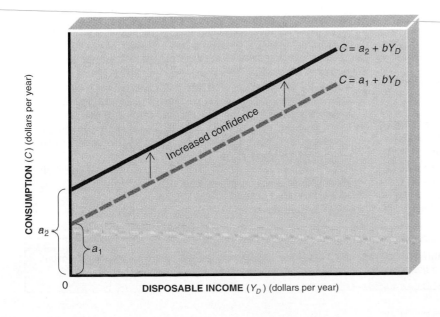

FIGURE 9.5
Shifts in the Consumption Function

Consumers' willingness to spend current income is affected by their confidence in the future. If consumers become more optimistic, autonomous consumption may increase from a_1 to a_2. This change will shift the entire consumption function upward.

FIGURE 9.6
Shifts vs. Movements: The 1990–1991 Recession

Incomes declined and consumer confidence fell during the 1990–1991 recession. The income decline prompted a movement along the initial consumption function from point *f* to point *g*. The fall in confidence shifted the entire consumption function downward (point *g* to point *h*).

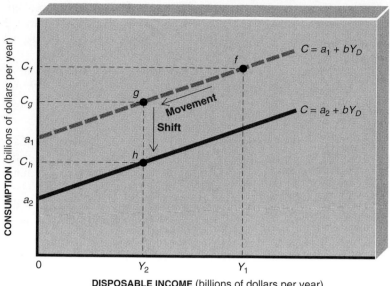

Shifts of Aggregate Demand. Shifts of the consumption function are reflected in shifts of the aggregate demand curve. Consider again an upward shift of the consumption function. An increase in consumer spending at any given income level implies an increase in aggregate demand as well. Recall that the aggregate demand curve depicts how much real output will be demanded at various price levels, *with income held constant.* When the consumption function shifts upward, households spend more of their income. Hence,

- *An* **upward** *shift of the consumption function implies a* **rightward** *shift of the aggregate demand curve.*

U.S. Consumer Confidence Drops Again

Unsettling Events in U.S., Abroad Raise Concerns About Income and Jobs

U.S. consumers are starting to worry that global economic turmoil and President Clinton's impeachment battle will begin to affect their own fortunes.

For the third straight month, the Conference Board's measure of consumer confidence dropped in September, tumbling seven points to a reading of 126.0. It was the biggest decline since January. The index is down 12.2 points from its 29-year high in June.

"Tumultuous financial markets here and abroad and unsettling political developments in the U.S. have been major fac-

tors in curbing consumer confidence," said Lynn Franco of the Conference Board, a private research group in New York.

While other sectors of the U.S. economy have taken a hit from recent world-wide events—for example, the manufacturing sector is battling a decline in demand from troubled Asia countries—consumers have largely remained unscathed. Consumer spending, which accounts for two-thirds of total U.S. economic growth, remains solid. So analysis are closely watching confidence measures for a sign that spending could suddenly take a nosedive.

—Christina Duff

Analysis: Expectations of *future* income affect consumer spending. When consumer confidence in the future declines, autonomous spending drops and the consumption function shifts downward.

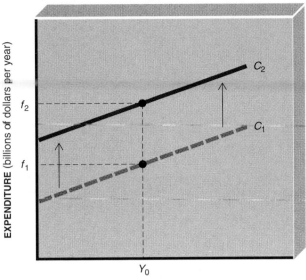

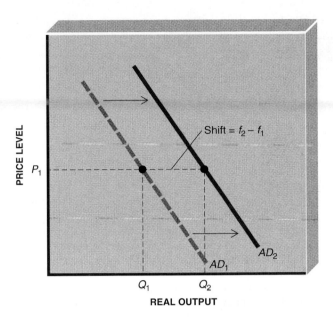

FIGURE 9.7
AD Effects of Consumption Shifts

An upward shift of the consumption function implies that households want to spend more of their income. Here consumption at the income level Y_0 increases from f_1 to f_2. This increased expenditure is reflected in a rightward shift of the aggregate demand curve. At the initial price level P_1 consumers demanded Q_1 output. At that same price level, consumers now demand additional output equal to $f_2 - f_1$. (*Note:* Both income and the price level are being held constant here.)

- *A **downward** shift of the consumption function implies a reduction (a **leftward** shift) in aggregate demand.*

These relationships are illustrated in Figure 9.7.

A change in consumer confidence is only one factor that might shift the consumption function. Anything that changes the value of autonomous consumption will shift the consumption function. *Shift factors include a*

Shift Factors

- *Change in consumer confidence (expectations)*
- *Change in wealth*
- *Change in credit conditions*
- *Change in tax policy*

Wealth Effect. The stock market boom of 1996–1999 greatly increased the value of household wealth. As their wealth increased, consumers felt they could spend more of their current income. According to the 1999 estimates of the Council of Economic Advisers, this "wealth effect" added 1 percentage point to the average propensity to consume in 1997 and 1998. This behavioral change was reflected in an upward shift of the consumption function.

Notice the emphasis on *change* in each shift factor. A large amount of accumulated wealth will influence autonomous consumption. But autonomous consumption won't *change* unless the value of wealth does. When the stock market gains of 1997–1998 increased the value of household wealth, the savings rate *fell* into *negative* territory (see NEWS); households were *dis*saving. How come? Because households decided their greater wealth enabled them to spend more and save less from each dollar of income. This "wealth effect" *shifted* the consumption function upward.

The same emphasis on *change* applies to other shift factors. A *change* in tax rates or interest rates is what *shifts* the consumption function up or down. These same changes therefore shift the aggregate demand curve left or right (Figure 9.7).

Savings Rate Hits Negative Territory

Spending Tops Income for 1st Time Since `59

Americans spent more money buying goods and services than they received in after-tax income in September, resulting in a negative national personal savings rate for the first time since 1959, when the monthly figures were first published.

The savings rate, which measures the share of disposable personal income left after people make their purchases, fell into negative territory as such spending increased a robust 0.5 percent and personal income rose by a much weaker 0.2 percent in September, the Commerce Department reported yesterday. . . .

The savings rate has been falling for years as households increased their spending faster than their disposable incomes were rising. Many analysts say consumers have been encouraged to spend so much by the soaring value of U.S. stocks—the so-called wealth effect—which has provided many individuals with capital gains, which are not counted by the Commerce Department as part of current disposable income.

Many stockholders may not have actually cashed in their gains, but as the value of their stock portfolios has increased rapidly they have become comfortable spending more and saving less from their paychecks and other income, the analysts say.

—John M. Berry

The Washington Post, Nov. 3, 1998, p. E1. © 1998, The Washington Post. Reprinted with permission. www.washingtonpost.com

Analysis: When household wealth increases, people save less and consume more out of current income. This "wealth effect" shifts up the consumption function. In 1998 the shift was so strong that households were *dis*saving.

LEAKAGES AND INJECTIONS

The potential for shifts of the consumption function heightens concern for the stability of the macro economy. Keynes used the consumption function to illustrate why it might be difficult to achieve or sustain full employment.

Consumer Saving

full-employment GDP: The total market value of final goods and services that could be produced in a given time period at full employment; potential GDP.

Suppose for the moment that we were fortunate enough to be producing at the rate of **full-employment GDP**—that is, the value of all final goods and services produced at full employment. For convenience, we'll assume that full-employment GDP adds up to $3 trillion per year. At this rate of output, we'd be generating an equivalent amount of income, as every dollar spent on production ends up in someone's pocket (see Chapter 5). In Figure 9.8 we designate this level of annual income Y_F (income at full employment). For simplicity, let's assume for the moment that there's no government—and thus no taxes—and that *all* income is received by consumers. Under these assumptions, disposable income (Y_D) and GDP are identical. Thus we can relate the rate of consumer spending directly to *total* output.

Some inkling of potential problems in maintaining full employment should already be evident. We've observed that consumers typically don't spend all their income; instead, they save some fraction of it. If all income isn't spent, the movement of income around the circular flow (Figure 5.2) isn't continuous; on the contrary, **the circular flow leaks.** Saving is a primary cause of such **leakage**—part of the income flow that doesn't return directly to product markets as spending on final goods and services.

leakage: Income not spent directly on domestic output but instead diverted from the circular flow, for example, saving, imports, taxes.

Total Output at Full Employment. If we're receiving $3 trillion worth of income at full employment (Y_F), then $3 trillion worth of output is being produced. Thus the horizontal axis of Figure 9.8 tells us not only how much income will be available for spending but also the value of goods and services that will be for sale in product markets.

As before, *we use the 45 degree line to illustrate all points where spending equals income.* All points on this line are equidistant from the vertical and horizontal axes. Point Z_F on that line reminds us how much output is being supplied to the market at

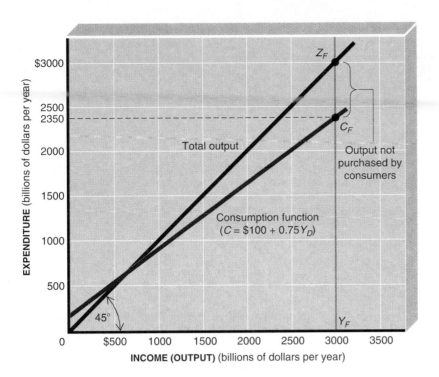

full employment; it has the same dollar value as Y_F. Were consumers to spend that
much income, all output would be sold.

Consumer Spending at Full Employment. To find out how much output will actually be demanded at Y_F, we need to look at spending behavior. The consumption function tells us how much consumers will wish to spend at different income levels, including full-employment GDP.

Suppose the aggregate consumption function is $100 billion per year $+ 0.75Y_D$, as
illustrated in Figure 9.8. Using this function, we can determine desired consumption
when total income equals Y_F. When we substitute $3000 billion for Y_D, we observe
what the annual rate of consumer spending at full employment (C_F) is:

$$C_F = \$100 \text{ billion} + 0.75 \ (\$3000 \text{ billion})$$
$$= \$2350 \text{ billion}$$

We find the same value in Figure 9.8 by moving up from point Y_F on the horizontal
(income) axis to the consumption function and noting the value of consumer spending
($2350 billion) at that juncture.

The message relayed by this consumption function is straightforward. If business
firms produce goods and services at the rate of $3 trillion per year (and that much in-
come), consumers will demand only $2350 billion per year. In short, the rate of pro-
duction at Y_F ($3000 billion per year) will exceed the rate of consumer expenditure
($2350 billion).

Why aren't consumers buying all the goods and services produced? Because they
choose to *save* some of their income. Saving isn't necessarily bad, but it does present
a potential problem. Some of the output produced isn't being purchased by consumers.
Unless other market participants, such as business, government, and foreigners, buy
this unsold output, goods will pile up on producer shelves. As undesired inventory accumulates, producers will reduce the rate of output and unemployment will rise. This
is the problem Japan confronted in 1995 (see WORLD VIEW on the next page). Because neither business firms nor the government stepped in to close the consumer-
spending gap, Japan's economy fell into a recession that lasted 4 years.

Prices in Japan Are Dropping but Consumers Aren't Buying

TOKYO—In Akihabara, a bustling hive of stores and sidewalk stalls that offer every consumer electronic product imaginable, wide-screen TV sets are selling for $1,200 these days, about $200 less than a year ago. Stereo prices have dropped by 22 percent and VCRs by 12 percent.

In Tokyo department stores, something similar is going on. Lipstick, for example, is down from $50 to $35 a tube. And at the upscale Sports Connection fitness club, the required $4,000 security deposit has been cut by half. . . .

Prices are falling all over Japan and people have a term for it—*kakaku hakai* or "price destruction." It's a situation Americans haven't known on an extended basis since the Great Depression—Tokyo's consumer price index declined 0.5 percent in August alone.

In a land of $30 pizzas, $60 melons, and $100 jeans, one would expect a national shopping spree to begin.

But it hasn't happened. Many Japanese fear for their jobs and are saving as much as they can. Those who do have money and confidence in their jobs worry they will be cheating themselves if they buy now, because they expect prices to go down further.

Indeed, many Japanese, ordinary ones and economists alike, see the declining prices and consumers' refusal to buy as threatening efforts to end their country's four-year recession.

—Sandra Sugawara

The Washington Post, Sept. 30, 1995, p. H1. © 1995, The Washington Post. Reprinted with permission. www.washingtonpost.com

Analysis: Consumer spending is affected by income and expectations. If expectations worsen, spending may fall, even if prices are declining.

Imports and Taxes

Saving isn't the only source of leakage. ***Imports also represent leakage from the circular flow.*** When consumers buy imported goods, their spending leaves (that is, leaks out of) the domestic circular flow and goes to foreign producers.

In the real world, ***taxes are a form of leakage as well.*** A lot of revenue generated in market sales gets diverted into federal, state, and local government coffers. Sales taxes are taken out of the circular flow in product markets. Then payroll taxes and income taxes are taken out of wages. Households never get the chance to spend any of that income.

Business Saving

The business sector also keeps part of the income generated in product markets. Some revenue is set aside to cover the costs of maintaining, repairing, and replacing plant and equipment. The revenue held aside for these purposes is called a depreciation allowance. In addition, businesses tend to keep some part of total profit (retained earnings) for other business uses rather than turn all profits over to the business owners, for example, dividends to stockholders. The total value of depreciation allowances and retained earnings is called **gross business saving.** Whatever businesses "save" in these forms represents further leakage from the circular flow—income that doesn't automatically flow directly back into product markets.

gross business saving: Depreciation allowances and retained earnings.

Disposable vs. Total Income

Taxes and business saving reduce the value of the income stream before it reaches households in the form of *disposable* income. As a result, households start out with less income (Y_D) than the value of total output (Y). This is illustrated by the leakages in Figure 9.9. As a result of those leaks, consumers don't have enough disposable income to buy all the output produced, even if they wanted to. In 1998, for example, disposable income was only $5.8 trillion out of $8.5 trillion of total income. This implies that consumers alone weren't able to demand enough output to maintain full employment at current price levels. When consumers in turn increase the leakage with saving and imports, the circular flow is still further reduced.

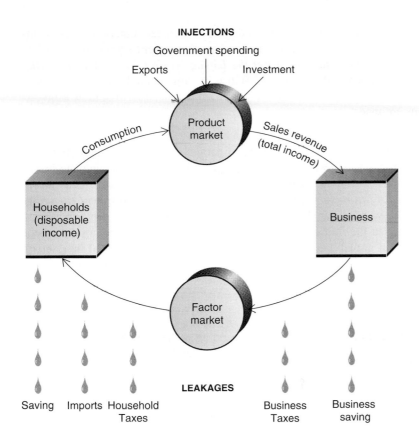

INJECTIONS

Government spending

Exports   Investment

FIGURE 9.9
Leakages and Injections

The income generated in production doesn't return completely to product markets in the form of consumer spending. Consumer saving, imports, taxes, and business saving all leak from the circular flow. If this leakage isn't offset, some of the output produced will remain unsold.

Business investment, government purchases of goods and services, and exports inject spending into the circular flow. The focus of macro concern is whether desired injections will offset desired leakage at full employment.

Although leakage from the circular flow is a potential source of unemployment problems, we shouldn't conclude that the economy will sink as soon as consumers start saving some of their income, but a few imports, or pay their taxes. Consumers aren't the only ones who buy goods and services in product markets; business firms and government agencies also contribute to total spending. So do international consumers who buy our exports. So before we run out into the streets screaming "The circular flow is leaking!", we need to look at what other market participants are doing.

The top half of Figure 9.9 completes the picture of the circular flow by depicting **injections** of new spending. When businesses buy plant and equipment, they add to the dollar value of product market sales. Government purchases and exports also inject spending into the product market. These ***injections of investment, government, and export spending help offset leakage from saving, imports, and taxes.*** As a result, there may be enough aggregate demand to maintain full employment even if consumers aren't spending every dollar of income. Before we conclude that leakage will leave some goods unsold, we need to determine how much spending will be injected into the circular flow from nonconsumer spending.

INVESTMENT

Investment spending is a major injection into the income stream. Business firms purchase new plant and equipment to expand or upgrade their output capabilities; such purchases are called *fixed investment*. Firms also acquire inventories of goods that can be used to satisfy consumer demands; such expenditures are called *inventory investment*. Residential construction is also counted in investment statistics because houses and apartment buildings continue to "produce" housing services for decades. All these forms of **investment** represent a demand for output.

Injections into the Circular Flow

injection: An addition of spending to the circular flow of income.

investment: Expenditures on (production of) new plant, equipment, and structures (capital) in a given time period, plus changes in business inventories.

Because investment spending represents a demand for current output, it might compensate for the leakage created by consumer saving. *Investment represents an injection into the circular flow that may offset the leakage caused by consumer saving.* But how much investment will take place? Will it be large enough to offset the leakage due to consumer saving? To answer this question, we need to look at how investment decisions are made.

Expectations

Expectations play a critical role in investment decisions. No firm wants to purchase new plant and equipment unless it is convinced people will later buy the output produced by that plant and that equipment. Nor do producers want to accumulate inventories of goods unless they expected consumers to eventually buy them. Thus *favorable expectations of future sales are a necessary condition for investment spending.*

No one is entirely sure what shapes investors' expectations. Essentially, it's a question of confidence in the future course of economic events. Whatever raises investor hopes for economic growth and increased sales will stimulate additional investment. Favorable tax or budget policy, new inventions, or unanticipated sales increases can all raise investor expectations. On the other hand, an unwelcome event—a rail strike or an oil shortage, for example—may shake investors' faith in the course of economic events.

Interest Rates

A second determinant of desired investment spending is the rate of interest. Business firms often borrow money in order to purchase plant and equipment. The higher the rate of interest, the costlier it is to invest. Accordingly, we anticipate a lower rate of investment spending when interest rates are high, more investment at lower rates (*ceteris paribus*).

Figure 9.10 summarizes the influence of expectations and interest rates on investment demand. The curve I_1 tells us how much investment spending business firms will want to undertake at various interest rates, given some set of expectations about future sales and profits. Within this context, we see that lower rates of interest lead to higher rates of investment (compare points *A* and *B*).

Curves I_2 and I_3 illustrate the impact on investment demand of a *change* in expectations. If investors suddenly foresee improved prospects for sales and profits, they'll be more eager to invest. They'll borrow *more* money at any given interest rate and use it to buy plant and equipment. This increased willingness to borrow is illustrated by a

FIGURE 9.10
Investment Demand

The rate of desired investment depends on expectations, the rate of interest, and innovation. A *change* in expectations will *shift* the investment-demand curve. With given expectations, a change in the rate of interest will lead to *movements* along the existing investment-demand curve. In this case, an increase in investment beyond $150 billion per year (point *A*) may be caused by lower interest rates (point *B*) or improved expectations (point *C*). Keynes emphasized the role of investor expectations in maintaining full-employment spending.

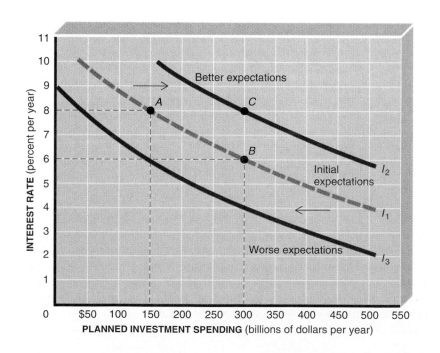

rightward *shift* of the investment curve to I_2 (that is, greater investment at any given interest rate). Conversely, should investors' faith in the future be shaken, expectations will worsen and the investment curve will shift to the left (I_3). This appeared to be the case at the end of 1998 (see NEWS).

A third determinant of investment is changes in technology and innovation. When scientists learned how to miniaturize electronic circuitry, an entire new industry of electronic calculators, watches, and other goods sprang to life. In this case, the demand for investment goods shifted to the right as a result of improved miniaturized circuits and imaginative innovation (the use of the new technology in pocket calculators). More recently, technological advances and cost reductions have stimulated an investment spree in laptop computers, cellular phones, video conferencing, fiber-optic networks, and anything associated with the Internet.

Technology and Innovation

Because the demand for investment goods is so heavily influenced by expectations, interest rates, technology, and innovation, Keynes concluded that it *isn't* very sensitive to current levels of income. This explains why businesses often continue to purchase new plant and equipment even in economic downturns. To the extent that investment isn't affected by short-run changes in national income, we may regard investment spending as *autonomous*—that is, *not* dependent on current income. This is in marked contrast to the demand for consumer goods, much of which Keynes asserted was directly determined by the level of current income.

Autonomous Investment

As long as investment spending *isn't* sensitive to the rate of current income, the investment function may be drawn as a horizontal line in Figure 9.11, which has current income on the horizontal axis. Notice that the assumed rate of investment spending is $150 billion per year, regardless of the level of total income. Remember our assumption that **the rate of desired investment spending depends on expectations, the rate of interest, and technology, but not on the current level of income.**

IN THE NEWS

Pessimism Tends to Hit Capital Spending

WASHINGTON—The evidence accumulates, day by day, that business optimism in America is fading. The executive sound bites are sounding dreary. So are the poll results of top managers; one from the Conference Board last week said business sentiment has sunk to a seven-year low.

What really matters, though, isn't psychology but economics. This is budget season in companies across the land. As sentiment turns negative, cutbacks proliferate.

Next on the chopping block is likely to be capital spending, one of the driving engines of economic growth through the 1990s expansion, by some measures accounting for as much as 25% of the growth of gross domestic product.

More than just investment in bricks and mortar, U.S. corporations have spent hugely on business equipment, labor-saving machinery and new generations of computer systems, which have triggered a huge boom in technology companies and consulting firms.

Chances are, the next few months will bring delays, cancellations and scaled-back versions of many such corporate expansion plans.

Overcapacity, world-wide product gluts and falling prices will account for some of these cancellations. Global gluts were already a problem in small autos, steel, semiconductors, commodity chemicals and other industries 18 months ago. But the downturn in Asian demand has made overcapacity a dire and obvious problem for companies around the world.

Looking ahead, world economic growth is hardly cause for expecting a rebound in capital spending next year. The International Monetary Fund recently reduced its projection for world economic growth in 1999 to 2.5% from 3.7%. Some academic economists believe that is still a generous forecast, pegging next year's growth at just 1%. And while only a fraction of economists predict a U.S. recession in 1999, most expect slow growth.

—Bernard Wysocki Jr.

The Wall Street Journal, Oct. 26, 1998, p. 1. Reprinted by permission of *The Wall Street Journal*, © 1998 Dow Jones & Company, Inc. All Rights Reserved Worldwide. www.wsj.com

Analysis: Business investment is based more on expected future sales than on current sales and income. When expectations for future growth diminish, investment spending drops.

FIGURE 9.11
Aggregate Expenditure

The aggregate expenditure curve shows how much market participants want to spend at different income levels. Three sources of spending—investment, government, and net exports—aren't dependent on current income. They're illustrated by horizontal lines. Consumption spending is, however, dependent on current income, as reflected in the marginal propensity to consume. Hence aggregate expenditure—$C + I + G + (X - IM)$—rises with income.

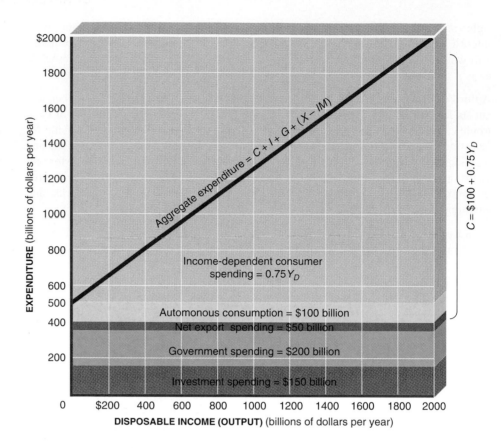

To determine the desired rate of investment at full employment (or any other rate of output), we must refer back to Figure 9.10, check the current rate of interest, and see how much investment businesses desire to undertake. For the moment we'll assume that the rate of interest is 8 percent and thus that the desired rate of investment spending is $150 billion per year (point *A* in Figure 9.10). Hence the investment function in Figure 9.10 begins at $150 billion on the vertical axis and has a zero slope as it extends to the right.

GOVERNMENT AND EXPORT SPENDING

We now know how much consumers and investors will spend at various income levels. That gives us a lot of predictive power. But what about the other two components of aggregate expenditure? How much will the government spend? How much output will global participants buy?

Government Spending

At present, the government sector (federal, state, and local) spends more than $1.5 trillion a year on goods and services. How much it spends, however, isn't directly related to income. True, the government gets most of its revenue from the taxes it extracts out of the circular flow. But tax revenues aren't income. Furthermore, government spending decisions aren't limited by available tax receipts, particularly federal spending, which is often financed in part by budget deficits (borrowed funds). It often applies to state and local government spending as well, especially when these governments can borrow money in financial markets.

At this point we aren't examining *how* government spending decisions are made; all we want to determine here is whether they're dependent on current income. If they're not, government spending is *autonomous* and may be illustrated with a horizontal line in Figure 9.11. This representation simply affirms that ***government spending decisions*** *are made independently of current income.* In Figure 9.11 it's assumed that the government has decided to spend $200 billion a year. We add this amount on top of investment spending. Hence combined investment (I) and government spending (G) totals $350 billion a year in Figure 9.11. Notice again that the level of $I + G$ does not vary with income.

Figure 9.11 also recognizes that a country's net export sales are part of aggregate spending. How much will foreigners spend? That depends largely on how much income they receive *in their own countries.* The level of export sales isn't very sensitive to changes in domestic (U.S.) incomes. Hence net export sales too are largely autonomous and can be represented by a horizontal line. In Figure 9.11 it's assumed that net exports add another $50 billion to total spending. Thus we have an autonomous spending base of $400 billion, built of investment ($150 billion), government ($200 billion), and net export ($50 billion) expenditures.

Net Exports

AGGREGATE EXPENDITURE

We've already seen (Figure 9.8) that consumption is sensitive to changes in current income; the consumption function slopes upward. Now we place the consumption function on top of the $I + G + (E - IM)$ spending base. The consumption function in Figure 9.11 is the same one we assumed earlier; that is,

$$C = \$100 + 0.75Y$$

This consumption function lies $100 billion above the $I + G + (E - IM)$ base. It now intercepts the vertical axis at $500 billion. From that point on, aggregate expenditure and consumption rise at the same place. This means that *the aggregate expenditure curve and the consumption function have the same slope.* In Figure 9.12 (next page) *disposable* income is on the horizontal axis. Hence the slope of both the aggregate expenditure curve and the consumption function is equal to the marginal propensity to consume (0.75 in this case).

Once we have all the components of spending on a single graph, we can predict the total spending behavior of market participants. *The aggregate expenditure curve tells us how much market participants desire to spend at different income levels.*

The critical message of the aggregate expenditure curve is that the rate of desired spending varies with the economy's level of output and income. How then can we be certain that the level of expenditure will be compatible with our full-employment and price-stability goals? Keynes used the aggregate expenditure curve to demonstrate that the economy might not perform as hoped.

Consider the expenditure behavior illustrated in Figure 9.12. In this figure output is again represented by Y_F, at $3 trillion. This is the rate of output that ensures full employment. Thus our goal is to keep the economy at Y_F. Will this happen? In trying to answer that question we simplify the analysis a bit by ignoring the distinction between *total* income and *disposable* income, making consumer spending directly dependent on *total* income (Y).[1]

aggregate expenditure: The rate of total expenditure desired at alternative levels of income, *ceteris paribus.*

Expenditure Equilibrium

---

[1]In principle, we first have to determine how much *disposable* income is generated by any given level of *total* income, then use the consumption function to determine how much consumption occurs. If Y_D is a constant percentage of Y, this two-step computation boils down to

$$Y_D = dY$$

where d = the share of total income received as disposable income, and

$$C = a + b(dY)$$
$$= a + (b \times d)Y$$

The term ($b \times d$) is the marginal propensity to consume out of *total* income.

FIGURE 9.12
Expenditure Equilibrium

There's only one rate of output at which desired expenditure equals the value of output. This expenditure equilibrium occurs at point E, where the aggregate expenditure and 45 degree lines intersect. At this equilibrium, $2000 billion of output is produced and willingly purchased.

At full-employment output ($Y_F =$ $3000), aggregate expenditure is only $2750 billion. This spending shortfall leaves $250 billion of output unsold. The difference between full-employment output (point g) and desired spending at full employment (point f) is called the recessionary gap.

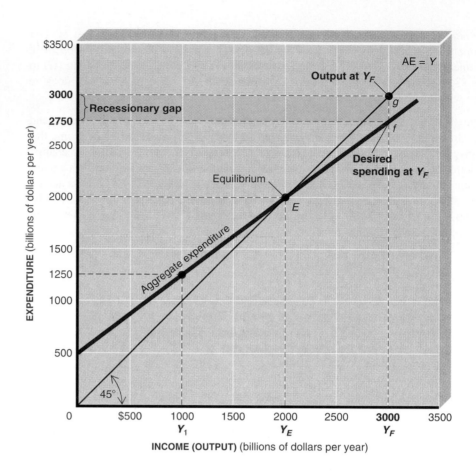

At Income (output) of:	Consumers Desire to Spend	+	Investors Desire to Spend	+	Governments Desire to Spend	+	Net Export Spending	=	Aggregate Expenditure
$ 500	$ 475		$150		$200		$50		$ 875
1000	850		150		200		50		1250
1500	1225		150		200		50		1625
2000	1600		150		200		50		2000
2500	1975		150		200		50		2375
3000	2350		150		200		50		2750
3500	2725		150		200		50		3125

Recessionary Gap. Figure 9.12 doesn't offer much optimism about maintaining full employment Y_F. Suppose we initially produced Y_F amount of output, with full employment. How much of that output would market participants buy? According to Figure 9.12, aggregate spending at Y_F would add up (in billions) to:

$$\text{Consumer spending at } Y_F = \$100 + 0.75(\$3000) = \$2350$$
$$\text{Investment spending at } Y_F \qquad\qquad\qquad = \$ 150$$
$$\text{Government spending at } Y_F \qquad\qquad\quad = \$ 200$$
$$\text{Net export spending at } Y_F \qquad\qquad\qquad = \$ \underline{\ 50}$$
$$\text{Aggregate spending at } Y_F \qquad\qquad\qquad = \$2750$$

This rate of spending is illustrated by point f in Figure 9.12. It represents the total amount of spending market participants desire to undertake when the economy is fully employed.

The economy illustrated in Figure 9.12 is in trouble. If full employment were achieved, it wouldn't last. At full employment, $3000 billion of output would be produced. But only $2750 of output would be sold. Because desired leakages exceed desired injections, there isn't enough aggregate demand at current price levels to sustain full employment. As a result, $250 billion of unsold output piles up in warehouses and on store shelves. That unwanted inventory pileup is a harbinger of trouble.

The difference between full-employment output and desired spending at full employment is called a **recessionary gap.** Not enough output is willingly purchased at full employment to sustain the economy. Producers may react to the spending shortfall by cutting back on production and laying off workers.

recessionary gap: The amount by which aggregate spending at full employment falls short of full-employment output.

A Single Equilibrium. You might wonder whether the desired spending of market participants would ever be exactly equal to the value of output. After all, leakage from the circular flow of income always occurs. However, at some rate of output new injections might exactly offset that leakage. In that case, aggregate spending would equal the value of output.

Figure 9.12 illustrates where this **expenditure equilibrium** exists. Recall the significance of the 45 degree line in that figure. The 45 degree line represents all points where expenditure *equals* income. At any point on this line there would be no difference between total spending and the value of output.

expenditure equilibrium: The rate of output at which desired spending equals the value of output.

The aggregate expenditure curve crosses the 45 degree line only once, at point E. At that point, therefore, desired spending is *exactly* equal to the value of output. In Figure 9.12 this equilibrium occurs at an output rate of $2000 billion. Notice in the accompanying table how much market participants desire to spend at that rate of output. We have

Consumer spending at	$Y_E = \$100 + 0.75(\$2000)$	$= \$1600$
Investment spending at	Y_E	$= \$\ 150$
Government spending at	Y_E	$= \$\ 200$
Net export spending at	Y_E	$= \$\ \ \ 50$
Aggregate expenditure at	Y_E	$= \$2000$

At Y_E we have spending behavior that's completely compatible with the rate of production. At this equilibrium rate of output, no goods remain unsold. At that one rate of output where desired spending and the value of output are exactly equal, an expenditure equilibrium exists. At that equilibrium producers have no incentive to change the rate of output because they're selling everything they produce.

Unfortunately, the equilibrium depicted in Figure 9.12 isn't the one we hoped to achieve. At Y_E the economy is well short of its full-employment goal (Y_F). This shortfall in equilibrium output is a symptom of market failure.

The expenditure equilibrium won't always fall short of the economy's productive capacity. Indeed, market participants' spending desires could also *exceed* the economy's full-employment potential. This might happen if investors, the government, or foreigners wanted to buy more output or if the consumption function shifted upward. In such circumstances an **inflationary gap** would exist. An inflationary gap arises when market participants want to buy *more* output than can be produced at full employment (see Figure 9.13). Notice that the expenditure equilibrium in Figure 9.13 exceeds that value of full-employment output. The resulting scramble for goods may start a bidding war that pushes price levels even higher. This would be another symptom of macro failure.

Macro Failure

inflationary gap: The amount by which aggregate spending at full employment exceeds full-employment output.

FIGURE 9.13
An Inflationary Gap

Market participants might want to purchase more goods and services than the economy can produce. At full employment (Y_F) desired aggregate expenditure (AE_F) exceeds full-employment output by the amount $AE_h - AE_F$. That inflationary gap will cause the price level to rise as market participants compete for available output.

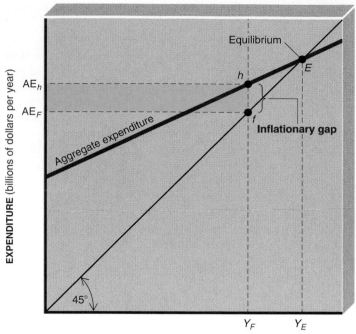

INCOME (OUTPUT) (billions of dollars per year)

THE ECONOMY TOMORROW

Doomed to Macro Failure?

Keynes' analysis of spending behavior led him to conclude that macro failure was likely in a market-driven economy. ***Because market participants make independent spending decisions, there's no reason to expect that the sum of their expenditures will generate the right amount of aggregate demand.*** Instead, there's a high likelihood that we'll confront an imbalance between desired spending and full-employment output levels—that is, too much or too little aggregate demand.

The implications of such imbalances aren't encouraging. If desired spending at full employment is less than the rate of production, some workers won't be needed and unemployment will spread. Such an imbalance—a recessionary gap—is the origin of **cyclical unemployment.** This contingency is illustrated in Figure 9.14a. Notice that equilibrium GDP falls short of the full-employment level of output. Keynes' depiction of the circular flow and independent spending decisions explains how this might happen.

cyclical unemployment: Unemployment attributable to a lack of job vacancies, that is, to an inadequate level of aggregate demand.

When desired spending at full employment exceeds production, a different problem emerges. In this case, consumers and investors begin competing with each other for available goods and services. Production can't be expanded beyond full-employment output without exerting upward pressure on prices. As a consequence, competition for available goods and services drives prices upward, setting in motion a **demand-pull inflation.** This contingency is illustrated in Figure 9.14b. The price level rises from P^* to P_E as market participants scramble to buy more than the economy can produce at full employment (Q_F). Once again, the Keynesian depiction of independent spending decisions by consumers, investors, governments, and export markets explains how such an imblance between aggregate demand and supply might occur.

demand-pull inflation: An increase in the price level initiated by excessive aggregate demand.

Although unemployment and inflation may arise from other causes (examined later), the potential imbalances we've described here are a potent source of macro failure. What we've observed is that ***market-driven decisions on how much to produce and***

(a) Cyclical unemployement:
too little demand

(b) Demand-pull inflation:
too much demand

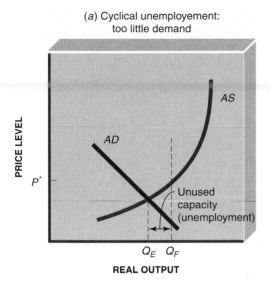

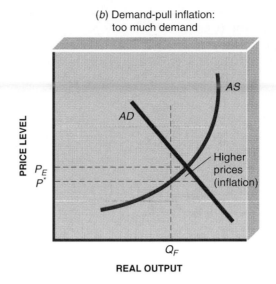

FIGURE 9.14
Macro Failures

The Keynesian explanation of spending behavior tells us why ag-gregate demand and supply might not intersect at desired out-put or price levels. If market participants want to spend less than full-employment output at current price levels, cyclical unem-ployment (part *a*) may result. If aggregate spending exceeds the value of output, demand-pull inflation (part *b*) may result.

how much to spend may leave our macro-economic goals unsatisfied. Full employ-ment and price stability will be attained only if desired aggregate expenditure at full employment turns out to be exactly equal to full-employment output. That seems like a most unlikely event, however, given the number of market participants involved.

An imbalance between aggregate expenditure and full-employment output doesn't necessarily doom the economy to macro failure. The seriousness of a spending-output imbalance also depends on how markets *respond* to that imbalance. If markets "self-correct," as classical economists believed, then spending imbalances will shrink. On the other hand, if markets don't self-correct—as Keynes argued—then the economy tomorrow is doomed to macro failure unless the government intervenes. Whether we should rely on the market or the government for macro stability thus hinges on how markets respond to spending imbalances. We examine those responses in the next chapter.

SUMMARY

- Macro failure occurs when the desired rate of spend-ing at full employment isn't equal to the value of full-employment output, causing unemployment or inflation. To determine whether such a spending imbalance might occur, we must assess the spending plans of consumers (C), investors (I), the government (G), and foreign buy-ers (net exports = $X - IM$).
- Consumer spending is affected by nonincome (au-tonomous) factors and current income, as summarized in the consumption function: $C = a + bY_D$.

- Autonomous consumption (a) depends on wealth, expec-tations, taxes, credit, and price levels. Income-dependent consumption depends on the marginal propensity to con-sume (MPC), the b in the consumption function.
- The consumption function shifts up or down when au-tonomous influences such as wealth and expectations change. Shifts of the consumption function at a constant price level are reflected in shifts of the aggregate demand curve.
- Consumer saving is the difference between disposable in-

come and consumption (that is, $S = Y_D - C$). All disposable income is either spent (C) or saved (S).

- Consumer saving represents leakage from the circular flow, that is, income not directly returned to product markets. Imports, taxes, and business saving also cause leakage.
- To maintain the circular flow at a desired level, leakages must be offset with injections of new spending. Such injections come from investment, government spending, and exports.
- Aggregate expenditure at full employment (AE$_F$) must equal full-employment output (Y_F) if full employment and price stability are to be maintained. If AE$_F$ is less than Y_F, a recessionary gap leaves output unsold. If AE$_F$ exceeds Y_F, an inflationary gap exists. Such gaps imply that aggregate demand is too high or too low.
- An expenditure equilibrium occurs where total desired spending equals the value of output. Keynes emphasized that this equilibrium may not achieve macro goals.
- A spending imbalance at full employment will cause unemployment or inflation. How serious these problems become depends on how the market responds to the initial imbalance.

Key Terms

aggregate demand
aggregate supply
equilibrium (macro)
consumption
disposable income
saving
average propensity to consume (APC)

marginal propensity to consume (MPC)
marginal propensity to save (MPS)
consumption function
dissaving
full-employment GDP
leakage
gross business saving

injection
investment
aggregate expenditure
recessionary gap
expenditure equilibrium
inflationary gap
cyclical unemployment
demand-pull inflation

Questions for Discussion

1. What percentage of last months' income did you spend? How much more would you spend if you won a $1000 lottery prize? Why might your average and marginal propensities to consume differ?
2. Why do rich people have a higher marginal propensity to save than poor people?
3. What events might change consumer confidence? (See NEWS, page 176.)
4. The NEWS item on page 183 implies that business investment isn't affected by current sales. Are current sales really ignored in investment decisions? How might changes in current sales affect expectations or the rate of desired investment?
5. Why wouldn't market participants always want to buy all the output produced?
6. Business saving can be used to finance new investment. Why doesn't this always occur? What else do firms do with their retained earnings and depreciation allowances?
7. How do households "dissave"? Can everyone dissave at the same time?
8. If an inflationary gap exists, what will happen to business inventories? How will producers respond?
9. **Web Activity** Draw the circular flow from Figure 9.9 in the text. Find the current dollar figure for consumption, exports, government spending, investment, and imports at www.bea.gov/bea/dn/niptbl-d.htm. Fill in the dollar amounts on your diagram.
10. **Web Activity** At the White House Economic Statistics Briefing room—www.whitehouse.gov/fsbr/esbr.html—find data on interest rates and different types of investment during the past several quarters. What relationship would you expect to see between investment and interest rates? What might have happened to expectations about the economy's future to change the relationship?

Problems for Chapter 9 appear at the back of the book.

10

Self-Adjustment
or Instability?

John Maynard Keynes took a dim view of a market-driven macro economy. He emphasized that (1) macro failure is likely to occur in such an economy, and worse yet, (2) macro failure isn't likely to go away. As noted earlier, the first prediction wasn't all that controversial. The classical economists had conceded the possibility of occasional recession or inflation. In their view, however, the economy would quickly self-adjust, restoring full employment and price stability. Keynes' second proposition challenged this view. The most distinctive—and frightening—proposition of Keynes' theory was that there'd be no automatic self-adjustment; the economy could stagnate in *persistent* unemployment or be subjected to *continuing* inflation.

Chapter 9 demonstrated how the economy can end up producing less output than its full-employment potential. This chapter focuses more closely on the *adjustment process* that changes macro outcomes. We're especially concerned with the following questions:

- What forces might derail the economy from its full-employment track?
- How will consumers and investors respond to a sudden imbalance between spending and output?
- What macro outcomes will these responses create?

EMERGENCE OF A
RECESSIONARY GAP

To see how the economy adjusts to macro failure, imagine an economy initially at full employment, as illustrated in Figure 10.1. As before, the behavior of market participants is summarized with **aggregate demand** and **aggregate supply** curves. The real value of output is indicated on the horizontal axis, with Q_F designating full-employment GDP.

The economy depicted in Figure 10.1 is in a state of near bliss. Aggregate demand and aggregate supply intersect to create an **equilibrium GDP** that's exactly equal to full-employment GDP. This economy is enjoying both full employment and price stability (at P_0).

One important characteristic of equilibrium is that the injections into the circular flow must be exactly equal to the leakages. Such a flow balance is the essence of any equilibrium. If the flows weren't equal, aggregate spending in the

Initial Equilibrium

FIGURE 10.1
Full-Employment Equilibrium

Aggregate demand and supply might intersect at full-employment output (Q_F), with price stability (at P_0). What happens, though, if this full-employment equilibrium is displaced by a short-run change in spending behavior?

aggregate demand (AD): The total quantity of output demanded at alternative price levels in a given time period, *ceteris paribus*.
aggregate supply (AS): The total quantity of output producers are willing and able to supply at alternative price levels in a given time period, *ceteris paribus*.
equilibrium GDP: The rate of real output at which aggregate demand equals aggregate supply.

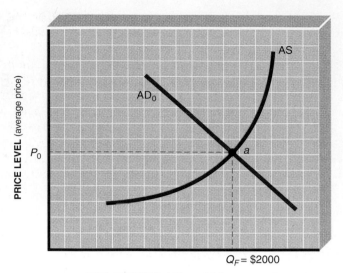

REAL OUTPUT (in billions of dollars per year)

economy would be either expanding or contracting. The intersection at point *a* in Figure 10.1 indicates that the economy has stabilized its spending flows.

Figure 10.2 depicts the various leakages and injections that affect the circular flow of income. To simplify the analysis we focus on only two flows: the investment injections and the consumer-saving leakage. In doing so, we're implicitly assuming that all the other flows balance out one another. In this case, only a change in consumer or investor behavior can derail equilibrium GDP.

In the real world, a GDP equilibrium could be upset by a sudden change in any spending or leakage component. Our primary interest, however, is to see how a purely private economy might get into trouble and how private market forces might get it out (self-adjust). Hence, the focus on consumption and investment not only simplifies the analysis but also helps us focus on the heart of the self-adjustment debate.

In the initial equilibrium (Q_F) in Figure 10.1, we assume the following spending behavior:

$$C = \$1600 \text{ billion}$$
$$S = \$\ 400 \text{ billion}$$
$$I = \$\ 400 \text{ billion}$$

Notice that the rate of consumer saving ($400 billion) is exactly equal to the rate of investment in this macro equilibrium. What we want to assess is how this happy economy would fare if the balance of expenditure and saving flows were upset.

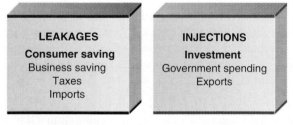

FIGURE 10.2
Leakages and Injections

Macro stability depends on the balance between injections and leakages. Of these, consumer saving and business investment are the primary sources of (im)balance in a wholly private and closed economy. Hence the relationship between saving and investment reveals whether a market-driven economy will "self-adjust" to full employment and price stability.

A change in investment behavior might well upset this apple cart. The full-employment equilibrium we've depicted includes $400 billion of investment spending at current prices. But investment spending is notoriously fickle. Look at the quarterly variations in investment that occurred just before and during the 1990–1991 recession (Figure 10.3). From one quarter to the next, investment spending fell by more than 5 percent and increased by as much as 7 percent. Such abrupt changes are hardly consistent with a steady flow of investment. Consumer spending also varies from quarter to quarter, but isn't nearly as volatile.

Suppose the rate of investment were suddenly to drop from $400 billion to $300 billion. This would disrupt the balance of savings and investment that previously existed at full employment. Now consumers are saving more ($400 billion) than businesses are investing ($300 billion). What will happen to the economy when this imbalance emerges?

We can use Figure 10.4 to illustrate the immediate consequences of the decline in investment. Previously, market participants were ready and willing to buy $2000 billion of output at current prices (the price level P_0). Now, however, only $1900 billion is demanded at that price level (point *d*). Hence, the ***initial impact of a decline in***

A Decline in Investment

CYBER NOTE

Check the U.S. Bureau of Economic Activity (BEA) Web site at www.stat-usa.gov/ebbdata/ei.txt to see how much seasonally adjusted investment has varied in percentage terms over the past six quarters.

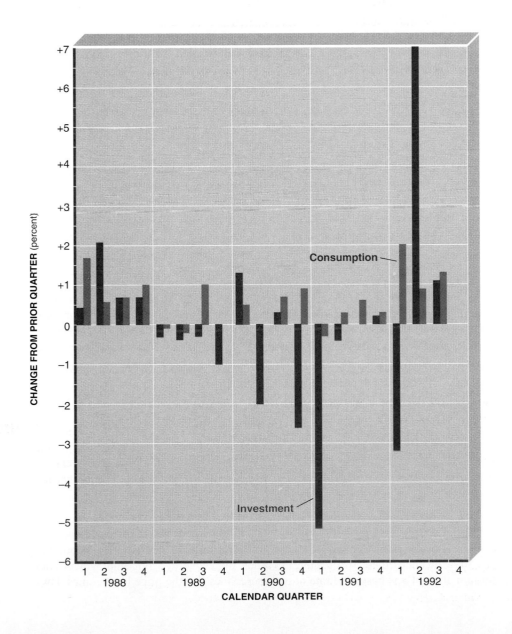

FIGURE 10.3
Volatile Investment Spending

Investment spending fluctuates more than consumption. Shown here are the quarter-to-quarter changes in the real rate of spending for fixed investment (excluding inventory changes) and total consumption. Notice the sharp drop in investment spending just prior to the recession that began in July 1990.

Source: *Economic Report of the President, 1993* (quarterly data seasonally adjusted).

FIGURE 10.4
AD Shift

When investment spending drops, aggregate demand shifts to the left. In the short run, this causes output and the price level to fall. The initial equilibrium at *a* is pushed to a new equilibrium at point *b*.

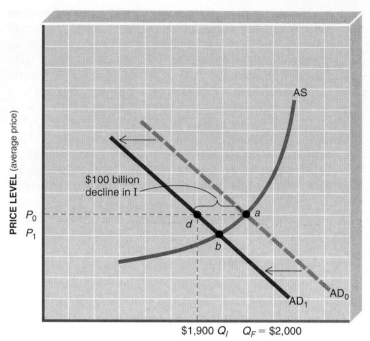

REAL OUTPUT (in billions of dollars per year)

investment is illustrated by a leftward shift of the aggregate demand curve. A recessionary gap has emerged in which aggregate demand falls short of full-employment output at current prices.

Undesired Inventory

When a recessionary gap emerges, producers are unable to sell all the goods that they'd hoped to. The goods don't disappear, however; the unsold goods pile up on producers' shelves as additional inventory. In the auto industry, the unsold goods accumulate on dealers' lots (see NEWS). Producers don't want this added inventory, but they're stuck with it. Ironically, this additional inventory is counted as part of investment spending. (Recall that our definition of investment spending includes changes in business inventories.) This additional inventory is clearly undesired, as producers had planned on selling these goods.

To keep track of these unwanted changes in investment, we **distinguish** desired *(or planned) investment from* **actual** *investment. Desired* investment represents purchases of new plant and equipment plus any desired changes in business inventories. By contrast, *actual* investment represents purhases of new plant and equipment plus *actual* changes in business inventories, desired or otherwise. In other words,

$$\text{Actual investment} = \text{desired investment} + \text{undesired investment}$$

If actual investment at full employment equals desired investment, producers' plans have been fulfilled. No imbalance exists between the rates of expenditure and production at full employment. By contrast, *a recessionary gap implies that producers' expectations haven't been fulfilled: Actual investment exceeds desired investment and excess (undesired) inventories are piling up.*

Falling Output and Prices

How are business firms likely to react when they see undesired inventory piling up on car lots and store shelves? Most likely they'll start cutting prices in an attempt to increase the rate of sales. Producers are also likely to reduce the rate of new output. Figure 10.4 illustrates these two responses. When the economy's full-employment equilibrium at point *a* is upset, the rate of output declines and the price level comes down.

CYBER NOTE

At the Economics Briefing Room of the White House at www.whitehouse.gov/fsbr/output.html, find current data on output.

Inventory Buildup Could Pose Threat for Some Big Companies

Heard on the Street

NEW YORK—It *is* possible to have too much of a good thing.

Especially inventory. When business inventories are on the rise while sales are slackening, it's a classic harbinger of recession—and it's exactly what happened in September.

Autos, metals and even a big retailer here and there are already showing signs of inventory problems, analysts say. GM has the fattest inventories of the Big Three auto makers, as the nearby table shows. . . .

Other industries where inventory problems are starting to crop up included appliances and building materials, plus some segments of the paper, chemicals and capital-equipment industries, says A. Gary Shilling, a New York economist.

With the economy slowing, inventories of the nation's manufacturers, retailers and wholesalers in September edged up 0.2% from August to $791.82 billion, as sales slipped 0.3% to $524.58 billion. So far, business inventories are holding at a respectable ratio of 1.51 times sales. But if sales keep declining while inventories rise further, the pattern would be a recessionary one.

—John R. Dorfman

The Wall Street Journal, Nov. 28, 1989, p. C1. Reprinted by permission of *The Wall Street Journal*, © 1989 Dow Jones & Company, Inc. All Rights Reserved Worldwide. www.wsj.com

Acres of Unsold Cars

Dealer inventories on Oct. 31, as calculated by Ronald A. Glantz of Montgomery Securities. He uses a year-to-date selling rate to gauge supplies on dealer lots.

	Unsold Days' Supply		Percent above Normal*
	Cars	Trucks	
General Motors	70 days	87 days	18%
Chrysler	69	88	17
Ford	63	76	5

*Normal defined as a 20-year average for cars and trucks combined.

Analysis: When desired spending falls short of current production, unwanted inventory piles up. This undesired investment causes producers to reduce the rate of output in the next period.

If no other changes were to occur, the economy would gravitate toward a new equilibrium at point *b*. At point *b*, the rate of output (Q_1) is less than the full-employment level (Q_F) and the price level has fallen from P_0 to P_1.

Figure 10.4 doesn't paint a pretty picture of an economy beset by a decline in investment. Keynes argued, however, that the picture painted by Figure 10.4 is far too optimistic! As Keynes saw it, the GDP gap created by a decline in investment will widen as the shock of reduced investment spending reverberates around the circular flow. In this scenario, the problems created by a short-term drop in autonomous spending *multiply* rather than dissipate over time.

THE MULTIPLIER PROCESS

The emergence of a GDP gap is a critical turning point in the economy's performance. As we've seen, the gap emerges when investment behavior changes for the worse. A gap could, in fact, emerge if *any* component of aggregate demand declined. A drop in exports, a cutback in government spending, or a decline in autonomous consumption could create the same kind of imbalance.

The critical question for macro stability is how market participants respond to this imbalance. We've already observed that *business firms* are likely to reduce prices and cut the rate of output. But what about *consumers?* How are they going to be affected by the production cutbacks? How is their spending behavior likely to change?

Household Incomes

So far we've treated the production cutbacks that accompany a GDP gap as a rather abstract problem. But the reality is that when production is cut back, people suffer. When producers decrease the rate of output, workers lose their jobs or face pay cuts, or both. The accumulation of undesired auto inventories in 1989 (see NEWS item on inventory buildup) soon led to a wave of layoffs in that industry (see NEWS). As workers get laid off or have their wages cut, household incomes decline. Thus, *a reduction in investment spending implies a reduction in household incomes.*

Income-Dependent Consumption

We saw in Chapter 9 the kind of threat a reduction in household income poses. Those consumers who end up with less income won't be able to purchase as many goods and services as they did before. As a consequence, the total value of goods and services demanded will fall further, leading to still larger stocks of unsold goods, more job layoffs, and further reductions in income. It's this sequence of events—called the *multiplier process*—that makes a recessionary gap so frightening. What starts off as a relatively small spending shortfall quickly snowballs into a much larger problem.

We can see the multiplier process at work by watching what happens to the $100 billion gap as it makes its way around the circular flow (Figure 10.5). At first (step 1), the only thing that happens is that unsold goods appear (in the form of undesired inventories). Producers adjust to this problem by cutting back on production and laying off workers or reducing wages and prices (step 2). In either case, consumer income falls $100 billion per year shortly after the recessionary gap emerges (step 3).

How will consumers respond to this drop in disposable income? *If disposable income falls, we expect consumer spending to drop as well.* In fact, the consumption function tells us just how much spending will drop. The **marginal propensity to consume (MPC)** is the critical variable in this process. Since we've specified that $C = \$100$ billion $+ 0.75Y$, we anticipate that consumers will reduce their spending by $0.75 for every $1.00 of lost income. In the present example, the loss of $100 billion of annual income will induce consumers to reduce their rate of spending by $75 billion per year ($0.75 \times \$100$ billion). This drop in spending is illustrated by step 4 in Figure 10.5.

marginal propensity to consume (MPC): The fraction of each additional (marginal) dollar of disposable income spent on consumption; the change in consumption divided by the change in disposable income.

IN THE NEWS

Layoffs at Big Three Spreading

DETROIT—Robert Stempel came to the North American International Auto Show to talk about electric cars, supercharged engines and sleek styling.

Instead, the General Motors Corp. president got question after question this week about the health of the auto industry, which is caught in its biggest spasm of layoffs since the early 1980s. Finally, Stempel grew exasperated. The Big Three will emerge from their latest slump, he said summarily, "when the customers come back to the showrooms."

Tell that to the quarter of the nation's autoworkers—133,500—who have been getting layoff notices since December from automakers struggling to cut production to meet falling demand. Some of those workers are being idled for as little as a week, but several thousand at GM will be out of work "indefinitely," along with 1,700 Chrysler workers. Auto executives refuse to rule out more "down weeks" in the near future. Meantime, sales continue to drag: On Thursday GM reported that its December car sales were off 27.6% from December 1988; Ford's fell 28.4%; and Chrysler's were down 31.2%.

The layoffs touch almost every corner of the country.

—James Cox and James R. Healey

USA Today, Jan. 5, 1990, p. 1B. Copyright 1990, USA TODAY. Reprinted with permission. www.usatoday.com

Analysis: The pileup of inventories in the auto industry (see NEWS item on inventory buildup), led to job layoffs. The displaced autoworkers curtailed *their* consumption and caused layoffs in other industries.

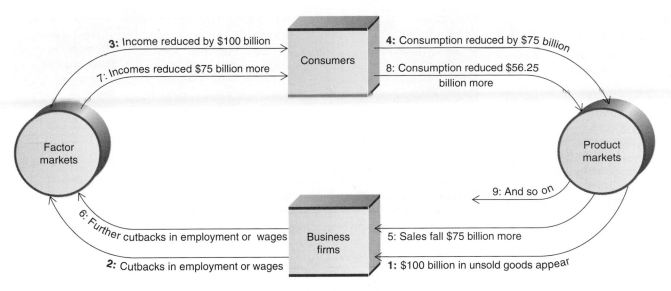

FIGURE 10.5
The Multiplier Process

A recessionary gap (step 1) may lead to a cutback in production and income (step 2). A reduction in total income (step 3) will in turn lead to a reduction in consumer spending (step 4). These additional cuts in spending cause a further decrease in income, leading to additional spending reductions, and so on. This sequence of adjustments is referred to as the "multiplier process."

The multiplier process doesn't stop here. A reduction in consumer spending quickly translates into more unsold output (step 5). As additional goods pile up on producers' shelves, we anticipate further cutbacks in production, employment, and disposable income (step 6).

As disposable incomes are further reduced by job layoffs and wage cuts (step 7), more reductions in consumer spending are sure to follow (step 8). Again the marginal propensity to consume (MPC) tells us how large such reductions will be. With an MPC of 0.75, we may expect spending to fall by another $56.25 billion per year (0.75 × $75 billion).

The multiplier process continues to work until the reductions in income and sales become so small that no one's market behavior is significantly affected. We don't have to examine each step along the way because all the steps begin to look alike once we've gone around the circular flow a few times. We can foresee how large an impact the multiplier process will ultimately have. Each time the multiplier process works its way around the circular flow, the reduction in spending equals the previous drop in income multiplied by the MPC. Accordingly, by pressing a few keys on a calculator, we can produce a sequence of events like that depicted in Table 10.1 on the next page.

The impact of the multiplier is devastating. The ultimate reduction in real spending resulting from the initial drop in investment isn't $100 billion per year but $400 billion! Even if one is accustomed to thinking in terms of billions and trillions, this is a huge drop in demand. What the multiplier process demonstrates is that the dimensions of an initial spending gap greatly understate the severity of the economic dislocations that will follow in its wake. ***The decline in spending will be much larger than the initial (autonomous) spending decrease.*** This was evident in the recession of 1990–1991, when layoffs snowballed from industry to industry (see NEWS, page 199), ultimately leaving 10 million people unemployed.

The ultimate impact of an AD shift on total spending can be determined by computing the change in income and consumption at each cycle of the circular flow, for an infinite number of cycles. This is the approach summarized in Table 10.1, with each

The Multiplier

CYBER NOTE

Do sports teams create multiplier effects for cities? Read about this at www.brook.edu/pub/review/summer97/noll.htm.

TABLE 10.1
The Multiplier Cycles

The circular flow of income implies that an initial change in income will lead to cumulative changes in consumer spending and income. Here, an initial income loss of $100 billion (first cycle) causes a cutback in consumer spending in the amount of $75 billion (second cycle). At each subsequent cycle, consumer spending drops by the amount MPC × prior change in income. Ultimately, total spending (and income) falls by $400 billion, or 1/(1 − MPC) × initial change in spending.

Spending Cycles	Change in This Cycle's Spending and Income (billions per year)	Cumulative Decrease in Spending and Income (billions per year)
First cycle: recessionary gap emerges	$100.00	$100.00 } ΔI
Second cycle: consumption drops by MPC × $100	75.00	175.00
Third cycle: consumption drops by MPC × $75	56.25	231.25
Fourth cycle: consumption drops by MPC × $56.25	42.19	273.44
Fifth cycle: consumption drops by MPC × $42.19	31.64	305.08 } ΔC
Sixth cycle: consumption drops by MPC × $31.64	23.73	328.81
Seventh cycle: consumption drops by MPC × $23.73	17.80	346.61
Eighth cycle: consumption drops by MPC × $17.80	13.35	359.95
⋮	⋮	⋮
*n*th cycle and beyond		400.00

multiplier: The multiple by which an initial change in aggregate spending will alter total expenditure after an infinite number of spending cycles; 1/(1 − MPC).

row representing a spending cycle. The entire computation can be simplified considerably by using a single figure, the multiplier. The **multiplier** tells us the extent to which the rate of total spending will change in response to an initial change in the flow of expenditure. The multiplier summarizes the sequence of steps described in Table 10.1.[1] In its simplest form, the multiplier can be computed as:

$$\text{Multiplier} = \frac{1}{1 - \text{MPC}}$$

In our example, the initial change in spending occurs when investment drops by $100 billion per year at full-employment output ($2000 billion per year). Table 10.1 indicates that this gap will lead to a $400 billion reduction in the rate of total spending at the current price level. Using the multiplier, we arrive at the same conclusion by observing that

$$
\begin{aligned}
\text{Total change in spending} &= \text{multiplier} \times \text{initial change in aggregate spending} \\
&= \frac{1}{1 - \text{MPC}} \times \$100 \text{ billion per year} \\
&= \frac{1}{1 - 0.75} \times \$100 \text{ billion per year} \\
&= 4 \qquad\quad \times \$100 \text{ billion per year} \\
&= \$400 \text{ billion per year}
\end{aligned}
$$

In other words, *the cumulative decrease in total spending ($400 billion per year) resulting from the appearance of a recessionary gap at full employment is equal to the gap ($100 billion per year) multiplied by the multiplier (4).* More generally, we may observe that the larger the fraction (MPC) of income respent in each round of the circular flow, the greater the impact of any change in spending on cumulative aggregate

[1]The multiplier summarizes the geometric progression $1 + \text{MPC} + \text{MPC}^2 + \text{MPC}^3 + \ldots + \text{MPC}^n$, which equals $1/(1 - \text{MPC})$ when *n* becomes infinite.

IN THE NEWS

Job Losses Spreading

The recession of 1990–1991 started with a slowdown in consumer spending. Producers responded by cutting back production and laying off workers. Some of the larger layoffs are listed in the table:

Company	Product	Month of Layoff	Number of Workers Laid Off
McDonnell Douglas	Aircraft	July 1990	15,000
Ford Motor Co.	Autos	August 1990	7,500
USAir	Airline	August 1990	1,500
Harley-Davidson	Motorcycles	September 1990	180
Saks Fifth Avenue	Retail	October 1990	700
Zenith	Televisions	October 1990	1,500
Philips N.V.	Electronics	October 1990	35,000
Unisys	Computers	October 1990	5,000
New York City	Government	November 1990	5,500
Chrysler	Autos	November 1990	6,200
General Motors	Autos	November 1990	7,600
MCI	Communications	November 1990	1,500
Sears	Retail	November 1990	20,000
Goodyear Tire and Rubber Co.	Tires	March 1991	1,100
IBM	Computers	March 1991	10,000
GTE Corp.	Communications	May 1991	4,900
Eastman Kodak	Photography	August 1991	3,000
Deere & Co.	Equipment	November 1991	2,100

Analysis: Few industries escape damage from a recession. Spending slowdowns spread from industry to industry in a multiplier-like way. Job layoffs reduce disposable income and consumption.

demand. The cumulative process of spending adjustments can also have worldwide effects. As the WORLD VIEW on the next page illustrates, the 1997–1998 recession in Asia caused U.S. firms to cut back output and lay off workers.

EQUILIBRIUM REVISITED

The key features of the Keynesian adjustment process are

- **Producers cut output and employment when output exceeds desired spending.**
- **The resulting loss of income causes a decline in consumer spending.**
- **Declines in consumer spending lead to further production cutbacks, more lost income, and still less consumption.**

Figure 10.6 illustrates the ultimate impact of the multiplier process. Notice that the AD curve shifts *twice*. The first shift—from AD_0 to AD_1—represents the $100 billion drop in investment spending. As we saw earlier in Figure 10.4, this initial shift of aggregate demand will start the economy moving toward a new equilibrium at point *b*.

Along the way, however, the multiplier kicks in and things get worse. *The decline in household income caused by investment cutbacks sets off the multiplier process,*

CYBER NOTE

JWT Communications tracks ongoing layoffs. To see how widespread layoffs are in any time period, visit www.hrlive.com/layoff.

Sequential AD Shifts

U.S. Manufacturers Continue to Suffer From Impact of Asian Economic Crisis

WASHINGTON—Although many other sectors of the economy are thriving, U.S. manufacturers continue to suffer from the effects of the Asian crisis.

A new survey conducted by the National Association of Purchasing Management paints a bleak picture of manufacturing, which represents about 20% of the total output of goods and services of the U.S. economy.

"Asia is having an impact . . . on our customer base, and the domestic industrial slowdown is certainly very real," said Peter Browning, chief executive of Sonic Product Co., a Hartsville, S.C., packaging concern. The company's sales still are growing, he said, but at a slower pace . . .

The Federal Reserve's measure of industrial production grew at a weak 0.18% in the third quarter. Exports of U.S. goods in the first nine months of 1998 were down 1% from the same period of 1997, after growing 10% the year before.

Among U.S. manufacturers, steel and farm-equipment producers have been hardest hit. U.S. steel producers have been roiled by a surge in imported steel that has hammered profit margins. Farm-equipment makers have been hit by a double-whammy: a downturn in foreign and domestic demand . . .

The industrial slowdown has put pressure on manufacturers to control costs and prompted some to announce layoffs, including such big-name companies at **Monsanto** Co. and **Deere**. Big mergers, such as this week's marriage of **Exxon** Corp. and **Mobil** Corp., are likely to lead to further job losses.

Citing the Asian economic crisis, **Boeing** Corp. plans to cut production rates for some of its commercial-airplane programs. In addition, the company said it plans to eliminate 48,000 jobs by the end of the year 2000—38,000 of them by the end of next year.

—Alejandro Bodipo-Memba and Carl Quintanilla

The Wall Street Journal, Dec. 2, 1998, p 2. Reprinted by permission of *The Wall Street Journal,* © 1998 Dow Jones & Company, Inc. All Rights Reserved Worldwide. www.wsj.com

Analysis: Multiplier effects can spill over national borders. The 1997–1998 downturn in Asia reduced demand for U.S. exports, setting off a sequence of domestic layoffs.

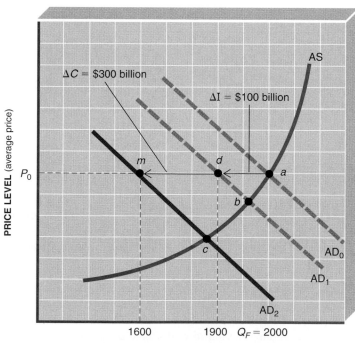

FIGURE 10.6
Multiplier Effects

A decline in investment spending reduces household income, setting off negative multiplier effects. Hence the *initial* shift of AD_0 to AD_1 is followed by a *second* shift from of AD_1 to AD_2. The second shift represents reduced consumption.

causing a secondary shift of the AD curve. We measure these multiplier effects at the initial price level of P_0. With a marginal propensity to consume of 0.75, we've seen that induced consumption declines by $300 billion when autonomous investment declines by $100 billion. In Figure 10.6 this is illustrated by the *second* shift of the aggregate demand curve, from AD_1 to AD_2. Notice that the horizontal distance between AD_1 and AD_2 is $300 billion.

Although aggregate demand has fallen (shifted) by $400 billion, real output doesn't necessarily drop that much. *The impact of a shift in aggregate demand is reflected in both output and price changes.* This is evident in Figure 10.7, which is a close-up view of Figure 10.6. When AD shifts from AD_0 to AD_2, the macro equilibrium moved down the sloped AS curve to point c. At point c the new equilibrium output is Q_E and the new price level is P_E.

Price and Output Effects

Real GDP Gap. As long as the aggregate supply curve is upward-sloping, the shock of any AD shift will be spread across output and prices. In Figure 10.7, the net effect on real output is shown as the real GDP gap. The *real GDP gap equals the difference between the equilibrium real output (Q_E) and full-employment real output (Q_F).* It repesents the amount by which the economy is underproducing during a recession. This is a classic case of **cyclical unemployment.**

GDP gap (real): The difference between full-employment GDP and equilibrium GDP.

cyclical unemployment: Unemployment attributable to a lack of job vacancies, that is, to an inadequate level of aggregate demand.

Short-Run Inflation-Unemployment Trade-Offs

Figure 10.7 not only illustrates how much output declines when AD falls but also provides an important clue about the difficulty of restoring full employment. Suppose the real GDP gap were $200 billion, as illustrated in Figure 10.8. How much more AD would we need to get back to full employment?

Upward-Sloping AS. Suppose aggregate demand at the current price level (P_E) were to increase by exactly $200 billion, as illustrated by the shift to AD_3. Would that get us back to full-employment output? Not according to Figure 10.8. *When AD increases, both output and prices go up.* Because the AS curve is upward-sloping, the $200

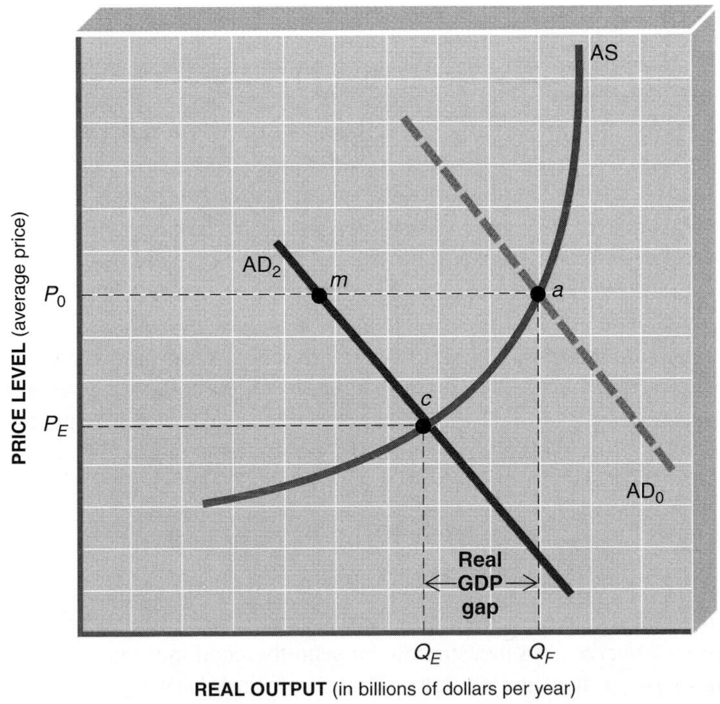

FIGURE 10.7
Real GDP Gap

The real GDP gap is the difference between equilibrium real output (Q_E) and full-employment real output (Q_F). It represents the lost output due to a recession.

FIGURE 10.8
The Unemployment-Inflation Trade-Off

If the short-run AS curve is upward-sloping, an AD increase will raise output *and* prices. If AD increases by the amount of the GDP gap only (AD_2 to AD_3), full employment (Q_f) won't be reached. Macro equilibrium moves to point *g*, not point *f*.

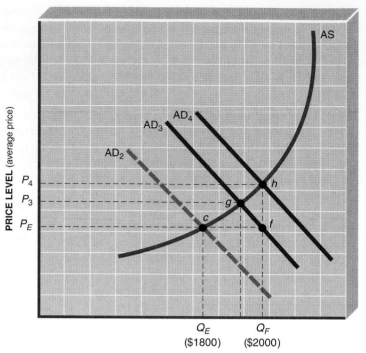

REAL OUTPUT (in billions of dollars per year)

billion AD shift moves the new macro equilibrium to point *g* rather than point *f*. We'd like to get to point *f* with full employment and price stability. But as demand picks up, producers are likely to raise prices. This leads us up the AS curve to point *g*. At point *g*, we're still short of full employment and have experienced a bit of inflation (an increased price level). *So long as the short-run AS is upward-sloping, there's a trade-off between unemployment and inflation.* We can get lower rates of unemployment (more real output) only if we accept some inflation.

"Full" vs. "Natural" Unemployment. The short-term trade-off between unemployment and inflation is the basis for the definition of "full" employment. We don't define full employment as *zero* unemployment; we define it as the rate of unemployment *consistent with price stability*. As noted in Chapter 6, **full employment** is typically defined as a 4 to 6 percent rate of unemployment. What the upward-sloping AS curve tells us is that *the closer the economy gets to capacity output, the greater the risk of inflation.* To get back to full employment in Figure 10.8, aggregate demand would have to increase to AD_4, with the price level rising to P_4.

Not everyone accepts this notion of full employment. As we saw in Chapter 8, neoclassical and monetarist economists prefer to focus on *long*-run outcomes. In their view, the long-run AS curve is vertical (see Figure 8.12). In that long-run context, there's no unemployment-inflation trade-off: An AD shift doesn't change the "natural" (institutional) rate of unemployment but does alter the price level.

full employment: The lowest rate of unemployment compatible with price stability; variously estimated at between 4 and 6 percent unemployment.

ADJUSTMENT TO AN INFLATIONARY GAP

As we're observed, a sudden imbalance in spending flows can have a cumulative effect on macro outcomes that's larger than the initial imbalance. This multiplier process works both ways: Just as a *decrease* in investment can send the economy into a recessionary tailspin, an *increase* in investment might initiate an inflationary spiral.

Figure 10.9 illustrates the consequences of a sudden jump in investment spending. We start out again in the happy equilibrium (point *a*), where full employment (Q_F) and price stability (P_0) prevail. Initial spending consists of

$$C = \$1600 \text{ billion}$$
$$I = 400 \text{ billion}$$

Increased Investment

Then investors suddenly decide to step up the rate of investment. Perhaps their expectations for future sales have risen. Maybe new technology has become available that compels firms to modernize their facilities. Whatever the reason, investors decide to raise the level of investment from $400 billion to $500 billion at current price levels. This change in investment spending shifts the aggregate demand curve from AD_0 to AD_5 (a horizontal shift of $100 billion).

Inventory Depletion. One of the first things you'll notice when AD shifts like this is that available inventories shrink. Investors can step up their *spending* quicker than firms can increase their *production*. A lot of the increased investment demand will have to be satisfied from existing inventory. When this happens, *desired* investment (including desired inventory) will fall below actual investment. The decline in inventory is a signal to producers that it might be a good time to raise prices a bit. Thus, ***inventory depletion is a warning sign of impending inflation.*** As the economy moves up from point *a* to point *r* in Figure 10.9, that inflation starts to become visible.

Household Incomes

Whether or not prices start rising quickly, household incomes will get a boost from the increased investment. Producers will step up the rate of output to rebuild inventories and supply more investment goods, e.g., equipment and structures. To do so, they'll hire more workers or extend working hours. The end result for workers will be fatter paychecks.

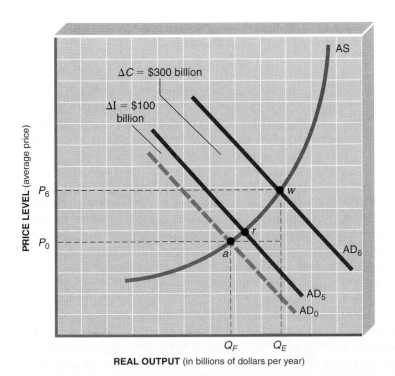

FIGURE 10.9
Demand-Pull Inflation

An increase in investment or other autonomous spending sets off multiplier effects shifting AD to the right. AD shifts to the right *twice,* first (AD_0 to AD_5) because of increased investment, then (AD_5 to AD_6) because of increased consumption. The increased AD moves the economy up the short-run AS curve, causing inflation.

Induced Consumption

What will households do with these heftier paychecks? By now, you know what the consumer response to more income will be. The marginal propensity to consume prompts an increase in consumer spending. Eventually, consumer spending increases by a *multiple* of the income change. In this case, the consumption increase is $300 billion (see Table 10.1).

Figure 10.9 illustrates the secondary shift of AD caused by multiplier-induced consumption. Notice how the AD curve shifts a second time, from AD_5 to AD_6.

A New Equilibrium

demand-pull inflation: An increase in the price level initiated by excessive aggregate demand.

The ultimate impact of the investment surge is reflected in the new equilibrium at point *w*. As before, the shift of AD has affected both real output and prices. Real output does increase beyond the "full-employment" level, but it does so only at the expense of accelerating inflation. This is a classic case of **demand-pull inflation.** The initial increase in investment was enough to kindle a little inflation. The multiplier effect worsened the problem by forcing the economy further along the ever-steeper AS curve.

THE ECONOMY TOMORROW

Maintaining Consumer Confidence

The Keynesian analysis of leakages, injections, and the multiplier paints a fairly grim picture of the prospects for macro stability. *The basic conclusion of the Keynesian analysis is that the economy doesn't self-adjust:* Instead, small disturbances of macro equilibrium may mushroom into bigger macro problems. Worse yet, the economy may end up stabilizing at price or output levels far removed from our macro goals of full employment and price stability.

This chapter emphasized how a sudden change in investment might set off the multiplier process. Investors aren't the only potential culprits, however. A sudden change in government spending or exports could just as easily get the multiplier ball rolling. In fact, the whole process could originate with a change in *consumer* spending.

Consumer Confidence

Recall the two components of consumption: *autonomous* consumption and *induced* consumption. These two components may be expressed as

$$C = a + bY$$

We've seen that autonomous consumption is influenced by *non*income factors, including consumer confidence. What's more, consumer confidence can change abruptly. (See NEWS in Chapter 9, page 176.) When it does, the value of *a* in the consumption function will change and the consumption function itself will shift. A change in consumer confidence might also change the marginal propensity to consume, the *b* in the equation.

The reverberation of a change in consumer confidence will cause *two* shifts of the AD curve. The first shift will be due to the effect of changed consumer confidence on *autonomous* consumption. The second shift will result from the multiplier effects on *induced* consumption. This is exactly the kind of dilemma that prolonged the Japanese recession (see WORLD VIEW). As the outlook got gloomier, Japanese households decided to decrease autonomous consumption and reduce the marginal propensity to consume. Unfortunately, their attempt to save more and spend less worsened Japan's recession.

The Official View: Always A Rosy Outlook

Because consumer spending vastly outweighs any other component of aggregate demand, the threat of abrupt changes in consumer behavior is serious. Recognizing this, public officials strive to maintain consumer confidence in the economy tomorrow, even when such confidence might not be warranted. That's what Japanese officials were doing in 1998, described in the WORLD VIEW. That's also why President Hoover,

Thrift Shift—The More the Japanese Save for a Rainy Day, The Gloomier It Gets

Stuffing Yen Into the Drawer

A decade ago, when Japan was considered economically mighty and the U.S. was struggling, many economists agreed that a big reason for the disparity was savings: The thrifty Japanese had plenty to invest in their future, the wanton Americans too little.

Today, the average Japanese family puts away more than 13% of its income, the average American family 4%. Yet Japan is in the tank while the U.S. prospers.

Is saving no longer an economic virtue and profligacy no longer a vice? Did Benjamin Franklin get it all wrong? Maybe not—but it isn't as simple as Franklin's Poor Richard's Almanac made it seem:

An economy can save too much.

Japan is the first major developed country since World War II to confront the "paradox of thrift," the condition John Maynard Keynes worried about, where bad times lead individuals to save more, suppressing overall demand and making a country even worse off.

But these days, the pressing savings crisis is in Tokyo. Interest rates on bank deposits run below 1%, and still "households are saving too much," says Kengo Inoue, a Bank of Japan economist. "That's depressing demand and, over time, corporate investment." That, in turn, has become a drag on all of Asia.

So the Japanese government nudges its citizens to live it up. The Finance Ministry, concerned that families would simply tuck away a recent $500-a-household income-tax cut, launched a media blitz to advise people on how to spend the money.

—Jacob M. Schlesinger and David P. Hamilton

Analysis: When Japanese consumers became more pessimistic about their economy, they started saving more and spending less. This shifted AD leftward and deepened the recession. Government officials urged them to spend more.

bank officials, and major brokerage houses tried to assure the public in 1929 that the outlook was still rosy. (Look back at the first few pages of Chapter 8). The "rosy outlook" is still the official perspective on the economy tomorrow. The White House is always upbeat about prospects for the economy. If it weren't—if it were even to hint at the possibility of a recession—consumer and investor confidence might wilt. Then the economy might turn ugly really fast.

SUMMARY

- A change in autonomous behavior shifts the aggregate demand curve, creating an imbalance between spending and production.
- An initial change in spending affects household incomes and starts a multiplier process, that is, induced changes in consumption.
- The multiplier itself is equal to $1/(1 - MPC)$. It indicates the cumulative change in demand that follows an initial (autonomous) disruption of spending flows.
- As long as the short-run aggregate supply curve slopes upward, AD shifts will affect both real output and prices.

- The Keynesian theory of the adjustment process suggests that the economy may not self-adjust to either inflation or unemployment. On the contrary, the economy may stabilize at an equilibrium that leaves too much unemployment or inflation.
- The real GDP gap measures the amount by which equilibrium GDP falls short of full-employment GDP.
- Sudden changes in consumer confidence would destabilize the economy. To avoid this, policymakers always maintain a rosy outlook.

Key Terms

aggregate demand

aggregate supply

equilibrium GDP

marginal propensity to consume

multiplier

GDP gap (real)

cyclical unemployment

full employment

demand-pull inflation

Questions for Discussion

1. What factors might prompt the business sector to reduce planned investment spending?
2. Why wouldn't investment and saving flows at full employment always be equal?
3. When unwanted inventories pile up in retail stores, how is production affected? What are the steps in this process?
4. How can equilibrium output exceed full-employment output (as in Figure 10.9)?
5. How might the auto industry job losses described in the NEWS feature on page 196 affect incomes in the clothing and travel industries?
6. How can an economy overcome cyclical unemployment?
7. Web Activity How bad was the Great Depression in the United States? Check how long it lasted at www.nber.org/cycles.html. Find out how much real GDP and business investment fell at www.bea.doc.gov, and chart the unemployment rate for the period at www.bls.gov.
8. Web Activity At the U.S. Congressional Budget Office—www.cbo.gov—find Current Economic Projections. Look at the projections for the next 10 years' change in real output and the price level. How do they expect these statistics to change from the current level? Draw AD and AS curves to show what this office predicts will happen to the U.S. economy.

Problems for Chapter 10 appear at the back of the book.

Fiscal Policy Options

The government's tax and spending activities influence economic outcomes. Keynesian theory emphasizes the inherent instability of a market economy and the necessity of using federal tax and spending power (fiscal policy) to stabilize the macro economy. Chapters 11 and 12 look closely at these issues.

11

Fiscal Policy

The Keynesian theory of macro instability is practically a mandate for government intervention. From a Keynesian perspective, too little aggregate demand causes unemployment; too much aggregate demand causes inflation. Since the market itself won't correct these imbalances, the federal government must. Keynes concluded that the government must intervene to manage the level of aggregate demand. This implies increasing aggregate demand when it's deficient and decreasing aggregate demand when it's excessive.

This chapter examines some tools the federal government can use to alter macroeconomic outcomes. The questions we confront are

- Can government spending and tax policies help ensure full employment?
- What policy actions will help fight inflation?
- What are the risks of government intervention?

As we'll see, the government's tax and spending activities affect not only the *level* of output and prices but the *mix* of output as well.

TAXES AND SPENDING

Article I of the U.S. Constitution empowers Congress "to lay and collect taxes, duties, imposts and excises, to pay the debts and provide for the common defense and general welfare of the United States." Up until 1915, however, the federal government collected few taxes and spent little. In 1902, the federal government employed fewer than 350,000 people and spent a mere $650 million. Today, the federal government employs nearly 5 million people and spends more than $1.8 trillion a year.

Government Revenue

The tremendous expansion of the federal government in this century started with the Sixteenth Amendment to the U.S. Constitution (1913); it extended the government's taxing power to *incomes*. Prior to that, most government revenue came from taxes on imports, whiskey, and tobacco. Once the federal government got the power to tax incomes, it had the revenue base to finance increased expenditure.

Today the federal government collects over $1.8 trillion a year in tax revenues. Nearly half of that revenue comes from individual income taxes (see Figure 4.7). Social Security payroll taxes are the second largest revenue sources, followed at a distance by corporate income taxes. The customs, whiskey, and tobacco taxes on which the federal government depended in 1902 now count for very little.

In 1902, federal government expenditures mirrored tax revenues: Both were very small. Today, things are very different. The federal government now spends virtually all of its much larger tax revenues. In some years Uncle Sam even borrows additional funds to pay for federal spending. In Chapter 12 we look at the implications of budget surpluses and deficits. In this chapter we focus on how government spending *directly* affects **aggregate demand.**

Purchases vs. Transfers. To understand how government spending affects aggregate demand, we must again distinguish between government *purchases* and *income transfers.* Government spending on defense, highways, and health care entail the purchase of goods and services in product markets; they're part of aggregate demand. By contrast, the government doesn't buy anything when it mails out Social Security checks. Those checks simply transfer income from taxpayers to retired workers. **Income transfers** don't become part of aggregate demand until the transfer recipients decide to spend that income.

As we observed in Chapter 4 (see Figure 4.5), less than half of all federal government spending entails the purchase of goods and services. Everything else in the federal budget is either an income transfer or an interest payment on the national debt.

The federal government's tax and spending powers give it a great deal of influence over aggregate demand. The government can alter aggregate demand by

- Purchasing more or fewer goods and services
- Raising or lowering taxes
- Changing the level of income transfers

Fiscal policy entails the use of these various budget levers to influence macroeconomic outcomes. ***From a macro perspective the federal budget is a tool that can change aggregate demand and macroeconomic outcomes.*** Figure 11.1 puts this tool into the framework of the basic AS/AD model.

Government Expenditure

aggregate demand: The total quantity of output demanded at alternative price levels in a given time period, *ceteris paribus.*

income transfer: Payments to individuals for which no current goods or services are exchanged, such as Social Security, welfare, unemployment benefits.

Fiscal Policy

fiscal policy: The use of government taxes and spending to alter macroeconomic outcomes.

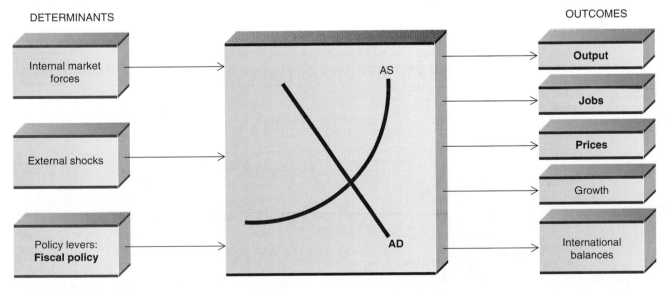

FIGURE 11.1
Fiscal Policy

Fiscal policy refers to the use of the government tax and spending powers to alter macro outcomes. Fiscal policy works principally through shifts of the aggregate demand curve.

Although fiscal policy can be used to pursue any of our economic goals, we begin our study by exploring its potential to ensure full employment. We then look at its impact on inflation. Along the way we also observe the potential of fiscal policy to alter the mix of output and the distribution of income.

FISCAL STIMULUS

Suppose that the economy is in a recession, as illustrated in Figure 11.2. **Macro equilibrium** occurs at Q_E, where $5.6 trillion of output is being produced. Full-employment GDP occurs at Q_F, where the real value of output is $6 trillion. Accordingly, the economy depicted in Figure 11.2 confronts a **real GDP gap** of $400 billion.

equilibrium (macro): The combination of price level and real output that is compatible with both aggregate demand and aggregate supply.

GDP gap (real): The difference between full-employment GDP and equilibrium GDP.

Keynesian Strategy

The Keynesian model of the adjustment process helps us not only understand how an economy can get into such trouble but also see how it might get out. Keynes emphasized how the aggregate demand curve *shifts* with changes in spending behavior. He also emphasized how new injections of spending into the circular flow multiply into much larger changes in total spending. From a Keynesian perspective, then, the way out of recession is obvious: Get someone to spend more on goods and services. Should desired spending increase, the aggregate demand curve would *shift* to the right, leading the economy out of recession. That additional spending impetus could come from increased government purchases or from tax cuts that induce increased consumption or investment. Such a **fiscal stimulus** might propel the economy out of recession.

fiscal stimulus: Tax cuts or spending hikes intended to increase (shift) aggregate demand.

Although the general strategy for Keynesian fiscal policy is clear, the scope of desired intervention isn't so evident. Two strategic policy questions must be addressed:

- By how much do we want to shift the AD curve to the right?
- How can we induce the desired shift?

The Fiscal Target

At first glance, the size of the desired AD shift might seem obvious. If the GDP gap is $400 billion, why not just increase aggregate demand by that amount?

The Naive Keynesian Model. Keynes thought that policy might just work. The intent of the expansionary fiscal policy is to achieve full employment. In Figure 11.3, this goal would be attained at point *b*. When the AD curve shifts rightward by $400 billion, the new AD_2 curve in fact passes through point *b*, creating the possibility of achieving our full-employment goal.

Will the economy move so easily from point *a* to point *b*? Only under very special conditions. The economy would move from point *a* to point *b* in Figure 11.3 only if the **aggregate supply** curve were horizontal. In other words, we'd achieve full em-

aggregate supply: The total quantity of output producers are willing and able to supply at alternative price levels in a given time period, *ceteris paribus.*

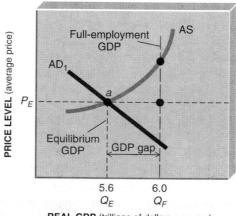

FIGURE 11.2
The Policy Goal

If the economy is in a recessionary equilibrium like point *a*, the policy goal is to increase output to full employment (Q_F). Keynes urged the government to use its tax and spending powers to shift the AD curve rightward.

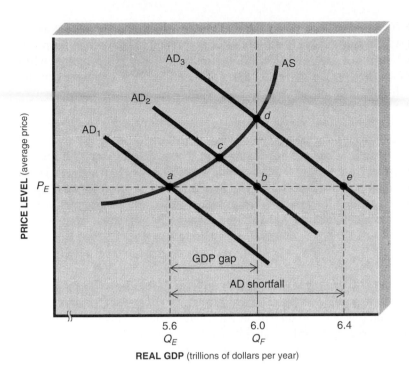

FIGURE 11.3
The AD Shortfall

If aggregate demand increased by the amount of the GDP gap, which is the shift from AD$_1$ to AD$_2$, equilibrium would occur at point c, leaving the economy short of full employment (Q_F). (Some of the increased demand pushes up prices instead of output.) To reach full-employment equilibrium (point d), the AD curve must shift to AD$_3$, thereby eliminating the entire AD shortfall. The AD shortfall—the horizontal distance between point a and point e—is the fiscal policy target for achieving full employment.

ployment with the shift to AD$_2$ only if prices didn't rise when the economy expanded. This is the expectation of the naive Keynesian model. In fairness to Keynes, we must recall that he developed this approach during the Great Depression, when prices were *falling*. No one was worried that prices would rise if demand increased.

Price-Level Changes. Even in today's economy, prices may not rise every time aggregate demand increases. Over some ranges of real output, the AS curve may actually be horizontal. Eventually, however, we expect the AS curve to slope upward. When it does, any increase in aggregate demand affects both real output *and* prices. In those circumstances, an increase in aggregate demand doesn't translate dollar-for-dollar into increased real GDP. Instead, *when the AD curve shifts to the right, the economy moves up the aggregate supply (AS) curve, not horizontally to the right.* As a result, both real output *and* the price level change.

Figure 11.3 illustrates the consequences of the upward-sloping aggregate supply curve. Suppose we actually increased aggregate demand by $400 billion, an amount equal to the initial GDP gap. When the aggregate demand curve shifts from AD$_1$ to AD$_2$, the economy moves to the macro equilibrium at point c, not to point b. As demand picks up, we expect cost pressures to increase, pushing the price level up the upward-sloping AS curve. At point c, the AS and AD$_2$ curves intersect, establishing a new equilibrium. At that equilibrium, the price level is higher than it was initially (P_E). Real output is higher as well but still short of the full-employment target. Hence, the naive Keynesian policy fails to achieve full employment. To do better, we must recognize that *shifting (increasing) aggregate demand by the amount of the GDP gap will achieve full employment only if the price level doesn't rise.*

The AD Shortfall. Although the naive Keynesian approach doesn't work, we needn't forsake fiscal policy. Figure 11.3 simply tells us that the naive Keynesian policy prescription probably won't cure our unemployment ills. It also suggests, however, that a *larger* dose of fiscal stimulus might just work. *So long as the AS curve slopes upward, we must increase aggregate demand by more than the size of the GDP gap in order to achieve full employment.*

AD shortfall: The amount of additional aggregate demand needed to achieve full employment after allowing for price-level changes.

Figure 11.3 illustrates this new policy target. The **AD shortfall** is the amount of additional aggregate demand needed to achieve full employment after allowing for price-level changes. Notice in Figure 11.3 that full employment (Q_F) is achieved only when the AD curve intersects the AS curve at point d. To get there, the aggregate demand curve must shift from AD_1 all the way to AD_3. That third aggregate demand curve passes through point e as well. Hence aggregate demand must increase until it passes through point e. This *horizontal distance between point* **a** *and point* **e** *in Figure 11.3 measures the AD shortfall.* Aggregate demand must increase (shift) by the amount of the AD shortfall in order to achieve full employment. Thus *the AD shortfall is the fiscal target.* In Figure 11.3 the AD shortfall amounts to $800 billion ($0.8 trillion). That's how much additional aggregate demand is required to reach full employment (Q_F).

Were we to increase AD by enough to attain full employment, it's apparent in Figure 11.3 that prices would increase as well. We examine this dilemma later; for the time being we focus on the policy options for increasing aggregate demand by the desired amount.

More Government Spending

The simplest way to shift aggregate demand is to increase government spending. If the government were to step up its purchases of tanks, highways, schools, and other goods, the increased spending would add directly to aggregate demand. This would shift the aggregate demand curve rightward, moving us closer to full employment. Hence *increased government spending is a form of fiscal stimulus.*

Multiplier Effects. It isn't necessary for the government to make up the entire shortfall in aggregate demand. Suppose that the fiscal target was to increase aggregate demand by $800 billion. That target coincides with the AD shortfall illustrated in Figure 11.3. Were government spending to increase by that amount, the AD curve would actually shift *beyond* point e in Figure 11.3. In that case we'd quickly move from a situation of *inadequate* aggregate demand (point a) to a situation of *excessive* aggregate demand.

The origins of this apparent riddle lie in the circular flow of income. When the government buys more goods and services, it creates additional income for market participants. The recipients of this income will in turn spend it. Hence each dollar gets spent and respent many times. This is the multiplier adjustment process we encountered in Chapter 10. As a result of this process, *every dollar of new government spending has a multiplied impact on aggregate demand.*

multiplier: The multiple by which an initial change in aggregate spending will alter total expenditure after an infinite number of spending cycles; $1/(1 - MPC)$.

How much "bang" the economy gets for each government "buck" depends on the value of the **multiplier.** Specifically,

$$\text{Total change in spending} = \text{multiplier} \times \text{new spending injection}$$

marginal propensity to consume (MPC): The fraction of each additional (marginal) dollar of disposable income spent on consumption; the change in consumption divided by the change in disposable income.

The multiplier adds a lot of punch to fiscal policy. Suppose that households have a **marginal propensity to consume** equal to 0.75. In this case, the multiplier would have a value of 4 and each dollar of new government expenditure would increase total expenditure by $4.

Figure 11.4 illustrates that leveraged impact of government spending. Aggregate demand shifts from AD_1 to AD_2 when the government buys an additional $200 billion of output. Multiplier effects then increase consumption spending by $600 billion. This additional consumption shifts aggregate demand further, to AD_3. Thus *the impact of fiscal stimulus on aggregate demand includes both the new government spending and all subsequent increases in consumer spending triggered by the additional government outlays.* In Figure 11.4, the shift from AD_1 to AD_3 includes

AD_1 to AD_2: Shift due to $200 billion injection of new government spending
AD_2 to AD_3: Shift due to multiplier-induced increase in consumption ($600 billion)

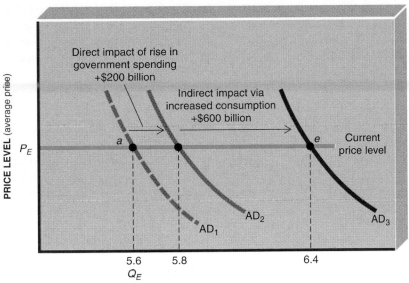

Direct impact of rise in
government spending
+$200 billion

Indirect impact via
increased consumption
+$600 billion

PRICE LEVEL (average price)

P_E

a

e

Current
price level

AD₁

AD₂

AD₃

5.6   5.8   6.4

Q_E

REAL OUTPUT (trillions of dollars per year)

FIGURE 11.4
Multiplier Effects

Fiscal stimulus will set off the multiplier process. As a result of this, aggregate demand will increase (shift) in two distinct steps: (1) the initial fiscal stimulus (AD_1 to AD_2) and (2) induced changes in consumption (AD_2 to AD_3). In this case, a $200 billion increase in government spending causes an $800 billion increase in real aggregate demand.

As a result of these initial and multiplier-induced shifts, aggregate demand increases by $800 billion. Thus

$$\text{Increase in AD} = \text{multiplier} \times \text{fiscal stimulus}$$

This equation is identical to the one above, but expressed in the terminology of fiscal policy. The "fiscal stimulus" is the "new spending injection" that sets the multiplier process in motion.

The Desired Stimulus. Multiplier effects make changes in government spending a powerful policy lever. The multiplier also increases the risk of error, however. Whereas too little fiscal stimulus may leave the economy in a recession, too much can rapidly lead to excessive spending and inflation. This was the dilemma President Clinton confronted in his first year. He believed a $60 billion stimulus was necessary to achieve full employment but feared that so much stimulus might accelerate inflation. He decided that $20 billion was safer.

If we knew the exact dimensions of aggregate demand, as in Figure 11.3, we could easily calculate the required increase in the rate of government spending. The general formula for computing the *desired* stimulus is a simple rearrangement of the earlier formula:

$$\text{Desired fiscal stimulus} = \frac{\text{desired AD increase}}{\text{the multiplier}}$$

In the economy in Figure 11.3, we assumed the policy goal was to increase aggregate demand by the amount of the AD shortfall ($800 billion). Accordingly, we conclude that

$$\text{Desired fiscal stimulus} = \frac{\$800 \text{ billion}}{4}$$

$$= \$200 \text{ billion}$$

In other words, a $200 billion increase in government spending at the current price level would be enough fiscal stimulus to close the $800 billion AD shortfall and achieve full employment.

In practice, we rarely know the exact size of the shortfall in aggregate demand. The multiplier is also harder to calculate when taxes and imports enter the picture. Nevertheless, the foregoing formula does provide a useful rule of thumb for determining how much fiscal stimulus is needed to achieve any desired increase in aggregate demand. Such calculations helped the Japanese government decide how much fiscal stimulus was needed in 1998 to propel the Japanese economy out of recession (see WORLD VIEW).

Tax Cuts

CYBER NOTE

To see what happened to real GDP in Japan after the 1998 fiscal stimulus, check out GDP data at the Web site of Japan's Statistics Bureau at www.stat.go.jp/16.htm.

disposable income: After-tax income of consumers; personal income less personal taxes.

Although injections of government spending can close a GDP gap, increased government purchases aren't the only way to get there. The increased demand required to raise output and employment levels from Q_E to Q_F could emerge from increases in autonomous consumption or investment as well as from increased government spending. It could also come from abroad, in the form of increased demand for our exports. In other words, any Big Spender would help, whether from the public sector or the private sector. Of course, the reason we're initially at Q_E instead of Q_F in Figure 11.3 is that consumers and investors have chosen *not* to spend as much as required for full employment.

Consumer and investor decisions are subject to change. Moreover, fiscal policy can encourage such changes. Congress not only buys goods and services but also levies taxes. By lowering taxes, the government increases the **disposable income** of the private sector. This was the objective of the 1997 fiscal stimulus that gave families a tax credit for their children (see NEWS). By putting $18 billion more after-tax income into the hands of consumers, Congress hoped to stimulate (shift) the consumption components of aggregate demand.

Taxes and Consumption. A tax cut directly increases the disposable income of consumers. The question here, however, is how a tax cut affects *spending*. By how much will consumption increase for every dollar of tax cuts?

The answer lies in the marginal propensity to consume. Consumers won't spend every dollar of tax cuts; they'll *save* some of the cut and spend the rest. The MPC tells us how the tax-cut dollar will be split between saving and spending. If the MPC is 0.75, consumers will spend $0.75 out of every tax-cut $1.00. In other words.

$$\text{Initial increase in consumption} = \text{MPC} \times \text{tax cut}$$

WORLD VIEW

Japan Proposes $124B Stimulus

Buckling to pressure to help rescue its Asian neighbors from recession, Japan Thursday promised to fire up its dormant economy with $124 billion in government spending and tax cuts.

However, world financial markets, by hardly reacting, expressed skepticism that Japan will either not follow through, or its people will save any windfall as they try to recover wealth lost in fallen stock and real estate markets.

U.S. Ambassador to Japan Thomas Foley reserved judgment until more details are released. The package is expected to include public works spending, tax breaks for education and a plan aimed at boosting the stock market.

—Del Jones

USA Today, Mar. 27, 1998, p. 1B. Copyright 1998, USA TODAY. Reprinted with permission. www.usatoday.com

Analysis: Japan's economy fell into a recession in the late 1990s. To spur more production, the Japanese government adopted a fiscal stimulus plan that included major increases in government spending.

A $500 Tax Credit for Children

The Taxpayer Relief Act of 1997 brought a lot of tax relief for families with children. The biggest tax cut in the 1997 legislature package is a $500 tax credit for each child under 17. Married couples with less than $110,000 of adjusted gross income can claim the entire $500 credit. Families with higher incomes will get smaller credits for each child.

The Congressional Budget Office estimates that the new "Kiddie Credit" will save taxpayers $18 billion in taxes.

Source: Congressional Budget Office, September, 1997. www.cbo.gov

Analysis: Tax cuts increase disposable income and spur consumer spending. President Clinton hoped to stimulate the economy by reducing income taxes paid by families with children. The "Kiddie Credit" served this purpose.

If taxes were cut by $200 billion, the resulting spree would amount to

$$\text{Initial increase in consumption} = 0.75 \times \$200 \text{ billion}$$

$$= \$150 \text{ billion}$$

Hence *the effect of a tax cut that increases disposable incomes is to stimulate consumer spending.* A tax cut therefore shifts the aggregate demand curve to the right.

The initial consumption spree induced by a tax cut starts the multiplier process in motion. The new consumer spending creates additional income for producers and workers, who will then use the additional income to increase their own consumption. This will propel us along the multiplier path already depicted in Figure 11.4. The cumulative change in total spending will be

$$\text{Cumulative change in spending} = \text{multiplier} \times \text{initial change in consumption}$$

In this case, the cumulative change is

$$\text{Cumulative change in spending} = \frac{1}{1 - \text{MPC}} \times \$150 \text{ billion}$$

$$= 4 \times \$150 \text{ billion}$$

$$= \$600 \text{ billion}$$

Here again we see that the multiplier increases the impact on aggregate demand of a fiscal policy stimulus. There's an important difference here, though. When we increased government spending by $200 billion, aggregate demand increased by $800 billion. When we cut taxes by $200 billion, however, aggregate demand increases by only $600 billion. Hence *a tax cut contains less fiscal stimulus than an increase in government spending of the same size.*

The lesser stimulative power of tax cuts is explained by consumer saving. Only part of a tax cut gets spent. Consumers save the rest. This is evident in Figure 11.5, which illustrates the successive rounds of the multiplier process. Notice that the tax cut is used to increase both consumption and saving, according to the MPC. Only that part of the tax cut that's used for consumption enters the circular flow as a spending injection. Hence *the initial spending injection is less than the size of the tax cuts.* By contrast, every dollar of government purchases goes directly into the circular flow. Accordingly, tax cuts are less powerful than government purchases because the initial *spending* injection is smaller.

FIGURE 11.5
The Tax Cut Multiplier

Only part of a tax cut is used to increase consumption; the remainder is saved. Accordingly, the initial spending injection is less than the tax cut. This makes tax cuts less stimulative than government purchases of the same size.

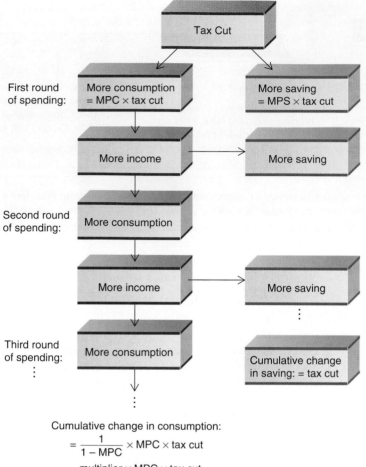

Cumulative change in consumption:

$$= \frac{1}{1 - MPC} \times MPC \times \text{tax cut}$$

$$= \text{multiplier} \times MPC \times \text{tax cut}$$

This doesn't mean we can't close the AD shortfall with a tax cut. It simply means that the desired tax cut must be larger than the required stimulus. It remains true that

$$\text{Desired fiscal stimulus} = \frac{\text{desired AD increase}}{\text{the multiplier}}$$

We now have to allow for the fact that the initial increase in consumption will only be

$$\text{Initial consumption stimulus} = MPC \times \text{tax cut}$$

Hence if we want to use a consumer tax cut to close a GDP gap, we have

$$\text{Desired tax cut} = \frac{\text{desired fiscal stimulus}}{MPC}$$

In the economy in Figure 11.3 we assumed that the desired stimulus is $200 billion and the MPC equals 0.75. Hence the desired tax cut is

$$\text{Desired tax cut} = \frac{\$200 \text{ billion}}{0.75} = \$267 \text{ billion}$$

By cutting taxes $267 billion, we directly increase disposable income by the same amount. Consumers then increase their rate of spending $200 billion (0.75 × $267 billion); they save the remaining $67 billion. As the added spending enters the circular flow, it starts the multiplier process, ultimately increasing aggregate demand by $800 billion per year.

This comparison of government purchases and tax cuts clearly reveals their respective power. What we've demonstrated is that *a dollar of tax cuts is less stimulative than a dollar of government purchases.* This doesn't mean that tax cuts are undesirable, just that they need to be larger than the desired injection of spending. Another implication of the evident leakage from tax cuts is that tax increases don't "offset" government spending of equal value. This unexpected result is described in Table 11.1.

Taxes and Investment. A tax cut may also be an effective mechanism for increasing investment spending. As we observed in Chapter 9, investment decisions are guided by expectations of future profit. If a cut in corporate taxes raises potential after-tax profits, it should encourage additional investment. Once an increase in the rate of investment spending enters the circular flow, it has a multiplier effect on total spending like that which follows an initial change in consumer spending.

Tax cuts designed to stimulate consumption (C) and investment (I) have been used frequently. In 1963 President John F. Kennedy announced his intention to reduce taxes in order to stimulate the economy, citing the fact that the marginal propensity to

Many taxpayers and politicians demand that any new government spending be "balanced" with new taxes. Such balancing "at the margin," it's asserted, will keep the budget deficit from rising, while avoiding further economic stimulus.

However, changes in government spending (G) are more powerful than changes in taxes (T) or transfers. This implies that an increase in G apparently "offset" with an equal rise in T will actually increase aggregate demand.

To see how this curious result comes about, suppose that the government decided to spend $50 billion per year on a new fleet of space shuttles and to pay for them by raising income taxes by the same amount. Thus

$$\text{Change in } G = + \$50 \text{ billion per year}$$
$$\text{Change in } T = + \$50 \text{ billion per year}$$
$$\text{Change in budget balance} = 0$$

How will this "pay-as-you-go" (balanced) budget initiative affect total spending?

The increase in the rate of government spending represents a new injection of $50 billion. But households will have to reduce their consumption in order to pay the new taxes. The marginal propensity to consume (MPC) tells us how much consumption will be reduced when disposable income falls. The initial reduction in annual consumer spending equals MPC × 50 billion.

The reduction in consumption is therefore less than the increase in government spending, implying a net increase in *aggregate* spending. The *initial* change in aggregate spending brought about by this balanced budget expenditure is

$$\text{Initial increase in government spending} = \$50 \text{ billion}$$
$$\text{less Initial reduction in consumer spending} = \text{MPC} \times \$50 \text{ billion}$$
$$\text{Net initial change in total spending} = (1 - \text{MPC})\$50 \text{ billion}$$

Like any other changes in the rate of spending, this initial increase in aggregate spending will start a multiplier process in motion. The *cumulative* change in expenditure will be much larger, as indicated by the multiplier. In this case, the cumulative (ultimate) change in total spending is

$$\frac{\text{The}}{\text{multiplier}} \times \frac{\text{initial change}}{\text{in spending per year}} = \frac{\text{cumulative change}}{\text{in total spending}}$$

$$\frac{1}{1 - \text{MPC}} \times (1 - \text{MPC})\$50 \text{ billion} = \$50 \text{ billion}$$

Thus the balanced budget multiplier is equal to 1. In this case, a $50 billion increase in annual government expenditure combined with an equivalent increase in taxes increases aggregate demand by $50 billion per year.

TABLE 11.1
The Balanced Budget Multiplier

An increase in government spending "paid for" by a tax cut of equal size shifts aggregate demand. This box explains why.

consume for the average U.S. family at that time appeared to be exceptionally high. His successor, Lyndon Johnson, concurred with Kennedy's reasoning. Johnson agreed to "shift emphasis sharply from expanding federal expenditure to boosting private consumer demand and business investment." He proceeded to cut personal and corporate taxes $11 billion. President Johnson proclaimed that "the $11 billion tax cut will challenge American businessmen, investors, and consumers to put their enlarged incomes to work in the private economy to expand output, investment, and jobs." He added, "I am confident that our private decision makers will rise to this challenge." They apparently did, because $C + I$ increased $33 billion in 1963 and another $46 billion in 1965 (in part as a result of multiplier effects, of course).

The largest tax cut in history was initiated by President Ronald Reagan. In 1981 Congress cut personal taxes $250 billion over a 3-year period and cut business taxes another $70 billion. The resulting increase in disposable income stimulated consumer spending and helped push the economy out of the 1981–1982 recession. When the economy slowed down at the end of the 1980s, President Bush proposed to cut the capital gains tax, hoping to stimulate investment. President Clinton also embraced the notion of tax incentives for investment. He favored a tax credit for new investments in plant and equipment. If such credits increase the level of investment, multiplier effects will create additional jobs for many years. As the accompanying NEWS illustrates, the job-creation effects of such a tax cut might still be visible 6 years later.

Increased Transfers

A third fiscal policy option for stimulating the economy is to increase transfer payments. If Social Security recipients, welfare recipients, unemployment insurance beneficiaries, and veterans get larger benefit checks, they'll have more disposable income to spend. The resulting increase in consumption will boost aggregate demand.

Increased transfer payments don't, however, increase injections dollar-for-dollar. Here again, we have to recognize that consumers will save some of their additional transfer

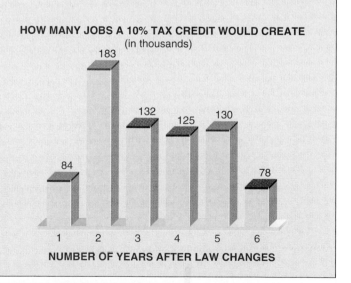

Tax Tips for the Next President

Bill Clinton will probably promote his promised investment tax credit—likely 10%—as a way to stimulate the economy fast. . . .

If Clinton goes for a 10% incremental credit for targeted investments, it will cost $76 billion in lost taxes over six years and raise capital equipment spending by $64 billion, according to Boston Co. Economic Advisors, a forecasting firm. President Allen Sinai predicts the investments would create 732,000 jobs over the same period. The chart shows the pace at which Sinai thinks that they would open up.

—Ann Reilly Dowd

HOW MANY JOBS A 10% TAX CREDIT WOULD CREATE (in thousands)

Analysis: A tax-induced increase in investment will have multiplier effects on aggregate demand. As a result, it creates jobs for several years as increased incomes get spent and respent.

payments; only part (MPC) of the additional income will be injected into the spending stream. Hence ***the initial fiscal stimulus of increased transfer payments is***

Initial fiscal stimulus (injection) = MPC × increase in transfer payments

This initial stimulus sets the multiplier in motion, shifting the aggregate demand curve further to the right.

FISCAL RESTRAINT

The objective of fiscal policy isn't always to increase aggregate demand. At times the economy is already expanding too fast and **fiscal restraint** is more appropriate. In these circumstances, policymakers are likely to be focused on inflation, not unemployment. Their objective will be to *reduce* aggregate demand, not to stimulate it.

The means available to the federal government for restraining aggregate demand emerge again from both sides of the budget. The difference here is that we use the budget tools in reverse. We now want to reduce government spending, increase taxes, or decrease transfer payments.

As before, our first task is to determine how much we want aggregate demand to fall. To determine this, we must consult Figure 11.6. The initial equilibrium in this case occurs at point E_1 where the AS and AD_1 curves intersect. At that equilibrium the unemployment rate falls below the rate consistent with full employment (Q_F) and we produce the output Q_1. The resulting strains on production push the price level to P_E, higher than we're willing to accept. Our goal is to maintain the price level at P_F, which is consistent with our notion of full employment *and* price stability.

In this case, we have a *negative* GDP gap—that is, equilibrium GDP exceeds full-employment GDP by the amount $Q_1 - Q_F$, or \$200 billion. If we want to restore price stability (P_F), however, we need to reduce aggregate demand by *more* than this GDP gap. The **aggregate demand excess** takes into account potential changes in the price level. Observe that *the AD excess exceeds the GDP gap.* In Figure 11.6, the AD excess equals the horizontal distance from E_1 to point f, which amounts to \$400 billion. This excess aggregate demand is our fiscal policy target. To restore price stability, we

fiscal restraint: Tax hikes or spending cuts intended to reduce (shift) aggregate demand.

The Fiscal Target

AD excess: The amount by which aggregate demand must be reduced to achieve full-employment equilibrium after allowing for price-level changes.

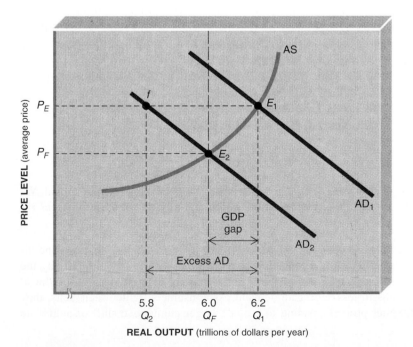

FIGURE 11.6
Excess Aggregate Demand

Too much aggregate demand (AD_1) causes the price level to rise (P_E) above its desired level (P_F). To restore price stability, the AD curve must shift leftward by the entire amount of the excess AD (here shown as $Q_1 - Q_2$). In this case the excess AD amounts to \$400 billion. If AD shifts by that much (from AD_1 to AD_2), the excess AD is eliminated and equilibrium moves from E_1 to E_2.

must shift the AD curve leftward until it passes through point f. The AD_2 curve does this. The shift to AD_2 moves the economy to a new equilibrium at E_2. At E_2 we have less output but also a lower price level (less inflation).

Knowing the dimensions of excess aggregate demand, we can compute the desired fiscal restraint as

$$\text{Desired fiscal restraint} = \frac{\text{desired AD reduction}}{\text{the multiplier}} = \frac{\text{excess AD}}{\text{the multiplier}}$$

In other words, first we determine how far we want to shift the AD curve. Generally, the desired AD reduction will equal the excess AD. Then we compute how much government spending or taxes must be changed to achieve the desired shift.

Budget Cuts

The first option to consider is budget cuts. By how much should we reduce government expenditure on goods and services? The answer is simple in this case: We first calculate the desired fiscal restraint, as computed above. Then we cut government expenditure by that amount.

The excess AD in Figure 11.6 amounts to $400 billion. If we assume a marginal propensity to consume of 0.75, the multiplier equals 4. In these circumstances the desired fiscal restraint is

$$\text{Desired fiscal restraint} = \frac{\text{excess AD}}{\text{the multiplier}}$$

$$= \frac{400 \text{ billion}}{4}$$

$$= 100 \text{ billion}$$

What would happen to aggregate demand if the federal government cut that much spending out of, say, the defense budget? Such a military cutback would throw a lot of aerospace employees out of work. Thousands of workers would get smaller paychecks, or perhaps none at all. These workers would be forced to cut back on their own spending, thereby reducing the consumption component of aggregate demand. Hence aggregate demand would take two hits: first a cut in government spending, then induced cutbacks in consumer spending. The accompanying NEWS feature highlights the impact of this multiplier process.

The marginal propensity to consume again reveals the power of the multiplier process. If the MPC is 0.75, the consumption of aerospace workers will drop by $75 billion when the government cutbacks reduce their income by $100 billion. (The rest of the income loss will be covered by a reduction in saving.)

From this point on the story should sound familiar. The $100 billion government cutback will ultimately reduce consumer spending by $300 billion. The total drop in spending is thus $400 billion. Like their mirror image, ***budget cuts have a multiplied effect on aggregate demand.*** The total impact is equal to

$$\text{Cumulative reduction in spending} = \text{multiplier} \times \text{initial budget cut}$$

This cumulative reduction in spending would eliminate excess aggregate demand. We conclude, then, that ***the budget cuts should equal the size of the desired fiscal restraint.***

Tax Hikes

Tax increases can also be used to shift the aggregate demand curve to the left. The direct effect of a tax increase is a reduction in disposable income. People will pay the higher taxes by reducing their consumption and depleting their savings. The reduced consumption results in less aggregate demand. As consumers tighten their belts, they set off the multiplier process, leading to a much larger cumulative shift of aggregate demand.

Economy Is Already Feeling the Impact of Federal Government's Spending Cuts

WASHINGTON—Skeptical about the federal government's pledge to tighten its belt? Consider this: It already has, and that's one reason the economy is so sluggish.

Federal purchases of goods and services dropped 3.3% in 1992, the first decline in three years and the largest in almost 20. Behind the decline were huge defense cutbacks: These purchases tumbled more than 6.0% during the year.

But nondefense purchases are showing signs of shrinking, too. For two years in a row their rate of increase has slowed, and in the second quarter of this year they actually fell 1.8%. . . .

The economy has felt the pinch. Kurl Karl of the WEFA Group, economic consultants based in suburban Philadelphia, estimates that cuts in purchases by the federal government knocked as much as 0.5 percentage point off the gross domestic product last year, costing roughly 400,000 jobs, and will probably do the same in 1993.

"Government cuts in defense spending have definitely been a drag" on the economy, says Jim O'Sullivan, economist with Morgan Guaranty in New York.

—Lucinda Harper

The Wall Street Journal, Aug. 18, 1993, p. A2. Reprinted by permission of *The Wall Street Journal,* © 1993 Dow Jones & Company, Inc. All Rights Reserved Worldwide. www.wsj.com

Analysis: Reductions in governmental spending on goods and services directly decrease aggregate demand. Multiplier effects induce additional cutbacks in consumption, further reducing aggregate demand.

Because people pay higher tax bills by reducing both consumption and saving (by MPC and MPS, respectively) *taxes must be increased more than a dollar to get a dollar of fiscal restraint.* This leads us to the following guideline:

$$\frac{\text{Desired increase}}{\text{in taxes}} = \frac{\text{desired fiscal restraint}}{\text{MPC}}$$

In other words, changes in taxes must always be larger than the desired change in leakages or injections. How much larger depends on the marginal propensity to consume. In this case

$$\frac{\text{Desired}}{\text{fiscal constraint}} = \frac{\text{excess AD}}{\text{the multiplier}}$$

$$= \frac{400 \text{ billion}}{4}$$

$$= 100 \text{ billion}$$

Therefore, the appropriate tax increase is

$$\frac{\text{Desired}}{\text{tax hike}} = \frac{\$100 \text{ billion}}{\text{MPC}}$$

$$= \frac{\$100 \text{ billion}}{0.75}$$

$$= \$133 \text{ billion}$$

Were taxes increased by this amount, consumers would reduce their consumption by $100 billion (= 0.75 × $133 billion). This cutback in consumption would set off the multiplier, leading to a cumulative reduction in spending of $400 billion. In Figure 11.6, aggregate demand would shift from AD_1 to AD_2.

Tax increases have been used to "cool" the economy on several occasions. In 1968, for example, the economy was rapidly approaching full employment and Vietnam War expenditures were helping to drive up prices. Congress respond by imposing a 10 percent surtax (temporary additional tax) on income, which took more than $10 billion in purchasing power away from consumers. Resultant multiplier effects reduced spending in 1969 over $20 billion and thus helped restrain price pressures.

In 1982 there was great concern that the 1981 tax cuts had been excessive and that inflation was emerging. To reduce that inflationary pressure, Congress withdrew some of its earlier tax cuts, especially those designed to increase investment spending. The net effect of the Tax Equity and Fiscal Responsibility Act of 1982 was to increase taxes roughly $90 billion for the years 1983 to 1985. This shifted aggregate demand leftward, thus reducing price-level pressures.

Reduced Transfers

The third option for fiscal restraint is to reduce transfer payments. *A cut in transfer payments works like a tax hike, reducing the disposable income of transfer recipients.* The appropriate size of the transfer cut can be computed exactly as the desired tax increase in the preceding formula.

Although transfer cuts have the same fiscal impact as a tax hike, they're seldom used. An outright cut in transfer payments has a direct and very visible impact on recipients, including the aged, the poor, the unemployed, and the disabled. Hence this policy option smacks of "balancing the budget on the backs of the poor." In practice, *absolute* cuts in transfer payments are rarely proposed. Instead, this lever is sometimes used to reduce the rate of increase in transfer benefits. This is what President Clinton and Senate Republicans had in mind in 1995 when they suggested that cost-of-living adjustments to future Social Security benefits might be reduced. This kind of policy also reduces inflationary pressures, but much more gradually.

FISCAL GUIDELINES

A Primer: Simple Rules

The essence of fiscal policy entails deliberate shifting of the aggregate demand curve. The steps required to formulate fiscal policy are straightforward:

- Specify the amount of the desired AD shift.
- Select the policy tools needed to induce the desired shift.

As we've seen, the fiscal policy toolbox contains a variety of tools for managing aggregate demand. When the economy is in a slump, the government can stimulate the economy with more government purchases, tax cuts, or an increase in transfer payments. When the economy is overheated, the government can reduce inflationary pressures by reducing government purchases, raising taxes, and cutting transfer payments. Table 11.2 summarizes the policy options and the desired use of each.

A Warning: Crowding Out

The fiscal policy guidelines in Table 11.2 are a useful guide. However, they neglect a critical dimension of fiscal policy. Notice that we haven't said anything about how the government is going to *finance* its expenditures. Suppose the government wanted to stimulate the economy with a $50 billion increase in federal purchases. How would it pay for those purchases? If the government raised taxes for this purpose, the fiscal stimulus would be largely offset by resultant declines in consumption and investment. If, instead, the government *borrows* the money from the private sector, less credit may be available to finance consumption and investment, again creating an offsetting reduction in private demand. In either case, government spending may "crowd out" some private expenditure. If this happens, some of the intended fiscal stimulus may be offset by the **crowding out** of private expenditure. We examine this possibility further in Chapter 12 when we look at the budget deficits and surpluses that accompany fiscal policy.

crowding out: A reduction in private-sector borrowing (and spending) caused by increased government borrowing.

Time Lags

Another limitation on fiscal policy is *time.* In the real world it takes time to recognize that the economy is in trouble. A blip in the unemployment or inflation rate may not signal a trend. Before intervening, we may want to be more certain that a recessionary

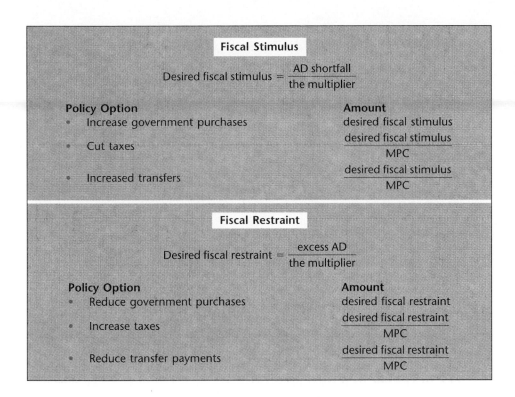

Fiscal Stimulus

$$\text{Desired fiscal stimulus} = \frac{\text{AD shortfall}}{\text{the multiplier}}$$

Policy Option	Amount
• Increase government purchases	desired fiscal stimulus
• Cut taxes	$\dfrac{\text{desired fiscal stimulus}}{\text{MPC}}$
• Increased transfers	$\dfrac{\text{desired fiscal stimulus}}{\text{MPC}}$

Fiscal Restraint

$$\text{Desired fiscal restraint} = \frac{\text{excess AD}}{\text{the multiplier}}$$

Policy Option	Amount
• Reduce government purchases	desired fiscal restraint
• Increase taxes	$\dfrac{\text{desired fiscal restraint}}{\text{MPC}}$
• Reduce transfer payments	$\dfrac{\text{desired fiscal restraint}}{\text{MPC}}$

TABLE 11.2
Fiscal Policy Primer

The goal of fiscal policy is to eliminate GDP gaps by shifting the AD curve rightward (to reduce unemployment) or leftward (to curb inflation). The desired shifts may be measured by the AD shortfall or the AD excess. In either case the desired fiscal initiative is equal to the desired shift divided by the multiplier. Once the size of the desired stimulus or restraint is known, the size of the appropriate policy options is easily calculated.

or inflationary gap is emerging. Then it will take time to develop a policy strategy and to get Congress to pass it. Once implemented, we'll have to wait for the many steps in the multiplier process to unfold. In the best of circumstances the fiscal policy rescue may not arrive for quite a while. In the meantime, the very nature of our macro problems could change if the economy is hit with other internal or external shocks.

Before putting too much faith in fiscal policy, we should also remember who designs and implements tax and spending initiatives: the U.S. Congress. Once a tax or spending plan arrives at the Capitol, politics take over. However urgent fiscal restraint might be, members of Congress are reluctant to sacrifice any spending projects in their own districts. And if taxes are to be cut, they want *their* constituents to get the biggest tax savings. And no one in Congress wants a tax hike or spending cut *before* the election. This kind of pork barrel politics can alter the content and timing of fiscal policy.

Pork Barrel Politics

CYBER NOTE

To review the latest budget data, go to the Congressional Budget Office at www.cbo.gov. CNN (www.cnn.com) is a good source for budget news.

THE ECONOMY TOMORROW

The guidelines for fiscal policy don't say anything about how the government spends its revenue or whom it taxes. The important thing is that the right amount of spending take place at the right time. In other words, insofar as our stabilization objectives are concerned, the content of total spending is of secondary interest; the level of spending is the only thing that counts.

But it does matter, of course, whether federal expenditures are devoted to military hardware, urban transit systems, or tennis courts. Our economic goals include not only full employment and price stability but also a desirable mix of output, an equitable distribution of income, and adequate economic growth. These other goals are directly affected by the content of total spending. The relative emphasis on, and sometimes exclusive concern for, stabilization objectives—to the neglect of related GDP content—has been designated by Joan Robinson as the "second crisis of economic theory." She explains:

The Concern for Content

The "Second Crisis"

For a liberal viewpoint of the content of federal spending, go to the Center on Budget and Policy Priorities at www.cbpp.org/the. For a conservative perspective, go to the National Center for Policy Analysis at www.public-policy.org/~ncpa.

The first crisis arose from the breakdown of a theory which could not account for the *level* of employment. The second crisis arises from a theory that cannot account for the *content* of employment.

Keynes was arguing against the dominant orthodoxy which held that government expenditure could not increase employment. He had to prove, first of all, that it could. He had to show that an increase in investment will increase consumption—that more wages will be spent on more beer and boots whether the investment is useful or not. He had to show that the secondary increase in real income [the multiplier effect] is quite independent of the object of the primary outlay. Pay men to dig holes in the ground and fill them up again if you cannot do anything else.

There was an enormous orthodox resistance to this idea. The whole weight of the argument had to be on this one obvious point.

The war was a sharp lesson in Keynesism. Orthodoxy could not stand up any longer. Government accepted the responsibility to maintain a high and stable level of employment. Then economists took over Keynes and erected the new orthodoxy. Once the point had been established, the question should have changed. Now that we all agree that government expenditure can maintain employment, we should argue about what the expenditure should be for. Keynes did not *want* anyone to dig holes and fill them.[1]

The alternatives to paying people for digging and filling holes in the ground are virtually endless. With over $1.8 trillion to spend each year, the federal government has great influence not only on prices and employment but also on the degree to which our other goals are fulfilled.

The kinds of expenditures and taxes that are appropriate at any given time depend on the values and perceived needs of society, and no structured blueprint can be provided in an economics textbook. We can, however, highlight two major issues.

Public vs. Private Spending

Fiscal policy can be directed toward private expenditure ($C + I$) or toward public expenditure (G). If G is increased, the public sector grows relative to the private sector. In this case, the government increases its influence over the dimensions of our economic and social welfare. If C and I are stimulated, the result will be exactly the opposite. The share of government purchases in total expenditure has actually risen dramatically over time, from only 2 percent in 1902 to 18 percent in the 1990s.

Whether one-fifth of total output is too much or too little depends on opportunity cost. A military force of 1.4 million men and women is "too big" from an economic perspective only if we value the forgone private production and consumption more highly than we value the added strength of our defenses. The government has gone "too far" if the highway it builds is less desired than the park and homes it implicitly replaced. In these and all cases, the assessment of bigness must come back to a comparison of what's given up with what's received.

There's also a question of individual freedom here. As the government share of output grows, there are fewer options for individual initiative. If people become more dependent on government for jobs, incomes, and goods and services, they also lose a degree of political freedom. Hence the choice of fiscal policy levers may affect the economy tomorrow in many different ways.

Output Mixes Within Each Sector

In addition to choosing whether to increase public or private spending, fiscal policy must also consider the specific content of spending within each sector. Suppose we determine that stimulation of the private sector is preferable to additional government spending as a means of promoting full employment. We still have many choices. We could, for example, cut corporate taxes, cut individual taxes, reduce excise taxes, or increase Social Security benefits. Each alternative implies a different mix of consumption and investment and a different distribution of income. When congressional Republicans proposed to cut the capital gains tax, for example, President Clinton objected that such a cut would unfairly benefit wealthy taxpayers. He preferred a tax cut that

[1]From "The Second Crisis of Economic Theory," by Joan Robinson, *American Economic Review,* May 1972, p. 6. Used by permission of American Economic Association.

Budget Highlights

Here are some of the major items in the $500 billion spending measure for fiscal 1999:

- **Education:** $1.1 billion to help local school districts hire teachers to reduce class size.
- **Agriculture:** $6 billion emergency package to help farmers hurt by low crop prices.
- **Emergency spending:** $20 billion in all for so-called emergencies, including the agriculture aid and $7.9 billion for the military. Funds also would help upgrade government computers for the year 2000, deal with storm damage and beef up security for embassies and other federal buildings.
- **Taxes:** $9.2 billion worth of tax credits for businesspeople, the self-employed and farmers extended.

- **IMF:** $17.9 billion for the International Monetary Fund, at the president's request. Republicans won language to ensure future IMF loans would be more open to public scrutiny.
- **Drugs:** $690 million in emergency spending for the interdiction of illicit drugs, a GOP proposal.
- **Congress:** $100 million to build a visitors center at the Capitol.
- **Medical research:** A 14%, $1.9 billion increase for the National Institutes of Health for research into diabetes, cancer, genetic medicine and AIDS.
- **Global warming:** A 25% increase, to more than $1 billion, to fight global warming.

USA Today, Oct. 16, 1998, p. 6A. Copyright 1998 USA TODAY. Reprinted with permission. www.usatoday.com

Analysis: A $500 billion budget can significantly alter the content of output. These are only nine specific items from the 1600-page 1999 budget.

would benefit the average worker. As President Clinton saw it, the same amount of economic stimulus could be achieved with very different distributional consequences.

The 1997 tax credit for children (see NEWS page 215) likewise wasn't just a response to the level of spending; it was also viewed as a mechanism for strengthening *family* ties. Indeed, in the Republican party's Contract with America, the child tax credit proposal was part of "The American Dream Restoration Act." The child-based tax credit was seen as a mechanism for achieving *social* as well as macroeconomic goals.

The content of public-sector spending can also be altered to pursue multiple goals. Once an appropriate level of government spending is chosen, we still have to decide what to spend it on. Defense spending was reduced sharply when the Cold War ended. That didn't reduce government expenditure, however. On the contrary, Congress found lots of ways to spend the so-called peace dividend. The 1999 federal budget included over 1600 pages of specific spending items, a few of which are noted in the NEWS above. Any such changes in the *mix* of output—not just the *level* of output—will affect the quality of life in the economy tomorrow.

SUMMARY

- The Keynesian explanation of macro instability requires government intervention to shift the aggregate demand curve to achieve the desired rate of output. Fiscal policy refers to the use of the government's tax and spending powers to achieve desired macro outcomes.

- Options for fiscal stimulus include increasing government purchases, reducing taxes, and raising income transfers.
- Fiscal restraint may originate in reductions in government purchases, increases in taxes, or cuts in income transfers.

- Government purchases add directly to aggregate demand; taxes and transfers have an indirect effect by inducing changes in consumption and investment. This makes changes in government spending more powerful per dollar than changes in taxes or transfers.
- Fiscal policy initiatives have a multiplied impact on total spending and output. An increase in government spending, for example, will result in more disposable income, which will be used to finance further consumer spending.

- The objective of fiscal policy is to close GDP gaps. To do this, the aggregate demand curve must shift by more than the size of the GDP gap to compensate for changing price levels. The desired shift is equal to the aggregate demand shortfall (or excess).
- Changes in government spending and taxes alter the content of GDP and thus influence what to produce. Fiscal policy affects the relative size of the public and private sectors as well as the mix of output in each sector.

Key Terms

aggregate demand	aggregate supply	fiscal restraint
income transfer	AD shortfall	AD excess
fiscal policy	multiplier	crowding out
equilibrium (macro)	marginal propensity to consume	
GDP gap (real)	(MPC)	
fiscal stimulus	disposable income	

Questions for Discussion

1. How can you tell if the economy is in equilibrium? How could you estimate the GDP gap?
2. Will an extra $20 billion per year spent on housing have the same impact on the economy as an extra $20 billion spent on interstate highways? Explain.
3. What happens to aggregate demand when transfer payments and the taxes to pay them both rise?
4. What other fiscal actions might have the same impact as the child tax credit? (See NEWS page 215.)
5. Will consumers always spend the same percentage of any tax cut? Why might they spend more or less than usual?
6. How does the slope of the AS curve affect the size of the AD shortfall? If the AS curve were horizontal, how large would the AD shortfall be in Figure 11.3?

7. Web Activity Look at the tax cut of 1981 and the Tax Relief Act of 1987 at www.cbo.gov/showdoc.cfm?index=1049sequence=0&from=5. What was the purpose of both tax changes? Were the tax policies designed to be countercyclical fiscal policies?
8. Web Activity The U.S. federal budget is the focal point for debate on the role of government. Identify a liberal argument in favor of increased government spending at the Center on Budget and Policy Priorities at www.cbpp.org/the. Identify a conservative argument against increased government spending at the National Center for Policy Analysis at www.public-org/~ncpa. For each side, give one possible counterargument to the position taken.

Problems for Chapter 11 appear at the back of the book.

Deficits, Surpluses, and Debt

The news was startling: Congress had actually balanced the federal budget. The year was 1998—a pivotal year in the history of the budget because it was the first year in a generation that the federal government had spent less money than it took in. In a White House ceremony celebrating that milestone, President Clinton hailed the budget *surplus* as one of his administration's greatest achievements. Newt Gingrich, then the Speaker of the U.S. House of Representatives, also lauded the surplus but asserted that the Republican-led Congress, not President Clinton, deserved credit for holding the line on government spending.

But the really amazing thing about the budget surplus was that hardly anyone outside Washington paid much attention. The financial markets didn't get excited, and the general public yawned at the news. How could this be? For decades the public had clamored for balanced budgets. Every year the "federal deficit" was cited in public opinion polls as one of the country's most urgent economic problems; 9 out of 10 Americans had even said they favored amending the Constitution to *require* Congress to balance the budget every year. In 1997, that proposal came within one vote of passing the U.S. Senate.

So why all the yawns? Did the public decide that Uncle Sam's budget balance wasn't really all that important? Were they disappointed that the economic landscape hadn't changed all that much when the budget surplus was attained? Had the evils of a budget deficit been exaggerated?

In this chapter we look closer at how government spending is *financed*. What happens to the budget balance when the budget is used as a policy lever to expand or contract the economy? What effect, if any, does a resulting deficit or surplus have on the economy? Should we applaud a surplus? Fear a deficit? To answer these questions we focus on three issues:

- How do deficits and surpluses arise?
- What harm (good) do deficits (surpluses) cause?
- Who will pay off the accumulated national debt?

As we'll see, the answers to these questions add another dimension to fiscal policy debates.

U.S. Deficits Not Unusually Large

Although the U.S. budget deficits receive the most attention, deficit spending is a common feature of fiscal policy. As these figures reveal, New Zealand was the only major country that had a budget surplus in 1995; other countries had budget deficits that were at least as large, in relation to GDP, as that of the United States.

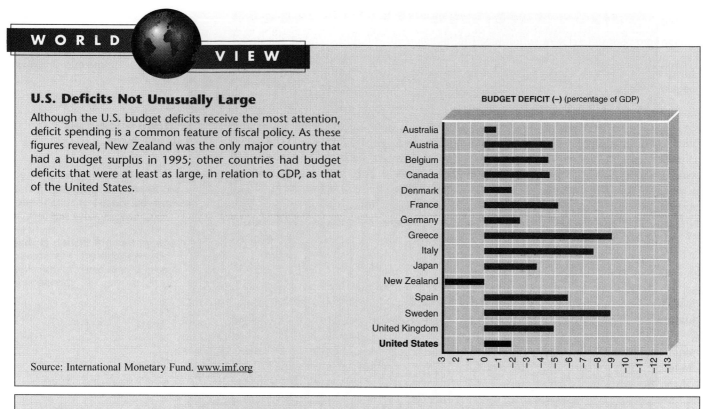

BUDGET DEFICIT (–) (percentage of GDP)

Source: International Monetary Fund. www.imf.org

Analysis: To compare U.S. deficits to those of other industrialized countries, we must adjust for differences in size by forming the *ratio* of deficits to GDP. By this measure, U.S. deficits haven't been that large.

---

fiscal year (FY): The 12-month period used for accounting purposes; begins October 1 for the federal government.

At the beginning of each year, the president and Congress put together a budget blueprint for the next **fiscal year (FY).** They don't start from scratch, however. Most budget line items reflect commitments made in earlier years. In FY 1998, for example, the federal budget included $376 billion in Social Security benefits. The FY 1998 budget also provided for $21 billion in veterans benefits, $244 billion for interest payments on the national debt, and many billions more for completion of projects begun in previous years. Short of repudiating all prior commitments, there's little that Congress or the president can do to alter these expenditures in any given year. *To a large extent, current revenues and expenditures are the result of decisions made in prior years.* In this sense, much of each year's budget is considered "uncontrollable."

discretionary fiscal spending: Those elements of the federal budget not determined by past legislative or executive commitments.

At present, uncontrollables account for roughly 80 percent of the federal budget. This leaves only 20 percent for **discretionary fiscal spending**—that is, spending decisions not "locked in" by prior legislative commitments. In recent years, rising interest payments and increasing entitlements (Social Security, Medicare, civil service pensions, etc.) have reduced the discretionary share of the budget even further. This doesn't mean that discretionary fiscal policy is no longer important; it simply means that the potential for *changing* budget outlays is much smaller than it might first appear. Yet, the ability to *change* tax or spending levels is the force behind Keynesian fiscal policy. Recall that deliberate changes in government spending or taxes are the essence of **fiscal restraint** and **fiscal stimulus.** If most of the budget is uncontrollable, those policy levers are less effective.

fiscal restraint: Tax hikes or spending cuts intended to reduce (shift) aggregate demand.
fiscal stimulus: Tax cuts or spending hikes intended to increase (shift) aggregate demand.

Automatic Stabilizers. Most of the uncontrollable line items in the federal budget have another characteristic that directly affects budget deficits: their value *changes* with economic conditions. Consider unemployment insurance benefits. The unemployment insurance program, established in 1935, provides that persons who lose their jobs will receive some income (an average of $197 per week) from the government (see Chapter 6). The law establishes the *entitlement* to unemployment benefits but not the amount to be spent in any year. Each year's expenditure depends on how many workers lose their jobs and qualify for benefits. In 1991, for example, outlays for unemployment benefits increased by $8 billion. That increase in federal spending wasn't the result of any new policy decisions. Spending went up simply because more workers lost their jobs in the 1990–1991 recession. The spending increase was *automatic,* not *discretionary.*

Welfare benefits also increased by $5 billion in 1991. This increase in spending also occurred automatically in response to changing economic conditions. As more people lost jobs and used up their savings, they turned to welfare for help. They were *entitled* to welfare benefits according to eligibility rules already written; no new congressional or executive action was required to approve this increase in government spending.

Notice that outlays for unemployment compensation and welfare benefits increase when the economy goes into recession. This is exactly the kind of fiscal policy that Keynes advocated. The increase in **income transfers** helps offset the income losses due to recession. These increased transfers therefore act as **automatic stabilizers**—injecting new spending into the circular flow during economic contractions. Conversely, transfer payments decline when the economy is expanding and fewer people qualify for unemployment or welfare benefits. Hence, no one has to pull the fiscal policy lever to inject more or less entitlement spending into the circular flow; much of it happens automatically.

Automatic stabilizers also exist on the revenue side of the federal budget. Income taxes constitute an important stabilizer because they move up and down with the value of spending and output. As we've observed, if household incomes increase, a jump in consumer spending is likely to follow. The resultant multiplier effects might create some demand-pull inflation. The tax code lessens this inflationary pressure. When you get more income, you have to pay more taxes. Hence, income taxes siphon off some of the increased purchasing power that might have found its way to product markets. Progressive income taxes are particularly effective stabilizers, as they siphon off increasing proportions of purchasing power when incomes are rising and decreasing proportions when aggregate demand and output are falling.

Automatic stabilizers imply that policymakers don't have total control of each year's budget. On the contrary, ***the size of the federal deficit is sensitive to expansion and contraction of the macro economy.***

Table 12.2 shows just how sensitive the budget is to cyclical forces. When the unemployment rate rises 1 percent, tax revenues decline $37 billion. As the economy slows, people also turn to the government for additional income support: Unemployment benefits and other transfer payments increase by $5 billion. As a consequence, the budget deficit widens by $42 billion.

Inflation also affects the budget deficit. Because Social Security benefits are automatically adjusted to inflation, federal outlays increase as the price level rises. This added expenditure is offset, however, by inflation-swollen tax receipts. Both Social Security payroll taxes and corporate profit taxes rise automatically with inflation. These offsetting expenditure and revenue effects almost cancel out each other: Table 12.2 shows that a 1-point increase in the inflation rate *shrinks* the deficit by only $4 billion.

The most important implication of Table 12.2 is that neither the president nor the Congress has complete control of the federal deficit. ***Actual budget deficits and surpluses may arise from economic conditions as well as policy.*** Perhaps no one learned this better than President Reagan. In 1980 he campaigned on a promise to balance the budget. The 1981–1982 recession, however, caused the actual deficit to soar. The president later had to admit that actual deficits aren't solely the product of "big spenders" in Washington.

income transfers: Payments to individuals for which no current goods or services are exchanged, such as Social Security, welfare, unemployment benefits.

automatic stabilizer: Federal expenditure or revenue item that automatically responds countercyclically to changes in national income, like unemployment benefits, income taxes.

Cyclical Deficits

IN THE NEWS

Fiscal Policy in the Great Depression

In 1931 President Herbert Hoover observed, "Business depressions have been recurrent in the life of our country and are but transitory." Rather than proposing fiscal stimulus, Hoover complained that expansion of public-works programs had unbalanced the federal budget. In 1932 he proposed *cutbacks* in government spending and *higher* taxes. In his view, the "unquestioned balancing of the federal budget . . . is the first necessity of national stability and is the foundation of further recovery."

Franklin Roosevelt shared this view of fiscal policy. He criticized Hoover for not balancing the budget, and in 1933, warned Congress that "all public works must be considered from the point of view of the ability of the government treasury to pay for them."

As the accompanying figure shows, the budget deficit persisted throughout the Great Depression. But these deficits were the result of a declining economy, not stimulative fiscal policy. The structural deficit actually *decreased* from 1931 to 1933 (see figure), thereby restraining aggregate spending at a time when producers were desperate for increasing sales. Only when the structural deficit was expanded tremendously by spending during World War II did fiscal policy have a decidedly positive effect. Federal defense expenditures jumped from $2.2 billion in 1940 to $87.4 billion in 1944!

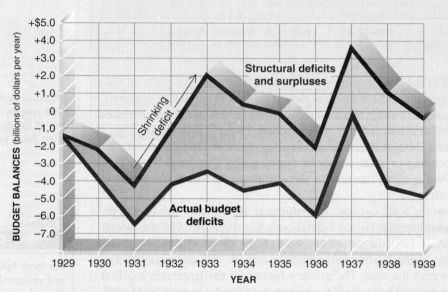

Source: Adapted from E. Cary Brown, "Fiscal Policy in the Thirties: A Reappraisal," *American Economic Review,* Dec. 1956, Table 1. Used by permission of American Economic Association.

Analysis: From 1931 to 1933, the structural deficit decreased from $4.5 billion to a $2 billion *surplus*. This fiscal restraint reduced aggregate demand and deepened the Great Depression.

ECONOMIC EFFECTS OF DEFICITS

No matter what the origins of budget deficits, most people are alarmed by them. Should they be? What are the *consequences* of budget deficits?

Crowding Out

crowding out: A reduction in private-sector borrowing (and spending) caused by increased government borrowing.

We've already encountered one potential consequence of deficit financing: *If the government borrows funds to finance deficits, the availability of funds for private-sector spending may be reduced.* This is the **crowding-out** problem first noted in Chapter 11. If crowding out occurs, the increase in government expenditure will be at least partially offset by reductions in consumption and investment.

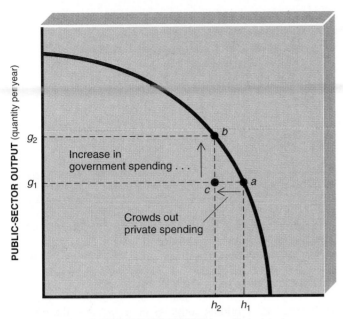

FIGURE 12.2
Crowding Out

If the economy is fully employed, an increase in public-sector expenditure (output) will reduce private-sector expenditure (output). In this case a deficit-financed increase in government expenditure moves the economy from point *a* to point *b*. In the process the quantity $h_1 - h_2$ of private-sector output is crowded out to make room for the increase in public-sector output (from g_1 to g_2). If the economy started at point *c*, however, with unemployed resources, crowding out need not occur.

If the economy were at full employment, crowding out would be inevitable. At full employment, we'd be on the production possibilities curve, using all available resources. As Figure 12.2 reminds us, additional government purchases can occur only if private-sector purchases are reduced. In real terms, ***crowding out implies less private-sector output.***

Crowding out is complete only if the economy is at full employment. If the economy is in recession, it's possible to get more public-sector output (like highways, schools, defense) without cutbacks in private-sector output. This possibility is illustrated by the move from point *c* to point *b* in Figure 12.2.

What Figure 12.2 emphasizes is that ***the risk of crowding out is greater the closer the economy is to full employment.*** This implies that deficits are less appropriate at high levels of employment but less worrisome at low levels of employment, which is consistent with the Keynesian notion of using fiscal restraint when inflationary pressures rise.

Even if crowding out does occur, that doesn't mean that deficits are necessarily too big. Crowding out simply reminds us that there's an **opportunity cost** to government spending. We still have to decide whether the private-sector output crowded out by government expenditure is more or less desirable than the increased public-sector output. The deficits of the 1980s financed a substantial military buildup and an increase in private consumption. Private investment spending stagnated, however. Hence the deficits were desirable only if the resulting change in the mix of output was itself desired.

President Clinton agreed that deficit reduction was desirable. He also, however, defended government expenditure on education, training, and infrastructure as public "investment." He believed crowding out wasn't necessarily an unwelcome outcome, especially if the government expenditures were well targeted.

Opportunity Cost

opportunity cost: The most desired goods or services that are forgone in order to obtain something else.

ECONOMIC EFFECTS OF SURPLUSES

The economic effects of budget *surpluses* are the mirror image of those for deficits.

When the government takes in more revenue than it spends, it adds to leakage in the circular flow. But Uncle Sam doesn't hide the surplus under a mattress. And the sums involved (such as $70 billion in 1998) are too large to put in a bank. Were the

Crowding In

government to buy corporate stock with the budget surplus, it would effectively be nationalizing private enterprises. So where does the surplus go?

There are really only four potential uses for a budget surplus, namely,

- **Cut taxes**
- **Increase income transfers**
- **Save it (pay down after debt)**
- **Spend it**

IN THE NEWS

Clinton Surplus Plan Seeks to Trim Debt

WASHINGTON—President Clinton's State of the Union address last night was an attempt to define how Congress should use mounting budget surpluses for years to come. His declared goal: save most of the funds to pay down the national debt, not for higher spending or tax cuts.

Many economists endorse the idea, saying it would boost America's savings rate and raise long-term growth prospects. But Mr. Clinton's ability to accomplish that goal depends on a few big "ifs."

Will the new rosy forecasts for huge budget surpluses materialize? And if so, will politicians really have the discipline to let them accumulate in the trust funds instead of spending them on popular programs, sweeter benefits or always-welcome tax cuts?

Skepticism abounds. "I consider the possibility quite remote that the government can run a surplus of trillions of dollars for decades without using it to increase benefits or for other things," said Stanford University Prof. Michael Boskin, President Bush's former top economist. "I worry that there will be unbelievable pressure to spend it."

The debt reduction is linked with Mr. Clinton's broader strategy of shoring up Social Security and Medicare. In his speech, he endorsed locking up in the trust funds for the two entitlement programs about three-quarters of the roughly $4.5 trillion in the federal budget surpluses projected over the next 15 years. As a result, the government's overall borrowing from the public would be reduced by that amount.

Tax Cuts Not Targeted

Only about one-tenth of those surpluses would be used for higher spending on defense, education and the like. None would go to big tax cuts.

—Jacob M. Schlesinger

The Wall Street Journal, Jan. 20, 1999, p. A2. Reprinted by permission of *The Wall Street Journal*, © 1999 Dow Jones & Company, Inc. All Rights Reserved Worldwide. www.wsj.com

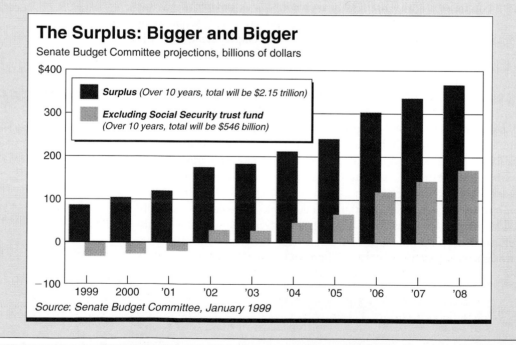

The Surplus: Bigger and Bigger

Senate Budget Committee projections, billions of dollars

■ **Surplus** *(Over 10 years, total will be $2.15 trillion)*

▨ **Excluding Social Security trust fund**
(Over 10 years, total will be $546 billion)

Source: Senate Budget Committee, January 1999

Analysis: A budget surplus must be spent, given back in tax relief, or used to repay national debt. Paying down debt now makes it potentially easier to finance future outlays, including Social Security benefits.

The first two options effectively wipe out the surplus by changing budget outlays or receipts. In either case, taxpayers end up with more disposable income, enabling them to purchase more goods and services, thus changing the public-private mix of output.

The third option ("save it") entails paying back accumulated debt. This has a similar but less direct **crowding-in** effect. If Uncle Sam pays off some of his accumulated debt, households that were holding that debt will end up with more money. If they use that money to buy goods and services, then private-sector output will expand.

Even people who haven't lent any money to Uncle Sam will benefit from the debt reduction. When the government reduces its level of borrowing, it takes pressure off market interest rates. As interest rates drop, consumers will be more willing and able to purchase big-ticket items such as cars, appliances, and houses, thus changing the mix of output in favor of private-sector production.

The fourth option, simply spending the surplus on government-purchased goods and services, wipes out the surplus and enlarges the relative size of government.

Taxpayers usually favor the first option: tax cuts. Just prior to the 1998 elections, that's exactly what the Republican-led Congress proposed. To head off that proposal, President Clinton insisted that Congress "save Social Security first" (see NEWS). This seemed to suggest that Congress could somehow "bank" the surplus until the Social Security fund begins to run short of funds (about the year 2013). In reality, saving Social Security would amount to using the surplus to pay off some of the national debt.

Like crowding out, the extent of crowding in depends on the state of the economy. In a recession, a surplus-induced decline in interest rates isn't likely to stimulate much spending. If consumer and investor confidence are low, even a surplus-financed tax cut might not lift private-sector spending much.

crowding in: An increase in private-sector borrowing (and spending) caused by decreased government borrowing.

Cyclical Sensitivity

THE ACCUMULATION OF DEBT

Deficit financing isn't a new phenomenon in U.S. politics. On the contrary, the United States started out in debt. The Continental Congress needed to borrow money in 1777 to continue fighting the Revolutionary War. The Congress tried to raise tax revenues and even printed new money (the Continental dollar) in order to buy needed food, tents, guns, and ammunition. But by the winter of 1777, these mechanisms for financing the war were failing. To acquire needed supplies, the Continental Congress plunged the new nation into debt.

As with today's deficits, the Continental Congress acknowledged its loans by issuing bonds. Today the U.S. Treasury is the fiscal agent of the U.S. government. The Treasury collects tax revenues, signs checks for federal spending, and—when necessary—borrows funds to cover budget deficits. When the Treasury borrows funds, it issues **Treasury bonds;** these are IOUs of the federal government. People buy bonds—lend money to the U.S. Treasury—because bonds pay interest and are a very safe haven for idle funds.

The total stock of all outstanding bonds represents the **national debt.** It's equal to the sum total of our accumulated deficits, less net repayments in years when a budget surplus existed. In other words, *the national debt is a stock of IOUs created by annual deficit flows.* Whenever there's a budget deficit, the national debt increases. In years when a budget surplus exists, the national debt can be pared down.

The United States began accumulating debt as soon as independence was declared. By 1783, the United States had borrowed over $8 million from France and $250,000 from Spain. Most of these funds were secretly obtained to help finance the Revolutionary War.

During the period 1790–1812, the United States often incurred debt but typically repaid it quickly. The War of 1812, however, caused a massive increase in the national debt. With neither a standing army nor an adequate source of tax revenues to acquire one, the U.S. government had to borrow money to repel the British. By 1816 the

Debt Creation

Treasury bonds: Promissory notes (IOUs) issued by the U.S. Treasury.

national debt: Accumulated debt of the federal government.

Early History, 1776–1900

national debt was over $129 million. Although that figure seems tiny by today's standards, it amounted to 13 percent of national income in 1816.

1835–1836: Debt-Free! After the War of 1812, the U.S. government used recurrent budget surpluses to repay its debt. These surpluses were so frequent that the U.S. government was completely out of debt by 1835. In 1835 and again in 1836, the government had neither national debt nor a budget deficit. The dilemma in those years was how to use the budget *surplus!* Since there was no accumulated debt, the option of using the surplus to reduce the debt didn't exist. In the end, Congress decided simply to distribute the surplus funds to the states. That was the last time the U.S. government was completely out of debt.

The Mexican-American War (1846–1848) necessitated a sudden increase in federal spending. The deficits incurred to fight that war caused a fourfold increase in the debt. That debt was pared down the following decade. Then the Civil War (1861–1865) broke out, and both sides needed debt financing. By the end of the Civil War the North owed over $2.6 billion, or approximately half its national income. The South depended more heavily on newly printed Confederate currency to finance its side of the Civil War, relying on bond issues for only one-third of its financial needs. When the South lost, however, neither Confederate currency nor Confederate bonds had any value.[2]

The Twentieth Century

The Spanish-American War (1898) also increased the national debt. But all prior debt was dwarfed by World War I, which increased the national debt from 3 percent of national income in 1917 to 41 percent at the war's end.

The national debt declined during the 1920s because the federal government was consistently spending less revenue than it took in. Budget surpluses disappeared quickly when the economy fell into the Great Depression, however, and the cyclical deficit widened (see NEWS, "Fiscal Policy during the Great Depression").

World War II. The most explosive jump in the national debt occurred during World War II, when the government had to mobilize all available resources. Rather than raise taxes to the fullest, the U.S. government restricted the availability of consumer goods. With consumer goods rationed, consumers had little choice but to increase their saving. Uncle Sam encouraged people to lend their idle funds to the U.S. Treasury by buying U.S. war bonds. The resulting bond purchases raised the national debt from 45 percent of GDP in 1940 to over 125 percent of GDP in 1946 (see Figure 12.3).

The Korean War (1950–1953) added little to the national debt. The Vietnam War (1965–1972), however, increased the debt by over $100 billion, largely owing to the refusal of President Lyndon Johnson or Congress to raise taxes to pay for that war (see Chapter 19).

The 1980s. During the 1980s the national debt jumped again—by nearly $2 *trillion.* This 10-year increase in the debt exceeded all the net debt accumulation since the country was founded. This time, however, the debt increase wasn't war-related. Instead, the debt explosion of the 1980s originated in recessions (1980–1982 and 1990–1991) and massive tax cuts (1981–1984). The recessions caused big jumps in the cyclical deficit while the Reagan tax cuts and military buildup caused the structural deficit to jump fourfold in only 4 years (1982–1986). The combination of the cyclical and structural forces caused huge annual deficits (see Table 12.3) that tripled the national debt in a single decade (Table 12.4).

---

[2]In anticipation of this situation, European leaders had forced the South to guarantee most of its loans with cotton. When the South was unable to repay its debts, these creditors could sell the cotton they had held as collateral. But most holders of Confederate bonds or currency received nothing.

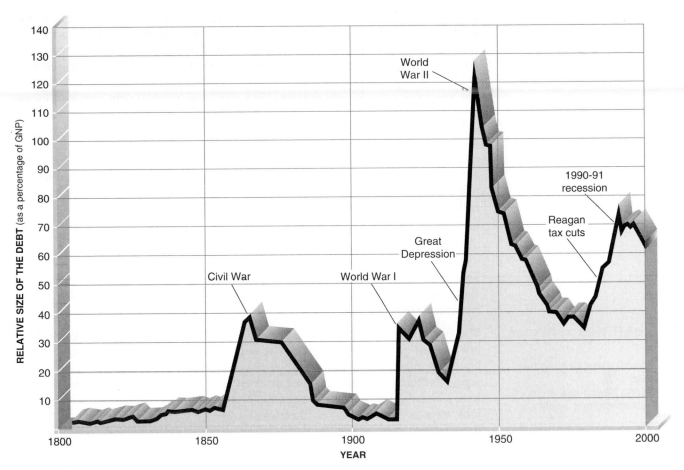

FIGURE 12.3
Historical View of the Debt/GDP Ratio

From 1790 to 1917, the national debt exceeded 10 percent of GDP only during the Civil War years. After 1917, however, the debt ratio grew sharply. World War I, the Great Depression, and World War II all caused major increases in the debt ratio. The tax cuts of 1981–1984 caused a further increase in the debt/GDP ratio.

Source: Office of Management and Budget.

Year	Total Debt Outstanding (millions of dollars)	Year	Total Debt Outstanding (millions of dollars)
1791	75	1920	24,299
1800	83	1930	16,185
1810	53	1940	42,967
1816	127	1945	258,682
1820	91	1960	286,331
1835	0	1970	370,919
1850	63	1980	914,300
1865	2678	1985	1,827,500
1890	1122	1990	3,163,000
1900	1263	1995	5,076,000
1915	1191	1999	5,594,000

Source: Office of Management and Budget.

TABLE 12.4
The Mounting Debt

It took nearly a century for the national debt to reach $1 trillion. Then the debt tripled in a mere decade. By 1996 the accumulated debt exceeded $5 trillion.

The 1990s. The early 1990s continued the same trend. Discretionary federal spending increased sharply in the first 2 years of the Bush administration. The federal government was also forced to bail out hundreds of failed savings and loan associations. Although taxes were raised a bit and military spending was cut back, the structural deficit was little changed. Then the recession of 1990–1991 killed any chance of achieving smaller deficits. In only 4 years (1988–1992) the national debt increased by another $1 trillion.

In 1993 the Clinton administration persuaded Congress to raise taxes, thereby reducing the structural deficit. Continuing recovery from the 1990–1991 recession also reduced the cyclical deficit (see Table 12.3). Nevertheless, the budget deficits of 1993–1996 pushed the national debt to over $5 trillion. After a couple of years of budget surplus, the accumulated debt still exceeded $5 trillion in 1999, which works out to nearly $20,000 of debt for every American citizen.

WHO OWNS THE DEBT?

To the average citizen, the accumulated national debt is both incomprehensible and frightening. Who can understand debts that are measured in *trillions* of dollars? Who can ever be expected to pay them?

Liabilities = Assets

liability: An obligation to make future payment; debt.
asset: Anything having exchange value in the marketplace; wealth.

The first thing to note about the national debt is that it represents not only a liability but an asset as well. When the U.S. Treasury borrows money, it issues bonds. Those bonds are a **liability** for the federal government since it then has a later obligation to repay. But those same bonds are an **asset** to the people who hold them. Bondholders have a claim to future repayment and can even convert that claim into cash by selling their asset in the bond market. Therefore, *national debt creates as much wealth (for bondholders) as liabilities (for the U.S. Treasury).* Neither money nor any other form of wealth disappears when the government borrows money.

The fact that total bond assets equal total bond liabilities is of little consolation to taxpayers confronted with $5 trillion of national debt and worry when, if ever, they'll be able to repay it. The fear that either the U.S. government or its taxpayers will be "bankrupted" by the national debt always lurks in the shadows. How legitimate is that fear?

Ownership of the Debt

Figure 12.4 shows who owns the bonds the U.S. Treasury has issued. One of the largest bondholders is the U.S. government itself: *Federal agencies hold roughly 50 percent of all outstanding Treasury bonds.* The Federal Reserve System, an independent agency of the U.S. government, acquires Treasury bonds in its conduct of monetary policy (see Chapters 14 and 15). Other agencies of the U.S. government also purchase bonds. The Social Security Administration, for example, maintains a trust fund balance to cover any shortfall between monthly payroll tax receipts and retirement benefits. Most of that balance is held in the form of interest-bearing Treasury bonds. Thus one arm of the federal government (the U.S. Treasury) owes another arm (the U.S. Social Security Administration) a significant part of the national debt. Because Social Security has been accumulating huge annual reserves in recent years, it's now the largest holder of the national debt.[3]

State and local governments hold another 8 percent of the national debt. This debt, too, arises when state and local governments use their own budget surpluses to purchase interest-bearing Treasury bonds.

The general public owns *directly* only about 7 percent of the national debt. This private wealth is in the form of familiar U.S. savings bonds or other types of Treasury bonds. Even more private wealth is held *indirectly*. As Figure 12.4 shows, over 23 per-

[3]Beginning in the year 2013, the flow of Social Security funds will reverse, with annual benefit outlays exceeding payroll tax revenues. This will require the U.S. Treasury to start repaying the debt held by the Social Security Trust Fund. To do that, the federal government will have to increase other taxes or reduce other spending.

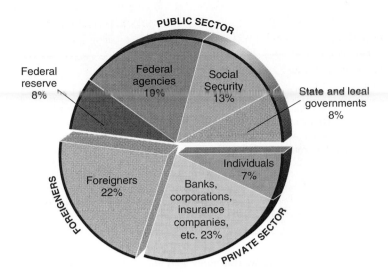

PUBLIC SECTOR

Federal
reserve
8%

Federal
agencies
19%

Social
Security
13%

State and local
governments
8%

Individuals
7%

Foreigners
22%

Banks,
corporations,
insurance
companies,
etc. 23%

FOREIGNERS

PRIVATE SECTOR

cent of the national debt is held by banks, insurance companies, money-market funds, corporations, and other institutions. All this wealth is ultimately owned by the people who have deposits at the bank or in money market funds, who own stock in corporations, or who are insured by companies that hold Treasury bonds. Thus *U.S. households hold almost one-third of the national debt, either directly or indirectly.*

All the debt held by U.S. households, institutions, and government entities is referred to as **internal debt.** As Figure 12.4 illustrates, approximately 78 percent of the national debt is internal. In other words, we owe most of the national debt to ourselves.

The remaining 22 percent of the national debt is held by foreign banks, corporations, households, and governments. U.S. Treasury bonds are attractive to global participants because of their relative security, the interest they pay, and the general acceptability of dollar-denominated assets in world trade. All the bonds held by foreign households and institutions is referred to as **external debt.**

internal debt: U.S. government debt (Treasury bonds) held by U.S. households and institutions.

external debt: U.S. government debt (Treasury bonds) held by foreign households and institutions.

BURDEN OF THE DEBT

It may be comforting to know that most of our national debt is owned internally, and much of it by the government itself. Figure 12.4 won't still the fears of most taxpayers, however, especially those who don't hold any Treasury bonds. From their perspective, the total debt still looks frightening.

How much of a "burden" the debt really represents isn't so evident. There's been almost no reduction in the national debt since you were born. As we've observed in most years the federal government has borrowed *more* money to finance deficits, adding to the debt. Prior to 1998, the last year in which the federal government reduced the national debt—that is, paid some of it off—was 1957, and that lone repayment reduced the total debt by less than a billion dollars. Since then, as debts have become due, the federal government has simply borrowed new funds to pay them off. New bonds have been issued to replace old bonds. This **refinancing** of the debt is a routine feature of the U.S. Treasury's debt management (see NEWS next page).

The ability of the U.S. Treasury to refinance its debt raises an intriguing question. What if the debt could be eternally refinanced? What if no one *ever* demanded to be "paid off" more than others were willing to lend Uncle Sam? Then the national debt would truly grow forever.

Two things are worrisome about this scenario. First, eternal refinancing seems like a chain letter that promises to make everyone rich. In this case, the chain requires that

Refinancing

refinancing: The issuance of new debt in payment of debt issued earlier.

IN THE NEWS

News: Analysis

Treasury to Raise Cash with Sale of $9 Billion in Forty-Two-Day Bills

WASHINGTON—The Treasury says it will sell about $9 billion in 42-day cash-management bills today to raise all new cash.

In addition, the department said it will raise $1.48 billion in new cash in its regular weekly bill offering Monday by selling about $27.0 billion in short-term bills to redeem $25.53 billion in maturing bills.

The minimum denomination for the cash-management bills is $10 million. Non-competitive bids must be received by noon EST today at Federal Reserve banks or branches. Competitive tenders must be received by 1 P.M. EST.

The Wall Street Journal, Mar. 13, 1996. p. C20. Reprinted by permission of *The Wall Street Journal*, © 1996 Dow, Jones & Company, Inc. All Rights Reserved Worldwide. www.wsj.com

Analysis: When debt obligations become due, the Treasury "refinances" them by issuing new bonds and notes. Using this process, the Treasury is always paying off old debt but incurring new debt.

people hold ever-larger portions of their wealth in the form of Treasury bonds. People worry that the chain will be broken and that they'll be forced to repay all the outstanding debt. Parents worry that the scheme might break down in the next generation, unfairly burdening their own children or grandchildren.

Aside from its seeming implausibility, the notion of eternal refinancing seems to defy a basic maxim of economics, namely, that "there ain't no free lunch." Eternal refinancing makes it look as though government borrowing has no cost, as though federal spending financed by the national debt is really a free lunch.

There are two flaws in this way of thinking. The first relates to the interest charges that accompany debt. The second, and more important, oversight relates to the real economic costs of government activity.

Debt Service

debt service: The interest required to be paid each year on outstanding debt.

With over $5 trillion in accumulated debt, the U.S. government must make enormous interest payments every year. **Debt service** refers to these annual interest payments. In FY 1999, the U.S. Treasury paid nearly $240 billion in interest charges. These interest payments are a large and "uncontrollable" component of the federal budget. As such, they force the government to reduce outlays for other purposes or to finance a larger budget each year. In this respect, *interest payments restrict the government's ability to balance the budget or fund other public-sector activities.*

Although the debt-servicing requirements may pinch Uncle Sam's spending purse, the real economic consequences of interest payments are less evident. Who gets the interest payments? What economic resources are absorbed by those payments?

As noted, most of the nation's outstanding debt is internal—that is, owned by domestic households and institutions. Therefore, most interest payments are made to people and institutions within the United States. *Most debt servicing is simply a redistribution of income from taxpayers to bondholders.* In many cases, the taxpayer and bondholder are the same person. In all cases, however, the income that leaks from the circular flow in the form of taxes to pay for debt servicing returns to the circular flow as interest payments. Total income is unchanged. Thus debt servicing may not have any direct effect on aggregate demand.

Debt servicing also has little impact on the real resources of the economy. The collection of additional taxes and the processing of interest payments require the use of some land, labor, and capital. But the value of the resources used for the processing of debt service is trivial—a tiny fraction of the interest payments themselves. This means that *interest payments themselves have virtually no direct opportunity cost.* The

CYBER NOTE

Find out about the U.S. Treasury government bills, notes, and bonds at www.publicdebt.treas.gov/of/ofaucrt.htm.

amount of goods and services available for other purposes is virtually unchanged as a result of debt servicing.

If debt servicing absorbs few economic resources, can we conclude that the national debt really does represent a free lunch? Unfortunately not. But the concept of opportunity cost does provide a major clue about the true burden of the debt and who bears it.

Opportunity costs are incurred only when real resources (factors of production) are used. The amount of that cost is measured by the other goods and services that could have been produced with those resources, but weren't. As noted earlier, the *process* of debt servicing absorbs few resources and so has negligible opportunity cost. To understand the true burden of the national debt, we have to look at what that debt financed. *The true burden of the debt is the opportunity cost of the activities financed by the debt.* To assess that burden, we need to ask what the government did with the borrowed funds.

Government Purchases. Suppose Congress decides to upgrade our naval forces and borrows $10 billion for that purpose. What's the opportunity cost of that decision? The economic cost of the fleet upgrade is measured by the goods and services forgone in order to build more ships. The labor, land, and capital used to upgrade the fleet can't be used to produce something else. We give up the opportunity to produce another $10 billion worth of private goods and services when Congress upgrades the fleet.

The economic cost of the naval buildup is unaffected by the method of government finance. Whether the government borrows $10 billion or increases taxes by that amount, the forgone civilian output will still be $10 billion. *The opportunity cost of government purchases is the true burden of government activity, however financed.* The decision to finance such activity with debt rather than taxes doesn't materially alter that cost.

Transfer Payments. Suppose the government uses debt financing to pay for increased transfer payments rather than the purchase of real goods and services. What would be the burden of debt in this case?

Note first that transfer payments entail few real costs. Income transfers entail a redistribution of income from the taxpayer to the transfer recipient. The only direct costs of those transfer payments are the land, labor, and capital involved in the administrative process of making that transfer. Those direct costs tend to be so trivial that they can be ignored. Whatever changes in output or prices occur because of transfer payments result from *indirect* behavioral responses. If taxpayers or transfer recipients respond to transfers by working, saving, or investing less, the economy may suffer. These important *indirect* effects must be distinguished from the *direct* cost of the transfers, which are minimal. As a result, the amount of income transferred isn't a meaningful measure of economic burden. Hence the debt that originated in deficit-financed income transfers can't be viewed as a unique "burden" either.

Although the national debt poses no special burden to the economy, the transactions it finances have a substantial impact on the basic questions of WHAT, HOW, and FOR WHOM to produce. The core issue of what mix of output to produce is influenced by how much deficit spending the government undertakes. The funds obtained by borrowing allow the federal government to bid for scarce resources. Private investors and consumers will have less access to loanable funds and be less able to acquire incomes or goods. The larger the deficit, the more the private sector gets "squeezed." Hence deficit financing allows the government to obtain more resources and change the mix of output. In general, *deficit financing tends to change the mix of output in the direction of more public-sector goods.*

As noted earlier, the deficits of the 1980s helped finance a substantial military buildup. The same result could have been financed with higher taxes. Taxes are more visible and always unpopular, however. By borrowing rather than taxing, the federal government's claim on scarce resources is less apparent. Either financing method allows the public sector to expand at the expense of the private sector. This resource reallocation reveals the true burden of the debt: ***The burden of the debt is really the opportunity cost (crowding out) of deficit-financed government activity.*** How large that burden is depends on how many unemployed resources are available and the behavioral responses of consumers and investors to increased government activity. Note too that that "burden" must be compared to whatever benefits society gets from government activity.

EXTERNAL DEBT

We observed earlier that most of America's national debt is *internal*—that is, held by U.S. households, institutions, and government agencies. Everything we've said about the burden of the debt and income redistributions applies fully to this internal debt. External debt, however, presents some special opportunities and problems.

No Crowding Out

When we borrow funds from abroad, we increase our ability to consume, invest, and finance government activity. In effect, other nations are lending us the income necessary to *import* more goods. If we can buy more imports with borrowed funds (without offsetting exports), then our real income will exceed our production possibilities. As Figure 12.5 illustrates, external borrowing allows us to enjoy a mix of output that lies *outside* our production possibilities curve. Specifically, ***external financing allows us to get more public-sector goods without cutting back on private-sector production.*** As we use external debt to increase government spending, we move from point *a* to point *d* in Figure 12.5. Imported goods and services eliminate the need to cut back on private-sector activity, a cutback that would otherwise force us to point *b* (see Figure 12.2). The additional imports financed by external debt eliminate this opportunity cost of increased government spending. The initial burden of that spending is relieved by foreign lenders. The move from point *a* to point *d* reflects the additional imports financed by external debt.[4]

External financing appears to offer the proverbial free lunch. It would be a free lunch if foreign lenders were willing to accumulate U.S. Treasury bonds forever. They would

---

[4]The imports needn't be public-sector goods. If enough consumer goods are imported to maintain private-sector activity at the rate h_1, the domestic resources idled by imports can be used to increase public-sector production.

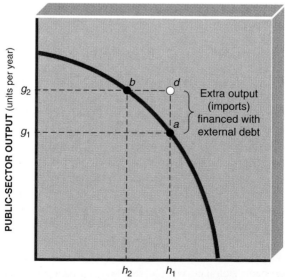

FIGURE 12.5
External Financing

A closed economy must forsake some private-sector output in order to increase public-sector output (see Figure 12.2). External financing temporarily eliminates that opportunity cost. Instead of having to move from *a* to *b*, external borrowing allows us to move from *a* to *d*. At point *d* we have more public output and no less private output.

then own stacks of paper (Treasury bonds), and we'd consume some of their output (our imports) each year. *As long as outsiders are willing to hold U.S. bonds, external financing imposes no real cost.* No goods or services are given up to pay for the additional output received.

Foreign investors may not be willing to hold U.S. bonds indefinitely, however. At some point they'll want to collect their bills. To do this, they'll cash in (sell) their bonds, then use the proceeds to buy U.S. goods and services. When this happens, the United States will be *exporting* goods and services to pay off its debts. Recall that the external debt was used to acquire imported goods and services. Hence *external debt must be repaid with exports of real goods and services.*

Repayment

DEFICIT AND DEBT LIMITS

Although external and internal debts pose very different problems, most policy discussions overlook these distinctions. In policy debates, the aggregate size of the national debt is the focal concern. The key policy questions are whether and how to limit or reduce the national debt.

The only way to stop the growth of the national debt is to eliminate the budget deficits that create debt. The first step in debt reduction, therefore, is a balanced annual budget. A balanced budget will at least stop the debt from growing further. **Deficit ceilings** are explicit limitations on the size of the annual budget deficit. A deficit ceiling of zero compels a balanced budget.

The Balanced Budget and Emergency Deficit Control Act of 1985—popularly referred to as the Gramm-Rudman-Hollings Act—was the first explicit attempt to force the federal budget into balance. The essence of the Gramm-Rudman Act was simple:

- First, it set a lower ceiling on each year's deficit, until budget balance was achieved.
- Second, it called for automatic cutbacks in spending if Congress failed to keep the deficit below the ceiling.

The original Gramm-Rudman law required Congress to pare the deficit from over $200 billion in FY 1985 to zero (a balanced budget) by 1991. But Congress wasn't willing to cut spending and increase taxes enough to meet those targets. And the Supreme Court declared that the "automatic" mechanism for spending cuts was unconstitutional.

Congress amended the Gramm-Rudman-Hollings Act in 1987. The immediate effect of the revision was to postpone the balanced-budget ceiling for 6 years, until 1993. This extension was to give Congress and the president more time to agree on a deficit-cutting strategy. President Reagan was opposed to tax hikes or cuts in defense spending. The Democrat-controlled Congress was opposed to cuts in nondefense spending. These opposing views left little room for deficit reduction. In the end, the only thing they could agree on was to ignore the newly revised rule for "automatic" spending cuts. The national debt kept growing.

In 1990, President Bush and the Congress developed a new set of rules for reducing the deficit. They first acknowledged that they lacked total control of the deficit. At best, Congress could close the *structural* deficit by limiting discretionary spending or raising taxes. The Budget Enforcement Act (BEA) of 1990 laid out a plan for doing exactly this. The BEA set separate limits on defense spending, discretionary domestic spending, and international spending. It also required that any new spending initiative be offset with increased taxes or cutbacks in other programs.

The Budget Enforcement Act was successful in reducing the structural deficit somewhat (see Table 12.1). Despite that effort, the total deficit continued to grow due to recession, slow recovery, and continuing bank bailouts. The spending limits established in the BEA were renewed in 1993. Nevertheless, continued growth of (nondiscretionary) entitlement spending on Social Security, Medicare, and Medicaid kept the deficit high.

Deficit Ceilings

deficit ceiling: An explicit, legislated limitation on the size of the budget deficit.

The Republican party's 1994 Contract with America included a provision for balancing the budget by the year 2002. The contract didn't establish specific deficit ceilings for the intervening years, however. Moreover, Congress discovered that the budget couldn't be balanced just by reducing discretionary spending; cutbacks in entitlements growth was a prerequisite to budget balance.

Frustrations with continuing budget deficits and apparent "Washington gridlock" renewed calls for a constitutional amendment that would *require* Congress to balance the budget. In 1995, The U.S. Senate voted down that notion, adding to a string of historical rejections (see NEWS). Few people believed that such an absolute deficit ceiling was either enforceable (given the cyclical sensitivity of revenues and expenditure) or desirable (given the potential need for fiscal stimulus).

By the end of 1995, both President Clinton and congressional Republicans vowed to balance the budget within the foreseeable future. But they couldn't agree on a target date for budget balancing (the Republicans wanted 2002, Clinton wanted three additional years), much less on specific spending cutbacks. The impasse was broken by continued expansion of the economy and the related decline in the cyclical budget. By 1998, President Clinton and the Republican Congress were arguing about how to use the emerging budget surplus.

CYBER NOTE

For a discussion of deficits and deficit-reduction efforts, visit the White House at www.access.gpo. gov/su_docs/budget99/guide/guide. html and click on "Deficits and the Debt."

Debt Ceilings

debt ceiling: An explicit, legislated limit on the amount of outstanding national debt.

Explicit **debt ceilings** are another mechanism for curbing the national debt. They're at best a substitute for deficit ceilings, however. If a limit is set on the national debt, the only way to stay within that limit is to reduce or eliminate the annual federal deficit.

Despite this evident shortcoming, debt ceilings are frequently invoked in Congress. If a debt ceiling is in place, the U.S. government must cease activity when that ceiling is reached. This causes an immediate operational crisis, with government workers suspended, income transfers withheld, and all but critical federal functions disrupted. This disruption typically lasts less than 24 hours and is often averted completely at the last minute when Congress raises the debt ceiling a bit further. Like deficit ceilings, debt ceilings are intended to force political compromises on specific issues.

IN THE NEWS

News: Analysis

The Balanced Budget Amendment: A History of Rejection

WASHINGTON, D.C.—Last week's Senate rejection of the balanced-budget amendment didn't surprise political historians. The battle over a constitutional amendment has been fought repeatedly, always with the same outcome.

1935: The First Attempt

Congress first proposed using a balanced-budget amendment to put the brakes on FDR's New Deal. The Great Depression dried up tax revenues at the same time FDR was increasing public works and welfare spending. In 1935 a balanced-budget amendment was proposed in Congress and rejected. In 1936 a proposed constitutional limit on per capita national debt met the same fate.

1975: The Convention Call

In 1975 the National Taxpayers Union tried an end-run around Congress. If 34 state legislatures call for a Constitutional Convention, the Constitution can be amended without Congress' initiative. Only 31 states issued the call, and this grass-roots effort floundered.

A Decade of Defeats

The quest for a balanced-budget amendment returned to the halls of Congress in the 1980s. Votes were taken in 1982, 1985, 1990, 1992, 1994, 1995, and again in 1996. The amendment was rejected every time. This year's vote was no different, even though the margin of defeat was only one vote.

Economy Today News Flash, March 1997. © The McGraw-Hill Companies.

Analysis: Although the notion is popular, constitutional limits on budget deficits have been rejected repeatedly. Critics emphasize that cyclical forces render deficit ceilings unenforceable and undesirable.

THE ECONOMY TOMORROW

Our Grandchildren's Burden?

Although deficits and debt appear to be routine features of fiscal policy, they're still regarded with fear and suspicion. People repeatedly blame deficits and the national debt for an assortment of economic ills: inflation, unemployment, slow growth, high interest rates, trade problems, and more. As Herbert Stein, President Nixon's chairman of the Council of Economic Advisers, observed, budget deficits get blamed for just about any economic outcomes people don't like.

One of the most persistent objections to deficits is that they pass the burden of debt on to future generations. Deficits, it's said, allow us to live beyond our means by "mortgaging" the future (see cartoon). In this view, it's our grandchildren, not we, who'll end up bearing the burden of the debt. If this "generational accounting" is true, this would suggest hard times in the economy of tomorrow.

What Burden?

To assess this argument we must recall the nature of the debt "burden." ***The burden of any government activity is its opportunity cost, as measured by private goods and services forgone.*** As we observed earlier, if the government uses deficit financing to upgrade the naval fleet, the costs of that activity are the real goods and services that are crowded out in the production process.

Notice also *when* that cost is incurred. If the fleet is upgraded this year, then the opportunity cost is incurred this year. It's only while resources are actually being used by the Navy that we give up the opportunity to use them elsewhere. Opportunity costs are incurred at the time a government activity takes place, not when the resultant debt is paid. In other words, ***the primary burden of the debt is incurred when the debt-financed activity takes place.***

If the entire naval construction program is completed this year, what costs are borne next year? None. The land, labor, and capital available next year can be used for whatever

"What's this I hear about you adults mortgaging my future?"

From *The Wall Street Journal*—permission, Cartoon Features Syndicate.

Analysis: The fear that present generations are passing the debt burden to future generations is exaggerated.

purposes are then desired. Once the new ships are built, no further resources are allocated to their construction. The real costs of ship construction can't be postponed until a later year. In other words, the real burden of the debt can't be passed on to future generations. On the contrary, future generations will benefit from the sacrifices made today to build ships, parks, highways, dams, and other public-sector projects. Future taxpayers will be able to *use* these projects without incurring the opportunity costs of their construction.

Economic Growth

Although future generations may benefit from current government spending, they may also be adversely affected by today's opportunity costs. Of particular concern is the possibility that government deficits might crowd out private investment. Investment is essential to enlarging our production possibilities and attaining higher living standards in the future. If federal deficits and debt-servicing requirements crowd our private investment, the rate of economic growth will slow, leaving future generations with less productive capacity than they would otherwise have. Thus *if debt-financed government spending crowds out private investment, future generations will bear some of the debt burden.* Their burden will take the form of smaller-than-anticipated productive capacity.

There's no certainty that such crowding out will occur. Also, any reduction in private investment may be offset by public works (such as highways, schools, defense systems) that benefit future generations. So future generations may not suffer a net loss in welfare even if the national debt slows private investment and economic growth. From this perspective, *the whole debate about the burden of the debt is really an argument over the* **optimal mix of output.** If we permit more deficit spending, we're promoting more public-sector activity. On the other hand, limits on deficit financing curtail growth of the public sector. Battles over deficits and debts are a proxy for the more fundamental issue of private versus public spending.

optimal mix of output: The most desirable combination of output attainable with existing resources, technology, and social values.

Repayment

All this sounds a little too neat. Won't future generations have to pay interest on the debts we incur today? And might they even have to pay off some of the debt?

We've already observed that the collection of taxes and processing of interest payments absorbs relatively few resources. Hence, the mechanism of repayment entail little burden.

Notice also who *receives* future interest payments. When we die, we leave behind not only the national debt but also the bonds that represent ownership of that debt. Hence future grandchildren will be both taxpayers *and* bondholders. If interest payments are made 30 years from today, only people who are alive and holding bonds at that time will receive interest payments. *Future interest payments entail a redistribution of income among taxpayers and bondholders living in the future.*

The same kind of redistribution occurs if and when our grandchildren decide to pay off the debt. Tax revenues will be used to pay off the debt. The debt payments will go to people then holding Treasury bonds. The entire redistribution will occur among people living in the future.

External Debt

The nature of opportunity costs makes it difficult but not impossible to pass the debt burden on to future generations. The exception is the case of external debt. Recall that external financing eliminates current opportunity costs by allowing us to consume more output than we currently produce (see Figure 12.5). At some date in the future, however, foreign bondholders will want, to collect on Uncle Sam's IOUs. If at that time they use the dollars they receive to buy U.S. goods (our exports), less output will be available for domestic use. This exported future output represents the real cost of government activity initially financed by external debt. Hence the burden of external debt *can* be passed on to future generations.

There's no certainty that foreign lenders (bondholders) will ever want to redeem their bonds for U.S. products. They too may choose to accept refinancing, thus postponing any debt collection. Even if they cash in their bonds, they may choose to save or invest in the United States rather than spend their dollars on our exports. Finally, as inflation drives up the average U.S. price level, foreign bondholders will discover that their bonds have less and less purchasing power. Over time, then, inflation reduces the potential real cost of external debt. That cost may nevertheless be more than citizens of the economy tomorrow wish to pay.

SUMMARY

- Budget imbalances result from both discretionary fiscal policy (structural deficits and surpluses) and cyclical changes in the economy (cyclical deficits and surpluses).
- Fiscal restraint is measured by the reduction in the structural deficit; fiscal stimulus occurs when the structural deficit increases.
- Automatic stabilizers increase federal spending and reduce tax revenues during recessions. When the economy expands, they have the reverse effect, thereby shrinking the cyclical deficit.
- Deficit financing of government expenditure may crowd out private investment and consumption. The risk of crowding out increases as the economy approaches full employment. If investment becomes the opportunity cost of increased government spending, economic growth may slow.
- Crowding-in refers to the increase in private-sector output made possible by a decline in government borrowing.
- Each year's deficit adds to the national debt. The national debt grew sporadically until World War II and then sky-

rocketed. A string of huge deficits in the 1980s and 1990s increased the national debt to over $5 trillion.
- Every dollar of national debt represents a dollar of assets to the people who hold U.S. Treasury bonds. Most U.S. bonds are held by government agencies, U.S. households, and U.S. banks, insurance companies, and other institutions.
- The real burden of the debt is the opportunity cost of the activities financed by the debt. That cost is borne at the time the deficit-financed activity takes place. The benefits of debt-financed activity may extend into the future.
- External debt permits the public sector to expand without reducing private-sector output. External debt also makes it possible to shift some of the real debt burden on to future generations.
- Deficit and debt ceilings are largely symbolic efforts to force consideration of real tradeoffs, to restrain government spending, and to change the mix of output.

Key Terms

fiscal policy	automatic stabilizer	asset
deficit spending	cyclical deficit	internal debt
budget deficit	structural deficit	external debt
budget surplus	crowding out	refinancing
fiscal year (FY)	opportunity cost	debt service
discretionary fiscal spending	crowding in	deficit ceiling
fiscal restraint	Treasury bonds	debt ceiling
fiscal stimulus	national debt	optimal mix of output
income transfers	liability	

Questions for Discussion

1. Who paid for the Revolutionary War? Did the deficit financing initiated by the Continental Congress pass the cost of the war on to future generations?
2. In what ways do future generations benefit from this generation's deficit spending? Cite three examples.
3. What's considered "too much" debt or "too large" a deficit? Are you able to provide any guidelines for deficit or debt ceilings?
4. If deficit spending "crowds out" some private investment, could future generations be worse off? If external

financing eliminates crowding out, are future generations thereby protected?

5. A constitutional amendment has been proposed that would require Congress to balance the budget each year. Is it possible to balance the budget each year? Is it desirable?

6. What should the government do with a budget surplus?

7. By how much did defense spending increase in 1940 to 1944? (See back endpapers of this book.) What was crowded out?

8. How long would it take to pay off the national debt? How would the economy be affected?

9. Web Activity Summarize liberal and conservative views on a constitutional requirement to balance the federal budget. For the liberal position, go to www.epn.org/balance/html. For the conservative position, go to www.concordcoalition.org.

10. Web Activity What is the future of Social Security? Currently Social Security is the largest holder of the national debt, a surplus that will increase and then fall as baby boomers retire. Visit the Social Security Administration for a summary of the problem and what could be done: www.ssa.gov/pubs/10055.htm. Look at the selections in the "Choices Lie Ahead" section. Which solution makes the most sense?

Problems for Chapter 12 appear at the back of the book.

Monetary Policy Options

Monetary policy tries to alter macro outcomes by managing the amount of money available in the economy. By changing the money supply and/or interest rates, monetary policy seeks to shift aggregate demand in the desired direction. Chapters 13 through 15 illustrate these concepts.

13

Money and Banks

Sophocles, the ancient Greek playwright, had very strong opinions about the role of money. As he saw it, "Of evils upon earth, the worst is money. It is money that sacks cities, and drives men forth from hearth and home; warps and seduces native intelligence, and breeds a habit of dishonesty."

In modern times, people may still be seduced by the lure of money and fashion their lives around its pursuit. Nevertheless, it's hard to imagine an economy functioning without money. Money affects not only morals and ideals but also the way an economy works.

This and the following two chapters examine the role of money in the economy today. We begin with a very simple question:

- What is money?

As we'll discover, money isn't exactly what you might think it is. There's a lot more money in the economy than there is cash. And there's a lot more income around than money. So money is something quite different from either cash or income. Once we've established the characteristics of money, we go on to ask:

- How is money created?
- What role do banks play in the circular flow of income and spending?

In Chapter 14 we look at how the Federal Reserve System controls the amount of money created. In Chapter 15 we look at the implications for monetary policy, another policy lever in our basic macro model.

WHAT IS "MONEY"?

To appreciate the significance of money for a modern economy, imagine for a moment that there were no such thing as money. How would you get something for breakfast? If you wanted eggs for breakfast, you'd have to tend your own chickens or go see Farmer Brown. But how would you pay Farmer Brown for his eggs? Without money, you'd have to offer him some goods or services that he could use. In other words, you'd have to engage in primitive **barter**—the direct exchange of one good for another—in order to get eggs for breakfast. You'd get those eggs only if Farmer Brown happened to want the particular goods or services you had to offer.

Analysis: When the Russian ruble lost its value, people would no longer accept it in payment. Market transactions had to be bartered, a clumsy and inefficient process.

The use of money greatly simplifies market transactions. It's a lot easier to exchange money for eggs at the supermarket than to go into the country and cut hay or lay sod every time you crave some eggs. Our ability to use money in market transactions, however, depends on the grocer's willingness to accept money as a *medium of exchange*. The grocer sells eggs for money only because he can use the same money to pay his help and buy the goods he himself desires. He too can exchange money for goods and services.

barter: The direct exchange of one good for another, without the use of money.

Without money, the process of acquiring goods and services would be much more difficult and time-consuming. This was evident when the value of the Russian ruble plummeted. Trading goods for Farmer Brown's eggs seems simple compared to the complicated barter deals Russian factories had to negotiate when paper money was no longer accepted (see WORLD VIEW). And Russian workers certainly would've preferred to be paid in cash rather than in bras and coffins.

THE MONEY SUPPLY

Although markets can't function well without money, they can get along without *dollars*. Just one example of money is U.S. dollars. In the early days of colonial America, there were no U.S. dollars; a lot of business was conducted with Spanish and Portuguese gold coins. Later, people used Indian wampum, then tobacco, grain, fish, and furs as mediums of exchange. Throughout the colonies, gunpowder and bullets were frequently used for small change. These forms of money weren't as convenient as U.S. dollars, but they did the job.

Many Types of "Money"

CYBER NOTE

For a brief history of coins and to learn how coins are made, visit the U.S. mint at www.usmint.gov.

This historical perspective on money highlights its essential characteristics. *Anything that serves all the following purposes can be thought of as money:*

- *Medium of exchange:* is accepted as payment for goods and services (and debts).
- *Store of value:* can be held for future purchases.
- *Standard of value:* serves as a yardstick for measuring the prices of goods and services.

All the items used during the colonial days satisfied these conditions and were thus properly regarded as money.

After the colonies became an independent nation, the U.S. Constitution prohibited the federal government from issuing paper money. Money was instead issued by state-chartered banks. Between 1789 and 1865 over 30,000 different paper bills were issued by 1600 banks in 34 states. People often preferred to get paid in gold, silver, or other commodities rather than in one of these uncertain currencies.

The first paper money the federal government issued consisted of $10 million worth of "greenbacks," printed in 1861 to finance the Civil War. The National Banking Act of 1863 gave the federal government permanent authority to issue money.

Modern Concepts

The "greenbacks" we carry around today aren't the only form of "money" we use. Most people realize this when they offer to pay for goods with a check rather than cash. People do distinguish between "cash" and "money," and for good reason. The "money" you have in a checking account can be used to buy goods and services or to pay debts, or it can be retained for future use. In these respects, your checking account balance is as much a part of your "money" as are the coins and dollars in your pocket or purse. You can access your balance by writing a check or using an ATM or debit card. People in fact use checks more often than cash for purchases over $50 (see NEWS). Checks are more convenient than cash because they eliminate trips to the bank. Checks are also safer: Lost or stolen cash is gone forever; checkbooks and credit cards are easily replaced at little or no cost. We might use checks even more frequently if everyone accepted them.

IN THE NEWS

News: Analysis

Purchase Plans

When asked what method of payment they use for purchases of selected sizes, these percentages of surveyed U.S. adults said:

	Cash	Check	Credit Card	Other
$1–$50	70%	24%	5%	1%
$51–$100	35	42	21	2
$101–$250	22	43	32	2
Above $250	18	42	34	3

Note: Numbers may not total 100% because of no response or rounding.

Source: *The Wall Street Journal,* Nov. 23, 1987, p. 29. Reprinted by permission of *The Wall Street Journal.* © 1987 Dow Jones & Company, Inc. All Rights Reserved Worldwide. www.wsj.com

Analysis: Check, credit cards, and cash are used in market exchanges but only checking account balances and cash are counted as "money." Credit cards simply postpone payment with money.

There's nothing unique about cash, then, insofar as the market is concerned. ***Checking accounts can and do perform the same market functions as cash.*** Accordingly, we must include checking account balances in our concept of **money.** The essence of money isn't its taste, color, or feel but, rather, its ability to purchase goods and services.

money: Anything generally accepted as a medium of exchange.

Credit cards are another popular medium of exchange. As the preceding NEWS reveals, people use credit cards for about one-third of all purchases over $100. This use is not sufficient, however, to qualify credit cards as a form of "money." Credit card balances must be paid by check or cash. The same holds true for balances in online electronic credit accounts ("E-cash"). Electronic purchases on the Internet (see NEWS) or online services are ultimately paid by withdrawals from a bank account (by check or computer). Online payment mechanisms and credit cards are a payment *service,* not a final form of payment (credit card companies charge fees and interest for this service). The cards themselves are not a store of value, in contrast to cash or bank account balances.

IN THE NEWS

Furniture Chain Won't Take Cash

One retail chain is just saying no to cash.

The Scan furniture chain, which has 10 stores in Maryland and Virginia, has stopped accepting cash because of concerns about employee security.

Two employees were shot and seriously wounded two weeks ago in a robbery attempt at a Maryland store.

A consultant advised the company to adopt a no-cash policy. It did. Now Scan finds itself the newest and most glaring example of the USA's movement toward becoming a cashless society.

Scan does less than 3% of its annual business in cash, explains CEO J. Russell Daily. "To protect customers and employees from senseless violence, we decided to stop taking cash." Signs at the entrance and checkout counter spell out the policy. The stores will get rid of cash registers, too. . . .

—Bruce Horovitz

USA Today, June 23, 1995, p. 13. Copyright 1995, USA TODAY. Reprinted with permission. www.usatoday.com

How to Send Real Money over the Internet

When you hit the jackpot at an online casino, don't expect a stream of quarters to pour out of your floppy drive. You won't find cold, hard cash in the ethereal online world. . . .

So how do you exchange money online? Several enterprising companies are trying to answer that question, struggling to establish themselves as the exchequers of the networked world. DigiCash, First Virtual Holdings, Checkfree and NetChex already have systems that are up and running, some for real money, others in Monopoly-money mode.

The basic idea of all these systems is the same: you authorize an online bank to take, say, $500 out of your credit-card or checking account, and the bank converts the money to electronic cash that can be spent at any site on the Internet—provided the site accepts it. Chances are it will. Online sales (including payments with traditional credit cards) topped $200 million last year and are expected to reach $1 billion this year. Some experts forecast that as much as 25% of U.S. consumer products will be purchased electronically by the turn of the century.

—Joshua Quittner

Time, June 12, 1996, p. 64. Copyright 1995, Time Inc. Reprinted by permission. www.time.com

Analysis: Cash payments entail security risks. Some people prefer to use new payment options created by the Information Highway. E-cash is a payment ***service,*** however, not a true form of money.

The Diversity of Bank Accounts. To determine how much money is available to purchase goods and services, we need to count up all our coins and currency—as well as our bank account balances. This effort is complicated by the variety of bank accounts people have. In addition to simple no-interest checking accounts at full-service banks, people have bank accounts that pay interest, offer automatic transfers, require minimum holding periods, offer overdraft protection, or limit the number of checks that can be written. People also have "bank" accounts in credit unions, brokerage houses, and other nontraditional financial institutions.

Although all bank account balances can be spent, they're not all used the same way. People use regular checking accounts all the time to pay bills or make purchases. But consumers can't write checks on most savings accounts. And few people want to cash in a certificate of deposit just to go to the movies. Hence *some bank accounts are better substitutes for cash than others.*

M1: Cash and Transactions Accounts

money supply (M1): Currency held by the public, plus balances in transactions accounts.

transactions account: A bank account that permits direct payment to a third party, for example, with a check.

Several different measures of money have been developed to accommodate the diversity of bank accounts and other payment mechanisms. The narrowest definition of the **money supply** is designated **M1,** *which includes*

- *Currency in circulation*
- *Transactions-account balances*
- *Traveler's checks*

As Figure 13.1 indicates, the largest component of this basic money supply (M1) is **transactions-account balances,** which are the balances in bank accounts that are readily accessed by check. Most people refer to these simply as "checking accounts." The term "transactions account" is broader, however, including NOW accounts, ATS accounts, credit union share drafts, and demand deposits at mutual savings banks. *The distinguishing feature of all transactions accounts is that they permit direct payment to a third party (by check or debit card),* without requiring a trip to the bank to make a special withdrawal. Because of this feature, transactions accounts are the readiest substitutes for cash in market transactions. Traveler's checks issued by nonbank firms such

FIGURE 13.1
Composition of the Money Supply

Cash is a small part of the money supply. People also have easy access to transactions-account balances and various savings account balances that are counted in measures of the money supply (M1 and M2). Because people hold so much money in money market mutual funds and savings (time-deposit) accounts, M2 is over three times larger than M1.

Source: Federal Reserve (January 1999 data).

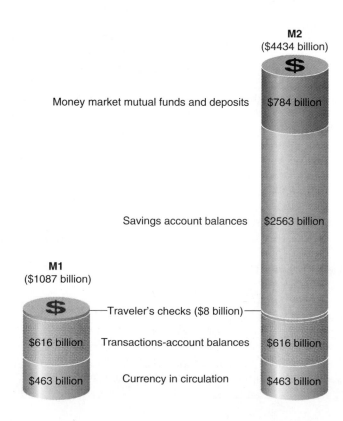

as American Express can also be used directly in market transactions, just like good old-fashioned cash.

Transactions accounts aren't the only substitute for cash. People can and do dip into savings accounts on occasion. People sometimes even cash in their certificates of deposit in order to buy something, despite the interest penalty associated with early withdrawal. And banks have made it easy to transfer funds from one type of account to another. Savings accounts can be transformed into transactions accounts with a phone call or computer instruction, such as automatic overdraft protection. As a result, *savings account balances are almost as good a substitute for cash as transactions-account balances.*

Another popular way of holding money is to buy shares of money market mutual funds. Deposits into money market mutual funds are pooled and used to purchase interest-bearing securities such as Treasury bills. The interest rates paid on these funds are typically higher than those paid by banks. Moreover, the deposits made into the funds can often be withdrawn immediately, just like those in transactions accounts. When interest rates are high, deposits move out of regular transactions accounts into these money-market mutual funds in order to earn a higher return.

Additional measures of the money supply have been constructed to account for the possibility of using savings account balances, money market mutual funds, and various other deposits to finance everyday spending. The most widely watched money measure is **M2,** which includes all of M1 *plus* balances in savings accounts, money market mutual funds, and some CDs ("time deposits"). As Figure 13.1 shows, M2 is over three times as large as M1. Table 13.1 summarizes the content of these and two other measures of money.

Our concern about the specific nature of money stems from our broader interest in **aggregate demand.** What we want to know is how much purchasing power consumers have, since this will affect their ability to purchase goods and services. What we've observed, however, is that money isn't so easily defined. How much spending power people have depends not only on the number of coins in their pockets but also on their willingness to write checks, make trips to the bank, or convert other assets into cash.

M2: M1 + Savings Accounts, etc.

M2 money supply: M1 plus balances in most savings accounts and money market mutual funds.

aggregate demand: The total quantity of output demanded at alternative price levels in a given time period, *ceteris paribus.*

Measure	Components
M1	Currency in circulation outside of bank vaults
	Demand deposits at commercial banks
	NOW and ATS accounts
	Credit union share drafts
	Demand deposits at mutual savings banks
	Traveler's checks (nonbank)
M2	M1 plus:
	Savings accounts
	Time deposits of less than $100,000
	Money market mutual funds
M3	M2 plus:
	Time deposits larger than $100,000
	Repurchase agreements
	Overnight Eurodollars
L	M3 plus other liquid assets, for example:
	Treasury bills
	U.S. savings bonds
	Bankers' acceptances
	Term Eurodollars
	Commercial paper

TABLE 13.1
Alternative Measures of the Money Supply

Measures of the money supply are intended to gauge the extent of purchasing power held by consumers. But the extent of purchasing power depends on how accessible assets are and how often people use them. The various money supply measures reflect variations in the liquidity and accessibility of assets.

In an increasingly complex financial system, the core concept of "money" isn't easy to pin down. Nevertheless, the official measures of the money supply (particularly M1 and M2) are fairly reliable benchmarks for gauging how much purchasing power market participants have.

CREATION OF MONEY

Once we've decided what money is, we still have to explain where it comes from. Part of the explanation is simple. Currency must be printed. Some nations use private printers for this purpose, but all U.S. currency is printed by the Bureau of Engraving and Printing in Washington, D.C. Coins come from the U.S. mints located in Philadelphia and Denver. As we observed in Figure 13.1, however, currency is a small fraction of our total money supply. So we need to look elsewhere for the origins of most money. Specifically, where do all the transactions accounts come from? How do people acquire transactions deposits? How does the total amount of such deposits—and therefore the money supply of the economy—change?

Deposit Creation

Most people assume that all transactions-account balances come from cash deposits. But this isn't the case. Direct deposits of paychecks, for example, are carried out by computer, not by the movement of cash (see cartoon). Moreover, the employer who issues the paycheck probably didn't make any cash deposits. It's more likely that she covered those paychecks with customers' checks that she deposited or with loans granted by the bank itself.

The ability of banks to lend money opens up a whole new set of possibilities for creating money. *When a bank lends someone money, it simply credits that individual's bank account.* The money appears in an account just as it would with a cash deposit. And the owner of the account is free to spend that money as with any positive balance. Hence, *in making a loan, a bank effectively creates money because transactions-account balances are counted as part of the money supply.*

To understand the origins of our money supply then, we must recognize two basic principles:

- Transactions-account balances are a large portion of our money supply.
- Banks can create transactions-account balances by making loans.

deposit creation: The creation of transactions deposits by bank lending.

The following two sections examine this process of **deposit creation** more closely. We determine how banks actually create deposits and what forces might limit the process of deposit creation.

Bank Regulation. Banks' deposit-creation activities are regulated by the government. The most important agency in this regard is the Federal Reserve System. The Fed puts

BANK   DIRECT DEPOSIT DEPT.

YOU SEE, WITH DIRECT DEPOSIT OF YOUR PAYCHECK WE COMPLETELY DO AWAY WITH THE ILLUSION THAT YOU ACTUALLY EVER SEE ANY OF YOUR MONEY.

Analysis: People see very little of their money—most deposits and loans are computer entries in the banking system.

limits on the amount of bank lending, thereby controlling the basic money supply. Table 13.2 describes the functions of a bank. Chapter 14 discusses the structure and functions of the Fed; here we focus on the process of deposit creation itself.

A Monopoly Bank

Suppose, to keep things simple, that there's only one bank in town, University Bank. Imagine also that you've been saving some of your income by putting loose change into a piggy bank. Now, after months of saving, you break the bank and discover that your thrift has yielded $100. You immediately deposit this money in a new checking account at University Bank. How will this deposit affect the money supply?

Your initial deposit will have no immediate effect on the money supply. The coins in your piggy bank were already counted as part of the money supply (M1 and M2) because they represented cash held by the public. ***When you deposit cash or coins in a bank, you're simply changing the composition of the money supply.*** The public (you) now holds $100 less of coins but $100 more of transactions deposits. Accordingly, no money is created by the demise of your piggy bank (the initial deposit). This accounting outcome is reflected in the following "T account" of University Bank and the composition of the money supply:

University Bank		Money Supply	
Assets	Liabilities	Cash held by the public	−$100
+$100 in coins	+$100 in deposits	Transactions deposits at bank	+$100
		Change in M	0

The T account shows that your coins are now held by University Bank. In exchange, the bank has credited your checking account $100. This balance is a liability for the bank since it must allow you to withdraw the deposit on demand.

Type of Bank	Characteristics
Commercial banks	The nearly 10,000 commercial banks in the United States provide a full range of banking services, including savings ("time") and checking accounts and loans for all purposes. They hold nearly all demand deposits and nearly half of total savings deposits.
Savings and loan associations	Begun in 1831 as a mechanism for pooling the savings of a neighborhood in order to provide funds for home purchases, which is still the basic function of such banks. The nearly 600 S&Ls channel virtually all their savings deposits into home mortgages.
Mutual savings banks	Originally intended to serve very small savers (like the Boston Five Cents Savings Bank). They now use their deposits for a wider variety of purposes, including investment bonds and "blue chip" stocks. Almost all the 738 mutual savings banks are located in only five states: New York, Massachusetts, Connecticut, Pennsylvania, and New Jersey.
Credit unions	A cooperative society formed by individuals bound together by some common tie, such as a common employer or labor union. Credit union members hold savings accounts and enjoy access to the pooled savings of all members. Most credit union loans are for consumer purchases. Although there are close to 12,000 credit unions in the United States, they hold less than 5 percent of total savings deposits.

TABLE 13.2
What Is a Bank?

The essential functions of a bank are to

- Accept deposits
- Offer drafts (check writing privileges)
- Make loans

In the United States, roughly 25,000 "depository institutions" fulfill these functions. These "banks" are typically classified into four general categories, even though most "banks" (and many other financial institutions) now offer similar services.

The total money supply is unaffected by your cash deposit because two components of the money supply change in opposite directions. This initial deposit is just the beginning of the money creation process, however. Banks aren't in business for your convenience; they're in business to earn a profit. To earn a profit on your deposit, University Bank will have to put your money to work, which means using your deposit as the basis for making a loan to someone who's willing to pay the bank interest for use of money. If the function of banks was merely to store money, they wouldn't pay interest on their accounts or offer free checking services. Instead, you'd have to pay them for these services. Banks pay you interest and offer free (or inexpensive) checking because they can use your money to make loans that earn interest.

The Initial Loan. Typically, a bank doesn't have much difficulty finding someone who wants to borrow money. Many firms and individuals have expenditure desires that exceed their current money balances and are eager to borrow money. The question is: How much money can a bank lend? Can it lend your entire deposit? Or must University Bank keep some of your coins in reserve, in case you want to withdraw them?

To answer this question, suppose that University Bank decided to lend the entire $100 to Campus Radio. Campus Radio wants to buy a new antenna but doesn't have any money in its own checking account. To acquire the antenna, Campus Radio must take out a loan.

When University Bank agrees to lend Campus Radio $100, it does so by crediting the account of Campus Radio. Instead of giving Campus Radio $100 cash, University Bank simply adds $100 to Campus Radio's checking account balance. That is, the loan is made with a simple bookkeeping entry as follows:

University Bank		Money Supply	
Assets	Liabilities	Cash held by the public	no change
$100 in coins	$100 your account balance	Transactions deposits at bank	+$100
$100 in loans	$100 Campus Radio Account	Change in M	+$100

This simple bookkeeping procedure has important implications. When University Bank lends $100 to the Campus Radio account, it "creates" money. Keep in mind that transactions deposits are counted as part of the money supply. Moreover, Campus Radio can use this new money to purchase its desired antenna, without worrying that its check will bounce.

Or can it? Once University Bank grants a loan to Campus Radio, both you and Campus Radio have $100 in your checking accounts to spend. But the bank is holding only $100 of **reserves** (your coins). In other words, the increased account balance obtained by Campus Radio doesn't limit your ability to write checks. There's been a net *increase* in the value of transactions deposits, but no increase in bank reserves.

Secondary Deposits. What happens if Campus Radio actually spends the $100 on a new antenna? Won't this "use up" all the reserves held by the bank, endangering your check writing privileges? The answer is no.

Consider what happens when Atlas Antenna receives the check from Campus Radio. What will Atlas do with the check? Atlas could go to University Bank and exchange the check for $100 of cash (your coins). But Atlas may prefer to deposit the check in its own checking account at University Bank (still the only bank in town). This way, Atlas not only avoids the necessity of going to the bank (it can deposit the check by mail) but also keeps its money in a safe place. Should Atlas later want to spend the money, it can simply write a check. In the meantime, the bank continues to hold its entire reserves (your coins), and both you and Atlas have $100 to spend.

Fractional Reserves. Notice what's happened here. The money supply has increased by $100 as a result of deposit creation (the loan to Campus Radio). Moreover, the bank

bank reserves: Assets held by a bank to fulfill its deposit obligations.

has been able to support $200 of transaction deposits (your account and either the Campus Radio or Atlas account) with only $100 of reserves (your coins). In other words, ***bank reserves are only a fraction of total deposits.*** In this case, University Bank's reserves (your $100 in coins) are only 50 percent of total deposits. Thus the bank's **reserve ratio** is 50 percent, rather than 100 percent—that is,

reserve ratio: The ratio of a bank's reserves to its total transactions deposits.

$$\frac{\text{Reserve}}{\text{ratio}} = \frac{\text{bank reserves}}{\text{total deposits}}$$

The ability of University Bank to hold reserves that are only a fraction of total deposits results from two facts: (1) people use checks for most transactions, and (2) there's no other bank. Accordingly, reserves are rarely withdrawn from this monopoly bank. In fact, if people *never* withdrew their deposits and *all* transactions accounts were held at University Bank, University Bank wouldn't need any reserves. In this most unusual case, University Bank could make as many loans as it wanted. Every loan it made would increase the supply of money.

In reality, many banks are available, and people both withdraw cash from their accounts and write checks to people who have accounts in other banks. In addition, bank lending practices are regulated by the Federal Reserve System. ***The Federal Reserve System requires banks to maintain some minimum reserve ratio.*** This reserve requirement directly limits banks' ability to grant new loans.

Required Reserves. The potential impact of Federal Reserve requirements on bank lending can be readily seen. Suppose that the Federal Reserve had imposed a minimum reserve requirement of 75 percent on University Bank. Such a requirement would have prohibited University Bank from lending $100 to Campus Radio. That loan would have resulted in $200 of deposits, supported by only $100 of reserves. The actual ratio of reserves to deposits would have been 50 percent ($100 of reserves ÷ $200 of deposits), which would have violated the Fed's assumed 75 percent reserve requirement. A 75 percent reserve requirement means that University Bank must hold **required reserves** equal to 75 percent of *total* deposits, including those created through loans.

required reserves: The minimum amount of reserves a bank is required to hold; equal to required reserve ratio times transactions deposits.

The bank's dilemma is evident in the following equation:

$$\frac{\text{Required}}{\text{reserves}} = \frac{\text{minimum reserve}}{\text{ratio}} \times \frac{\text{total}}{\text{deposits}}$$

To support $200 of total deposits, University Bank would need to satisfy this equation:

$$\frac{\text{Required}}{\text{reserves}} = 0.75 \times \$200 = \$150$$

But the bank has only $100 of reserves (your coins) and so would violate the reserve requirement if it increased total deposits to $200 by lending $100 to Campus Radio.

University Bank can still issue a loan to Campus Radio. But the loan must be less than $100 in order to keep the bank within the limits of the required reserve formula. Thus ***a minimum reserve requirement directly limits deposit-creation possibilities.*** It's still true, however, as we'll now illustrate, that the banking system, taken as a whole, can create multiple loans (money) from a single deposit.

Table 13.3 illustrates the process of deposit creation in a multibank world with a required reserve ratio. In this case, we assume that legally required reserves must equal at least 20 percent of transactions deposits. Now when you deposit $100 in your checking account, University Bank must hold at least $20 as required reserves.[1]

A Multibank World

---

[1]The reserves themselves may be held in the form of cash in the bank's vault but are usually held as credits with one of the regional Federal Reserve banks.

TABLE 13.3
Deposit Creation

Excess reserves (step 1) are the basis of bank loans. When a bank uses its excess reserves to make a loan, it creates a deposit (step 2). When the loan is spent, a deposit will be made some-where else (step 3). This new deposit creates additional excess reserves (step 3) that can be used for further loans (step 4, etc.). The process of deposit creation continues until the money supply has increased by a multiple of the initial deposit.

Step 1: You deposit cash at University Bank. The deposit creates $100 of reserves, $20 of which are designated as required reserves.

University Bank

Assets		Liabilities	
Required reserves	$ 20	Your deposit	$100
Excess reserves	80		
Total	$100		100

Banking System

Change in Transactions Deposits	Change in M
+$100	$ 0

Step 2: The bank uses its excess reserves ($80) to make a loan to Campus Radio. Total deposits now equal $180. The money supply has increased.

University Bank

Assets		Liabilities	
Required reserves	$ 36	Your account	$100
Excess reserves	64	Campus Radio account	80
Loans	80		
Total	$180	Total	$180

Banking System

Δ Deposits	Δ M
+$ 80	+$ 80

Step 3: Campus Radio buys an antenna. This depletes Campus Radio's account but increases Atlas's balance. Eternal Savings gets $80 of reserves when the Campus Radio check clears.

University Bank

Assets		Liabilities	
Required reserves	$ 20	Your account	$100
Excess reserves	0	Campus Radio account	0
Loan	80		
Total	$100	Total	$100

Eternal Savings

Assets		Liabilities	
Required reserves	$ 16	Atlas Antenna account	$80
Excess reserves	64		
Total	$ 80	Total	$80

Banking System

Δ Deposits	Δ M
$ 0	$ 0

Step 4: Eternal Savings lends money to Herman's Hardware. Deposits, loans, and M all increase by $64.

University Bank

Assets		Liabilities	
Required reserves	$ 20	Your account	$100
Excess reserves	0	Campus Radio account	0
Loan	80		
Total	$100		$100

Eternal Savings

Assets		Liabilities	
Required reserves	$ 29	Atlas Antenna account	$ 80
Excess reserves	51	Herman's Hardware account	64
Loans	64		
	$144		$144

Banking System

Change in Transaction Deposits	Change in M
+$ 64	+$ 64

⋮

nth step: Some bank lends $1.00

	+ 1	+ 1

Cumulative Change in Banking System

Bank Reserves	Transactions Deposits	Money Supply
+$100	+$500	+$400

Excess Reserves. The remaining $80 the bank obtains from your deposit is regarded as **excess reserves.** These reserves are "excess" in that your bank is *required* to hold in reserve only $20 (equal to 20 percent of your initial $100 deposit):

$$\frac{\text{Excess}}{\text{reserves}} = \frac{\text{total}}{\text{reserves}} - \frac{\text{required}}{\text{reserves}}$$

excess reserves: Bank reserves in excess of required reserves.

The $80 of excess reserves isn't required and may be used to support additional loans. Hence the bank can now lend $80. In view of the fact that banks earn profits (interest) by making loans, we assume that University Bank will try to use these excess reserves as soon as possible.

To keep track of the changes in reserves, deposit balances, and loans that occur in a multibank world we'll have to do some bookkeeping. For this purpose we'll again use the same balance sheet, or "T account," that banks themselves use. On the left side of the balance sheet, a bank lists all its assets. *Assets* are things the bank owns or is owed by others, including cash held in a bank's vaults, IOUs (loan obligations) from bank customers, reserve credits at the Federal Reserve (essentially the bank's own deposits at the central bank), and securities (bonds) the bank has purchased.

On the right side of the balance sheet a bank lists all its liabilities. *Liabilities* are things the bank owes to others. The largest liability is represented by the deposits of bank customers. The bank owes these deposits to its customers and must return them "on demand."

Table 13.3 also shows the use of balance sheets. Notice how the balance of University Bank now looks immediately after it receives your initial deposit (step 1, Table 13.3). Your deposit of coins is entered on both sides of University's balance sheet. On the left side, your deposit is regarded as an asset, because your piggy bank's coins have an immediate market value and can be used to pay off the bank's liabilities. The coins now appear as *reserves*. The reserves these coins represent are further divided into required reserves ($20, or 20 percent of your deposit) and excess reserves ($80).

On the right side of the balance sheet, the bank reminds itself that it has an obligation (liability) to return your deposit when you so demand. Thus the bank's accounts balance, with assets and liabilities being equal. In fact, **a bank's books must always balance because all the bank's assets must belong to someone (its depositors or its owners).**

University Bank wants to do more than balance its books, however; it wants to earn profits. To do so, it will have to make loans—that is, put its excess reserves to work. Suppose that it lends $80 to Campus Radio.[2] As step 2, Table 13.3 illustrates, this loan alters both sides of University Bank's balance sheet. On the right-hand side, the bank creates a new transactions deposit for (credits the account of) Campus Radio; this item represents an additional liability (promise to pay). On the left-hand side of the balance sheet, two things happen. First, the bank notes that Campus Radio owes it $80 ("loans"). Second, the bank recognizes that it's now required to hold $36 in *required* reserves, in accordance with its higher level of transactions deposits ($180). (Recall we're assuming that required reserves are 20 percent of total transactions deposits.) Since its total reserves are still $100, $64 is left as *excess* reserves. Note again that **excess reserves are reserves a bank isn't required to hold.**

Changes in the Money Supply. Before examining further changes in the balance sheet of University Bank, consider again what's happened to the economy's money supply during these first two steps. In the first step, you deposited $100 of cash in your checking account. This initial transaction didn't change the value of the money supply. Only the composition of the money supply (M1 or M2) was affected ($100 less cash held by the public, $100 more in transactions accounts).

CYBER NOTE

Find the most recent data on total bank reserves, borrowed reserves, excess reserves, and required reserves at the U.S. Federal Reserve: www.bog.frb.fed.us/releases/H3.

---

[2]Because of the Fed's assumed minimum reserve requirement (20 percent), University Bank can now lend only $80 rather than $100, as before.

Not until step 2—when the bank makes a loan—does all the excitement begin. In making a loan, the bank automatically increases the total money supply by $80. Why? Because someone (Campus Radio) now has more money (a transactions deposit) than it did before, *and no one else has any less*. And Campus Radio can use its money to buy goods and services, just like anybody else.

This second step is the heart of money creation. Money effectively appears out of thin air when a bank makes a loan. To understand how this works, you have to keep reminding yourself that money is more than the coins and currency we carry around. Transactions deposits are money too. Hence *the creation of transactions deposits via new loans is the same thing as creating money.*

More Deposit Creation. Suppose again that Campus Radio actually uses its $80 loan to buy an antenna. The rest of Table 13.3 illustrates how this additional transaction leads to further changes in balance sheets and the money supply.

In step 3, we see that when Campus Radio buys the $80 antenna, the balance in its checking account at University Bank drops to zero because it has spent all its money. As University Bank's liabilities fall (from $180 to $100), so does the level of its required reserves (from $36 to $20). (Note that required reserves are still 20 percent of its remaining transactions deposits). But University Bank's excess reserves have disappeared completely! This disappearance reflects the fact that Atlas Antenna keeps *its* transactions account at another bank (Eternal Savings). When Atlas deposits the check it received from Campus Radio, Eternal Savings does two things: First it credits Atlas's account by $80. Second, it goes to University Bank to get the reserves that support the deposit.[3] The reserves later appear on the balance sheet of Eternal Savings as both required ($16) and excess ($64) reserves.

Observe that the money supply hasn't changed during step 3. The increase in the value of Atlas Antenna's transactions-account balance exactly offsets the drop in the value of Campus Radio's transactions account. Ownership of the money supply is the only thing that has changed.

In step 4, Eternal Savings takes advantage of its newly acquired excess reserves by making a loan to Herman's Hardware. As before, the load itself has two primary effects. First, it creates a transactions deposit of $64 for Herman's Hardware and thereby increases the money supply by the same amount. Second, it increases the required level of reserves at Eternal Savings. (To how much? Why?)

THE MONEY MULTIPLIER

By now it's perhaps obvious that the process of deposit creation won't come to an end quickly. On the contrary, it can continue indefinitely, just like the income multiplier process in Chapter 10. Indeed, people often refer to deposit creation as the money multiplier process, with the **money multiplier** expressed as the reciprocal of the required reserve ratio.[4] That is

money multiplier: The number of deposit (loan) dollars that the banking system can create from $1 of excess reserves; equal to 1 ÷ required reserve ratio.

$$\frac{\text{Money}}{\text{multiplier}} = \frac{1}{\text{required}\atop\text{reserve ratio}}$$

Figure 13.2 illustrates the money multiplier process. When a new deposit enters the banking system, it creates both excess and required reserves. The required reserves rep-

---

[3]In actuality, banks rarely "go" anywhere; such interbank reserve movements are handled by bank clearinghouses and regional Federal Reserve banks. The effect is the same, however. The nature and use of bank reserves are discussed more fully in Chapter 14.

[4]The money multiplier $(1/r)$ is the sum of the infinite geometric progression $1 + (1 - r) + (1 - r)^2 + (1 - r)^3 + \cdots + (1 - r)^\infty$.

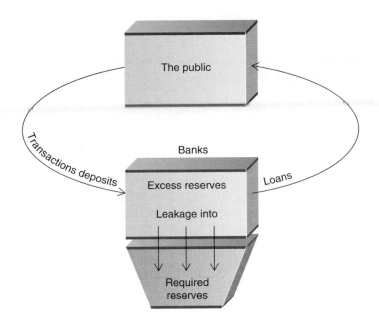

FIGURE 13.2
The Money Multiplier Process

Part of every new bank deposit leaks into required reserves. The rest—excess reserves—can be used to make loans. These loans, in turn, become deposits elsewhere. The process of money creation continues until all available reserves become required reserves.

resent leakage from the flow of money since they can't be used to create new loans. Excess reserves, on the other hand, can be used for new loans. Once those loans are made, they typically become transactions deposits elsewhere in the banking system. Then some additional leakage into required reserves occurs, and further loans are made. The process continues until all excess reserves have leaked into required reserves. Once excess reserves have completely disappeared, the total value of new loans will equal initial excess reserves multiplied by the money multiplier.

The potential of the money multiplier to create loans is summarized by the equation

$$\begin{array}{c}\text{Excess} \\ \text{reserves} \\ \text{of banking} \\ \text{system}\end{array} \times \begin{array}{c}\text{money} \\ \text{multiplier}\end{array} = \begin{array}{c}\text{potential} \\ \text{deposit creation}\end{array}$$

Notice how the money multiplier worked in our previous example. The value of the money multiplier was equal to 5, since we assumed that the required reserve ratio was 0.20. Moreover, the initial level of excess reserves was $80, as a consequence of your original deposit (step 1). According to the money multiplier, then, the deposit-creation potential of the banking system was

$$\begin{array}{c}\text{Excess reserves} \\ (\$80)\end{array} \times \begin{array}{c}\text{money multiplier} \\ (5)\end{array} = \begin{array}{c}\text{potential} \\ \text{deposit} \\ \text{creation (\$400)}\end{array}$$

When all the banks fully utilized their excess reserves at each step of the money multiplier process, the ultimate increase in the money supply was in fact $400 (see the last row in Table 13.3).

While you're struggling through Table 13.3, notice the critical role that excess reserves play in the process of deposit creation. A bank can make additional loans only if it has excess reserves. Without excess reserves, all of a bank's reserves are required, and no further liabilities (transactions deposits) can be created with new loans. On the other hand, a bank with excess reserves can make additional loans. In fact,

Excess Reserves as Lending Power

• *Each bank may lend an amount equal to its excess reserves and no more.*

As such loans enter the circular flow and become deposits elsewhere, they create new excess reserves and further lending capacity. As a consequence,

* ***The entire banking system can increase the volume of loans by the amount of excess reserves multiplied by the money multiplier.***

By keeping track of excess reserves, then, we can gauge the lending capacity of any bank or, with the aid of the money multiplier, the entire banking system.

Table 13.4 summarizes the entire money multiplier process. In this case, we assume that all banks are initially "loaned up"—that is, without any excess reserves. The money multiplier process begins when someone deposits $100 in cash into a transactions account at Bank *A*. If the required reserve ratio is 20 percent, this initial deposit creates $80 of excess reserves at Bank *A* while adding $100 to total transactions deposits.

If Bank *A* uses its newly acquired excess reserves to make a loan that ultimately ends up in Bank *B*, two things happen: Bank *B* acquires $64 in excess reserves (0.80 × $80), and total transactions deposits increase by another $80.

The money multiplier process continues with a series of loans and deposits. When the twenty-sixth loan is made (by bank *Z*), total loans grow by only $0.30 and trans-

TABLE 13.4

The Money Multiplier at Work

The process of deposit creation continues as money passes through different banks in the form of multiple deposits and loans. At each step, excess reserves and new loans are created. The lend- ing capacity of this system equals the money multiplier times ex- cess reserves. In this case, initial excess reserves of $80 create the possibility of $400 of new loans when the reserve ratio is 0.20 (20 percent).

Required reserves = 0.20	Change in Transactions Deposits	Change in Total Reserves	Change in Required Reserves	Change in Excess Reserves	Change in Lending Capacity
If $100 in cash is deposited in Bank *A*, Bank *A* acquires	$100.00	$100.00	$20.00	$80.00	$80.00
If loan made and deposited elsewhere, Bank *B* acquires	80.00	80.00	16.00	64.00	64.00
If loan made and deposited elsewhere, Bank *C* acquires	64.00	64.00	12.80	51.20	51.20
If loan made and deposited elsewhere, Bank *D* acquires	51.20	51.20	10.24	40.96	40.96
If loan made and deposited elsewhere, Bank *E* acquires	40.96	40.96	8.19	32.77	32.77
If loan made and deposited elsewhere, Bank *F* acquires	32.77	32.77	6.55	26.27	26.22
If loan made and deposited elsewhere, Bank *G* acquires	26.22	26.22	5.24	20.98	20.98
. . .	.	.	.	.	.
If loan made and deposited elsewhere, Bank *Z* acquires	0.38	0.38	0.08	0.30	0.30
Cumulative, through Bank *Z*	$498.80	$100.00	$99.76	$0.24	$398.80
. . .	.	.	.	.	.
And if the process continues indefinitely	$500.00	$100.00	$100.00	$0.00	$400.00

A $100 cash deposit creates $400 of new lending capacity when the required reserve ratio is 0.20. Initial excess reserves are $80 (= $100 deposit − $20 required reserves). The money multiplier is 5 (= 1 ÷ 0.20). New lending potential equals $400 (= $80 excess reserves × 5).

actions deposits by an equal amount. Should the process continue further, the *cumulative* change in loans will ultimately equal $400, that is, the money multiplier times initial excess reserves. The money supply will increase by the same amount.

BANKS AND THE CIRCULAR FLOW

The bookkeeping details of bank deposits and loans are rarely exciting and often confusing. But they do demonstrate convincingly that banks can create money. In that capacity, *banks perform two essential functions for the macro economy:*

- *Banks transfer money from savers to spenders by lending funds (reserves) held on deposit.*
- *The banking system creates additional money by making loans in excess of total reserves.*

In performing these two functions, banks change the size of the money supply—that is, the amount of purchasing power available for buying goods and services. Market participants may respond to these changes in the money supply by altering their spending behavior and shifting the aggregate demand curve.

Figure 13.3 is a simplified perspective on the role of banks in the circular flow. As before, income flows from product markets through business firms to factor markets and returns to consumers in the form of disposable income. Consumers spend most of their income but also save (don't spend) some of it.

The leakage represented by consumer saving is a potential source of stabilization problems, particularly unemployment. If additional spending by business firms, foreigners, or governments doesn't compensate for consumer saving at full employment, a recessionary gap will emerge, creating unemployment (see Chapters 9 and 10). Our interest here is in the role the banking system can play in encouraging such additional spending.

Suppose for the moment that *all* consumer saving was deposited in piggy banks rather than depository institutions (banks) and that no one used checks. Under these circumstances, banks couldn't transfer money from savers to spenders by holding deposits and making loans.

Financing Injections

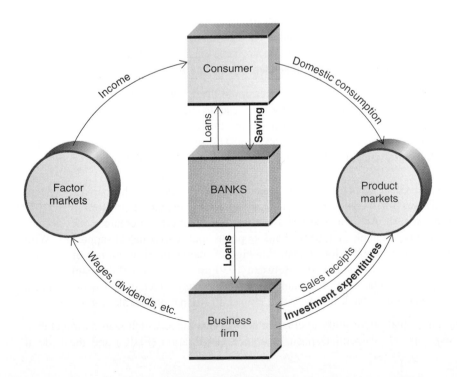

FIGURE 13.3
Banks in the Circular Flow

Banks help transfer income from savers to spenders by using their deposits to make loans to business firms and consumers who want to spend more money than they have. By lending money, banks help maintain any desired rate of aggregate spending.

In reality, a substantial portion of consumer saving *is* deposited in banks. These and other bank deposits can be used as the basis of loans, thereby returning purchasing power to the circular flow. In fact, the primary economic function of banks isn't to store money but to transfer purchasing power from savers to spenders. They do so by lending money to businesses for new plant and equipment, to consumers for new homes or cars, and to government entities that desire greater purchasing power. Moreover, because the banking system can make *multiple* loans from available reserves, banks don't have to receive all consumer saving in order to carry out their function. On the contrary, *the banking system can create any desired level of money supply if allowed to expand or reduce loan activity at will.*

Constraints on Deposit Creation

There are three major constraints on the deposit creation of the banking system.

Deposits. The first constraint is the willingness of consumers and businesses to continue using and accepting checks rather than cash in the marketplace. If people preferred to hold cash rather than checkbooks, banks wouldn't be able to acquire or maintain the reserves that are the foundation of bank lending activity.

Borrowers. The second constraint on deposit creation is the willingness of consumers, businesses, and governments to borrow the money that banks make available. The chain of events we've observed in deposit creation depends on the willingness of Campus Radio to borrow $80, of Herman's Hardware to borrow $64, and so on. If no one wanted to borrow any money, deposit creation would never begin. By the same reasoning, if all excess reserves aren't borrowed (lent), deposit creation won't live up to its theoretical potential.

Regulation. The third major constraint on deposit creation is the Federal Reserve System. As we've observed, the Fed may limit deposit creation by imposing reserve requirements. These and other tools of monetary policy are discussed in Chapter 14.

THE ECONOMY TOMORROW

When Banks Fail

The power of banks to create money originates in the *fractional reserve* system. As we've observed, a bank holds reserves that are a small fraction of its liabilities, implying that no bank could pay off its customers if they all sought to withdraw their deposits at one time.

Bank Panics

In earlier times, banks did experience occasional "runs" when depositors would rush to withdraw their funds. Such depositor runs usually began when word spread that a particular bank was running low on cash and might close. Depositor runs became self-fulfilling confirmation of a bank's insolvency. The resulting bank closing wiped out customer deposits, curtailed bank lending, and often pushed the economy into recession.

During the Great Depression there was widespread fear that the banking system would collapse. Borrowers weren't able to repay their loans and depositors were withdrawing more cash. As their reserves dwindled, banks' ability to create money evaporated. Suddenly, a chunk of money (bank deposits and loans) just disappeared. With little cash coming in and a lot of cash flowing out, banks quickly ran out of cash reserves and had to shut their doors. Between 1930 and 1933 over 9000 banks failed. To prevent total collapse of the banking system, newly elected president Franklin Roosevelt declared a "bank holiday" that closed all the nation's banks for 1 week.

Deposit Insurance

Congress used that opportunity to create a deposit insurance which would protect customer deposits. The Federal Deposit Insurance Corporation (FDIC) and the Federal

Savings and Loan Insurance Corporation (FSLIC) were created in 1933 and 1934 to ensure depositors that they'd get their money back even it their bank failed. The guarantee of insured deposits eliminated the motivation for deposit runs. If a bank closed, the federal government would step in and repay deposits.

The S&L Crisis

Federal deposit insurance provided a foundation for public confidence in the banking system. It didn't, however, ward off bank failures. In some respects, deposit insurance even contributed to bank failures. By insuring deposits, the federal government eliminated a major risk for bank customers. Depositors no longer had to concern themselves with the soundness of a bank's lending practices; their deposits were insured. This created the opportunity for bank owners to engage in riskier loans that had greater profit potential.

During the 1970s, accelerating inflation pushed interest rates up. To attract deposits, banks had to offer higher rates of interest on customer deposits. Many of their loans, however, were already set at lower interest rates. This was particularly true for savings and loan associations (S&Ls), which traditionally lent most of their funds in long-term home mortgages. Suddenly, they were stuck earning low interest rates on long-term mortgages while paying high interest rates on short-term deposits. This was a recipe for failure.

The woes of the S&Ls were exacerbated by increased competition from new financial institutions (like money market mutual funds) that enticed deposits away from S&Ls. Sharp downturns in oil prices and real estate also weakened borrowers' ability to repay their loans. These and other forces caused more than half the S&Ls that existed in 1970 to disappear by 1990. In 1988, more banks failed (200) than in any year since the Great Depression. The 1990–1991 recession pushed still more banks into insolvency (see NEWS).

Bank Bailouts

The FSLIC and FDIC averted bank panics by paying off depositors in failed banks. So many S&Ls failed, however, that the FSLIC itself ran out of funds. Congress had to appropriate ever larger sums of money to bail out the banks. In 1992 alone, over $60 billion was spent on bank bailouts.

When the federal government steps in to pay insured deposits, it also assumes control of a failing bank. The government then tries to arrange a merger or acquisition with a stronger bank. In the process, the federal government acquires some or all of the outstanding loans of the failed bank. The Resolution Trust Corporation (RTC) was created in 1989 to manage these loans. The RTC tried to collect outstanding loans or sell the properties (such as office buildings, shopping centers, homes) that were

IN THE NEWS

First City Fails

First City Bancorp, which owns 20 Texas banks hurt by bad loans, was declared insolvent Friday. Regulators say First City is the largest bank failure this year and the eighth-largest ever. Sen. Don Riegle, D-Mich., says the failure is significant because it's the second time the bank has been bailed out. In 1988, the Federal Deposit Insurance Corp. gave First City $977 million to protect depositors' money. The banks will reopen today under government control until a buyer is found. But FDIC will guarantee only 80% of deposits that exceed the $100,000 insurance limit at four of the 20 banks.

USA Today, Nov. 2, 1992, p. B1. Copyright 1992, USA TODAY. Reprinted with permission. www.usatoday.com

Analysis: When a bank fails, the FDIC (or SAIF for savings banks) steps in to guarantee that deposited funds will be returned to depositors. The government then tries to sell the bank or its remaining assets (loans).

financed with those loans. Part of the huge outlays for bank bailouts in the early 1990s were offset by the proceeds from these RTC property sales.

Banks will continue to compete for deposits and loans in the economy tomorrow. They'll have the advantage of deposit insurance [provided by the FDIC and the renamed Savings Association Insurance Fund (SAIF)] in attracting new funds. Congress, however, has set more stringent requirements on the types of loans and investments banks can make. It has also forced bank owners to put more of their own funds at risk. The intent of these changes is to improve the financial stability of banks while assuring the public that their deposits are safe—even in banks with only fractional reserves.

SUMMARY

- In a market economy, money serves a critical function in facilitating exchanges and specialization, thus permitting increased output. "Money" refers to any medium that's generally accepted in exchange.
- Because people use bank account balances to buy goods and services, such balances are also regarded as money. The money supply M1 includes cash plus transactions-account (checkable) deposits. M2 adds savings account balances and other deposits to form a broader measure of the money supply.
- Banks have the power to create money by making loans. In making loans, banks create new transactions deposits, which become part of the money supply.
- Banks' ability to make loans—create money—depends on their reserves. Only if a bank has excess reserves—reserves greater than those required by federal regulation—can it make new loans.
- As loans are spent, they create deposits elsewhere, making it possible for other banks to make additional loans.

- The money multiplier (1 ÷ required reserve ratio) indicates the total value of deposits that can be created by the banking system from excess reserves.
- The role of banks in creating money includes the transfer of money from savers to spenders as well as deposit creation in excess of deposit balances. Taken together, these two functions give banks direct control over the amount of purchasing power available in the marketplace.
- The deposit-creation potential of the banking system is limited by government regulation. It's also limited by the willingness of market participants to hold deposits or borrow money.
- When banks fail, the federal government (FDIC or SAIF) guarantees to pay deposits. To reduce bank failures, bank owners are now required to put more of their own assets at risk.

Key Terms

barter
money
transactions account
money supply (M1, M2)

aggregate demand
deposit creation
bank reserves
reserve ratio

required reserves
excess reserves
money multiplier

Questions for Discussion

1. How are an economy's production possibilities affected when workers are paid in bras and coffins rather than cash? (See WORLD VIEW page 253 about bartering in Russia.)
2. What percentage of your monthly spending do you pay with (*a*) cash, (*b*) check, (*c*) credit card, and (*d*) automatic transfers. How do you pay off the credit card balance? How do your payment choices compare with the

NEWS summary on page 254? How does your use of cash compare with the composition of the money supply (Figure 13.1)?
3. If you can purchase airline tickets with online computer services, should your electronic account be counted in the money supply? Explain.
4. Does the fact that your bank keeps only a fraction of your account balance in reserve make you uncomfort-

able? Why don't people rush to the bank and retrieve their money? What would happen if they did?

5. If people never withdrew cash from banks, how much money could the banking system potentially create? Could this really happen? What might limit deposit creation in this case?

6. If all banks heeded Shakespeare's admonition "Neither a borrower nor a lender be," what would happen to the circular flow?

7. How does federal deposit insurance encourage greater risk taking by banks? Could the banking system function without government deposit insurance? How?

8. If Internet E-cash systems (NEWS page 255) could make loans, how would the money supply be affected?

9. Why did Scan decide to stop accepting cash in payment for furniture (NEWS page 255)?

10. Web Activity Find historical data for M1 and M2 at the Federal Reserve, at www.bog.frb.fed.us/releases/H6/hist. During the past year, which measure of the money supply has increased the least? The most? Based on what you have learned about the difference between M1 and M2, what might explain why one type of money is increasing faster than the other?

11. Web Activity Take the Money Challenge at the St. Louis Fed at www.stls.frb.org/education/econed3.html. Print your answers and bring them to class. Which question is most important for U.S. economic policy. Why?

Problems for Chapter 13 appear at the back of the book.

14

The Federal Reserve System

We've seen how money is created. We've also gotten a few clues about how the government limits money creation and thus influences aggregate demand. This chapter examines the mechanics of government control more closely. The basic issues addressed are

- How does the government control the amount of money in the ecomomy?
- Which government agency is responsible for exercising this control?
- How are banks and bond markets affected by the government's policies?

Most people have a ready answer for the first question. The popular view is that the government controls the amount of money in the economy by printing more or fewer dollar bills. But we've already observed that the concept of "money" isn't so simple. In Chapter 13 we demonstrated that banks, not the printing presses, create most of our money. In making loans, banks create transactions deposits that are counted as part of the money supply.

Because bank lending activities are the primary source of money, the government must regulate bank lending if it wants to control the amount of money in the economy. That's exactly what the Federal Reserve System does. The Federal Reserve System—the "Fed"—not only limits the volume of loans that the banking system can make from available reserves; it can also alter the amount of reserves banks hold.

The Federal Reserve System's control over the supply of money is the key mechanism of **monetary policy.** The potential of this policy level to alter macro outcomes is examined in Chapter 15, where the way changes in the supply of money can alter the rate of unemployment, the rate of inflation, or both are discussed. For the time being, however, we focus on the tools available for implementing monetary policy.

STRUCTURE OF THE FED

In the absence of any government regulation, the supply of money would be determined by individual banks. Moreover, individual depositors would bear all the risks of bank failures. In fact, this is the way the banking system operated until 1914. The money supply was subject to abrupt changes, and consumers frequently lost their savings in recurrent bank failures.

A series of bank failures resulted in a severe financial panic in 1907. Millions of depositors lost their savings, and the economy was thrown into a tailspin. In the wake of this panic, a National Monetary Commission was established to examine ways of restructuring the banking system. The mandate of the commission was to find ways to avert recurrent financial crises. After 5 years of study, the commission recommended the creation of a Federal Reserve System. Congress accepted the commission's recommendations, and President Wilson signed the Federal Reserve Act in December 1913.

monetary policy: The use of money and credit controls to influence macroeconomic outcomes.

Federal Reserve Banks

The core of the Federal Reserve System consists of 12 Federal Reserve banks. Each bank acts as a central banker for the private banks in its region. In this role, the Fed banks perform the following services:

- *Clearing checks between private banks.* Suppose the Bank of America in San Francisco receives a deposit from one of its customers in the form of a share draft written on the New York State Employees Credit Union. The Bank of America doesn't have to go to New York to collect the cash or other reserves that support that draft. Instead, the Bank of America can deposit the draft (check) at its account with the Federal Reserve Bank of San Francisco. The Fed then collects from the Credit Union. This vital clearinghouse service saves the Bank of America and other private banks a great deal of time and expense in processing the 70 *billion* checks that are written every year.
- *Holding bank reserves.* Notice that the Fed's clearinghouse service was facilitated by the fact that the Bank of America and the New York Employees Credit Union had their own accounts at the Fed. As we noted before, banks are *required* to hold some minimum fraction of their deposits in reserve. Only a small amount of reserves is held as cash in a bank's vaults. The rest is held in reserve accounts at the regional Federal Reserve banks. These accounts at the Fed provide greater security and convenience for bank reserves and also enable the Fed to monitor the actual level of bank reserves.
- *Providing currency.* Before every major holiday there's a great demand for cash. People want some pocket money during holidays and know that it's difficult to cash checks on weekends or holidays, especially if they're going out of town. After the holiday is over, most of this cash is returned to the banks, typically by the stores, gas stations, and restaurants that benefited from holiday spending. Because banks hold very little cash in their vaults, they turn to the Fed to meet these sporadic cash demands. A private bank can simply call the regional Federal Reserve bank and order a supply of cash, to be delivered (by armored truck) before a weekend or holiday. The cash will be deducted from the bank's own account at the Fed. When all the cash comes back in after the holiday, the bank can reverse the process, sending the unneeded cash back to the Fed.
- *Providing loans.* The Federal Reserve banks may also loan reserves to private banks. This practice, called "discounting," is examined more closely here.

CYBER NOTE

Who runs the Fed? Read profiles of the governors at www.bogfrb.fed.us/FOMC/minutes.

The Board of Governors

At the top of the Federal Reserve System's organization chart (Figure 14.1) is the Board of Governors, which is responsible for setting monetary policy. The Board, located in Washington, D.C., consists of seven members (governors), appointed by the president of the United States and confirmed by the U.S. Senate. Board members are appointed for 14-year terms and can't be reappointed. Their exceptionally long appointments are intended to give the Fed governors a measure of political independence. They're not beholden to any elected official and will hold office longer than any president.

The intent of the Fed's independence is to keep control of the nation's money supply beyond the immediate reach of politicians (especially members of Congress, elected for 2-year terms). The designers of the Fed system feared that political control of monetary policy would cause wild swings in the money supply and macro instability. Critics argue, however, that the Fed's independence makes it unresponsive to the majority will.

FIGURE 14.1
Structure of the Federal Reserve System

The Fed's broad policies are determined by the 7-member Board of Governors. The 12 Federal Reserve banks provide central banking services to individual banks in their respective regions. The Federal Open Market Committee directs Federal Reserve transactions in the money market. Various committees offer formal and informal advice to the Board of Governors.

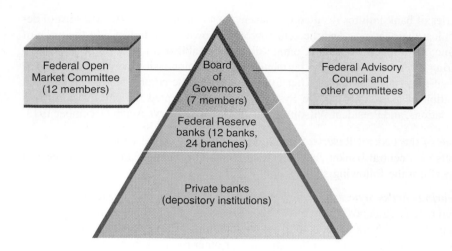

The president selects one of the governors to serve as chairman of the Board for 4 years. Alan Greenspan was first appointed as chairman by President Reagan, then reappointed for a second 4-year term by President Bush in 1991, and again by President Clinton in 1996. Chairman Greenspan is the primary spokesperson for Fed policy and reports to Congress every 6 months on the conduct of monetary policy.

The Federal Open Market Committee (FOMC)

A key arm of the Board is the Federal Open Market Committee (FOMC), which is responsible for the Fed's daily activity in financial markets. The FOMC plays a critical role in determining the level of reserves held by private banks. The membership of the FOMC includes all 7 governors and 5 of the 12 regional Reserve bank presidents. The FOMC meets in Washington, D.C., every 4 or 5 weeks throughout the year to review the economy's performance. It decides whether the economy is growing fast enough (or too fast) and then adjusts monetary policy as needed.

MONETARY TOOLS

money supply (M1): Currency held by the public, plus balances in transactions accounts.
M2 money supply: M1 plus balances in most savings accounts and money market mutual funds.

Our immediate interest isn't in the structure of the Federal Reserve but the way the Fed is able to alter the **money supply.** The Fed's control of the money supply is exercised by use of three policy instruments:

- Reserve requirements
- Discount rates
- Open market operations

Reserve Requirements

required reserves: The minimum amount of reserves a bank is required to hold; equal to required reserve ratio times transactions deposits.

We emphasized the need for banks to maintain some minimal level of reserves. As noted in Chapter 13, the Fed requires private banks to keep some stated fraction of their deposits "in reserve." These **required reserves** are held either in the form of actual vault cash or, more commonly, as credits (deposits) in the bank's "reserve account" at a regional Federal Reserve bank. *By changing the reserve requirements, the Fed can directly alter the lending capacity of the banking system.*

Recall that the banking system's ability to make additional loans—create deposits—is determined by two factors: (1) the amount of excess reserves banks hold and (2) the money multiplier. Both factors are directly influenced by the Fed's required reserve ratio.

Suppose, for example, that banks hold $100 billion of transactions deposits and total reserves of $30 billion. Assume too that the minimum reserve requirement is 20 percent. Under these circumstances, banks are holding more reserves than they have to. Recall that

$$\frac{\text{Required}}{\text{reserves}} = \frac{\text{required}}{\text{reserve ratio}} \times \frac{\text{total}}{\text{deposits}}$$

so, in this case

$$\text{Required reserves} = 0.20 \times \$100 \text{ billion}$$

$$= \$20 \text{ billion}$$

Banks are *required* to hold \$20 billion in reserve to meet Federal Reserve regulations. They're actually holding \$30 billion, however. The \$10 billion difference between actual and required reserves is **excess reserves**—that is,

$$\text{Excess reserves} = \text{total reserves} - \text{required reserves}$$

excess reserves: Bank reserves in excess of required reserves.

The existence of excess reserves implies that banks aren't fully utilizing their lending powers. With \$10 billion of excess reserves and the help of the **money multiplier** the banks *could* lend an additional \$50 billion.

The potential for additional loans is calculated as

$$\text{Available lending capacity of banking system} = \text{excess reserves} \times \text{money multiplier}$$

money multiplier: The number of deposit (loan) dollars that the banking system can create from \$1 of excess reserves; equal to 1 ÷ required reserve ratio.

or, in this case,

$$\$10 \text{ billion} \times \frac{1}{0.20} = \$50 \text{ billion of unused lending capacity}$$

That is, the banking system could create another \$50 billion of money (transactions-account balances) without any additional reserves.

A simple way to confirm this—and thereby check your arithmetic—is to note what would happen to total deposits if the banks actually made further loans. Total deposits would increase to \$150 billion in this case (the initial \$100 billion plus the new \$50 billion), an amount that could be supported with \$30 billion in reserves (20 percent of \$150 billion).

But what if the Fed doesn't want the money supply to increase this much? Maybe prices are rising and the Fed wants to restrain rather than stimulate total spending in the economy. Under such circumstances, the Fed would want to restrict the availability of credit (loans). Does it have the power to do so? Can the Fed reduce the lending capacity of the banking system?

The answer to both questions is clearly yes. ***By raising the required reserve ratio, the Fed can immediately reduce the lending capacity of the banking system.***

Table 14.1 summarizes the impact of an increase in the required reserve ratio. In this case, the required reserve ratio is increased from 20 to 25 percent. Notice that this change in the reserve requirement has no effect on the amount of deposits in the banking system (row 1, Table 14.1) or the amount of total reserves (row 2). They remain at

	Required Reserve Ratio	
	20 Percent	**25 Percent**
1. Total deposits	\$100 billion	\$100 billion
2. Total reserves	30 billion	30 billion
3. Required reserves	20 billion	25 billion
4. Excess reserves	10 billion	5 billion
5. Money multiplier	5	4
6. Unused lending capacity	\$ 50 billion	\$ 20 billion

TABLE 14.1
The Impact of an Increased Reserve Requirement

An increase in the required reserve ratio reduces both excess reserves (row 4) and the money multiplier (row 5). As a consequence, changes in the reserve requirement have a substantial impact on the lending capacity of the banking system (row 6).

$100 billion and $30 billion, respectively. What the increased reserve requirement does affect is the way those reserves can be used. Before the increase, only $20 billion in reserves was *required,* leaving $10 billion of *excess* reserves. Now, however, banks are required to hold $25 billion (0.25 × $100 billion) in reserves, leaving them with only $5 billion in excess reserves. Thus an increase in the reserve requirement immediately reduces excess reserves, as illustrated in row 4, Table 14.1.

There's also a second effect. Notice what happens to the money multiplier (1 ÷ reserve ratio). Previously it was 5(1 ÷ 0.20); now it's only 4(1 ÷ 0.25). Consequently, a higher reserve requirement not only reduces excess reserves but diminishes their lending power as well.

A change in the reserve requirement, therefore, hits banks with a triple whammy. *A change in the reserve requirement causes a change in*

- *Excess reserves*
- *The money multiplier*
- *The lending capacity of the banking system*

These changes lead to a sharp reduction in bank lending power. Whereas the banking system initially had the power to increase the volume of loans by $50 billion ($10 billion of excess reserves × 5), it now has only $20 billion ($5 million × 4) of unused lending capacity, as noted in the last row in Table 14.1

Changes in reserve requirements are a powerful weapon for altering the lending capacity of the banking system. The Fed uses this power sparingly, so as not to cause abrupt changes in the money supply and severe disruptions of banking activity. From 1970 to 1980, for example, reserve requirements were changed only twice, and then by only half a percentage point each time (for example, from 12.0 to 12.5 percent). The Fed cut the reserve requirement from 12 to 10 percent in 1992 to increase bank profits and encourage more lending (see NEWS). Smaller banks have a lower reserve requirement (3 percent), which gives them a competitive advantage.

The Discount Rate

Banks have a tremendous incentive to maintain their reserves at or close to the minimum established by the Fed. Bank reserves held at the Fed earn no interest, but loans and bonds do. Hence a profit-maximizing bank seeks to keep its excess reserves as low as possible, preferring to put its reserves to work. In fact, banks have demonstrated an uncanny ability to keep their reserves close to the minimum federal requirement. As Figure 14.2 illustrates, the only time banks held huge excess reserves was in the

IN THE NEWS

Fed Cuts Deposit-Reserve Requirements

Reduction Is the Latest Bid to Bolster Bank Profits and Encourage Lending

WASHINGTON—The Federal Reserve Board, in another attempt to shore up bank profits so bankers will be more willing to lend, reduced the fraction of deposits that must be held as reserves.

The Fed cut to 10% from 12% the percentage of checking account deposits that banks are required to hold as reserves.

Because reserves must be in cash or in accounts that don't pay any interest, the change will add between $300 million and $600 million to bank industry profits.

—David Wessel

The Wall Street Journal, Feb. 19, 1992, p. A2. Reprinted by permission of *The Wall Street Journal,* © 1992 Dow Jones & Company, Inc. All Rights Reserved Worldwide. www.wsj.com

Analysis: A reduction in the reserve requirement transforms some of the banking system's required reserves into excess reserves, thus increasing potential lending activity and profits. It also increases the size of the money multiplier.

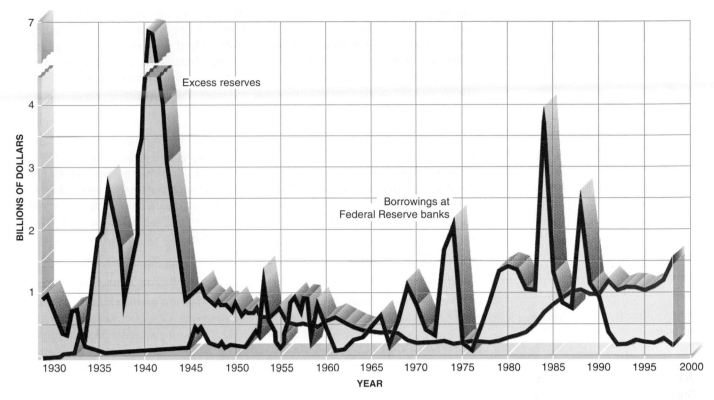

FIGURE 14.2
Excess Reserves and Borrowings

Excess reserves represent unused lending capacity. Hence banks strive to keep excess reserves at a minimum. One exception to this practice occurred in the Great Depression, when banks were hesitant to make any loans. In trying to minimize excess reserves, banks occasionally fall short of required reserves. At such times they may borrow from other banks (the federal funds market), or they may borrow reserves from the Fed. Borrowing from the Fed is called "discounting."

Great Depression of the 1930s. The banks didn't want to make any more loans and were fearful of panicky customers withdrawing their deposits.

Because banks continually seek to keep excess reserves at a minimum, they run the risk of falling below reserve requirements. A large borrower may be a little slow in repaying a loan, or the rate of deposit withdrawals and transfers may exceed expectations. At such times a bank may find that it doesn't have enough reserves to satisfy Fed requirements.

Banks could ensure continual compliance with reserve requirements by maintaining large amounts of excess reserves. But that's an unprofitable procedure, and a profit-maximizing bank will seek other alternatives.

The Federal Funds Market. A bank that finds itself short of reserves can turn to other banks for help. If a reserve-poor bank can borrow some reserves from a reserve-rich bank, it may be able to bridge its temporary deficit and satisfy the Fed. *Reserves borrowed by one bank from another are referred to as "federal funds" and are lent for short periods, usually overnight.* Although trips to the federal funds market—via telephone and computer—will usually satisfy Federal Reserve requirements, such trips aren't free. The lending bank will charge interest (the **"federal funds rate"**) on its interbank loan.[1] The use of the federal funds market to satisfy Federal Reserve requirements also depends on other banks having excesss reserves to lend.

federal funds rate: The interest rate for interbank reserve loans.

[1]An overnight loan of $1 million at 6 percent interest (per year) costs $165 in interest charges plus any service fees that might be added. Banks make multimillion-dollar loans in the federal funds market.

Sale of Securities. Another option available to reserve-poor banks is the sale of securities. Banks use some of their excess reserves to buy government bonds, which pay interest. If a bank needs more reserves to satisfy federal regulations, it may sell these securities and deposit the proceeds at the regional Federal Reserve bank. Its reserve position is thereby increased. This option also involves distinct costs, however, both in forgone interest-earning opportunities and in the possibility of capital losses when the bond is offered for quick sale.

Discounting. A third option for avoiding a reserve shortage lies in the structure of the Federal Reserve System itself. The Fed not only establishes certain rules of behavior for banks but also functions as a central bank, or banker's bank. Banks maintain accounts with the regional Federal Reserve banks, much the way you and I maintain accounts with a local bank. Individual banks deposit and withdraw "reserve credits" from these accounts, just as we deposit and withdraw dollars. Should a bank find itself short of reserves, it can go to the Fed's "discount window" and borrow some reserves. This process is called **discounting.** Discounting means the Fed is lending reserves directly to private banks.[2]

> **discounting:** Federal Reserve lending of reserves to private banks.

The Fed's discounting operation provides private banks with an important source of reserves, but not without cost. The Fed too charges interest on the reserves it lends to banks, a rate of interest referred to as the **discount rate.**

> **discount rate:** The rate of interest the Federal Reserve charges for lending reserves to private banks.

The discount window is a mechanism for directly influencing the size of bank reserves. *By raising or lowering the discount rate, the Fed changes the cost of money for banks and therewith the incentive to borrow reserves.* At high discount rates, borrowing from the Fed is expensive. High discount rates also signal the Fed's desire to restrain the money supply and an accompanying reluctance to lend reserves. Low discount rates, on the other hand, make it profitable to acquire additional reserves and exploit one's lending capacity to the fullest. Low discount rates also indicate the Fed's willingness to support credit expansion. The accompanying WORLD VIEW illustrates how Japan's central bank used this policy lever in 1998 to encourage more borrowing and spending.

Open Market Operations

Reserve requirements and discount window operations are important tools of monetary policy. But they don't come close to open market operations in day-to-day impact on the money supply. *Open market operations are the principal mechanism for directly altering the reserves of the banking system.* Since reserves are the lifeblood of the banking system, open market operations are of immediate and critical interest to private banks and the larger economy.

Portfolio Decisions. To appreciate the impact of open market operations, you have to think about the alternative uses for idle funds. Just about all of us have some idle funds, even if they amount to just a few dollars in our pocket or a minimal balance in our checking account. Other consumers and corporations have great amounts of idle funds, even millions of dollars at any time. Here we're concerned with what people decide to do with such funds.

People (and corporations) don't hold all their idle funds in transactions accounts or cash. Idle funds are also used to purchase stocks, build up savings account balances, and purchase bonds. These alternative uses of idle funds are attractive because they promise some additional income in the form of interest, dividends, or capital appreciation, such as higher stock prices. Deciding where to place idle funds is referred to as the **portfolio decision.**

> **portfolio decision:** The choice of how (where) to hold idle funds.

---

[2]In the past, banks had to present loan notes to the Fed in order to borrow reserves. The Fed "discounted" the notes by lending an amount equal to only a fraction of their face value. Although banks no longer have to present loans as collateral, the term "discounting" endures.

Japan's Central Bank Cuts Rates
Move Made in Bid to Aid Economy

TOKYO, Sept. 9—Japan's central bank tonight unexpectedly cut its short-term interest rates, which were already at rock bottom, in an attempt to stabilize the nation's fragile financial system and halt the rapid slide of the world's second-largest economy.

The Bank of Japan, in a statement released tonight, said it took the action "to prevent the economy from falling into a deflationary spiral," which some analysts read as an extraordinary admission of the danger faced by the Japanese economy.

Japan's economy is in recession, stalled by falling consumer demand, business investment and prices. The economy is de-teriorating rapidly, experts say, because the ailing Japanese banking system is unable to lend fresh capital to businesses.

Financial analysts said the cut in interest rates would do little to reignite the economy because interest rates were already so low, and were not the cause of the credit crunch.

The bank reduced its target rate for overnight loans among banks to 0.25 percent from slightly under 0.5 percent. By comparison, the U.S. federal funds rate is 5.5 percent.

—Sandra Sugawara

The Washington Post, Sept. 10, 1998, p. C1. © 1998, The Washington Post. Reprinted with permission. www.washingtonpost.com

Analysis: A rate cut encourages banks to borrow more reserves from the central bank (in the United States, the Fed). Those borrowed reserves enable banks to make more loans to business and consumers.

Hold Money or Bonds? The Fed's open market operations focus on one of the portfolio choices people make: whether to deposit idle funds in bank accounts or purchase government bonds. In essence, the Fed attempts to influence this choice by making bonds more or less attractive, as circumstances warrant, thereby inducing people to move funds from banks to bond markets or vice versa. In the process, reserves either enter or leave the banking system, thereby altering the lending capacity of banks.

Figure 14.3 depicts the general nature of the Fed's open market operations. As we first observed in Chapter 13 (Figure 13.2), the process of deposit creation begins when people deposit money in the banking system. But people may also hold their assets in the form of bonds. The Fed's objective is to alter this portfolio decision by buying or selling bonds. ***When the Fed buys bonds from the public, it increases the flow of deposits (reserves) to the banking system. Bond sales by the Fed reduce the flow.***

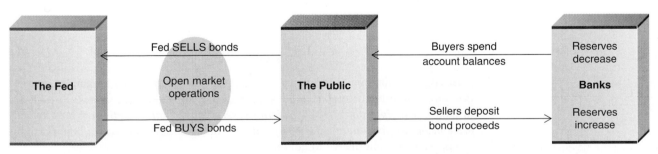

FIGURE 14.3
Open Market Operations

People may hold assets in the form of bank deposits (money) or bonds. When the Fed buys bonds from the public, it increases the flow of deposits (and reserves) to the banks. When the Fed sells bonds, it diminishes the flow of deposits and therewith the banks' capacity to lend (create money).

The Bond Market. To understand how open market operations work, let's look closer at the bond market. Not all of us buy and sell bonds, but a lot of consumers and corporations do: Daily volume in bond markets exceeds $100 billion. What's being exchanged in this market, and what influences decisions to buy or sell?

In our discussion thus far, we've portrayed banks as intermediaries between savers and spenders. Banks aren't the only mechanism available for transferring purchasing power from nonspenders to spenders. Funds are lent and borrowed in bond markets as well. In this case, a corporation may borrow money directly from consumers or other institutions. When it does so, it issues a bond as proof of its promise to repay the loan. A **bond** is simply a piece of paper certifying that someone has borrowed money and promises to pay it back at some future date. In other words, a bond is nothing more than an IOU. In the case of bond markets, however, the IOU is typically signed by a giant corporation or a government agency, rather than a friend. It's therefore more widely accepted by lenders.

Because most corporations and government agencies that borrow money in the bond market are well known and able to repay their debts, their bonds are actively traded. If I lend $1000 to General Motors on a 10-year bond, for example, I don't have to wait 10 years to get my money back; I can resell the bond to someone else at any time. If I do, that person will collect the face value of the bond (plus interest) from GM when it's due. The actual purchase and sale of bonds take place in the bond market. Although a good deal of the action occurs on Wall Street in New York, the bond market has no unique location. Like other markets we've discussed, the bond market exists whenever and however bond buyers and sellers get together.

Bond Yields. People buy bonds because bonds pay interest. If you buy a General Motors bond, GM is obliged to pay you interest during the period of the loan. For example, an 8 percent 2005 GM bond in the amount of $1000 states that GM will pay the bondholder $80 interest annually (8 percent of $1000) until 2005. At that point the initial $1000 loan will be repaid.

The current **yield** paid on a bond depends on the promised interest rate (8 percent in this case) and the actual purchase price of the bond. Specifically,

$$\text{Yield} = \frac{\text{annual interest payment}}{\text{price paid for bond}}$$

If you pay $1000 for the bond, then the current yield is

$$\text{Yield} = \frac{\$80}{\$1000} = 0.08, \text{ or } 8\%$$

which is the same as the interest rate printed on the face of the bond. But what if you pay only $900 for the bond? In this case, the promised interest rate remains at 8 percent, but the *yield* jumps to

$$\text{Yield} = \frac{\$80}{\$900} = 0.089, \text{ or } 8.9\%$$

Buying a $1000 bond for only $900 might seem like too good a bargain to be true. But bonds are often bought and sold at prices other than their face value (see NEWS). In fact, *a principal objective of Federal Reserve open market activity is to alter the price of bonds, and therewith their yields.* By doing so, the Fed makes bonds a more or less attractive alternative to holding money.

Open Market Activity. The basic premise of open market activity is that participants in the bond market will respond to changes in bond prices and yields. As we've observed, the less you pay for a bond, the higher its yield. Accordingly, the Fed can induce people to buy bonds by offering to sell them at a lower price, for example, a

bond: A certificate acknowledging a debt and the amount of interest to be paid each year until repayment; an IOU.

yield: The rate of return on a bond; the annual interest payment divided by the bond's price.

Zero-Coupon Bonds

Conventional bonds make interest payments each year, often quarterly. However, some bonds pay no current interest. Because so-called zero-coupon bonds make no interest payments, they have a *current* yield of zero. In effect, a zero-coupon bond accumulates interest payments, paying them all at once when the bond comes due. The *yield to maturity* on such bonds is implied by the difference between the purchase price and the face value of the bond. A $1000 "zero" due in 10 years, for example, might cost only $400 today. You lend $400 now and get back $1000 in 10 years. The implied yield to maturity is approximately 9 percent.

Analysis: The yield (return) on a bond depends not only on annual interest payments but also on the difference between the price paid for the bond and its face (payoff) value.

$1000, 8 percent bond for only $900. Similarly, the Fed can induce people to sell bonds by offering to buy them at higher prices. In either case, the Fed hopes to move reserves into or out of the banking system. In other words, **open market operations** entail the purchase and sale of government securities (bonds) for the purpose of altering the flow of reserves into and out of the banking system.

open market operations: Federal Reserve purchases and sales of government bonds for the purpose of altering bank reserves.

Open Market Purchases. Suppose the Fed wants to increase the money supply and therefore desires to provide the banking system with additional reserves. To do so, it must persuade people to deposit a larger share of their financial assets in banks and hold less in other forms, particularly government bonds. If the Fed offers to pay a higher price for bonds, it will effectively lower bond yields. The higher prices and lower yields will reduce the attractiveness of holding bonds. If the price offered by the Fed is high enough, people will sell some of their bonds to the Fed and deposit some or all of the proceeds of the sale in their bank accounts. This influx of money into bank accounts will directly increase bank reserves.

Figure 14.4 illustrates the dynamics of open market operations in more detail. When the Fed buys a bond from the public, it pays with a check written on itself. The bond seller must deposit the Fed's check in his bank account if he wants to use part of the proceeds or simply to hold the money for safekeeping. The bank, in turn, deposits the

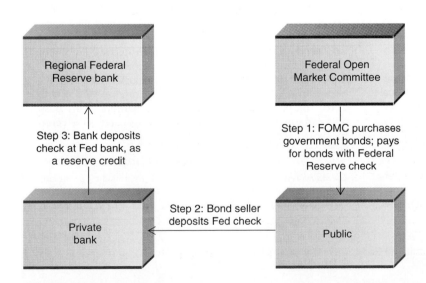

FIGURE 14.4
An Open Market Purchase

The Fed can increase bank reserves by buying government securities from the public. The Fed check used to buy securities (step 1) gets deposited in a private bank (step 2). The bank returns the check to the Fed (step 3), thereby obtaining additional reserves. To decrease bank reserves, the Fed would sell securities, thus reversing the flow of reserves.

check at a regional Federal Reserve bank, in exchange for a reserve credit. The bank's reserves are directly increased by the amount of the check. Thus *by buying bonds, the Fed increases bank reserves.* These reserves can be used to expand the money supply still further, as banks put their newly acquired reserves to work making loans.

Open Market sales. Should the Fed desire to slow the growth in the money supply, it can reverse the whole process. Instead of offering to *buy* bonds, the Fed in this case will try to *sell* bonds. If it sets the price sufficiently low—so that bond yields are sufficiently high—individuals, corporations, and government agencies will convert some of their transactions deposits into bonds. When they do so, they write a check, paying the Fed for the bonds.[3] The Fed then returns the check to the depositor's bank, taking payment through a reduction in the bank's reserve account. The reserves of the banking system are thereby diminished, as is the capacity to make loans. Thus *by selling bonds, the Fed reduces bank reserves.*

The Fed Funds Rate. A market signal of these changing reserve flows is provided by the federal funds rate. Recall that "feds funds" are excess reserves traded among banks. If the Fed pumps more reserves into the banking system (by buying bonds), the interest rate charged for overnight reserve loans—the federal funds rate—will decline. Conversely, if the Fed is reducing bank reserves (by selling bonds), the federal funds rate will increase. Hence, the federal funds rate is a highly visible signal of Federal Reserve open market operations. When Alan Greenspan reduced the fed funds rate twice in October 1998, the financial markets interpreted the move as a clear signal of monetary stimulus (see NEWS).

CYBER NOTE

How has the federal funds rate changed in the past 8 weeks? What does it signal about Federal Reserve activity? For data on the fed funds rate visit the Fed's Web site www.federalreserve.gov.

[3]In actuality, the Fed deals directly with only 36 "primary" bond dealers. These intermediaries then trade with each other, "secondary" dealers, financial institutions, and individuals. These additional steps don't significantly alter the flow of funds depicted here.

IN THE NEWS

News: Analysis

Fed Chairman Cuts Rates Quarter Point

Greenspan's Decision Sparks Stock and Bond Rallies; Blue Chips Surge 330.58

WASHINGTON—Delighting stock and bond markets and underscoring his concerns about what he has called the "scary psychology" in financial markets, Federal Reserve Chairman Alan Greenspan cut short-term interest rates by a quarter of a percentage point.

The surprise move, which came less than three weeks after the Fed's last rate cut, reflects both Fed worries about unusual conditions in the bond market, where even top-grade corporate borrowers are having some trouble raising money, and a sense at the Fed that it may have goofed by cutting short-term rates by only a quarter of a percentage point on Sept. 29.

After consulting other Fed officials around midday yesterday—but without asking for a formal vote—Mr. Greenspan reduced the Fed's target for the important federal-funds rate, at which banks lend to each other, to 5% from 5.25%. The last time Mr. Greenspan exercised his authority in this fashion was in April 1994, when he raised interest rates.

At the same time, the Fed's board of governors voted 5-0 to cut the largely symbolic discount rate—at which the Fed itself lends to banks—by 0.25 percentage point to 4.75%. One seat on the Fed board is vacant, and Governor Edward Gramlich had to leave the meeting before the vote was taken.

Immediately after the Fed move, a number of big banks cut their prime rates to 8% from 8.25%, including **Chase Manhattan** Corp., **U.S. Bancorp, Norwest** Corp. and **Banc One** Corp. The prime rate serves as a benchmark for many business and some consumer loans, so borrowers across the country should see some drop in borrowing costs because of the Fed's act.

—David Wessel and Jacob M. Schlesinger

The Wall Street Journal, Oct. 19, 1998, p. A2. Reprinted by permission of *The Wall Street Journal*; © 1998 Dow Jones & Company, Inc. All Rights Reserved Worldwide. www.wsj.com

Analysis: A cut in the federal funds rate indicates that the Fed is increasing bank reserves, thereby decreasing market interest rates.

Volume of Activity. To appreciate the significance of open market operations, you need a sense of the magnitudes involved. The volume of trading in U.S. government securities exceeds $100 billion per day. The Fed alone owned $450 billion worth of government securities at the beginning of 1999 and bought or sold enormous sums daily. Thus open market operations involve tremendous amounts of money and, by implication, potential bank reserves. Each $1 of reserves represents something like $10 of potential lending capacity (via the money multiplier). Thus open market operations can have a profound impact on the money supply.

INCREASING THE MONEY SUPPLY

The three major instruments of monetary policy are reserve requirements, discount rates, and open market operations. The Fed can use these levers individually or in combination to change the money supply. This section illustrates the use of each tool to attain a specific policy goal.

Suppose the policy goal is to increase the money supply from an assumed level of $340 billion to $400 billion. In surveying the nation's banks, the Fed discovers the facts shown in Table 14.2. On the basis of the facts presented in Table 14.2, it's evident that

- The banking system is "loaned up." Because excess reserves are zero, there's no additional lending capacity.
- The required reserve ratio must be equal to 25 percent, because this is the current ratio of required reserves ($60 billion) to total deposits ($240 billion).

Accordingly, if the Fed wants to increase the money supply, it will have to pump additional reserves into the banking system or lower the reserve requirement. *To increase the money supply the Fed can*

- *Lower reserve requirements*
- *Reduce the discount rate*
- *Buy bonds*

Lowering the reserve requirements is an expedient way of increasing the lending capacity of the banking system. But by how much should the reserve requirement be reduced?

Recall that the Fed's policy objective is to increase the money supply from $340 billion to $400 billion, an increase of $60 billion. If the public isn't willing to hold any additional cash, this entire increase in money supply will have to take the form of added transactions deposits. In other words, total deposits will have to increase from $240 billion to $300 billion. These additional deposits will have to be *created* by the banks, in the form of new loans to consumers or business firms.

If the banking system is going to support $300 billion in transactions deposits with its *existing* reserves, the reserve requirement will have to be reduced from 25 percent; thus

$$\frac{\text{Total reserves}}{\text{Desired level of deposits}} = \frac{\$60 \text{ billion}}{\$300 \text{ billion}} = 0.20$$

Lowering Reserve Requirements

Item	Amount
Cash held by public	$100 billion
Transactions deposits	240 billion
Total money supply (M1)	$340 billion
Required reserves	$ 60 billion
Excess reserves	0
Total reserves of banks	$ 60 billion
U.S. bonds held by public	$460 billion
Discount rate	7 percent

TABLE 14.2
How to Increase the Money Supply

The accompanying data depict a banking system that has $340 billion of money (M1) and no further lending capacity (excess reserves = 0). To enlarge M1 to $400 billion, the Fed can (1) lower the required reserve ratio, (2) reduce the discount rate, or (3) buy bonds held by the public.

At the moment the Fed lowers the minimum reserve ratio to 0.20, *total* reserves won't change. The bank's potential lending power will change, however. Required reserves will drop to $48 billion (0.20 × $240 billion), and excess reserves will jump from zero to $12 billion. These new excess reserves imply an additional lending capacity:

$$\underset{(\$12 \text{ billion})}{\text{Excess reserves}} \times \underset{(5)}{\text{money multiplier}} = \underset{(\$60 \text{ billion})}{\text{unused lending capacity}}$$

If the banks succeed in putting all this new lending power to work—actually make $60 billion in new loans—the Fed's objective of increasing the money supply will be attained.

Lowering the Discount Rate

The second monetary tool available to the Fed is the discount rate. We assumed it was 7 percent initially (see Table 14.2). If the Fed lowers this rate, it will become cheaper for banks to borrow reserves from the Fed. The banks will be more willing to borrow (cheaper) reserves so long as they can make additional loans to their own customers at higher interest rates. The profitability of discounting depends on the *difference* between the discount rate and the interest rate the bank charges its loan customers. The Fed increases this difference when it lowers the discount rate.

There's no way to calculate the appropriate discount rate without more detailed knowledge of the banking system's willingness to borrow reserves from the Fed. Nevertheless, we can determine how much reserves the banks *must* borrow if the Fed's money supply target is to be attained. The Fed's objective is to increase transactions deposits by $60 billion. If these deposits are to be created by the banks—and the reserve requirement is unchanged at 0.25—the banks will have to borrow an additional $15 billion of reserves ($60 billion divided by 4, the money multiplier).

Buying Bonds

The Fed can also get additional reserves into the banking system by buying U.S. bonds in the open market. As Table 14.2 indicates, the public holds $460 billion in U.S. bonds, none of which are counted as part of the money supply. If the Fed can persuade people to sell some of these bonds, bank reserves will surely rise.

To achieve its money supply target, the Fed will offer to buy $15 billion of U.S. bonds. It will pay for these bonds with checks written on its own account at the Fed. The people who sold the bonds will deposit these checks in their own transactions accounts. As they do so, they'll directly increase bank deposits and reserves by $15 billion.

Is $15 billion of open market purchases enough? Yes. The $15 billion is a direct addition to transactions deposits, and therefore to the money supply. The additional deposits bring in $15 billion of reserves, only $3.75 billion of which is required (0.25 × $15 billion). Hence the new deposits bring in $11.25 billion of excess reserves, which themselves create an additional lending capacity:

$$\underset{(\$11.25 \text{ billion})}{\text{Excess reserves}} \times \underset{(4)}{\text{money multiplier}} = \underset{(\$45 \text{ billion})}{\text{unused lending capacity}}$$

Thus the $15 billion of open market purchases will eventually lead to a $60 billion increase in M1 as a consequence of both direct deposits ($15 billion) and subsequent loan activity ($45 billion).

DECREASING THE MONEY SUPPLY

All the tools used to increase the money supply can also be used to decrease it. *To reduce the money supply, the Fed can*

- *Raise reserve requirements*
- *Increase the discount rate*
- *Sell bonds*

On a week-to-week basis the Fed does occasionally seek to reduce the total amount of cash and transactions deposits held by the public. These are minor adjustments, however, to broader policies. A growing economy needs a steadily increasing supply of money to finance market exchanges. Hence the Fed rarely seeks an outright reduction in the size of the money supply. What it does do is regulate the *rate of growth* in the money supply. When the Fed wants to slow the rate of consumer and investor spending, it restrains the *growth* of money and credit. Although many people talk about "reducing" the money supply, they're really talking about slowing its rate of growth. A rising fed funds rate is a convenient signal of the Fed's intent.

THE ECONOMY TOMORROW

The policy tools at the Fed's disposal imply tight control of the nation's money supply. By altering reserve requirements, discount rates, or open market purchases, the Fed apparently has the ability to increase or decrease the money supply at will. But the Fed's control is far from complete. The nature of "money," as well as our notion of what a "bank" is, keeps changing. As a result, the Fed has to run pretty fast just to stay in place.

Before 1980 the Fed's control of the money supply wasn't only incomplete but actually weakening. The Fed didn't have authority over all banks. Only one-third of all commercial banks were members of the Federal Reserve System and subject to its regulations. In addition, all savings and loan associations and other savings banks remained outside the Federal Reserve System. These banks were subject to regulations of state banking commissions and other federal agencies but not to Federal Reserve requirements. As a consequence, a substantial quantity of money and near-money lay beyond the control of the Fed.

To increase the Fed's control of the money supply, Congress passed the Depository Institutions Deregulation and Monetary Control Act of 1980. Commonly referred to simply as the Monetary Control Act, that legislation called for a complete restructuring of the U.S. banking system. Its principal objectives were to (1) extend the Fed's control of the money supply and (2) encourage greater competition in the banking industry.

The Monetary Control Act subjects *all* commercial banks, S&Ls, savings banks, and most credit unions to Fed regulation. All depository institutions now have to satisfy new (and lower) Fed reserve requirements. All depository institutions also enjoy access to the Fed's discount window. These reforms (phased in over a period of 7 years) obliterated the distinction between member and nonmember banks and greatly strengthened the Fed's control of the banking system.

Ironically, **as the Fed's control of the banks was increasing, the banks themselves were declining in importance.** Banks are part of a larger financial services industry that provides deposit, credit, and payment services. Many of these services are provided by financial institutions other than banks. These "nonbank" financial institutions have grown in importance while traditional banks have declined in number and importance.

Accepting and holding deposits is a core bank function. Consumers can also place idle funds in money market mutual funds (MMMF), however. MMMFs typically pay higher interest rates than traditional bank accounts and also permit limited check writing privileges. They thus serve as a potential substitute for traditional banks. Many brokerage houses also offer to hold idle cash in interest-earning accounts for their stock and bond customers.

Nonbanks are also competing against banks for loan business; 30 percent of all consumer loans are now made through credit cards. Banks themselves were once the primary source of credit cards. Now corporate giants like AT&T, GM, Sears, and American Airlines offer nonbank credit cards. Large corporations also offer loans to consumers who want to buy their products and even extend loans to unaffiliated businesses.

Insurance companies and pension funds also use their vast financial resources to make loans. The Teachers Insurance and Annuity Association (TIAA)—the pension

Is the Fed Losing Control?

Monetary Control Act

Decline of Traditional Banks

The Globalization of Money

About two-thirds of the $460 billion in U.S. currency in circulation is now held abroad. Transactions accounts also cross international borders with ease. All it takes is a couple of entries on a computer and some electronic bookkeeping.

Over $1.2 trillion of money is transmitted by bank wire every day, in billions of separate transactions. Most of these transactions go through one of two clearinghouses, the Fed's "Fedwire" system or CHIPS (the Clearing House Interbank Payments System), which specializes in international finance. These clearinghouses move money so efficiently that the same dollar can be used seven times in a day—in seven different countries!

The network of international wire transfers has globalized money. "Eurodollars" are dollar deposits kept in European banks. These dollars may be used in Europe—perhaps to finance a British purchase of French champagne. Or U.S. corporations may borrow Eurodollars to finance investments at home or abroad. In either case, a couple of electronic signals is all it takes to move the money across international borders.

The globalization of money markets increased in January 1990, when U.S. banks received permission to accept deposits in foreign currency. On top of that, international credit cards provide worldwide access to cash and credit.

The globalization of money makes it more difficult for the Fed to control the money supply. If "tight" money policies make domestic credit less available, U.S. firms can turn to Eurodollars or other foreign markets. Electronic outflows can similarly frustrate the Fed's attempts to increase the domestic money supply.

Analysis: The Fed's control of the money supply depends on its ability to regulate bank reserves and lending. The movement of money across international borders weakens this control.

fund for college professors—has lent over $10 billion directly to corporations. Many insurance companies provide long-term loans for commercial real estate.

Foreign banks, corporations, and pension funds may also extend credit to American businesses. They may also hold deposits of U.S. dollars abroad (for example, Eurodollars). As the accompanying WORLD VIEW illustrates, money travels easily across national borders.

All this credit and deposit activity by global and nonbank institutions competes with traditional banks. And the nonbanks are winning the competition. In the past 20 years, the share of all financial institution assets held by banks has dropped from 37 percent to 27 percent, which means that banks are less important than they once were. It also implies that the Fed will have to focus more on nonbank financial institutions if it wants to maintain control of the money supply in the economy tomorrow.

SUMMARY

- The Federal Reserve System controls the nation's money supply by regulating the loan activity (deposit creation) of private banks (depository institutions).
- The core of the Federal Reserve System is the 12 regional Federal Reserve banks, which provide check-clearance, reserve deposit, and loan ("discounting") services to individual banks. Private banks are required to maintain minimum reserves on deposit at one of the regional Federal Reserve banks.
- The general policies of the Fed are set by its Board of Governors. The Board's chair is selected by the U.S. president and confirmed by the Senate. The chair serves as

the chief spokesperson for monetary policy. The general policies of the Fed are carried out by the Federal Open Market Committee (FOMC), which directs open market sales and purchase of U.S. bonds.

- The Fed has three basic tools for changing the money supply. By altering the reserve requirement, the Fed can immediately change both the quantity of excess reserves in the banking system and the money multiplier, which limits banks' lending capacity. By altering discount rates (the rate of interest charged by the Fed for reserve borrowing), the Fed can also influence the amount of reserves maintained by banks. Finally, and most important, the Fed can increase or decrease the reserves of the banking system by buying or selling government bonds, that is, by engaging in open market operations.

- When the Fed buys bonds, it causes an increase in bank reserves (and lending capacity). When the Fed sells bonds, it induces a reduction in reserves (and lending capacity).

- The federal funds (interest) rate is a market signal of Fed open market activity and intentions.
- In the 1980s the Fed gained greater control of the banking system. Global and nonbank institutions such as pension funds, insurance companies, and nonbank credit services have grown in importance, however, making control of the money supply more difficult.

Key Terms

monetary policy	money multiplier	portfolio decision
money supply (M1, M2)	federal funds rate	bond
required reserves	discounting	yield
excess reserves	discount rate	open market operations

Questions for Discussion

1. Why do banks want to maintain as little excess reserves as possible? Under what circumstances might banks want to hold excess reserves? (*Hint:* see Figure 14.2.)

2. Why do people hold bonds rather than larger savings account or checking account balances? Under what circumstances might they change their portfolios, moving their funds out of bonds into bank accounts?

3. What is the current price and yield of U.S. Treasury bonds? Of General Motors bonds? (Check the financial section of your daily newspaper.) What accounts for the difference?

4. Why did the stock and bond markets rally so strongly when the Fed cut the federal funds rate? (See NEWS page 282.)

5. Why might the Fed want to decrease the money supply?

6. Why would a zero-coupon bond (see NEWS page 281) have a lower price than a bond paying annual interest?

7. Why might Japanese consumers and investors *not* respond to the discount-rate cut described in the WORLD VIEW page 279?

8. Web Activity At www.bog.frb.fed.us/centralbanks.htm you'll find links to the home pages for the central banks of major industrialized countries. Visit the sites for two central banks other than U.S. ones. Find at least one difference between each foreign central bank and the U.S. Federal Reserve. Find at least one similarity.

9. Web Activity Find the most recent testimony of the Chairman of the Federal Reserve Board of Governors at www.federal.reserve.gov/BoardDocs/Testimony/Current. What does it indicate about the Fed's current monetary policy? What economic conditions is the Fed attempting to remedy or improve? Do you agree with current Fed policy?

Problems for Chapter 14 appear at the back of the book.

15

Monetary Policy

So what if the Federal Reserve System controls the nation's money supply. Why is this significant? Does it matter how much money is available? Will the money supply affect our ability to achieve full employment, price stability, or any other macroeconomic goal?

Vladimir Lenin thought so. The first communist leader of the Soviet Union once remarked that the best way to destroy a society is to destroy its money. If a society's money became valueless, it would no longer be accepted in exchange for goods and services in product markets. As a consequence, people would resort to barter, and the economy's efficiency would be severely impaired. Adolf Hitler tried unsuccessfully to use this weapon against Great Britain during World War II. His plan was to counterfeit British currency, then drop it from planes flying over England. He believed that the sudden increase in the quantity of money, together with its suspect origins, would render the British pound valueless.

Even in peacetime, the quantity of money in circulation will influence its value in the marketplace. Moreover, access to credit (bank loans) is a basic determinant of spending behavior. Consequently, control over the money supply implies an ability to influence macroeconomic outcomes.

But how much influence does the money supply have on macro performance? Specifically,

- What's the relationship between the money supply and aggregate demand?
- How can the Fed use its control of the money supply to alter macro outcomes?
- How effective is monetary policy, compared to fiscal policy?

Economists offer very different answers to these questions. Some argue that changes in the money supply directly affect macro outcomes; others argue that the effects of such changes are indirect and less certain.

Paralleling these arguments about *how* **monetary policy** works are debates over the relative effectiveness of monetary and fiscal policy. Some economists argue that monetary policy is more effective than fiscal policy; others contend the reverse is true. This chapter examines these different views of money and assesses their implications for fiscal and monetary policy.

THE MONEY MARKET

The best place to learn how monetary policy works is the money *market*. You must abandon any mystical notions you may harbor about money and view it like any other commodity that's traded in the marketplace. Like other goods, there's a supply of money and a demand for money. Together they determine the "price" of money, or the **interest rate.**

At first glance, it may appear strange to call interest rates the price of money. But, when you borrow money, the "price" you pay is measured by the interest rate you're charged. When interest rates are high, money is "expensive." When interest rates are low, money is "cheap."

Even people who don't borrow must contend with the price of money. Money, as we've seen, comes in many different forms. A common characteristic of all money is that it can be held as a store of value. People hold cash and maintain positive balances in various bank accounts for this purpose. Most of the money in our common measures of **money supply (M1, M2)** is in the form of bank balances. There's an opportunity cost associated with such money balances, however. Money held in transactions accounts earns little or no interest. Money held in savings accounts and money market mutual funds does earn interest, but usually at relatively low rates. By contrast, money used to buy bonds or stocks or to make loans is likely to earn a higher interest rate of return.

The Price of Money. The nature of the "price" of money should be apparent: People who hold *cash* are forgoing an opportunity to earn interest. So are people who hold money in checking accounts that pay no interest. In either case, forgone interest is the opportunity cost (price) of money people choose to hold. How high is that price? It's equal to the market rate of interest.

Money held in interest-paying bank accounts does earn some interest. In this case, the opportunity cost of holding money is the *difference* between the prevailing rate of interest and the rate paid on deposit balances. As is the case with cash and regular checking accounts, opportunity cost is measured by the forgone interest.

Once we recognize that money does have a price, we can easily formulate a demand for money. As is the case with all goods, the **demand for money** is simply a schedule (or curve) showing the quantity of money demanded at alternative prices (interest rates).

The decision to hold (demand) money balances is a **portfolio decision.** While at first glance it might seem irrational to hold money balances that pay little or no interest, there are many good reasons for doing so.

Transactions Demand. Even people who've mastered the principles of economics hold money. They do so because they want to buy goods and services. In order to transact business in product or factor markets, we need money in the form of either cash or a positive bank account balance. ATM cards don't work unless there's money in the bank. Payment by "E-cash" also requires a supporting bank balance. Even when we use credit cards, we're only postponing the date of payment by a few weeks or so. Accordingly, we recognize the existence of a basic **transactions demand for money.**

Precautionary Demand. Another reason people hold money is their fear of the proverbial rainy day. A sudden emergency may require money purchases over and above normal transactions needs. Moreover, such needs may arise when the banks are closed or in a community where one's checks aren't accepted. Also, future income is uncertain and may diminish unexpectedly. Therefore, people hold a bit more money (cash or bank account balances) than they anticipate spending. This **precautionary demand for money** is the extra money being held as a safeguard against the unexpected.

---

monetary policy: The use of money and credit controls to influence macroeconomic outcomes.

interest rate: The price paid for the use of money.

Money Balances

money supply (M1): Currency held by the public, plus balances in transactions accounts.

money supply (M2): M1 plus balances in most savings accounts and money market mutual funds.

The Demand for Money

demand for money: The quantities of money people are willing and able to hold at alternative interest rates, *ceteris paribus.*

portfolio decision: The choice of how (where) to hold idle funds.

transactions demand for money: Money held for the purpose of making everyday market purchases.

precautionary demand for money: Money held for unexpected market transactions or for emergencies.

Speculative Demand. People also hold money for speculative purposes, so they can respond to financially attractive opportunities. Suppose you were interested in buying stocks or bonds but hadn't yet picked the right ones, or regarded their present prices as too high. In such circumstances, you might want to hold some money so that you could later buy a "hot" stock or bond at a price you think attractive. Thus you'd be holding money in the hope that a better financial opportunity would later appear. In this sense, you'd be *speculating* with your money, forgoing present opportunities to earn interest in the hope of hitting a real jackpot later. These money balances represent a **speculative demand for money.**

speculative demand for money: Money held for speculative purposes, for later financial opportunities.

The Market Demand Curve. These three motivations for holding money combine to create a *market demand* for money. The question is, what shape does this demand curve take? Does the quantity of money demanded decrease sharply as the rate of interest rises? Or do people tend to hold the same amount of money, regardless of its price?

People do cut down on their money balances when interest rates rise. At such times, the opportunity cost of holding money is simply too high, which explains why so many people move their money out of transactions deposits (M1) and into money market mutual funds (M2) when interest rates are extraordinarily high (for example, in 1980–1982). Corporations are even more careful about managing their money when interest rates rise. Better money management requires watching checking account balances more closely and even making more frequent trips to the bank, but the opportunity costs are worth it.

Figure 15.1 illustrates the total market demand for money. Like nearly all demand curves, the market demand curve for money slopes downward. The downward slope indicates that *the quantity of money people are willing and able to hold (demand) increases as interest rates fall* (ceteris paribus).

Equilibrium

Once a money demand curve and a money supply curve are available, the action in money markets is easy to follow. Figure 15.1 summarizes this action. The money demand curve in Figure 15.1 reflects existing demands for holding money. The money supply curve is drawn at an arbitrary level of g_1. In practice, its position depends on Federal Reserve policy (Chapter 14), the lending behavior of private banks, and the willingness of consumers and investors to borrow money.

FIGURE 15.1
Money Market Equilibrium

All points on the market demand curve represent the quantity of money people are willing to hold at a specific interest rate. The equilibrium interest rate occurs at the intersection (E_1) of the money supply and money demand curves. At that rate of interest, people are willing to hold as much money as is available. At any other interest rate (for example, 9 percent), the quantity of money people are *willing* to hold won't equal the quantity available, and people will adjust their portfolios.

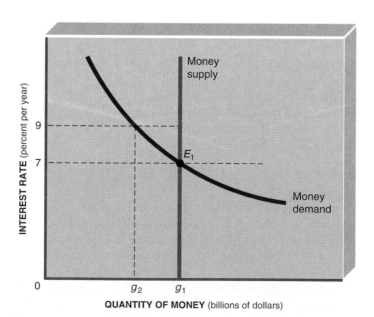

The intersection of the money demand and money supply curves (E_1) establishes an **equilibrium rate of interest.** Only at this interest rate is the quantity of money supplied equal to the quantity demanded. In this case, we observe that an interest rate of 7 percent equates the desires of suppliers and demanders.

At any rate of interest other than 7 percent, the quantity of money demanded wouldn't equal the quantity supplied. Look at the imbalance that exists, for example, when the interest rate is 9 percent. At that rate, the quantity of money supplied (g_1) exceeds the quantity demanded (g_2). All the money (g_1) must be held by someone, of course. But the demand curve indicates that people aren't *willing* to hold so much money at that interest rate (9 percent). People will adjust their portfolios by moving money out of cash and bank accounts into bonds or other assets that offer higher returns. This will tend to lower interest rates (recall that buying bonds tends to lower their yields). As interest rates drop, people are willing to hold more money. Ultimately we get to E_1, where the quantity of money demanded equals the quantity supplied. At that equilibrium, people are content with their portfolio choices.

The equilibrium rate of interest is subject to change. As we saw in Chapter 14, the Federal Reserve System can alter the money supply through changes in reserve requirements, changes in the discount rate, or open market operations. By implication, then, *the Fed can alter the equilibrium rate of interest.*

Figure 15.2 illustrates the potential impact of monetary policy on the equilibrium rate of interest. Assume that the money supply is initially at g_1 and the equilibrium interest rate is 7 percent. The Fed then increases the money supply to g_2 by lowering the reserve requirement, reducing the discount rate, or, most likely, purchasing additional bonds in the open market. This expansionary monetary policy brings about a new equilibrium, at E_2. At this intersection, the market rate of interest is only 6 percent. Hence, by increasing the money supply, the Fed tends to lower the equilibrium rate of interest. To put the matter differently, people are *willing* to hold larger money balances only at lower interest rates.

Were the Fed to reverse its policy and reduce the money supply, interest rates would rise. You can see this result in Figure 15.2 by observing the change in the rate of interest that occurs when the money supply *shrinks* from g_2 to g_1.

Federal Funds Rate. As we noted in Chapter 14, the most visible market signal of the Fed's activity is the **federal funds rate.** When the Fed injects or withdraws reserves

equilibrium rate of interest: The interest rate at which the quantity of money demanded in a given time period equals the quantity of money supplied.

Changing Interest Rates

federal funds rate: The interest rate for interbank reserve loans.

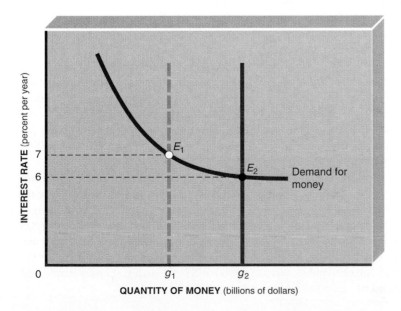

FIGURE 15.2
Changing the Rate of Interest

Changes in the money supply tend to alter the equilibrium rate of interest. In this case, an increase in the money supply (from g_1 to g_2) lowers the equilibrium rate of interest (from 7 percent to 6 percent).

TABLE 15.1
The Hierarchy of Interest Rates

Interest rates reflect the risks and duration of loans. Because risks and loan terms vary greatly, dozens of different interest rates are available. Here are a few of the more common rates as of February 1999.

Interest Rate	Type of Loan	Rate
Discount rate	Reserves lent to banks by Fed	4.75%
Federal funds rate	Interbank reserves, overnight	4.63%
Prime rate	Bank loans to blue chip corporations	7.75%
Mortgage rate	Loans for house purchases; up to 30 years	6.69%
Auto loan	Financing of auto purchase	8.62%
Consumer installment credit	Loans for general purposes	13.75%
Credit cards	Financing of unpaid credit card purchases	15.69%

Source: Federal Reserve

from the banking system (via open market operations), the interest rate on interbank loans is most directly affected. Any change in the federal funds rate, moreover, is likely to affect a whole hierarchy of interest rates (see Table 15.1).

INTEREST RATES AND SPENDING

A change in the interest rate isn't the end of this story. The ultimate objective of monetary policy is to alter macroeconomic outcomes: prices, output, employment. This requires a change in aggregate demand. Hence the next question is how changes in interest rates affect consumer, investor, government, and net export spending.

Monetary Stimulus

aggregate demand: The total quantity of output demanded at alternative price levels in a given time period, *ceteris paribus*.

Consider first a policy of monetary stimulus. The goal of monetary stimulus is to increase **aggregate demand.** A mechanism for doing so is lower interest rates.

Investment. Will lower interest rates encourage spending? In Chapter 9 we observed that investment decisions are sensitive to the rate of interest. Specifically, we demonstrated that lower rates of interest reduce the cost of buying plant and equipment, making investment more profitable. Accordingly, a lower rate of interest should result in a higher rate of desired investment spending, as shown by the movement down the investment-demand curve in Figure 15.3*b*.

CYBER NOTE

Compare the interest rates in Table 5.1 with today's rates at www.stls.frb.org.

Aggregate Demand. The increased investment brought about by lower interest rates represents an injection of new spending into the circular flow. That jump in spending will kick off multiplier effects and result in an even larger increase in aggregate demand. Figure 15.3*c* illustrates this increase by the rightward *shift* of the aggregate demand curve. Market participants, encouraged by lower interest rates, are now willing to buy more output at the prevailing price level.

Consumers too may change their behavior when interest rates fall. As interest rates fall, mortgage payments decline. Monthly payments on home equity and credit card balances may also decline. As the NEWS story illustrates, these lower interest changes can free up billions of dollars. This increased net cash flow and lower interest rates may encourage consumers to buy new cars, appliances, or other "big-ticket" items. State and local governments may also conclude that lower interest rates increase the desirability of bond-financed public works (see NEWS). All such responses would add to aggregate demand.

(a) An increase in the money supply lowers the rate of interest

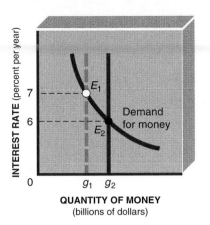

(b) A reduction in the rate of interest stimulates investment

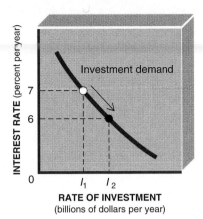

(c) More investment increases aggregate demand (including multiplier effects)

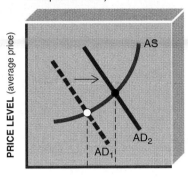

FIGURE 15.3
Monetary Stimulus

An increase in the money supply may reduce interest rates and encourage more investment. The increase in investment will trigger multiplier effects that increase aggregate demand by an even larger amount.

IN THE NEWS

Lower Rates Send a Flood of Cash into the Economy

It's bonanza time for borrowers. Although the economy is still stalled, lower rates are starting to put big bucks into the pockets of homeowners, businesses, and even governments. Calculations by *Business Week* and others show that the current level of interest rates could add about $27 billion to the economy in 1992 (table). That's more money than most tax-cutting schemes now talked about in Washington.

The biggest winners from lower rates, of course, are homeowners. Since last summer, the interest rate on one-year Treasury bills, to which many adjustable-rate mortgages are pegged, has fallen by two percentage points. Fixed-rate mortgages, too, have fallen, leading to a tidal wave of refinancings. Borrowers could see their housing costs fall by some $22 billion in 1992, estimates Richard W. Peach, an economist at the Mortgage Bankers Assn. . . .

Companies stand to gain plenty, too. . . . Based on past experience, the fall in interest rates since last summer could save corporations $10 billion, which could give a nice boost to profits.

Even deficit-ridden governments, big borrowers in the 1980s, are cashing in on the fall in interest rates.

What Lower Rates Add to the Economy (Effects in 1992 in billions of dollars)*

Consumer Rates	
Mortgage cost	$22
Other debt	2
(Credit cards, home equity and auto loans)	
Interest income	−15
(Certificates of deposit and other savings)	

Business Borrowing Costs	
Corporate debt	10

Government Borrowing Costs	
Federal	7
State and local	1
Total	$27

*Assuming interest rates stay at current levels

DATA: Mortgage Bankers Assn.; Donaldson, Lufkin & Jenrette; *Business Week,* Feb. 3, 1992, p. 16.

Analysis: Lower interest rates reduce debt-servicing costs, freeing up income for new purchases. Lower interest rates also make new purchases more affordable.

From this perspective, *the Fed's objective of stimulating the economy is achieved in three distinct steps:*

- *An increase in the money supply*
- *A reduction in interest rates*
- *An increase in aggregate demand*

Quantitative Impact. Just how much stimulus can monetary policy create? According to Fed Chairman Alan Greenspan, the impact of monetary policy can be impressive:

$$\text{Greenspan's policy guide:} \quad \frac{\text{1/10 point reduction in}}{\text{long-term interest rate}} = \frac{\text{\$10 billion}}{\text{fiscal stimulus}}$$

By this rule of thumb, a full point reduction in interest rates would increase aggregate demand just as much as a $100 billion injection of new government spending. This is the kind of stimulus Europe was hoping for when interest rates were cut in 1998 (see WORLD VIEW).

Monetary Restraint

Like fiscal policy, monetary policy is a two-edged sword, at times seeking to increase aggregate demand and at other times trying to restrain it. When inflation threatens, the objective of monetary policy is to reduce the rate of total spending, which puts the Fed in the position of "leaning against the wind." If successful, the resulting reduction in spending will keep aggregate demand within the dimensions of our production possibilities.

Higher Interest Rates. The mechanics of monetary policy designed to combat inflation are similar to those used to fight unemployment; only the direction is reversed. In this case, we seek to discourage spending by increasing the rate of interest. The Fed can push interest rates up by selling bonds, increasing the discount rate, or increasing the reserve requirement. All these actions reduce the money supply and help establish a new and higher equilibrium rate of interest.

The ultimate objective of a restrictive monetary policy is to reduce aggregate demand. For monetary restraint to succeed, spending behavior must be responsive to interest rates.

WORLD VIEW

Interest Rates Cut in Europe

11 Euro Nations Try to Stimulate Growth

PARIS, Dec. 3—The central banks of the 11 European countries that will merge their currencies into one in less than a month unexpectedly cut interest rates today in a coordinated response to sagging economic growth.

Political officials in France, Germany and elsewhere praised the rate reductions.

"These decisions, by their nature, reinforce the confidence in the European economy on the eve of the launch of the euro," said Yves-Thibault de Silguy, European Union commissioner for monetary affairs. . . .

Although the Federal Reserve has eased U.S. rates three times since financial markets slumped this fall—and is not likely to follow the European actions with more cuts in the near future—France and Germany had not reduced rates for two years. Most other European nations have been cutting interest rates lately to bring them into line with those of France and Germany before the new currency is born on Jan. 1. . . .

Interest rate reductions stimulate the economy by reducing the cost of borrowing, encouraging consumers to buy and businesses to invest. But if the economy becomes overstimulated, prices rise too much. The European Central Bank, like all central banks, must balance the desire for growth with the need to avoid spurring inflation.

—Anne Swardson

The Washington Post, Dec. 4, 1998, p A31. © 1998, The Washington Post. Reprinted with permission. www.washingtonpost.com

Analysis: Central banks (like the Fed) use interest rate reductions to stimulate more spending. If successful, monetary stimulus will accelerate short-run economic growth.

Reduced Aggregate Demand. Figure 15.3 showed the impact of interest rates on investment and aggregate demand. If the interest rate rises from 6 to 7 percent, investment declines from I_2 to I_1 and aggregate demand shifts *leftward*. At higher rates of interest, many marginal investments will no longer be profitable. Likewise, many consumers will decide that they can't afford the higher monthly payments associated with increased interest rates; purchases of homes, cars, and household appliances will be postponed. State and local governments may also decide to cancel or postpone bond-financed projects. Thus *monetary restraint is achieved with*

- *A decrease in the money supply*
- *An increase in interest rates*
- *A decrease in aggregate demand*

The resulting leftward shift of the aggregate demand curve lessens inflationary pressures.

POLICY CONSTRAINTS

The mechanics of monetary policy are simple enough. They won't always work as well as we might hope. Several constraints can limit the Fed's ability to alter the money supply, interest rates, or aggregate demand.

Reluctant Lenders. The process of monetary constraint begins with an increase in the money supply. The Fed, however, doesn't have direct control of the money supply. The Fed can increase bank reserves and even alter the money multiplier. The banks themselves, however, must expand the money supply by making new loans (deposit creation). If the banks instead choose to accumulate excess reserves, the money supply won't increase as much as intended. This happened in 1992, when the Fed was trying to stimulate the economy but banks were reluctant to increase their loan activity. Banks were trying to shore up their own equity and were wary of making any new loans that might not get repaid in a weak economy. During the Great Depression banks also held onto their excess reserves instead of using them for new loans (recall Figure 14.2).

Liquidity Trap. Even if the money supply *does* expand, interest rates may not fall. The possibility that interest rates may not respond to changes in the money supply is illustrated by the liquidity trap. When interest rates are low, the opportunity cost of holding money is cheap. At such times people may decide to hold all the money they can get, waiting for income-earning opportunities to improve. Bond prices, for example, may be high and their yields low. Buying bonds at such times entails the risk of capital losses (when bond prices fall) and little reward (since yields are low). Accordingly, market participants may decide just to hold any additional money the Fed supplies. At this juncture—a phenomenon Keynes called the **liquidity trap**—further expansion of the money supply has no effect on the rate of interest. The horizontal section of the money demand curve in Figure 15.4a (next page) portrays this situation.

What happens to interest rates when the initial equilibrium falls into this trap? Nothing at all. Notice that the equilibrium rate of interest doesn't fall when the money supply is increased from g_1 to g_2 (Figure 15.4a). People are willing to hold all that additional money without a reduction in the rate of interest.

Low Expectations. Even if we're able to avoid a liquidity trap, we've no assurance that desired spending will increase as expected. Keynes put great emphasis on *expectations*. Recall that investment decisions are motivated not only by interest rates but by expectations as well. During a recession—when unemployment is high and the rate of spending low—corporations have little incentive to expand production capacity. With little expectation of future profit, investors are likely to be unimpressed by "cheap money" (low interest rates) and may decline to use the lending capacity that banks make available.

CYBER NOTE

For an official explanation of monetary policy, with links to relevant data, visit the Minneapolis Fed at http://woodrow.mpls.frb.fed.us/info/policy.

Constraints on Monetary Stimulus

liquidity trap: The portion of the money demand curve that is horizontal; people are willing to hold unlimited amounts of money at some (low) interest rate.

(a) A liquidity trap can stop interest rates from falling

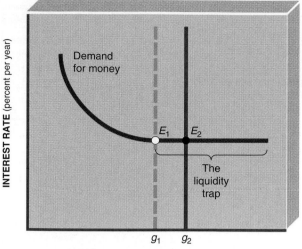

(b) Inelastic investment demand can also impede monetary policy

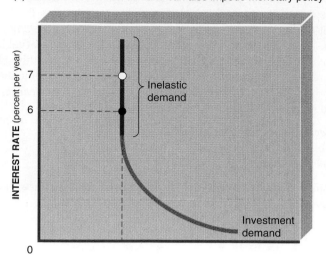

FIGURE 15.4
Constraints on Monetary Stimulus

(a) **Liquidity trap** If people are willing to hold unlimited amounts of money at the prevailing interest rate, increases in the money supply won't push interest rates lower. A liquidity trap—the horizontal segment of the money demand curve—prevents interest rates from falling.

(b) **Inelastic Demand** A lower interest rate won't always stimulate investment. If investors have unfavorable expectations for future sales, small reductions in interest rates may not alter their investment decisions. Here the rate of investment remains constant when the interest rate drops from 7 to 6 percent. This kind of situation blocks the second step in the Keynesian approach to monetary policy (see Figure 15.3*b*).

Investment demand that's slow to respond to the stimulus of cheap money is said to be *inelastic* because it won't expand. Consumers too are reluctant to borrow when current and future income prospects are uncertain or distinctly unfavorable. Accordingly, even if the Fed is successful in lowering interest rates, there's no assurance that lower interest rates will stimulate borrowing and spending. Such a reluctance to spend was evident in 1992. Although the Fed managed to push interest rates down to 20-year lows, investors and consumers preferred to pay off old debts rather than incur new ones (see NEWS).

Monetary stimulus was even less effective in Japan in 1998. When the Japanese central bank cut the discount rate from an extraordinary low $1/2$ percent to an unheard of $1/4$ percent, no one responded. In the lengthening recession Japanese consumers were trying to save more of their money and producer expectations were glum. So even *really* cheap loans didn't budge the aggregate demand curve.

The vertical portion of the investment demand curve in Figure 15.4 illustrates the possibility that investment spending may not respond to changes in the rate of interest. Notice that a reduction in the rate of interest from 7 percent to 6 percent doesn't increase investment spending. In this case, businesses are simply unwilling to invest any more funds. As a consequence, aggregate spending doesn't rise. The Fed's policy objective remains unfulfilled, even though the Fed has successfully lowered the rate of interest. Recall that the investment demand curve may also *shift* if expectations change. If expectations worsened, the investment demand curve would shift to the left and might result in even *less* investment at 6 percent interest (see Figure 15.4*b*).

Limits on
Monetary Restraint

Expectations. Expectations could also limit the effectiveness of monetary restraint. In pursuit of "tight" money, the Fed could drain bank reserves and force interest rates

Rate Cuts' Limited Real Life Impact

Other Fears Fuel Consumer Caution

Margit Hunt, a lawyer, and her fiancé, Kirk Nahra, another lawyer, have been looking for a house in the Washington area for a year. During that period, the Federal Reserve has lowered interest rates five times.

None of those reductions, not even the one in the Fed's discount rate announced yesterday, has made it possible for the young couple to buy. . . .

With interest rates at their lowest levels in nearly 20 years in some cases, the textbooks say the economy ought to be listening. Consumers should be increasing their purchases of cars and houses as lower rates reduce the cost; businesses should be investing more in new factories and equipment as borrowing gets cheaper. . . .

But so far at least, the response has been unenthusiastic. And economic experts, consumers and business executives interviewed yesterday said that the latest reduction is not likely to trigger much more spending or investing. It is not that rates are not low enough, it is that rates are not the issue.

"Confidence is lacking and that is not going to be addressed simply by lowering interest rates," said Irwin L. Kellner, chief economist for Manufacturers Hanover Trust Co.

—Anne Swardson

The Washington Post, Nov. 7, 1991, p. B10. © 1991, The Washington Post. Reprinted with permission. www.washingtonpost.com

Analysis: Interest rate cuts are supposed to stimulate investment and consumption. But gloomy expectations may deter people from borrowing and spending.

higher. Yet market participants might continue to borrow and spend. High expectations for rising sales and profits might overwhelm high interest rates in investment decisions. Consumers too might believe that future incomes will be sufficient to cover larger debts and higher interest charges. Both groups might foresee accelerating inflation that would make even "high" interest rates look cheap in the future.

Global Money. Market participants might also tap global sources of money. If money gets too tight in domestic markets, business may borrow funds from foreign banks or institutions. GM, Disney, Exxon, and other multinational corporations can borrow funds from foreign subsidiaries, banks, and even bond markets. As we saw in Chapter 14, market participants can also secure funds from nonbank sources in the United States. These nonbank and global lenders make it harder for the Fed to restrain aggregate demand.

How Effective? In view of all these constraints on monetary policies, some observers have concluded that monetary policy is an undependable policy lever. Keynes, for example, emphasized that monetary policy wouldn't be very effective in ending a deep recession. He believed that the combination of reluctant bankers, the liquidity trap, and low expectations would render monetary stimulus ineffective. Using monetary policy to stimulate the economy in such circumstances would be akin to "pushing on a string." Alan Greenspan came to much the same conclusion in September 1992 when he said that further Fed stimulus would be ineffective in accelerating a recovery from the 1990–1991 recession. He believed, however, that earlier cuts in interest rates would help stimulate spending once banks, investors, and consumers gained confidence in the economic outlook.

The limitations on monetary restraint aren't considered as serious. The Fed has the power to reduce the money supply. If the money supply shrinks far enough, the rate of spending will have to slow down.

THE MONETARIST PERSPECTIVE

The Keynesian view of money emphasizes the role of interest rates in fulfilling the goals of monetary policy. *In the Keynesian model, changes in the money supply affect macro outcomes primarily through changes in interest rates.* The three-step sequence of (1) money supply change, (2) interest rate movement, and (3) aggregate demand shift makes monetary policy subject to several potential uncertainties.

An alternative view of money downplays the role of interest rates and makes the outcomes of monetary policy more certain. Ironically, monetarists, as they're known, also conclude that monetary stimulus isn't effective, but monetary restraint is. In their view, monetary policy has little impact on real output and unemployment levels but a far more powerful and certain impact on the price level than Keynes surmised.

The Equation of Exchange

equation of exchange: Money supply (*M*) times velocity of circulation (*V*) equals level of aggregate spending (*P* × *Q*).

income velocity of money (*V*): The number of times per year, on average, a dollar is used to purchase final goods and services; $PQ \div M$.

Monetarists assert that the potential of monetary policy can be expressed in a simple equation called the **equation of exchange,** written as

$$MV = PQ$$

where *M* refers to the quantity of money in circulation and *V* to its **velocity** of circulation. Total spending in the economy is equal to the average price (*P*) of goods times the quantity (*Q*) of goods sold in a period. This spending is financed by the supply of money (*M*) times the velocity of its circulation (*V*).

Suppose, for example, that only two participants are in the market and that the money supply consists of one crisp $20 bill. What's the limit to total spending in this case? If you answer "$20," you haven't yet grasped the nature of the circular flow. Suppose I begin the circular flow by spending $20 on eggs, bacon, and a gallon of milk. The money I spend ends up in Farmer Brown's pocket because he is the only other market participant. Once in possession of the money, Farmer Brown may decide to satisfy his long-smoldering desire to learn something about economics and buy one of my books. If he acts on that decision, the $20 will return to me. At that point, both Farmer Brown and I have sold $20 worth of goods. Hence $40 of total spending has been financed with one $20 bill.

As long as we keep using this $20 bill to buy goods and services from each other, we can continue to do business. Moreover, the faster we pass the money from hand to hand during any period of time, the greater the value of sales each of us can register. If the money is passed from hand to hand eight times, then I'll be able to sell $80 worth of textbooks and Farmer Brown will be able to sell $80 worth of produce during that period, for a total nominal output of $160. The quantity of money in circulation and the velocity with which it travels (changes hands) in product markets will always be equal to the value of total spending and income. The relationship is summarized as

$$M \times V = P \times Q$$

In this case, the *equation of exchange* confirms that

$$\$20 \times 8 = \$160$$

The value of total sales for the year is $160.

Monetarists use the equation of exchange to simplify the explanation of how monetary policy works. There's no need, they argue, to follow the effects of changes in *M* through the money markets to interest rates and further to changes in aggregate spending. The basic consequences of monetary policy are evident in the equation of exchange. The two sides of the equation of exchange must always be in balance. Hence we can be absolutely certain that *if* **M** *increases, prices* **(P)** *or output* **(Q)** *must rise, or* **V** *must fall.*

The equation of exchange is an incontestable statement of how the money supply is related to macro outcomes. The equation itself, however, says nothing about which variables will respond to a change in the money supply. The *goal* of monetary policy is to change the macro outcomes on the right side of the equation. It's *possible,* however, that a change in M might be offset with a reverse change in V, leaving P and Q unaffected. Or it could happen that the *wrong* macro outcome is affected. Prices (P) might rise, for example, when we're trying to increase real output (Q).

Stable Velocity

Monetarists add some important assumptions to transform the equation of exchange from a simple identity to a behavioral *model* of macro performance. The first assumption is that the velocity of money (V) is stable. How fast people use their money balances depends on the institutional structure of money markets and people's habits. Neither the structure of money markets nor people's habits are likely to change when M is altered. Accordingly, an increase in M won't be offset by a reduction in V. Instead, the impact of an increased money supply will be transmitted to the right-hand side of the equation of exchange, which means that *total spending must rise if the money supply* **(M)** *grows and* **V** *is stable.*

Money Supply Focus

From a monetarist perspective, there's no need to trace the impacts of monetary policy through interest rate movements. The focus on interest rates is a uniquely Keynesian perspective. Monetarists claim that interest rate movements are secondary to the major thrust of monetary policy. *As monetarists see it, changes in the money supply must alter total spending, regardless of how interest rates move.*

A monetarist perspective leads to a wholly different strategy for the Fed. Because interest rates aren't part of the monetarist explanation of how monetary policy works, the Fed shouldn't try to manipulate interest rates (see NEWS); instead, it should focus on the money supply itself. Monetarists also argue that the Fed can't really control interest rates well since they depend on both the supply of and the demand for money. What the Fed *can* control is the supply of money, and the equation of exchange clearly shows that money matters.

"Natural" Unemployment

Some monetarists add yet another perspective to the equation of exchange. They assert that not only V but Q as well is stable. If this is true, then changes in the money supply (M) would affect only prices (P).

What does it mean for Q to be stable? The argument here is that the quantity of goods produced is primarily dependent on production capacity, labor market efficiency,

---

IN THE NEWS

Monetarists Reject Focus on Lowering Rates

A group of monetarist economists urged the . . . administration and the Federal Reserve yesterday to stop trying to encourage faster economic growth by insisting on lower interest rates.

The group, known as the Shadow Open Market Committee, said that the gross national product, adjusted for inflation, has grown during the past two years at a $2\frac{1}{2}$ percent annual rate, only slightly less than its average for the last 100 years.

"Efforts to force interest rates lower, to depreciate the dollar and to stimulate the economy to head off protectionist (trade) legislation are based on the mistaken belief that we have learned how to stimulate now and prevent inflation later," the committee said in a statement issued after one of its semiannual meetings in New York. . . .

The Shadow Committee, headed by economists Allan H. Meltzer of Carnegie-Mellon University and Karl Brunner of the University of Rochester, was formed more than a decade ago to provide economic analysis and policy recommendations from a monetarist point of view.

—John M. Berry

The Washington Post, Sept. 23, 1986, p. C1. © 1986, The Washington Post. Reprinted with permission. www.washingtonpost.com

Analysis: Monetarists reject the notion that lower interest rates will necessarily stimulate aggregate demand. What matters is the supply of money, not the rate of interest.

natural rate of unemployment: Long-term rate of unemployment determined by structural forces in labor and product markets.

and other "structural" forces. These structural forces establish a **"natural" rate of unemployment** that's fairly immune to short-run policy intervention. This is the *long-run* aggregate supply curve we first encountered in Chapter 8. From this perspective, there's no reason for producers to depart from this "natural" rate of output when the money supply increases. Producers are smart enough to know that both prices and costs will rise when spending increases. Hence rising prices won't create any new profit incentives for increasing output. Firms will just continue producing at the "natural" rate with higher (nominal) prices and costs. As a result, increases in aggregate spending—whether financed by more M or faster V—aren't likely to alter real output levels. Q will stay constant.

If the quantity of real output is in fact stable, then P is the only thing that can change. Thus *the most extreme monetarist perspective concludes that changes in the money supply affect prices only.* As the "simple economics" in the accompanying cartoon suggests, a decrease in M should directly reduce the price level. When M *increases,* total spending rises, but the higher nominal value of spending is completely absorbed by higher prices. In this view, monetary policy affects only the rate of inflation. This is the kind of money-driven inflation that bedeviled George Washington's army (see NEWS).

Figure 15.5 illustrates the extreme monetarist argument in the context of aggregate supply and demand. The assertion that real output is fixed at the natural rate of unemployment is reflected in the vertical aggregate supply curve. With real output stuck at Q^*, any increase in aggregate demand directly raises the price level.

Monetarist Policies

At first glance, the monetarist argument looks pretty slick. Keynesians worry about how the money supply affects interest rates, how interest rates affect spending, and how spending affects output. By contrast, monetarists point to a simple equation ($MV = PQ$) that produces straightforward responses to monetary policy.

There are fundamental differences between the two schools here, not only about how the economy works but also about how successful macro policy might be. To appreciate those differences, consider monetarist responses to inflationary and recessionary gaps.

Fighting Inflation. Consider again the options for fighting inflation. The objective of policy is to reduce aggregate spending. From a Keynesian perspective, the way to achieve this reduction is to shrink the money supply and drive up interest rates. But monetarists argue that nominal interest rates are already likely to be high. Furthermore, if an effective anti-inflation policy is adopted, interest rates will come *down,* not go up.

Real vs. Nominal Interest. To understand this monetarist conclusion, we have to distinguish between *nominal* interest rates and *real* ones. Nominal interest rates are the ones we actually see and pay. When a bank pays $5\frac{1}{2}$ percent interest on your bank account, it's quoting (and paying) a nominal rate.

Analysis: If the money supply shrinks (or its growth rate slows), price levels will rise less quickly.

"Not Worth a Continental": The U.S. Experience with Hyperinflation

The government of the United States had no means to pay for the Revolutionary War. Specifically, the federal government had no power to levy taxes that might transfer resources from the private sector to the public sector. Instead, it could only request the states to levy taxes of their own and contribute them to the war effort. The states were not very responsive, however: state contributions accounted for only 6 percent of federal revenues during the war years.

To pay for needed weapons and soldiers, the federal government had only two other options, either (1) borrow money or (2) create new money. When loans proved to be inadequate, the Continental Congress started issuing new paper money—the "Continental" dollar—in 1775. By the end of 1779, Congress had authorized issuance of over $250 million in Continental dollars.

At first the paper money enabled George Washington's troops to acquire needed supplies, ammunition, and volunteers. But soon the flood of paper money inundated product markets. Wholesale prices of key commodities skyrocketed. Commodity prices *doubled* in 1776, in 1777, and again in 1778. Then prices increased *tenfold* in the next two years.

Many farmers and storekeepers refused to sell goods to the army in exchange for Continental dollars. Rapid inflation had taught them that the paper money George Washington's troops offered was nearly worthless. The expression "not worth a Continental" became a popular reference to things of little value.

The states tried price controls and even empowered themselves to seize needed war supplies. But nothing could stop the inflation fueled by the explosive increase in the money supply. Fortunately, the war ended before the economy collapsed. After the war, the U.S. Congress established a new form of money, and in 1787 it empowered the federal government to levy taxes and mint gold and silver coins.

From Sidney Ratner, James H. Soltow, and Richard Sylla, *The Evolution of the American Economy.* © 1979 by Basic Books; 2nd ed., Macmillan, 1993. Reprinted by permission of the authors.

Analysis: Rapid expansion of the money supply will push the price level up. As inflation accelerates, money becomes less valuable.

Real interest rates are never actually seen and rarely quoted. These are "inflation-adjusted" rates. Specifically, the **real interest rate** equals the nominal rate *minus* the anticipated rate of inflation; that is,

$$\begin{array}{ccc} \text{Real} & \text{nominal} & \text{anticipated} \\ \text{interest} = & \text{interest} - & \text{inflation} \\ \text{rate} & \text{rate} & \text{rate} \end{array}$$

real interest rate: The nominal rate of interest minus anticipated inflation rate.

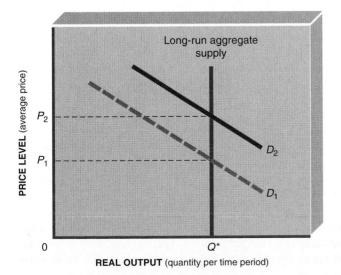

FIGURE 15.5
The Monetarist View

Monetarists argue that the rate of real output is set by structural factors. Furthermore, firms aren't likely to be fooled into producing more just because prices are rising if costs are rising just as much. Hence long-run aggregate supply remains at the "natural" level Q*. Any increases in aggregate demand, therefore, raise the price level (inflation) but not output.

Recall what inflation does to the purchasing power of the dollar: As inflation continues, each dollar purchases fewer goods and services. As a consequence, dollars borrowed today are of less real value when they're paid back later. The real rate of interest reflects this inflation adjustment.

Suppose you lend someone $100 at the beginning of the year, at 8 percent interest. You expect to get more back at the end of the year than you start with. That "more" you expect refers to *real* goods and services, not just dollar bills. Specifically, you anticipate that when the loan is repaid with interest at the end of the year, you'll be able to buy more goods and services than you could at the beginning. This expectation of a *real* gain is at least part of the reason for making a loan.

Your expected gain won't materialize, however, if all prices rise by 8 percent during the year. If the inflation rate is 8 percent, you'll discover that $108 buys you no more at the end of the year than $100 would have bought you at the beginning. Hence you'd have given up the use of your money for an entire year without any real compensation. In such circumstances, the *real* rate of interest turns out to be zero; that is,

$$\begin{matrix} \text{Real} \\ \text{interest} \\ \text{rate} \end{matrix} = \begin{matrix} 8\% \text{ nominal} \\ \text{interest} \\ \text{rate} \end{matrix} - \begin{matrix} 8\% \text{ inflation} \\ \text{rate} \end{matrix}$$

$$= 0\%$$

The nominal rate of interest, then, really has two components: (1) the real rate of interest, and (2) an inflation adjustment. If the real rate of interest was 4 percent and an inflation rate of 9 percent was expected, the nominal rate of interest would be 13 percent. If inflationary expectations *improved,* the *nominal* interest rate would *fall.* This is evident in the rearranged formula:

$$\begin{matrix} \text{Nominal} \\ \text{interest rate} \end{matrix} = \begin{matrix} \text{real} \\ \text{interest rate} \end{matrix} + \begin{matrix} \text{anticipated rate} \\ \text{of inflation} \end{matrix}$$

If the real interest rate is 4 percent and anticipated inflation falls from 9 to 6 percent, the nominal interest rate would decline from 13 to 10 percent.

A central assumption of the monetarist perspective is that the real rate of interest is fairly stable. This is a critical point. ***If the real rate of interest is stable, then changes in the nominal interest rate reflect only changes in anticipated inflation.*** From this perspective, high nominal rates of interest are a symptom of inflation, not a cure. Indeed, high nominal rates may even look cheap if inflationary expectations are worsening faster than interest rates are rising (see NEWS).

Consider the implications of all this for monetary policy. Suppose we want to close an inflationary gap. Monetarists and Keynesians alike agree that a reduced money supply (*M*) will deflate total spending. But Keynesians rely on a "quick fix" of *higher* interest rates to slow consumption and investment spending. Monetarists, by contrast, assert that nominal interest rates will *fall* if the Fed tightens the money supply. Once market participants are convinced that the Fed is going to reduce money supply growth, inflationary expectations diminish. When inflationary expectations diminish, nominal interest rates will begin to fall.

Notice the difference in *timing* between these two views. In the Keynesian view, interest rates respond quickly to changes in the money supply. In the monetarist view, interest rates respond more slowly (and in the opposite direction). Nominal rates fall only after market participants are convinced that the Fed will pursue monetary restraint. Therefore, ***monetarists advocate steady and predictable changes in the money supply.***

Fighting Unemployment. The link between anticipated inflation and nominal interest rates also constrains expansionary monetary policy. The Keynesian cure for a recession is to expand *M* and lower interest rates. But monetarists fear that an increase

IN THE NEWS

Money Is Free!

"Money's not tight, it's cheap. It's free!"

So says one of our most articulate friends along Wall Street. The point is that short-term interest rates, horrendous as they are, are below the short-term inflation rate, horrendous as it is. The August numbers showed a six-month inflation rate of 9.4%, for example, while six months earlier the prime interest rate was 8.0%. If you borrowed and paid back in cheaper dollars, you got your money for free.

We relate the quote because we have the impression a lot of folks in Washington don't realize how those of us out here in the real world look at these matters. In particular, the observation ought to be of interest to the Federal Reserve's Open Market Committee, which meets today to set money growth targets for both the next two months and the next year.

Out here in the real world, folks know free money when they see it. That is why interest rates will not go down, nor the dollar recover meaningfully, until inflation is reduced. And the longer the Fed delays in starting to curb money growth, the higher price the nation will have to pay before inflation is ultimately brought under control.

The Wall Street Journal. Reprinted by permission of *The Wall Street Journal,* © 1978 Dow Jones & Company, Inc. All Rights Reserved Worldwide. www.wsj.com

Analysis: Monetarists argue that changes in nominal interest rates have little effect on investment. In their view, *real* (inflation-adjusted) interest rates determine investment behavior.

in M will lead—via the equation of exchange—to higher P. If everyone believed this would happen, then an unexpectedly large increase in M would immediately raise people's inflationary expectations. Nominal interest rates would go up, not down, when the money supply was increased!

From a monetarist perspective, expansionary monetary policies aren't likely to lead us out of a recession. On the contrary, such policies might double our burden by heaping inflation on top of our unemployment woes. The rate of real output and employment is more dependent on structural characteristics of the economy than on changes in the money supply. All monetary policy should do is ensure a stable and predictable rate of growth in the money supply. Then people could concentrate on real production decisions without worrying so much about fluctuating prices.

THE CONCERN FOR CONTENT

Monetary policy, like fiscal policy, can affect more than just the *level* of total spending. We must give some consideration to the impact of Federal Reserve actions on the *content* of the GDP if we're going to be responsive to the "second crisis" of economic theory.[1]

Both Keynesians and monetarists agree that monetary policy will affect nominal interest rates. When interest rates change, not all spending decisions will be affected equally. Investment decisions that are highly sensitive to interest rates are more susceptible to monetary policy than others. The construction industry, especially the residential housing market, stands out in this respect. The sensitivity of housing costs to interest rate changes forces the construction industry to bear a disproportionate burden of restrictive monetary policy. Accordingly, when the Fed pursues a policy of tight money—high interest rates and limited lending capacity—it not only restrains total

The Mix of Output

[1]See the quotation from Joan Robinson in Chapter 11, calling attention to the exclusive focus of economists on the *level* of economic activity (the "first crisis"), to the neglect of content (the "second crisis").

spending but reduces the share of housing in that spending. Utility industries, public works projects, and state and local finances are also disproportionately affected by monetary policy.

In addition to altering the content of demand and output, monetary policy affects the competitive structure of the market. When money is tight, banks must ration available credit among loan applicants. Large and powerful corporations aren't likely to run out of credit because banks will be hesitant to incur their displeasure and lose their business. Thus General Motors and IBM stand a much better chance of obtaining tight money than does the corner grocery store. Moreover, if bank lending capacity becomes too small, GM and IBM can always resort to the bond market and borrow money directly from the public. Small businesses seldom have such an alternative.

Income Redistribution

Monetary policy also affects the distribution of income. When interest rates fall, borrowers pay smaller interest charges. On the other hand, lenders get smaller interest payments. Hence a lower interest rate redistributes income from lenders to borrowers. When interest rates declined sharply in 1998, home owners refinanced their mortgages and saved billions of dollars in interest payments. The decline in interest rates, however, *reduced* the income of retired persons, who depend heavily on interest payments from certificates of deposit, bonds, and other assets.

THE ECONOMY TOMORROW

Which Lever to Pull?

 Our success in managing the macro economy of tomorrow depends on pulling the right policy levers at the right time. But which levers should be pulled? Keynesians and monetarists offer very different prescriptions for treating an ailing economy. Can we distill some usable policy guidelines from this discussion?

The Policy Levers

The equation of exchange is a convenient summary of the differences between Keynesian and monetarist perspectives. There's no disagreement about the equation itself: aggregate spending ($M \times V$) *must* equal the value of total sales ($P \times Q$). *What Keynesians and monetarists argue about is which of the policy levers—**M** or **V**—is likely to be effective in altering aggregate spending.*

- *Monetarists* point to changes in the money supply (M) as the principal lever of macroeconomic policy. They assume V is reasonably stable.
- *Keynesian* fiscal policy *must* rely on changes in the velocity of money (V) because tax and expenditure policies have no direct impact on the money supply.

Crowding Out

The extreme monetarist position that *only* money matters is based on the assumption that the velocity of money (V) is constant. *If **V** is constant, changes in total spending can come about only through changes in the money supply.* There are no other policy levers on the left side of the equation of exchange.

Think about an increase in government spending designed to stimulate the economy. How does the government pay for this fiscal policy initiative? Monetarists argue that there are only two ways to pay for this increased expenditure (G): The government must either raise additional taxes or borrow more money. If the government raises taxes, the disposable income of consumers will be reduced, and private spending will fall. On the other hand, if the government borrows more money to pay for its expenditures, there will be less money available for loans to private consumers and investors. In either case, more government spending (G) implies less private spending (C or I). Thus *increased G effectively "**crowds out**" some C or I,* leaving total spending unchanged. From this viewpoint, fiscal policy is ineffective; it can't even shift the aggregate demand curve. At best, fiscal policy can change the composition of demand and thus the mix of output. Only changes in M (monetary policy) can shift the aggregate spending curve.

crowding out: A reduction in private-sector borrowing (and spending) caused by increased government borrowing.

Milton Friedman, formerly of the University of Chicago, champions the monetarist view with this argument:

I believe that the state of the government budget matters; matters a great deal—for some things. The state of the government budget determines what fraction of the nation's income is spent through the government and what fraction is spent by individuals privately. The state of the government budget determines what the level of our taxes is, how much of our income we turn over to the government. The state of the government budget has a considerable effect on interest rates. If the federal government runs a large deficit, that means the government has to borrow in the market, which raises the demand for loanable funds and so tends to raise interest rates.

If the government budget shifts to a surplus, that adds to the supply of loanable funds, which tends to lower interest rates. It was no surprise to those of us who stress money that enactment of the surtax was followed by a decline in interest rates. That's precisely what we had predicted and what our analysis leads us to predict. But—and I come to the main point—in my opinion, the state of the budget by itself has no significant effect on the course of nominal income, on inflation, on deflation, or on cyclical fluctuations.[2]

Keynesians reply that the alleged constant velocity of money is a monetarist's pipe dream. Some even argue that the velocity of money is so volatile that changes in V can completely offset changes in M, leaving us with the proposition that money doesn't matter.

The liquidity trap illustrates the potential for V to change. Keynes argued that people tend to accumulate money balances—slow their rate of spending—during recessions. A slowdown in spending implies a reduction in the velocity of money. Indeed, in the extreme case of the liquidity trap, the velocity of money falls toward zero. Under these circumstances, changes in M (monetary policy) won't influence total spending. The velocity of money falls as rapidly as M increases. On the other hand, increased government spending (fiscal policy) can stimulate aggregate spending by putting idle money balances to work (thereby increasing V). Changes in fiscal policy will also influence consumer and investor expectations, and thereby further alter the rate of aggregate spending.

Tables 15.2 and 15.3 on the next page summarize these different perspectives on fiscal and monetary policy. The first table evaluates fiscal policy from both Keynesian and monetarist viewpoints. The central issue is whether and how a change in government spending *(G)* or taxes *(T)* will alter macroeconomic outcomes. Keynesians assert that aggregate spending will be affected as the velocity of money (V) changes. Monetarists say no, because they anticipate an unchanged V.

How Fiscal Policy Works: Two Views

If aggregate spending isn't affected by a change in G or T, then fiscal policy won't affect prices (P) or real output (Q). Thus, monetarists conclude that fiscal policy isn't a viable tool for combating either inflation or unemployment. By contrast, Keynesians believe V will change and that output and prices will respond accordingly.

Insofar as interest rates are concerned, monetarists recognize that nominal interest rates will be affected (read Friedman's quote again) but *real* rates won't be because real interest rates depend on real output and growth, both of which are seen as immune to fiscal policy. Keynesians see less impact on nominal interest rates and more on real interest rates.

What all this boils down to is this: Fiscal policy, by itself, will be effective only if it can alter the velocity of money. ***How well fiscal policy works depends on how much the velocity of money can be changed by government tax and spending decisions.***

Table 15.3 is a similar summary of monetary policy. This time the positions of monetarists and Keynesians are reversed, or nearly so. Monetarists say a change in M must alter total spending ($P \times Q$) because V is stable. Keynesians assert that V may vary,

How Monetary Policy Works: Two Views

[2]Milton Friedman and Walter W. Heller, *Monetary vs. Fiscal Policy* (New York: Norton, 1969), pp. 50–51.

TABLE 15.2

How Fiscal Policy Matters: Monetarist vs. Keynesian Views

Monetarists and Keynesians have very different views on the impact of fiscal policy. Monetarists assert that changes in government spending (*G*) and taxes (*T*) don't alter the velocity of money (*V*). As a result, fiscal policy alone can't alter total spending. Keynesians reject this view, arguing that *V* is changeable. They claim that tax cuts and increased government spending increase the velocity of money and so alter total spending.

Do Changes in *G* or *T* Affect:	Monetarist View	Keynesian View
1. Aggregate demand?	No (stable *V* causes crowding out)	Yes (*V* changes)
2. Prices?	No (aggregate demand not affected)	Maybe (if at capacity)
3. Real output?	No (aggregate demand not affected)	Yes (output responds to demand)
4. Nominal interest rates?	Yes (crowding out)	Maybe (may alter demand for money)
5. Real interest rates?	No (determined by real growth)	Yes (real growth and expectations may vary)

so they aren't convinced that monetary policy will always work. The heart of the controversy is again the velocity of money. Monetary policy works as long as *V* is stable, or at least predictable. ***How well monetary policy works depends on how stable or predictable V is.***

Once the central role of velocity is understood, everything else falls into place. Monetarists assert that prices but not output will be directly affected by a change in *M* because the right-hand side of the equation of exchange contains only two variables (*P* and *Q*), and one of them (*Q*) is assumed unaffected by monetary policy. Keynesians, by contrast, aren't so sure prices will be affected by *M,* or that real output won't be. It all depends on *V* and the responsiveness of *P* and *Q* to changes in aggregate spending.

Finally, monetarists predict that nominal interest rates will respond to changes in *M,* although they're not sure in what direction. It depends on how inflationary expectations adapt to changes in the money supply. Keynesian economists aren't so sure nominal interest rates will change but are sure about the direction if they do.

TABLE 15.3

How Money Matters: Monetarist vs. Keynesian Views

Because monetarists believe that *V* is stable, they assert that changes in the money supply (*M*) must alter total spending. But all the monetary impact is reflected in prices and nominal interest rates; *real* output and interest rates are unaffected.

Keynesians think that *V* is variable and thus that changes in *M* might *not* alter total spending. If monetary policy does alter aggregate spending, however, Keynesians expect all outcomes to be affected.

Do Changes in *M* Affect:	Monetarist View	Keynesian View
1. Aggregate demand?	Yes (*V* stable)	Maybe (*V* may change)
2. Prices?	Yes (*V* and *Q* stable)	Maybe (*V* and *Q* may change)
3. Real output?	No (rate of unemployment determined by structural forces)	Maybe (output responds to demand)
4. Nominal interest rates?	Yes (but direction unknown)	Maybe (liquidity trap)
5. Real interest rates?	No (depends on real growth)	Maybe (real growth may vary)

Tables 15.2 and 15.3 highlight the velocity of money as a critical determinant of policy impact. The critical question appears to be whether V is stable or not. Why hasn't someone answered this simple question and resolved the debate over fiscal versus monetary policy?

Long-Run Stability. The velocity of money (V) turns out, in fact, to be quite stable over long periods of time. Over the past 30 years the velocity of money (M2) has averaged about 1.64, as Figure 15.6 illustrates. Moreover, the range of velocity has been fairly narrow, extending from a low of 1.56 in 1987 to a high of 2.05 in 1997. Monetarists conclude that the historical pattern justifies the assumption of a stable V.

Short-Run Instability. Keynesians reply that monetarists are farsighted and so fail to see significant short-run variations in V. The difference between a velocity of 1.56 and velocity of 2.05 translates into hundreds of billions of dollars in aggregate demand. Moreover, there's a pattern to short-run variations in V: velocity tends to decline in recessions (see Figure 15.6). These are precisely the situations in which fiscal stimulus (increasing V) would be appropriate.

The differing views of Keynesians and monetarists clearly lead to different conclusions about which policy lever to pull.

Monetarist Advice. The monetarists' policy advice to the Fed is straightforward. *Monetarists favor fixed money supply targets.* They believe that V is stable in the long run and unpredictable in the short run. Hence the safest course of action is to focus

Is Velocity Stable?

Money Supply Targets

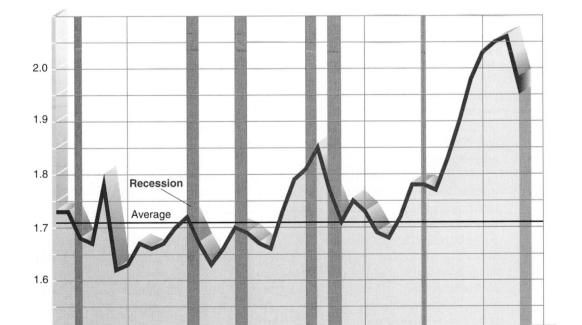

RATIO OF GDP TO M2

FIGURE 15.6
The Velocity of M2

The velocity of money (the ratio of GDP to M2) averages about 1.64. However, V appears to decline in recessions. Keynes urged the use of fiscal stimulus to boost V. Monetarists caution that short-run changes in V are too unpredictable.

Source: Congressional Budget Office.

on *M.* All the Fed has to do is announce its intention to increase the money supply by some fixed amount (such as 3 percent per year), then use its central banking powers to hit that money growth target. The fiscal policy lever should be left alone.

Keynesian Advice. *Keynesians reject fixed money supply targets,* favoring more flexibility in control of the money supply. In their view, a fixed money supply target would render monetary policy useless in combating cyclical swings of the economy. Keynesians prefer the risks of occasional policy errors to the "straitjacket" of a fixed money supply target. *Keynesians advocate targeting interest rates, not the money supply.* Keynesians also advocate liberal use of the fiscal policy lever.

The Fed's Eclecticism. For a brief period (1979–1982) the Fed adopted the monetarists' policy of fixed money supply targets. On Oct. 6, 1979, the chairman of the Fed (Paul Volcker) announced that the Fed would begin focusing on the money supply exclusively, without worrying about interest rates. The Fed's primary goal was to reduce inflation, which was then running at close to 14 percent a year. To slow the inflationary spiral, the Fed decided to limit sharply growth of the money supply.

The Fed succeeded in reducing money supply growth and the inflationary spiral. But its tight-money policies sent interest rates soaring and pushed the economy into a deep recession (1981–1982). Exactly 3 years after adopting the monetarist approach, the Fed abandoned it.

In place of a strict monetarist approach,[3] the Fed has adopted an eclectic mixture of monetarist and Keynesian policies. For many years the Fed announced targets for money supply growth. But the targets were very broad and not very stable. At the beginning of 1986, for example, the Fed set a target of 3 to 8 percent growth for M1. That wide target gave it plenty of room to adjust to changing interest rates and cyclical changes. But the Fed actually missed the target by a mile—M1 increased by 15 percent in 1986. In explaining this mile-wide miss to Congress, Chairman Volcker emphasized pragmatism. "Success," he asserted, "will not be measured by whether or not we meet some preordained, arbitrary target: but by our macroeconomic performance. Since the economy was growing steadily in 1987, and inflation wasn't increasing, he concluded that monetary policy had been a success. He concluded his testimony by telling Congress that the Fed would no longer set targets for M1 but would instead keep an eye on broader money supply measures (M2 and M3; see Table 13.1) and interest rates. Nobel Laureate Paul Samuelson provided a glib explanation of this approach by noting that "God gave us two eyes so we can keep one on the money supply and the other on interest rates."

Fed watchers say that Alan Greenspan not only uses both eyes but also some personal radar to track the economy and formulate monetary policy. In early 1990 he refused to set a target for growth of the narrowly defined money supply (M1) and set very wide targets (3 to 7 percent) for broader measures of the money supply (M2). For 1993 the Fed set a very broad target range for M2 growth (2 to 6 percent). By midyear it was evident the Fed couldn't even hit that target. Rather than establish yet another target, however, the Fed chairman told Congress that M2 growth was an unreliable policy guide. A more eclectic mix of indicators—including several measures of both the money supply and interest rates—was more appropriate. Greenspan told Congress. The Fed must be flexible enough, he said, to adjust to changing economic conditions. In his view, the Fed can't be bound to any one theory but must instead use a mix of money supply and interest rate adjustments to attain desired macro outcomes. As Greenspan himself concluded, "The Federal Reserve specializes in precision guesswork."

---

[3]The Fed's policy of 1979–1982 was not strict monetarism. Although the Fed emphasized money supply targets, it allowed the money supply to fluctuate much more than strict monetarists prescribed.

SUMMARY

- The essence of monetary policy lies in the Federal Reserve's control over the money supply. By altering the money supply, the Fed can determine the amount of purchasing power available.
- There are sharp disagreements about how monetary policy works. Keynesians argue that monetary policy works indirectly, through its effects on interest rates and spending. Monetarists assert that monetary policy has more direct and more certain impacts, particularly on price levels.
- In the Keynesian view, the demand for money is important. This demand reflects desires to hold money (in cash or bank balances) for transactions, precautionary, and speculative purposes. The interaction of money supply and money demand determines the equilibrium rate of interest.
- From a Keynesian perspective, the impact of monetary policy on the economy occurs in three distinct steps. (1) Changes in the money supply alter the equilibrium rate of interest. (2) Changes in the interest rate alter the rate of investment expenditure. (3) The change in desired investment alters (shifts) aggregate demand.
- For Keynesian monetary policy to be fully effective, interest rates must be responsive to changes in the money supply, and investment spending must be responsive to changes in interest rates. Neither condition is assured. In a liquidity trap, people are willing to hold unlimited amounts of money at some low rate of interest. The in-

  terest rate won't fall below this level as the money supply increases. Also, investor expectations of sales and profits may override interest rate considerations in the investment decision.
- The monetarist view of monetary policy is simpler, and it builds on the equation of exchange ($MV = PQ$). Monetarists assert that the velocity of money (V) is stable, so that changes in M must influence ($P \times Q$). Monetarists focus on the money supply; Keynesians, on interest rates.
- Some monetarists also argue that the level of real output (Q) is set by structural forces, as illustrated by the vertical, long-run aggregate supply curve. Q is therefore insensitive to changes in aggregate spending. If both V and Q are constant, changes in M directly affect P.
- Monetary policy attempts to influence total expenditure by changing M and will be fully effective only if V is constant. Fiscal policy attempts to influence total expenditure by changing V and will be fully effective only if M doesn't change in the opposite direction. The controversy over the effectiveness of fiscal versus monetary policy depends on whether the velocity of money (V) is stable or instead is subject to policy influence.
- The velocity of money is more stable over long periods of time than over short periods. Keynesians conclude that this makes fiscal policy more powerful in the short run. Monetarists conclude that the unpredictability of short-run velocity makes *any* short-run policy risky.

Key Terms

monetary policy
interest rate
money supply (M1, M2)
demand for money
portfolio decision
transactions demand for money

precautionary demand for money
speculative demand for money
equilibrium rate of interest
aggregate demand
liquidity trap
equation of exchange

income velocity of money (V)
natural rate of unemployment
real interest rate
crowding out

Questions for Discussion

1. What proportions of your money balance are held for transactions, precautionary, and speculative purposes? Can you think of any other purposes for holding money?
2. Why do high interest rates so adversely affect the demand for housing and yet have so little influence on the demand for strawberries?
3. If the Federal Reserve banks mailed everyone a brand-new $100 bill, what would happen to prices, output, and

   income? Illustrate your answer by using the equation of exchange.
4. Can there be any inflation without an increase in the money supply? How?
5. Suppose the Fed wanted to reduce aggregate demand (to fight inflation) and the president wanted to increase total expenditure (to fight unemployment). What kind of action would each take? What effects would their combined actions have on GDP?

6. How might the existence of multiplier effects increase the risk of inflation when interest rates are cut, as described in the WORLD VIEW on page 294?

7. According to the NEWS on page 301, what caused the U.S. price level to double in 1776?

8. How can money be truly "free" if you have to pay interest on loans? (See NEWS on page 303.)

9. Web Activity Go to http://epn.org/prospect/25/25galb.html for a critique of Federal Reserve policy. What is the author's view of the use of natural rate of unemployment to guide Fed policy? Do you agree with the author? Do you think the Fed should persue a low inflationary goal more vigorously than a full-employment goal?

10. Web Activity At www.federalreserve.gov/release/h6/hist/h6hist1.txt, the Federal Reserve Site, choose one year from each of the past three decades and record data for M1, M2, and M3. For each year, why are the three velocities different? Do you note a trend? What might explain the trend?

Problems for Chapter 15 appear at the back of the book.

Supply-Side Options

F iscal and monetary levers attempt to alter macro outcomes by managing aggregate demand. Supply-side policies focus on possibilities for shifting the aggregate *supply* curve instead. They also tend to emphasize the importance of long-run economic growth instead of focusing exclusively on short-run stability. Chapters 16 and 17 examine these policies.

16

Supply-Side Policy: Short-Run Options

Fiscal and monetary policies focus on the *demand* side of the macro economy. The basic premise of both approaches is that macro goals can be achieved by shifting the aggregate demand curve. The aggregate demand curve isn't the only game in town, however; there's an aggregate supply curve as well. Why not focus instead on possibilities for shifting the aggregate *supply* curve?

Any policies that alter the willingness or ability to supply goods at various price levels will shift the aggregate supply curve. This chapter identifies some of those policy options and examines how they affect macro outcomes. The focus is on two questions:

- How does the aggregate supply curve affect macro outcomes?
- How can the aggregate supply curve be shifted?

As we'll see, the aggregate supply curve plays a critical role in determining how difficult it is to achieve the goals of full employment and price stability.

AGGREGATE SUPPLY

The impetus for examining the supply side of the macro economy sprang up in the stagflation of the 1970s. **Stagflation** occurs when both unemployment *and* inflation increases at the same time. From 1973 to 1974, for example, consumer price inflation surged from 8.7 to 12.3 percent. At the same time, the unemployment rate jumped from 4.9 to 5.6 percent. How could this happen? *No shift of the aggregate demand curve can increase inflation and unemployment at the same time.* If aggregate demand increases (shifts right), the price level may rise but unemployment should decline with increased output. If aggregate demand decreases (shifts left), inflation should subside but unemployment increase. In other words, most demand-side theories predict that inflation and unemployment move in *opposite* directions in the short run. When this didn't happen, an alternative explanation was sought. The explanation was found on the supply side of the macro economy. Two critical clues were (1) the shape of the **aggregate supply** curve and (2) potential AS shifts.

SHAPE OF THE AS CURVE

As we've seen, the basic short-run objective of fiscal and monetary policy is to attain full employment and price stability. The strategy is to shift the aggregate demand curve to a more favorable position. In earlier chapters we examined several reasons policy-makers might *not* be able to shift the AD curve. Now, however, we'll assume Congress and/or the Fed *can* shift the AD curve in the desired way. Then the question turns to the *response* of producers to an aggregate demand shift.

The response of producers to an AD shift is expressed in the slope and position of the aggregate supply curve. Until now we've used a generally upward-sloping curve to depict aggregate supply, but we have to recognize that other supply responses are possible.

stagflation: The simultaneous occurrence of substantial unemployment and inflation.
aggregate supply: The total quantity of output producers are willing and able to supply at alternative price levels in a given time period, *ceteris paribus.*

Three Views of AS

Figure 16.1 (next page) illustrates three very different supply behaviors. Part (*a*) depicts what we've called the "naive" Keynesian view. Recall that Keynes was primarily concerned with the problem of unemployment. He didn't think there was much risk of inflation in the depths of a recession. He expected producers to increase output, not prices, when aggregate demand expanded. This expectation is illustrated by a *horizontal* AS curve. When fiscal or monetary stimulus shifts the AD curve rightward, output (Q) rises but not the price level (P). Only when capacity (Q^*) is reached do prices start rising abruptly.

The monetarist view of supply behavior is very different. In the most extreme monetarist view, real output remains at its "natural" rate, regardless of fiscal or monetary interventions. Rising prices don't entice producers to increase output because costs are likely to rise just as fast. They instead make output decisions based on more fundamental factors like technology and market size. The AS curve is *vertical* because output doesn't respond to changing price levels. (This is the long-run AS curve we first encountered in Chapter 8.) With a vertical AS curve, only prices can respond to a shift in aggregate demand. In Figure 16.1*b*, the AS curve is anchored at the natural rate of unemployment Q_N. When aggregate demand increases from AD_4 to AD_5, the price level (P) rises, but output (Q) is unchanged.

Figure 16.1*c* blends these Keynesian and monetarist perspectives into a hybrid AS curve. At low rates of output, the curve is nearly horizontal; at high rates of output, the AS curve becomes nearly vertical. In the broad middle of the AS curve, the curve slopes gently upward. In this area, shifts of aggregate demand affect *both* prices and output. The message of this hybrid AS curve is that the outcomes of fiscal and monetary policy depend on how close the economy is to full employment. *The closer we are to capacity, the greater the risk that fiscal or monetary stimulus will spill over into price inflation.*

The Inflation-Unemployment Trade-Off

Until now we've used the upward-sloping AS curve depicted in Figure 16.1*c* to characterize producer behavior. Because it allows for varying output/price responses at different levels of economic activity, the AS curve in Figure 16.1*c* is generally regarded as the most realistic for short-run outcomes. However, the upward-sloping section of the AS curve in Figure 16.1*c* has some disturbing implications. Because both prices and output respond to demand-side shifts, the economy can't attain both full employment and price stability at the same time—at least not with fiscal and monetary policies. Consider the simple geometry of policy stimulus and restraint.

Demand Stimulus. Monetary and fiscal stimulus shift the aggregate demand curve rightward. This demand-side effect is evident in all three graphs in Figure 16.1. However, *all rightward shifts of the aggregate demand curve increase both prices and output if the aggregate supply curve is upward-sloping.* This implies that fiscal and monetary efforts to reduce unemployment will also cause some inflation.

Demand Restraint. Monetary and fiscal restraint shift the aggregate demand curve leftward. If the aggregate supply curve is upward-sloping, *leftward shifts of the aggregate demand curve cause both prices and output to fall.* Therefore, fiscal and monetary efforts to reduce inflation will also increase unemployment.

FIGURE 16.1
Contrasting Views of Aggregate Supply

(a) **Keynesian AS** In the simple Keynesian model, the rate of output responds fully and automatically to increases in demand until full employment (Q^*) is reached. If demand increases from AD_1 to AD_2, equilibrium GDP will expand from Q_1 to Q^*, without any inflation. Inflation becomes a problem only if demand increases beyond capacity—to AD_3, for example.

(b) **Monetarist AS** Monetarists assert that changes in the money supply affect prices but not output. They regard aggregate supply as a fixed quantum, at the long run, "natural" rate of unemployment (here noted as Q_N). Accordingly, a shift of demand (from AD_4 to AD_5) can affect only the price level (from P_4 to P_5).

(c) **Hybrid AS** The consensus view incorporates Keynesian and monetarist perspectives but emphasizes the upward slope that dominates the middle of the AS curve. When demand increases, both price levels and the rate of output increase. Hence the slope and position of the AS curve limit the effectiveness of fiscal and monetary policies.

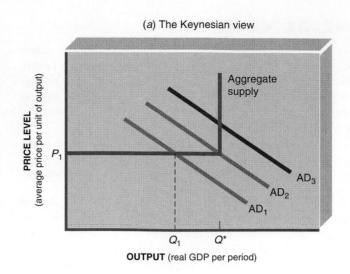

(a) The Keynesian view

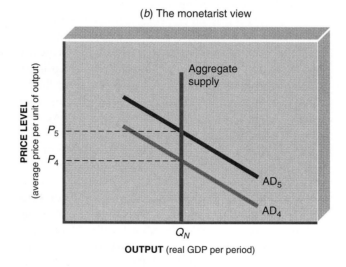

(b) The monetarist view

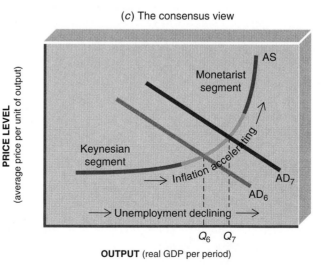

(c) The consensus view

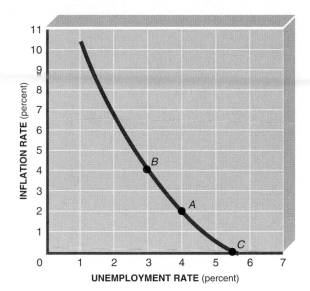

FIGURE 16.2
The Phillips Curve

The Phillips curve illustrates a trade-off between full employment and price stability. In the 1960s it appeared that efforts to reduce unemployment rates below 5.5 percent (point *C*) led to increasing rates of inflation (points *A* and *B*). Inflation threatened to reach unacceptable heights long before everyone was employed.

The Phillips Curve. The message of the upward-sloping aggregate supply curve is clear: *Demand-side policies alone can never succeed completely; they'll always cause some unwanted inflation or unemployment.*

Our macro track record provides ample evidence of this dilemma. Consider, for example, our experience with unemployment and inflation during the 1960s, as shown in Figure 16.2. This figure shows a **Phillips curve** indicating that prices (*P*) generally started rising before the objective of expanded output (*Q*) had been completely attained. Inflation struck before full employment was reached.

The Phillips curve was developed by a New Zealand economist, Alban W. Phillips, to summarize the relationship between unemployment and inflation in England for the years 1826–1957.[1] The Phillips curve was raised from the status of an obscure graph to that of a policy issue by the discovery that the same kind of relationship apparently existed in other countries and at other times. Paul Samuelson and Robert Solow of the Massachusetts Institute of Technology were among the first to observe that the Phillips curve was a reasonable description of U.S. economic performance for the years 1900–1960. For the post–World War II years in particular, Samuelson and Solow noted that an unemployment rate of 4 percent was likely to be accompanied by an inflation rate of approximately 2 percent. This relationship is expressed by point *A* in Figure 16.2. By contrast, lower rates of unemployment were associated with higher rates of inflation, as at point *B*. Alternatively, complete price stability appeared attainable only at the cost of an unemployment rate of 5.5 percent (point *C*). A seesaw kind of relationship existed between inflation and unemployment: When one went up, the other fell.

The trade-off between unemployment and inflation originates in the upward sloping AS curve. Figure 16.3a illustrates this point. Suppose the economy is initially at equilibrium *A*, with fairly stable prices but low output. When aggregate demand expands to AD$_2$, prices rise along with output, so we end up with higher inflation but less unemployment. This is also shown in Figure 16.3b by the move from point *a* to point *b* on the Phillips curve. The move from point *a* to point *b* indicates a decline in unemployment (more output) but an increase in inflation (higher price level). If demand is increased further, to AD$_3$, a still lower unemployment rate is achieved, but at the cost of higher inflation (point *c*).

Phillips curve: An historical (inverse) relationship between the rate of unemployment and the rate of inflation; commonly expresses a trade-off between the two.

[1] A. W. Phillips, "The Relationship Between Unemployment and the Rate of Change of Money Wage Rates in the United Kingdom, 1826–1957," *Economica,* November 1958. Phillips's paper studied the relationship between unemployment and *wage* changes rather than *price* changes; most later formulations (and public policy) focus on prices.

(a) Increases in aggregate demand cause . . .

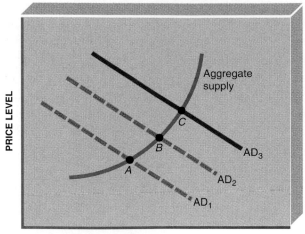

(b) A trade-off between unemployment and inflation.

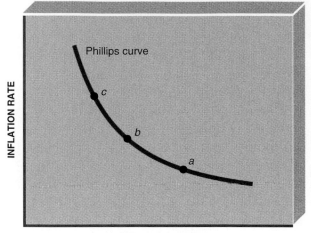

FIGURE 16.3
The Phillips Curve Trade-Off

If the aggregate supply curve slopes upward, increases in aggregate demand always cause both prices and output to rise. Thus higher inflation becomes a cost of achieving lower unemploy-

ment. In (a), increased demand moves the economy from point *A* to point *B*. At *B*, unemployment is lower, but prices are higher. This trade-off is illustrated on the Phillips curve in (b). Each point on the Phillips curve represents a different AS/AD equilibrium from the graph on the left.

SHIFTS OF THE AS CURVE

The unemployment inflation trade-off implied by the upward-sloping AS curve is not etched in stone. Many economists argue that the economy can attain lower levels of unemployment without higher inflation. This certainly appeared to be the case in the 1990s: Unemployment rates fell sharply from 1992 to 1999 without any increase in inflation. How could this have happened? There's no AD shift in any of part of Figure 16.1 that would reduce both unemployment *and* inflation.

Rightward AS Shifts:
All Good News

Only a rightward shift of the AS curve can reduce unemployment and inflation at the same time (see Figure 16.4). When aggregate supply increases from AS_1 to AS_2, macro equilibrium moves from E_1 to E_2. At E_2 real output is higher, so the unemployment rate must be lower. At E_2 the price level is also lower, indicating reduced inflation. Hence, a rightward shift of the AS curve offers the best of two worlds—something aggregate *demand* shifts (Figure 16.1) can't do.

Phillips Curve Shift. As we saw in Figure 16.3, the Phillips curve is a direct by-product of the AS curve. Accordingly, *when the AS curve shifts, the Phillips curve shifts as well.* As Figure 16.5 illustrates, the Phillips curve shifts to the left, the opposite of the AS shift in Figure 16.4. No new information is conveyed here. The Phillips curve simply focuses more directly on the implied change in the unemployment-inflation trade-off. *When the Phillips curve shifts to the left, the unemployment-inflation trade-off eases.*

The Misery Index. To keep track of simultaneous changes in unemployment and inflation, Arthur Okun developed the "misery index"—a simple sum of the inflation and unemployment rates. As the NEWS feature on page 318 illustrates, macro misery diminished substantially during the first Reagan administration (1981–1984). President Clinton also benefited from a leftward shift of the Phillips curve.

Leftward AS Shifts:
All Bad News

Whereas rightward AS Shifts appear to be a dream come true, leftward AS shifts are a real nightmare. Imagine in Figure 16.4 that the AS shift is reversed, that is, from AS_2

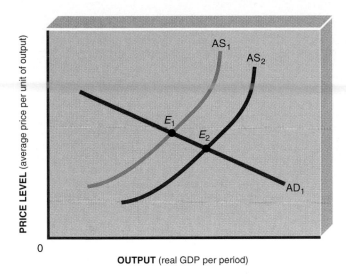

FIGURE 16.4
Shifts of Aggregate Supply

A rightward AS shift (AS_1 to AS_2) reduces both unemployment and inflation. A leftward shift has the opposite effect, creating stagflation.

to AS_1. What would happen? Output would decrease and prices would rise, exactly the kind of dilemma depicted in the cartoon on page 319. In other words, nothing would go in the right direction. This would be rampant stagflation.

A natural disaster can trigger a leftward shift of the AS curve, especially in smaller nations. In 1998, Hurricane Mitch struck Central America with a vengeance, killing upward of 10,000 people. In addition, Honduras' most important industry—bananas— was virtually wiped out, and even the banana trees themselves were destroyed (see WORLD VIEW page 319). This supply-side shock diminished the capacity for future production.

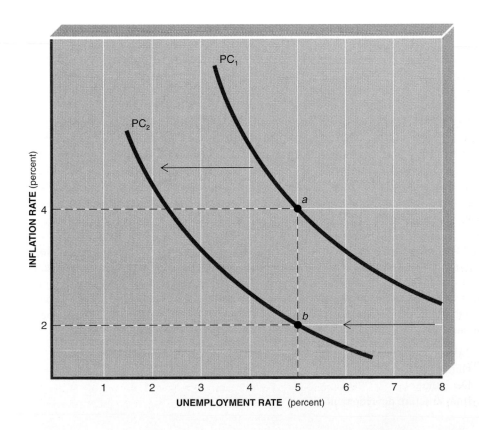

FIGURE 16.5
A Phillips Curve Shift

If the Phillips curve shifts leftward, the short-run unemployment inflation trade-off eases. With PC_1, 5 percent unemployment ignites 4 percent inflation (point *a*). With PC_2, 5 percent unemployment causes only 2 percent inflation (point *b*).

IN THE NEWS

The Misery Index

Unemployment is a problem and so is inflation. Being burdened with both problems at the same time is real misery.

The late Arthur Okun proposed measuring the extent of misery by adding together the inflation and unemployment rates. He called the sum of the two rates the "discomfort index." Political pundits quickly renamed it the "misery index."

In essence, the misery index is a measure of stagflation—the simultaneous occurrence of inflation and unemployment. In 1980, the misery index peaked at 19.6 percent as a result of high inflation (12.5 percent) as well as high unemployment (7.1 percent). Stagflation—and the misery it causes—has since receded markedly.

Source: *Economic Report of the President, 1999.*

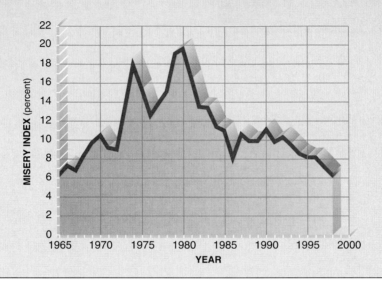

Analysis: Stagflation refers to the simultaneous occurrence of inflation and unemployment. The "misery index" combines both problems into a single measure.

CYBER NOTE

To update the misery index, retrieve data on unemployment and inflation from the U.S. Bureau of Labor Statistics at www.bls.gov/eag.table.html.

In a large economy like that of the United States, leftward shifts of aggregate supply are less dramatic. When the Organization of Petroleum Exporting Countries (OPEC) abruptly raised oil prices and limited exports to the United States, many industries experienced higher production costs and resource shortages, which reduced the ability and willingness to supply output at given price levels. The end result was an increase in both inflation and unemployment. This increase caused the big increase in macro misery during the years 1975–1989, as depicted in the NEWS feature, "The Misery Index."

Policy Levers

What the foregoing graphs demonstrate is *that rightward shifts of the aggregate supply curve always generate desirable macro outcomes.* The next question, of course, is how to shift the aggregate supply curve in the desired (rightward) direction. Supply-side economists look for clues among the forces that influence the supply-side response to changes in demand. Among those forces, the following policy options have been emphasized:

- Tax incentives for saving, investment, and work
- Human capital investment
- Deregulation
- Infrastructure development

WORLD VIEW

Mitch Left Honduras a Republic Without Bananas

LA CEIBITA, Honduras—Against all odds, Tropical Storm Mitch did not claim any lives among the 1,200 workers and residents of La Ceibita, a plantation town that is owned and managed by one of the largest private employers in Honduras, Cincinnati-based Chiquita Brands International. Throughout the country, flooding and landslides caused by Mitch killed perhaps 6,000 people, and another 4,000 in neighboring Nicaragua.

But the sense of relief felt by survivors such as Rodas, who has worked for Chiquita since he was 9, has largely been supplanted by worry about the future. Banana industry and government officials said that flooding destroyed not just the banana crop, but the plants themselves—in other words, virtually the entire banana industry in Honduras. The damage has already thrown thousands of people out of work and is expected to wipe out $255 million in annual banana exports over the next two years before the industry might begin to recover.

"This is by far the most devastating loss the industry has encountered in the last 25 years," said Steven Warshaw, Chiquita's president and chief operating officer. "We think all or close to all of our production of bananas is destroyed. . . ."

Chiquita officials in Honduras, which is the world's fourth-largest banana producer and exports about 6 billion bananas a year, said the company lost nearly 11 million plants on its 17,300 acres. Countrywide, government officials said, about 90 percent of the industry was destroyed, or more than 27 million plants.

The destruction was not confined to bananas, or to Honduras. Agriculture across Central America, where large portions of the impoverished populations rely on farming, was devastated by Mitch, which drowned crops with up to six feet of rain.

—John Ward Anderson

The Washington Post, Nov. 19, 1998, p. A39. © 1998, The Washington Post. Reprinted with permission. www.washingtonpost.com

Analysis: A natural disaster that destroys production capabilities shifts the aggregate supply curve to the left, which reduces output and raises price levels.

The Great Divide

Analysis: Leftward shifts of the aggregate supply curve push price levels up and output down. The remedy for such stagflation is a rightward shift of aggregate supply.

All these policies have the potential to change supply decisions *independently* of any changes in aggregate demand. If they're effective, they'll result in a rightward shift of the aggregate supply curve and an *improved* trade-off between unemployment and inflation.

TAX INCENTIVES

The most renowned supply-side policy option for improving the unemployment-inflation trade-off was the "supply-side" tax cuts of the early 1980s. Tax cuts are of course a staple of Keynesian economics. But tax cuts take on a whole new role on the supply side of the economy. *In Keynesian economics, tax cuts are used to increase aggregate demand.* By putting more disposable income in the hands of consumers, Keynesian economists seek to increase expenditure on goods and services. Output is expected to increase in response. From a Keynesian perspective, the form of the tax cut is not very important, as long as disposable income increases.

The supply side of the economy encourages a different view of taxes. Taxes not only alter disposable income but also affect the incentives to work and produce. High tax rates destroy the incentives to work and produce, so they end up reducing total output. Low tax rates, by contrast, allow people to keep more of what they earn and so stimulate greater output. *The direct effects of taxes on the supply of goods are the concern of supply-side economists.* Figure 16.6 shows the difference between demand-side and supply-side perspectives on tax policy.

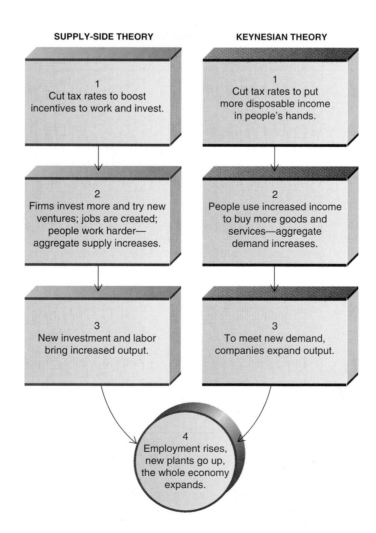

FIGURE 16.6
Two Theories for Getting the Economy Moving

Keynesians and supply-siders both advocate cutting taxes to reduce unemployment. But they have very different views on the kind of tax cuts required and the impact of any cuts enacted.

Marginal Tax Rates

Supply-side theory places special emphasis on *marginal* tax rates. The **marginal tax rate** is the tax rate imposed on the last (marginal) dollar of income received. In our progressive income tax system, marginal tax rates increase as more income is received. Uncle Sam takes a larger share out of each additional dollar earned. In 1999, the highest marginal tax rate on personal income was 39.6 percent (see NEWS). But that top rate has varied from a low of 12 percent to a shocking high of 91 percent. Wouldn't you expect that kind of variation in tax rates to affect supply decisions?

marginal tax rate: The tax rate imposed on the last (marginal) dollar of income.

Labor Supply. The marginal tax rate influences the financial incentive to *increase* one's work. *If the marginal tax rate is high, there's less incentive to work more;* Uncle Sam will get most of the added income. Confronted with high marginal tax rates, workers may choose to stay home rather than work as extra shift. Families may decide that it doesn't pay to send both parents into the labor market. When marginal tax rates are low, by contrast, those extra work activities generate bigger increases in disposable income.

Investment. High marginal tax rates discourage not only work effort but **investment** as well. Business investment is motivated by the desire for profits. But the profitability of an investment depends in part on taxes. If Uncle Sam imposes a high tax rate on business profits, the payoff to investors will be diminished. Potential investors may decide to consume their income or to purchase tax-free bonds rather than to invest in plant and equipment. If that happens, total investment will decline and output will suffer. Accordingly, *if high tax rates discourage investment, aggregate supply will be constrained.*

investment: Expenditures on (production of) new plant, equipment, and structures (capital) in a given time period, plus changes in business inventories.

IN THE NEWS

Taxes Off the Top

The tax rate for the richest 1 percent of U.S. taxpayers has ranged from 12 percent in 1916 to 91 percent during the post–World War II years. It is now at 39.6 percent, higher than a decade ago but relatively low by postwar standards.

The Washington Post, Feb. 19, 1998, p. H1. © 1998, The Washington Post. Reprinted with permission. www.washingtonpost.com

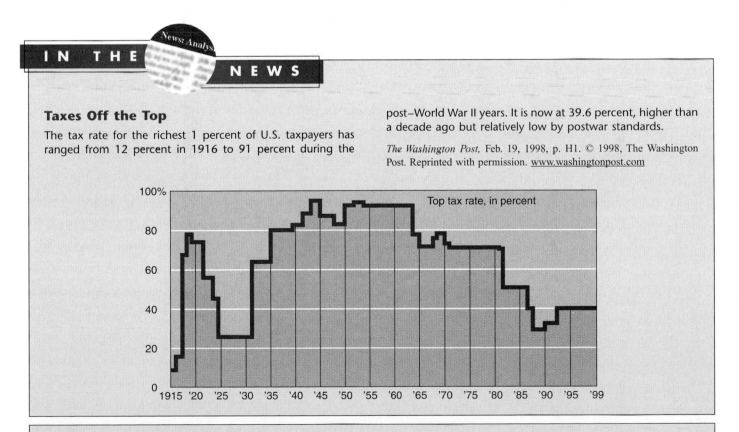

Analysis: The top marginal tax rate on income has varied from a low of 12 percent to a high of 91 percent. Supply-side theory emphasizes how these varying tax rates affect work, investment, and production decisions, that is, aggregate supply.

Tax-Induced Supply Shifts

If tax rates affect supply decisions, then *changes* in tax rates will shift aggregate supply. Specifically, supply-siders conclude that ***a reduction in marginal tax rates will shift the aggregate supply curve to the right.*** The increased supply will come from two sources: more work effort and more investment. This increased willingness to produce will reduce the rate of unemployment. The additional output will also help reduce inflationary pressures. Thus we end up with less unemployment *and* less inflation.

tax rebate: A lump-sum refund of taxes paid.

From a supply-side perspective, the form of the tax cut is critical. For example, **tax rebates** are a one-time windfall to consumers and have no effect on marginal tax rates. As a consequence, disposable income rises, but not the incentives for work or production. Rebates directly affect only the demand side of the economy.

To stimulate aggregate *supply,* tax *rates* must be reduced, particularly at the margin. These cuts can take the form of reductions in personal income tax rates or reductions in the marginal tax rates imposed on businesses. In either case, the lower tax rates will give people a greater incentive to work, invest, and produce. This was the motivation for the Reagan tax cuts of 1981–1984.

Table 16.1 illustrates the distinction between Keynesian and supply-side tax cuts. Under both tax systems (*A* and *B*), a person earning $200 pays $80 in taxes before the tax cut and $60 after the tax cut. But under system *A,* the marginal tax rate is always 50 percent, which means that Uncle Sam is getting half of every dollar earned above $100. By contrast, system *B* imposes a marginal tax rate of only 30 percent—$0.30 of every dollar above $100 goes to the government. Under system *B,* people have a greater incentive to earn more than $100. Although both systems raise the same amount of taxes, system *B* offers greater incentives to work extra hours and produce more output.

TABLE 16.1
Average vs. Marginal Tax Rates

The same amount of taxes can be raised via two very different systems. Here a person earning $200 pays $80 in taxes under either system (*A* or *B*). Thus the *average* tax rate (total tax ÷ total income) is the same in both cases ($80 ÷ $200 = 40%). But the *marginal* tax rates are very different. System *A* has a high marginal rate (50%), whereas system *B* has a low marginal tax rate (30%). System *B* provides a greater incentive for people to earn over $100.

			Tax Rate		
Tax System	**Initial Tax Schedule**	**Tax on Income of $200**	**Average**	**Marginal**	**Disposable Income**
A	$30 + 50% of income over $100	$80	40%	50%	$120
B	$50 + 30% of income over $100	$80	40%	30%	$120

Initial Alternatives

The average tax rate could be cut to 30 percent under either system. Under both systems, the revised tax would be $60 and disposable income would be increased to $140. Keynesians would be happy with either form of tax cut. But supply-siders would favor system *B* because the lower marginal tax rate gives people more incentive to earn higher incomes.

			Tax Rate		
Tax System	**Revised Tax Schedule**	**Tax on Income of $200**	**Average**	**Marginal**	**Disposable Income**
A	$10 + 50% of income over $100	$60	30%	50%	$140
B	$30 + 30% of income over $100	$60	30%	30%	$140

Alternative Forms of Tax Cut

Virtually all economists agree that tax rates influence people's decisions to work, invest, and produce. But the policy-relevant question is, how much influence do taxes have? Do reductions in the marginal tax rate shift the aggregate supply curve far to the right? Or are the resultant shifts quite small?

The expected response of labor and capital to a change in tax rates is summarized by the **tax elasticity of supply.** Like other elasticities, this one measures the proportional response of supplies to a change in price (in this case, a tax rate). Specifically, the tax elasticity of supply is the percentage change in quantity supplied divided by the percentage in tax rates, that is,

$$\text{Tax elasticity of supply} = \frac{\% \text{ change in quantity supplied}}{\% \text{ change in tax rate}}$$

Normally we expect quantity supplied to go up when tax rates go down. Elasticity (E) is therefore negative, although it's usually expressed in absolute terms (without the minus sign). The (absolute) value of E is typically greater than zero, since we expect *some* response to a tax cut. The policy issue boils down to the question of how large E actually is.

If the tax elasticity of supply were large enough, a tax cut might actually *increase* tax revenues. Suppose the tax elasticity were equal to 1.5. In that case a tax cut of 10 percent would cause output supplied to increase by 15 percent ($= 1.5 \times 10\%$). Such a large increase in the tax base (income) would result in *more* taxes being paid even though the tax *rate* was reduced. One of President Reagan's economic advisers, Arthur Laffer, actually thought such an outcome was possible. He predicted that tax revenues would increase after the Reagan supply-side tax cuts were made. In reality, the tax elasticity of supply turned out to be much smaller (around 0.15) and tax revenues fell substantially. The aggregate supply curve *did* shift to the right, but not very far, when marginal tax rates were cut.

The evidently low tax elasticity of supply helped President Clinton convince Congress to *increase* marginal tax rates in 1993. Although opponents objected that higher tax rates would reduce work and investment, the Clinton administration pointed out that any leftward shift of aggregate supply was likely to be small.

Supply-side economists respond that their tax-cut proposals have important *long-run* effects that aren't immediately apparent. On the demand side, an increase in income translates very quickly into increased spending. On the supply side, things don't happen so fast. It takes time to construct new plants and equipment. People are also slow to respond to new work and investment incentives. Hence the full benefits of supply-side tax cuts—or the damage done by tax hikes—won't be immediately visible.

Of particular concern to supply-side economists is the rate of saving in the economy. Demand-side economists emphasize spending and tend to treat **saving** as a leakage problem. Supply-siders, by contrast, emphasize the importance of saving for financing investment and economic growth. At full employment, a greater volume of investment is possible only if the rate of consumption is cut back. In other words, additional investment requires additional saving. Hence **supply-side economists favor tax incentives that encourage saving as well as greater tax incentives for investment.** This kind of perspective contrasts sharply with the Keynesian emphasis on stimulating consumption, as the cartoon on the next page emphasizes.

In the early 1980s Congress greatly increased the incentives for saving. First, banks were permitted to increase the rate of interest paid on various types of savings accounts. Second, the tax on earned interest was reduced. Finally, new forms of tax-free savings were created, for example, Individual Retirement Accounts, or IRAs.

Despite these incentives, the U.S. savings rate declined during the 1980s. Household savings dropped from 6.2 percent of disposable income in 1981 to a low of 2.5 percent in 1987. Neither the tax incentive nor the high interest rates that prevailed in the early 1980s convinced Americans to save more.

Tax Elasticity of Supply

tax elasticity of supply: The percentage change in quantity supplied divided by the percentage change in tax rates.

Savings Incentives

saving: That part of disposable income not spent on current consumption; disposable income less consumption.

CYBER NOTE

The U.S. Bureau of Economic Analysis (BEA) maintains quarterly data on the personal saving rate of U.S. households. See "Overview of the U.S. Economy" at www.bea.doc.gov.

Analysis: In the short run, consumer saving may reduce aggregate demand. However, saving also finances increased investment, which is essential to long-run growth.

Investment Incentives

An alternative lever for shifting aggregate supply is to offer tax incentives for investment. The 1981 tax cuts focused on *personal* income tax rates. By contrast, President Bush advocated cutting capital gains taxes. These are taxes levied on the increase in the value of property, such as land, buildings, and corporate stock, when it's sold. Lower capital gains taxes, Bush argued, would encourage people to start businesses or invest in them.

President Clinton also emphasized the need for investment incentives. His very first proposal for stimulating the economy was a temporary investment tax credit. People who invested in new plant and equipment would receive a tax credit equal to 10 percent of their investment. In effect, Uncle Sam would pay for part of any new investment by demanding less taxes. Because the credit is available only to those who make new investments, it's a particularly efficient lever for shifting the aggregate supply curve. President Clinton withdrew the investment-credit proposal, however, when he decided that deficit reduction was a higher priority.

CYBER NOTE

Find out ways to save taxes at www.irs.ustreas.gov.

HUMAN CAPITAL INVESTMENT

A nation's ability to supply goods and services depends on its *human* capital as well as its *physical* capital. If the size of the labor force increased, more output could be produced in any given price level. Similarly, if the *quality* of the workforce were to increase, more output could be supplied at any given price level. In other words, increases in **human capital**—the skills and knowledge of the workforce—add to the nation's potential output.

human capital: The knowledge and skills possessed by the workforce.

A mismatch between the skills of the workforce and the requirements of new jobs is a major cause of the unemployment-inflation trade-off. When aggregate demand increases, employers want to hire more workers. But the available (unemployed) workers may not have the skills employers require. This is the essence of **structural unemployment.** The consequence is that employers can't increase output as fast as they'd like to. Prices, rather than output, increase.

Structural Unemployment

structural unemployment: Unemployment caused by a mismatch between the skills (or location) of job seekers and the requirements (or location) of available jobs.

The larger the skills gap between unemployed workers and the requirements of emerging jobs, the worse will be the Phillips curve trade-off. To improve the trade-off, the skills gap must be reduced. This is another supply-side imperative. ***Investments in human capital reduce structural unemployment and shift the aggregate supply curve rightward.***

Worker Training

The tax code is a policy tool for increasing human capital investment as well as physical capital investment. In this case tax credits are made available to employers who offer more worker training. Such credits reduce the employer's after-tax cost of training.

President Clinton proposed even stronger incentives for employer-based training. He wanted to *require* employers to spend at least 1.5 percent of their total payroll costs on training activities. Those employers who didn't provide training activities directly would have to pay an equivalent sum into a public training fund. This "play-or-pay" approach would force employers to invest in the human capital of their employees. The higher costs of the play-or-pay approach might shift the aggregate supply curve to the left and actually *worsen* the unemployment-inflation trade-off, however. If those mandatory investments increased **labor productivity,** the aggregate supply curve would later shift to the right. But there's a risk of misallocating training resources and ending up worse off. Ultimately, the Clinton administration chose not to *require* more training but instead to *encourage* more training with moral suasion and tax incentives.

labor productivity: Amount of output produced by a worker in a given period of time; output per hour.

Education Spending

Another way to increase human capital is to expand and improve the efficacy of the education system. President Bush encouraged local school systems to become more competitive. He suggested they experiment with vouchers that would allow students to attend the school of their choice. Schools would then have to offer services that attracted voucher-carrying students. Those schools that didn't compete successfully wouldn't have enough funds (vouchers) to continue.

President Clinton advocated a more conventional approach. He urged Congress to allocate more funds to the school system, particularly programs for preschoolers, like Head Start, and disadvantaged youth. He acknowledged the potential value of vouchers in increasing school quality but wanted to limit their use to public schools. If successful, these efforts will shift the aggregate supply curve rightward. They're more likely to develop human capital gradually, however, than to spur short-term economic growth.

Affirmative Action

Lack of skills and experience aren't the only reasons it's sometimes hard to find the "right" workers. The mismatch between employed workers and jobs is often less a matter of skills than of race, gender, or age. In other words, discrimination can create an artificial barrier between job seekers and available job openings.

If discrimination tends to shift the aggregate supply curve leftward, then reducing discriminatory barriers should shift it to the right. Equal opportunity programs are thus a natural extension of a supply-side approach to macro policy. However, critics are also quick to point out the risks inherent in government regulation of hiring decisions. From a supply-side perspective, laws that forbid discrimination are welcome and should be enforced. But aggressive affirmative action programs that require employers to hire specific numbers of women or minority workers limit productive capabilities and can lead to excessive costs.

Transfer Payments

Welfare programs also discourage workers from taking available jobs. Unemployment and welfare benefits provide a source of income when a person isn't working. Although these **transfer payments** are motivated by humanitarian goals, they also inhibit labor supply. Transfer recipients must give up some or all of their welfare payments when they take a job, which makes working less attractive and therefore reduces the number of available workers. The net result is a leftward shift of the aggregate supply curve.

In 1996, Congress reformed the nation's core welfare program. The supply-side emphasis of that reform was manifest in the very title of the reform legislation: the

transfer payments: Payments to individuals for which no current goods or services are exchanged, like Social Security, welfare, unemployment benefits.

Personal Responsibility and Work Opportunity Act. Congress set time limits on how long people can draw welfare benefits. The act also required recipients to engage in job-related activities like job search and training. As a result of that legislation, well over 1 million adults were expected to leave welfare and go to work, thereby increasing aggregate supply.

Recognizing that income transfers reduce aggregate supply doesn't force us to eliminate all welfare programs. Welfare programs are also intended to serve important social needs. The AS/AD framework reminds us, however, that the structure of such programs will affect aggregate supply. With over 60 million Americans receiving income transfers, the effect on aggregate supply can be significant.

DEREGULATION

Government intervention affects the shape and position of the aggregate supply curve in other ways. The government intervenes directly in supply decisions by *regulating* employment and output behavior. In general, such regulations limit the flexibility of producers to respond to changes in demand. Government regulation also tends to raise production costs. The higher costs result not only from required changes in the production process but also from the expense of monitoring government regulations and filling out endless government forms. Thomas Hopkins, a Rochester Institute of Technology economist, estimates that the total costs of regulation exceed $500 billion a year. These added costs of production shift the aggregate supply curve to the left.

Factor Markets

Government intervention in factor markets increases the cost of supplying goods and services in many ways.

Minimum Wages. Minimum wage laws are one of the most familiar forms of factor-market regulation. The Fair Labor Standards Act of 1938 required employers to pay workers a minimum of 25 cents per hour. Over time, Congress has increased the coverage of that act and the minimum wage itself repeatedly.

The goal of the minimum wage law is to ensure workers a decent standard of living. But the law has other effects as well. By prohibiting employers from using lower-paid workers, it limits the ability of employers to hire additional workers. Teenagers, for example, may not have enough skills or experience to merit the federal minimum wage. Employers may have to rely on more expensive workers rather than hire unemployed teenagers. In the absence of a minimum wage, employers would hire and train more teenagers and other low-skill workers. With minimum wage requirements, the costs of production increase.

Here again the issue is not whether minimum wage laws serve any social purposes but how they affect macro outcomes. By shifting the aggregate supply curve leftward, minimum wage laws make it more difficult to achieve full employment with stable prices.

Mandatory Benefits. Government-directed fringe benefits have the same kind of effect on aggregate supply. One of the first bills President Clinton signed into law was the Family and Medical Leave Act, which requires all businesses with 50 or more employees to grant leaves of absence for up to 12 weeks. The employer must continue to pay health benefits during such absences and must also incur the costs of recruiting and training temporary replacements. The General Accounting Office estimated this would add nearly $700 million per year to payroll costs (see NEWS). These added payroll costs add to the costs of production, making producers less willing to supply output at any given price level. When President Clinton signed it in February 1993, *The Wall Street Journal* called the act "Job Destruction Bill Number 1" because of its impact on aggregate supply.

IN THE NEWS

Effect of Family Leave Bill

A federal study says 2.5 million people would benefit from the federal Family and Medical Leave bill at a total estimated cost to employers of $674 million the first year. The number benefiting from various provisions, and employer cost of each:

Provision	Potential Beneficiaries	Employer Cost (in millions)
Birth or adoption of child	908,000	$244
Seriously ill child	64,000	$19
Seriously ill parent	177,000	$80
Temporary medical leave	659,000	$90
Seriously ill spouse	731,000	$241
Total	2,539,000	$674

Highlights of the Bill

Focus: Businesses with 50 or more workers must give employees up to 12 weeks of unpaid leave yearly to care for a new baby or sick family member.
Effect: Only about 5% of U.S. businesses would be included, but they employ about 40% of all workers.

USA Today, Feb. 3, 1993, p. 5A. Copyright 1993, USA TODAY. Reprinted with permission. www.usatoday.com

Analysis: By requiring employers to provide specific fringe benefits, the government increases the cost of doing business. The higher costs of production shift the aggregate supply curve leftward.

Occupational Health and Safety. Government regulation of factor markets extends beyond wages and benefits. The government also sets standards for workplace safety and health. The Occupational Safety and Health Administration (OSHA), for example, sets limits on the noise levels at work sites. OSHA's Noise Exposure Standard limits the average sound level to 90 decibels for 8 hours, 92 decibels for 6 hours, 95 decibels for 3 hours, and so forth, up to a maximum of 115 decibels for 15 minutes or less. If noise levels exceed these limits, the employer is required to adopt administrative or engineering controls to reduce the noise level. Personal protection of workers (such as earplugs or earmuffs), although much less costly, will suffice only if source controls are not feasible. All such regulations are intended to improve workers' welfare. In the process, however, these regulations raise the costs of production and inhibit supply responses.

The government's regulation of factor markets tends to raise production costs and inhibit supply. The same is true of regulations imposed directly on product markets, as the following examples illustrate.

Transportation Costs. At the federal level, various agencies regulate the output and prices of transportation services. Until 1984 the Civil Aeronautics Board (CAB) determined which routes airlines could fly and how much they could charge. The Interstate Commerce Commission (ICC) has had the same kind of power over trucking, interstate bus lines, and railroads. The routes, services, and prices for ships (in U.S. coastal waters and foreign commerce) have been established by the Federal Maritime Commission. In all these cases, the regulations constrained the ability of producers to respond to increases in demand. Existing producers couldn't increase output at will, and

Product Markets

new producers were excluded from the market. Hence the rate of output was kept too low and prices too high.

Similar problems continue to inflate intrastate trucking costs. All but eight states limit the routes, the loads, and the prices of intrastate trucking companies. These regulations promote inefficient transportation and protect producer profits. The net cost to the economy is at least $8 billion, or about $128 a year for a family of four.

Many cities and counties also limit the number of taxicabs and regulate their prices. The net effect of such regulation is to limit competition and drive up the cost of transportation.

Food and Drug Standards. The Food and Drug Administration (FDA) has a broad mandate to protect consumers from dangerous products. In fulfilling this responsibility, the FDA sets health standards for the content of specific foods. A hot dog, for example, can be labeled as such only if it contains specific mixtures of skeletal meat, pig lips, snouts, and ears. By the same token, a milk chocolate bar is a milk chocolate bar, according to the FDA, only if it

> contains not less than 3.66 percent by weight of milk fat, not less than 12 percent by weight of milk solids, and not less than 10 percent by weight of chocolate liquor as calculated by subtracting from the weight of chocolate liquor used the weight of cacao fat therein and the weights therein of alkali and seasoning ingredients, if any, multiplying the remainder by 2.2, dividing the result by the weight of the finished milk chocolate, and multiplying the quotient by 100.

The FDA also sets standards for the testing of new drugs and evaluates the test results. In all three cases, the goal of regulation is to minimize health risks to consumers.

Like all regulation, however, the FDA standards entail real costs. The tests required for new drugs are expensive and time-consuming. Getting a new drug approved for sale can take years of effort and require a huge investment. The net results are that (1) fewer new drugs are brought to market and (2) those that do reach the market are more expensive than they would have been in the absence of regulation. In other words, the aggregate supply of goods is shifted to the left.

Other examples of government regulation are commonplace. The Environmental Protection Agency (EPA) regulates auto emissions, the discharge of industrial wastes, and water pollution. The U.S. Congress restricts foreign imports and raises their prices. The Federal Trade Commission (FTC) limits firms' freedom to increase their output or advertise their products.

CYBER NOTE

For the EPA's assessment of how its own regulations affect the U.S. economy, go to www.epa.gov/oppe/eaed/eedhmpg.htm.

CYBER NOTE

The Cato Institute, a conservative Washington, D.C., think tank, publishes lots of studies on regulatory costs; visit www.cato.org/research/reglt-st.html.

Reducing Costs

Many—perhaps most—of these regulatory activities are beneficial. In fact, all were originally designed to serve specific public purposes. As a result of such regulation, we do get safer drugs, cleaner air, and less deceptive advertising. We must also consider the costs involved, however. All regulatory activities impose direct and indirect costs. These costs must be compared to the benefits received. ***The basic contention of supply-side economists is that regulatory costs are now too high.*** To improve our economic performance, they assert, we must *deregulate* the production process, thereby shifting the aggregate supply curve to the right again.

During the past two decades, serious efforts to deregulate sectors of the private economy have occurred. As noted in Chapter 14, the Monetary Control Act of 1980 permitted domestic banks much greater flexibility in the prices and services they offered. Before then, the Securities and Exchange Commission had granted stockbrokers the same kind of flexibility. The Airline Deregulation Act of 1978 ended regulation of airline routes and fares as of 1983. The trucking and oil and gas industries were also substantially deregulated in the 1980s. The electric utility industry, cable, and local telephone services were deregulated during the 1990s.

Easing Trade Barriers

Government regulation of international trade also affects aggregate supply. If the supply of imports is restricted by quotas or tariffs, U.S. producers end up paying higher prices for parts, equipment, and raw materials. With imports restricted, demand pres-

"I blame government, labor, business, and my ex-wife."

Analysis: Because many constraints on aggregate supply contribute to stagflation, it's hard to single out any one cause (or cure).

sures are also more likely to push up domestic prices rather than output. A less restricted supply of imports would provide a "safety valve" for demand-pull inflation. Accordingly, "free-trade" pacts such as the North American Free Trade Agreement (NAFTA) tend to shift aggregate supply rightward.

INFRASTRUCTURE DEVELOPMENT

Another way to reduce the costs of supplying goods and services is to improve the nation's **infrastructure**, that is, the transportation, communications, judicial, and other systems that bind the pieces of the economy into a coherent whole. The interstate highway system, for example, enlarged the market for producers looking for new sales opportunities. Improved air traffic controls and larger airports have also made international markets and factors of production readily accessible. Without interstate highways and international airports, the process of supplying goods and services would be more localized and much more expensive.

It's easy to take infrastructure for granted until you have to make do without it. In recent years, U.S. producers have rushed into China, Russia, and Eastern Europe looking for new profit opportunities. What they discovered is that even simple communication is difficult where telephones are scarce and unreliable. In China there's only 1 telephone for every 100 people; Russia has 12. By contrast, the United States has 76 phones for every 100 people. Cars and taxicabs are almost as hard to locate in Russia or China, and conference facilities are primitive. There are few established clearinghouses for marketing information, and labor markets are fragmented and localized. Getting started sometimes requires doing everything from scratch.

Although the United States has a highly developed infrastructure, it too could be improved. There are roads and bridges to repair, more airports to be built, faster rail systems to construct, and space-age televideo networks to install. Spending on this kind of infrastructure will not only increase aggregate demand (fiscal stimulus) but also shift aggregate supply.

infrastructure: The transportation, communications, education, judicial, and other institutional systems that facilitate market exchanges.

THE ECONOMY TOMORROW

The output of the U.S. economy depends not only on *private* investment but on *public* investment as well. The infrastructure of transportation, communications, and environmental systems all affect the nation's production possibilities. As we look to the future, we have to wonder whether that

Rebuilding America

infrastructure will satisfy the needs of the economy tomorrow. If it doesn't, it will become increasingly difficult and costly to increase output. Inadequate infrastructure would not only worsen short-term macro outcomes but also impair our ability to compete in world markets.

Declining Infrastructure Investment

The United States has over $2 trillion worth of public, nonmilitary infrastructure, including highways, bridges, sewage systems, buildings, hospitals, and schools. Like private capital (business plant, equipment, and structures), this *public* capital contributes to our production possibilities.

Investment in public infrastructure slowed down in the 1970s and 1980s. As Figure 16.7 shows, the rate of infrastructure investment peaked at around 3.5 percent of GDP in the mid-1960s. It then declined steadily to a low of about 0.5 percent of GDP in the early 1980s. As a result of this decline in spending, the United States has barely been able to *maintain* existing infrastructure, much less *expand* it. Studies by Alan Aschauer and others suggest that **declining infrastructure investment has reduced actual and potential output.** In other words, crumbling infrastructure has shifted the aggregate supply curve leftward.

Not everyone agrees that the nation's infrastructure is actually "crumbling." Accident rates on the roads, rails, and in the air have been declining. Moreover, the quality of interstate roads—including the 155,000-mile National Highway system—has improved significantly since 1980. But everyone agrees that **the transportation system isn't keeping up with a growing economy.** Highway traffic is increasing at 2.5 percent a year, while airline passenger traffic is rising at closer to 4 percent a year. To accommodate this growth, we need more and better transportation systems.

The Cost of Delay

The failure to expand the infrastructure could prove costly. The U.S. Department of Transportation estimates that people now spend nearly 800 *million* hours a year in traffic delays. If the nation's highways don't improve, those delays will skyrocket to 3.9 *billion* hours a year a decade from now. That's a lot of labor resources to leave idle. Moreover, cars stuck on congested highways waste a lot of gasoline: nearly 3 billion gallons a year.

Delays in air travel impose similar costs. The Federal Aviation Administration says air travel delays increase airline operating costs by over $2 billion a year and idle over $3 billion worth of passenger time. That time imposes a high opportunity cost in forgone business transactions and shortened vacations. Ultimately, all these costs are reflected in lower productivity, reduced output, and higher prices.

FIGURE 16.7
Declining Infrastructure Investment

Relative investments in civilian infrastructure dropped sharply in the 1970s and early 1980s. The investment ratio peaked about 3.5 percent of GDP in the mid-1960s and plummeted to only 0.5 percent in 1981–1982.

Source: David Alan Aschauer, "Infrastructure: America's Third Deficit." *Challenge,* March/April 1991. Reprinted with permission of publisher, M. E. Sharpe, Inc.

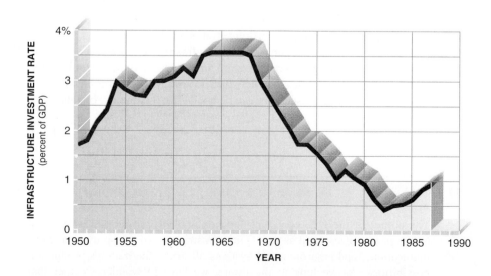

To alleviate these constraints on aggregate supply, Congress voted to accelerate infrastructure spending. The Surface Transportation Act of 1991 raised federal spending to over $50 billion a year. Among the public investments:

The Rebuilding Process

- *Highways:* Highway construction and rehabilitation
- *Air traffic control:* Modernization of the air traffic control system
- *Weather service:* Modernization of the weather service (new satellites, a supercomputer)
- *Maglev trains:* Research on magnetically levitated ("maglev") trains that can travel at 300 miles per hour and are environmentally clean
- *Smart cars and highways:* Research and testing of cars and highways outfitted with radar, monitors, and computers to reduce congestion and accidents

Other legislation authorized more spending on sewage systems, access to space (for example, the space shuttle), modernization of the postal service, and construction of more hospitals, prisons, and other buildings. These infrastructure improvements increase aggregate supply, improving both short- and long-run economic outcomes. To keep track of such activity, the GDP accounts now distinguish government *investment* spending from government *consumption* spending.

SUMMARY

- Fiscal and monetary policies seek to attain full employment and price stability by altering the level of aggregate demand. Their success, however, depends on microeconomic responses, as reflected in the price and output decisions of market participants.
- The market's response to shifts in demand is reflected in the shape and position of the aggregate supply curve. If the curve slopes upward, a trade-off between unemployment and inflation exists. The Phillips curve illustrates the trade-off.
- If the aggregate supply curve shifts to the left, the trade-off between unemployment and inflation worsens. Stagflation—a combination of substantial inflation and unemployment—results. This is illustrated by rightward shifts of the Phillips curve.
- Supply-side policies attempt to alter price and output decisions directly. If successful, they'll shift the aggregate supply curve to the right. Such a shift implies less inflation *and* less unemployment.
- Marginal tax rates are a major concern of supply-side economists. High tax rates discourage extra work, investment, and saving. A reduction in marginal tax rates should shift aggregate supply to the right.
- The tax elasticity of supply measures the response of quantity supplied to changes in tax rates. Empirical evidence suggests that tax elasticity is low and that short-run shifts of the aggregate supply curve are therefore small.
- Investments in human capital increase productivity and therefore shift aggregate supply also. Workers training and education enhancement are policy levers.
- Government regulation often raises the cost of production and limits output. Deregulation is intended to reduce costly restrictions on price and output behavior, thereby shifting aggregate supply to the right.
- Public infrastructure is part of the economy's capital resources. Investments in infrastructure (such as transportation systems) facilitate market exchanges and expand production possibilities.

Key Terms

stagflation
aggregate supply
Phillips curve
marginal tax rate
investment

tax rebate
tax elasticity of supply
saving
human capital
structural unemployment

labor productivity
transfer payments
infrastructure

Questions for Discussion

1. Why might prices rise when aggregate demand increases? What factors might influence the extent of price inflation?
2. What were the unemployment and inflation rates last year? Where would they lie on Figure 16.5? Can you explain the implied shift from curve PC$_2$?
3. If you were suddenly to start earning $20,000 per year, how much of that income would you have to pay in taxes? Include not only federal income taxes but Social Security and any state and local taxes as well. A what tax rate would you stop working?
4. Why would mandatory *unpaid* family leave (see NEWS page 327) raise production costs?
5. Testing procedures required by the U.S. Food and Drug Administration raise the cost and price of drugs. Should we eliminate such requirements in order to ease infla-

tionary pressures? How about the regulation of hot dog content?
6. How do each of the following infrastructure items affect aggregate supply? (*a*) highways, (*b*) schools, (*c*) sewage systems, (*d*) courts and prisons.
7. Web Activity Find the inflation rates and unemployment rates for each year in the 1960s and 1980s at www.bls.gov. Construct a Phillips Curve for each decade. Do you see a pattern?
8. Web Activity How much does the typical U.S. household pay in taxes? Researchers disagree. Compare the findings of a group that maintains federal taxes have gone up quickly at www.taxfoundation.org with a group that maintains federal taxes haven't gone up quickly at www.cbpp.org. What policy recommendations does each group make based on its different reading of the data?

Problems for Chapter 16 appear at the back of the book.

Growth and Productivity: Long-Run Possibilities

17

Economic growth is the fundamental determinant of the long-run success of any nation, the basic source of rising living standards, and the key to meeting the needs and desires of the American people.

—*Economic Report of the President, 1992*

Imagine a world with no fax machines, no cellular phones, no miniaturized televisions, and no digital sound. Such a world actually existed—and only 25 years ago! At the time, personal computers were still on the drawing board, and laptops weren't even envisioned. Web sites were a place where spiders gathered, not locations in the Internet. Home video hadn't been seen, and no one had yet popped any microwave popcorn. Biotechnology hadn't yet produced any blockbuster drugs, and people wore the same pair of athletic shoes for a wide variety of sports.

New products are evidence of economic progress. Over time, we produce not only *more* goods and services but also *new* and *better* goods and services. In the process, we get richer: Our material living standards rise.

Rising living standards aren't inevitable, however. According to World Bank estimates, over 3 *billion* people—more than half the world's population—continue to live in abject poverty. Worse still, living standards in many of the poorest countries have *fallen* in the last decade. Living standards also fell in Eastern Europe when communism collapsed and a painful transition to market economies began. Those living in the former Soviet bloc countries are counting on the power of free markets to jump-start their economies and raise living standards.

This chapter takes a longer-term view of U.S. economic performance. Chapters 8 to 16 were concerned with the business cycle—that is, *short-run* variations in output and prices. This chapter looks at the prospects for *long-run* growth and considers three questions:

- How important is economic growth?
- How does an economy grow?
- Is continued economic growth possible? Is it desirable?

We develop answers to these questions by first examining the nature of economic growth and then examining its sources and potential limits.

THE NATURE OF GROWTH

Economic growth refers to increases in the output of the economy. But there are two distinct ways in which output increases, and they have very different implications for our economic welfare.

Short-Run Changes in Capacity Utilization

production possibilities: The alternative combinations of final goods and services that could be produced in a given time period with all available resources and technology.

The easiest kind of growth comes from increased use of our productive capabilities. At any given moment there's a limit to an economy's potential output. This limit is determined by the quantity of resources available and our technological know-how. We've illustrated these short-run limits with a **production possibilities** curve, as in Figure 17.1a. By using all our available resources and our best expertise, we can produce any combination of goods and services on our production possibilities curve.

We don't always take full advantage of our productive capacity. The economy often produces a mix of output that lies *inside* our production possibilities, like point A in Figure 17.1a. When this happens, a major short-run goal of macro policy is to achieve full employment—to move us from point A to some point on the production possibilities curve (such as point B). In the process, we produce more output.

Long-Run Changes in Capacity

Once we're fully utilizing our productive capacity, further increases in output are attainable only if we *expand* that capacity. To do so we have to *shift* the production possibilities outward, as in Figure 17.1b. Such shifts imply an increase in *potential* GDP—that is, our productive capacity.

economic growth: An increase in output (real GDP); an expansion of production possibilities.

Over time, increases in capacity are critical. Short-run increases in the utilization of existing capacity can generate only modest increases in output. Even "high" unemployment rates, such as 7 percent, leave little room for increased output. *To achieve large and lasting increases in output we must push our production possibilities outward.* For this reason, economists often define **economic growth** in terms of changes in *potential* GDP.

The unique character of economic growth can also be illustrated with aggregate supply and demand curves. Figure 17.2 depicts both a sloped, *short-run* AS curve and a vertical, *long-run* AS curve. In the short run, macro stabilization policies try to shift the AD curve to a more desirable price-output equilibrium. Such demand-side policies are unlikely to change the country's long-run capacity to produce, however. At best they move the macro equilibrium to a more desirable point on the *short-run* AS curve (for example, from E_1 to E_2 in Figure 17.2).

Our productive capacity may increase nevertheless. If it does, the "natural" long-run AS curve will also shift. In this framework, *economic growth implies a rightward shift of the long-run aggregate supply curve.* Should that occur, the economy will be

FIGURE 17.1
Two Types of Growth

Increases in output may result from increased use of existing productive capacity or from increases in that capacity itself. In part (*a*) the initial mix of output at point A doesn't make full use of our production possibilities. Hence we can get more output by employing more of our available resources or using them more efficiently. This is illustrated by point B (or any other point on the curve). Once we're on the production possibilities curve, we can get more output only by *increasing* our productive capacity. This is illustrated by the *shift* of the production possibilities curve in part (*b*).

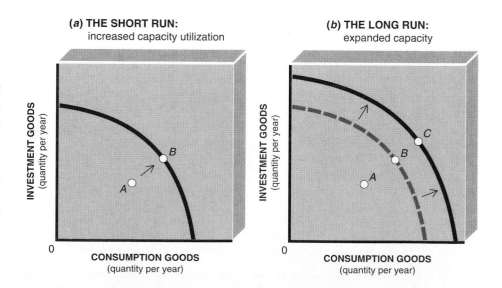

(a) THE SHORT RUN: increased capacity utilization

(b) THE LONG RUN: expanded capacity

INVESTMENT GOODS (quantity per year)

CONSUMPTION GOODS (quantity per year)

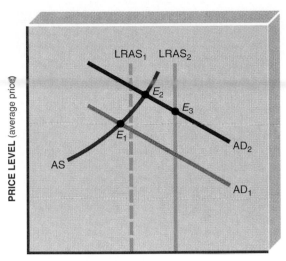

FIGURE 17.2
Shifts of Long-Run Supply

Macro stabilization policies try to shift the aggregate demand curve (e.g., from AD_1 to AD_2) to achieve greater output and employment. The vertical long-run AS curve implies that these efforts will have no lasting impact on the "natural" rate of output, however. To achieve economic growth, the long-run aggregate supply curve must be shifted to the right (e.g., from $LRAS_1$ to $LRAS_2$)

able to produce still more output with less inflationary pressure (e.g., as at E_3 in Figure 17.2).

Notice we refer to *real* GDP, not *nominal* GDP, in our concept of economic growth. Nominal GDP can rise even when the quantity of goods and services falls, as was the case in 1991. The total quantity of goods and services produced in 1991 was less than the quantity produced in 1990. Nevertheless, prices rose enough in 1991 to keep nominal GDP growing.

Real GDP refers to the actual quantity of goods and services produced. Real GDP avoids the distortions of inflation by adjusting for changing prices. By using 1992 prices as a **base period,** we observe that real GDP fell from $6139 billion in 1990 to only $6079 billion in 1991. Since then real GDP has increased substantially.

MEASURES OF GROWTH

Typically, changes in real GDP are expressed in percentage terms, as a growth *rate.* The **growth rate** is simply the change in real output between two periods divided by total output in the base period. The percentage decline in real output during 1991 was thus $60 billion ÷ $6139 billion, or 1 percent. By contrast, real output grew in 1992 by 2.7 percent.

Figure 17.3 illustrates the recent growth experience of the U.S. economy. In the 1960s real GDP grew by an average of 4.1 percent per year. Economic growth slowed to only 2.8 percent in the 1970s however, with actual output declines in 3 years. The steep recession of 1982, as seen in Figure 17.3, reduced GDP growth in the 1980s to an even lower rate: 2.5 percent per year. The 1990s started out even worse, with negligible growth in 1990 and a recession in 1991. The economy performed better after that, however. For the decade as a whole, output growth averaged close to 2.3 percent a year.

Slowing Growth. Even with the improved performance of the late 1990s, a general decline in decade-specific growth rates is apparent. Figure 17.4 illustrates this gradual but persistent slowing of the growth process.

The growth slowdown has sparked a lot of concern. Ultimately, our future living standards will depend on the rate of economic growth. The challenge now is to increase the growth rate to previous levels. Indeed, a lot of observers say we shouldn't even be satisfied with 2.5 percent growth (the average of the 1980s) but instead strive for a 3.5 percent growth (see NEWS).

Nominal vs. Real GDP

real GDP: The value of final output produced in a given period, adjusted for changing prices.
base period: The time period used for comparative analysis; the basis for indexing, e.g., of price changes.

The Growth Rate

growth rate: Percentage change in real output from one period to another.

CYBER NOTE

The U.S. Bureau of Economic Analysis (BEA) maintains quarterly data on real GDP growth in their "overview of the U.S. economy" at www.bea.doc.gov.

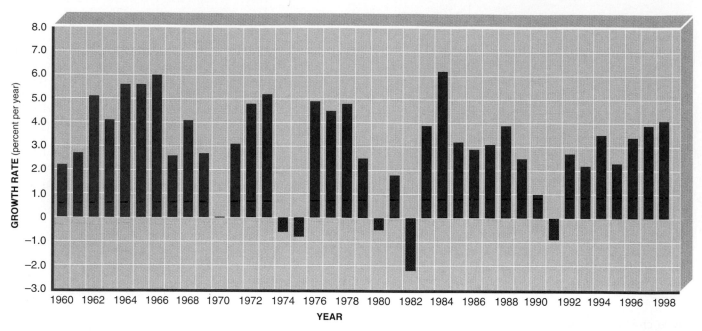

FIGURE 17.3
Recent U.S. Growth Rates

Total output typically increases from one year to another. The focus of policy is on the growth *rate,* that is, how fast real GDP increases from one year to the next.

Source: *Economic Report of the President, 1999.*

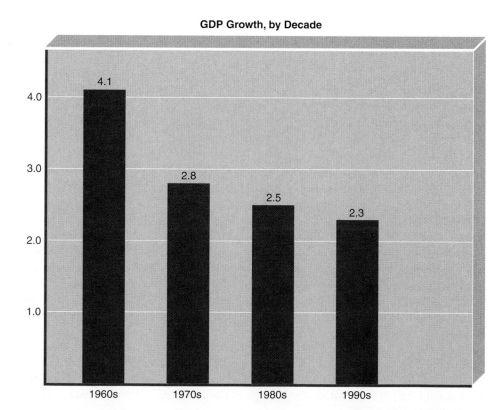

FIGURE 17.4
The Growth Slowdown

Since the 1960s, the U.S. GDP growth rate has been slipping. The policy challenge is to explain—and reverse—this growth slowdown.

Source: U.S. Department of Commerce.

GDP Growth, by Decade

The Great Growth Debate: 2.5 Percent or 3.5 Percent?

How fast can the economy grow? Most mainstream economists believe total output can grow at a rate of only $2^1/_2$ percent a year. That allows for 1.2 percent growth in the labor-force and 1.3 percent productivity growth. Recent gains in productivity have inspired higher forecasts, however—annual growth rates of 3.5 percent or better.

If the mainstream view is correct, real GDP will double in 28 years or so. If the optimists are correct, output will double every 20 years.

The rate of capacity growth will also affect fiscal and monetary policy. If the slower growth track (2.5 percent) is projected, policymakers are likely to exercise fiscal and monetary restraint any time the economy speeds up. If faster growth is deemed possible, Washington won't be so quick to curb spending or raise interest rates at every economic upturn. To keep slow growth from becoming a self-fulfilling prophecy, the business sector will have to demonstrate that productivity gains of 2.5 percent or more per year are sustainable.

Source: Adapted from *Economic Report of the President, 1995.*

Analysis: Increases in long-run aggregate supply create more leeway for noninflationary fiscal stimulus. To achieve that growth, productivity must advance.

The Exponential Process. At first blush, the "challenge" of raising the growth rate from 2.3 to 2.5 percent or even to 3.5 percent may appear neither difficult nor important. Indeed, the whole subject of economic growth looks rather dull when you discover that "big" gains in economic growth are measured in fractions of a percent. However, this initial impression isn't fair. First, even one year's "low" growth implies lost output. If we had just *maintained* output in 1991 at its 1990 level—that is, "achieved" a *zero* growth rate rather than a 1 percent decline—we would have had $60 billion more worth of goods and services, which works out to over $200 worth of goods and services per person. Lots of people would have liked that extra output.

Second, economic growth is a *continuing* process. Gains made in one year accumulate in future years. It's like interest you earn at the bank: If you leave your money in the bank for several years, you begin to earn interest on your interest. Eventually you accumulate a nice little bankroll.

The process of economic growth works the same way. Each little shift of the production possibilities curve broadens the base for future GDP. As shifts accumulate over many years, the economy's productive capacity is greatly expanded. Ultimately we discover that those "little" differences in annual growth rates generate tremendous gains in GDP.

This cumulative process, whereby interest or growth is compounded from one year to the next, is called an "exponential process." The NEWS feature highlights the implications of this process. At growth rates of 2.5 percent, GDP doubles in 28 years. With 3.5 percent growth, GDP doubles in only 20 years. In a single generation the *difference* between 2.5 percent growth and 3.5 percent growth amounts to $5 trillion of output a year. That *difference* is about two-thirds of this year's total output. From this longer-term perspective, the difference between 2.5 percent and 3.5 percent growth begins to look very meaningful.

The exponential process might look even more meaningful if we translate it into *per capita* terms. We can do so by looking at GDP *per capita* rather than total GDP. **GDP per capita** is simply total output divided by total population. In 1998 the total output

GDP per capita: Total GDP divided by total population; average GDP.

GDP per Capita: A Measure of Living Standards

of the U.S. economy was $8.5 trillion. Since there were 270 million of us to share that output, GDP per capita was

$$\underset{(1998)}{\text{GDP per capita}} = \frac{\$8.5 \text{ trillion of output}}{270 \text{ million people}} = \$31,481$$

This does not mean that every man, woman, and child in the United States received $31,481 worth of goods and services in 1998; it simply indicates how much output was potentially available to the "average" person. GDP per capita is often used as a basic measure of our standard of living.

Growth in GDP per capita is attained only when the growth of output exceeds population growth. In the United States, this condition is usually achieved. Even when *total* GDP growth slowed in the 1970s and 1980s, *per capita* GDP kept rising because the U.S. population was growing by only 1 percent a year. Hence even relatively slow economic growth of 2.5 percent a year was enough to keep raising living standards.

The developing nations of the Third World aren't so fortunate. Many of these countries bear both slower *economic* growth and faster *population* growth. They have a difficult time *maintaining* living standards, much less increasing them. Ethiopia, for example, is one of the poorest countries in the world, with GDP per capita of roughly $500 (see WORLD VIEW in Chapter 2, page 28). Yet its population continues to grow rapidly (2.3 percent per year), putting constant pressure on living standards. The population of Nigeria grew by an average of 2.9 percent per year in the 1990s, while GDP grew at a slower rate of only 2.7 percent (see Table 2.1). As a consequence, GDP per capita *declined* nearly 0.3 percent per year.

By comparison with these countries, the United States has been most fortunate. Our GDP per capita has more than doubled since 1960s, despite several recessions. This means that the average person today has twice as many goods and services as the average person had a generation ago.

What about the future? Will we continue to enjoy substantial gains in living standards? Many Americans harbor great doubts. A 1996 poll revealed that 54 percent of adults believe their children's living standards will be below today's level. That would happen only if population growth outstrips GDP growth. That seems most unlikely; it all depends on how fast output continues to grow in relation to population. Table 17.1 indicates some more optimistic possibilities. If GDP per capita continues to grow at 1.5 percent per year—as it did in the 1990s—it will take 47 years to double our standard of living. If GDP per capita grows just 1 percent faster, say, by 2.5 percent per year, our standard of living will double in only 30 years.

The potential increases in living standards depicted in Table 17.1 won't occur automatically. Someone is going to have to produce more output if we want GDP per capita

CYBER NOTE

Find growth rates of various countries at www.bea.doc.gov/bea/dn/0898nip3/tab2b.htm.

GDP per Worker: A Measure of Productivity

TABLE 17.1
The Rule of 72

Small differences in annual growth rates cumulate into large differences in GDP. Shown here are the number of years it would take to double GDP per capita at various net growth rates. "Net" growth refers to the GDP growth rate minus the population growth rate.

Doubling times can be approximated by the "rule of 72." Seventy-two divided by the growth rate equals the number of years it takes to double.

Net Growth Rate (percent)	Doubling Time (years)
0.0	Never
0.5	140
1.0	70
1.5	47
2.0	35
2.5	30
3.0	24
3.5	20
4.0	18

to rise. One reason our living standard rose in the 1980s is that the labor force grew faster than the population. Those in the World War II baby boom had reached maturity and were entering the **labor force** in droves. At the same time, more women took jobs outside the home. As a consequence, the number of workers grew faster than the population, increasing GDP per capita.

labor force: All persons over age 16 who are either working for pay or actively seeking paid employment.

The employment rate can't increase forever. At the limit, everyone would be in the labor market, and no further workers could be found. Further increases in GDP per capita could only come from increases in output *per worker.*

The most common measure of **productivity** is output per labor-hour, which is simply the ratio of total output to the number of hours worked. As noted earlier, total GDP in 1998 was $8.5 trillion. In that same year the labor force was employed for a total of 237 billion hours. Hence the average worker's productivity was

productivity: Output per unit of input, for example, output per labor-hour.

$$\frac{\text{Labor}}{\text{productivity}} = \frac{\text{total output}}{\text{total labor-hours}}$$

$$= \frac{\$8.5 \text{ trillion}}{237 \text{ billion}}$$

$$= \$36 \text{ per hour}$$

The increase in our GDP per capita in recent decades is directly related to the higher productivity of the average U.S. worker. The average worker today produces twice as many goods and services than the average worker did in 1960.

The Productivity Slowdown. For economic growth to continue, the productivity of the average U.S. worker must rise still further. In the 1970s and 1980s, however, productivity growth slowed considerably (see Figure 17.5). The annual increase in productivity averaged 3.3 percent in the 1960s, then fell to 2.2 percent in the 1970s. In the 1980s and 1990s the growth of productivity was even slower, averaging just over 1 percent a year. This productivity slowdown caused people to wonder if the American "growth machine" was wearing out.

CYBER NOTE

The U.S. Bureau of Labor Statistics (BLS) maintains quarterly data on labor productivity at www.bls.gov/datahome.htm.

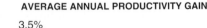

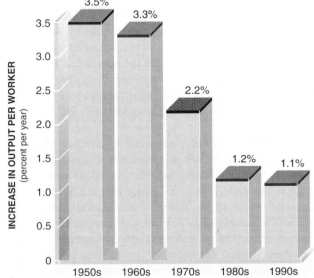

FIGURE 17.5
The Productivity Slowdown

Increases in output per worker are the ultimate source of rising living standards. In the 1970s, 1980s, and 1990s productivity continued to increase, but at ever slower rates. This "productivity slowdown" has limited economic growth.

Source: U.S. Bureau of Labor Statistics.

SOURCES OF GROWTH

The arithmetic of economic growth is simple. Future output growth depends on two factors:

$$\text{Growth rate of total output} = \text{Growth rate of labor force} + \text{Growth rate of productivity}$$

Accordingly, how fast GDP increases in the future depends on how fast the labor force grows and how fast productivity advances. Since the long-run growth of the labor force has stabilized at around 1.2 percent, the real uncertainty about future economic growth originates in the unpredictability of productivity advances. Will output per worker increase at the snail's pace of only 1 percent a year or at much faster rates of 2, 3, or 4 percent per year?

To assess the potential for U.S. productivity gains, we need to examine the sources of productivity improvement. ***The sources of productivity gains include***

- *Higher skills—an increase in labor skills*
- *More capital—an increase in the ratio of capital to labor*
- *Technological advance—the development and use of better capital equipment and products*
- *Improved management—better use of available resources in the production process*

Human-Capital Investment

Continuing advances in education and skills training have greatly increased the quality of U.S. labor. In 1950 less than 8 percent of all U.S. workers had completed college. Today nearly 30 percent of the workforce has completed 4 years of college. There has also been a substantial increase in vocational training, both in the public sector and by private firms.

In the 1970s these improvements in the quality of individual workers were offset by a change in the composition of the labor force. As we observed in Chapters 6 and 16, the proportion of teenagers and women in the labor force grew tremendously in the 1960s and 1970s. These baby boomers and their mothers contributed to higher output. Because teenagers and women (re)entering the labor market generally have less job experience than adult men, however, *average* productivity fell.

This phenomenon reversed itself in the 1990s, as the baby boomers entered their prime working years. The increased productivity of the workforce is not a reflection of the aging process itself. Rather, the gains in productivity reflect the greater **human-capital** investment associated with more schooling and more on-the-job learning.

human capital: The knowledge and skills possessed by the workforce.

Physical-Capital Investment

The knowledge and skills a worker brings to the job don't completely determine his or her productivity. A worker with no tools, no computers, and no machinery won't produce much even if she has a Ph.D. Similarly, a worker with outmoded equipment won't produce as much as an equally capable worker equipped with the newest machines and the best technology. From this perspective, ***a primary determinant of labor productivity is the rate of capital investment.*** In other words, improvements in output per *worker* depend in large part on increases in the quantity and quality of *capital* equipment (see WORLD VIEW).

The efforts of the average U.S. worker are presently augmented with over $100,000 of invested capital. This huge capital endowment is a prime source of high productivity. To *increase* productivity, however, the quality and quantity of capital available to the average worker must continue to increase. This is occurring, but at a slower pace. While labor-force growth accelerated in the 1970s, the growth of capital slowed. As Table 17.2 indicates, the capital stock increased by 4.1 percent per year in the late 1960s. In the 1970s, however, the growth of capital slowed to only 2.5 percent per year, and in the early 1980s it slowed even further. The stock of capital was still growing faster than the labor force (compare columns 1 and 2), but the difference was getting smaller. As a consequence, productivity growth declined (see column 3).

WORLD VIEW

Comparative Investment and Growth

Investment in new plant and equipment is essential for economic growth. In general, countries that allocate a larger share of output to investment will grow more rapidly. In the 1990s China had the highest growth rate and one of the highest investment rates.

Country	Investment as Percentage of GDP (average, 1990–1996)	Growth Rate of GDP (average, 1990–1997)
China	39	10.2
Thailand	41	7.4
Singapore	35	6.6
India	24	5.6
United States	17	2.4
Great Britain	16	1.6

Source: International Monetary Fund. www.imf.org

Analysis: Investment increases production possibilities. Countries that devote a larger share of output to investment tend to grow faster.

Saving and Investment Rates. The dependence of productivity gains on capital investment puts a new perspective on consumption and saving. In the short run, the primary concern of macroeconomic policy is to balance aggregate demand and aggregate supply. In this context, savings are a form of leakage that requires offsetting injections of investment or government spending. From the longer-run perspective of economic growth, saving and investment take on added importance. ***Savings aren't just a form of leakage but a basic source of investment financing.*** If we use all our resources to produce consumer, export, and public-sector goods, there won't be any investment. In that case, we might not face a short-run stabilization problem—our productive capacity might be fully utilized—but we'd confront a *growth* problem. Indeed, if we consumed our entire output, our productive capacity would actually shrink since we wouldn't even be replacing worn-out plant and equipment. We must have at least enough savings to finance **net investment.**

net investment: Gross investment less depreciation.

	Average Annual Percentage Change In:		
Period	Labor Stock	Capital Stock	Output per Labor-Hour
1959–1965	0.9	3.8	3.3
1965–1969	1.2	4.1	2.2
1969–1973	0.4	3.5	2.6
1973–1979	1.6	2.5	0.8
1979–1985	1.6	2.2	0.9

Source: *Economic Report of the President, 1988.*

TABLE 17.2
Average Annual Growth Rate of Labor, Capital, and Productivity, 1959–1985

In the 1970s the rate of capital growth slowed while the rate of labor growth increased. As a consequence, productivity gains declined. These trends were reversed in the late 1980s.

Actual saving and investment rates have been quite low in the United States. In the 1960s and 1970s, consumers saved 7 to 8 percent of their disposable income. Consumer saving rates then dropped in the 1980s, hitting a low of 3.2 percent in 1987. The household saving rate fell even further in the 1990s, actually turning *negative* in the third quarter of 1998. Continued financing of investment was made possible only by the emergence of a federal budget surplus and a continuing inflow of foreign investment. These added sources of investment financing permitted the U.S. economy to continue growing. We can't rely on foreign savings forever, however. In fact, interest and dividends paid to international participants for past financial investments now reduce the net inflow of foreign savings. To increase the future rate of investment, Americans will have to save and invest more themselves.

Management Training

Resources, however good and abundant, must be organized into a production process and managed. Hence entrepreneurship and the quality of continuing management are also major determinants of economic growth.

It's difficult to characterize differences in management techniques or to measure their effectiveness. However, much attention has been focused in recent years on the alleged shortsightedness of U.S. managers. The rumor is that U.S. firms focus too narrowly on short-term profits, neglecting long-term gains in productivity. They also emphasize quantity over quality of output. And they fail to include workers in key decisions, thus depriving themselves of important insights and goodwill. By contrast, firms in Japan and elsewhere concentrate on longer-term gains, quality control, and strong bonds between labor and management. As a consequence, Japanese firms enjoy remarkably good labor and customer relations, intense worker loyalty, and faster productivity gains.

If all these accusations about U.S. corporate management were true, the U.S. economy would surely be in a sorry state. At best, these contrasts between management practices serve as precautionary tales. The time horizons used for developing investment and production plans can affect long-run growth prospects. Management-labor relations can also materially affect productivity. As well, management familiarity with *global* markets will affect a firm's ability to grow and prosper in both foreign and domestic markets. Corporations in the United States spend billions of dollars on management training to help keep company executives up to speed on these and other determinants of long-run productivity. Such investments in managerial talent are another source of economic growth.

Research and Development

A fourth and vital source of productivity advance is research and development (R&D), a broad concept that includes scientific research, product development, innovations in production techniques, and the development of management improvements. R&D activity may be a specific, identifiable activity such as in a research lab, or it may be part of the process of "learning by doing." In either case, the insights developed from R&D generally lead to new products and cheaper ways of producing them. Over time, R&D is credited with the greatest contributions to economic growth. In his study of U.S. growth during the period 1929–1982, Edward Denison concluded that 26 percent of *total* growth was due to "advances in knowledge" (see Table 17.3 next page).

CYBER NOTE

The National Science Foundation tracks R & D spending. Visit www.nsf.gov/sbe/srs/nprdr/start.hml.

New Growth Theory. The evident contribution of "advances in knowledge" to economic growth has spawned a new perspective called "new growth theory." "Old growth theory," it is said, emphasized the importance of bricks and mortar, that is, saving and investing in new plant and equipment. By contrast, "new" growth theory emphasizes the importance of investing in ideas. Paul Romer, a Stanford economist, asserts that new ideas and the spread of knowledge are the primary engines of growth. Unfortunately, neither Romer nor anyone else is exactly sure how one spawns new ideas or best disseminates knowledge. The only evident policy lever appears to be the support of research and development, a staple of "old" growth theory.

There's an important link between R&D and capital investment. As noted earlier, part of each year's gross investment compensates for the depreciation of existing plant and

Source	Percentage Contribution to Output Growth
More inputs	
Additional labor	34
Additional capital	17
	51
Productivity advances	
Education of labor	13
Advances in knowledge	26
Improved resource allocation	8
Economies of scale	8
	55
Miscellaneous	−6
	100

Source: Edward F. Denison, *Trends in American Economic Growth, 1929–1982* (Washington, D.C.: Brookings Institution, 1985).

TABLE 17.3
The Sources of U.S. Growth

From 1929 to 1982 total output grew by 3.2 percent annually. More than half of this growth was due to improvements in our technological and managerial capabilities. In the 1980s productivity advances were even more important in increasing output. Such productivity improvements have shifted our production-possibilities curve outward, increasing GDP per capita as well.

equipment. However, new machines are rarely identical to the ones they replace. Instead, new capital equipment tends to embody improved technology. Indeed, the availability of improved technology is often a major motivation for new investment, long before old machines have literally worn out. From this perspective, R&D and capital investment make a *joint* contribution to productivity advance. The possibility of Internet communication becomes a reality only when the necessary computer networks are developed.

POLICY LEVERS

Once the sources of growth are known, policies for accelerating long-run economic growth can be developed. Although the pace of economic growth is primarily set by market forces, government policy may be able to affect that pace. Most of the policy options are distinctly *micro* in nature, although *macro* policy decisions are also important.

Increasing Human-Capital Investment

Governments at all levels already play a tremendous role in human-capital development by building, operating, and subsidizing schools. The quantity and quality of continuing investments in America's schools will have a major effect on future productivity. Government policy also plays an *indirect* role in schooling decisions by offering subsidized college loans. Favorable tax treatment of college expenses would also include the incentives for human-capital investments.

Immigration policy is also a determinant of the nation's stock of human capital. At least 1 million immigrants enter the United States every year. The Immigration Act of 1990 reserves 140,000 legal immigrant visas for persons with desired occupational skills, such as nurses. By regulating the number and skills of immigrants, the federal government can affect the size and quality of the U.S. labor force. As the WORLD VIEW on the next page explains, Canada's immigration policy is designed explicitly to raise the skill level of the labor force.

CYBER NOTE

The U.S. Immigration and Naturalization Service (INS) maintains a profile of immigrants, including their occupational skills. Visit http://ins.usdoj.gov/stats/index.html.

As in the case of human capital, the possibilities for increasing physical-capital investment are also many and diverse.

Increasing Physical-Capital Investment

Investment Incentives. The tax code is a mechanism for stimulating investment. Faster depreciation schedules, tax credits for new investments, and lower business tax rates all encourage increased investment in physical capital.

WORLD VIEW

Barriers to Entry

Huddled masses, beware. Americans are fed up not only with illegal immigrants but with legal ones, too. As Congress revs up the immigration debate again, some would-be reformers are pressing for an overhaul of U.S. admissions criteria. They want to cut down on the number of newcomers to the U.S. on family-unification visas by creating a point system that measures applicants' potential for contributing to the economy. The criteria: education, job skills, and English-language abilities. . . .

Alan Simpson (R-Wyo.), chairman of the Senate subcommittee on immigration, plans to introduce a bill this summer that would establish a point system in the U.S. It would mimic procedures employed by two of the world's largest immigrant nations, Canada and Australia, which admit about half of their newcomers using the point system.

But in the U.S., such wholesale change is unnecessary. Today's immigrants aren't lacking skills and education . . . By some measures, they're better equipped than U.S. natives. Besides, negotiating the measurements used to gauge potential success in America would hardly be a politically tenable process.

—Catherine Yang

Reprinted from May 29, 1995, issue of *Business Week* by special permission, copyright © 1995 by The McGraw-Hill Companies. www.businessweek.com

In 1993, almost half of Canada's immigrants entered on a point system, having scored a total of 70 points or more in the following areas:

Maximum Score

Education/Training	34
Work Experience/Occupation	18
English/French	15
Job Offer	10
Age	10
Personal Suitability	10
Demographic Factor*	8

*Adjusted annually to reflect immigration policy.

Source: Department of Citizenship and Immigration of Canada.

Analysis: Immigrant flows affect a nation's stock of human capital. Can or should immigrants be selected on the basis of human-capital traits?

Savings Incentives. In principle, the government can also deepen the savings pool that finances investment. Here again, the tax code offers some policy levers. Tax preferences for Individual Retirement Accounts and other pension savings may increase the marginal propensity to save or at least redirect savings flows to longer-term investments.

Infrastructure Development. The government also directly affects the level of physical capital through its public works spending. As we observed in Chapter 16, the $2 trillion already invested in bridges, highways, airports, sewer systems, and other infrastructure is an important part of America's capital stock.

Fiscal Responsibility. In addition to these many supply-side interventions, the government's *macro* policies may also affect the rate of investment and growth. Of particular interest in this regard is the federal government's budget deficits. As we've seen, budget deficits may be a useful mechanism for attaining short-run macro stability. Those same deficits, however, may have negative long-run effects. If Uncle Sam borrows more funds from the national savings pool, other borrowers may end up with less. As we saw in Chapter 12, there's no guarantee that federal deficits will result in the **crowding out** of private investment. Let's recognize the risk of such an outcome, however. Hence *fiscal and monetary policies must be evaluated in terms of their impact not only on (short-run) aggregate demand but also on long-run aggregate supply.*

crowding out: A reduction in private-sector borrowing (and spending) caused by increased government borrowing.

The position of the long-run AS curve also depends on a broader assessment of the economic outlook. Expectations are a critical factor in both consumption and investment behavior. People who expect to lose their job next year are unlikely to buy a new car or house this year. Likewise, if investors expect interest rates to jump next year, they may be less willing to initiate long-run capital projects.

Maintaining Stable Expectations

A sense of political and economic stability is critical to any long-run current trend. Within that context, however, specific perceptions of government policy may also alter investment plans. Investors may look to the Fed for a sense of monetary stability. They may be looking for a greater commitment to long-run price stability than to short-run adjustments of aggregate demand. In the fiscal policy area the same kind of commitment to long-run fiscal discipline rather than to short-run stimulus may be sought. Such possibilities imply that macro policy must be sensitive to long-run expectations. It also implies that short-run goals may at times conflict with longer-run growth and investment objectives.

Last, but not least, the prospects for economic growth depend on the institutional context of a nation's economy. We first encountered this proposition in Chapter 1. In the WORLD VIEW on page 14, nations were ranked on the basis of an Index of Freedom. Studies have shown how greater economic freedom—secure property rights, open trade, lower taxes, less regulation—typically fosters faster growth. In less regulated economies there's more scope for entrepreneurship and more opportunity to invest. Recognizing this, nations around the world, from India to China, to Russia, to Latin America, have deregulated industries, privatized state enterprises, and promoted more open trade and investment.

Institutional Context

THE ECONOMY TOMORROW

Suppose we pulled all the right policy levers and were able to keep the economy on a fast-paced growth track. Could the economy keep growing forever? Wouldn't we use up all available resources and ruin the environment in the process? How much long-term growth is really possible—or even desirable?

Limitless Growth?

The prospect of an eventual limit to economic growth originated in the eighteenth-century warnings of the Reverend Thomas Malthus. Malthus argued that continued economic growth was impossible because food production couldn't keep pace with population growth. His dire projections earned the economics profession its characterization as the "dismal science."

The Malthusian Formula for Destruction

When Malthus first issued his warnings, in 1798, the population of England (including Wales) was about 9 million. Annual production of barley, oats, and related grains was approximately 162 million bushels, and wheat production was around 50 million bushels, just about enough to feed the English population (a little had to be imported from other countries). Although the relationship between food and population was satisfactory in 1798, Malthus reasoned that starvation was not far off. First of all, he observed that "population, when unchecked, goes on doubling itself every 25 years, or increases in a geometrical ratio."[1] Thus, he foresaw the English population increasing to 36 million people by 1850, 144 million by 1900, and more than 1 billion by 1975, unless some social or natural restraints were imposed on population growth.

Limits to Food Production

One natural population check that Malthus foresaw was a scarcity of food. England had only a limited amount of land available for cultivation and was already farming the most fertile tracts. Before long, all available land would be in use and only improvements in agricultural productivity (output per acre) could increase food supplies. Some productivity increases were possible, Malthus concluded, but "the means of subsistence, under circumstances the most favorable to human industry, could not possibly be made to increase faster than in an arithmetical ratio."[2]

With population increasing at a *geometric* rate and food supplies at an *arithmetic* rate, the eventual outcome is evident. Figure 17.6 illustrates how the difference between a **geometric growth** path and an **arithmetic growth** path ultimately leads to starvation. As Malthus calculated it, per capita wheat output would decline from 5.5 bushels in 1800 to only 1.7 bushels in 1900 (Figure 17.5*b*). This wasn't enough food to feed the English people. According to Malthus' projections, either England died off about 100 years ago, or it has been maintained at the brink of starvation for more than a century only by recurrent plagues, wars, or the kind of "moral restraint" that's commonly associated with Victorian preachments.

Malthus' logic was impeccable. As long as population increased at a geometric rate while output increased at an arithmetic rate, England's doomsday was as certain as two plus two equals four. Malthus' error was not in his logic but in his empirical assumptions. He didn't know how fast output would increase over time, any more than we know whether people will be wearing electronic wings in the year 2203. He had to make an educated guess about future productivity trends. He based his estimates on his own experiences at the very beginning of the Industrial Revolution. As it turned

geometric growth: An increase in quantity by a constant proportion each year.

arithmetic growth: An increase in quantity by a constant amount each year.

[1]Thomas Malthus, *An Essay on the Principle of Population* (1798; reprint ed., Homewood, Ill.: Richard D. Irwin, 1963), p.4.
[2]Ibid, p. 5.

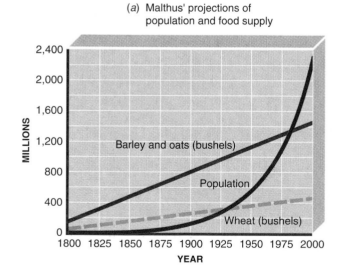

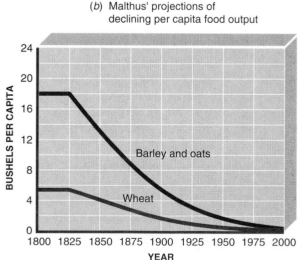

(*a*) Malthus' projections of population and food supply

(*b*) Malthus' projections of declining per capita food output

FIGURE 17.6
The Malthusian Doomsday

By projecting the growth rates of population and food output into the future, Malthus foresaw England's doomsday. At that time, the amount of available food per capita would be too small to sustain human life. Fortunately, Malthus overestimated population growth and underestimated productivity growth.

Source: Mathus' arithmetic applied to actual data for 1800 (see text).

out (fortunately), he had no knowledge of the innovations that would change the world, and he grossly underestimated the rate at which productivity would increase. ***Output, including agricultural products, has increased at a geometric rate, not at the much slower arithmetic rate foreseen by Malthus.*** As we observed earlier, U.S. output has grown at a long-term rate of roughly 3 percent a year. This *geometric* growth has doubled output every 25 years or so. That rate of economic growth is more than enough to raise living standards for a population growing by only 1 percent a year.

As Yale historian Paul Kennedy has suggested, maybe Malthus' doomsday predictions were just premature, not wrong. Maybe growth will come to a screeching halt when we run out of arable land, water, oil, or some other vital resource.

Resource Constraints

Malthus focused on arable land as the ultimate resource constraint. Other doomsday prophets have focused on the supply of whale oil, coal, oil, potatoes and other "essential" resources. All such predictions ignore the role of markets in both promoting more efficient uses of scarce resources and finding substitutes for them. If, for example, the world were really running out of oil, what would happen to oil prices? Oil prices would rise substantially, prompting consumers to use oil more efficiently and prompting producers to develop alternative fuel sources. If productivity and the availability of substitutes increase fast enough, the price of "scarce" resources might actually fall rather than rise. This possibility prompted a famous "Doomsday bet" between University of Maryland business professor Julian Simon and Stanford ecologist Paul Ehrlich. In 1980, Paul Ehrlich identified five metals that he predicted would become so scarce as to slow economic growth. Simon wagered that the price of those metals would actually *decline* over the ensuing decade as productivity and available substitutes increased. In 1990, their prices had fallen, and Ehrlich paid Simon for the bet.

The market's ability to circumvent resource constraints would seem to augur well for our future. Doomsayers warn, though, that other limits to growth will emerge, even in a world of "unlimited" resources and unending productivity advance. The villain this time is pollution. Over 20 years ago, Paul Ehrlich warned about this second problem:

Environmental Destruction

> Attempts to increase food production further will tend to accelerate the deterioration of our environment, which in turn will eventually *reduce* the capacity of the Earth to produce food. It is not clear whether environmental decay has now gone so far as to be essentially irreversible; it is possible that the capacity of the planet to support human life has been permanently impaired. Such technological "successes" as automobiles, pesticides, and inorganic nitrogen fertilizers are major contributors to environmental deterioration.[3]

The "inevitability" of environmental destruction led G. Evelyn Hutchinson to conclude in 1970 that the limits of habitable existence on earth would be measured "in decades."[4]

It's not difficult for anyone with the basic five senses to comprehend the pollution problem. Pollution is as close these days as the air we breathe. Moreover, we can't fail to observe a distinct tendency for pollution levels to rise along with GDP and population expansion. If one projects such pollution trends into the future, things are bound to look pretty ugly.

Although pollution is universally acknowledged to be an important and annoying problem, we can't assume that the *rate* of pollution will continue unabated. On the contrary, the growing awareness of the pollution problem has already led to significant abatement-policy efforts. The Environmental Protection Agency (EPA), for example, is unquestionably a force working for cleaner air and water. Indeed, active policies to curb pollution are as familiar as auto-exhaust controls and DDT bans. A computer programmed 10 or 20 years ago to project present pollution levels wouldn't have foreseen these abatement efforts and would thus have overestimated current pollution levels.

[3]Paul R. Ehrlich and Anne H. Ehrlich, *Population, Resources, Environment: Issues in Human Ecology,* 2nd ed. (San Francisco: W. H. Freeman, 1972), p. 442.
[4]Evelyn Hutchinson, "The Biosphere," *Scientific American,* September 1970, p. 53: Dennis L. Meadows et al., *The Limits to Growth* (New York: Universe Books, 1972), Chapter 4.

"And so, extrapolating from the best figures available, we see that current trends, unless dramatically reversed, will inevitably lead to a situation in which the sky will fall."

Analysis: Most doomsday predictions fail to recognize the possibilities for behavioral change—or the role of market incentives in encouraging it.

This isn't to say that we have in any final way "solved" the pollution problem or that we're even doing the best job we possibly can. It simply says that geometric increases in pollution aren't inevitable. There's simply no compelling reason why we have to continue polluting the environment; if we stop, another doomsday can be averted. Julian Simon was so confident of our ability to do so that he offered another doomsday wager in 1996. He offered a $100,000 bet that by any measure human well-being will improve in the next decade.

The Possibility of Growth

Julian Simon may have been right that there are no limits to growth, at least none emanating from resource constraints or pollution thresholds. As Robert Solow summed up the issue:

> My real complaint about the Doomsday school [is that] it diverts attention from the really important things that can actually be done, step by step, to make things better. The end of the world *is* at hand—the earth, if you take the long view, will fall into the sun in a few billion years anyway, unless some other disaster happens first. In the meantime, I think we'd be better off passing a strong sulfur-emissions tax, or getting some Highway Trust Fund money allocated to mass transit, or building a humane and decent floor under family incomes, or overriding President Nixon's veto of a strong Water Quality Act, or reforming the tax system, or fending off starvation in Bengal—instead of worrying about the generalized "predicament of mankind."[5]

Karl Marx expressed these same thoughts nearly a century earlier. Marx chastised "the contemptible Malthus" for turning the attention of the working class away from what he regarded as the immediate problem of capitalist exploitation to some distant and ill-founded anxiety about "natural" disaster.[6]

The Desirability of Growth

Let's concede, then, that continued, perhaps even "limitless" growth is *possible.* Can we also agree that it's *desirable?* Those of us who commute on congested highways, worry about global warming, breathe foul air, and can't find a secluded camping site may raise a loud chorus of no's. But before reaching a conclusion let's at least determine what it is people don't like about the prospect of continued growth. Is it really

[5]Robert M. Solow, "Is the End of the World at Hand?" *Challenge,* March 1973, p. 50.
[6]Cited by John Maddox in *The Doomsday Syndrome* (New York: McGraw-Hill, 1972), pp. 40 and 45.

economic growth per se that people object to, or instead the specific ways GDP has grown in the past? To state the question this way may provoke a few second thoughts.

First of all, let's distinguish very clearly between economic growth and population growth. Congested neighborhoods, dining halls, and highways are the consequence of too many people, not of two many goods and services. Indeed, if we had *more* goods and services—if we had more houses and transit systems—much of the population congestion we now experience might be relieved. Maybe if we had enough resources to meet our existing demands *and* to build a solar-generated "new town" in the middle of Montana, people might move out of the crowded neighborhoods of Chicago and St. Louis. Well, probably not, but at least one thing is certain; with fewer goods and services, more people will have to share any given quantity of output.

Which brings us back to the really essential measure of growth, GDP per capita. Are there any serious grounds for desiring *less* GDP per capita, a reduced standard of living? And don't say yes just because you think we already have too many cars on our roads or calories in our bellies. That argument refers to the *mix* of output again and doesn't answer the question of whether or not we want *any* more goods or services per person. Increasing GDP per capita can take a million forms, including the educational services you're now consuming. The rejection of economic growth per se implies that none of those forms is desirable.

SUMMARY

- Economic growth refers to increases in real GDP. Short-run growth may result from increases in capacity utilization (like less unemployment). In the long run, however, growth requires increases in capacity itself—rightward shifts on the long-run aggregate supply curve.
- GDP per capita is a basic measure of living standards. GDP per worker is a basic measure of productivity.
- The rate of economic growth is set by the growth rate of the labor force *plus* the growth rate of output per worker (productivity). Over time, increases in productivity have been the primary cause of rising living standards.
- Productivity gains comes from many sources, including better labor quality, increased capital investment, research and development, improved management, and supportive government policies.
- Supply-side policies increase both the short- and long-run capacity to produce. Monetary and fiscal policies may also affect capital investment and thus the rate of economic growth.

- The productivity slowdown of the late 1970s resulted from lower investment, a shift in the composition of the labor force, increases in government taxes and regulation, and other factors. Some of these forces were reversed in the early 1990s, but productivity advances were still slow.
- The argument that there are identifiable and imminent limits to growth—perhaps even a cataclysmic doomsday—are founded on one of two concerns: (1) the depletion of resources and (2) pollution of the ecosystem.
- The general weakness of doomsday arguments is that they regard existing patterns of resource use or pollution as unalterable. As a consequence, they consistently underestimate the possibilities for technological advance or adaptation. Even "optimistic" projections of technological possibilities turn out to be pessimistic.
- Continued economic growth is desirable as long as it brings a higher standard of living for people and an increased ability to produce and consume socially desirable goods and services.

Key Terms

production possibilities	GDP per capita	crowding out
economic growth	labor force	geometric growth
real GDP	productivity	arithmetic growth
base period	human capital	
growth rate	net investment	

Questions for Discussion

1. In what specific ways (if any) does a college education increase a worker's productivity?

2. Why don't we consume all our current output instead of sacrificing some present consumption for investment?

3. Should we grant immigration rights based on potential contributions to economic growth as Canada does? (See WORLD VIEW page 344.)

4. How might perceptions of growth potential affect monetary or fiscal policy decisions? Could short-term stabilization goals ever conflict with long-run growth goals?

5. In 1866 Stanley Jevons predicted that economic growth would come to a halt when England ran out of coal, a doomsday that he reckoned would occur in the mid-1970s. How did we avert that projection?

6. Fertility rates in the United States have dropped so low that we're approaching zero population growth, a condition that France has maintained for decades. How will this affect our economic growth? Our standard of living?

7. Is limitless growth really possible? What forces do you think will be most important in slowing or halting economic growth?

8. Would you accept Julian Simon's second (1996) doomsday wager? What dimensions of human well-being might worsen in 10 years?

9. Web Activity Research that is conducted at the World Bank focuses on economic growth. From the topic list at www.worldbank.org/research/projects.htm, choose a project that uses one of the terms identified in the book as a factor in economic growth. What does this abstract conclude about the relationship between this factor and economic growth?

10. Web Activity Compare productivity increases in the motion picture industry with the auto industry for the three most recent years at ftp://ftp.bls.gov/pub/special.requests/opt/dipts/oaeaiin.tex. How do you think output per worker is measured in each industry? Is productivity easier to measure in one industry than the other? Why?

Problems for Chapter 17 appear at the back of the book.

Current Policies

Macro theories often provide conflicting advice about whether and how the government ought to intervene. To make matters worse, the information needed to make a decision is typically incomplete. Politics muddies the waters too by changing priorities and restricting the use of policy levers. Finally, there's the inescapable reality that everything changes at once—there's no *ceteris paribus* in the real world. Chapters 18 and 19 consider these theories.

18

Global Macro

> In this global economy there is no such thing as a purely domestic policy.
> —President Bill Clinton
> American University, February 26, 1993

Two years after making that statement, President Clinton got a crash course in global macroeconomics. The Mexican economy took a nosedive in 1995: Unemployment rose, prices skyrocketed, and the value of the Mexican peso plunged. President Clinton and his economic advisers quickly realized that this turn of events wasn't simply a Mexican problem. Mexico is one of America's largest export markets. If the Mexican economy sinks into a recession, Mexican consumers and businesses won't be able to buy so many U.S.-made goods. The U.S. economy would suffer export losses and related job losses.

The financial markets of Mexico and the United States are also linked. When the peso collapsed, many Mexicans rushed to convert their currency into U.S. dollars. As they moved assets into American banks, U.S. bank reserves increased. This capital inflow made the Fed's job of controlling the money supply that much more difficult.

There was no way the United States could seal off its economy from the Mexican crisis. So long as resources, goods, and money can move across national borders, countries are economically interdependent. Ironically, the 1993 North American Free Trade Agreement (NAFTA) had increased the interdependence between Mexico and the United States. Therefore, helping Mexico, was also a way of helping the United States avert economic damage. This realization helped convince President Clinton to "bail out" Mexico with a multibillion-dollar loan. The U.S. Federal Reserve also helped control disruptions in currency flows and values.

The global economy was disrupted again with the 1997–1998 Asian crisis (see WORLD VIEW). American policymakers again had to assess how the U.S. economy would be affected by economic turmoil in Thailand, Malaysia, Indonesia, and Korea and then adjust domestic monetary and fiscal policies. The Brazilian monetary crisis of 1999 raised similar problems.

WORLD VIEW

Asia's Fall Starves U.S. Export Market

Feds: Slump Could Force Job Losses

Asia's financial turmoil has rolled across the USA, causing slumping exports and qualms about job losses in virtually every state, a Treasury Department report says. . . .

U.S. exports to Asia, which make up 30% of all exports, have dropped 11% in the past year. Agriculture is especially at risk: 40% of U.S. agricultural exports go to Asia, more than to any other region.

Exports to Asia support millions of jobs. And, the report says, export-related jobs in the USA pay an average 15% more than other jobs.

Key exports from the USA to Asia include medical equipment; food processing and packaging equipment; agricultural products such as grain, corn and wheat; and environmental pollution-control equipment, according to the Department of Commerce.

The U.S. economy remains robust, marked by low unemployment, inflation and interest rates. But some economists worry a global recession would slash exports and slow growth, sending the U.S. economy into a tailspin.

—Stephanie Armour

USA Today, Oct. 7, 1998, p. 3B. Copyright 1998, USA Today. Reprinted with permission. www.usatoday.com

Analysis: The flow of goods, labor, and money across national borders makes countries economically interdependent. A recession in Asia hurts U.S. exports and related jobs.

This chapter explores this global interdependence. Of particular concern are the following questions:

- How does the U.S. economy interact with the rest of the world?
- How does the rest of the world affect U.S. macro outcomes?
- How does global interdependence limit macro policy options?

As we'll see, international transactions significantly affect U.S. economic performance and policy.

INTERNATIONAL TRADE

Japanese cars are the most visible reminders of America's global interdependence. American consumers purchase over 1 million cars from Japan each year and buy another million or so Toyotas, Nissans, Hondas, Mazdas, and Subarus produced in the United States. On the other side of the Pacific Ocean, Japanese auto workers are apt to wear Levis, sip Coca-Cola, and grab a quick meal at McDonald's.

The motivations for international trade are explained at length in Chapter 35. Also discussed in Chapter 35 are the *microeconomic* demands for greater protection from "unfair" imports. What concerns us here is how such trade affects our domestic *macro* performance. Does trade help or hinder our efforts to attain full employment, price stability, and economic growth?

We first noticed in Chapter 9 that **imports** are a source of **leakage** in the circular flow. The income that U.S. consumers spend on Japanese cars *could* be spent in America. When that income instead leaks out of the circular flow, it limits domestic spending and related **multiplier** effects.

The basic macro model can be expanded easily to include this additional leakage. In a closed (no-trade) economy, total income and domestic spending are always equal—that is,

$$\text{Closed economy: } C + I + G = Y$$

Imports as Leakage

imports: Goods and services purchased from international sources.
leakage: Income not spent directly on domestic output but instead diverted from the circular flow, such as saving, imports, taxes.
multiplier: The multiple by which an initial change in aggregate spending will alter total expenditure after an infinite number of spending cycles.

When some goods are sold as exports and others can be purchased from abroad, however, this equality no longer holds. In an open economy, we have to take account of imports and exports; that is,

$$\text{Open economy}: C + I + G + X = Y + IM$$

where X refers to exports and IM to imports. ***In an open economy, the combined spending of consumers, investors, and the government may not equal domestic output.*** Total spending is augmented by the demand for exports, and the supply of goods is increased by imports.

Although imported goods may be desired, their availability complicates macro policy. Increases in aggregate spending are supposed to boost domestic output and employment. With imports, however, the link between spending and output is weakened. ***Part of any increase in income will be spent on imports.*** This fraction is called the **marginal propensity to import (MPM).** Like its cousin, the **marginal propensity to save (MPS),** the marginal propensity to import

- Reduces the initial impact on domestic demand of any income change
- Reduces the size of the multiplier

Table 18.1 illustrates the impact of imports on the Keynesian multiplier process. The process starts with an increase of $10 billion in new government spending. This injection directly adds $10 billion to consumer income (assuming an economy with no income taxes).

The successive panels of Table 18.1 illustrate the sequence of events that follows. In the closed economy, consumers have only two uses for their income: to spend it on domestic consumption ($B1$) or to save it ($B2$). We assume here the marginal propensity to save is 0.10. Hence consumers save $1 billion and spend the remaining $9 billion on domestic consumption.

In an open economy, consumers have one other choice. They may spend their income on domestic goods ($B1$), save it ($B2$), or spend it on imported goods ($B3$). In Table 18.1 we assume that the marginal propensity to import is 0.10. Hence consumers use their additional $10 billion of income the following way:

$8 billion spent on domestic consumption
$1 billion saved
$1 billion spent on imports

marginal propensity to import (MPM): The fraction of each additional (marginal) dollar of disposable income spent on imports.
marginal propensity to save (MPS): The fraction of each additional (marginal) dollar of disposable income not spent on consumption; $1 - MPC$.

TABLE 18.1
Imports as Leakage

Import leakage reduces the initial spending impact of autonomous changes in consumer income. Continuing import leakage reduces the size of the multiplier as well. In this case, the ultimate impact of added government spending is cut in half by import leakage: Aggregate demand increases by $50 billion rather than $100 billion in response to a $10 billion increase in government spending.

Action	Cumulative Change in Aggregate Demand	
	Closed Economy	Open Economy
A. Government spends additional $10 billion	+ $10 billion	+ $10 billion
B. Consumers use added $10 billion of income for:		
1. Domestic consumption	+ $9 billion	+ $8 billion
2. Saving (MPS = 0.1)	($1 billion)	($1 billion)
3. Imports (MPM = 0.1)	0	($1 billion)
C. Multiplier	$\frac{1}{MPS} = 10$	$\frac{1}{MPS + MPM} = 5$
D. Additional multiplier-induced consumption = $C \times B1$	+ $90 billion	+ $40 billion
E. Cumulative change = $A + D$	+ $100 billion	+ $50 billion

In the open economy only $8 billion rather than $9 billion is initially spent on domestic consumption. Thus *imports reduce the initial spending impact of added income.*

Import leakage continues through every round of the circular flow. As a consequence, *imports also reduce the value of the multiplier.* In this case, the multiplier is reduced from 10 to 5.

To see how this change in the multiplier comes about, note that *the value of the multiplier depends on the extent of leakage.* The most general form of the multiplier is

$$\text{Generalized multiplier} = \frac{1}{\text{leakage fraction}}$$

In a closed (no trade) and private (no taxes) economy, the multiplier takes the familiar Keynesian form:

$$\begin{matrix}\text{Closed economy} \\ \text{multiplier} \\ \text{(without taxes)}\end{matrix} = \frac{1}{\text{MPS}}$$

In this case, consumer saving is the only form of leakage. Therefore, the marginal propensity to save (MPS) is the entire leakage fraction. In Table 18.1 the closed-economy multiplier is equal to 10 (see panel *C*).

Once we open the economy to trade, we have to contend with additional leakage. In an open economy, leakage results from the MPS *and* the MPM. Thus the generalized multiplier becomes:

$$\begin{matrix}\text{Open economy} \\ \text{multiplier} \\ \text{(without taxes)}\end{matrix} = \frac{1}{\text{MPS} + \text{MPM}}$$

Imports act just like saving leakage, decreasing the multiplier bang of each autonomous buck. In Table 18.1 (panel *C*),

$$\text{Open economy multiplier} = \frac{1}{\text{MPS} + \text{MPM}} = \frac{1}{0.1 + 0.1} = \frac{1}{0.2} = 5$$

The consequences of these different multipliers are striking. Panel *D* shows that additional consumption of $90 billion is induced in the closed economy. By comparison, the open economy generates only $40 billion of additional consumption.

The last panel of Table 18.1 summarizes the consequences for aggregate demand. The cumulative increase in aggregate demand is

$$\begin{matrix}\text{Cumulative change} \\ \text{in aggregate demand}\end{matrix} = \begin{matrix}\text{initial change} \\ \text{in spending}\end{matrix} \times \begin{matrix}\text{income} \\ \text{multiplier}\end{matrix}$$

In this example, the initial injection of spending is the $10 billion spent by the government. In the closed economy, this injection leads to a $100 billion increase in aggregate demand (panel *E*). In the open economy, the same injection increases aggregate demand only $50 billion! This end result is also illustrated in Figure 18.1, which shows how imports limit the shift of aggregate demand. The smaller shift that occurs in the open economy results in a smaller increase in equilibrium real GDP. In this sense *imports, by increasing leakage, reduce the impact of fiscal stimulus.* Notice in Figure 18.1 the much larger induced consumption in the closed economy. The fiscal stimulus shifts aggregate demand to AD_4 in the closed economy but only to AD_3 in the open economy. The end result is less of an increase in domestic output (and less inflationary pressure as well).

Exports as Injections

Were imports our only link to the rest of the world, we might be tempted to erect a wall around "Fortress America" to preserve our output and employment levels. But international trade is a two-way street. Whereas we import goods and services from the rest of the world, other countries buy our **exports.** Thus *export sales inject spending into our circular flow at the same time that imports cause leakage from it.*

exports: Goods and services sold to foreign buyers.

FIGURE 18.1
Imports Reduce Multiplier Effects

The amount of additional demand created by a fiscal stimulus depends on the marginal propensity to import. In a closed economy (MPM = 0) aggregate demand increases from AD_1 to AD_4. In an open economy (MPM > 0) imports limit spending on domestic goods, shifting aggregate demand only to AD_3.

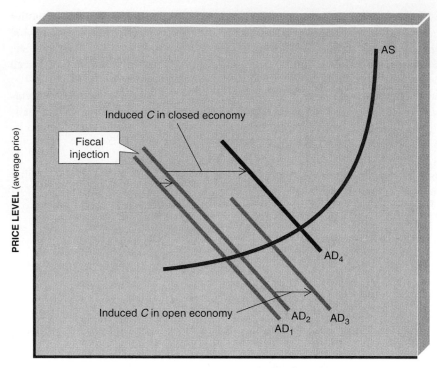

REAL OUTPUT (INCOME) (dollars per time period)

Any changes in exports are regarded as autonomous, since export sales depend primarily on the income and spending behavior of foreigners. Hence *a change in export demand causes a shift of the aggregate demand curve.* Like any other injection, an increase in export demand would set off a chain of multiplier effects. In other words, small changes in exports generate larger (multiplied) shifts of aggregate demand. This was a distinct risk for the U.S. economy in the 1997–1998 Asian crisis; a reduction in American exports to Asia could have snowballed into very large job losses (see WORLD VIEW page 353).

TRADE IMBALANCES

With exports adding to aggregate spending, and imports subtracting from the circular flow, the net impact of international trade on the domestic economy comes down to a question of balance. *What counts is the difference between exports (injections) and imports (leakages).* If exports and imports were exactly equal, there would be no net stimulus or leakage from the rest of the world.

A convenient way of emphasizing the offsetting effects of exports and imports is to rearrange the income identity to

$$C + I + G + (X - IM) = Y$$

net exports: The value of exports minus the value of imports: $(X - IM)$.

where $(X - IM)$ equals **net exports.**

If exports and imports were always equal, the term $(X - IM)$ would disappear and we could focus on domestic spending behavior. But why would we expect imports and exports to be equal? We now know that even *domestic* injections such as investment aren't likely to equal domestic leakages like saving. Indeed, the core macro stability problem arises because investment and saving decisions are made by different people and for very different reasons. There's no *a priori* reason to expect those outcomes to be identical.

The same problem affects international trade. Foreign decisions about how much to spend on American exports are made outside U.S. borders. Decisions in the United States about how much to spend on imports are made by American consumers, investors, and government agencies. Because these sets of shoppers are so isolated from one another, it seems unlikely that exports will ever equal imports. Instead, we have to expect a trade imbalance.

There are specific terms for characterizing trade imbalances. A **trade surplus** exists when America is exporting more goods and services than it's importing—that is, when net exports $(X - IM)$ are positive. When net exports are negative, imports have exceeded exports and the United States has incurred a **trade deficit.** In 1998 the United States had a trade deficit of $168 billion. That deficit implies that U.S. consumers, investors, and government agencies were buying $168 billion more output in 1998 than American factories and offices were producing.

A trade deficit isn't all bad. After all, when imports exceed exports, we end up consuming more than we're producing. In effect, *a trade deficit permits domestic living standards to exceed domestic output.* It's almost like getting something for nothing—the proverbial "free lunch."

Although the additional consumption a trade deficit permits may be enjoyed, a negative trade flow may have unwelcome effects as well. A trade deficit represents net leakage. That leakage may frustrate attempts to attain full employment. As we observed (Figure 18.1), import leakage necessitates a larger fiscal injection to reach any particular spending goal. Larger injections may not be possible, especially if *budget* deficit concerns limit government initiatives.

Crowding Out Net Exports. One reason people worry about budget deficits is that increased government spending may supplant private investment and consumption. This is the **crowding-out** problem we encountered in Chapter 12. It takes on a new dimension in an open economy. In an open economy, increased government purchases need not reduce private-sector spending—even at full employment! Increased imports can satisfy the increase in aggregate demand. Thus in an open economy *an increase in imports can reduce domestic crowding out.*

The elbow room imports provide relieves some of the worries about federal *budget* deficits. New concerns arise, however, about *trade* deficits. As imports increase, our net export position deteriorates. Hence *in an open economy fiscal stimulus tends to crowd out net exports by boosting imports.* Indeed any fiscal stimulus intended to boost domestic output will also *worsen* the trade deficit! Consumers will spend some fraction of their additional income—the marginal propensity to import (MPM)—on imports. These added imports will widen the trade gap. Thus *the objective of reducing the trade deficit may conflict with the goal of attaining full employment.*

At other times our trade and domestic goals might be more compatible. Suppose we were approaching full employment and were more concerned about inflation than about unemployment. In this context, we might welcome some net import leakage. In this case, import leakage would act as a "safety valve" to help keep the economy from overheating. Restrictive fiscal policies would help close both the domestic inflationary gap and the trade gap (deficit).

A trade surplus can create similar problems. The additional spending implied by positive net exports may fuel inflationary pressures. If the economy is overheating, the policy objective is to restrain aggregate spending. But fiscal and monetary policies don't directly affect the incomes, expectations, or tastes of foreign consumers. Foreign spending on U.S. goods may continue unabated, even as domestic monetary and fiscal restraint "squeezes" domestic consumers and investors. Indeed, domestic monetary and fiscal restraint will have to be harder, just to offset continuing export demand.

Worse yet, the trade surplus may grow in response to restrictive macro policies. Domestic consumers, squeezed by monetary and fiscal restraint, will reduce purchases of

trade surplus: The amount by which the value of exports exceeds the value of imports in a given time period (positive net exports).
trade deficit: The amount by which the value of imports exceeds the value of exports in a given time period (negative net exports).

Macro Effects

CYBER NOTE

To track changes in the U.S. trade balance, see the import and export data in the "Overview of the Economy" the Bureau of Economic Analysis maintains at <u>www.bea.doc.gov</u>.

crowding out: A reduction in private-sector borrowing (and spending) caused by increased government borrowing.

imported goods. On the other hand, if fiscal and monetary restraint reduces domestic inflation, foreigners may increase their export purchases. Here again, ***trade goals and domestic macro goals may conflict.***

Foreign Perspectives

Who cares if our trade balance worsens? Why don't we just focus on our domestic macro equilibrium and ignore any trade imbalances that result? If we ignored trade imbalances, we wouldn't have a goal conflict and could achieve our domestic policy goals.

Unfortunately, our trading partners have their own policy objectives and may not be content to ignore our trade imbalances. ***If the United States has a trade deficit, other countries must have a trade surplus.*** This is simple arithmetic. Its implications are potentially worrisome, however. The rest of the world might not be happy about shipping us good than they're getting in return. In real economic terms, they'd be picking up the tab for our "free lunch." Their exports would be financing a higher standard of living for us than our output alone permitted. At the same time, their living standards would be less than their output made possible. These disparities could cause tension. In addition, foreign nations might also be concerned about inflationary pressures of their own and so resist additional demand for their exports (our imports).

The whole notion of macro equilibrium gets much more complicated when we adopt these global views. From a global perspective, ***we can't focus exclusively on domestic macro goals and ignore international repercussions.*** If our trade balance upsets other economies, foreign nations may respond with their own macro and trade initiatives. These responses, in turn, would affect America's trade flows and so alter domestic outcomes. A *global* macro equilibrium would be attained only when no trading partner had reason to change macro or trade policy.

A Policy Constraint

From a macro perspective, our basic objective in both an open and a closed economy remains the same: to find the optimal balance of aggregate demand and aggregate supply. Trade flows may help or hinder this effort, depending on the timing, size, and source of the trade imbalance. Sudden *changes* in trade flows can create an external shock that upsets macro policy goals (see WORLD VIEW). All we know for certain is

- Imports and exports alter the rate and composition of aggregate spending.
- Trade flows may help or impede domestic macro policy attain its objectives.
- Macro policy decisions need to take account of international trade repercussions.

Thus international trade adds an important new wrinkle to macro policy decision making.

INTERNATIONAL FINANCE

Our global interactions with the rest of the world are further complicated by international money flows. Money flows across international borders as easily as goods and services. In fact, money *must* move across borders to pay for imports and exports. In addition, people move money across borders to get bigger profits, higher interest rates, or more security. Like trade in goods and services, these international money flows alter macro outcomes and complicate macro decision making.

Capital Inflows

In 1998, over $500 billion of foreign capital flowed into the United States. A lot of this capital inflow was used to purchase U.S. bonds. The Treasury bonds were attractive to international investors for two reasons. First, real interest rates in the U.S. economy were relatively high, making them a more attractive investment than foreign bonds. Second, the U.S. economy looked more prosperous and more politically stable than many other places, making Treasury bonds appear more secure. Corporate bonds, stocks and other U.S. investments also looked attractive, for much the same reasons. So people and institutions around the world moved some of their funds into U.S. markets, creating a tremendous capital inflow.

The profits of U.S. corporations operating abroad added to that capital inflow. When

U.S. firms build plants abroad, they anticipate earning profits they can bring home. Over time, U.S. multinational firms have accumulated a sizable share of world markets, giving them a regular inflow of international profits. McDonald's, for example, operates more than 20,000 restaurants in 89 countries. Profits from its foreign outlets add to America's capital inflow.

Money flows out of the United States to the rest of the world for the same purposes. Most of the outflow is used to pay for U.S. imports. In addition, U.S. investors may seek to invest in foreign countries and so need to buy foreign land, labor, and capital. And U.S. households and institutions may be attracted to overseas *financial* investments, for example, foreign bonds or stocks. Some people simply want to keep their money in Swiss banks to avoid scrutiny or evade taxes. Finally, the U.S. government

Capital Outflows

WORLD VIEW

Oil Shocks

In 1973 and again in 1979 the Organization of Petroleum Exporting Countries (OPEC) sharply increased crude oil prices. The price of oil quadrupled in 1973 and doubled again in 1979. The resulting "shock" to macro equilibrium caused both higher unemployment and more inflation in oil-importing nations.

Inflationary Impact

In mid-1973 the world price of OPEC oil was about $3.30 per barrel. OPEC pushed the price up to $12 a barrel almost overnight and ultimately to over $30 a barrel. The increase in the price of oil set the stage for cost-push inflation. Industries using oil to fuel their machines or heat their furnaces were hit with an increase in production costs. These higher costs shifted the aggregate *supply* curve to the left, as in the accompanying figure.

Recessionary Impact

The leftward shift of the aggregate supply curve not only pushed the average price level up (to P_2) but also reduced output (to Q_2). In the United States, the reduction in total domestic output was aggravated by price controls on domestic oil and gas. As a consequence, many manufacturers were forced to shut down because they couldn't get the oil they were willing and able to purchase. Others shut down because higher fuel costs made continued production unprofitable.

Decreased Consumption

Although the most visible effects of the 1973 and 1979 oil shocks were inflation and shortages, the greatest threat lay on the demand side of product and factor markets. The OPEC price boosts forced consumers to spend more of their income on foreign oil imports. In 1973 the United States was spending approximately $10 billion a year on imported oil. After the

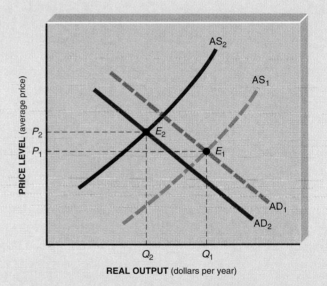

REAL OUTPUT (dollars per year)

The higher prices of imported oil increased production costs. As a consequence, producers were less able or willing to sell output at any given price. The domestic aggregate supply curve shifted to the left (from AS_1 to AS_2).

The increased leakage caused by higher oil import prices also curtailed demand for domestic goods. Aggregate demand shifted from AD_1 to AD_2. The U.S. economy ended up with higher prices and less employment.

OPEC price increase, however, our annual import bill suddenly jumped to $25 billion. This sudden increase in import leakage left consumers with less income to spend on domestic output. Thus the aggregate *demand* curve also shifted to the left.

Analysis: Abrupt changes in the price or availability of imported goods will alter domestic output and spending. Such external shocks can worsen domestic inflation and unemployment.

spends money in foreign countries to maintain American defenses, operate embassies, encourage economic development, and provide emergency relief. All these motivations cause a dollar outflow.

Part of the dollar outflow is also prompted by foreign investors and institutions. We already noted that a motivation for capital *inflows* is the desire for U.S.-based investments and profits. As interest and profits accumulate, foreign investors may want to retrieve some of their assets. Those repatriated interest and profit payments are part of the capital *outflows*. If the relative attractiveness of investments in the United States diminishes, even more foreign capital will flow out. When the U.S. stock market crashed in October 1987, many foreign investors took their money and ran.

CAPITAL IMBALANCES

capital deficit: The amount by which the capital outflow exceeds the capital inflow in a given time period.

capital surplus: The amount by which the capital inflow exceeds the capital outflow in a given time period.

Like trade flows, capital flows won't always be balanced. At times the outflow of dollars will exceed the inflow, and the United States will experience a **capital deficit.** At other times, the balance may be reversed, leaving the United States with a **capital surplus.** In 1998 the United States had a capital surplus of more than $200 billion.

The huge capital surplus of 1998 is directly related to the huge trade deficit in that same year. When we import more than we export, we're effectively buying foreign goods and services on credit. The bulk of that "credit" is derived from the net inflow of foreign capital. The net inflow of money prompted by foreign investors creates a pool of funds that can be used to purchase foreign goods and services. If the capital inflow were smaller, our ability to purchase imports would be less, too. The reverse of this is true as well. If Americans weren't buying so many imports, foreigners wouldn't have as many dollars to invest in U.S. banks, corporations, and property. Thus *capital imbalances are directly related to trade imbalances.*

Macro Effects

Capital imbalances are a problem for monetary policy. The essence of monetary policy is control of the money supply. When money is able to move across international borders at will, control of the money supply becomes much more difficult.

Suppose inflationary forces are building and the Fed wants to reduce money supply growth. To do so, it might engage in open market operations, with the objective of net selling. By selling bonds, the Fed would seek to draw reserves out of the banking system and thereby slow money supply growth. The bond sales will also tend to raise interest rates and thus dampen both consumer and investor spending. This now-familiar sequence of events is illustrated on the left side of Figure 18.2.

The figure also illustrates how an open economy complicates monetary policy. The higher interest rates caused by the Fed's bond sales attract foreign investors. As the return on U.S. bonds increases, the inflow of foreign capital will accelerate. This will frustrate the Fed's goal of reducing money supply growth and tend to put downward pressure on domestic interest rates. The Fed will have to work harder (for example, sell more bonds) to achieve any desired money supply target.

Exchange Rates

An important feature of Figure 18.2 is the box marked "higher value of dollar." When we purchase goods and services from foreign countries, we must exchange our dollars for foreign currency. The Japanese workers who make Toyotas, for example, are paid in yen. Their willingness to supply cars is based on how many yen, not dollars, they'll receive. Thus we must first exchange dollars for yen before we can import Toyotas. When you travel abroad, you do these exchanges yourself, typically at banks, hotels, or special foreign exchange offices. When you stay at home and buy imported goods, someone else handles the exchange for you.

Whether you or some middleperson does the exchange is irrelevant. What matters is how many yen you get for your dollars. The more yen you get, the more Toyotas and other Japanese goods you're able to buy. In other words, *if the dollar's value in the world markets is high, imports are cheap.*

The impact of a cut in the money supply:

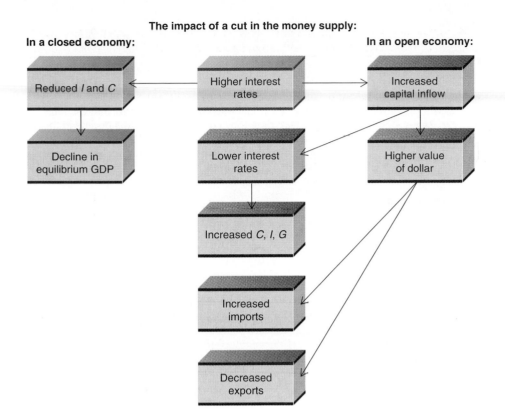

FIGURE 18.2
International Constraints on Monetary Policy

A reduction in the money supply is intended to reduce consumption and investment spending and thereby relieve inflationary pressures. If the money supply reduction increases domestic interest rates, however, it may trigger additional capital inflow. That increased capital inflow will frustrate monetary policy by increasing the money supply and holding down interest rates. The capital inflow will also tend to increase the value of the U.S. dollar and so widen the trade deficit.

The dollar's value in international trade is reflected in the **exchange rate.** The exchange rate is simply the price (value) of one currency, measured in terms of another. The exchange rate prevailing at any time reflects the interplay of trade and capital flows and all their determinants. (Foreign exchange markets are examined in Chapter 36.) What matters here is that exchange rates *change,* often in response to monetary and fiscal policy.

In Figure 18.2, restrictive monetary policy causes domestic interest rates to rise. These higher interest rates make U.S. bonds more attractive and so increase capital inflow from the rest of the world. To buy Treasury bonds, however, foreign investors need dollars. As they clamor to exchange their yen, marks, francs, and pounds for dollars, the value (price) of the dollar will increase. A higher dollar means that you can get more yen for every dollar. Imports thus become cheaper, and so Americans buy more of them. On the other hand, a stronger (more expensive) dollar makes U.S. exports costlier for foreign consumers, and so they buy fewer American products. The end result is a widening trade gap.

Similar kinds of global obstacles can impede policies of monetary stimulus. When interest rates increase abroad, the Fed risks a capital outflow if it *reduces* interest rates at home. This is the dilemma that constrained monetary policy in 1992 (see WORLD VIEW).

International capital flows add yet another complication to macro policy. The very existence of international capital flows weakens the Fed's ability to control the money supply. Furthermore, the goals of domestic monetary policy may conflict with international commitments. This conflict has been particularly evident in the European Union, where the domestic goals of the separate EU nations are often in conflict with their joint desire to forge a common market (see The Economy Tomorrow later in this chapter).

exchange rate: The price of one country's currency expressed in terms of another's; the domestic price of a foreign currency.

Capital Flows—Another Policy Constraint

Germany Lifts Discount Rate to 8.75%, Putting Squeeze on Already Weak Dollar

The German Bundesbank raised its highly visible discount rate to the highest level since 1931 to underscore its inflation-fighting resolve, a move that had ripple effects throughout Europe and pushed down the already weak U.S. dollar.

Although Italy, the Netherlands and Austria quickly followed with rate increases of their own, the surprisingly large 0.75 percentage point increase in the German rate to 8.75% was crafted to minimize international repercussions. "We wanted to accomplish something domestically without causing complications on the international front," said Bundesbank President Helmut Schlesinger.

But with the dollar flirting with postwar lows, some analysts said further declines in the U.S. currency could make the Fed-

eral Reserve uneasy about cutting short-term interest rates again. "The last time they cut rates, there was a decline in the dollar," said Scott Pardee, chairman of Yamaichi Securities (America) Inc., and a former Fed staffer. "It's becoming more of a constraint." . . .

A lower dollar tends to make U.S. goods cheaper overseas, helping U.S. exports, which have been one of the few bright spots in the U.S. economy of late. But it also tends to push up import prices and add to inflationary pressures. For that reason, the Fed usually tries to avoid a declining dollar.

—David Wessel and Terence Roth

Analysis: Global differences in interest rates encourage international capital flows. When foreign interest rates rise, the Fed has less leeway to lower U.S. interest rates.

International capital flows create one more problem. In addition to all our other macro worries, we now have to be concerned about

- The flow of capital into and out of the country
- The effect of capital imbalances on domestic macro performance
- How macro policy will affect international capital flows, exchange rates, and trade balances

PRODUCTIVITY AND COMPETITIVENESS

The global dimensions of the economy add a whole new layer of complexity to macro policy. One might reasonably wonder whether international trade and finance is really worth all the trouble. Couldn't we get along just as well without the rest of the world?

Specialization

Perhaps. But we wouldn't be able to drink much coffee. Or spend summer vacations in Europe. Or buy Japanese cars and Mexican beer.

To decide whether international trade and finance is worth all the trouble, we have to consider how international exchanges affect our standard of living. One obvious advantage of trade is that it gives us access to goods and services we don't or can't produce at home, such as coffee, vacations abroad, bananas, and Italian shoes. These *imported goods and services broaden our consumption possibilities.*

Most of the goods and services we import *could* be produced at home. Cars and shoes are made in America as well as abroad, as is a small quantity of coffee and bananas (in Hawaii). Even more coffee and bananas *could* be produced in the United States if we invested enough in greenhouses that duplicated tropical conditions. Home-grown coffee and bananas would turn out to be terribly expensive, however, so we're better off importing them. This leaves domestic resources available for the production of other goods that we can more easily grow (corn), manufacture (computers), or build (houses). In other words, we're better off *specializing* in the production of things we do relatively well and *trading* with other nations for the rest of the goods and services we desire. This is the principle of **comparative advantage** we first encountered in Chapter 2. In essence, it recommends that we produce what we do best and trade with other nations for goods they produce best. *Specialization among countries increases world efficiency and output, making all nations richer.*

Chapter 35 demonstrates the benefits of international specialization (the theory of comparative advantage). At this juncture we may note that the same principles that motivate *individuals* to specialize and then exchange their goods and services also motivate *nations* to specialize and then exchange their goods and services in international trade. In both cases, **productivity** and total output increase.

The increased output and productivity that specialization makes possible isn't the only benefit of international trade. *Trade stimulates improvements in productivity.* The presence of foreign producers keeps domestic producers on their toes. To compete in international markets, domestic producers must reduce costs and increase efficiency.

In recent years America's huge trade deficits have provoked questions about the competitiveness of U.S. producers. The excess of imports over exports suggests to many people that America isn't producing goods of the quality and value that consumers demand. Productivity may have lagged in some U.S. industries. And other nations inevitably become more efficient in producing certain goods and services. But the trade gap isn't a general indictment of U.S. competitiveness.

As we've observed, international trade and capital flows are interrelated, and both are directly influenced by exchange rates. In the early 1980s, the relative attractiveness of America's capital markets led to a surge of capital inflows and a higher exchange rate for the U.S. dollar. Between 1981 and 1985 the world value of the U.S. dollar rose by 50 percent, which made all American goods more expensive in international markets. To *maintain* their prices in international markets. U.S. producers would have had to cut costs enough to offset that increase in the dollar's value. Although American productivity increased faster than foreign productivity in those years, few U.S. producers could stay ahead of the rising dollar. The resulting increase in the trade deficit was a product of the rising dollar, not of a decline in U.S. productivity. The same thing happened again during the period 1996–1999, when the value of the dollar and the trade deficit both jumped.

Although a trade gap isn't necessarily evidence of declining competitiveness, it does draw policy attention to productivity issues. Productivity improvements are essential to economic growth and rising living standards. If a trade gap stimulates fiscal, monetary, and supply-side policies that foster productivity advances, then the economy may be better off as a result. By the same token, trade gaps remind us that policies that restrain productivity improvements (research, innovation, and investment) also have international consequences.

GLOBAL COORDINATION

As all countries begin to acknowledge the international dimensions of their economies, the desire for coordination grows. The coordination is pursued both through formal institutions and informal "understandings" among the major industrialized nations.

The most visible institution for global coordination is the International Monetary Fund (IMF).The IMF is sort of a bankers' United Nations. All nations contribute funds to the IMF, which then uses those funds to assist nations whose currency is in trouble. When Thailand devalued its currency (the *baht*) in July 1997, for example, the

comparative advantage: The ability of a country to produce a specific good at a lower opportunity cost than its trading partners.

productivity: Output per unit of input, for example, output per labor-hour.

Competitiveness

CYBER NOTE

The U.S. Bureau of Labor Statistics (BLS) assembles international comparisons of manufacturing productivity (also published in the *Monthly Labor Review*); visit www.bls.gov/flshome.htm.

IMF

currencies of other Asian nations also plunged. As we noted earlier (see WORLD VIEW, page 353), this Asian crisis threatened U.S. exports as well as those of other nations. There was a distinct threat that the "Asian flu" would become a global contagion. To keep the Asian flu from spreading, the IMF lent more than $100 billion to Thailand, Korea, Indonesia, and other Asian nations. The IMF also loaned Brazil over $40 billion in 1998–1999 to avoid a "Latin flu" from spreading to other South American nations and the global economy.

Although the IMF often provides global "first aid," IMF assistance typically comes with strings attached, such as insisting that a debtor nation alter its domestic monetary fiscal or trade policies as a condition of an IMF bailout. Such intrusions into domestic macro policy are often resented, especially when they entail high political costs in the debtor nation.

CYBER NOTE

For a summary of IMF activities and recent bailouts visit www.imf.org.

Group of Seven

The seven largest industrial countries (the United States, Japan, Canada, Germany, France, Italy, and Great Britain) attain a less formal mode of global coordination. The finance economic ministers of these nations meet periodically to assess the global outlook and coordinate macro policy. Although the Group of Seven (the G-7) has no formal apparatus for joint actions, any informal agreements it reaches can have a substantial effect on global trade and capital flow. Reaching agreement isn't always easy, however. In late 1997, most nations wanted the United States to reduce interest rates, thereby slowing capital outflows from Asia and Latin America. The Fed, however, was still concerned about the prospect of inflation in the fully employed U.S. economy, so it resisted the demand for lower interest rates (see NEWS). Not until the Asian crisis began affecting U.S. financial and export markets did the Fed relent and reduce the discount and federal funds rates. When the Fed or Congress has to choose between domestic or global priorities, global concerns typically come in second.

Global interests will never fully displace national policy priorities. However, even limited global coordination helps smooth out some of the rough spots of macro performance in an increasingly interdependent world.

IN THE NEWS

Greenspan Says Global Rate Cut Isn't Planned

Fed Chief Provides No Clue About a U.S. Reduction Despite Slowing Growth

WASHINGTON—Federal Reserve Chairman Alan Greenspan quashed speculation that he is working with other central bankers around the world to cut interest rates.

"I can safely say that at the moment there is no endeavor to coordinate interest-rate cuts," he told Congress yesterday.

Mr. Greenspan also did little to encourage investors looking for further hints of an imminent rate cut in the U.S. He didn't even raise the topic in his prepared remarks before the House Banking Committee yesterday, and touched on the question only indirectly in the question and answer session.

The Fed chairman had touched off hopes that U.S. monetary policy would be eased in a speech early this month about the risks to the American economy from the Asia crisis. Talk of a broader global move intensified earlier this week with an unusual joint statement by the Group of Seven finance ministers and central bankers about the need to stimulate worldwide growth.

—Jacob M. Schlesinger

The Wall Street Journal, Sept. 17, 1998, p. A2. Reprinted by permission of *The Wall Street Journal,* © 1998 Dow Jones & Company, Inc. All Rights Reserved Worldwide. www.wsj.com

Analysis: Global priorities may conflict with domestic policy priorities. When they do, domestic priorities usually prevail.

THE ECONOMY TOMORROW

A Global Currency?

The New Euro

On January 1, 1999, 11 European nations adopted a simple currency, the *euro*. That wasn't an easy or quick policy decision. As the accompanying WORLD VIEW notes, the quest for a common European currency began in the Middle Ages. The latest push for the euro began over 40 years ago. In view of this history, one has to wonder why a single European currency has been sought and why it has taken so long to attain.

The allure of a common currency is that it facilitates trade and capital flows across national borders. A common currency eliminates the uncertainties and added costs of diverse currencies. European businesses spent nearly $13 billion a year just on currency conversions. Exchange rate fluctuation also impeded cross-border business transactions, which is why the U.S. Congress created a national currency to replace the hundreds of state and private bank currencies that existed prior to 1863.

Macro Coordination

There's a huge difference, however, between creating a common *national* currency (the U.S. dollar) and a common *cross-national* currency like the euro. The 50 states that make up the United States share a common set of laws, monetary institutions, and government. The 11 nations of the European Union (EU) don't even share a common language, much less governmental authority. Accordingly, in creating a common currency, they're agreeing to submerge some national interests in favor of broader European goals. **To maintain a common currency, nations must maintain common macro policies.**

Germany, for example, has been particularly vigilant about inflation, while Italy has given higher priority to reducing unemployment. As a result, Germany monetary

WORLD VIEW

The Long History of Europe's Single Currency

- **Middle Ages:** Feudal rulers frequently try to unify coins with trading partners.
- **1865–1927:** "Latin coin union" (France, Belgium, Italy, Switzerland, and Greece) undermined by policy rows.
- **1872–1924:** "Scandinavian coin union" (Sweden, Norway, and Denmark) works smoothly for a time but eroded by World War I.
- **1957:** European Community's founding Treaty of Rome provides for coordination of economic and monetary policies.
- **1970:** "Werner Plan" seeks to achieve monetary union by 1980, but is derailed by international oil crisis.
- **1972:** European nations link currencies in 'snake' that limits fluctuations.
- **1979:** Founding of European Monetary System tying exchange rates.
- **1987:** Single European Act fixed objective of monetary union in a treaty for first time.

- **1989:** Delores Report outlines three-stage plan for monetary union.
- **1991:** EC head of state agree in Maastricht, the Netherlands, to create a monetary union in 1997 or 1999.
- **1993:** After currency turmoil-ejects Britain and Italy from exchange-rate mechanism, fluctuation bands are widened.
- **1994:** Founding of European Monetary Institute, forerunner of a European central bank.
- **1995:** EU governments agree they won't be able to meet the 1997 deadline.
- **1998:** Using 1997 data, EU rules which nations can participate in monetary union.
- **1999:** Parities of currencies are irrevocably fixed, European central bank takes over monetary policy.
- **2002:** Notes and coins in new currency issued to public.

Analysis: The adoption of a common currency requires nations to give up control of monetary policy. Few countries are willing to do so.

policy tended to be tighter (more restrictive) than Italian monetary policy. When they adopt a common currency, Germany and Italy and the other 9 EU members will have to find a middle ground for monetary policy. If unemployment or growth rates vary significantly across the 11 EU nations, such a middle ground may be politically difficult to establish.

Recognizing these obstacles, the 11 EU nations hedged on their commitment to a common currency. Although the euro is now the official currency of the 11 nations, each country will maintain its own currency for at least 3 years. In fact, no euros will even circulate publicly until at least 2002. And although the EU nations established a new European central bank, the central banks of the member nations are still functioning. In effect, the EU nations agreed to a "trial marriage" for the euro and are now assessing their willingness to pursue common fiscal monetary and trade policies. If they succeed, more nations may adopt the euro. But no one really expects a single global currency to become a reality in the economy tomorrow. As long as individual countries and regions have different economic problems, priorities, and institutions, a bit of global coordination is the best we can hope for.

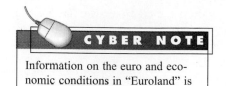

CYBER NOTE

Information on the euro and economic conditions in "Euroland" is posted at http://europa.eu.int.

SUMMARY

- The United States exports about 11 percent of total output and imports an even larger percentage. This international trade ties our macro performance to that of the rest of the world.

- Imports represent leakage from the circular flow and so tend to reduce equilibrium GDP. The marginal propensity to import also diminishes the multiplier impact of fiscal and monetary policies.

- Exports represent added spending on domestic output and so tend to increase equilibrium GDP. This added demand may conflict with restrictive macro policy objectives.

- Trade imbalances occur when exports and imports are unequal. Trade deficits imply that we're consuming more output than we're producing. Trade surpluses indicate the opposite.

- Fiscal stimulus increases imports and crowds out net exports. The resulting increase in the trade deficit may constrain policy options.

- Capital imbalances occur when the inflow of capital doesn't equal the outflow of capital. Capital surpluses help finance trade deficits but may also conflict with macro policy goals at home or abroad.

- International trade and capital flows place additional constraints on macro policy. Macro policy must both anticipate and respond to changes in trade and capital flows.

- The benefits of international trade and capital markets are the broadening of consumption possibilities and the enhanced productivity they promote. Productivity advances arise from specialization in production and from the competitive pressure of foreign producers and markets.

- In adopting a common currency, EU nations hope to broaden markets and accelerate productivity and growth. To maintain that currency, they may have to submerge some national priorities.

Key Terms

imports
leakage
multiplier
marginal propensity to
    import (MPM)
marginal propensity
    to save (MPS)

exports
net exports
trade surplus
trade deficit
crowding out
capital deficit
capital surplus

exchange rate
comparative advantage
productivity

Questions for Discussion

1. How is the U.S. economy affected by (*a*) a recession in Mexico, (*b*) stimulative monetary policies in Mexico, (*c*) a drop in the value of the peso?

2. Suppose investors in other countries increased their purchases of U.S. corporate stock. How would this influx of capital affect the U.S. economy?

3. Why is it unrealistic to expect trade flows to be balanced?

4. Farmers in the United States export about one-third of their major crops. What would happen to U.S. farmers if foreign consumers stopped buying American food? What would happen to our macro equilibrium?

5. Japan imports most of the raw materials it uses in the production of finished goods. If the international prices of raw materials rose sharply, how would Japan's economy be affected? Would Japanese exports be affected?

6. How would a tax cut in the United States affect international capital and trade flows?

7. Why did the Fed reject an interest rate cut in September 1998? (See NEWS page 364.) How would an interest rate cut have (*a*) relieved the Asian crisis? (*b*) hurt the U.S. economy?

8. Web Activity What comparative advantages does your state have? Check out your state's "trade map" at www.csis.org/nge/trade/ustrade.html. What are your state's major exports? Why do you think your state has a comparative advantage in those products? How much does your state export? What countries are the top export markets for your state?

9. Web Activity Go to http://europa.eu.int/geninfo/key_en.htm for the latest information on the European Union. Read about the current key issues. Is the European Union succeeding in its "trial marriage" to adopt a common currency and common fiscal, monetary, and trade policies?

Problems for Chapter 18 appear at the back of the book.

Theory and Reality

There is no one solution. It isn't just a question of the budget. It isn't just the question of inflationary labor rates. It isn't just the question of sticky prices. It isn't just the question of what the Government does to keep prices up or to make regulations that tend to be inflationary. It isn't just the weather or just the drought.

It is all these things. The interaction of these various factors is what is so terribly difficult for us to understand and, of course, what is so terribly difficult for us to deal with.

—Former Secretary of the Treasury W. Michael Blumenthal

Macroeconomic theory is supposed to explain the business cycle and show policymakers how to control it. But something is obviously wrong. Despite our relative prosperity, we haven't consistently achieved the goals of full employment, price stability, and vigorous economic growth. All too often, either unemployment or inflation surges higher unexpectedly or economic growth slows down. No matter how hard we try to manipulate it, the business cycle seems to go its own stubborn way.

What accounts for this gap between the promises of economic theory and the reality of economic performance? Are the theories inadequate? Or is sound economic advice being ignored?

Many people blame the economists. They point to the conflicting advice of Keynesians, monetarists, and supply-siders and wonder what theory is supposed to be followed. If economists themselves can't agree, it is asked, why should anyone else listen to them?

Not surprisingly, economists see things a bit differently. First, they point out, the **business cycle** isn't as bad as it used to be. Since World War II, the economy has had many ups and downs, but none of the downs has been as severe as the Great Depression or earlier catastrophes. Second, economists complain that "politics" often takes precedence over good economic advice. Politicians are reluctant, for example, to raise taxes, cut spending, or slow money growth in order to control inflation. Their concern is winning the next election, not solving the country's economic problems.

IN THE NEWS

Class Over; Clinton Faces Real Test Now

LITTLE ROCK—President-elect Clinton was praised for a dazzling display of knowledge and listening skills at his two-day economic conference, but his dilemma hasn't changed: How does he fix this mess?

As Carol Bartz, of Autodisk in Sausalito, Calif., told Clinton: "So much for consensus. You are a very smart man. Get on with making decisions as fast as you can."

But the decisions and solutions for economic woes, outlined in 19 hours of televised economic give-and-take over two days, aren't quite so easy. And Clinton got an earful of conflicting evidence. . . .

He listened to passionate defenses of both a short-term burst of government spending and deficit-cutting measures.

But Clinton stuck fiercely, as is his habit, to a middle ground that may mildly please everyone or not please anyone at all.

Amid praise for how Clinton ran the conference as a kind of economics classroom, the participants' passion for drastic action—on all sides of the political spectrum—contains the seeds of political nightmares. . . .

"This is a very tough call," Clinton said. "This is the major economic policy decision we're going to have to make."

—Bill Nichols

USA Today, Dec. 16, 1992, p. 4A. Copyright 1992, USA TODAY. Reprinted with permission. www.usatoday.com

Analysis: The reality of decision making is that someone has to select and implement a policy even in the face of conflicting advice and uncertainty about the state of the economy.

When President Jimmy Carter was in office, he anguished over another problem: the complexity of economic decision making. In the real world, neither theory nor politics can keep up with all our economic goals. As President Carter observed: "We cannot concentrate just on inflation or just on unemployment or just on deficits in the federal budget or our international payments. Nor can we act in isolation from other countries. We must deal with all of these problems simultaneously and on a worldwide basis."

As if the burdens of a continuously changing world weren't enough, the president must also contend with sharply differing economic theories and advice, a slow and frequently hostile Congress, a massive and often unresponsive bureaucracy, and a complete lack of knowledge about the future. No one was more acutely aware of these dilemmas than Bill Clinton just after his election victory when he had to put theory to practice (see NEWS).

This chapter confronts these and other frustrations of the real world head on. In so doing, we provide answers to the following questions:

- What's the ideal "package" of macro policies?
- How well does our macro performance live up to the promises of that package?
- What kinds of obstacles prevent us from doing better?

The answers to these questions may shed some light on a broader concern that has long troubled students and policymakers alike, namely, "If economists are so smart, why is the economy always in such a mess?"

business cycle: Alternating periods of economic growth and contraction.

POLICY LEVERS

Table 19.1 summarizes the macroeconomic tools available to policymakers. Although this list is brief, we hardly need a reminder at this point of how powerful each instrument can be. Every one of these major policy instruments can significantly change our answers to the basic economic questions of WHAT, HOW, and FOR WHOM to produce.

TABLE 19.1
The Policy Levers

Economic policymakers have access to a variety of policy instruments. The challenge is to choose the right tools at the right time. The mix of tools required may vary from problem to problem.

Type of Policy	Policy Instruments
Fiscal	Tax cuts and increases
	Changes in government spending
Monetary	Open market operations
	Reserve requirements
	Discount rates
Supply-side	Tax incentives for investment and saving
	Deregulation
	Human-capital investment
	Infrastructure development
	Free trade
	Immigration

Fiscal Policy

fiscal policy: The use of government taxes and spending to alter macroeconomic outcomes.

CYBER NOTE

The Library of Congress maintains a summary of recent congressional tax legislation at http://thomas.loc.gov.

The basic tools of **fiscal policy** are contained in the federal budget. Tax cuts are supposed to stimulate spending by putting more income in the hands of consumers and businesses. Tax increases are intended to curtail spending and reduce inflationary pressures. Table 19.2 summarizes some of the major tax changes of recent years.

The expenditure side of the federal budget is another fiscal policy tool. From a Keynesian perspective, increases in government spending raise aggregate demand and so encourage more production. A slowdown in government spending is supposed to restrain aggregate demand and lessen inflationary pressures.

Who Makes Fiscal Policy? As we first observed in Chapter 11, changes in taxes and government spending originate both in economic events and explicit policy decisions. When the economy slows, tax revenues decline, and government spending increases

1981	Economic Recovery Tax Act	3-year consumer tax cut of $213 billion; $59 billion of business tax cuts
1982	Tax Equity and Fiscal Responsibility Act	Raised business, excise, and income taxes by $100 billion over 3 years
1983	Social Security Act Amendments	Increased payroll taxes and cut future retirement benefits
1984	Deficit Reduction Act	Increased income, business, and excise taxes by $50 billion over 3 years
1985	Gramm-Rudman-Hollings Act	Required a balanced budget by 1991; authorized automatic spending cuts
1986	Tax Reform Act	Major reduction in tax rates coupled with broadening of tax base
1990	Budget Enforcement Act	Limits set on discretionary spending; pay-as-you-go financing required for new initiatives
1993	Clinton "New Direction"	Tax increases and spending cuts to achieve $300 billion deficit reduction between 1994 and 1997
1994	Contract with America	Republican-led Congress cuts spending, sets 7-year target for balanced budget
1997	Balanced Budget Act Taxpayer Relief Act	Package of tax cuts and spending cuts to balance budget by 2002
1998	Budget Surplus	Strong economy pushes budget into surplus

TABLE 19.2
Fiscal Policy Milestones

automatically. Conversely, when real GDP grows, tax revenues automatically rise, and government transfer payments decline. These **automatic stabilizers** are a basic countercyclical feature of the federal budget. They don't represent active fiscal policy. On the contrary, *fiscal policy refers to deliberate changes in tax or spending legislation.* These changes can be made only by the U.S. Congress. Every year the president proposes specific budget and tax changes, negotiates with Congress, then accepts or vetoes specific acts that Congress has passed. The resulting policy decisions represent "discretionary" fiscal policy. Those policy decisions expand or shrink the **structural deficit** and thus give the economy a shot of **fiscal stimulus** or **fiscal restraint.**

The policy arsenal described in Table 19.1 also contains monetary tools. The tools of **monetary policy** include open market operations, discount rate changes, and reserve requirements.

As we saw in Chapter 15, there are disagreements over how these monetary tools should be used. Keynesians believe that interest rates are the critical policy lever. In their view, the money supply should be expanded or curtailed in order to achieve whatever interest rate is needed to shift aggregate demand. Monetarists, on the other hand, contend that the money supply itself is the critical policy lever and that it should be expanded at a steady and predictable rate. This policy, they believe, will ensure price stability and a **natural rate of unemployment.**

Who Makes Monetary Policy? Actual monetary policy decisions are made by the Federal Reserve's Board of Governors. Twice a year the Fed provides Congress with a broad overview of the economic outlook and monetary objectives. The Fed's assessment of the economy is updated each month at meetings of the Federal Open Market Committee (FOMC). The FOMC decides which monetary policy levers to pull.

Table 19.3 depicts milestones in recent monetary policy. Of particular interest is the October 1979 decision to adopt a pure monetarist approach. This involved an exclusive focus on the money supply, without regard for interest rates. After interest rates soared and the economy appeared on the brink of a depression, the Fed abandoned the

automatic stabilizer: Federal expenditure or revenue item that automatically responds countercyclically to changes in national income—such as unemployment benefits, income taxes.

structural deficit: Federal revenues at full employment minus expenditures at full employment under prevailing fiscal policy.

Monetary Policy

fiscal stimulus: Tax cuts or spending hikes intended to increase (shift) aggregate demand.

fiscal restraint: Tax hikes or spending cuts intended to reduce (shift) aggregate demand.

monetary policy: The use of money and credit controls to influence macroeconomic outcomes.

natural rate of unemployment: Long-term rate of unemployment determined by structural forces in labor and product markets.

October 1979	Fed adopts monetarist approach, focusing exclusively on money supply; interest rates soar
March 1980	Fed imposes direct credit controls
July 1982	Deep into recession, Fed votes to ease monetary restraint
October 1982	Fed abandons pure monetarist approach and expands money supply rapidly
May 1983	Fed reverses policy and begins slowing money supply growth
1985	Fed relaxes money supply grip with cuts in discount rate and more open market purchases
1987	Fed abandons money supply targets as policy guides. Money supply growth decreases; discount rate increased
1989	Greenspan announces goal of "zero inflation," exercises more monetary restraint
1991	Deep in recession, the Fed begins to ease monetary restraint culminating in a full-point drop in discount rate in December
1993	Greenspan announces he's "satisfied" with pace of recovery, advises Congress to reduce deficit
1994	Fed slows M2 growth to 1 percent; raises federal funds rate by 3 percentage points as economy nears full employment
1995	Greenspan trumpets "soft landing" and eases monetary restraint
1998	Fed cuts discount and federal fund rates to cushion U.S. economy from Asian crisis

TABLE 19.3
Monetary Policy Milestones

monetarist approach and again began keeping an eye on both interest rates (the Keynesian focus) and the money supply.

Monetarists contend that the Fed never fully embraced their policy. The money supply grew at a very uneven pace in 1980, they argue, not at the steady, predictable rate that they demanded. Nevertheless, the policy shifts of 1979 and 1982 were distinctive and had dramatic effects.

Also of interest in Table 19.3 is the Fed's brief imposition of credit controls in 1980. After the Fed tightened the money supply, it attempted to ensure that the available money would be allocated to the "right" uses, particularly business investment. It tried to ensure this outcome by restricting consumer credit. The credit controls restrained borrowing so much, however, that they further threatened the economy. The controls were lifted a few months later.

In 1987 the Fed discarded M1 as a reliable policy target, arguing that changing banking practices (deregulation) had made it too volatile. Shortly thereafter, Alan Greenspan replaced Paul Volcker as chairman of the Fed and began to reduce money supply growth. Greenspan vowed to keep a tight rein on money supply growth in order to eliminate inflation. He hoped that his public commitment to "zero inflation" would also reduce inflationary expectations.

The Fed's renewed tightness helped push the economy into another recession (1990–1991). In the early months of the recession, Chairman Greenspan kept asserting that economic recovery was imminent. Months later the Fed belatedly decided that recovery wasn't right around the corner and that monetary stimulus might be necessary. Throughout 1991 the Fed repeatedly eased monetary policy, culminating in a decisive, full-point cut in the discount rate in December. During a period of 15 months (September 1990–December 1991), the Fed cut the discount rate in half. During the same period the prime rate of interest dropped from 10 to 6 percent. This monetary ease was a decisive factor in ending the 1990–1991 recession.

Real output grew by more than 2 percent in 1993 and even faster in 1994. As the economy approached full employment, the Fed began to worry about inflation again. Money supply growth was slowed in 1994 and interest rates were pushed up. The Fed was hoping that this mild monetary restraint would create a "soft landing" for the economy, that is, a slowdown in growth without an outright reduction in output (recession). The Fed stuck with this course until October 1998, when the effects of the Asian crisis on U.S. exports and financial markets became more visible. The Fed then cut interest rates to keep the economy growing.

Supply-Side Policy

supply-side policy: The use of tax incentives, (de)regulation, and other mechanisms to increase the ability and willingness to produce goods and services.

Supply-side theory offers the third major set of policy tools. The focus of **supply-side policy** is to provide incentives to work, invest, and produce. Of particular concern are high tax rates and regulations that reduce supply incentives. Supply-siders argue that marginal tax rates and government regulation must be reduced in order to get more output without added inflation.

In the 1980s tax rates were reduced dramatically. The maximum marginal tax rate on individuals were cut from 70 to 50 percent in 1981, and then still further, to 28 percent, in 1987. The 1980s also witnessed major milestones in the deregulation of airlines, trucking, telephone service, and other industries (see Table 19.4).

Some of the momentum toward less regulation was reversed during the 1990s. New regulatory costs on business were created by the Americans with Disabilities Act, the 1990 amendments to the Clean Air Act, and the Family Leave Act of 1993. All three laws provide important benefits to workers or the environment. At the same time, however, they also make supplying goods and services more expensive.

The Clinton administration broadened supply-side efforts to include infrastructure development and increased investment in human capital (through education and skill training programs). These activities increase the capacity to produce and so shift the aggregate supply curve rightward. The Clinton administration also toughened environ-

TABLE 19.4
Supply-Side Milestones

1978	Airline Deregulation Act	Phased out federal regulations of airline routes, fares, and entry
1980	Motor Carrier Act	Eliminated federal restrictions on entry, routes, and fares in trucking industry
1981	Economic Recovery Tax Act	Decreased marginal tax rates by 30 percent
1982	AT&T breakup	AT&T monopoly on local phone service ended via antitrust action
1986	Tax Reform Act	Eliminated many tax preferences but sharply reduced marginal tax rates
1989	Fair Labor Standards Act amended	Congress increases minimum wage to $3.80 in 1990 and $4.25 in 1991
1990	Social Security Act amendments	Payroll tax increased to 7.65 percent
1990	Americans with Disabilities Act	Required employers to provide greater access for disabled individuals
1990	Immigration Act	Increased immigraton, especially for high-skill workers
1990	Clean Air Act amendments	Increased pollution control requirements
1991	Surface Transportation Act	Accelerated highway and rail improvements
1993	Rebuild America Program	Increased spending on infrastructure and human-capital investment
	Family Leave Act	Requires employers to provide unpaid leaves of absence for workers
	NAFTA	North American trade barriers lowered
1994	GATT renewed	World trade barriers lowered
1996	Telecommunications Act	Permits greater competition in cable and telephone industries
1996–1997	Minimum Wage Hike	Minimum wage jumps from $4.25 to $5.15 per hour
1996	Personal Responsibility and Work Opportunity Act	Requires more welfare recipients to work
1997	Taxpayer Relief Act	Created tuition tax credits and other supply incentives

mental regulation, however, and sought legislation that would require employers to provide more training and fringe benefits (like health insurance), initiatives that shift the aggregate supply curve leftward.

Who Makes Supply-Side Policy? Because tax rates are a basic tool of supply-side policy, fiscal and supply-side policies are often intertwined. When Congress changes the tax laws, it almost always alters marginal tax rates and thus changes production incentives. Notice, for example, that tax legislation appears in Table 19.4 as well as in Table 19.2. The Taxpayer Relief Act of 1997 not only changed total tax revenues (fiscal policy) but also restructured production and investment incentives (supply-side policy).

Supply-side and fiscal policies also interact on the outlay side of the budget. The Surface Transportation Act of 1991, for example, authorized accelerated public works spending (fiscal stimulus) on infrastructure development (increase in supply capacity). President Clinton's Rebuild America program also affected both aggregate demand and aggregate supply. *Deciding whether to increase spending is a fiscal policy decision; deciding how to spend may entail supply-side policy.*

Regulatory policy is also fashioned by Congress. The president and executive agencies play a critical role in this supply-side area in the day-to-day decisions on how to interpret and enforce regulatory policies.

IDEALIZED USES

These fiscal, monetary, and supply-side tools are potentially powerful levers for controlling the economy. In principle, they can cure the excesses of the business cycle. To see how, let's review their use in three distinct macroeconomic settings.

Case 1: Recession

GDP gap (real): The difference between full-employment GDP and equilibrium GDP.

multiplier: The multiple by which an initial change in aggregate spending will alter total expenditure after an infinite number of spending cycles; 1/(1 − MPC).

When output and employment levels fall far short of the economy's full-employment potential, the mandate for public policy is clear. Total spending must be increased so that producers can sell more goods, hire more workers, and move the economy toward its productive capacity. At such times the most urgent need is to put people to work and close the **real GDP gap.**

How should people be put to work? Pure Keynesians emphasize the need to increase aggregate demand by cutting taxes or boosting government spending. The resulting stimulus will set off a **multiplier** reaction. If the initial stimulus and multiplier are large enough, the GDP gap can be eliminated, propelling the economy to full employment.

Modern Keynesians acknowledge that monetary policy might also help. Specifically, increases in the money supply may lower interest rates and thus give investment spending a further boost. All these actions can be taken simultaneously. To give the economy a really powerful stimulus, we might want to cut taxes, increase government spending, and expand the money supply all at the same time. This is what the Japanese government did in 1998 to jump-start their economy (see WORLD VIEW). By taking such sweeping action, policymakers hope to increase consumer confidence, raise investor expectations, and induce still greater spending and output.

Monetarists proceed differently. First, they see no point in toying with the federal budget. In the pure monetarist model, changes in taxes or government spending may

WORLD VIEW

Japan's Ruling Party Offers Stimulus Package

Associated Press

TOKYO, Nov. 12 (Thursday)—Prime Minister Keizo Obuchi's ruling party outlined plans today for Japan's biggest stimulus package ever in an attempt to jumpt-start the country's anemic economy. . . .

The centerpiece of party's package calls for $82 billion in public-works-related spending through next March and $33 billion in income tax cuts next year.

With the addition of corporate tax cuts and other tax relief measures, it will likely total a record $148 billion. . . .

The government has faced intense pressure both from opposition parties at home and foreign trade partners such as the United States to deal with record unemployment, soaring bankruptcies and deeply shaken consumer confidence.

Japan estimates its gross domestic product will contract by 1.8 percent for the current fiscal year, which ends March 31, 1999. The economy shrank 0.7 percent last year.

On Tuesday, Clinton singled out Japan—as he often has in recent months—as the key to reviving economic growth in Asia and pulling the region out of the financial crisis that is beginning to be felt on American soil. . . .

The party also recommended a novel idea designed to get consumers to spend more—the distribution of government-issue coupons worth about $164 to the elderly and families with young children.

The Washington Post, Nov. 12, 1998, p. F3. © 1998, The Washington Post. Reprinted with permission. www.washingtonpost.com

Analysis: In a deep and prolonged recession, a nation may have to pursue a variety of stimulative policies simultaneously.

alter the mix of output, but not its level. So long as the **velocity of money (V)** is constant, fiscal policy doesn't matter. In this view, the appropriate policy response to a recession is patience. As sales and output slow, interest rates decline, and new investment will be stimulated.

Supply-siders emphasize the need to improve production incentives. They urge cuts in marginal tax rates on investment and labor. They also look for ways to reduce government regulation. Finally, they urge that any increase in government spending (fiscal stimulus) focus on long-run capacity expansion such as infrastructure development.

An overheated economy provides as clear a policy mandate as does a sluggish one. In this case, the task of policy is to restrain aggregate spending until the rate of total expenditure is compatible with the productive capacity of the economy. This entails shifting the aggregate demand curve to the left. Keynesians would do this by raising taxes and cutting government spending. Keynesians would also see the desirability of increasing interest rates to curb investment spending.

Monetarists would simply cut the money supply. In their view, the short-run aggregate supply curve is unknown and unstable. The only predictable response is reflected in the vertical, long-run aggregate supply curve. According to this view, changes in the money supply alter prices, not output. Inflation is seen simply as "too much money chasing too few goods." Monetarists would turn off the money spigot. The Fed's job in this situation isn't only to reduce money supply growth but to convince market participants that a more cautious monetary policy will be continued. This was the intent of Chairman Greenspan's public commitment to zero inflation.

Supply-siders would point out that inflation implies both "too much money" and "not enough goods." They'd look at the supply side of the market for ways to expand productive capacity. In a highly inflationary setting, they'd propose more incentives to save. The additional savings would automatically reduce consumption while creating a larger pool of investable funds. Supply-siders would also cut taxes and regulations that raise production costs and lower import barriers that keep out cheaper foreign goods.

Although serious inflations and recessions provide clear mandates for economic policy, there's a vast gray area between these extremes. All too often the economy suffers from both inflation and unemployment at the same time, a condition called **stagflation.** The simultaneous pressure of both unemployment and inflation greatly complicates decision making. If aggregate demand were stimulated to reduce unemployment, the resultant pressure on prices might fuel the existing inflation. And if fiscal and monetary restraints were used to reduce inflationary pressures, unemployment might worsen. In such a situation, there are no simple solutions.

Knowing the causes of stagflation will help achieve the desired balance. If prices are rising before full employment is reached, some degree of structural unemployment is likely to occur. An appropriate policy response might include more vocational training in skill-shortage areas as well as a redirection of aggregate demand toward labor-surplus sectors.

High tax rates or costly regulations might also contribute to stagflation. If either constraint exists, high prices (inflation) may not be a sufficient incentive for increased output. In this case, reductions in tax rates and regulation might help reduce both unemployment and inflation, which is the basic goal of supply-side policies.

Stagflation may also arise from a temporary contraction of aggregate supply that both reduces output and drives up prices. In this case, neither structural unemployment nor excessive demand is the culprit. Rather, an "external shock" (such as a natural disaster) or an abrupt change in world trade (such as an oil embargo) is likely to be the cause of the policy dilemma. Accordingly, none of our familiar policy tools is likely to provide a complete "cure." In most cases the economy simply has to adjust to a temporary setback.

velocity of money (V): The number of times per year, on average, that a dollar is used to purchase final goods and services; $PQ \div M$.

Case 2: Inflation

Case 3: Stagflation

stagflation: The simultaneous occurrence of substantial unemployment and inflation.

Analysis: There are different theories about when and how the government should "fix" the economy. Policymakers must decide which advice to follow in specific situations.

Fine Tuning

fine tuning: Adjustments in economic policy designed to counteract small changes in economic outcomes; continuous responses to changing economic conditions.

The apparently inexhaustible potential of public policy to alter the economy's performance has often generated optimistic expectations about the efficacy of fiscal, monetary, and supply-side tools. In the early 1960s such optimism pervaded even the highest levels of government. Those were the days when prices were relatively stable, unemployment rates were falling, the economy was growing rapidly, and preparations were being made for the first trip into space. The potential of economic policy looked great indeed. It was also during the 1960s that a lot of people (mostly economists) spoke of the potential for **fine tuning,** or altering economic outcomes to fit very exacting specifications. Flexible responses to changing market conditions, it was argued, could ensure fulfillment of our economic goals. The prescription was simple: When unemployment is the problem, simply give the economy a jolt of fiscal or monetary stimulus; when inflation is worrisome, simply apply the fiscal or monetary brakes. To fulfill our goals for content and distribution, we simply pick the right target for stimulus or restraint. With a little attention and experience, the right speed could be found and the economy guided successfully down the road to prosperity.

THE ECONOMIC RECORD

The economy's track record doesn't live up to the high expectations of "fine tuning." To be sure, the economy has continued to grow and we've attained an impressive standard of living. We can't lose sight of the fact that our per capita income greatly exceeds the realities and even the expectations in most other countries of the world. Nevertheless, we must also recognize that our economic history is punctuated by periods of recession, high unemployment, inflation, and recurring concern for the distribution of income and mix of output.

The graphs in Figure 19.1 provide a quick summary of the gap between the theory and reality of economic policy. The Employment Act of 1946 committed the federal government to macro stability. It's evident that we haven't kept that commitment. In the 1970s we rarely came close. Although we approached all three goals in the mid-1980s, our achievements were short-lived. Economic growth ground to a halt in 1989, and the economy slipped into yet another recession in 1990. Although inflation stayed low, unemployment rates jumped.

The economy performed very well again from 1992 to 1999. As the milennium approached, however, there were signs that GDP growth was slowing. Fears of another recession began to surface.

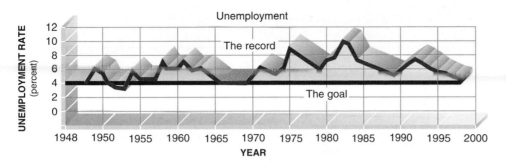

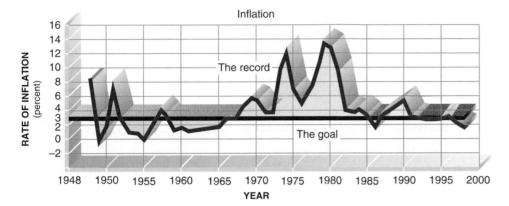

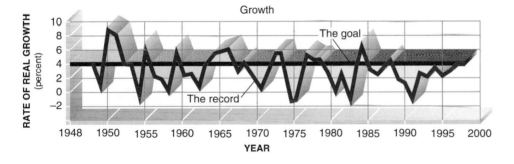

FIGURE 19.1
The Economic Record

The Full Employment and Balanced Growth Act of 1978 established specific goals for unemployment (4 percent), inflation (3 percent), and economic growth (4 percent). We've rarely attained those goals, however, as these graphs illustrate. Measurement, design, and policy implementation problems help explain these shortcomings.

Source: *Economic Report of the President, 1999.*

Looking back over the entire postwar period, the record includes 9 years of outright recession (actual declines in output) and another 18 years of **growth recession** (growth of less than 3 percent). Moreover, the distribution of income in 1998 looked virtually identical to that of 1946, and over 30 million people were still officially counted as poor in the later year.

The economic performance of the United States was better than that of other Western nations in the 1990s. The economies of most countries didn't grow as fast as the U.S. economy in the 1990s. But, as the WORLD VIEW on the next page shows, some countries did a better job of restraining prices.

When one looks at the specific policy initiatives of various administrations, the gap between theory and practice is even larger. The Fed's decision to reduce the money supply on repeated occasions during the Great Depression was colossally perverse. Only slightly less so was the Fed's decision to expand the money supply rapidly in 1978, despite evidence that inflationary pressures were already building up. During 1980–1981 and again in 1989–1990, the Fed slowed money supply growth much more and far longer than was justified. As a consequence, the economy suffered two consecutive recessions in the early 1980s and another one in the early 1990s.

On the fiscal side of the ledger, we must recall President Roosevelt's timid efforts to expand aggregate demand during the Great Depression. Also worth remembering is

growth recession: A period during which real GDP grows, but at a rate below the long-term trend of 3 percent.

Macro Performance in the 1990s

The performance of the U.S. economy in the 1990s was better than most developed economies. Japan had the greatest success in restraining inflation (1.2 percent) but suffered from sluggish growth (1.5 percent per year). The United States grew faster and also experienced less unemployment than most European countries.

Performance (annual average percentage)	U.S.	Japan	Germany	United Kingdom	France	Italy	Canada
Real growth	2.4	1.5	2.4	1.6	1.8	1.4	1.8
Inflation	3.0	1.2	2.5	3.9	2.0	4.1	2.2
Unemployment	5.8	3.0	9.0	7.3	11.2	11.4	9.7

Source: International Monetary Fund. www.imf.org

Analysis: Macroeconomic performance varies a lot, both over time and across countries. In the 1990s, U.S. economic performance was above average on most measures.

President Johnson's refusal to "pay" for the Vietnam War by either raising taxes or cutting nonmilitary expenditures. The resulting strain on the economy's capacity kindled inflationary pressures that lasted for years. For his part, President Carter increased labor costs (higher payroll taxes and minimum wages), farm prices, and government spending at a time when inflation was a foremost policy concern. President Reagan made his share of mistakes too, including the pursuit of deep budget cuts in the early stages of a recession. President Bush ignored the recession for an entire year, believing that "self-adjustment" would ensure recovery. That mistake cost him his job.

President Clinton pushed through a tax increase in 1993 that helped subdue the recovery from the 1990–1991 recession. He also caused the aggregate supply curve to shift upward by forcing employers to pay higher labor costs. Repeated policy flip-flops also undermined investor and consumer confidence in Washington's ability to manage the economy.

WHY THINGS DON'T ALWAYS WORK

There's plenty of blame to go around for all the blemishes on our economic record. Some people blame the Fed, others blame Congress, still others blame Japan or Mexico. Some forces, however, constrain economic policy even when no one is specifically to blame. In this regard, we can distinguish *four obstacles to policy success:*

- *Goal conflicts*
- *Measurement problems*
- *Design problems*
- *Implementation problems*

Goal Conflicts   The first factor to take note of is potential conflicts in policy priorities. President Clinton had to confront this problem his first day in office. He had pledged to create new jobs by increasing public infrastructure spending and offering a middle-class tax cut. He had also promised to reduce the deficit, however. This created a clear goal conflict.

In the end, President Clinton had to settle for a smaller increase in infrastructure spending and a tax *increase.*

Most macro goal conflicts originate in the trade-off between unemployment and inflation. Should we try to cure inflation, unemployment, or just a bit of both? Answers are likely to vary. Unemployed people put the highest priority of attaining full employment. Labor unions press for faster economic growth. Bankers, creditors, and people on fixed incomes demand an end to inflation.

This goal conflict is often institutionalized in the decision-making process. The Fed is traditionally viewed as the guardian of price stability. The president and Congress worry more about people's jobs and government programs, so they are less willing to raise taxes or cut spending.

Distributional goals may also conflict with macro objectives. Anti-inflationary policies may require cutbacks in programs for the poor, the elderly, or needy students. These cutbacks may be politically impossible (see NEWS). Likewise, tight-money policies may be viewed as too great a burden for small businesses.

Although the policy levers in Table 19.1 are powerful, they can't grant all our wishes. Since we still live in a world of scarce resources, ***all policy decisions entail opportunity costs,*** which means that we'll always be confronted with trade-offs. The best we can hope for is a set of compromises that yields *optimal* outcomes, not ideal ones.

Measurement Problems

One reason firefighters are pretty successful in putting out fires before entire cities burn down is that fires are highly visible phenomena. But such visibility isn't characteristic of economic problems. An increase in the unemployment rate from 5 to 6 percent, for example, isn't the kind of thing you notice while crossing the street. Unless you work in the unemployment insurance office or lose your own job, the increase in unemployment isn't likely to attract your attention. The same is true of prices; small increases in product prices aren't likely to ring many alarms. Hence both inflation and unemployment may worsen considerably before anyone takes serious notice. Were we as slow and ill-equipped to notice fires, whole neighborhoods would burn before someone rang the alarm.

IN THE NEWS

Deficit-Cutting Wilts in Heat from Voters: Entitlements Remain Mostly Off-Limits

In April, Sen. Pete V. Domenici (R-N.M.) suggested a plan for digging out of the massive federal deficit. His idea seemed modest on its face but was revolutionary by Washington standards.

Domenici proposed capping cost-of-living increases in entitlement programs, the automatic spending engines such as Medicaid, Medicare and federal retirement that are exempt from annual congressional review. . . .

Even before his proposal took shape, more than 3,000 New Mexico constituents sent him identical postcards opposing any effort to cap entitlement programs.

The National Council of Senior Citizens dubbed the plan "the most outrageous attack on the elderly we have seen in years." The Veterans of Foreign Wars expressed "shock and outrage." Milk producers accused Domenici of trying to balance the budget "on the back of farmers."

That was enough for the Senate, which voted 69 to 28 to reject the proposal. . . .

—Eric Pianin

The Washington Post, Aug. 4, 1992, p. 1. © 1992, The Washington Post. Reprinted with permission. www.washingtonpost.com

Analysis: Changes in economic policy inevitably alter incomes and stir political opposition. Cuts in spending are particularly difficult to enact.

Measurement problems are a very basic policy constraint. To formulate appropriate economic policy, we must first determine the nature of our problems. To do so, we must measure employment changes, output changes, price changes, and other macro outcomes. The old adage that governments are willing and able to solve only those problems they can measure is relevant here. Indeed, before the Great Depression, a fundamental barrier to public policy was the lack of statistics on what was happening in the economy. One lasting benefit of that experience is that we now try to keep informed on changing economic conditions. The information at hand, however, is always dated and incomplete. *At best, we know what was happening in the economy last month or last week.* The processes of data collection, assembly, and presentation take time, even in this age of high-speed computers. The average recession lasts about 11 months, but official data generally don't even confirm the existence of a recession until 8 months after a downturn starts! The recession of 1990–1991 was no exception (see NEWS).

Forecasts. In an ideal world, policymakers wouldn't only respond to economic problems that occur but would also anticipate their occurrence. If we foresee an inflationary GDP gap emerging, for example, we want to take immediate action to keep aggregate spending from increasing. That is, the successful firefighter not only responds to a fire but also looks for hazards that might start one.

Unfortunately, economic policymakers are again at a disadvantage. Their knowledge of future problems is even worse than their knowledge of current problems. *In designing policy, policymakers must depend on economic forecasts,* that is, informed guesses about what the economy will look like in future periods.

Macro Models. Those guesses are often based on complex computer models of how the economy works. These models—referred to as *econometric macro models*—are mathematical summaries of the economy's performance. The models try to identify the key determinants of macro performance and then show what happens to macro outcomes when they change.

An economist "feeds" the computer two essential inputs. One is a quantitative model of how the economy allegedly works. A Keynesian model, for example, includes equations that show multiplier spending responses to tax cuts. A monetarist model shows that tax cuts raise interest rates, not total spending ("crowding out"), and a supply-side model stipulates labor-supply and production responses. The computer can't tell which theory is right; it just predicts what it's programmed to see. In other words, the computer sees the world through the eyes of its economic master.

CYBER NOTE

For an overview of the forecasting model the Congressional Budget Office uses, visit www.cbo.gov and search for the 1998 report, "Description of Economic Models."

IN THE NEWS

News: Analysis

This Just In: Recession Ended 21 Months Ago

WASHINGTON—Here's proof that economics is an inexact science. An official panel of economists determined today that the nation's ninth postwar recession ended a month before they realized it had started. And it took 21 months to sort all this out.

The dating committee of the National Bureau of Economic Research declared today that the recession had ended in March 1991—the month before it even announced there was a recession. The committee determined in April 1991 that the recession had begun in the previous July.

—Robert D. Hershey, Jr.

The New York Times, Dec. 23, 1992, p. D1. Copyright © 1992 by The New York Times Company. Reprinted by permission. www.nytimes.com

Analysis: In the absence of timely information, today's policy decisions are inevitably based on yesterday's perceptions.

The second essential input in a computer forecast is the assumed values for critical variables. A Keynesian model, for example, must specify how large a multiplier to expect. All the computer does is carry out the required mathematical routines, once it's told that the multiplier is relevant and what its value is. It can't discern the true multiplier any better than it can pick the right theory.

Given the dependence of computers on the theories and perceptions of their economic masters, it's not surprising that computer forecasts often differ greatly. It's also not surprising that they're often wrong. Even policymakers who are familiar with both economic theory and computer models can make some pretty bad calls. In January 1990, Fed Chairman Alan Greenspan assured Congress that the risk of a recession was as low as 20 percent. Although he said he "wouldn't bet the ranch" on such a low probability, he was confident that the odds of a recession were below 50 percent; 5 months after his testimony, the 1990–1991 recession began.

Leading Indicators. Given the complexity of macro models, many people prefer to use simpler tools for divining the future. One of the most popular is the Index of Leading Economic Indicators. The leading indicators are things we can observe today that are frequently related to future events. One of the 11 leading indicators, for example, is orders for new equipment. Those orders should trigger future production.

Unfortunately, equipment orders and the other leading indicators (see Table 19.5) aren't wholly reliable forecasting tools, either. Equipment orders might be canceled. Or producers might be unwilling or unable to fill those orders quickly. In either event, today's orders *wouldn't* result in tomorrow's output.

Crystal Balls. In view of the fragile foundations and spotty record of computer and index-based forecasts, many people shun them altogether, preferring to use their own "crystal balls." The Foundation for the Study of Cycles has identified 4000 different crystal balls that people use to gauge the health of the economy, including the ratio of used-car to new-car sales (it rises in recession); the number of divorce petitions (it rises

CYBER NOTE

The Dismal Sciences company assembles economic forecasts and a broad array of economic statistics, along with user-friendly commentary. You can visit the company at www.dismal.com.

Indicator	Expected Impact
1. Average workweek	Hours worked per week typically increase when greater output and sales are expected.
2. Unemployment claims	Initial claims for unemployment benefits reflect changes in industry layoffs.
3. Delivery times	The longer it takes to deliver ordered goods, the greater the ratio of demand to supply.
4. Credit	Changes in business and consumer borrowing indicate potential purchasing power.
5. Materials prices	When producers step up production they buy more raw materials, pushing their prices higher.
6. Equipment orders	Orders for new equipment imply increased production capacity and higher anticipated sales.
7. Stock prices	Higher stock prices reflect expectations of greater sales and profits.
8. Money supply	Faster growth of the money supply implies a pickup in aggregate demand.
9. New orders	New orders for consumer goods trigger increases in production and employment.
10. Building permits	A permit represents the first step in housing construction.
11. Inventories	Companies build up inventory when they anticipate higher sales.

TABLE 19.5
The Leading Economic Indicators

Everyone wants a crystal ball to foresee future economic events. In reality, forecasters must reckon with very crude predictors of the future. One of the most widely used predictors is the Index of Leading Economic Indicators, which includes 11 factors believed to predict economic activity 3 to 6 months in advance. Changes in the leading indicators are used to forecast changes in GDP.

The leading indicators rarely move in the same direction at the same time. They're weighted together to create the index. Up-and-down movements of the index are reported each month by the nonprofit Conference Board.

in bad times); animal population cycles (they peak just before economic downturns); and even the optimism/pessimism content of popular music (a reflection of consumer confidence). Corporate executives claim that such crystal balls are as valuable as professional economic forecasts. In a Gallup survey of CEOs, most respondents said economists' forecasts had little or no influence on company plans or policies. The head of one large company said, "I go out of my way to ignore them." The general public apparently shares this view, giving higher marks to the forecasts of sportswriters and weather forecasters than to those of economists.

Economic forecasters defend themselves in two ways. First, they note that economic policy decisions are inevitably based on anticipated changes in the economy's performance. The decision to stimulate or restrain the economy can't be made by a flip of a coin; *someone* must try to foresee the future course of the economy. Second, forecasters claim that their quantitative approach is the only honest one. Because forecasting models require specific behavioral assumptions and estimates, they force people to spell out their versions of the future. Less rigorous ("gut feeling") approaches are too ambiguous and often inconsistent.

These are valid arguments. Still, one must be careful to distinguish the precision of computers from the inevitable uncertainties of their spoon-fed models. The basic law of the computer is GIGO: garbage in, garbage out. If the underlying models and assumptions are no good, the computer's forecasts won't be any better.

Policy and Forecasts. The task of forecasting the economic future is made still more complex by the interdependency of forecasts, policy decisions, and economic outcomes (see Figure 19.2). First a forecast is made, based on current economic conditions, likely disturbances to the economy, and anticipated economic policy. These forecasts are then used to project likely budget deficits and other policy variables. Congress and the president react to these projections by revising fiscal, monetary, or supply-side policies. These changes, in turn, alter the basis for the initial forecasts.

This interdependence among forecasts, budget projections, and policy decisions was superbly illustrated in the early months of President Reagan's first term. A principal theme of Ronald Reagan's 1980 election campaign was the need to balance the federal budget. When he took office, his plan for balancing the budget included big cuts in both taxes and government spending. Congress resisted this approach, however, for fear that the tax cuts would accelerate inflation. The Congressional Budget Office and others foresaw a strong economy in 1981 and urged Congress to reject massive tax cuts.

CYBER NOTE

To review the latest forecasts of 50 noted economists, see the Blue Chip average at www.bluechippubs.com.

FIGURE 19.2
The Mutual Dependence of Forecasts and Policy

Because tax revenues and government spending are sensitive to economic conditions, budget projections must rely on economic forecasts. The budget projections may alter policy decisions, however, and so change the basis for the initial forecasts. This interdependence between macro forecasts, budget projections, and policy decisions is virtually inevitable.

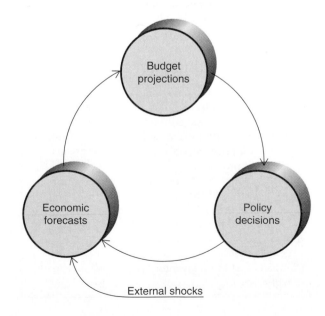

By the time Congress finally approved a scaled-down tax cut, the economy had actually entered a recession, but no one knew it. Indeed, President Reagan was still demanding further spending cuts in November 1981. Only a few weeks later the president and Congress belatedly realized that the country was in a deep recession. They then began talking about the need to postpone further spending cuts and accelerate planned tax reductions.

In 1995, a changed forecast by the Congressional Budget Office (CBO) caused similar policy turmoil. President Clinton and congressional Republicans were deadlocked over the details of a balanced budget plan. In the midst of their negotiations, CBO changed its economic forecasts, projecting faster growth than previously foreseen. Faster growth would reduce the cyclical deficit, narrowing budget differences between the White House and Capitol Hill. Observers criticized the timing of the revised forecast, however, and pointed to CBO's reputation for excessively optimistic projections (see NEWS).

These forecasting episodes illustrate two major points about fine tuning. First, it may be possible to fine-tune an economy if we know what problems exist and how serious they're likely to become. Second, it reminds us that we seldom have such good information. Thus, we're likely to fail as often as we succeed.

Assume for the moment that we somehow are able to get a reliable forecast of where the economy is headed. The outlook, let's suppose, is bad. Now we're in the driver's seat to steer the economy past looming dangers. We need to chart our course—to design an economic plan. What action should we take? Which theory of macro behavior should guide us? How will the marketplace respond to any specific action we take?

Suppose, for example, that we adopt a Keynesian approach to ending a recession. Specifically, we cut income taxes to stimulate consumer spending. How do we know

CYBER NOTE

For the latest CBO and Office of Management and Budget (OMB) macro forecasts visit www.cbo.gov and www.whitehouse.gov/WH/EOP/OMB/html/ombhome.html.

Design Problems

Wishful Thinking? The Rosy Forecasts of CBO and OMB

Congress and the president need forecasts of future GDP and future budget deficits to make informed decisions on fiscal policy. Those forecasts are prepared by the Office of Management and Budget (OMB) for the president and by the Congressional Budget Office (CBO) for the Congress.

Like private forecasters, the CBO and OMB have dismal track records in divining the future. The accompanying table shows by how far OMB and CBO missed the mark on forecasts of

GDP growth and the federal budget deficit for the period 1977–1994. On average, they erred by 1 percentage point for annual growth—an error margin of 40 percent. They also erred by $40 to $45 billion on annual deficit projections.

CBO and OMB errors don't appear to be random. On the contrary, both offices tend to overstate economic growth and underestimate budget deficts. These rosy outlooks are always welcomed by the president and Congress, since they make budget decisions appear easier. Wishful thinking, in other words, may be part of the job.

Economic Growth Forecasts 1977–1994			Budget Deficit Forecasts 1977–1994		
Average Error	Frequency of Underestimates	Frequency of Overestimates	Average Error	Frequency of Underestimates	Frequency of Overestimates
CBO 0.9%	33%	67%	$40 billion	60%	40%
OMB 1.0%	39%	61%	$45 billion	80%	20%

Analysis: The executive (OMB) and legislative (CBO) branches both have incentives to overestimate future economic growth and underestimate future budget deficits.

that consumers will respond as anticipated? In 1998, Japanese households used their tax cut to increase *savings* rather than consumption (see WORLD VIEW). As a result, the intended fiscal stimulus didn't materialize. Such behavioral responses will frustrate even the best-intentioned policy. The successful policymaker needs a very good crystal ball, one that will also foretell how market participants are going to respond to any specific actions taken.

Implementation Problems

Measurement and design problems can break the spirit of even the best policymaker (or the policymaker's economic advisers). Yet measurement and design problems are only part of the story. A good idea is of little value unless someone puts it to use. Accordingly, to understand fully why things go wrong, we must also consider the difficulties of *implementing* a well-designed policy.

Congressional Deliberations. Suppose that the president and his Council of Economic Advisers (perhaps in conjunction with the National Economic Council, the secretary of the Treasury, and the director of the Office of Management and Budget) decide that the rate of aggregate spending is slowing down. A tax cut, they believe, is necessary to stimulate demand for goods and services. Can they simply go ahead and cut tax rates? No, because only the Congress can legislate tax changes. Once the president decides on the appropriate policy, he must ask Congress for authority to take the required action, which means a delay in implementing policy, and possibly no policy at all.

At the very least, the president must convince Congress of the wisdom of his proposed policy. The tax proposal must work its way through separate committees of both the House of Representatives and the Senate, get on the congressional calendar, and be approved in each chamber. If there are important differences in Senate and House versions of the tax-cut legislation, they must be compromised in a joint conference. The modified proposal must then be returned to each chamber for approval.

WORLD VIEW

Japanese Tighten Belts

Many Plan to Save, Not Spend, Tax Cut

CHIBA, Japan—The proof is not in the pudding. It's in the soy sauce.

Every day just about every Japanese person uses soy sauce, on rice and fish and chicken and in cooking. Yuzaburo Mogi, family patriarch of the famous Kikkoman brand, can tell by people's soy sauce-buying habits that his nation's economy is in deep trouble.

"Food companies are usually not hit by recession, but this time we are having trouble," said Mogi, whose family has been making soy sauce for more than 300 years. "People who usually buy expensive soy sauce are buying cheaper sauce. And people who bought our cheaper soy sauce are now buying other brands."

The declining soy sauce index is a useful indicator to explain why one of the world's richest countries is in so much trouble. The heart of why the economy is expected to shrink for the first time in a quarter-century is simple: People are spending less. . . .

Prime Minister Ryutaro Hashimoto aimed a $30 billion rescue effort directly at consumers last week. He proposed a tax cut that would give a typical household as much as $500 this year and again next year.

But housewives, retirees and salarymen in this Tokyo suburb are not impressed with Hashimoto's rescue. They said it will not move them to spend more.

In hours of discussions, they talked about why they started saving more: fear that more jobs will be lost and wages cut, distrust of the government's ability to correct structural problems in the economy and a growing feeling that if they do not look out for themselves, no one will.

—Mary Jordan and Kevin Sullivan

The Washington Post, April 14, 1998, p. 1. © 1998, The Washington Post. Reprinted with permission. www.washingtonpost.com

Analysis: The success of macro policy depends on how market participants respond to policy initiatives. Japanese consumers didn't follow the Keynesian script.

The same kind of process applies to the outlay side of the budget. Once the president has submitted his budget proposals (in January), Congress reviews them, then sets its own spending goals. After that, the budget is broken down into 13 different categories, and a separate appropriations bill is written for each one. These bills spell out in detail how much can be spent and for what purposes. Once Congress passes them, they go to the president for acceptance or veto.

Budget legislation requires Congress to finish these deliberations by October 1 (the beginning of the federal fiscal year), but Congress rarely meets this deadline. In most years the budget debate continues well into the fiscal year. In some years, the budget debate isn't resolved until the fiscal year is nearly over! The final budget legislation is typically more than 1000 pages long and so complex that few people understand all its dimensions.

Time Lags. This description of congressional activity isn't an outline for a civics course; rather, it's an important explanation of why economic policy isn't fully effective. *Even if the right policy is formulated to solve an emerging economic problem, there's no assurance that it will be implemented. And if it's implemented, there's no assurance that it will take effect at the right time.* Once of the most frightening prospects for economic policy is that a policy design intended to serve a specific problem will be implemented much later, when economic conditions have changed. This isn't a remote danger. According to Christina Romer and Paul Romer, the Fed doesn't pull the monetary-stimulus lever until a recession is under way, and Congress is even slower in responding to an economic downturn. Indeed, a U.S. Treasury Department study concluded that every postwar fiscal stimulus package was enacted well after the end of the recession it was intended to cure!

Figure 19.3 is a schematic view of why macro policies don't always work as intended. There are always delays between the time a problem emerges and the time it's recognized. There are additional delays between recognition and response design, between design and implementation, and finally between implementation and impact. Not only may mistakes be made at each juncture, but even correct decisions may be overcome by changing economic conditions.

We can illustrate the processes in Figure 19.3 by considering how the income surtax of 1968 came about. The expansion of the Vietnam War in July 1965 added something like $15 billion to aggregate demand at a time when the economy was already fully employed.[1] To offset resulting inflationary pressures, the president and Congress initiated some fiscal restraint, including the restoration of excise taxes on cars and telephones. Much stronger action was necessary, however. But President Lyndon Johnson insisted that the escalation of the war was temporary. From his perspective, the imposition of stronger fiscal restraints was tantamount to an admission that the war

[1]This figure includes multiplier effects through the first quarter of 1966.

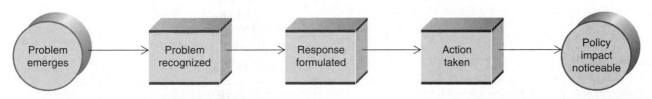

FIGURE 19.3
Policy Response: A Series of Time Lags

Even the best-intentioned economic policy can be frustrated by time lags. It takes time for a problem to be recognized, time to formulate a policy response, and still more time to implement that policy. By the time the policy begins to affect the economy, the underlying problem may have changed.

wouldn't be won quickly. Only after another 18 months of war did the administration propose further action. In January 1967 President Johnson called for a 6 percent surtax to corrrect the "imbalances created by the special pressures of Vietnam procurement."[2] Thus the problem that emerged in July 1965 wasn't recognized until 1966, and a response wasn't formulated until January 1967. Compounding these delays was the reluctance of Congress to help finance an undeclared war. Congress didn't take the requested action until June 1968. Thus there was a 3-year lag between the time the problem emerged and the policy response. In the interim, inflationary pressures worsened.

Politics vs. Economics. The delayed fiscal response to accelerated Vietnam expenditures also illustrates the very first barrier to policy implementation: *goal conflicts.* Just as the design of policy is compromised by conflicting interests, so too is the implementation of those designs. Especially noteworthy in this regard is the potential conflict of economic policy with political objectives. The conflict that existed between President Johnson's war objectives and his economic objectives is obvious. More generally, observers have noted that the president and Congress are reluctant to impose fiscal restraints (tax increases or budget cutbacks) in election years, regardless of economic circumstances. Fiscal restraint is never popular.

The tendency of Congress to hold fiscal policy hostage to electoral concerns has created a pattern of short-run stops and starts—a kind of policy-induced business cycle. Indeed, some argue that the business cycle has been replaced with the political cycle: The economy is stimulated in the year of an election and then restrained in the postelection year. President Clinton was no exception to this pattern. In the election campaign of 1992 he promised a tax cut. Yet in his first year of office he *raised* taxes instead. In the 1995–1996 election campaign he again proposed to *cut* taxes (see NEWS).

[2]*Economic Report of the President,* 1967, pp. 5 and 9.

IN THE NEWS

News: Analysis

For Clinton, the Politics of a Tax Cut Are Sure to Clash with the Economics

WASHINGTON—Can Bill Clinton, looking for ways to boost his popularity, resist taking a bite from the tax-cut apple?

Administration officials acknowledge that President Clinton will be tempted by his advisers this fall with a proposal to revive his broken campaign promise to cut taxes for middle-class families.

So far, the question hasn't been formally discussed in a White House preoccupied with health care, crime, Haiti and Cuba. But Clinton advisers are talking informally about the wisdom of a tax cut. For the record, White House spokesmen say only: "We haven't ruled it out."

Conflicting Views

When the debate is joined in the fall, it is likely to pit some of Mr. Clinton's political advisers, who like the politics of a tax cut, against some of his economic advisers, who dislike the economics. . . .

The economic team also will warn that the possibility of a bidding war between Mr. Clinton and congressional Republicans to see who can propose the biggest tax cut for the middle class will unsettle financial markets and the Federal Reserve, threatening higher interest rates that could retard the economy before a tax reduction could get through Congress.

—David Wessel

The Wall Street Journal, Sept. 6, 1994, p. A3. Reprinted by permission of *The Wall Street Journal,* © 1994 Dow Jones & Company, Inc. All Rights Reserved Worldwide. www.wsj.com

Analysis: Political survival requires policymakers to offer tax cuts and avoid tax hikes in election years. After the election, economic conditions may require a different approach.

The conflict between the urgent need to get reelected and the necessity to manage the economy results in a seesaw kind of instability.

In theory, the political independence of the Fed's Board of Governors provides some protection from ill-advised but politically advantageous policy initiatives. In practice, however, the Fed's relative obscurity and independence may backfire. The president and the Congress know that if they don't take effective action against inflation—by raising taxes or cutting government spending—the Fed can and will take stronger action to restrain aggregate demand. This is a classic case of having one's cake and eating it to. Elected officials win votes for not raising taxes or cutting some constituent's favorite spending program. They then take credit for any reduction in the rate of inflation brought about by Federal Reserve policies. To top it off, Congress and the president can also blame the Fed for driving up interest rates or starting a recession if monetary policy becomes too restrictive!

Finally, we must recognize that policy design is obstructed by a certain lack of will. Neither people on the street nor elected public officials focus constantly on economic goals and activities. Even students enrolled in economics courses have a hard time keeping their minds on the economy and its problems. The executive and legislative branches of government, for their part, are likely to focus on economic concerns only when economic problems become serious or voters demand action. Otherwise, policymakers are apt to be complacent about economic policy as long as economic performance is within a "tolerable" range of desired outcomes.

THE ECONOMY TOMORROW

In view of the goal conflicts and the measurement, design, and implementation problems that policymakers confront, it's less surprising that things sometimes go wrong than that things so often work out right. The maze of obstacles through which theory must pass before it becomes policy explains a great many of our collective shortcomings. On this basis alone, we may conclude that ***consistent fine tuning of the economy isn't compatible with either our design capabilities or our decision-making procedures.*** We have exhibited a strong capability to avoid major economic disruptions in the last four decades. We haven't, however, been able to make all the minor adjustments necessary to fulfill our goals completely. As Arthur Burns, former chairman of the Fed's Board of Governors, said:

> There has been much loose talk of "fine tuning" when the state of knowledge permits us to predict only within a fairly broad level the course of economic development and the results of policy actions.[3]

Some critics of economic policy take this argument a few steps further. If fine tuning isn't really possible, they say, we should abandon discretionary policies altogether and follow fixed rules for fiscal and monetary intervention.

As we saw in Chapter 15, pure monetarism would require the Fed to increase the money supply at a constant rate. Critics of fiscal policy would require the government to maintain balanced budgets, or at least to offset deficits in sluggish years with surpluses in years of high growth. Such rules would prevent policymakers from over- or understimulating the economy, and the risks of economic instability would be reduced.

Milton Friedman has been one of the most persistent advocates of fixed policy rules. With discretionary authority, Friedman argues,

> the wrong decision is likely to be made in a large fraction of cases because the decision-makers are examining only a limited area and not taking into account the cumulative consequences

Hands On or Hands Off?

Hands Off

[3]*Newsweek,* Aug. 27, 1973, p. 4.

of the policy as a whole. On the other hand, if a general rule is adopted for a group of cases as a bundle, the existence of that rule has favorable effects on people's attitudes and beliefs and expectations that would not follow even from the discretionary adoption of precisely the same policy on a series of separate occasions.[4]

The case for a hands-off policy stance is based on practical, not theoretical, arguments. Everyone agrees that flexible, discretionary policies *could* result in better economic performance. But Friedman and others argue that the practical requirements of monetary and fiscal management are too demanding and thus prone to failure. Moreover, required policies may be compromised by political pressures.

rational expectations: Hypothesis that people's spending decisions are based on all available information, including the anticipated effects of government intervention.

New Classical Economics. Monetarist critiques of discretionary policy are echoed by a new perspective refered to as new classical economics (NCE). Classical economists saw no need for discretionary macro policy. In their view, the private sector is inherently stable and government intervention serves no purpose. New classical economics reaches the same conclusion. As Robert Barro, a proponent of NCE, put it: "It is best for the government to provide a stable environment, and then mainly stay out of the way."[5] Barro and other NCE eonomists based this laissez-faire conclusion on the intriguing notion of **rational expectations.** This notion contends that people make decisions on the basis of all available information, including the *future* effects of *current* government policy.

Suppose, for example, that the Fed decided to increase the money supply in order to boost output. If people had rational expectations, they'd anticipate that this money supply growth will fuel inflation. To protect themselves, they'd immediately demand higher prices and wages. As a result, the stimulative monetary policy would fail to boost real output. (Monetarists reach the same conclusion but for different reasons; for monetarists, the countervailing forces are technological and institutional rather than rational expectations.)

Discretionary fiscal policy could be equally ineffective. Suppose Congress accelerated government spending in an effort to boost aggregate demand. Monetarists contend that the accompanying increase in the deficit would push interest rates up and crowd out private investment and consumption. New classical economists again reach the same conclusion via a different route. They contend that people with rational expectations would anticipate that a larger deficit now will necessitate tax increases in later years. To prepare for later tax bills, consumers will reduce spending now, thereby saving more. This "rational" reduction in consumption will offset the increased government expenditure, thus rendering fiscal policy ineffective.

If the new classical economists are right, then the only policy that works is one that surprises people—one that consumers and investors don't anticipate. But a policy based on surprises isn't very practical. Accordingly, New Classical economists conclude that minimal policy intervention is best. This conclusion provides yet another guideline for policy decisions (see Table 19.6 for a roster of competing theories).

Hands On

Proponents of a hands-on policy strategy acknowledge the possibility of occasional blunders. They emphasize, however, the greater risks of doing nothing when the economy is faltering. Some proponents of the quick fix even turn the new classical economics argument on its head. Even the "wrong" policy, they argue, might be better than doing nothing if enough market participants believed that *change* implied *progress.* They cite the jump in consumer confidence that followed the election of Bill Clinton, who had emphasized the need for a *change* in policy but hadn't spelled out the details of that change. The surge in confidence itself stimulated consumer purchases, even before President Clinton took office.

[4]Milton Friedman, *Capitalism and Freedom* (Chicago: University of Chicago Press, 1962), p. 53.
[5]Robert Barro, "Don't Fool with Money, Cut Taxes," *The Wall Street Journal,* Nov. 21, 1991, p. A14.

Keynesians	Keynesians believe that the private sector is inherently unstable and likely to stagnate at low levels of output and employment. They want the government to use tax cuts and government spending to increase demand and output.
Modern ("neo") Keynesians	Post–World War II followers of Keynes worry about inflation as well as recession. They urge budgetary restraint to cool an overheated economy. They also use monetary policy to change interest rates.
Monetarists	The money supply is their only heavy hitter. By changing the money supply, they can raise or lower the price level. Pure monetarists shun active policy, believing that it destabilizes the otherwise stable private sector. Output and employment gravitate to their "natural" levels.
Supply-siders	Incentives to work, invest, and produce are the key to their plays. Cuts in marginal tax rates and government regulation are used to expand production capacity, thereby increasing output and reducing inflationary pressures.
New classical economists	They say fine tuning won't work because once the private sector realizes what the government is doing, it will act to offset it. They also question the credibility of "quick-fix" promises. They favor steady, predictable policies.
Marxists	Marxists contend that the failures of the economy are inherent in its capitalist structure. The owners of capital won't strive for full employment or a more equitable income distribution. Workers, without any capital, have little incentive to excel. This team proposes starting a new game, with entirely different rules.

TABLE 19.6
Who's on First? Labeling Economists

It sometimes hard to tell who's on what side in economic debates. Although some economists are proud to wear the colors of monetarists, Keynesians, or other teams, many economists shun such allegiances. Indeed, economists are often accused of playing on one team one day and on another team the next, making it hard to tell which team is at bat. To simplify matters, this guide may be used for quick identification of the players. Closer observation is advised, however, before choosing up teams.

Policy activists don't rely on random changes, however, and certainly don't want to pull the wrong policy levers. There's enough consensus, they argue, about economic principles to ensure that the right choices are made most of the time. They also point to the historical record. Our economic track record may not be perfect, but the historical record of prices, employment, and growth has improved since active fiscal and monetary policies were adopted. Without flexibility in the money supply and the budget, they argue, the economy would be less stable and our economic goals would remain unfulfilled.

The historical evidence for discretionary policy is ambiguous. Victor Zarnowitz showed that the U.S. economy has been much more stable since 1946 than it was in earlier periods (1875–1918 and 1919–1945).[6] Recessions have gotten shorter and economic expansions longer. But a variety of factors—including a shift from manufacturing to services, a larger government sector, and automatic stabilizers—have contributed to this improved macro performance. The contribution of discretionary macro policy is less clear. It's easy to observe what actually happened but almost impossible to determine what would have occurred in other circumstances.

Finally, one must contend with the difficulties inherent in adhering to any fixed rules. How is the Fed, for example, supposed to maintain a steady rate of growth in the money supply? As we observed in Chapter 13, people move their funds back and forth between different kinds of "money." Also, the demand for money is subject to unpredictable shifts. To maintain a steady rate of growth in M2 or any other measure of

---

[6]Victor Zarnowitz, *Facts and Factors in the Recent Evolution of the Business Cycle in the United States* (Cambridge, Mass.: National Bureau of Economic Research, 1989).

money would require superhuman foresight and responses. As former Fed chairman Paul Volcker told Congress, it would be "exceedingly dangerous and in fact practically impossible to eliminate substantial elements of discretion in the conduct of Federal Reserve policy."

The same is true of fiscal policy. Government spending and taxes are directly influenced by changes in unemployment, inflation, interest rates, and growth. These automatic stabilizers make it virtually impossible to maintain any fixed rule for budget balancing. Moreover, if we eliminated the automatic stabilizers, we'd risk greater instability.

Modest Expectations

The clamor for fixed policy rules is more a rebuke of past policy than a viable policy alternative. We really have no choice but to pursue discretionary policies. Recognition of measurement, design, and implementation problems is important for an understanding of the way the economy functions. Even though it's difficult or even impossible to reach all our goals, we can't abandon conscientious attempts to get as close as possible to goal fulfillment. If public policy can create a few more jobs, a better mix of output, a little more growth and price stability, or an improved distribution of income, those initiatives are worthwhile.

SUMMARY

- The government possesses an array of macro policy levers, each of which can significantly alter economic outcomes. To end a recession, we can cut taxes, expand the money supply, or increase government spending. To curb inflation, we can reverse each of these policy levers. To overcome stagflation, we can combine fiscal and monetary levers with improved supply-side incentives.

- Although the potential of economic theory seems impressive, the economic record doesn't look so good. Persistent unemployment, recurring economic slowdowns, and nagging inflation suggest that the realities of policy-making are more difficult than theory implies.

- To a large extent, the "failures" of economic policy are a reflection of scarce resources and competing goals. Even when consensus exists, however, serious obstacles to effective economic policy remain. These obstacles include

(a) Measurement problems. Our knowledge of economic performance is always dated and incomplete.
(b) Design problems. We don't know exactly how the economy will respond to specific policies.
(c) Implementation problems. It takes time for Congress and the president to agree on an appropriate plan of action. Moreover, political needs may take precedence over economic needs.

For all these reasons, discretionary policy rarely lives up to its theoretical potential.

- Monetarists and new classical economists favor rules rather than discretionary macro policies. They argue that discretionary policies are unlikely to work and risk being wrong. Critics respond that discretionary policies are needed to cope with ever-changing economic circumstances.

Key Terms

business cycle	monetary policy	velocity of money (V)
fiscal policy	natural rate of	stagflation
automatic stabilizer	unemployment	fine tuning
structural deficit	supply-side policy	growth recession
fiscal stimulus	GDP gap (real)	rational expectations
fiscal restraint	multiplier	

Questions for Discussion

1. Why do policymakers respond so slowly to economic problems?

2. If policymakers have instant data on the economy's performance, should they respond immediately? Why or why not?

3. Suppose it's an election year and aggregate demand is growing so fast that it threatens to set off an inflationary movement. Why might Congress and the president hesitate to cut back on government spending or raise taxes, as economic theory suggests is appropriate?

4. In his fiscal 1991 budget, President Bush proposed increases in defense spending while arguing for cutbacks in total spending. Should military spending be subject to macroeconomic constraints? What programs should be expanded or contracted to bring about needed changes in the budget? Is this feasible?

5. Prior to assuming office, President-elect Clinton pledged to propose a tax credit for new investment during the first months of his administration. How might such an announcement affect the timing of investment decisions?

6. Suppose the government proposes to cut taxes while maintaining the current level of government expenditures. To finance this deficit, it may either (*a*) sell bonds to the public or (*b*) print new money (via Federal Reserve cooperation). What are the likely effects of each of these alternatives on each of the following? Would Keynesians, monetarists, and supply-siders give the same answers:
   (*a*) Interest rates
   (*b*) Consumer spending
   (*c*) Business investment
   (*d*) Aggregate demand

7. Suppose the economy is slumping into recession and needs a fiscal policy boost. Voters, however, are opposed to larger federal deficits. What should policymakers do?

8. The WORLD VIEW on page 374 describes Japanese efforts to stimulate their economy. What elements of that package represent (*a*) fiscal policy, (*b*) monetary policy, (*c*) supply-side policy?

9. Web Activity Debate continues today between supply-siders and new Keynesians. Identify one supply argument in papers from the Heritage Foundation at www.taxation.org. Identify one new Keynesian argument in articles available through the Electronic Policy Network at www.epn.org (click on Economic Policy).

10. Web Activity What's in the future? Go to http://wuecon.wustl.edu/econfaq/Consult/index.html and find three economic forecasts. How do they differ? Explain why you would be more confident with one of these forecasts. *Optional:* Look for "economic forecasts" with your Internet search engine. Remember that just about anyone can post economic forecasts on the Web. Using this method, find one forecast from a reputable source. Then find one forecast from a less "reputable" source and explain why you would have little confidence in this prediction.

Problems for Chapter 19 appear at the back of the book.

International Economics

Our interactions with the rest of the world have a profound impact on the mix of output (WHAT), the methods of production (HOW), and the distribution of income (FOR WHOM). Trade and global money flows can also affect the stability of the macro economy. Chapters 20 and 21 explore the nature of international trade and finance. Chapter 22 focuses on the problems of transforming a centrally planned economy into a more market-based global participant.

20

International Trade

The 1998 World Series between the New York Yankees and the San Diego Padres was played with Japanese gloves, baseballs made in Costa Rica, and Mexican bats. Most of the players were wearing shoes made in Korea, and half the games were played on artificial grass made in Taiwan. Baseball, it seems, has become something less than the "all-American" game.

Imported goods have made inroads into other activities as well. All DVDs and VCRs are imported, as are most televisions, fax machines, personal computers, and cell phones. Most of these imported goods could have been produced in the United States. Why did we purchase them from other countries? For that matter, why does the rest of the world buy computers, tractors, chemicals, airplanes, and wheat from us rather than produce such products for themselves? Wouldn't we all be better off relying on ourselves for the goods we consume (and the jobs we need) rather than buying and selling products in international markets? Or is there some advantage to be gained from international trade?

This chapter begins with a survey of the nature of international trade patterns—what goods and services we trade, and with whom. Then we address basic issues related to such trade:

- What benefit, if any, do we get from international trade?
- How much harm do imports cause, and to whom?
- Should we protect ourselves from "unfair" trade by limiting imports?

After examining the arguments for and against international trade, we draw some general conclusions about trade policy. As we'll see, international trade tends to increase *average* incomes, although it may diminish the job and income opportunities for specific industries and workers.

U.S. TRADE PATTERNS

Imports

In 1998, the United States imported more than $1 trillion in goods and services. These **imports** included the consumer items mentioned earlier as well as capital equipment, raw materials, and food. Table 20.1 is a sampler of the goods and services we purchase from foreign suppliers.

Although imports represent only 12 percent of total GDP, they account for larger shares of specific product markets. Coffee is a familiar example. Since all

Country	Imports from	Exports to
Australia	Beef Alumina Autos	Airplanes Computers Auto parts
Belgium	Jewelry Cars Optical glass	Cigarettes Airplanes Diamonds
Canada	Cars Trucks Paper	Auto parts Cars Computers
China	Toys Shoes Clothes	Fertilizer Airplanes Cotton
Germany	Cars Engines Auto parts	Airplanes Computers Cars
Japan	Cars Computers Telephones	Airplanes Computers Timber
Russia	Oil Platinum Artworks	Corn Wheat Oil seeds
South Korea	Shoes Cars Computers	Airplanes Leather Iron ingots and oxides

Source: U.S. Department of Commerce.

TABLE 20.1
A U.S. Trade Sampler

The United States imports and exports a staggering array of goods and services. Shown here are the top exports and imports with various countries. Notice that we export many of the same goods we import (such as cars and computers). What's the purpose of trading goods we produce ourselves?

coffee is imported, Americans would have a harder time staying awake without imports. Likewise, there'd be no aluminum if we didn't import bauxite, no chrome bumpers if we didn't import chromium, no tin cans without imported tin, and a lot fewer computers without imported components. We couldn't even play the all-American game of baseball without imports, since baseballs are no longer made in the United States!

We import *services* as well as *goods*. If you fly to Europe on British Airways you're *importing* transportation services. If you stay in a London hotel, you're *importing* lodging services. When you go to Barclay's Bank to cash traveler's checks, you're importing foreign financial services. These and other services now account for one-fifth of U.S. imports.

imports: Goods and services purchased from international sources.

While we're buying goods (merchandise) and services from the rest of the world, global consumers are buying our **exports**. In 1998, we exported $671 billion of goods, including farm products (wheat, corn, soybeans), tobacco, machinery (computers), aircraft, automobiles and auto parts, raw materials (lumber, iron ore), and chemicals (see Table 20.1 for a sample of U.S. merchandise exports). We also exported $260 billion of services (movies, software licenses, tourism, engineering, financial services, etc.).

Although the United States is the world's largest exporter of goods and services, exports represent a relatively modest fraction of our total output. As the WORLD VIEW illustrates, other nations export much larger proportions of their GDP. Jamaica is one of the most export-oriented countries, with tourist services pushing its export ratio to

Exports

exports: Goods and services sold to foreign buyers.

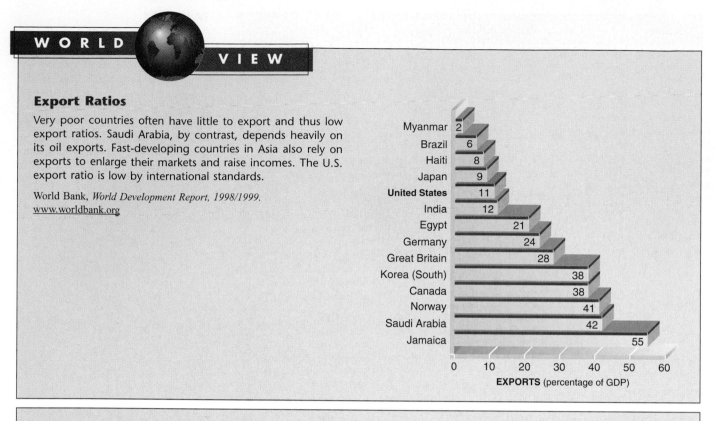

WORLD VIEW

Export Ratios

Very poor countries often have little to export and thus low export ratios. Saudi Arabia, by contrast, depends heavily on its oil exports. Fast-developing countries in Asia also rely on exports to enlarge their markets and raise incomes. The U.S. export ratio is low by international standards.

World Bank, *World Development Report, 1998/1999.*
www.worldbank.org

Country	Exports (percentage of GDP)
Myanmar	2
Brazil	6
Haiti	8
Japan	9
United States	11
India	12
Egypt	21
Germany	24
Great Britain	28
Korea (South)	38
Canada	38
Norway	41
Saudi Arabia	42
Jamaica	55

Analysis: The relatively low U.S. export ratio reflects the vast size of our domestic market and our relative self-sufficiency in food and resources. European nations are smaller and highly interdependent.

CYBER NOTE

Find the most recent trends in trade statistics at www.whitehouse.gov/fsbr/international.html.

55 percent. By contrast, Myanmar (Burma) has a largely agricultural economy, with few exports (other than opium and other drugs traded in the black market).

The low U.S. export ratio disguises our heavy dependence on exports in specific industries. We export 25 to 50 percent of our rice, corn, and wheat production each year, and still more of our soybeans. Clearly, a decision by international consumers to stop eating U.S. agricultural products could devastate a lot of American farmers. Such companies as Boeing (planes), Caterpillar Tractor (construction and farm machinery), Weyerhaeuser (logs, lumber), Eastman Kodak (film), Dow (chemicals), and Sun Microsystems (computer workstations) sell over one-fourth of their output in foreign markets. McDonalds sells hamburgers in 89 countries around the world; to do so, the company exports management and marketing services from the United States. The Walt Disney Company produces the most popular TV shows in Russia and Germany, pub-

TABLE 20.2
Trade Balances

Both merchandise (goods) and services are traded between countries. The United States typically has a merchandise deficit and a services surplus. When combined, an overall trade deficit remained in 1998.

Product Category	Exports (in billions of dollars)	Imports (in billions of dollars)	Surplus (Deficit) (in billions of dollars)
Merchandise	671	919	(248)
Services	260	181	79
Total Trade	931	1100	(169)

Source: U.S. Department of Commerce.

Country	Exports to (in billions of dollars)	Imports from (in billions of dollars)	Trade Balance (in billions of dollars)
Top Deficit Countries			
Japan	65.5	121.7	−56.1
China	12.9	62.6	−49.7
Germany	24.5	43.1	−18.7
Canada	151.8	168.2	−16.4
Mexico	71.4	85.9	−14.5
Top Surplus Countries			
Netherlands	19.8	7.3	+12.5
Australia	12.1	4.6	+7.5
Brazil	15.9	9.6	+6.3
Belgium and Luxembourg	14.1	8.2	+5.9
Hong Kong	15.1	10.3	+4.8

Source: Office of Trade & Economic Analysis.

TABLE 20.3
Bilateral Trade Balances

The U.S. trade deficit is the net result of bilateral deficits and surpluses. We had a very large trade deficit with Japan and China in 1998, for example, but small trade surpluses with the Netherlands, Brazil, Belgium, Australia, and Hong Kong. International trade is multinational, with surpluses in some countries being offset by trade deficits elsewhere.

lishes Italy's bestselling weekly magazine, and has the most popular tourist attraction in Japan (Tokyo Disneyland). The 500,000 foreign students attending U.S. universities are purchasing $5 billion of American educational services. All these activities are part of America's service exports.

Although we export a lot of products, we often have an imbalance in our trade flows. The trade balance is computed simply as the difference between the value of exports and imports; that is,

$$\text{Trade balance} = \text{exports} - \text{imports}$$

During 1998, we imported much more than we exported and so had a negative trade balance. A negative trade balance is called a **trade deficit.**

Although the overall trade balance includes both goods and services, these flows are usually reported separately, with the *merchandise* trade balance distinguished from the *services* trade balance. As Table 20.2 shows, the United States had a merchandise (goods) trade deficit of $248 billion in 1998 and a *services* trade *surplus* of $79 billion, leaving the overall trade balance in the red.

When the United States has a trade deficit with the rest of the world, other countries must have an offsetting **trade surplus.** On a global scale, imports must equal exports, since every good exported by one country must be imported by another. Hence *any imbalance in America's trade must be offset by reverse imbalances elsewhere.*

Whatever the overall balance in our trade accounts, bilateral balances vary greatly. Table 20.3 shows, for example, that our 1998 aggregate trade deficit ($169 billion) incorporated huge bilateral trade deficits with Japan and China. In the same year, however, we had trade surpluses with the Netherlands, Brazil, Belgium, Australia, and Hong Kong.

Trade Balances

trade deficit: The amount by which the value of imports exceeds the value of exports in a given time period.

trade surplus: The amount by which the value of exports exceeds the value of imports in a given time period.

MOTIVATION TO TRADE

Many people wonder why we trade so much, particularly since (1) we import many of the things we also export (like computers, airplanes, clothes), (2) we *could* produce many of the other things we import, and (3) we worry so much about trade imbalances. Why not just import those few things that we can't produce ourselves, and export just enough to balance that trade?

Specialization

Although it might seem strange to be importing goods we could produce ourselves, such trade is imminently rational. Our decision to trade with other countries arises from the same considerations that motivate individuals to specialize in production, satisfying their remaining needs in the marketplace. Why don't you become self-sufficient, growing all your own food, building your own shelter, recording your own songs? Presumably because you've found that you can enjoy a much higher standard of living (and better music) by producing only a few goods and buying the rest in the marketplace. When countries engage in international trade, they're expressing the same kind of commitment to specialization, and for the same reason: *Specialization increases total output.*

To demonstrate the economic gains from international trade, let's examine the production possibilities of two countries. We want to demonstrate that two countries that trade can together produce more output than they could in the absence of trade. If they can, *the gain from trade is increased world output and a higher standard of living in all trading countries.* This is the essential message of the *theory of comparative advantage.*

Production and Consumption Without Trade

production possibilities: The alternative combinations of final goods and services that could be produced in a given time period with all available resources and technology.

Consider the production and consumption possibilities of just two countries—say, the United States and France. For the sake of illustration, let's assume that both countries produce only two goods: bread and wine. Let's also set aside worries about the law of diminishing returns and the substitutability of resources, thus transforming the familiar **production possibilities** curve into a straight line, as in Figure 20.1.

The "curves" in Figure 20.1 suggest that the United States is capable of producing much more bread than France. With our greater abundance of labor, land, and other resources, we assume that the United States is capable of producing up to 100 zillion loaves of bread per year. To do so, we'd have to devote all our resources to that purpose. This capability is indicated by point *A* in Figure 20.1*a* and the accompanying production possibilities schedule. France (Figure 20.1*b*), on the other hand, confronts a *maximum* bread production of only 15 zillion loaves per year (point *G*) because it has little available land, less fuel, and fewer potential workers.

The capacities of the two countries for wine production are 50 zillion barrels for us (point *F*) and 60 zillion for France (point *L*), largely reflecting France's greater experience in tending vines. Both countries are also capable of producing alternative *combinations* of bread and wine, as evidenced by their respective production possibilities curves (points *B–E* for the United States and *H–K* for France).

consumption possibilities: The alternative combinations of goods and services that a country could consume in a given time period.

In the absence of contact with the outside world, the production possibilities curve for each country also defines its **consumption possibilities.** Without imports, neither country can consume more than it produces. Thus the only immediate issue in each country is which mix of output to choose—*what* to produce and consume—out of the domestic choices available.

Assume that Americans choose point *D* on their production possibilities curve, producing and consuming 40 zillion loaves of bread and 30 zillion barrels of wine. The French, on the other hand, prefer the mix of output represented by point *I* on *their* production possibilities curve. At that point they produce and consume 9 zillion loaves of bread and 24 zillion barrels of wine.

To assess the potential gain from trade, consider the *combined* output of the United States and France. In this case total world output (points *D* and *I*) comes to 49 zillion loaves of bread and 54 zillion barrels of wine. What we want to know is whether world output would increase if France and the United States abandoned their isolation and started trading. Could either country, or both, consume more output by engaging in a little trade?

Production and Consumption with Trade

Because both countries are saddled with limited production possibilities, trying to eke out a little extra wine and bread from this situation might not appear very promising.

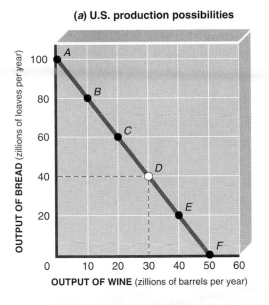

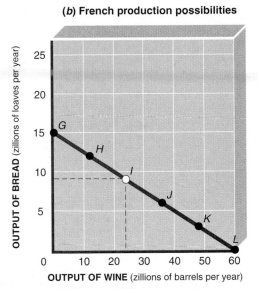

U.S. Production Possibilities				French Production Possibilities			
	Bread (zillions of loaves)	+	Wine (zillions of barrels)		Bread (zillions of loaves)	+	Wine (zillions of barrels)
A	100	+	0	G	15	+	0
B	80	+	10	H	12	+	12
C	60	+	20	I	9	+	24
D	40	+	30	J	6	+	36
E	20	+	40	K	3	+	48
F	0	+	50	L	0	+	60

FIGURE 20.1
Consumption Possibilities Without Trade

In the absence of trade, a country's consumption possibilities are identical to its production possibilities. The assumed production possibilities of the United States and France are illustrated in the graphs and the corresponding schedules. Before entering into trade, the United States chose to produce and consume at point *D*, with 40 zillion loaves of bread and 30 zillion barrels of wine. France chose point *I* on its own production possibilities curve. By trading, each country hopes to increase its consumption beyond these levels.

Such a conclusion is unwarranted, however. Take another look at the production possibilities confronting the United States, as reproduced in Figure 20.2 on the next page. Suppose the United States were to produce at point *C* rather than point *D*. At point *C* we could produce 60 zillion loaves of bread and 20 zillion barrels of wine. That combination is clearly possible, since it lies on the production possibilities curve. We didn't choose that point earlier because we assumed the mix of output at point *D* was preferable. The mix of output at point *C could* be produced, however.

We could also change the mix of output in France. Assume that France moved from point *I* to point *K*, producing 48 zillion barrels of wine and only 3 zillion loaves of bread.

Two observations are now called for. The first is simply that output mixes have changed in each country. The second, and more interesting, is that total world output

FIGURE 20.2
Consumption Possibilities with Trade

A country can increase its consumption possibilities through international trade. Each country alters its mix of domestic output to produce more of the good it produces best. As it does so, total world output increases, and each country enjoys more consumption. In this case, trade allows U.S. consumption to move from point D to point N. France moves from point I to point M.

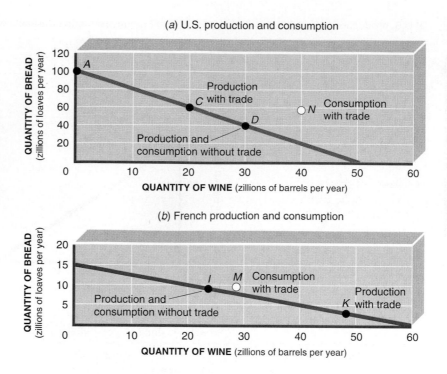

has increased. When the United States and France were at points *D* and *I*, their *combined* output consisted of

	Bread (zillions of loaves)	Wine (zillions of barrels)
U.S. (at point *D*)	40	30
France (at point *I*)	9	24
Total pretrade output	49	54

After moving along their respective production possibilities curves to points *C* and *K*, the combined world output becomes

	Bread (zillions of loaves)	Wine (zillions of barrels)
U.S. (at point *C*)	60	20
France (at point *K*)	3	48
Total output with trade	63	68

Total world output has increased by 14 zillion loaves of bread and 14 zillion barrels of wine. ***Just by changing the mix of output in each country, we've increased total world output.*** This additional output creates the potential for making both countries better off than they were in the absence of trade.

The United States and France weren't producing at points *C* and *K* before because they simply didn't want to *consume* those particular combinations of output. Nevertheless, our discovery that points *C* and *K* allow us to *produce* more output suggests that everybody can consume *more* if we change the mix of output in each country.

Suppose we're the first to discover the potential benefits from trade. Using Figure 20.2 as our guide, we suggest to the French that they move their mix of output from point *I* to point *K*. As an incentive for making such a move, we promise to give them 6 zillion loaves of bread in exchange for 20 zillion barrels of wine. This would leave them at point *M*, with as much bread to consume as they used to have, *plus* an extra 4 zillion barrels of wine. At point *I* they had 9 zillion loaves of bread and 24 zillion barrels of wine. At point *M* they can have 9 zillion loaves of bread and 28 zillion barrels of wine. Thus by altering their mix of output (from point *I* to point *K*) and then trading (point *K* to point *M*), the French end up with more goods and services than they had in the beginning. Notice in particular that this new consumption possibility (point *M*) lies *outside* France's domestic production possibilities curve.

The French will be quite pleased with the extra output they get from trading. But where does this leave us? Does France's gain imply a loss for us? Or do we gain from trade as well?

As it turns out, *both* the United States and France gain by trading. The United States, too, ends up consuming a mix of output that lies outside our production possibilities curve.

Note that at point *C* we *produce* 60 zillion loaves of bread per year and 20 zillion barrels of wine. We then export 6 zillion loaves to France. This leaves us with 54 zillion loaves of bread to consume. In return for our exported bread, the French give us 20 zillion barrels of wine. These imports, plus our domestic production, permit us to *consume* 40 zillion barrels of wine. Hence we end up *consuming* at point *N*, enjoying 54 zillion loaves of bread and 40 zillion barrels of wine. Thus by first changing our mix of output (from point *D* to point *C*), then trading (point *C* to point *N*), we end up with 14 zillion more loaves of bread and 10 zillion more barrels of wine than we started with! International trade has made us better off, too.

There's no sleight of hand going on here; the gains from trade are due to specialization in production. When each country goes it alone, it's a prisoner of its own production possibilities curve; it must make production decisions on the basis of its own consumption desires. When international trade is permitted, however, each country can concentrate on the exploitation of its production capabilities. ***Each country produces those goods it makes best and then trades with other countries to acquire the goods it desires to consume.***

The resultant specialization increases total world output. In the process, each country is able to escape the confines of its own production possibilities curve, to reach beyond it for a larger basket of consumption goods. ***When a country engages in international trade, its consumption possibilities always exceed its production possibilities.*** These enhanced consumption possibilities are emphasized by the positions of points *N* and *M outside* the production possibilities curves (Figure 20.2). If it weren't possible for countries to increase their consumption by trading, there'd be no incentive for trading, and thus no trade.

Mutual Gains

PURSUIT OF COMPARATIVE ADVANTAGE

Although international trade can make everyone better off, it's not so obvious which goods should be traded, or on what terms. In our previous illustration, the United States ended up trading bread for wine in terms that were decidedly favorable to us. Why did we export bread rather than wine, and how did we end up getting such a good deal?

The decision to export bread is based on **comparative advantage,** that is, the *relative* cost of producing different goods. Recall that we can produce a maximum of 100 zillion loaves of bread per year or 50 zillion barrels of wine. Thus the domestic **opportunity cost** of producing 100 zillion loaves of bread is the 50 zillion barrels of wine we forsake in order to devote our resources to bread production. In fact, at every point

comparative advantage: The ability of a country to produce a specific good at a lower opportunity cost than its trading partners.

Opportunity Costs

opportunity cost: The most desired goods or services that are forgone in order to obtain something else.

on the U.S. production possibilities curve (Figure 20.2*a*), the opportunity cost of a loaf of bread is $1/2$ barrel of wine. We're effectively paying half a barrel of wine to get a loaf of bread.

Although the cost of bread production in the United States might appear outrageous, even higher opportunity costs prevail in France. According to Figure 20.2*b,* the opportunity cost of producing a loaf of bread in France is a staggering 4 barrels of wine. To produce a loaf of bread, the French must use factors of production that could otherwise be used to produce 4 barrels of wine.

A comparison of the opportunity costs prevailing in each country exposes the nature of comparative advantage. The United States has a comparative advantage in bread production because less wine has to be given up to produce bread in the United States than in France. In other words, the opportunity costs of bread production are lower in the United States than in France. *Comparative advantage refers to the relative (opportunity) costs of producing particular goods.*

A country should specialize in what it's *relatively* efficient at producing, that is, goods for which it has the lowest opportunity costs. In this case, the United States should produce bread because its opportunity cost ($1/2$ barrel of wine) is less than France's (4 barrels of wine). Were you the production manager for the whole world, you'd certainly want each country to exploit its relative abilities, thus maximizing world output. Each country can arrive at that same decision itself by comparing its own opportunity costs to those prevailing elsewhere. *World output, and thus the potential gains from trade, will be maximized when each country pursues its comparative advantage.* Each country does so by exporting goods that entail relatively low domestic opportunity costs and importing goods that involve relatively high domestic opportunity costs.

Absolute Costs Don't Count

absolute advantage: The ability of a country to produce a specific good with fewer resources (per unit of output) than other countries.

In assessing the nature of comparative advantage, notice that we needn't know anything about the actual costs involved in production. Have you seen any data suggesting how much labor, land, or capital is required to produce a loaf of bread in either France or the United States? For all you and I know, the French may be able to produce both a loaf of bread and a barrel of wine with fewer resources than we're using. Such an **absolute advantage** in production might exist because of their much longer experience in cultivating both grapes and wheat, or simply because they have more talent.

We can envy such productivity, and even try to emulate it, but it shouldn't alter our production or trade decisions. All we really care about are *opportunity costs*—what we have to give up in order to get more of a desired good. If we can get a barrel of wine for less bread in trade than in production, we have a comparative advantage in producing bread. As long as we have a *comparative* advantage in bread production we should exploit it. It doesn't matter to us whether France could produce either good with fewer resources. For that matter, even if France had an absolute advantage in *both* goods, we'd still have a *comparative* advantage in bread production, as we've already confirmed. The absolute costs of production were omitted from the previous illustration because they were irrelevant.

To clarify the distinction between absolute advantage and comparative advantage, consider this example. When Charlie Osgood joined the Willamette Warriors football team, he was the fastest runner ever to play football in Willamette. He could also throw the ball farther than most people could see. In other words, he had an *absolute advantage* in both throwing and running that made all other football players look like second-string water boys. Without extolling Charlie's prowess any further, let it stand that Charlie would have made the greatest quarterback *or* the greatest end ever to play football. *Would have.* The problem was that he could play only one position at a time, just as our resources can be used to produce only one good at a time. Thus the Willamette coach had to play Charlie either as a quarterback or as an end. He reasoned that Charlie could throw only a bit farther than some of the other top quarterbacks but could far outdistance all the other ends. In other words, Charlie had a *comparative advantage* in running and was assigned to play as an end.

TERMS OF TRADE

It definitely pays to pursue one's comparative advantage by specializing in production. It may not yet be clear, however, how we got such a good deal with France. We're clever traders, but beyond that, is there any way to determine the **terms of trade,** the quantity of good *A* that must be given up in exchange for good *B*? In our previous illustration, the terms of trade were very favorable to us; we exchanged only 6 zillion loaves of bread for 20 zillion barrels of wine. The terms of trade were thus 6 loaves = 20 barrels.

terms of trade: The rate at which goods are exchanged; the amount of good *A* given up for good *B* in trade.

The terms of trade with France were determined by our offer and France's ready acceptance. But why did France accept those terms? France was willing to accept our offer because the terms of trade permitted France to increase its wine consumption without giving up any bread consumption. Our offer of 6 loaves for 20 barrels was an improvement over France's domestic opportunity costs. France's domestic possibilities required it to give up 24 barrels of wine in order to produce 6 loaves of bread (see Figure 20.2*b*). Getting bread via trade was simply cheaper for France than producing bread at home. France ended up with an extra 4 zillion barrels of wine.

Our first clue to the terms of trade, then, lies in each country's domestic opportunity costs. *A country won't trade unless the terms of trade are superior to domestic opportunities.* In our example, the opportunity cost of 1 barrel of wine in the United States is 2 loaves of bread. Accordingly, we won't export bread unless we get at least 1 barrel of wine in exchange for every 2 loaves of bread we ship overseas.

All countries want to gain from trade. Hence we can predict that *the terms of trade between any two countries will lie somewhere between their respective opportunity costs in production.* That is, a loaf of bread in international trade will be worth at least $1/2$ barrel of wine (the U.S. opportunity cost) but no more than 4 barrels (the French opportunity cost). In our example, the terms of trade ended up at 1 loaf = 3.33 barrels (that is, at 6 loaves = 20 barrels). This represented a very large gain for the United States and a small gain for France. Figure 20.3 on the following page illustrates this outcome and several other possibilities.[1]

Limits to the Terms of Trade

The Role of Markets and Prices

Relatively little trade is subject to such direct negotiations between countries. More often than not, the decision to import or export a particular good is left up to the market decisions of individual consumers and producers.

Individual consumers and producers aren't much impressed by such abstractions as comparative advantage. Market participants tend to focus on prices, always trying to allocate their resources in order to maximize profits or personal satisfaction. Consumers tend to buy the products that deliver the most utility per dollar of expenditure, while producers try to get the most output per dollar of cost. Everybody's looking for a bargain.

So what does this have to do with international trade? Well, suppose that Henri, an enterprising Frenchman, visited the United States before the advent of international trade and observed our market behavior. He noticed that bread was relatively cheap, while wine was relatively expensive—the opposite of the price relationship prevailing in France. These price comparisons brought to his mind the opportunity for making a fast franc. All he had to do was bring over some French wine and trade it in the United

---

[1]The kink in the consumption possibilities curve at point *Y* occurs because France is unable to produce more than 60 zillion barrels of wine.

FIGURE 20.3
Searching for the Terms of Trade

Assume the United States can produce 100 zillion loaves of bread per year (point *A*). If we reduce output to only 85 zillion loaves, we could move to point *X*. At point *X* we have 7.5 zillion barrels of wine and 85 zillion loaves of bread.

Trade increases consumption possibilities. If we continued to produce 100 zillion loaves of bread, we could trade 15 zillion loaves to France in exchange for as much as 60 zillion barrels of wine. This would leave us *producing* at point *A* but *consuming* at point *Y*. At point *Y* we have more wine and no less bread than we had at point *X*.

A country will end up on its consumption possibilities curve only if it gets *all* the gains from trade. It will remain on its production possibilities curve only if it gets *none* of the gains from trade. The terms of trade determine how the gains from trade are distributed, and thus at what point in the shaded area each country ends up.

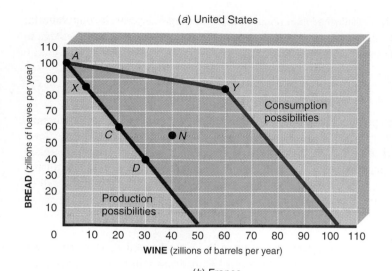

(a) United States

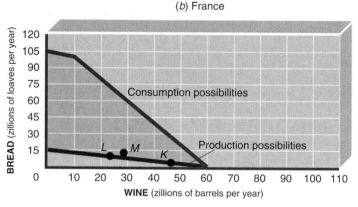

(b) France

States for a large quantity of bread. Then he could return to France and exchange the bread for a greater quantity of wine. *Alors!* Were he to do this a few times, he'd amass substantial profits.

Henri's entrepreneurial exploits won't only enrich him but will also move each country toward its comparative advantage. The United States ends up exporting bread to France and France ends up exporting wine to the United States, exactly as the theory of comparative advantage suggests. The activating agent isn't the Ministry of Trade and its 620 trained economists, but simply one enterprising French trader. He's aided and encouraged, of course, by consumers and producers in each country. American consumers are happy to trade their bread for his wines. They thereby end up paying less for wine (in terms of bread) than they'd otherwise have to. In other words, the terms of trade Henri offers are more attractive than the prevailing (domestic) relative prices. On the other side of the Atlantic, Henri's welcome is equally warm. French consumers are able to get a better deal by trading their wine for his imported bread than by trading with the local bakers.

Even some producers are happy. The wheat farmers and bakers in the United States are eager to deal with Henri. He's willing to buy a lot of bread and even to pay a premium price for it. Indeed, bread production has become so profitable in the United States that a lot of people who used to grow and mash grapes are now growing wheat and kneading dough. This alters the mix of U.S. output in the direction of more bread, exactly as suggested in Figure 20.2a.

In France the opposite kind of production shift is taking place. French wheat farmers are planting more grape vines so they can take advantage of Henri's generous purchases. Thus Henri is able to lead each country in the direction of its comparative advantage, while raking in a substantial profit for himself along the way.

Where the terms of trade and the volume of exports and imports end up depends partly on how good a trader Henri is. It will also depend on the behavior of the thousands of individual consumers and producers who participate in the market exchanges. In other words, trade flows depend on both the supply and the demand for bread and wine in each country. ***The terms of trade, like the price of any good, depends on the willingness of market participants to buy or sell at various prices.***

PROTECTIONIST PRESSURES

Although the potential gains from world trade are impressive, not everyone will smile at the Franco-American trade celebration. On the contrary, some people will be very upset about the trade routes that Henri has established. They'll not only boycott the celebration but actively seek to discourage us from continuing to trade with France.

Consider, for example, the winegrowers in western New York. Do you think they're going to be very happy about Henri's entrepreneurship? Americans can now buy wine more cheaply from France than they can from New York. Before long we may hear talk about unfair foreign competition or about the greater nutritional value of American grapes (see NEWS). The New York winegrowers may also emphasize the importance of maintaining an adequate grape supply and a strong wine industry at home, just in case of nuclear war.

Joining with the growers will be the farm workers and the other producers and merchants whose livelihood depends on the New York wine industry. If they're clever enough, the growers will also get the governor of the state to join their demonstration. After all, the governor must recognize the needs of his people, and his people definitely don't include the wheat farmers in Kansas who are making a bundle from international trade. New York consumers are of course benefiting from lower wine prices, but they're unlikely to demonstrate over a few cents a bottle. On the other hand, those few extra pennies translate into millions of dollars for domestic wine producers.

The wheat farmers in France are no happier about international trade than are the winegrowers in the United States. They'd dearly love to sink all those boats bringing wheat from America, thereby protecting their own market position.

Microeconomic Pressures

IN THE NEWS

Whining over Wine

A new type of wine bar has sprung up on Capitol Hill, and it's not likely to tickle the palate of a dedicated oenophile. California wine makers are hawking a bill that could slap higher tariffs on imported wine, and Congress shows some sign of becoming intoxicated with what the wine makers have to offer. First introduced last summer, the Wine Equity Act, as the measure is called, is already sponsored by 345 Congressmen and 60 Senators.

The wine makers aren't putting all their grapes into one bottle. Behind the scenes they have been making common cause with the American Grape Growers Alliance for Fair Trade, a group that represents many of the farmer cooperatives that supply domestic wineries. In a suit they filed with the Commerce Department and International Trade Commission in January, the growers complained that the Europeans, and particularly the Italians, are unfairly subsidizing the wine producers. If their suit is upheld, the ITC could impose stiff duties on the imports. The importers say there is no good evidence of substantial government subsidies.

Fortune, Feb. 20, 1984, p. 41. © 1984 Time Inc. All rights reserved. www.fortune.com

Analysis: Although trade increases consumption possibilities, imports typically compete with a domestic industry. The affected industries will try to restrict imports in order to preserve their own jobs and incomes.

If we're to make sense of trade policies, then, we must recognize one central fact of life: Some producers have a vested interest in restricting international trade. In particular, *workers and producers who compete with imported products—who work in import-competing industries—have an economic interest in restricting trade.* This helps explain why GM, Ford, and Chrysler are unhappy about auto imports and why workers in Massachusetts want to end the importation of Italian shoes. It also explains why textile producers in South Carolina think Taiwan and Korea are behaving irresponsibly when they sell cotton shirts and dresses in the United States.

Although imports typically mean fewer jobs and less income for some domestic industries, exports represent increased jobs and income for other industries. Producers and workers in export industries gain from trade. Thus on a microeconomic level, there are identifiable gainers and losers from international trade. *Trade not only alters the mix of output but also redistributes income from import-competing industries to export industries.* This potential redistribution is the source of political and economic friction.

We must be careful to note, however, that the microeconomic gains from trade are greater than the microeconomic losses. It's not simply a question of robbing Peter to enrich Paul. We must remind ourselves that consumers in general enjoy a higher standard of living as a result of international trade. As we saw earlier, trade increases world efficiency and total output. Accordingly, we end up slicing up a larger pie rather than just reslicing the same old smaller pie.

The gains from trade will mean nothing to workers who end up with a smaller slice of the (larger) pie. It's important to remember, however, that the gains from trade are large enough to make everybody better off. Whether we actually choose to distribute the gains from trade in this way is a separate question, to which we shall return shortly. Note here, however, that *trade restrictions designed to protect specific microeconomic interests reduce the total gains from trade.* Trade restrictions leave us with a smaller pie to split up.

Additional Pressures

Import-competing industries are the principal obstacle to expanded international trade. Selfish micro interests aren't the only source of trade restrictions, however. Other arguments are also used to restrict trade.

National Security. The national security argument for trade restrictions is twofold. We can't depend on foreign suppliers to provide us with essential defense-related goods, it is said, because that would leave us vulnerable in time of war. The machine tool industry used this argument to protect itself from imports. In 1991 the Pentagon again sided with the toolmakers, citing the need for the United States to "gear up military production quickly in case of war," a contingency that couldn't be assured if weapons manufacturers relied on imported lathes, milling machines, and other tools.

The second part of the national security argument relates to our export of defense-related goods. There's some doubt about the wisdom of shipping nuclear submarines or long-range missiles to a potential enemy, even for a high price. But here also the argument can be overextended as when we forbade the export to the former Soviet Union of sugar-coated cereals and of machinery for making pantyhose.

dumping: The sale of goods in export markets at prices below domestic prices.

Dumping. Another argument against free trade arises from the practice of **dumping.** Foreign producers "dump" their goods when they sell them in the United States at prices lower than those prevailing in their own country, perhaps even below the costs of production.

Dumping may be unfair to import-competing producers, but it isn't necessarily unwelcome to the rest of us. As long as foreign producers continue dumping, we're getting foreign products at very low prices. How bad can that be?! There's a legitimate worry, however. Foreign producers might hold prices down only until domestic producers are driven out of business. Then we might be compelled to pay the foreign producers higher prices for their products. In that case, dumping could consolidate market power and lead to monopoly-type pricing. The fear of dumping, then, is analogous to the fear of predatory pricing.

The potential costs of dumping are serious. It's not always easy to determine when dumping occurs, however. Those who compete with imports have an uncanny ability to associate any and all low prices with predatory dumping. Low import prices may also reflect greater productivity and lower costs. Lower import prices may also result from a drop in the value of the exporting country's currency. Thus responsible policy-makers must take special care to confirm that dumping has occurred before attempting to restrict trade. If it has, taxes or penalties can be imposed on the foreign producer. This is what Japan did when it concluded that Chinese producers were dumping steel ore (see WORLD VIEW).

Infant Industries. Dumping threatens to damage already established domestic industries. Even normal import prices, however, may make it difficult or impossible for a new domestic industry to develop. Infant industries are often burdened with abnormally high startup costs. These high costs may arise from the need to train a whole workforce and the expenses of establishing new marketing channels. With time to grow, however, an infant industry might experience substantial cost reductions and establish a comparative advantage. When this is the case, trade restrictions might help nurture an industry in its infancy. Trade restrictions are justified, however, only if there's tangible evidence that the industry can develop a comparative advantage reasonably quickly.

Improving the Terms of Trade. A final argument for restricting trade rests on how the gains from trade are distributed. As we observed, the distribution of the gains from trade depends on the terms of trade. If we were to buy fewer imports, foreign producers might lower their prices. If that happened, the terms of trade would move in our favor, and we'd end up with a larger share of the gains from trade.

One way to bring about this sequence of events is to put restrictions on imports, making it more difficult or expensive for Americans to buy foreign products. Such

WORLD VIEW

Japan Accuses China of Dumping, Will Impose Duties

TOKYO—For years, Japan has been accused of illegally "dumping" underpriced products on foreign markets. Now, for the first time, Tokyo is turning the tables, with dumping charges of its own.

On Friday, Japan's government said it will impose punitive duties on cheap Chinese steelmaking materials. . . .

MITI will impose duties of between 4.5% and 27.2% on ferrosilicon manganese exported by more than 100 Chinese producers. In 1991, China shipped to Japan 135,000 metric tons of the material, valued at $70 million.

MITI ruled that the Chinese exporters had hurt Japanese makers by unfairly underpricing their ferrosilicon manganese.

Chinese makers increased their share of Japan's market for the material to 39% in 1991 from 17% in 1989. . . .

Friday's decision was the first time Japan decided to impose dumping duties, but it has investigated dumping charges three times before, twice against South Korean textile exporters and once against Norwegian and French ferrosilicon makers.

—Jacob M. Schlesinger and Masayoshi Kanabayashi

The Wall Street Journal, Feb. 1, 1993, p. A6. Reprinted by permission of *The Wall Street Journal,* © 1993 Dow Jones & Company, Inc. All Rights Reserved Worldwide. www.wsj.com

Analysis: "Dumping" means that a foreign producer is selling exports at prices below cost or below prices in the home market. Dumping puts import-competing industries at a competitive disadvantage.

restrictions will reduce the volume of imports, thereby inducing foreign producers to lower their prices. Unfortunately, this kind of stratagem is available to everyone, so our trading partners are likely to follow suit. Retaliatory restrictions on imports, each designed to improve the terms of trade, will ultimately eliminate all trade and therewith all the gains people were competing for in the first place.

BARRIERS TO TRADE

The microeconomic losses associated with imports give rise to a constant clamor for trade restrictions. People whose jobs and incomes are threatened by international trade tend to organize quickly and air their grievances. The NEWS below depicts the efforts of farmers in Montana and North Dakota to limit imports of Canadian wheat and livestock. They hope to convince Congress to impose restrictions on imports. More often than not, Congress grants the wishes of these well-organized and well-financed special interests.

Embargoes

embargo: A prohibition on exports or imports.

The sure-fire way to restrict trade is simply to eliminate it. To do so, a country need only impose an embargo on exports of imports, or both. An **embargo** is nothing more than a prohibition against trading particular goods.

In 1951, Senator Joseph McCarthy convinced the U.S. Senate to impose an embargo on Soviet mink, fox, and five other furs. He argued that such imports helped finance world communism. Senator McCarthy also represented the state of Wisconsin, where most U.S. minks are raised. The Reagan administration tried to end the fur embargo in 1987 but met with stiff congressional opposition. By then, U.S. mink ranchers had developed a $120 million per year industry.

The United States has also maintained an embargo on Cuban goods since 1959, when Fidel Castro took power there. This embargo severely damaged Cuba's sugar industry and deprived American smokers of the famed Havana cigars. It also fostered the development of U.S. sugar beet and tobacco farmers, who now have a vested interest in maintaining the embargo.

Tariffs

tariff: A tax (duty) imposed on imported goods.

A more frequent trade restriction is a **tariff,** a special tax imposed on imported goods. Tariffs, also called "customs duties," were once the principal source of revenue for governments. In the eighteenth century, tariffs on tea, glass, wine, lead, and paper were

IN THE NEWS

Farmers Stage Protests over Import of Products

Farmers claiming that imports of Canadian grain and other agricultural products are depressing U.S. prices threatened on Tuesday more blockades at border crossings unless the U.S. government acts to slow the flow of goods.

Farmers also want Canadian wheat and livestock tested for diseases and additives that are banned here.

Blockades and other protests have appeared at various border crossings in North Dakota and Montana for several days.

In Montana, 20 long-haul truckers were ticketed Monday, the first day of a state crackdown on border inspections. And farmers in North Dakota dumped grain on U.S. Highway 281, stopping truck traffic for eight hours.

"We've got an oversupply of wheat, hogs and cattle already," said Curt Trulson, a farmer in Ross, N.D. "We don't need any more foreign commodities."

USA Today, Sept. 23, 1998, p. 3A. Copyright 1998, USA TODAY. Reprinted with permission. www.usatoday.com

Analysis: Import-competing industries cite lots of reasons for restricting trade. Their primary concern, however, is to protect their own jobs and profits.

imposed on the American colonies to provide extra revenue for the British government. The tariff on tea led to the Boston Tea Party in 1773 and gave added momentum to the American independence movement. In modern times, tariffs have been used primarily as a means to protect specific industries from import competition. The current U.S. tariff code specifies tariffs on 9219 different products—nearly 50 percent of all U.S. imports. Although the average tariff is only 5 percent, individual tariffs vary widely. The tariff on cars, for example, is only 2.5 percent, while polyester sweaters confront a 34.6 percent tariff.

The attraction of tariffs to import-competing industries should be obvious. *A tariff on imported goods makes them more expensive to domestic consumers, and thus less competitive with domestically produced goods.* Among familiar tariffs in effect in 1999 were $0.50 per gallon on Scotch whiskey and $1.17 per gallon on imported champagne. These tariffs made American-produced spirits look relatively cheap and thus contributed to higher sales and profits for domestic distillers and grape growers. In the same manner, imported baby clothes are taxed at 12.5 percent, maple sugar at 9.4 percent, golf shoes at 8.5 percent, and imported sailboats at 1.5 percent. In each case, domestic producers in import-competing industries gain. The losers are domestic consumers, who end up paying higher prices. The tariff on orange juice, for example, raises the price of drinking orange juice by $525 million a year. Tariffs also hurt foreign producers, who lose business, and world efficiency, as trade is reduced.

"Beggar-Thy-Neighbor." Microeconomic interests aren't the only source of pressure for tariff protection. Imports represent leakage from the domestic circular flow and a potential loss of jobs at home. In the same way, exports represent increased aggregate demand and more jobs. From this perspective, the curtailment of imports looks like an easy solution to the problem of domestic unemployment. Just get people to "buy American" instead of buying imported products, so the argument goes, and domestic output and employment will surely expand. Congressman Willis Hawley used this argument in 1930. He assured his colleagues that higher tariffs would "bring about the growth and development in this country that has followed every other tariff bill, bringing as it does a new prosperity in which all people, in all sections, will increase their comforts, their enjoyment, and their happiness."[2] Congress responded by passing the Smoot-Hawley Tariff Act of 1930, which raised tariffs to an average of nearly 60 percent, effectively cutting off most imports.

Tariffs designed to expand domestic employment are more likely to fail than to succeed. If a tariff wall does stem the flow of imports, it effectively transfers the unemployment problem to other countries, a phenomenon often referred to as "beggar-thy-neighbor." The resultant loss of business in other countries leaves them less able to purchase our exports. The imported unemployment also creates intense political pressures for retaliatory action. That's exactly what happened in the 1930s. Other countries erected trade barriers to compensate for the effects of the Smoot-Hawley tariff. World trade subsequently fell from $60 billion in 1928 to a mere $25 billion in 1938. This trade contraction increased the severity of the Great Depression (see WORLD VIEW).

Tariffs reduce the flow of imports by raising import prices. The same outcome can be attained more directly by imposing import **quotas,** restrictions on the quantity of a particular good that may be imported. The United States limits the quantity of ice cream imported from Jamaica to 950 gallons a year. Only 1.4 million kilograms of Australian cheddar cheese and no more than 7730 tons of Haitian sugar can be imported. Textile quotas are imposed on every country that wants to ship textiles to the U.S. market. According to the U.S. Department of State, approximately 12 percent of our imports are subject to import quotas.

CYBER NOTE

The tariff schedule for imported products is available online from the U.S. Customs Service. Go to www.customs.ustreas.gov and click on "Importing and Exporting," then "Rulings & Regulations."

Quotas

quota: A limit on the quantity of a good that may be imported in a given time period.

[2]*The New York Times,* June 15, 1930, p. 25.

"Beggar-Thy-Neighbor" Policies in the 1930s

President Herbert Hoover, ignoring the pleas of 1028 econo-mists to veto it, signed the Smoot-Hawley Tariff Act on June 17, 1930. It was a hollow celebration. The day before, antic-ipating the signing, the stock market suffered its worst col-lapse since November 1929, and the law quickly helped push the Great Depression deeper.

The new tariffs, which by 1932 rose to an all-time high of 59 percent of the average value of imports (today it's 5 per-cent), were designed to save American jobs by restricting for-eign competition. Economists warned that angry nations would retaliate, and they did.

- Spain passed the Wais tariff in July in reaction to U.S. tar-iffs on grapes, oranges, cork, and onions.
- Switzerland, objecting to new U.S. tariffs on watches, em-broideries, and shoes, boycotted American exports.
- Italy retaliated against tariffs on hats and olive oil with high tariffs on U.S. and French automobiles in June 1930.

- Canada reacted to high duties on many food products, logs, and timber by raising tariffs threefold in August 1932.
- Australia, Cuba, France, Mexico, and New Zealand also joined in the tariff wars.

From 1930 to 1931 U.S. imports dropped 29 percent, but U.S. exports fell even more, 33 percent, and continued their collapse to a modern-day low of $2.4 billion in 1933. World trade contracted by similar proportions, spreading unem-ployment around the globe.

In 1934 the U.S. Congress passed the Reciprocal Trade Agreements Act to empower the president to reduce tariffs by half the 1930 rates in return for like cuts in foreign duties on U.S. goods. The "beggar-thy-neighbor" policy was dead. Since then, the nations of the world have been reducing tariffs and other trade barriers.

World Bank, *World Development Report 1987;* and *The Wall Street Jour-nal,* Apr. 28, 1989. www.worldbank.org; www.wsj.com

Analysis: Tariffs inflict harm on foreign producers. If foreign countries retaliate with tariffs of their own, world trade will shrink and unemployment will increase in all countries.

Comparative Effects

equilibrium price: The price at which the quantity of a good de-manded in a given time period equals the quantity supplied.

Quotas, like all barriers to trade, reduce world efficiency and invite retaliatory action. Moreover, their impact can be even more damaging than tariffs. To see this, we may compare market outcomes in four different contexts: no trade, free trade, tariff-restricted trade, and quota-restricted trade.

Figure 20.4*a* depicts the supply-and-demand relationships that would prevail in an economy that imposed a trade *embargo* on foreign textiles. In this situation, the **equi-librium price** of textiles is completely determined by domestic demand and supply curves. The no-trade equilibrium price is p_1, and the quantity of textiles consumed is q_1.

Suppose now that the embargo is lifted. The immediate effect of this decision will be a rightward shift of the market supply curve, as foreign supplies are added to do-mestic supplies (Figure 20.4*b*). If an unlimited quantity of textiles can be bought in world markets at a price of p_2, the new supply curve will look like S_2 (infinitely elas-tic at p_2). The new supply curve (S_2) intersects the old demand curve (D_1) at a new equilibrium price of p_2 and an expanded consumption of q_2. At this new equilibrium, domestic producers are supplying the quantity q_d while foreign producers are supply-ing the rest ($q_2 - q_d$). Comparing the new equilibrium to the old one, we see that *free trade results in reduced prices and increased consumption.*

Domestic textile producers are unhappy, of course, with their foreign competition. In the absence of trade, the domestic producers would sell more output (q_1) and get higher prices (p_1). Once trade is opened up, the willingness of foreign producers to sell unlimited quantities of textiles at the price p_2 puts a lid on domestic prices.

Figure 20.4*c* illustrates what would happen to prices and sales if the United Textile Producers were successful in persuading the government to impose a tariff. Assume that the tariff raises imported textile prices from p_2 to p_3, making it more difficult for foreign producers to undersell domestic producers. Domestic production expands from

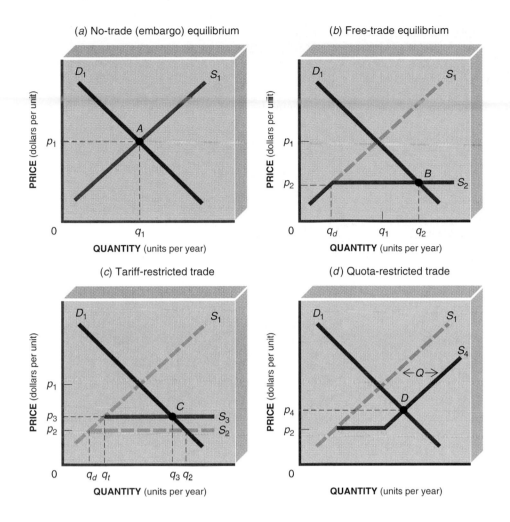

(a) No-trade (embargo) equilibrium

(b) Free-trade equilibrium

(c) Tariff-restricted trade

(d) Quota-restricted trade

FIGURE 20.4
The Impact of Trade Restrictions

In the *absence of trade,* the domestic price and sales of a good will be determined by domestic supply and demand curves (point *A* in part *a*). Once trade is permitted, the market supply curve will be altered by the availability of imports. With *free trade* and unlimited availability of imports at price p_2, a new market equilibrium will be established at world prices (point *B*).

Tariffs raise domestic prices and reduce the quantity sold (point *C*). *Quotas* put an absolute limit on imported sales and thus give domestic producers a great opportunity to raise the market price (point *D*).

q_d to q_1, imports are reduced from $q_2 - q_d$ to $q_3 - q_t$, and the market price of textiles rises. Domestic textile producers are clearly better off, whereas consumers and foreign producers are worse off. In addition, the U.S. Treasury will collect increased tariff revenues.

Now consider the impact of a textile *quota.* Suppose we eliminate tariffs but decree that imports can't exceed the quantity Q. Because the quantity of imports can never exceed Q, the supply curve is effectively shifted to the right by that amount. The new curve S_4 (Figure 20.4*d*) indicates that no imports will occur below the world price p_2 and above that price the quantity Q will be imported. Thus the *domestic* demand curve determines subsequent prices. Foreign producers are precluded from selling greater quantities as prices rise further. This outcome is in marked contrast to that of tariff-restricted trade (Figure 20.4*c*), which at least permits foreign producers to respond to rising prices. Accordingly, **quotas are a greater threat to competition than tariffs, because quotas preclude additional imports at any price.** The actual quotas on textile imports raise the prices of shirts, towels, and other textile products by 58 percent. As a result, a $10 shirt ends up costing consumers $15.80. All told, U.S. consumers end up paying an extra $25 billion a year for textile products. The next WORLD VIEW explains how quotas also prop up sugar prices and who benefits from that policy.

A slight variant of quotas has been used in recent years. Rather than impose quotas on imports, the U.S. government asks foreign producers to "voluntarily" limit their exports. These so-called **voluntary restraint agreements** have been negotiated with producers in Japan, South Korea, Taiwan, China, the European Union, and other countries.

CYBER NOTE

Differing views on the cost of sugar quotas are offered by Public Voice for Food and Health Policy at www.publicvoicedc.com and by the Sugar Alliance at www.sugaralliance.com.

voluntary restraint agreement (VRA): An agreement to reduce the volume of trade in a specific good; a "voluntary" quota.

Voluntary Restraint Agreements

"TELL ME AGAIN HOW THE QUOTAS ON JAPANESE CARS HAVE PROTECTED US"

—from HERBLOCK AT LARGE (Pantheon Books, 1987).

Analysis: Trade restrictions that protect import-competing industries also raise consumer prices.

WORLD VIEW

Sugar Quota a Sour Deal

Very little sugar cane is grown in the United States. Most domestically produced sugar comes from beet sugar. The rest of our sugar is imported from tropical countries.

The 12,000 domestic beet sugar growers have convinced Congress to protect their industry to ensure a secure supply of sugar in the event of a war. The U.S. Department of Agriculture guarantees the beet sugar growers a minimum of 18 cents per pound for their output. To keep prices at that level, the U.S. Congress limits sugar imports. As a result, domestic sugar prices are typically twice as high as world sugar prices. In 1998, the price of sugar in U.S. markets was 22 cents per pound, versus only 7 cents in world markets. This price

difference cost American consumers over $1.2 billion in 1998 alone. Foreign producers and workers who were excluded from the U.S. market also lost out. Between 1983 and 1990, over 400,000 workers in Caribbean nations lost their jobs as a result of shrinking U.S. sugar quotas.

Who benefits from these sugar quotas? The list includes

- The 12,000 American beet sugar farmers
- Producers of sugar substitutes (such as corn syrups)
- Those nations and producers that get a share of the U.S. quota
- Former and current members of Congress who receive fees and campaign contributions for perpetuating the sugar quota system

Analysis: Import quotas preclude increased foreign competition when domestic prices rise. Protected domestic producers enjoy higher prices and profits while consumers pay higher prices.

Korea, for example, agreed to reduce its annual shoe exports to the United States from 44 million pairs to 33 million pairs. Taiwan reduced its shoe exports from 156 million pairs to 122 million pairs per year. In 1989 China agreed to slow its exports of clothing, limiting its sales growth to 3 percent a year. For their part, the Japanese agreed to reduce sales of color TV sets in the United States from 2.8 million to 1.75 million per year. In 1989 President Bush extended voluntary restraint agreements on foreign steel exports, limiting imported steel to 18.4 percent of total U.S. sales. In 1996 President Clinton forced Canada to limit its exports of lumber to the United States, and in 1999 Russia reluctantly agreed to limit steel exports.

All these "voluntary export restraints," as they're often called, represent an informal type of quota. The only difference is that they're negotiated rather than imposed. But these differences are lost on consumers, who end up paying higher prices for these goods. The voluntary limit on Japanese auto exports to the United States alone cost consumers $15.7 billion in only 4 years.

Nontariff Barriers

Embargoes, export controls, tariffs, and quotas are the most visible barriers to trade, but they're only the tip of the iceberg. Indeed, the variety of protectionist measures that have been devised is testimony to the ingenuity of the human mind. At the turn of the century, the Germans were committed to a most-favored-nation policy, a policy of extending equal treatment to all trading partners. The Germans, however, wanted to lower the tariff on cattle imports from Denmark without extending the same break to Switzerland. Such a preferential tariff would have violated the most-favored-nation policy. Accordingly, the Germans created a new and higher tariff on "brown and dappled cows reared at a level of at least 300 meters above sea level and passing at least one month in every summer at an altitude of at least 800 meters." The new tariff was, of course, applied equally to all countries. But Danish cows never climb that high, so they weren't burdened with the new tariff.

With the decline in tariffs over the last 20 years, nontariff barriers have increased. The United States uses product standards, licensing restrictions, restrictive procurement practices, and other nontariff barriers to restrict roughly 15 percent of imports. Japan makes even greater use of nontariff barriers, restricting nearly 30 percent of imports in such ways. As the following WORLD VIEW notes, Japanese consumers pay dearly for these trade barriers.

WORLD VIEW

Japan's Price of Protection

One thing . . . often overlooked amid the volleys of rhetoric about our lopsided trade balance with Japan is the raw deal Japanese consumers are getting. According to a new report for the Institute for International Economics (IIE) by economists Yoko Sazanami, Shujiro Urata, and Hiroki Kawai, trade barriers cost Japanese consumers . . . between $75 billion and $110 billion in 1989, or between 3% and 4% of Japan's GNP. The industries getting the most protection are food and beverages, metals, machinery, chemicals, and textiles and apparel. On the whole, Japanese consumers effectively paid upwards of $600,000 for each job protected by barriers.

Fortune, Mar. 6, 1995, p. 48. © 1995 Time Inc. All rights reserved. www.fortune.com

Analysis: The cost of foreign trade barriers is largely borne by foreign consumers. They end up with a smaller selection of goods and with higher prices.

THE ECONOMY TOMORROW

An Increasingly Global Market

Proponents of free trade and representatives of special interests that profit from trade protection are in constant conflict. But most of the time the trade-policy deck seems stacked in favor of the special interests. Because the interests of import-competing firms and workers are highly concentrated, they're quick to mobilize politically. By contrast, the benefits of freer trade are less direct and spread over millions of consumers. As a consequence, the beneficiaries of freer trade are less likely to monitor trade policy—much less lobby actively to change it. Hence, the political odds favor the spread of trade barriers.

Multilateral Trade Pacts

Despite these odds, the long-term trend is toward *lowering* trade barriers, thereby increasing global competition. Two forces encourage this trend. The principal barrier to protectionist policies is worldwide recognition of the gains from freer trade. Since world nations now understand that trade barriers are ultimately self-defeating, they're more willing to rise above the din of protectionist cries and dismantle trade barriers. They diffuse political opposition by creating across-the-board trade pacts that seem to spread the pain (and gain) from freer trade across a broad swath of industries. Such pacts also incorporate multiyear timetables that give affected industries time to adjust.

The opposition of import-competing industries to these multilateral, multiyear trade pacts is countered by a second force: the interests of *export*-oriented industries and other multilateral firms. Barriers to auto imports from Japan may keep out cars produced by General Motors in that country. Tariffs on imported steel raise product costs for U.S.-based auto producers. Foreign retaliation to our trade barriers may hurt our own exports. Increasing awareness of such damage has created a political climate for freer trade.

Global Pacts: GATT and WTO

The granddaddy of the multilateral, multiyear free-trade pacts was the 1947 *General Agreement on Tariffs and Trade (GATT)*. Twenty-three nations pledged to reduce trade barriers and give all GATT nations equal access to their domestic markets.

Since the first GATT pact, seven more "rounds" of negotiations have expanded the scope of GATT: 117 nations signed the 1994 pact. As a result of these GATT pacts, average tariff rates in developed countries have fallen from 40 percent in 1948 to less than 4 percent today.

The 1994 GATT pact also created the *World Trade Organization (WTO)* to enforce free-trade rules. One of the first crises the WTO had to resolve was the "banana war" between the United States and Europe. The United States complained that the quotas of the European Union (EU) and its licensing rules (nontariff barriers) favored bananas imported from former colonies in Africa and the West Indies. American companies (Dole and Chiquita) were being unfairly handicapped in the 1.5 billion euro-banana market.

In September 1997 the WTO agreed that the EU's nontariff barriers on banana imports were discriminatory and ordered the EU nations to change them within 15 months. In January 1999, however, the United States complained that the new banana rules were no fairer than the old ones and threatened to retaliate with barriers against European exports. For the WTO the critical issue was who had the power to enforce free-trade rules: the WTO or industrial nations. On the brink of a "banana war," the EU revised its banana-licensing regulations a bit more and asked the WTO to resolve the 6-year-old dispute.

Regional Pacts: NAFTA and EU

Groups of nations have moved even faster toward open markets by developing regional trade pacts. In December 1992 the United States, Canada, and Mexico signed the *North American Free Trade Agreement (NAFTA)*, a 1000-page document covering more than 9000 products. The ultimate goal of NAFTA is to eliminate all trade barriers between these three countries. At the time of signing, intraregional tariffs averaged 11 percent

IN THE NEWS

NAFTA Reallocates Labor: Comparative Advantage at Work

More Jobs in These Industries		But . . .	Few Jobs in These Industries	
Agriculture	+10,600		Construction	−12,800
Metal products	+6,100		Medicine	−6,000
Electrical appliances	+5,200		Apparel	−5,900
Business services	+5,000		Lumber	−1,200
Motor vehicles	+5,000		Furniture	−400

Source: Congressional Budget Office.

The lowering of trade barriers between Mexico and the United States is changing the mix of output in both countries. New export opportunities create jobs in some industries while increased imports eliminate jobs in other industries. (Estimated gains and losses are during the first 5 years of NAFTA.)

Analysis: The specialization encouraged by free trade creates new jobs in export but reduces employment in import-competing industries. In the process, total world output increases.

in Mexico, 5 percent in Canada, and 4 percent in the United States. NAFTA requires that all tariffs between the three countries be eliminated within 15 years. The pact also requires the elimination of specific nontariff barriers.

The NAFTA-initiated reduction in trade barriers substantially increased trade flows between Mexico, Canada, and the United States. It also prompted a wave of foreign investment in Mexico, where both cheap labor and NAFTA access were available. Overall, NAFTA accelerated economic growth and reduced inflationary pressures in all three nations. Some industries (like construction and apparel) suffered from the freer trade, but others (like trucking, farming, and finance) reaped huge gains (see NEWS).

The *European Union (EU)* is another regional pact, but one that virtually eliminates national boundaries between 15 countries. The EU not only eliminates trade barriers but also enhances full intercountry mobility of workers and capital. In 1999, 11 of the EU nations also created a new currency (the euro) that will replace the German mark, the French franc, and other national currencies by 2002 (see WORLD VIEW, "What's in a Euro," in Chapter 21). In effect, Europe has become one large, unified market. As trade barriers continue to fall around the world, the global marketplace is likely to become more like an open bazaar as well. The resulting increase in competition should spur efficiency and growth in the economy tomorrow.

CYBER NOTE

To see how detailed a trade pact can be, access the NAFTA pact at www.nafta.net/naftagre.htm.

SUMMARY

- International trade permits each country to specialize in areas of relative efficiency, increasing world output. For each country, the gains from trade are reflected in consumption possibilities that exceed production possibilities.

- One way to determine where comparative advantage lies is to compare the quantity of good *A* that must be given up in order to get a given quantity of good *B* from domestic production. If the same quantity of *B* can be obtained for less *A* by engaging in world trade, we have a comparative advantage in the production of good *A*. Comparative advantage rests on a comparison of relative opportunity costs.

- The terms of trade—the rate at which goods are exchanged—are subject to the forces of international supply and demand. The terms of trade will lie somewhere between the opportunity costs of the trading partners. The terms of trade determine how the gains from trade are shared.
- Resistance to trade emanates from workers and firms that must compete with imports. Even though the country as a whole stands to benefit from trade, these individuals and companies may lose jobs and incomes in the process.
- Trade barriers take many forms. Embargoes are outright

prohibitions against import or export of particular goods. Quotas limit the quantity of a good imported or exported. Tariffs discourage imports by making them more expensive. Other nontariff barriers make trade too costly or time-consuming.

- Trade adjustment assistance is a mechanism for compensating people who incur economic losses as a result of international trade; it represents an alternative to trade restrictions.
- The World Trade Organization (WTO) seeks to reduce worldwide trade barriers. Regional accords such as the European Union (EU) and North American Free Trade Agreement (NAFTA) pursue similar objectives among fewer countries.

Key Terms

imports	comparative advantage	tariff
exports	opportunity cost	quota
trade deficit	absolute advantage	equilibrium price
trade surplus	terms of trade	voluntary restraint
production possibilities	dumping	agreement (VRA)
consumption possibilities	embargo	

Questions for Discussion

1. Suppose a lawyer can type faster than any secretary. Should the lawyer do her own typing? Can you demonstrate the validity of your answer?
2. What would be the effects of a law requiring bilateral trade balances?
3. If a nation exported much of its output but imported little, would it be better or worse off? How about the reverse, that is, exporting little but importing a lot?
4. How does international trade restrain the price behavior of domestic firms?
5. Suppose we refused to sell goods to any country that reduced or halted its exports to us. Who would benefit and who would lose from such retaliation? Can you suggest alternative ways to ensure import supplies?
6. Domestic producers often base their claim for import protection on the fact that workers in country X are paid substandard wages. Is this a valid argument for protection?
7. Based on the NEWS on page 415, how do U.S. furniture

manufacturers feel about NAFTA? How about farmers?
8. Who would gain or lose from the proposed Wine Equity Act? (See the NEWS page 405.)
9. What are the benefits of sugar quotas and auto VRAs? (See WORLD VIEW page 412). Could these goals be achieved more efficiently in other ways?
10. Web Activity How will NAFTA affect U.S. consumers? Find out the benefits for the United States at www.doc.gov/oca/nafta.htm. What additional information would you need to determine if the benefits are indeed as described?
11. Web Activity Find out about trade restrictions nearly every country uses at the Web site for the U.S. Department of State, Economic Policy and Trade Practices. Go to www.tradecompass.com/library/dos/ecopol. Choose one country for analysis. What type of trade restrictions does this country use? Who will benefit from these restrictions? Who might lose?

Problems for Chapter 20 appear at the back of the book.

International Finance

A sudden change in the value of the baht sparked an "Asian crisis" that sent shock waves all the way to Iowa hog farms. But many people there didn't even know what a baht was!

The Thai currency set off a global crisis in 1997–1998 that threw millions of people out of work, deprived millions more of basic necessities, sent world stock markets plunging, and destabilized governments. It also sent hog prices to a 40-year low, devastating farmers in the American Midwest. Besides not knowing that the baht is the national currency of Thailand, most people affected by the 1997–1998 crisis didn't have a clue as to how a change in the value of another currency could possibly affect Midwestern hog prices.

This chapter examines why and how changes in the value of national currencies can have such debilitating effects worldwide. In so doing, we focus on the following questions:

- What determines the value of one country's money as compared to the value of another's?
- What causes the international value of currencies to change?
- Should governments intervene to limit currency fluctuations?

EXCHANGE RATES: THE GLOBAL LINK

As we saw in Chapter 20, the United States exports and imports a staggering volume of goods and services. Although we trade with nearly 200 nations around the world, we seldom give much thought to where imports come from and much less to how we acquire them. Most of the time, all we want to know is which products are available and at what price.

Suppose you want to buy a Magnavox DVD player. You don't have to know that Magnavox players are produced by the Dutch company Philips Electronics. And you certainly don't have to fly to the Netherlands to pick it up. All you have to do is drive to the nearest electronics store; or you can just "click and buy" at the Internet's virtual mall.

But you may wonder how the purchase of an imported product was so simple. Dutch companies sell their products in euros, the new currency of Europe (see WORLD VIEW next page). But you purchase the DVD player in dollars. How is such an exchange possible?

There's a chain of distributions between your dollar purchase in the United States and the euro-denominated sale in the Netherlands. Somewhere along that

What's in a Euro?

European Union finance ministers met in Brussels yesterday and set the fixed conversion rates between the euro and currencies from the 11 nations participating in the shared new currency.

One Euro Is Worth:	
13.7603	Austrian shillings
40.3399	Belgian francs
2.203371	Dutch guilders
5.94573	Finnish markkaa
6.55957	French francs
1.95583	German marks
1,936.27	Italian lire
0.787564	Irish pounds
40.3399	Luxembourg francs
200.482	Portuguese escudos
166.386	Spanish pesetas

The U.S. dollar was set at $1.1685 to the euro. But that rate will begin to fluctuate when financial markets open Monday.

The Washington Post, Jan. 1, 1999, p.1. © 1998 The Washington Post. Reprinted with permission. www.washingtonpost.com

Analysis: In 1999 the euro became the common currency of 11 European nations. The U.S. price of European products now depends on the dollar price of the euro.

---

exchange rate: The price of one country's currency expressed in terms of another's; the domestic price of a foreign currency.

chain someone has to convert your dollars into euros. The critical question for everybody concerned is how many euros we can get for our dollars—that is, what the **exchange rate** is. If we can get 2 euros for every dollar, the exchange rate is 2 euros = 1 dollar. Alternatively, we could note that the price of a euro is 50 cents when the exchange rate is 2 to 1. Thus *an exchange rate is simply the price of one currency in terms of another.*

FOREIGN-EXCHANGE MARKETS

Most exchange rates are determined in foreign-exchange markets. Stop thinking of money as some sort of magical substance and instead view it as a useful commodity that can facilitate market exchanges. From that perspective, an exchange rate—the price of money—is subject to the same influences that determine all market prices: demand and supply.

The Demand for Dollars

When Daimler-Benz bought Chrysler in 1998, it paid $36 billion. When the Sony Corporation bought Columbia Pictures, it also needed dollars—over 3 billion of them! In both cases, the objective of the foreign investor was to acquire an American business. To attain their objectives, however, the buyers first had to buy *dollars.* The German and Japanese buyers had to exchange their own currency (marks and yen) for American dollars.

Canadian tourists also need American dollars. Few American restaurants or hotels will accept Canadian currency as payment for goods and services; they want to be paid in U.S. dollars. Accordingly, Canadian tourists must buy American dollars if they want to see the United States.

Europeans love iMac computers. The Apple Corporation, however, wants to be paid in U.S. dollars. Hence European consumers must exchange their currencies for U.S. dollars if they want an iMac. Individual consumers can spend francs, marks, lire, or the new euro at their local computer store. When they do so, however, they're initiating a series of market transactions that will end when Apple Corporation gets paid in U.S. dollars. In this case, some intermediary exchanges the European currency for American dollars.

Some foreign investors also buy U.S. dollars for speculative purposes. When the Russian ruble collapsed, American tourists could get great discounts from Russian vendors and restaurants by offering to pay with U.S. dollars. Russians feared that the value of the ruble would drop further and preferred to hold U.S. dollars. Barclay's Bank also speculates in dollars on occasions when it fears that the value of the British pound will drop.

All these motivations give rise to a demand for U.S. dollars. Specifically, *the market demand for U.S. dollars originates in*

- *Foreign demand for American exports*
- *Foreign demand for American investments*
- *Speculation*

Governments may also create a demand for dollars through currency "swaps" and other activities.

The Supply of Dollars

The *supply* of dollars arises from similar sources. On the supply side, however, it's Americans who are initiating the exchanges. Suppose you take a trip to Mexico. You'll need to buy Mexican pesos at some point. When you do, you'll be offering to *buy* pesos by offering to *sell* dollars. In other words, *the* **demand** *for foreign currency represents a* **supply** *of U.S. dollars.*

When Americans buy BMW cars, they also supply U.S. dollars. American consumers pay for their BMWs in dollars. Somewhere down the road, however, those dollars will be exchanged for European euros. At that exchange, dollars are being *supplied* and euros *demanded*.

American corporations demand foreign exchange too. General Motors builds cars in Germany, Coca-Cola produces Coke in China, Exxon produces and refines oil all over the world. In nearly every such case, the U.S. firm must first build or buy some plant and equipment, using another country's factors of production. This activity requires foreign currency and thus becomes another component of our demand for foreign currency.

We may summarize these market activities by noting that *the supply of dollars originates in*

- *American demand for imports*
- *American investments in foreign countries*
- *Speculation*

As on the demand side, government intervention can also contribute to the supply of dollars.

The Value of the Dollar

Whether American consumers will choose to buy a BMW depends partly on what the car costs. The price tag isn't always apparent in international transactions. Remember that the BMW producer and workers want to be paid in their own currency. Hence the *dollar* price of a BMW depends on two factors: (1) the German price of a BMW and

(2) the *exchange rate* between U.S. dollars and euros. Specifically, the U.S. price of a BMW is

$$\begin{matrix} \text{Dollar price} \\ \text{of BMW} \end{matrix} = \begin{matrix} \text{euro price} \\ \text{of BMW} \end{matrix} \times \begin{matrix} \text{dollar price} \\ \text{of euro} \end{matrix}$$

Suppose the BMW company is prepared to sell a BMW for 100,000 euros and that the current exchange rate is 2 euros = $1. At these rates, a BMW will cost you

$$\begin{matrix} \text{Dollar price} \\ \text{of BMW} \end{matrix} = 100{,}000 \text{ euros} \times \frac{\$1}{2 \text{ euros}}$$

$$= \$50{,}000$$

If you're willing to pay this much for a shiny new BMW, you may do so at current exchange rates.

Now suppose the exchange rate changes from 2 euros = $1 to 1 euro = $1. ***A higher dollar price for euros will raise the dollar costs of European goods.*** In this case, the dollar price of a euro increases from $0.50 to $1. At this new exchange rate, the BMW company is still willing to sell BMW's at 100,000 euros apiece. And German consumers continue to buy BMWs at that price. But this constant euro price now translates into a higher *dollar* price. Thus a BMW now costs you $100,000.

As the U.S. price of a BMW rises, the number of BMWs sold in the United States will decline. As BMW sales decline, the quantity of euros demanded may decline as well. Thus the quantity of foreign currency demanded declines when the exchange rate rises because foreign goods become more expensive and imports decline.[1] When the dollar price of European currencies actually increased in 1992, BMW decided to start producing cars in South Carolina. A year later Mercedes-Benz decided to produce cars in the United States as well. Sales of American-made BMWs and Mercedes don't depend on the exchange rate of the U.S. dollars.

The Supply Curve. These market responses suggest that the supply of dollars is upward-sloping. If the value of the dollar rises, Americans will be able to buy more euros. As a result, the dollar price of imported BMWs will decline. American consumers will respond by demanding more imports, thereby supplying a larger quantity of dollars. The supply curve in Figure 21.1 shows how the quantity of dollars supplied rises as the value of the dollar increases.

The Demand Curve. The demand for dollars can be explained in similar terms. Remember that the demand for dollars arises from the foreign demand for U.S. exports and investments. If the exchange rate moves from 2 euros = $1 to 1 euro = $1, the euro price of dollars will fall. As dollars become cheaper for Germans, all American exports effectively fall in price. Germans will buy more American products (including trips to DisneyWorld) and therefore demand a greater quantity of dollars. In addition, foreign investors will perceive in a cheaper dollar the opportunity to buy U.S. stocks, businesses, and property at fire-sale prices. Accordingly, they join foreign consumers in demanding more dollars. Not all these behavioral responses will occur overnight, but they're reasonably predictable over a brief period of time.

Equilibrium

equilibirum price: The price at which the quantity of a good demanded in a given time period equals the quantity supplied.

Given market demand and supply curves, we can predict the **equilibrium price** of any commodity, that is, the price at which the quantity demanded will equal the quantity supplied. This occurs in Figure 21.1 where the two curves cross. At that equilibrium, the value of the dollar (the exchange rate) is established. In this case, the euro price of the dollar turns out to be 0.86, the price prevailing in early 1999.

---

[1]The extent to which imports decline as the cost of foreign currency rises depends on the *price elasticity of demand.*

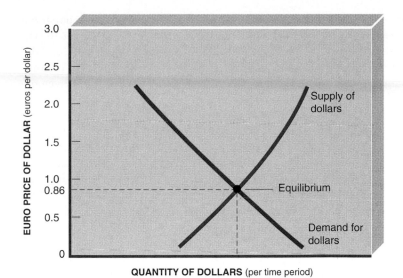

FIGURE 21.1
The Foreign-Exchange Market

The foreign-exchange market operates like other markets. In this case, the "good" bought and sold is dollars (foreign exchange). The price and quantity of dollars are determined by market supply and demand.

The value of the dollar can also be expressed in terms of other currencies. The WORLD VIEW displays a sampling of dollar exchange rates in 1999. (Notice how many Indonesian rupiah you could buy for $1 by then.) The *average* value of the dollar is a weighted mean of the exchange rates between the U.S. dollar and all these currencies. The value of the dollar is "high" when its foreign-exchange price is above recent levels, "low" when it is below recent averages.

WORLD VIEW

Foreign-Exchange Rates

Thursday, January 7, 1999—The New York foreign exchange selling rates below apply to trading among banks in amounts of $1 million and more, as quoted at 3 p.m. Eastern time by Dow Jones, Telerate, Inc., and other sources. Retail transactions provide fewer units of foreign currency per dollar.

Country	U.S. Dollar per Unit (dollar price of foreign currency)	Currency per U.S. Dollar (foreign price of U.S. dollar)
Brazil (real)	0.8269	1.2094
Britain (pound)	1.6548	0.6043
Canada (dollar)	0.6618	1.5111
China (renminbi)	0.1208	8.2788
Indonesia (rupiah)	0.0001	7962.50
Japan (yen)	0.0088	112.95
Mexico (peso)	0.1023	9.7750
Russia (ruble)	0.0428	23.390
Euroland (euro)	1.1626	0.8601

The Wall Street Journal, Jan. 7, 1999, p. A35. Reprinted by permission of *The Wall Street Journal,* © 1996 Dow Jones & Company, Inc. All Rights Reserved Worldwide. www.wsj.com

Analysis: The exchange rates between currencies are determined by supply and demand in foreign-exchange markets. The rates reported here represent the equilibrium exchange rates on a particular day.

The Balance of Payments

balance of payments: A summary record of a country's international economic transactions in a given period of time.

trade deficit: The amount by which the value of imports exceeds the value of exports in a given time period.

The equilibrium depicted in Figure 21.1 determines not only the *price* of the dollar but also a specific *quantity* of international transactions. Those transactions include the exports, imports, international investments, and other sources of dollar supply and demand. A summary of all those international money flows is contained in the **balance of payments**—an accounting statement of all international money flows in a given period of time.

Trade Balance. Table 21.1 depicts the U.S. balance of payments for 1998. Notice first how the millions of separate transactions are classified into a few summary measures. The trade balance is the difference between exports and imports of goods (merchandise) and services. In 1998 the United States imported $1.1 billion of goods and services but exported only $931 billion. This created a **trade deficit** of $169 billion. That trade deficit represents a net outflow of dollars to the rest of the world.

$$\text{Trade balance} = \text{exports} - \text{imports}$$

The excess supply of dollars created by the trade gap widened further by other net outflows. Profits from U.S. overseas investments ($243 billion) were less than the outgoing profits to foreign investors ($265 billion). The $22 billion difference in repatriated profits contributed to the net *supply* of dollars.

Current-Account Balance. The current-account balance is a subtotal in Table 21.1. It includes the merchandise, services, and investment balances as well as government grants and private transfers such as wages sent home by foreign citizens working in the United States.

$$\frac{\text{Current-account}}{\text{balance}} = \frac{\text{trade}}{\text{balance}} + \frac{\text{unilateral}}{\text{transfer}}$$

The current-account balance is the most comprehensive summary of our trade relations. As indicated in Table 21.1, the United States had a current-account deficit of $233 billion in 1998.

TABLE 21.1
The U.S. Balance of Payments, 1998

The balance of payments is a summary statement of a country's international transactions. The major components of that activity are the trade balance (merchandise exports minus merchandise imports), the current-account balance (trade, services, and transfers), and the capital-account balance. The net total of these balances must equal zero, since the quantity of dollars paid must equal the quantity received.

Item	Amount (in billions)
1. Merchandise exports	$671
2. Merchandise imports	(919)
3. Service exports	260
4. Service imports	(181)
Trade Balance (items 1–4)	−169
5. Income from U.S. overseas investments	243
6. Income outflow for foreign U.S. investments	(265)
7. Net U.S. government grants	(12)
8. Net private transfers and pensions	(30)
Current-Account Balance (items 1–8)	−233
9. U.S. capital inflow	564
10. U.S. capital outflow	(298)
11. Increase in U.S. official reserves	(8)
12. Increase in foreign official assets in U.S.	22
Capital-Account Balance (items 9–12)	236
13. Statistical discrepancy	3
Net Balance (items 1–13)	0

Source: U.S. Department of Commerce.

Capital-Account Balance. The current-account deficit is offset by the capital-account surplus. The capital-account balance takes into consideration assets bought and sold across international borders; that is,

$$\text{Capital-account balance} = \text{foreign purchases of U.S. asset} - \text{U.S. purchases of foreign assets}$$

As Table 21.1 shows, foreign consumers demanded $564 billion worth of dollars in 1998 to buy farms and factories as well as U.S. bonds, stocks, and other investments (item 9). This exceeded the flow of U.S. dollars going overseas to purchase foreign assets (item 10). In addition, the United States and foreign governments bought and sold dollars, creating an additional outflow of dollars (items 11 and 12).

The net capital inflows were essential in financing the U.S. trade deficit (negative trade balance). As in any market, the number of dollars demanded must equal the number of dollars supplied. Thus *the capital-account surplus must equal the current-account deficit.* In other words, there can't be any dollars left lying around unaccounted for. Item 13 in Table 21.1 reminds us that our accounting system isn't perfect—that we can't identify every transaction. Nevertheless, all the accounts must eventually "balance out":

$$\text{Net balance of payments} = \text{current-account balance} + \text{capital-account balance} = 0$$

That's the character of a market *equilibrium:* The quantity of dollars demanded equals the quantity of dollars supplied.

MARKET DYNAMICS

The interesting thing about markets isn't their character in equilibrium but the fact that prices and quantities are always changing in response to shifts in demand and supply. The U.S. demand for BMWs shifted overnight when Japan introduced a new line of sleek, competitively priced cars. The reduced demand for BMWs shifted the supply of dollars leftward. That supply shift raised the value of the dollar vis-á-vis the euro, as illustrated in Figure 21.2 on the next page. (It also increased the demand for Japanese yen, causing the yen value of the dollar to *fall.*)

Exchange-rate changes have their own terminology. **Depreciation** of a currency refers to the fact that one currency has become cheaper in terms of another currency. In our earlier discussion of exchange rates, for example, we assumed that the exchange rate between euros and dollars changed from 2 euros = $1 to 1 euro = $1, making the euro price of a dollar cheaper. In this case the dollar *depreciated* with respect to the euro.

The other side of depreciation is **appreciation,** an increase in value of one currency as expressed in another country's currency. *Whenever one currency depreciates, another currency must appreciate.* When the exchange rate changed from 2 euros = $1 to 1 euro = $1, not only did the euro price of a dollar fall, the dollar price of a euro rose. Hence the euro appreciated as the dollar depreciated.

Figure 21.3 following illustrates actual changes in exchange rates since 1973. During the 1970s the German mark and Japanese yen appreciated substantially relative to the U.S. dollar. At the same time, the British pound depreciated. Hence German and Japanese goods became more expensive, while the dollar price of British goods fell. These trends were reversed in the early 1980s, and then reversed again after 1985.

Also shown in Figure 21.3 is the trade-adjusted value of the U.S. dollar. This is the (weighted) average of all exchange rates for the dollar. In general, the dollar lost value in the late 1970s but recovered in the early 1980s. Between 1980 and 1984 the U.S. dollar appreciated over 50 percent. This appreciation greatly reduced the price of

CYBER NOTE

The latest statistics on the balance of payments are available from the Bureau of Economic Analysis at www.bea.doc.gov/bea/di1.htm.

Depreciation and Appreciation

depreciation (currency): A fall in the price of one currency relative to another.

appreciation: A rise in the price of one currency relative to another.

CYBER NOTE

How much is 100 Japanese yen worth in U.S. dollars? Find out at the currency converter at www.oanda.com/site/cc_index.shtml.

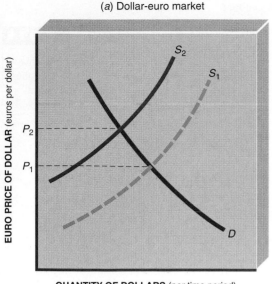

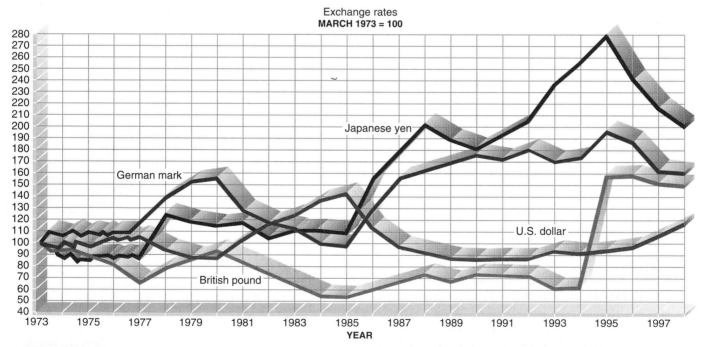

FIGURE 21.2
Shifts in Foreign-Exchange Markets

When the Japanese introduced luxury autos into the United States, the American demand for German cars fell. As a consequence, the supply of dollars in the dollar-euro market (part *a*) shifted to the left and the euro value of the dollar rose. At the same time, the increased American demand for Japanese cars shifted the dollar supply curve in the yen market (part *b*) to the right, reducing the yen price of the dollar.

FIGURE 21.3
Changing Exchange Rates

Since 1973, exchange rates have been flexible (not fixed). As a result, exchange rates have reflected international differences in unemployment, inflation, interest rates, and economic growth. The relatively strong growth of the U.S. economy in the mid-1980s raised the American demand for imports and, with it, the price of foreign currencies. This is reflected in the depreciation of the dollar, beginning in 1985. The trend reversed again in 1995.

Source: *Economic Report of the President, 1999.*

imports and thus increased their quantity. At the same time, the dollar appreciation raised the foreign price of U.S. exports and so reduced their volume. A huge trade deficit resulted.

The value of the dollar reversed course after 1985, falling sharply against the yen and the mark. This dollar depreciation set in motion forces that reduced the trade deficit in the late 1980s and early 1990s. Then the dollar appreciated again, slowing exports and increasing imports.

Market Forces

Exchange rates change for the same reasons that any market price changes: The underlying supply or demand (or both) has shifted. Among the more important sources of such shifts are

- *Relative income changes.* If incomes are increasing faster in country *A* than in country *B,* consumers in *A* will tend to spend more, thus increasing the demand for *B*'s exports and currency. *B*'s currency will appreciate.
- *Relative price changes.* If domestic prices are rising rapidly in country *A,* consumers will seek out lower-priced imports. The demand for *B*'s exports and currency will increase. *B*'s currency will appreciate.
- *Changes in product availability.* If country *A* experiences a disastrous wheat crop failure, it will have to increase its food imports. *B*'s currency will appreciate.
- *Relative interest rate changes.* If interest rates rise in country *A,* people in country *B* will want to move their deposits to *A.* Demand for *A*'s currency will rise and it will appreciate.
- *Speculation.* If speculators anticipate an increase in the price of *A*'s currency, for the preceding reasons or any other, they'll begin buying it, thus pushing its price up. *A*'s currency will appreciate.

foreign-exchange markets: Places where foreign currencies are bought and sold.

All these various changes are taking place every minute of every day, thus keeping **foreign-exchange markets** active. On an average day, over *$1 trillion* of foreign exchange is bought and sold in the market. Significant changes occur in currency values, however, only when several of these forces move in the same direction at the same time. This is what caused the Asian crisis of 1997–1998.

The Asian Crisis of 1997–1998

In July 1997, the Thai government decided the baht was overvalued and let market forces find a new equilibrium. Within days, the dollar prices of the baht plunged 25 percent. This sharp decline in the value of the Thai baht simultaneously increased the Thai price of the U.S. dollar. As a consequence, Thais could no longer afford to buy as many American products.

The devaluation of the baht had a domino effect on other Asian currencies. The plunge in the baht shook confidence in the Malaysian ringget, the Indonesian rupiah, and even the Korean won. People wanted to hold "hard" currencies like the U.S. dollar. As people rushed to buy U.S. dollars with their local currencies, the value of those currencies plunged. At one point the Indonesian rupiah had lost 80 percent of its dollar value, making U.S. exports five times more expensive for Indonesians. As a result, Indonesians could no longer afford to buy imported rice, machinery, cars, or pork. Indonesian students attending U.S. colleges could no longer afford to pay tuition (see WORLD VIEW). The sudden surge in prices and scarcity of goods led to street demonstrations and a change in government. Similar problems erupted throughout Southeast Asia.

The "Asian contagion" unfortunately wasn't confined to that area of the world. Hog farmers in the United States saw foreign demand for their pork evaporate. Koreans stopped taking vacations in Hawaii. Thai Airways canceled orders for Boeing jets. And Japanese consumers bought fewer Washington state apples and California oranges. Our fruit-growing states and many exporters in other nations lost sales. This loss of export markets slowed economic growth in the United States, Europe, Japan, and other nations.

CYBER NOTE

Check out the latest exchange rates for the euro and the rupiah at the New York Fed's Web site www.ny. frb.org/pihome/mktrates/forex12. shtml. By how much have the rates changed since January 1999 (see WORLD VIEW page 421)? Why?

Money Crisis Pulling Asian Students Home

The financial tsunami that swamped Asian economies in the last few months is sloshing back across the Pacific toward American colleges and universities, where thousands of Asian students are suddenly short of dollars.

Since last July, the Indonesian currency, the rupiah, has lost 80% of its value as measured against the U.S. dollar. A half-dozen Asian currencies have lost about half their value against the dollar.

That means, for example, that what would have been $20,000 in Korean money (the won) a year ago is now worth only $10,000. Consequently, Korean and Indonesian students—plus Malaysians, Thais, Singaporeans and Japanese—are struggling to pay their tuition bills. Some can't—so they're going home.

There are about 458,000 foreign students in the USA—about 3% of total higher education enrollment, according to the Institute of International Education, a nonprofit cultural exchange organization that conducts an annual census of foreign students. About 57% of the students are Asians.

USA Today, Feb. 18, 1998, p. 11A. Copyright 1998, USA TODAY. Reprinted with permission. www.usatoday.com

Analysis: When the foreign price of the U.S. dollar rises (dollar appreciation), American exports (including educational services) become more expensive, which causes a decline in enrollments (quantity demanded).

RESISTANCE TO EXCHANGE-RATE CHANGES

Given the scope and depth of the Asian crisis of 1997–1998, it's easy to understand why people crave *stable* exchange rates. The resistance to exchange-rate fluctuations originates in various micro and macro economic interests.

Micro Interests

The microeconomic resistance to changes in the value of the dollar arises from two general concerns. First, people who trade or invest in world markets want a solid basis for forecasting future costs, prices, and profits. Forecasts are always uncertain, but they're even less dependable when the value of money is subject to change. An American firm that invests $2 million in a ski factory in Sweden expects not only to make a profit on the production there but also to return that profit to the United States. If the Swedish krona depreciates sharply in the interim, however, the profits amassed in Sweden may dwindle to a mere trickle, or even a loss, when the kronor are exchanged back into dollars. Even the Nobel Prize loses a bit of its luster when the krona depreciates (see WORLD VIEW). From this view, the uncertainty associated with fluctuating exchange rates is an unwanted burden.

Even when the direction of an exchange rate move is certain, those who stand to lose from the change are prone to resist. *A change in the price of a country's money automatically alters the price of all its exports and imports.* When the Russian ruble plunged in 1998, for example, the dollar price of Russian steel plunged as well. This prompted U.S. steelmakers to accuse Russia of "dumping" steel (see NEWS). Steel companies and unions appealed to Washington to protect their sales and jobs.

Even in the country whose currency becomes cheaper, there'll be opposition to exchange-rate movements. When the U.S. dollar appreciates, Americans buy more foreign products. This increased U.S. demand for imports may drive up prices in other countries. In addition, foreign firms may take advantage of the reduced American competition by raising their prices. In either case, some inflation will result. The consumer's insistence that the government "do something" about rising prices may turn into a political force for "correcting" foreign-exchange rates.

Nobel Prize Was Nobler in October

STOCKHOLM—Winners of the four Nobel science awards said yesterday that the honor is more important than the money, so it does not matter much that each award has lost $242,000 in value since October.

"If we had been more intelligent, we would have done some hedging," said Gary S. Becker, 61, a University of Chicago professor and a Nobel economics laureate. Sweden's decision last month to let the krona float caused the prizes' value to drop from $1.2 million each when announced in October to $958,000 when King Carl XVI Gustaf presents them Thursday.

The recipients are Becker; American Rudolph A. Marcus, the chemistry laureate; Frenchman Georges Charpak, the physics laureate; and medicine prize winners Edmond Fischer and Edwin Krebs of the University of Washington in Seattle.

—Associated Press

Boston Globe, Dec. 8, 1992. Reprinted by permission of the Associated Press. www.ap.org

Analysis: Currency depreciation reduces the external value of domestic income and assets. The dollar value of the Nobel Prize fell when the Swedish krona depreciated.

Macro Interests

Any microeconomic problem that becomes widespread enough can turn into a macroeconomic problem. The huge U.S. trade deficits of the 1980s effectively exported jobs to foreign nations. Although the U.S. economy expanded rapidly in 1983–1985, the unemployment rate stayed high, partly because American consumers were spending more of their income on imports. Yet fear of renewed inflation precluded more stimulative fiscal and monetary policies.

The U.S. trade deficits of the 1980s were offset by huge capital-account surpluses. Foreign investors sought to participate in the U.S. economic expansion by buying land,

White House Weighs Steel Import Options

The Clinton administration, facing mounting anger in Congress and the steel industry over the flood of cheap steel imports, is scrambling to produce a report this week on the issue that goes beyond a simple compilation of actions already taken, administration officials said yesterday.

One option under consideration would involve steel-exporting countries limiting their shipments to the United States to avoid other, more severe import restrictions. Formal agreements of this sort, called voluntary export restraints, run afoul of World Trade Organization rules, and it wasn't clear yesterday how the administration might structure its approach to avoid legal pitfalls.

The last-minute jockeying reflected deep concern among White House officials—notably President Clinton himself—that the administration risked sparking a political firestorm if it appeared insensitive to the plight of the hard-hit industry and its workers, sources said.

Under the slogan "Stand Up for Steel," steel companies and the United Steelworkers of America have been campaigning vigorously for protection against cut-rate imports from countries affected by the global financial crisis, including Russia, Brazil, South Korea and Japan.

—Paul Blustein

The Washington Post, Jan. 7, 1999, p. E3. © 1999 The Washington Post. Reprinted with permission. www.washingtonpost.com

Analysis: Import-competing industries suffer when currency depreciations make imports cheaper. They want to be protected from "unfair" competition.

plant, and equipment and by lending money in U.S. financial markets. These capital inflows complicated monetary policy, however, and greatly increased U.S. foreign debt and interest costs.

U.S. a Net Debtor

The inflow of foreign investment also raised anxieties about "selling off" America. As Japanese and other foreign investors increased their purchases of farmland, factories, and real estate (e.g., Rockefeller Center), many Americans worried that foreign investors were taking control of the U.S. economy. A Gallup poll in 1989 revealed that Americans were much more worried about foreign economic domination than foreign military threats.

Fueling these fears was the dramatic change in America's international financial position. From 1914 to 1984 the United States had been a net creditor in the world economy. We owned more assets abroad than foreign investors owned in the United States. Our financial position changed in 1985. Continuing trade deficits and offsetting capital inflows transformed the United States into a net debtor in that year. Since then, foreigners have owned more U.S. assets than Americans own of foreign assets.

America's new debtor status can complicate domestic policy. A sudden flight from U.S. assets could severely weaken the dollar and disrupt the domestic economy. To prevent that from occurring, policymakers must consider the impact of their decisions on foreign investors. This may necessitate difficult policy choices.

There's a silver lining to this cloud, however. The inflow of foreign investment is a reflection of confidence in the U.S. economy. Foreign investors want to share in our growth and profitability. In the process, their investments (like BMW's auto plant) expand America's production possibilities and stimulate still more economic growth.

Foreign investors actually assume substantial risk when they invest in the United States. If the dollar falls, the foreign value of their U.S. investments will decline. Hence foreigners who've already invested in the United States have no incentive to start a flight from the dollar. On the contrary, a strong dollar protects the value of their U.S. holdings.

EXCHANGE-RATE INTERVENTION

Given the potential opposition to exchange-rate movements, governments often feel compelled to intervene in foreign-exchange markets. The intervention is usually intended to achieve greater exchange-rate stability. But such stability may itself give rise to undesirable micro- and macroeconomic effects.

Fixed Exchange Rates

gold standard: An agreement by countries to fix the price of their currencies in terms of gold; a mechanism for fixing exchange rates.

One way to eliminate fluctuations in exchange rates is to fix the rate's value. To fix exchange rates, each country may simply proclaim that its currency is "worth" so much in relation to that of other countries. The easiest way to do this is for each country to define the worth of its currency in terms of some common standard. Under a **gold standard,** each country determines that its currency is worth so much gold. In so doing, it implicitly defines the worth of its currency in terms of all other currencies, which also have a fixed gold value. In 1944, the major trading nations met at Bretton Woods, New Hampshire, and agreed that each currency was worth so much gold. The value of the U.S. dollar was defined as being equal to 0.0294 ounce of gold, while the British pound was defined as being worth 0.0823 ounce of gold. Thus the exchange rate between British pounds and U.S. dollars was effectively fixed at $1 = 0.357 pound, or 1 pound = $2.80 (or $2.80/0.0823 = $1/0.0294).

Balance-of-Payments Problems. It's one thing to proclaim the worth of a country's currency; it's quite another to *maintain* the fixed rate of exchange. As we've observed, foreign-exchange rates are subject to continual and often unpredictable changes in supply and demand. Hence two countries that seek to stabilize their exchange rate at some fixed value are going to find it necessary to compensate for such foreign-exchange market pressures.

Suppose the exchange rate officially established by the United States and Great Britain is equal to e_1, as illustrated in Figure 21.4. As is apparent, that particular exchange rate is consistent with the then-prevailing demand and supply conditions in the foreign-exchange market (as indicated by curves D_1 and S_1).

Now suppose that Americans suddenly acquire a greater taste for British cars and start spending more income on Jaguars and the like. Although Ford Motor owns Jaguar, the cars are still produced in Great Britain. Hence, as U.S. purchases of British goods increase, the demand for British currency will *shift* from D_1 to D_2 in Figure 21.4. Were exchange rates allowed to respond to market influences, the dollar price of a British pound would rise, in this case to the rate e_2. But government intervention has fixed the exchange rate at e_1. Unfortunately, at e_1, American consumers want to buy more pounds (q_D) than the British are willing to supply (q_s). The difference between the quantity demanded and the quantity supplied in the market at the rate e_1 represents a **market shortage** of British pounds.

The excess demand for pounds implies a **balance-of-payments deficit** for the United States: More dollars are flowing out of the country than into it. The same disequilibrium represents a **balance-of-payments surplus** for Britain, because its outward flow of pounds is less than its incoming flow.

Basically, there are only two solutions to balance-of-payments problems brought about by the attempt to fix exchange rates:

- Allow exchange rates to rise to e_2 (Figure 21.4), thereby eliminating the excess demand for pounds.
- Alter market supply or demand so that they intersect at the fixed rate e_1.

Since fixed exchange rates were the initial objective of policy, only the second alternative is of immediate interest.

The Need for Reserves. One way to alter market conditions would be for someone simply to supply British pounds to American consumers. The U.S. Treasury could have accumulated a reserve of foreign exchange in earlier periods. By selling some of those **foreign-exchange reserves** now, the Treasury could help to stabilize market conditions at the officially established exchange rate. The rightward shift of the pound supply curve in Figure 21.5 illustrates the sale of accumulated British pounds—and related purchase of U.S. dollars—by the U.S. treasury. (In 1998, the U.S. Treasury reduced foreign-exchange reserves by \$8 billion; see item 12 in Table 21.1.)

Although foreign-exchange reserves can be used to fix exchange rates, such reserves may not be adequate. Indeed, Figure 21.6 should be testimony enough to the fact that today's deficit isn't always offset by tomorrow's surplus. A principal reason that fixed exchange rates didn't live up to their expectations is that the United States had

market shortage: The amount by which the quantity demanded exceeds the quantity supplied at a given price; excess demand.

balance-of-payments deficit: An excess demand for foreign currency at current exchange rates.

balance-of-payments surplus: An excess demand for domestic currency at current exchange rates.

foreign-exchange reserves: Holdings of foreign exchange by official government agencies, usually the central bank or treasury.

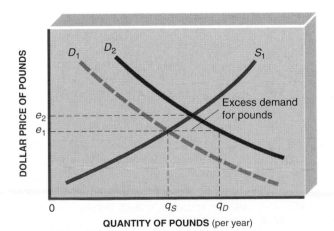

FIGURE 21.4
Fixed Rates and Market Imbalance

If exchange rates are fixed, they can't adjust to changes in market supply and demand. Suppose the exchange rate is initially fixed at e_1. When the demand for British pounds increases (shifts to the right), an excess demand for pounds emerges. More pounds are demanded (q_D) at the rate e_1 than are supplied (q_S). This causes a balance-of-payments deficit for the United States.

FIGURE 21.5
The Impact of Monetary Intervention

If the U.S. Treasury holds reserves of British pounds, it can use them to buy U.S. dollars in foreign-exchange markets. As it does so, the supply of pounds will shift to the right, to S_2, thereby maintaining the desired exchange rate, e_1. The Bank of England could bring about the same result by offering to buy U.S. dollars with pounds.

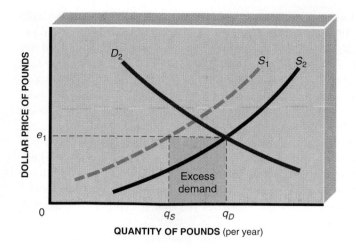

gold reserves: Stocks of gold held by a government to purchase foreign exchange.

balance-of-payments deficits for 22 consecutive years. This long-term deficit overwhelmed our stock of foreign-exchange reserves.

The Role of Gold. Gold reserves are a potential substitute for foreign-exchange reserves. As long as each country's money has a value defined in terms of gold, we can use gold to buy British pounds, thereby restocking our foreign-exchange reserves. Or we can simply use the gold to purchase U.S. dollars in foreign-exchange markets. In either case, the exchange value of the dollar will tend to rise. However, we must have **gold reserves** available for this purpose. Unfortunately, the continuing U.S. balance-of-payments deficits recorded in Figure 21.6 exceeded even the hoards of gold buried under Fort Knox. As a consequence, our gold reserves lost their credibility as a potential "guarantee" of fixed exchange rates.

Domestic Adjustments. The supply and demand for foreign exchange can also be shifted by changes in basic fiscal, monetary, or trade policies. With respect to trade policy, *trade protection can be used to prop up fixed exchange rates.* We could eliminate the excess demand for pounds (Figure 21.4), for example, by imposing quotas

FIGURE 21.6
The U.S. Balance of Payments, 1950–1973

The United States had a balance-of-payments deficit for 22 consecutive years. During this period, the foreign-exchange reserves of the U.S. Treasury were sharply reduced. Fixed exchange rates were maintained by the willingness of foreign countries to accumulate large reserves of U.S. dollars. However, neither the Treasury's reserves nor the willingness of foreigners to accumulate dollars was unlimited. In 1973, fixed exchange rates were abandoned.

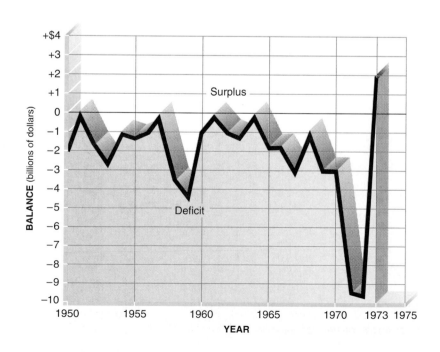

and tariffs on British goods. Such trade restrictions would reduce British imports to the United States and thus the demand for British pounds. In August 1971 President Nixon imposed an emergency 10 percent surcharge on all imported goods to help reduce the payments deficit that fixed exchange rates had spawned. Such restrictions on international trade, however, violate the principle of comparative advantage and thus reduce total world output. Trade protection also invites retaliatory trade restrictions.

Fiscal policy is another way out of the imbalance. An increase in U.S. income tax rates will reduce disposable income and have a negative effect on the demand for all goods, including imports. A reduction in government spending will have similar effects. In general, ***deflationary (or restrictive) policies help correct a balance-of-payments deficit by lowering domestic incomes and thus the demand for imports.***

Monetary policies in a deficit country could follow the same restrictive course. A reduction in the money supply will tend to raise interest rates. The balance of payments will benefit in two ways. The resultant slowdown in spending will reduce import demand. In addition, higher interest rates may induce international investors to move some of their funds into the deficit country. Such moves will provide immediate relief to the payments imbalance.[2] Russia tried this strategy in 1998, tripling key interest rates (to as much as 150 percent!). But even that wasn't enough to restore confidence in the ruble, which kept depreciating. Within 3 months of the monetary policy tightening, the ruble lost half its value.

A surplus country could help solve the balance-of-payments problem. By pursuing expansionary— even inflationary—fiscal and monetary policies, a surplus country could stimulate the demand for imports. Moreover, any inflation at home will reduce the competitiveness of exports, thereby helping to restrain the inflow of foreign demand. Taken together, such efforts would help reverse an international payments imbalance. The United States government has tried repeatedly to persuade Japan to pursue such expansionary policies.

Even under the best of circumstances, domestic economic adjustments entail significant costs. In effect, ***domestic adjustments to payments imbalances require a deficit country to forsake full employment and a surplus country to forsake price stability.*** These are sacrifices few countries are willing to make. Accordingly, balance-of-payments problems typically lead to protracted arguments about who should adjust, repeated hopes that the imbalances will go away, and frequent "crises" ending in exchange-rate adjustments. There's no easy way out of this impasse. Market imbalances caused by fixed exchange rates can be corrected only with abundant supplies of foreign-exchange reserves or deliberate changes in fiscal, monetary, or trade policies.

The Euro Fix. As noted earlier in the chapter, the 11 nations of the European Monetary Union (EMU) did fix their exchange rates in 1999 (WORLD VIEW page 418). They went far beyond the kind of exchange-rate fix we're discussing here. Members of the EMU have pledged to *eliminate* their national currencies, making the euro the common currency of "Euroland." When that happens, they won't have to worry about reserve balances or domestic adjustments. However, they'll have to reconcile their varied national interests to a single monetary authority, which may prove to be more difficult politically than balance-of-payments problems.

Balance-of-payments problems wouldn't arise in the first place if exchange rates were allowed to respond to market forces. Under a system of **flexible exchange rates** (often called "floating" exchange rates), the exchange rate moves up or down to choke off any excess supply of or demand for foreign exchange. Notice again in Figure 21.4

Flexible Exchange Rates

flexible exchange rates: A system in which exchange rates are permitted to vary with market supply-and-demand conditions; floating exchange rates.

---

[2]Before 1930, not only were foreign-exchange rates fixed, but domestic monetary supplies were tied to gold stocks as well. Countries experiencing a balance-of-payments deficit were thus forced to contract their money supply, and countries experiencing a payments surplus were forced to expand their money supply by a set amount. Monetary authorities were powerless to control domestic money supplies except by erecting barriers to trade. The system was abandoned when the world economy collapsed into the Great Depression.

"*Damn it! How can I relax, knowing that out there, somewhere, somehow, someone's attacking the dollar?*"

Analysis: A "weak" dollar reduces the buying power of American tourists.

that the exchange-rate move from e_1 to e_2 prevents any excess demand from emerging. *With flexible exchange rates, the quantity of foreign exchange demanded always equals the quantity supplied,* and there's no imbalance. For the same reason, there's no need for foreign-exchange reserves.

Although flexible exchange rates eliminate balance-of-payments and foreign-exchange reserves problems, they don't solve all of a country's international trade problems. *Exchange-rate movements associated with flexible rates alter relative prices and may disrupt import and export flows.* As noted before, depreciation of the dollar raises the price of all imported goods. The price increases may contribute to domestic cost-push inflation. Also, domestic businesses that sell imported goods or use them as production inputs may suffer sales losses. On the other hand, appreciation of the dollar raises the foreign price of U.S. goods and reduces the sales of American exporters. Hence *someone is always hurt (and others are helped) by exchange-rate movements.* The resistance to flexible exchange rates originates in these potential losses. Such resistance creates pressure for official intervention in foreign-exchange markets or increased trade barriers.

The United States and its major trading partners abandoned fixed exchange rates in 1973. Although exchange rates are now able to fluctuate freely, it shouldn't be assumed that they necessarily undergo wild gyrations. On the contrary, experience with flexible rates since 1973 suggests that some semblance of stability is possible even when exchange rates are free to change in response to market forces.

Speculation. One force that often helps maintain stability in a flexible exchange-rate system is speculation. Speculators often counteract short-term changes in foreign-exchange supply and demand. If an exchange rate temporarily rises above its long-term equilibrium, speculators will move in to sell foreign exchange. By selling at high prices and later buying at lower prices, speculators hope to make a profit. In the process, they also help stabilize foreign-exchange rates.

Speculation isn't always stabilizing, however. Speculators may not correctly gauge the long-term equilibrium. Instead, they may move "with the market" and help push exchange rates far out of kilter. This kind of destabilizing speculation sharply lowered the international value of the U.S. dollar in 1987, forcing the Reagan administration to intervene in foreign-exchange markets, borrowing foreign currencies to buy U.S. dollars. In 1997 the Clinton administration intervened for the opposite purpose: stemming the rise in the U.S. dollar.

Managed Exchange Rates. Governments can intervene in foreign-exchange markets without completely fixing exchange rates. That is, they may buy and sell foreign exchange for the purpose of *narrowing* rather than *eliminating* exchange-rate movements. Such limited intervention in foreign-exchange markets is often referred to as **managed exchange rates,** or, popularly, "dirty floats."

The basic objective of exchange-rate management is to provide a stabilizing force. The U.S. Treasury, for example, may use its foreign-exchange reserves to buy dollars when they're depreciating too much. Or it will buy foreign exchange if the dollar is rising too fast. From this perspective, exchange-rate management appears as a fail-safe system for the private market. Unfortunately, the motivation for official intervention is sometimes suspect. Private speculators buy and sell foreign exchange for the sole purpose of making a profit. But government sales and purchases may be motivated by other considerations. A falling exchange rate increases the competitive advantage of a country's exports. A rising exchange rate makes international investment less expensive. Hence a country's efforts to "manage" exchange-rate movements may arouse suspicion and outright hostility in its trading partners.

Although managed exchange rates would seem to be an ideal compromise between fixed rates and flexible rates, they can work only when some acceptable "rules of the game" and mutual trust have been established. As Sherman Maisel, a former governor of the Federal Reserve Board, put it, "Monetary systems are based on credit and faith: If these are lacking, a . . . crisis occurs."[3]

managed exchange rates: A system in which governments intervene in foreign-exchange markets to limit but not eliminate exchange-rate fluctuations; "dirty floats."

THE ECONOMY TOMORROW

 The world has witnessed a string of currency crises, including the one in Asia during 1997–1998, the Brazilian crisis of 1999, recurrent ruble crises in Russia, and periodic panics in Mexico and South America. In every instance, the country in trouble pleads for external help. In most cases a currency "bailout" is arranged, whereby global monetary authorities lend the troubled nation enough reserves (such as U.S. dollars) to defend its currency. Typically, the International Monetary Fund (IMF) heads the rescue party, joined by the central banks of the strongest economies.

The argument for currency bailouts typically rests on the domino theory. Weakness in one currency can undermine another. This seemed to be the case during the 1997–1998 Asian crisis. After the **devaluation** of the Thai baht, global investors began worrying about currency values in other Asian nations. Choosing to be "safe rather than sorry," they moved funds out of Korea, Malaysia, and the Philippines and invested in U.S. and European markets.

The initial baht devaluation also weakened the competitive trade position of these same economies. Thai exports became cheaper, diverting export demand from other Asian nations. To prevent loss of export markets, Thailand's neighbors felt they had to devalue as well. Speculators who foresaw these effects accelerated the domino effect by selling the region's currencies.

When Brazil devalued its currency (the *real*) in January 1999, global investors worried that a "samba effect" might sweep across Latin American (see WORLD VIEW next page). The domino effect could reach across the ocean and damage U.S. and European exports as well. Hence the industrial countries often offer a currency bailout as a form of self-defense.

Critics of bailouts argue that such interventions are ultimately self-defeating. They say that once a country knows for sure that currency bailouts are in the wings, it doesn't

Currency Bailouts

The Case for Bailouts

devaluation: An abrupt depreciation of a currency whose value was fixed or managed by the government.

The Case Against Bailouts

[3]Sherman Maisel, *Managing the Dollar* (New York: W. W. Norton, 1973), p. 196.

WORLD VIEW

Brazil's Ills Distress Continent

Money Crisis Shakes Investors' Confidence

BUENOS AIRES—Fallout from the continuing currency crisis in Brazil has sparked the most serious financial turmoil in Latin America since the Mexican peso crisis of four years ago, scaring away foreign investors and undermining growth after years of rapid gains.

In the days since Brazil, Latin America's largest nation, devalued its currency on Jan. 12, a number of leading economists have scaled back their forecasts for Latin American growth, predicting it will be flat or negative for the first half of 1999.

The "samba effect," as Brazil's impact on its neighbors is called, is exacerbating regional unemployment rates and sending already high interest rates climbing. Even more significantly, perhaps, it is eroding foreign investment and confi-

dence in the region amid fears that Brazil may default on its foreign debt despite government promises to the contrary.

To encourage investors to keep their money in Brazil, the central bank raised interest rates to stratospheric levels, with dire consequences for Brazilian borrowers. Economists predict that the world's eighth-largest economy will contract by 6 percent this year.

With the Brazilian real's value having fallen sharply, Brazil's neighbors, especially Argentina, are now discovering that one of their biggest markets has been closed off—essentially because of the weaker real, which has raised the price of imported goods in the nation of 165 million people.

—Anthony Faiola

The Washington Post, Feb. 1, 1999, p. 1. © 1999 The Washington Post. Reprinted with permission. www.washingtonpost.com

Analysis: When a nation devalues its currency, its imports become more expensive and its exports cheaper. These price changes disrupt trade flows of other nations. Devaluations also shake the confidence of global investors.

---

have to pursue the domestic policy adjustments that might stabilize its currency. A nation can avoid politically unpopular options such as high interest rates, tax hikes, or cutbacks in government spending. It can also turn a blind eye to trade barriers, monopoly power, lax lending policies, and other constraints on productive growth. Hence the expectation of readily available bailouts may foster the very conditions that cause currency crises.

Future Bailouts?

The decision to bail out a depreciating currency isn't as simple as it appears. To minimize the ill effects of bailouts, the IMF and other institutions typically require the crisis nation to pledge more prudent monetary, fiscal, and trade policies. Usually there's a lot of debate about what kinds of adjustments will be made—and how soon. As long as the crisis nation is confident of an eventual bailout, however, it has a lot of bargaining power to resist policy changes.

SUMMARY

- Money serves the same purposes in international trade as it does in the domestic economy, namely, to facilitate productive specialization and market exchanges. The basic challenge of international finance is to create acceptable standards of value from the various currencies maintained by separate countries.

- Exchange rates are the basic mechanism for translating the value of one national currency into the equivalent value of another. An exchange rate of $1 = 2 euros means

that one dollar is worth two euros in foreign-exchange markets.

- Foreign currencies have value because they can be used to acquire goods and resources from other countries. Accordingly, the supply of and demand for foreign currency reflect the demands for imports and exports, for international investment, and for overseas activities of governments.

- The balance of payments summarizes a country's international transactions. Its components are the trade balance, the current-account balance, and the capital-account balance. The current and capital accounts must offset each other.

• The equilibrium exchange rate is subject to any and all shifts of supply and demand for foreign exchange. If relative incomes, prices, or interest rates change, the demand for foreign exchange will be affected. A depreciation is a change in market exchange rates that makes one country's currency cheaper in terms of another currency. An appreciation is the opposite kind of change.

• Changes in exchange rates are often resisted. Producers of export goods don't want their currencies to rise in value (appreciate); importers and people who travel dislike it when their currencies fall in value (depreciate).

• Under a system of fixed exchange rates, changes in the supply and demand for foreign exchange can't be ex-

pressed in exchange-rate movements. Instead, such shifts will be reflected in excess demand for or excess supply of foreign exchange. Such market imbalances are referred to as balance-of-payments deficits or surpluses.

• To maintain fixed exchange rates, monetary authorities must enter the market to buy and sell foreign exchange. In order to do so, deficit countries must have foreign-exchange reserves. In the absence of sufficient reserves, a country can maintain fixed exchange rates only if it's willing to alter basic fiscal, monetary, or trade policies.

• Flexible exchange rates eliminate balance-of-payments problems and the crises that accompany them. But complete flexibility can lead to excessive changes. To avoid this contingency, many countries prefer to adopt managed exchange rates, that is, rates determined by the market but subject to government intervention.

Key Terms

exchange rate
equilibrium price
balance of payments
trade deficit
depreciation (currency)
appreciation
foreign-exchange markets

gold standard
market shortage
balance-of-payments deficit
balance-of-payments surplus

foreign-exchange reserves
gold reserves
flexible exchange rates
managed exchange rates
devaluation

Questions for Discussion

1. Why would a decline in the value of the dollar prompt foreign manufacturers such as BMW to build production plants in the United States?

2. How do changes in the foreign value of the U.S. dollar affect foreign enrollments at U.S. colleges (see WORLD VIEW page 434)?

3. How would rapid inflation in Canada alter our demand for travel to Canada and for Canadian imports? Does it make any difference whether the exchange rate between Canadian and U.S. dollars is fixed or flexible?

4. Under what conditions would a country welcome a balance-of-payments deficit? When would it *not* want a deficit?

5. In what sense do fixed exchange rates permit a country to "export its inflation"?

6. Why did the Mexican government have to restrain the economy after the peso devaluation?

7. If a nation's currency depreciates, are the reduced export prices that result "unfair"?

8. **Web Activity** Learn about Asian exchange rates at http://business-times.asial.com/sg. On the opening page or at "Money Matters," find an article about one country's exchange rate. In one sentence, summarize the effect described in this article. Then draw a demand and supply diagram for this currency, showing the predicted shift(s) in supply and demand.

9. **Web Activity** Find out possible benefits of the euro for European consumers at http://europa.eu.int/euro/html/page-dossier5.html?dossier=152&lang=5&page=1&nav=5. What are the possible problems? What does this study conclude about such problems?

Problems for Chapter 21 appear at the back of the book.

22

The New Capitalist Revolutions: Russia, China, Cuba

Fidel Castro's overthrow of the Cuban government in 1959 was a cinch. Popular resentment of the Batista regime, widespread poverty, and stark inequalities created a springboard for revolution: The Cuban people wanted drastic changes. Similar conditions spawned the first communist revolution in Russia (1917), the Chinese revolution (1948–1949), and other communist takeovers. In every case, the revolutionary fervor was fueled in part by the expectation that a change in the basic economic *system* was the surest route to greater economic well-being for the masses. In every case, the capitalist market system was dismantled and replaced with a centrally planned system of state ownership.

But the centrally planned economies didn't live up to their utopian promise. Seventy years after the revolution, the Moscow skyline was shabby and obscured by pollution. The average Soviet consumer was squashed in cramped housing and enjoyed few consumer durables—no telephone and no car. Even basics like soap, sugar, salt, and vodka were rationed. By official Soviet estimates, 40 percent of the population was desperately poor. Conditions in Cuba were even worse in 1995. People had to use ox carts for transportation because cars and fuel were so scarce. Electricity was available only 4 to 8 hours a day in rural areas and 10 to 12 hours in the cities. Basic consumer goods were rationed, and more desired products could be obtained only with U.S. dollars. Per capita income hovered around a skimpy $1300.

The failure of communism to deliver the goods that were promised set off a wave of radical political and economic changes throughout the communist world. The Soviet Union itself unraveled in 1991, sending 15 separate republics looking for new economic direction. In China, the government still maintains central control of the economy but has opened many sectors to capitalist innovation. Fidel Castro clings fiercely to the ideals of the revolution while seeking ways to integrate the Cuban economy into world markets. Former communist nations are reestablishing property rights, decontrolling prices, giving up state ownership, and pursuing other market reforms. Like most revolutions, this new *capitalist* revolution entails painful adjustments.

This chapter examines these structural changes, particularly the transformations from centrally planned to market-oriented economies. We start by looking at the grand design of the communist vision and then at the economic difficulties actually encountered. These are the key questions:

- What is the appeal of central planning?
- What are the basic problems of central planning?
- What impedes the transition to market economies?

In pursuing these questions, we also look at the trade-offs involved. The basic restructuring of an entire economy entails significant economic, social, and political costs. These costs are important in explaining why some communist countries (e.g., Russia) are slow to change and others (e.g., Cuba) resist change so fiercely.

THE PROMISE

Marx's Vision

Working with his good friend and later benefactor Friedrich Engels, Karl Marx described how capitalist systems would be destroyed. From his perspective, all history was a sequence of struggles between economic classes. In the words of the *Communist Manifesto,* "The history of all existing society is the history of class struggles. Freeman and slave, patrician and plebeian, lord and serf, guildmaster and journeyman, in a word, oppressor and oppressed." **Capitalist** systems, Marx claimed, followed the same pattern; only the class identities were changed. In this case, the oppressors—the capitalists—owned the means of production, and the oppressed—the proletariat—were their modern-day serfs.

capitalism: An economy in which the factors of production (such as land, capital) are owned by individuals; basic allocation decisions are made by market forces.

According to Marx's labor theory of value, all output was the product of the workers. Ownership of land and capital served only as a mechanism for "expropriating" part of labor's rightful income. A "natural" antagonism between workers and capitalists arose out of the capitalists' unrelenting quest for profits and the attendant desire to pay workers as little as possible. This continued exploitation would eventually drive the working class to revolt.

Once the capitalists were sent packing (if they were so fortunate), the working class itself, the proletariat, would take over the means of production. There'd be no more class strife, because there'd be only one class. Everyone would share equally in access to the means of production and the output it yielded. The abolition of private property implied that nobody would have the means of exploiting anybody else. The core motivating principles of the **communism** Marx envisioned would be "from each according to his ability, to each according to his need." In that idealized society, there'd be no central authority—no state—because the only function of a state was to express and pursue the interests of the dominant class. Since only one class would exist, in Marx's vision, no state would be necessary.

communism: A stateless, classless economy in which there's no private property and everyone shares in production and consumption according to individual abilities and needs.

The Socialist Transition

Marx wasn't very specific about exactly how a classless, stateless, communist society would function. His immediate concern was with the continuing exploitation of the working class, the widespread poverty, sickness, and degradation that he observed in the early stages of the Industrial Revolution. Marx died 25 years before the first successful communist revolution, and before he was able to complete *Das Kapital,* his voluminous study of the way capitalist systems functioned.[1]

Although he concentrated on the internal flaws of capitalism and the awakening of working class interests, Marx also provided some sketches of the kind of society that would follow the revolution. He foresaw that a central government (the state) would be required for some time to give direction to the new society. The proletariat wouldn't be prepared to embrace fully the basic tenets of communism, nor would it have the technical expertise required to organize the means of production. In the interim period, a central authority, a **socialist** state, would have to solidify class consciousness, reorganize property and production rights, and plan the transition to a truly communist

socialism: An economy in which all nonlabor means of production are owned by the state, which exercises control over resource allocation.

---

[1]Marx never forgave capitalism for driving him into the relentless research (most of it undertaken in the British Museum) and political activism that exhausted his finances and health. On publication of the first volume of *Das Kapital,* he wrote to Engels, "I hope that the bourgeoisie as long as they live will have cause to remember my carbuncles" (cited in *Fortune,* May 1946, p. 146).

society. As society moved along in that direction, the state would become increasingly unnecessary and would gradually wither away.

From Marx's perspective, then, the demise of capitalism would be succeeded by two further stages: socialism and communism. In both stages of development, the means of production would be publicly owned. Under socialism, however, the state would play an important role in allocating resources, and goods would be distributed in part according to each person's work effort. The economy would enter the final stage of development, communism, only after goods were in such abundance that everyone's needs could be satisfied. In that final stage—the communist utopia—people would work for the common good and wouldn't have to be prodded with the promise of personal gain.

The communist revolutions that later took place—in Russia in 1917, in China in 1949, and elsewhere—didn't follow Marx's scenario in every respect. Indeed, Marx would have been surprised to see the revolutions occur in countries as underdeveloped as Russia was in 1917, China in 1949, or Cuba in 1959. Nevertheless, most "communist" countries heeded Marx's admonition to exert strong central authority, to use the state as an instrument for reforming society and developing the economy. Indeed, most "communist" countries refer to themselves as "socialist," with communism expressed as a goal, not a description.

Read more about China at www.ita.doc.gov/bems/China.html. For more on Russia, see www.itaiep.doc.gov/bisnis.html.

CENTRAL PLANNING

The challenge of transforming capitalist economies into communist economies was daunting. Imagine that you've led a successful revolution and must now organize the economy to fulfill the revolution's goals. This is the kind of dilemma Vladimir Lenin and his comrades confronted in 1917, Mao Zedong in 1949, and Fidel Castro in 1959.

In general, you want to ensure greater equality for all the people, because that was a motivating force behind the revolution. And you want to improve the standard of living, both to satisfy revolutionary aspirations and to reassure the proletariat that they've bet on the right horse. Finally, you want to build up the country's defenses to protect yourself against counterrevolution from within and aggression from without. How are you going to attain these goals?

Production Possibilities

production possibilities: The alternative combinations of final goods and services that could be produced in a given time period with all available resources and technology.

The starting point for all planning is the concept of **production possibilities.** By adding up all of society's productive resources and surveying available technology, you could conceivably determine what production possibilities exist. The solid line in Figure 22.1 might be an adequate description of the possibilities for producing "consumption goods" and "investment goods."

FIGURE 22.1
Postrevolutionary Production Possibilities

All countries confront limited production possibilities. A revolution may even destroy capital, land, or labor, thus reducing immediate production possibilities (to the solid curve). Deciding what to produce with available resources and technology is a basic planning issue. To increase the production of consumer goods (say, from point *A* to point *B*) will require cutbacks in investment goods.

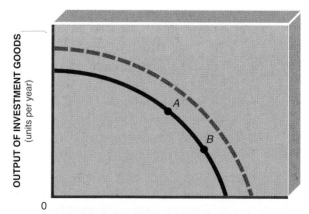

The first dilemma we confront is the fact that our production possibilities are no larger immediately after the revolution than they were just before it. In fact, they're probably smaller. A lot of buildings and equipment were destroyed in the revolt, many workers have been wounded, and most of the capitalists and their lackeys are either dead or have fled. At the time the communists took control of China in 1949, industrial output was one-half its prewar peak. The transportation system was partially destroyed, many skilled technicians and managers had fled, and the government's foreign-exchange reserves had been moved to Taiwan. In Cuba there was little physical destruction, but a mass exodus of doctors and other professionals during the period 1959–1962 curtailed production possibilities. Accordingly, our immediate production possibilities probably look more like the solid curve in Figure 22.1 than the larger, dashed one that prevailed earlier.

In the face of shrunken production possibilities, it's evident that we're going to have a difficult time delivering the resolution's promises. Any immediate improvement of living standards for the masses will have to come about through *redistribution* of output rather than from *added* output. It's unlikely, however, that there'll be sufficient stockpiles of basic goods—food, housing, clothes—to satisfy consumer demands through redistribution of existing output.[2]

What to Produce. The only viable option for increasing consumption levels is to change the mix of output. In the two-dimensional economy of Figure 22.1, this means cutting back on the production of **investment** goods. By altering the mix of output in favor of more consumption goods, an immediate improvement of living standards can be attained. This was a primary concern in Cuba, where the rural population lacked access to schools, healthcare, or even clean water. The Castro regime allocated more resources to those basic human needs, reducing the stock of resources available for investment. Such a change in the output mix is illustrated by the move from point *A* to point *B* in Figure 22.1.

investment: Expenditures on (production of) new plant, equipment, and structure (capital) in a given time period, plus changes in business inventories.

Although this move might deliver quickly on revolutionary promises, it poses difficulties for the years ahead. Some investment is needed simply to maintain and replace existing plant and equipment. Additional *net* investment is required to achieve **economic growth**—to *expand* our productive capacity. Accordingly, ***one of the most basic decisions central planners must confront is what proportion of resources to devote to investment and what proportion to present consumption.*** The trade-off is particularly difficult in a country where living standards are abnormally low and where we need to increase *both* consumption and investment. In principle, a nation might get external assistance in the form of foreign aid or loans to increase consumption and investment possibilities. But few capitalist banks are eager to lend funds to a communist revolution. So there are few options here.

economic growth: An increase in output (real GDP); an expansion of production possibilities.

In the Soviet Union, the decision was made to shift the mix of output in favor of investment, with investment rates as high as 30 percent of total output. This strategy accelerated economic growth but reduced already low living standards. Consumer goods were always in short supply, and basic necessities had to be rationed.

The political leaders of China decided that they couldn't afford such high rates of investment. In 1949 the Chinese people were on the brink of starvation. GDP per capita was less than $300 (in 1998 U.S. dollars). Thus China's leaders had to devote a larger share of total output to consumption, especially such basic foodstuffs as wheat, rice, and cooking oil. Less than 10 percent of total output was devoted to investment in the early postrevolutionary years. Only after minimal consumption standards were ensured did the share of output devoted to investment increase (to as high as 25 percent in the early 1970s).

---

[2]Following the Bolshevik revolution in 1917, the mansions of many Russian aristocrats and affluent capitalists were converted into multifamily dwellings; but the number of such mansions is obviously limited. Redistribution possibilities may have been slightly greater in China, where the landlord-gentry class had diverted a lot of output to personal consumption, including reserves of rice and other food.

Resource Allocation

Once a mix of output is chosen, it must be produced. This requires two key steps:

- Selecting production processes
- Allocating resources

If we want more machinery, for example, we have to decide how to produce it and must make sure we allocate sufficient resources to that process.

In a market economy, Adam Smith's "invisible hand" takes care of these problems. Individual producers seek out the best ways of producing various goods and then bid for scarce resources. The resulting competition tends to allocate resources to their most valuable use.

A purely socialist state can't rely on the invisible hand. A purely socialist state doesn't permit private ownership, profit accumulation, or "exploitive" wage relationships. Immediately after overthrowing the Batista regime, Castro's revolutionary government confiscated private property, voided rental contracts, expropriated foreign-owned assets, and collectivized large farms. Cuba also forbade anyone from hiring paid labor; everyone was to work for the state. From the government's perspective, market-directed resource allocations were too risky: Decisions made by market participants might not conform to the central plan (the designated output mix). ***In a socialist state, central planners assume the resource allocation responsibilities.*** They designate how many resources will go to each industry. The central planners also decide where every college graduate will work (see WORLD VIEW).

This resource allocation task is critical to the success of central planning—and fraught with complexity. Two-dimensional production possibilities curves will no longer suffice. Now we have to start thinking about all the inputs needed to produce each and every good.

Input-Output Analysis

The kind of input-output calculations required for efficient resource allocation would give you an unbelievable headache, even if you were equipped with high-speed computers. A sense of how painful such an effort might be is only suggested by Table 22.1, which indicates a few input-output relationships for the Soviet economy. Input-output

WORLD VIEW

Soviets Find Job for Every College Grad

MOSCOW—"It's like their wedding day," the university rector said happily.

A graduating senior disagreed. "It's terrible," he said. "Everyone is taking tranquilizers."

The occasion was the Day of Distribution, which is far more emotional than Graduation Day at the 900 or so institutions of higher learning in the Soviet Union. On the Day of Distribution, graduates get their first job assignments.

By the end of June, virtually all of the 800,000 young men and women graduating from universities and other university-level institutions will have met with a placement commission and will know which job is waiting for them.

The system is a creature of this country's planned economy.

In the United States, collegians choose their specialties and take their chances in the job market after graduation. In the Soviet Union, the system cranks out cars, bombs, and paper clips according to government decree, and it produces diplomas the same way.

"They give us money, we give them specialists," Arnold Koop, rector of Tartu University in Soviet Estonia, summed up. . . .

When they scrawl "I consent" at the bottom of the placement commission's decision, Soviet graduates technically commit themselves to work at their first job for at least three years, repaying the state for a free education.

But they resent the fact that many assigned jobs are far from home, in the provinces, where life is often primitive and their talents are sometimes not appreciated. And many wind up with jobs only remotely related to their studies.

—Dan Fisher

Los Angeles Times, June 17, 1980, p. 6. Copyright, 1980, Los Angeles Times. Reprinted by permission. www.latimes.com

Analysis: To ensure that the planned mix of output will be produced, central planners must assign people to specific jobs.

TABLE 22.1
Soviet Input-Output Relationships

Nothing can be produced unless the required inputs are available in the correct quantities. An input-output table such as this describes the production requirements of various goods. The production of one automobile, for example, requires inputs of 0.08503 unit of ferrous ores and metals, 0.02649 unit of nonferrous ores, and so on. Central planning agencies use such tables to determine what goods and services can be produced with available resources and technology.

Sector Number	Inputs	Automobiles	Tractors and Agricultural Machinery	Bread, Flour, and Confections	Electric and Thermal Power
1	Ferrous ores and metals	0.08503	0.13637	0.00024	0.00137
2	Nonferrous ores and metals	0.02649	0.01685	0.00018	0.00000
3	Coke products and refractory materials	0.00173	0.00382	0.00002	0.00024
4	Industrial metal products	0.00954	0.00828	0.00015	0.00089
5	Coal	0.00216	0.00187	0.00238	0.20491
6	Oil extraction and refining	0.00524	0.00475	0.00065	0.06132
7	Gas	0.00332	0.00303	0.00083	0.05900
8	Peat and oil shales	0.00019	0.00011	0.00014	0.02763
9	Electric and thermal power	0.01171	0.01935	0.00284	0.00153
10	Energy and power machinery	0.00021	0.00065	0.00001	0.00174
11	Electrical machinery and cable products	0.01705	0.01571	0.00026	0.00153
12	Metalworking machinery	0.00155	0.00229	0.00000	0.00000
13	Tools and dies	0.00272	0.00506	0.00009	0.00013
14	Precision instruments	0.00080	0.00147	0.00004	0.00048
15	Mining and metallurgical machinery	0.00000	0.00000	0.00000	0.00000
16	Pumps and compressors	0.00123	0.00122	0.00001	0.00012
17	Tractors and agricultural machinery	0.00026	0.18826	0.00001	0.00008
18	Bearings	0.00841	0.01723	0.00002	0.00009
19	Other machine building	0.02052	0.02061	0.00041	0.00307
20	Other metalworking	0.00585	0.01013	0.00061	0.00035
21	Repair of machinery	0.00101	0.00153	0.00053	0.00533
22	Abrasives	0.00106	0.00195	0.00001	0.00007
23	Synthetic resins and plastics	0.00240	0.00065	0.00004	0.00040
24	Paints and lacquers	0.00703	0.00626	0.00012	0.00029
25	Rubber and asbestos products	0.08596	0.03779	0.00017	0.00040
26	Woodworking	0.00677	0.01067	0.00401	0.00039
27	Paper and pulp	0.00173	0.00107	0.00225	0.00009
28	Construction materials	0.00136	0.00084	0.00023	0.00044
29	Glass and porcelain	0.00393	0.00074	0.00004	0.00016
30	Textiles	0.00621	0.00296	0.00083	0.00037
31	Sugar	0.00000	0.00006	0.05334	0.00000
32	Bread, flour, and confections	0.00000	0.00000	0.23885	0.00000
33	Crops	0.00002	0.00002	0.31794	0.00000
34	Transportation and communications	0.05446	0.06347	0.01214	0.00054
35	Trade and distribution	0.02239	0.00761	0.07199	0.00005

Source: U.S. Congress, *Soviet Economic Prospects for the Seventies,* a compendium of papers submitted to the Joint Economic Committee, June 27, 1973 (Washington, D.C.: U.S. Government Printing Office, 1973).

coefficients, as displayed in the table, indicate how much output from one industry will be required to provide inputs for another industry.

You can discover by reading down the column marked "Automobiles," for example, that the production of 1 ruble's worth of automobiles required 0.08503 ruble's worth of ferrous ores and metals, 0.02649 ruble's worth of nonferrous ores and metals, and so forth. Incredibly boring statistics, to be sure. But if you're in charge of allocating the people's resources, you'd better be certain that you allocate the right amount of resources to the production of such inputs.

Prices

market economy: An economy that relies on markets for basic decisions about WHAT to produce, HOW to produce it, and FOR WHOM to produce.

You might be thinking that markets and prices could help solve some of these problems. But such thoughts merely demonstrate that you haven't yet cleansed your mind of its bourgeois capitalist prejudices. It's of course true that *a basic function of prices in a **market economy** is to signal to producers and consumers that some products are relatively scarce or plentiful.* These signals are expected to call forth appropriate supply-and-demand responses. Thus one way to solve the resource allocation problem might be to let prices respond to shortages. If somebody in the Administration for Tires and Rubber Products messed up her homework and left us without enough tires, tire prices would rise. This price increase would provide an early warning of trouble and give tire producers a strong incentive to increase production. In this way, the tire shortage might be alleviated before it got too serious.

market mechanism: The use of market prices and sales to signal desired outputs (or resource allocations).

But such "efficiency" isn't welcome in a planned socialist economy. The **market mechanism** has been rejected for two reasons. First, were prices allowed to function as market signals, we could no longer be assured that our planning goals would be achieved. High prices might lure scarce resources into the production of low-priority consumer goods. Second, if prices and production are determined by the market, some producers might profit from market imbalances. This is a very serious matter: To suggest that market prices could help to solve our allocation problems is tantamount to condoning profiteering. Hence both the allocation of resources and the distribution of incomes are "threatened" by the market mechanism.

Distributing Output. Shall we completely abolish prices, then? No. Unless we're prepared to ration everything from basic resources to final consumer goods, prices are still needed. But central planners don't use prices the same way the capitalists do. *In a planned economy, prices are used to reconcile the mix of goods demanded to the centrally planned supply.* The mix of goods supplied is determined by the state plan. Prices aren't permitted to have an independent influence on resource allocation. Prices are used solely to control demand. Specifically, *high prices on luxury goods are used to limit the quantity demanded.* Those prices are maintained with high retail taxes, while producers are paid very little for their output of consumer goods. This strategy effectively dampens both consumer demand and producer incentives for low-priority goods.

The central planners also use *low* prices to ensure that everyone can afford basic staples. In China and the Soviet Union, for example, the prices of food, housing, and health services were kept very low. In Moscow, bread cost 15 cents a loaf in 1989, the price set by the central planners in 1954. Cuba decreed that rent may not exceed 10 percent of a household's income. Rent on a two-room apartment in China costs something like $100 a year and a visit to the doctor only 10 cents. Such *low prices for necessities are intended to assure everyone access to basic consumer goods.*

Measuring Performance. Centrally planned prices are also used as a convenient measure of efficiency. How can we know whether the People's Bicycle Factory at Tientsin is producing as many bicycles as it can with the resources made available to it? It would be a horrendous task to inventory all the separate inputs used and then to compare those input-output relationships with those of the People's Bicycle Factory at Kwangchow. And how do you know which factory is better serving the people if you can do no more than observe basic inputs and outputs? Say that the Tientsin factory produced 27 bikes last month and used 18 pounds of aluminum, 7 pounds of rubber, $1\frac{1}{2}$ gallons of lacquer, and 13 pounds of steel. At the same time the Kwangchow factory produced 33 bikes, using 21 pounds of aluminum, $6\frac{1}{2}$ pounds of rubber, 4 gallons of lacquer, and 12 pounds of steel. Some summary sort of measure is clearly necessary. Far better if we attach prices to all those inputs and simply see how much total cost goes into the production of so many bicycles. Prices will allow us to measure performance.

Insofar as planning objectives are concerned, the question of FOR WHOM is readily resolved. We want all our people to be equal, to enjoy the same standard of living—whatever their respective abilities. Disparities in income create jealousies, anxieties, and social friction. If such disparities are large enough, they can lead to conspicuous social stratification—that is, to socioeconomic *classes.* That's clearly inconsistent with the stateless, classless society Marx envisioned. Hence we'll strive to ensure that everyone receives a more equal share of total income. To ensure further that people don't use their income for purposes of indulgent consumption, we'll ration basic commodities equally among the people and price conspicuous consumption goods, such as automobiles, so high that there's little chance of anyone acquiring them.

Income Distribution

PROBLEMS OF IMPLEMENTATION

At this juncture, some problems inherent in implementing the communist vision of utopia should be evident.

To begin, we have to recognize just how complicated the planning process can become. The input-output relationships in Table 22.1 are just a hint of that complexity. ***The more specific output targets become, the more complex the central plans must be.*** In the Soviet Union, the central planning agency, Gosplan, established production targets for 70,000 items and set 200,000 prices each year. In Cuba, the central planning board, Juceplan, had to set production targets for thousands of factories and farms. One of the planners' foremost concerns was to confirm that all the planning details were *consistent*—that all inputs and outputs matched up in the style of Table 22.1. This is a complex and onerous task, fraught with opportunities for error.

Complexity

Suppose we were smart or lucky enough to work out all the details of a perfect central plan. What assurances do we have that the plan will be implemented? How are we going to persuade the workers, the farmers, and the managers to fulfill the specific objectives of our plans? They may not possess the same revolutionary zeal and farsightedness that we do. Input-output coefficients may mean as little to them as they do to economics students in capitalist societies. How then can we get the masses to contribute to output in the form and quantity we desire?

Incentives

In market economies, material rewards in the form of higher wages, prices, or profits are used as carrots to call forth the desired supply responses. Such an emphasis is clearly less appropriate for a socialist state. As we've emphasized, ***material incentives lead to income inequalities*** and nurture selfish interests rather than social interests.

Having rejected market incentives, central planners must find other ways to motivate workers. Typically, the only alternatives are exhortation or brute force. Neither alternative is an adequate substitute for material incentives, however. Neither "reeducation" campaigns nor forced labor (like forced collectivization of farms) will generate efficiency, much less creativity. Workers in state-owned enterprises find that it's easier—and no less rewarding—to just "get by" than to challenge production decisions or pursue innovation.

Recognizing this shortcoming, most communist governments experimented with material incentives. In the former Soviet Union, for example, workers were coaxed into "fulfilling and overfulfilling" plan targets by a variety of bonuses that equaled as much as 30 percent of take-home pay.

Cuba too experimented with material incentives. In 1979 the government suppplemented state-established wages with piece rates (*normas*); bonuses (*primas*) for "overfulfilling" plan targets, increasing exports, or reducing material or energy inputs; and profit sharing (*primios*). By 1985, however, all such pay supplements amounted to only

11 percent of basic wages. The Castro government also tried to encourage more construction activity by permitting Cubans to build, own, and sell their own homes.

Goal Conflicts. The use of even these limited material incentives conflicts with the egalitarian goals of communist ideology. Mao Zedong repeatedly denounced Soviet "revisionism." Mao made a much greater effort to rely exclusively on nonmaterial incentives. For over two decades, Chinese workers were urged to "develop the socialist economy, carry the revolution through to the end" by banners hung in every office and factory (together with photographs of Marx, Lenin, and Mao). Thoughts of personal gain were regarded as counterrevolutionary.

Such dedication was difficult to maintain. Over time, the Chinese leaders permitted limited use of material incentives (including private garden plots). But this was inconsistent with Mao's basic dictum that "politics must come before economics." This tension led to the Great Proletarian Cultural Revolution (1966–1969), a widespread and sometimes violent reaction to "creeping materialism." The Cultural Revolution was designed to reassert revolutionary ideals and communal aspirations.

Fidel Castro also despaired over the corrosive power of material incentives. Some Cubans were getting rich by building and selling houses, selling food or handicrafts at peasant markets, or earning workplace bonuses. Fearful that class distinctions were reemerging, Castro sought to "rebalance" moral and material incentives. In 1986 peasant markets were abolished, material incentives for labor were reduced, and the state decreed that all private housing sales would have to pass through a government agency at regulated prices. In 1994 the Cuban government confiscated cars, trucks, cash, and other property from hundreds of people who had become too successful. The Chinese government did the same thing when Chinese entrepreneurs became too successful in China's "enterprise zones."

Shortages

The socialist system of administered prices and moral incentives generated widespread shortages. In keeping with the central goal of equality, prices on food, fuel, electricity, and other consumer goods were set at very low levels. These low prices increased the quantity demanded. At the same time, the quantity supplied was fixed by the state. The market supply curve was effectively vertical, since (1) prices weren't allowed to rise, and (2) even if prices were raised, producers weren't permitted to profit therefrom.

Figure 22.2 illustrates the consequences of these nonmarket structures. In a market economy, the price of meat would reflect underlying supply and demand. In the figure, p_m would be the market price of meat. At that price, however, meat would be con-

FIGURE 22.2
Suppressed Inflation and Market Shortages

Socialist planners set low prices on basic consumer goods to ensure that everyone can afford them. At the controlled price (p_c), however, the quantity demanded (q_d) exceeds the supply fixed by the planners (q_s). In a market economy the resulting market shortage would push the price up to equilibrium (p_m). The central planners don't permit price increases, however. As a result, the inflationary pressure causes empty shelves, long lines, and black markets—all symptoms of suppressed inflation.

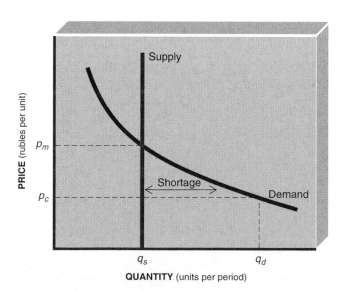

sumed only by those consumers who had a greater ability or willingness to pay. Material bonuses (wage inequalities) might result in unequal access to food. To avoid such inequality, the central planners set the price of meat at p_c. At that low price everyone can afford meat.

Not everyone gets meat, however. Socialist consumers confront a **market shortage:** The quantity demanded at p_c greatly exceeds the quantity supplied; thus the meat disappears from the stores long before everyone who's willing and able to buy it at the controlled price gets a chance to do so.

Cuba started rationing consumer staples in early 1962. As Table 22.2 indicates, the rationed allotments were pretty skimpy—just 5 eggs per month and only 2 pounds of chicken. Over 150 products were rationed this way. To get these products, every Cuban household had to register with the National Rationing Board and specify the store at which it would shop. The household then had to buy all its rationed products at that shop, paying government-set (very low) prices.

Suppressed Inflation. When prices are centrally controlled, prices don't rise to reflect these market imbalances. In fact, the planners take public credit for the absence of inflation. However, the imbalances have to show up somewhere. The inflationary pressures are manifest in empty shelves, long lines, and rationing—rather than higher prices. These are the symptoms of **suppressed inflation,** that is, inflationary imbalances reflected in nonprice forms. Suppressed inflation also spills over into black markets, where goods and services are exchanged at higher prices without official sanction. In Cuba, the government set up "parallel" markets where people could buy additional quantities of rationed goods from the government. The prices, however, were often 10 times higher than the administered prices for rationed goods. Cubans could also buy such "luxuries" as canned peaches, jam, or rum in these parallel markets. More often than not, Cubans still resorted to the black market, where better goods were available, though at far higher prices.

The shortages of consumer goods not only frustrate consumers but also weaken production incentives. Socialist countries introduced material bonuses to spur production. However, the basic allure of material bonuses isn't the money per se but the increased consumption implied by greater income. Hence *material incentives will fail if there's nothing to buy with the added income.*

Recall that the central planners determine the mix of output. They use material incentives only to coax more productivity from the workers. If successful, economic growth will accelerate and more output will be produced. But what about the supply of consumer goods? If the central planners are striving to increase investment or

market shortage: The amount by which the quantity demanded exceeds the quantity supplied at a given price; excess demand.

suppressed inflation: Inflationary imbalances reflected in nonprice forms (like market shortages and rationing) when prices aren't permitted to rise.

Involuntary Savings

Product	Monthly Adult Ration
Rice	6 pounds
Beef	3 pounds
Beans	1.5 pounds
Fish	1 pound
Chicken	2 pounds
Coffee	0.75 pounds
Eggs	5
Milk (fresh)	6 liters
Milk (condensed)	3 cans

Source: Jorge Perez-Lopez, *Cuba's Second Economy* (Transaction Publishers, 1995) (1962 allotments).

TABLE 22.2
Rationing in Cuba

Like other centrally planned economies, Cuba used rationing rather than the market mechanism to distribute scarce consumer goods. The table lists 9 of the more than 150 products rationed in Cuba.

involuntary saving: Consumer saving compelled by shortages of consumer goods.

defense output, the increased output may not include additional consumer goods. The workers will have fatter paychecks but nothing more to buy. Before long, they'll realize that the material rewards to extra effort are an illusion. As workers in many communist countries have observed: "We pretend to work and they pretend to pay us." Output stagnates and savings accumulate. Such **involuntary saving,** however, frustrates workers and ultimately undermines the bonus system.

Soviet planners began to grapple with this problem in the 1970s. The ninth 5-year plan (1971–1975) asserted that "the main task" was "to ensure a significant increase in the people's material and cultural standard of living."[3] That goal was submerged by defense needs in the tenth plan, however, and by investment needs (particularly new gas lines) in the eleventh plan. Consumers didn't again get priority until the twelfth plan (1986–1990). By that time, however, Soviet consumers had accumulated over 100 *billion* unspent and unwanted rubles. They couldn't even buy soap or salt with their rubles, much less consumer appliances, televisions, or a good pair of jeans. In these circumstances, Soviet people saw no purpose in working hard to accumulate still more rubles.

The same problem has afflicted Cuba. Workers accumulated pesos that have little or no market value. Basic consumer goods are rationed, and "luxury" goods are available only in black markets or state-run stores where U.S. dollars are the only accepted currency. Seeing no gain from continued work effort, workers signal their frustration with high rates of absenteeism. As workers withdraw from the labor force, production slows and shortages become even more acute.

Nonconvertible Currency

In principle, the shortage of consumer goods could be alleviated by imports. International trade, however, isn't so easy with central planning. To begin with, how are consumers to gain access to imported goods? Domestic production and prices are controlled by the state. There's no network of importers, distributors, and retail outlets for selling imported goods. Moreover, the viability of such a network would depend on profitability—an alien notion. Furthermore, if consumers could purchase imported goods, they might not buy the output produced by the state enterprises. They might even begin making unfavorable comparisons about the quality and price of imported and domestic products.

Fear of competition and a revulsion to profits aren't the only forces blocking imports. There's also the problem of *money.* How is the country to pay for imports? Centrally planned prices don't conform to market prices. Hence the currency of communist nations has no foundation in market realities. International consumers will have little opportunity or incentive to spend Soviet rubles, Chinese yuan, or Cuban pesos. If they take these currencies in payment, they may end up with the same involuntary savings accumulated by consumers in planned economies. To avert this fate, foreign producers will want to be paid in **hard currency**—U.S. dollars and other currencies that are widely exchanged in international markets.

hard currency: Any national currency widely accepted in payment in international markets.

But how will central planners or consumers in communist states acquire hard currency? Like other nations, they'll have to *export* goods to earn foreign exchange. But exports aren't part of the central plan. To produce exports, the central planners will have to divert scarce resources from domestic investment or consumption to export-producing industries. This will frustrate planning objectives. Furthermore, there's no guarantee that the goods produced for export will be sold, or at what price (the central planners can't control prices in world markets).

Bartered Trade. All these problems have tended to "close" communist economies to international markets. Most of their trade was among themselves and dictated by the central planners. The countries of Eastern Europe, for example, were expected to ship

---

[3]*Pravda,* Dec. 19, 1972, cited by Keith Bush in *Soviet Economic Prospects for the Seventies,* a compendium of papers submitted to the Joint Economic Committee of Congress, June 27, 1973.

specific quotas of food (Romania), machinery (East Germany), and manufactured goods (Hungary) to the Soviet Union. They were paid for these goods in rubles, at prices established by the central planners. These countries were then "permitted" to buy oil, natural gas, and other resources from the Soviet Union. These bilateral agreements were essentially forms of **barter,** in which specific goods were exchanged.

These bilateral barter deals severely limited the amount and content of trade that socialist countries could engage in. They also created the opportunity, however, to subsidize one trading partner at the expense of another. Russia, for example, "bought" Cuban sugar at administered prices that were up to ten times the world price. Russia then "sold" Cuba oil at administered prices that were *below* the world price. These extremely favorable terms of barter exchange effectively transferred income from Russia to Cuba. In fact, this implicit Russian subsidy was the principal source of Cuba's external income from 1961 until 1992.

Trade with the rest of the world was essentially limited to barter deals as well. Foreign producers who wanted to sell products or build factories in communist countries typically had to accept payment in kind—that is, in oil, coal, diamonds, or other natural resources. These barter arrangements greatly limited trading opportunities. As a result, the communist countries weren't in a position to exploit their **comparative advantage** and associated efficiencies. The relatively small East Germany economy (1990 population of 16 million; GDP of $211 billion), for example, produced 80 percent of the total variety of industrial goods available in the world. With greater specialization and trade, East Germany could have achieved greater efficiency and higher living standards.

barter: The direct exchange of one good for another, without the use of money.

comparative advantage: The ability of a country to produce a specific good at a lower opportunity cost than its trading partners.

THE COLLAPSE

With so many inherent inefficiencies, the collapse of communism seemed inevitable. However, the upheavals of 1989 were neither widely predicted nor easily explained. After all, the communist system, however creaky and inefficient, had functioned for over 70 years in the Soviet Union and over 40 years in Eastern Europe and China. Moreover, some of these countries had achieved remarkable economic growth in earlier years. Stalin's forced industrialization of its economy made the Soviet Union a world power. Cuba had succeeded in ensuring the basic human needs of its entire population. Even China had managed to raise the living standards of a billion people. These achievements were gradually overshadowed, however, by inherent inefficiencies and widening disparities with market-driven economies.

The failure to deliver an adequate supply of consumer goods was probably the most important cause of the breakdown in the central planning system. In the early stages of forced development, the "belt tightening" required of consumers was made palatable by the vision of a better future. But the promised higher consumption levels kept getting postponed. In the absence of tangible rewards, the motivation to work diminished. Declining oil and gold prices plus poor harvests in the 1980s made it increasingly difficult for the Soviet Union to even maintain, much less improve, living standards. Severe shortages of soap, sugar, matches, shoes, and fruit and vegetables in the late 1980s eliminated all pretense of improved living standards.

Once the Russian economy collapsed, the Cuban economy faltered as well. The Russian bartered-trade subsidy was an essential prop holding up the Cuban economy. The subsidy allowed Cuba to maintain and even increase living standards even while production became less and less efficient. The Russian subsidy declined sharply after 1989, however, and ended completely in 1992. Without Russian oil, Cuban factories had to shut down, electricity had to be shut off, and cars, buses, tractors, and trucks had to be abandoned. Cuba's annual output declined by at least 30 percent from 1989 to 1994. As it did, already skimpy rations of rice, beef, beans, and other staples (see Table 22.2) were cut back sharply. Thousands of Cubans fled the country, seeking refuge in the Guantanomo U.S. military base or risking a treacherous sea voyage to Florida.

THE MARKET TRANSITION

When the failures of communism became so evident, most centrally planned economies looked to the market mechanism to achieve more and better output. They embraced market reforms at very different speeds, however. Poland restructured its economy so quickly that its adjustment process was dubbed "shock therapy." In China, the process of structural transition was more gradual and is still far from complete. Russia has been whipsawed by the advances of *perestroika* (restructuring) and resurgent opposition to market reforms. As of 1999, Fidel Castro was still searching for market reforms that wouldn't violate the basic principles of the socialist revolution.

To make the transition from a centrally planned to a market-driven economy, all these countries must confront four basic reforms:

- Price reform
- Currency reform
- Private property
- Institutional reform

Price Reform

A key component of the transition to market economies is price reform. The distorted prices dictated by central planners generated the wrong market signals. For the market mechanism to function efficiently, price signals must reflect underlying supply-and-demand conditions. This requires an end to government-dictated prices. In all Eastern Europe and the countries of the former Soviet Union this has meant an end to artificially low prices for basic necessities. Higher prices for basic (subsidized) goods were needed to increase the quantity supplied and reduce the quantity demanded (see Figure 22.2).

Poland was the first communist nation to restructure its prices this way. Upon taking office, the new, Solidarity-led government abruptly eliminated price subsidies on most consumer goods. The price of bread rose 40 percent in the first week of January 1990. Ham prices went up 55 percent; electricity and cooking gas climbed 400 percent, and the price of gasoline doubled. Although these price increases immediately reduced the real wages of Polish workers, they also had a positive effect. Suddenly more goods appeared on Polish shelves. Overnight, shortages disappeared. Polish workers had to pay more for basic goods, but at least they could find them.

The Castro government has been reluctant to abolish administered prices, particularly for goods that serve basic human needs. Unregulated peasant markets were authorized in 1979, outlawed in 1986, and then sanctioned again in 1994. In these markets, the prices of produce and handicrafts are set by the forces of supply and demand. In 1994 the government also raised the administered price of cigars, alcohol, and electricity. However, prices for most consumer staples remain centrally controlled and far below equilibrium levels and rationing continues.

Currency Reform

Price reform is effective only if money has some established value. Raising bread prices by 40 percent, for example, won't change the quantity of bread demanded or supplied if all incomes and prices also increase by 40 percent. ***The objective of price reform is to change the real and relative prices of specific goods.*** To achieve this objective the supply of money must be limited. Otherwise inflation will accelerate and the price reforms will get lost in a wave of rising prices. In Russia, the inflation rate skyrocketed to more than 1000 percent per year when the government tried to ease the pain of price reform by expanding the money supply.

Cuba has tried to sidestep currency reform by permitting widespread use of U.S. dollars. Scarce consumer goods may be purchased in government-run dollar stores. Cuban citizens are also permitted to hold and trade in U.S. dollars. The government even pays some work-incentive bonuses in dollar coupons that can be used to buy goods in the dollar stores. Most of the U.S. dollars in circulation are sent to Cuban citizens by relatives in the United States or earned in export markets. By permitting the "dollarization" of the Cuban economy, the government is promoting more efficiency but undermining the foundation of administered (peso) prices.

Price and currency reforms are the foundation of the market mechanism. To function effectively, however, the market also had to offer *incentives*. This was the most difficult issue for communists. To encourage or even permit private gain was contrary to the very principles of socialism. As a practical matter, however, the new governments of Eastern Europe recognized that market incentives were the key to faster growth. This meant that **profits** would have to be permitted. It also implied that individuals, rather than the state, could own the means of production. Individuals, not only the state, would have to be permitted to buy and hold property, build and operate factories, hire and fire labor, and accumulate profits. In other words, communism would have to permit capitalism if it wanted more goods and services.

Privatizing land, homes, and industries is a formidable challenge in an economy where the state ostensibly owns everything. In Poland most farmland had stayed in private ownership under communist rule. In Albania collective farms were split up in 1992 through a process the World Bank called "spontaneous privatization." In the rest of Eastern Europe and the former Soviet republics, however, the delineation and sale of farmland and machinery posed great difficulties. The huge state-owned factories presented even more formidable problems. No one had the money to buy large enterprises. Nor did their inefficient methods make them attractive acquisitions.

Cuba confronts these same challenges. As of 1999, the state still owned all the means of production, including factories, farms, land, and machinery. Cuban citizens could own their own homes, but even their resale value was regulated by the government. Foreign investors were invited to "participate" in joint ventures but couldn't own Cuban property or even hire Cuban workers directly.

Even if private property were permitted, the state would have to legitimize ownership rights. Market economies need well-established and enforced rules of market behavior. People must be able to buy and sell property. They also need assurance that contracts will be enforced. While a legal and judicial infrastructure is taken for granted in Western market economies, centrally planned economies lacked the institutions and laws required to support private property and market transactions. As a result, the transition to market economies requires sweeping institutional reform of legal, financial, and economic systems.

Fidel Castro not only failed to make the necessary institutional reforms, he also displayed a wanton disregard for property rights. The confiscation of automobiles and other property in 1994, the forced price regulation on privately owned homes, the arbitrary revisions to foreign-investment contracts, and the refusal to negotiate compensation of seized prerevolutionary assets undermined confidence in ownership rights.

Much of the resistance to market reforms originates in the core issue of egalitarianism. ***The ultimate justification for communist rule wasn't economic efficiency but social justice.*** "From each according to his ability, to each according to his need" is a basic principle of communism. The inequalities spawned by private property and markets gave impetus to the communist movement. In prerevolutionary Cuba, 1 percent of the landowners owned nearly half of all farmland. The great majority of Cubans were desperately poor, illiterate, and often unemployed. The Castro regime redistributed incomes to the poor, reduced income gaps between rural and urban areas, and brought schools, hospitals, and healthcare to the entire population. These were notable achievements, of which Castro is rightfully proud. Moreover, the passion for egalitarianism hadn't dimmed. Accordingly, Castro has been loath to adopt any market reforms that might "betray the revolution." He fears that market-based incentives will again generate widening inequalities, destroying the very fabric of socialist society.

China had grappled with this trade-off many times. The Cultural Revolution of 1966–1976 was an explicit reaction to the inequalities and rewards spawned by material incentives. During that period, private entrepreneurs were humiliated, imprisoned, and "reeducated." These same forces reemerged in 1989–1990. The successes bred by the 1979 reforms created a new class of successful entrepreneurs and farmers. Increasing

Private Property

profit: The difference between total revenue and total cost.

Institutional Reform

Equity vs. Efficiency

inequalities, however, spurred envy and unrest. Greater economic freedom also ignited demands for more political freedom. A Marxian backlash against market reforms accused entrepreneurs of being "capitalist roaders." The Chinese government started backpedaling on reforms. Echoing the Cultural Revolution, the government initiated a reeducation campaign that gave socialist principles priority over material incentives. During the global Asian crisis of 1997–1998, both China and Russia tightened state control over their economies (see WORLD VIEW).

Security vs. Uncertainty

The broad goal of egalitarianism has very tangible dimensions in most socialist countries. Everyone is guaranteed a job, healthcare, a pension, and access to subsidized goods and services. This "cradle-to-grave" security is hard to give up. When East Germany started moving toward reunification with West Germany, many workers worried about their socialist pensions, healthcare, and other welfare benefits. Although the inefficiencies of central planning constrained the quality and quantity of social services, at least *some* benefits were guaranteed to socialist workers. The Castro regime fears that market-directed resources will rip holes in the social safety net that now ensures that everyone's basic human needs are met. An "efficient" market might fail to allocate healthcare, educational, and social services to those with little ability to pay. Just the *fear* of such a lapse might spawn social and political anxiety.

The prospect of explicit unemployment is particularly upsetting. Like other centrally controlled economies, Cuba had guaranteed everyone a job. The state-run factories and collective farms are directed to hire all labor-force participants, regardless of their pro-

WORLD VIEW

China Debates Whether to Slow Reforms

BEIJING—China's senior Communist leaders are cloistered in a military-run hotel here this week, trying to reach consensus on whether to slow down or speed up the country's economic reforms.

Just over a year ago, the country was engaged in restructuring its obsolete state enterprises, inadequate housing system and insolvent banks. Then the Asian economic crisis hit, and though China has weathered the crisis well so far, reform efforts have slowed. The crisis has, for example, put on hold reforms designed to protect private property, give private entrepreneurs equal access, along with state enterprises, to the stock market and bank loans, break up monopolies and broaden the number of state companies allowed to declare bankruptcy.

—Matt Forney and Ian Johnson

The Wall Street Journal, Dec. 10, 1998, A19.

Tightened State Controls Are Urged in Russia

MOSCOW—Russia's new economics chief called for tighter state control over the economy yesterday, saying rapid free-market reform had outpaced the country's ability to change and led to financial collapse.

The comments by Yuri Maslyukov, a first deputy prime minister in charge of economic policy, and a Communist, point to a change of direction as Russia grapples with its worst economic crisis since the collapse of the Soviet Union. The country's new prime minister, Yevgeny Primakov, has yet to reveal his blueprint for handling the crisis, and key cabinet posts, such as that of finance minister, are expected to be filled only by the end of this week.

"The movement toward a free market is inevitable," Mr. Maslyukov told Russian news agencies while on a visit to St. Petersburg. But, he added, "our speed and expectations have surpassed our real opportunities, and instead of a free market we have got crisis and collapse of our financial system. The role of the state must, of course, be increased."

—Betsy McKay

The Wall Street Journal, Sept. 23, 1998, P. A14.

Analysis: The adoption of market incentives conflicts with core values of socialism. This conflict creates political stress and occasional policy reversals.

ductivity. This job guarantee generates **disguised unemployment,** with bloated payrolls and low productivity. In Poland, over 400,000 workers lost their jobs when state enterprises were privatized. Still more workers became unemployed when East Germany sold or dismantled its 126 state monopoly enterprises. In 1996, one million Russian coal miners went on strike to protest pay cuts and potential job losses. In Cuba, the government itself estimates that 600,000 to 800,000 workers in state enterprises—as much as one-fourth of the civilian workforce!—are redundant. Castro doesn't see how he can jettison all these workers in the name of efficiency without betraying the socialist commitment to equality.

disguised unemployment: People are employed but contribute little or nothing to total output.

THE ECONOMY TOMORROW

Cuba After Castro

The reality for Cuba is that the choice between a command economy and a market economy no longer exists. The Cuban economy survived, even grew, in economic isolation only because of Russian subsidies. Russia was not only the principal buyer of Cuba's exports (sugar and nickel) but also the main supplier of needed oil, machinery, fertilizers, and other production inputs. When the Russian barter ended, Cuba's production possibilities contracted sharply.

Cuba can't restore, much less expand, its production possibilities without vital imports. To acquire needed fuel, fertilizers, spare parts, tractors, and machinery, Cuba needs access to hard currency. Ironically, the remittances of Cuban refugees living in the United States have provided temporary relief. The Cuban government has obtained those dollars by making desired consumer goods available only in 600 state-run dollar stores. In 1994 close to $1 billion was obtained this way, a sum that exceeded the net value of sugar exports. Even that amount can't begin to replace the value of bartered Russian imports, which exceeded $6 billion per year.

China stepped up its aid to Cuba in 1993 and has become one of the largest buyers of Cuban sugar. In 1995 Castro visited China to see how that country balances market and nonmarket structures and to seek greater economic assistance. The Chinese government hasn't been willing, however, to assume the subsidy burden Russia once bore.

That leaves Castro only one real option: hard-currency markets. To tap those markets, Castro has to pursue the price, currency, property, and structural reforms that foreign investors demand. Although a few investors and creditors are willing to do business with Cuba without such reforms, most aren't willing to assume such risks. The U.S. government is even more insistent that economic reforms be implemented before the door to U.S. markets is opened. Until then, the United States is maintaining a trade embargo that shuts Cuba out of its largest prerevolutionary market.

Can Castro go it alone and snub demands for economic reform? Not likely. Cuba doesn't have the natural resources, the capital stock, or the currency reserves required to rebuild its economy. A good sugar harvest can help sustain the economy; but even future sugar harvests are threatened by shortages of fertilizers, tractors, fuel, and other inputs. Cuba has to attract foreign investment and loans to keep even that economic lifeline operating. Otherwise Cuba's production possibilities will continue to shrink and its living standards decline. Recognizing these drawbacks, Castro has experimented with very limited price and limited reforms. But Castro's commitment to socialism is unshaken. As one of his top aides asserted in January 1999, "We are not a capitalist country, we are a socialist one. We are not in the process of a transition. We are not becoming a capitalist economy." Yet, increasing tourism and international communication is giving Cuba's citizens—two-thirds of whom were born after the 1959 revolution—a vivid picture of how far their living standards have fallen behind more market-oriented nations. As equality increasingly comes to mean that everyone is poor, Cubans will demand greater structural reforms, perhaps even a capitalist revolution.

SUMMARY

- Marx's vision of communism foresaw an egalitarian society in which individuals would selflessly contribute to output and everyone's material needs would be satisfied.
- To achieve the desired mix of output and distribution of income, the state owns and directs the means of production. Central planning is the key mechanism for deciding WHAT, HOW, and FOR WHOM in a socialist economy.
- Central planning requires detailed knowledge of input-output relationships. As the variety of goods and the specificity of production goals increase, the risk of miscalculation rises.
- Centrally planned prices are used to achieve specific planning goals, for example, to discourage consumption of luxury goods or ensure access to necessities. Resource allocations (production decisions) are determined by central planners, however; prices don't function as conventional market signals.

- The low quality and quantity of planned consumption output force consumers to accumulate involuntary savings. The lack of consumer goods also creates market shortages, long lines, and pressure for reform.
- Incentives are a basic problem in planned economies. Most socialist countries reluctantly adopted limited material incentives (like bonuses and garden plots) to spur production.
- To achieve greater efficiency and growth, most socialist economies are restructuring. The transition to a market-based economy requires price reforms, currency reform, market-based incomes, and the introduction of private property rights.
- The transition from command to market systems entails significant social, economic, and political costs. These short-run costs often dictate a slow transition with occasional policy reversals.

Key Terms

capitalism	market economy	barter
communism	market mechanism	comparative advantage
socialism	market shortage	profit
production possibilities	suppressed inflation	disguised unemployment
investment	involuntary saving	
economic growth	hard currency	

Questions for Discussion

1. Suppose that an increase in agricultural output were a major objective of economic policy. What policy tools would the U.S. Congress use to bring about this result? What tools would the Soviet Gosplan have used?
2. Why do communists reject use of the market mechanism to allocate resources or distribute goods?
3. The unavailability of consumer luxury items in the Soviet Union helped to equalize living standards. How will increased availability of consumer goods affect incentives and equality?
4. Would you plan to work less or choose to enter a different occupation if everyone were paid equal wages regardless of the work they do? What would be the incentive to work under such circumstances?

5. Who is hurt and who is helped by the dismantling of price controls on food? On housing?
6. If Cuba suddenly became a capitalist economy, why might living standards increase? Would anyone be worse off?
7. Web Activity What has happened to the Russian ruble recently? Find out at www.itaiep.doc.gov/bisnis/ruble/ruble.htm. Then go to www.itaiep.doc.gov/bisnis/country/rusfed.htm#Russia and find an explanation for the recent rise or fall of the ruble.
8. Web Activity How is the U.S. trade embargo affecting the Cuban economy? Find out at www.latinworld.com/caribe/cuba/economy.

Problems for Chapter 22 appear at the back of the book.

Note: Numbers in parentheses indicate the chapters in which the definitions appear.

absolute advantage: The ability of a country to produce a specific good with fewer resources (per unit of output) than other countries. (20)

AD excess: The amount by which aggregate demand must be reduced to achieve full-employment equilibrium after allowing for price-level changes. (11)

AD shortfall: The amount of additional aggregate demand needed to achieve full employment after allowing for price-level changes. (11)

adjustable-rate mortgage (ARM): A mortgage (home loan) that adjusts the nominal interest rate to changing rates of inflation. (7)

aggregate demand (AD): The total quantity of output demanded at alternative price levels in a given time period, *ceteris paribus.* (8)(9)(10)(11)(13)(15)

aggregate expenditure: The rate of total expenditure desired at alternative levels of income, *ceteris paribus.* (9)

aggregate supply (AS): The total quantity of output producers are willing and able to supply at alternative price levels in a given time period, *ceteris paribus.* (8)(9)(10)(11)(16)

antitrust: Government intervention to alter market structure or prevent abuse of market power. (4)

appreciation: A rise in the price of one currency relative to another. (21)

arithmetic growth: An increase in quantity by a constant amount each year. (17)

asset: Anything having exchange value in the marketplace; wealth. (12)

automatic stabilizer: Federal expenditure or revenue item that automatically responds countercyclically to changes in national income, like unemployment benefits, income taxes. (12)(19)

average propensity to consume (APC): Total consumption in a given period divided by total disposable income. (9)

balance of payments: A summary record of a country's international economic transactions in a given period of time. (21)

balance-of-payments deficit: An excess demand for foreign currency at current exchange rates. (21)

balance-of-payments surplus: An excess demand for domestic currency at current exchange rates. (21)

bank reserves: Assets held by a bank to fulfill its deposit obligations. (13)

barter: The direct exchange of one good for another, without the use of money. (13)(22)

base period: The time period used for comparative analysis; the basis for indexing, e.g., of price changes. (5)(7)(17)

bond: A certificate acknowledging a debt and the amount of interest to be paid each year until repayment; an IOU. (14)

bracket creep: The movement of taxpayers into higher tax brackets (rates) as nominal incomes grow. (7)

budget deficit: Amount by which government spending exceeds government revenue in a given time period. (12)

budget surplus: An excess of government revenues over government expenditures in a given time period. (12)

business cycle: Alternating periods of economic growth and contraction. (8)(19)

capital: Final goods produced for use in the production of other goods, e.g., equipment, structures. (1)

capital deficit: The amount by which the capital outflow exceeds the capital inflow in a given time period. (18)

capital-intensive: Production processes that use a high ratio of capital to labor inputs. (2)

capital surplus: The amount by which the capital inflow exceeds the capital outflow in a given time period. (18)

capitalism: An economy in which the factors of production (e.g., land, capital) are owned by individuals; basic allocation decisions are made by market forces. (22)

categorical grants: Federal grants to state and local governments for specific expenditure purposes. (4)

ceteris paribus: The assumption of nothing else changing. (1)(3)

communism: A stateless, classless economy in which there's no private property and everyone shares in production and consumption according to individual abilities and needs. (22)

comparative advantage: The ability of a country to produce a specific good at a lower opportunity cost than its trading partners. (2)(18)(20)(22)

complementary goods: Goods frequently consumed in combination; when the price of good *x* rises, the demand for good *y* falls, *ceteris paribus.* (3)(20)

Consumer Price Index (CPI): A measure (index) of changes in the average price of consumer goods and services. (7)

consumption: Expenditure by consumers on final goods and services. (9)

consumption function: A mathematical relationship indicating the rate of desired consumer spending at various income levels. (9)(10)

consumption possibilities: The alternative combinations of goods and services that a country could consume in a given time period. (20)

cost-of-living adjustment (COLA): Automatic adjustments of nominal income to the rate of inflation. (7)

crowding in: An increase in private-sector borrowing (and spending) caused by decreased government borrowing. (12)

crowding out: A reduction in private-sector borrowing (and spending) caused by increased government borrowing. (11)(12)(15)(17)(18)

cyclical deficit: That portion of the budget deficit attributable to unemployment or inflation. (12)

cyclical unemployment: Unemployment attributable to a lack of job vacancies, that is, to an inadequate level of aggregate demand. (6)(9)(10)

debt ceiling: An explicit, legislated limit on the amount of outstanding national debt. (12)

debt service: The interest required to be paid each year on outstanding debt. (12)

deficit ceiling: An explicit, legislated limitation on the size of the budget deficit. (12)

deficit spending: The use of borrowed funds to finance government expenditures that exceed tax revenues. (12)

deflation: A decrease in the average level of prices of goods and services. (7)

demand: The willingness and ability to buy specific quantities of a good at alternative prices in a given time period, *ceteris paribus.* (3)

demand curve: A curve describing the quantities of a good a consumer is willing and able to buy at alternative prices in a given time period, *ceteris paribus.* (3)

demand for money: The quantities of money people are willing and able to hold at alternative interest rates, *ceteris paribus.* (15)

demand-pull inflation: An increase in the price level initiated by excessive aggregate demand. (9)(10)

demand schedule: A table showing the quantities of a good a consumer is willing and able to buy at alternative prices in a given time period, *ceteris paribus.* (3)

deposit creation: The creation of transactions deposits by bank lending. (13)

depreciation: The consumption of capital in the production process; the wearing out of plant and equipment. (5)

depreciation (currency): A fall in the price of one currency relative to another. (21)

devaluation: An abrupt depreciation of a currency whose value was fixed or managed by the government. (21)

discount rate: The rate of interest the Federal Reserve charges for lending reserves to private banks. (14)

discounting: Federal Reserve lending of reserves to private banks. (14)

discouraged worker: An individual who isn't actively seeking employment but would look for or accept a job if one were available. (6)

discretionary fiscal spending: Those elements of the federal budget not determined by past legislative or executive commitments. (12)

disguised unemployment: People are employed but contribute little or nothing to total output. (22)

disposable income (DI): After-tax income of households; personal income less personal taxes. (5)(9)(11)

dissaving: Consumption expenditure in excess of disposable income; a negative saving flow. (9)

dumping: The sale of goods in export markets at prices below domestic prices. (20)

economic growth: An increase in output (real GDP); an expansion of production possibilities. (1)(2)(17)(22)

economics: The study of how best to allocate scarce resources among competing uses. (1)

efficiency: Maximum output of a good from the resources used in production. (1)

efficiency (technical): Maximum output of a good from the resources used in production. (1)

embargo: A prohibition on exports or imports. (20)

entrepreneurship: The assembling of resources to produce new or improved products and technologies. (1)

equation of exchange: Money supply *(M)* times velocity of circulation *(V)* equals level of aggregate spending *(P × Q)*. (15)(16)

equilibrium (macro): The combination of price level and real output that is compatible with both aggregate demand and aggregate supply. (8)(9)(11)

equilibrium GDP: The rate of real output at which aggregate demand equals aggregate supply. (10)

equilibrium price: The price at which the quantity of a good demanded in a given time period equals the quantity supplied. (3)(20)(21)

equilibrium rate of interest: The interest rate at which the quantity of money demanded in a given time period equals the quantity of money supplied. (15)

excess reserves: Bank reserves in excess of required reserves. (13)(14)

exchange rate: The price of one country's currency expressed in terms of another's; the domestic price of a foreign currency. (18)(21)

expenditure equilibrium: The rate of output at which desired spending equals the value of output. (9)(10)

exports: Goods and services sold to foreign buyers. (2)(5)(18)(20)

external debt: U.S. government debt (Treasury bonds) held by foreign households and institutions. (12)

externalities: Costs (or benefits) of a market activity borne by a third party; the difference between the social and private costs (benefits) of a market activity. (2)(4)

factor market: Any place where factors of production (e.g., land, labor, capital) are bought and sold. (3)

factors of production: Resource inputs used to produce goods and services, e.g., land, labor, capital, entrepreneurship. (1)(2)

federal funds rate: The interest rate for interbank reserve loans. (14)(15)

fine-tuning: Adjustments in economic policy designed to counteract small changes in economic outcomes; continuous responses to changing economic conditions. (19)

fiscal policy: The use of government taxes and spending to alter macroeconomic outcomes. (8)(11)(12)(19)

fiscal restraint: Tax hikes or spending cuts intended to reduce (shift) aggregate demand. (11)(19)

fiscal stimulus: Tax cuts or spending hikes intended to increase (shift) aggregate demand. (11)(19)

fiscal year (FY): The 12-month period used for accounting purposes; begins October 1 for the federal government. (12)

flexible exchange rates: A system in which exchange rates are permitted to vary with market supply-and-demand conditions; floating exchange rates. (21)

foreign-exchange markets: Places where foreign currencies are bought and sold. (21)

foreign-exchange reserves: Holdings of foreign exchange by official government agencies, usually the central bank or treasury. (21)

free rider: An individual who reaps direct benefits from someone else's purchase (consumption) of a public good. (4)

frictional unemployment: Brief periods of unemployment experienced by people moving between jobs or into the labor market. (6)

full employment: The lowest rate of unemployment compatible with price stability; variously estimated at between 4 and 6 percent unemployment. (6)(10)

full-employment GDP: The total market value of final goods and services that could be produced in a given time period at full employment; potential GDP. (8)(9)(10)

GDP deflator: A price index that refers to all goods and services included in GDP. (7)

GDP gap (real): The difference between full-employment GDP and equilibrium GDP. (10)(11)(19)

GDP per capita: Total GDP divided by total population; average GDP. (5)(17)

geometric growth: An increase in quantity by a constant proportion each year. (17)

gold reserves: Stocks of gold held by a government to purchase foreign exchange. (21)

gold standard: An agreement by countries to fix the price of their currencies in terms of gold; a mechanism for fixing exchange rates. (21)

government failure: Government intervention that fails to improve economic outcomes. (1)(4)

gross business saving: Depreciation allowances and retained earnings. (9)

gross domestic product (GDP): The total market value of all final goods and services produced within a nation's borders in a given time period. (2)(5)

gross investment: Total investment expenditure in a given time period. (5)

growth rate: Percentage change in real output from one period to another. (17)

growth recession: A period during which real GDP grows, but at a rate below the long-term trend of 3 percent. (8)(19)

hard currency: Any national currency widely accepted in payment in international markets. (22)

human capital: The knowledge and skills possessed by the workforce. (2)(16)(17)(22)

hyperinflation: Inflation rate in excess of 200 percent, lasting at least 1 year. (7)

imports: Goods and services purchased from international sources. (2)(5)(18)(20)

income quintile: One-fifth of the population, rank-ordered by income (e.g., top fifth). (2)

income transfers: Payments to individuals for which no current goods or services are exchanged, e.g., Social Security, welfare, unemployment benefits. (2)(11)(12)

income velocity of money *(V)*: The number of times per year, on average, a dollar is used to purchase final goods and services; $PQ \div M$. (15)

inflation: An increase in the average level of prices of goods and services. (4)(5)(7)(8)

inflation rate: The annual percentage rate of increase in the average price level. (7)

inflationary gap: The amount by which aggregate spending at full employment exceeds full-employment output. (9)(10)

infrastructure: The transportation, communications, education, judicial, and other institutional systems that facilitate market exchanges. (16)

injection: An addition of spending to the circular flow of income. (9)

interest rate: The price paid for the use of money. (15)

intermediate goods: Goods or services purchased for use as input in the production of final goods or in services. (5)

internal debt: U.S. government debt (Treasury bonds) held by U.S. households and institutions. (12)

investment: Expenditures on (production of) new plant, equipment, and structures (capital) in a given time period, plus changes in business inventories. (2)(5)(9)(16)(22)

involuntary saving: Consumer saving compelled by shortages of consumer goods. (22)

item weight: The percentage of total expenditure spent on a specific product; used to compute inflation indexes. (7)

labor force: All persons over age 16 who are either working for pay or actively seeking paid employment. (6)(17)

labor-force participation rate: The percentage of the population working or seeking employment. (6)

labor productivity: Amount of output produced by a worker in a given period of time; output per hour (or day, etc.). (16)

laissez faire: The doctrine of "leave it alone," of nonintervention by government in the market mechanism. (1)(8)

law of demand: The quantity of a good demanded in a given time period increases as its price falls, *ceteris paribus*. (3)(8)

law of supply: The quantity of a good supplied in a given time period increases as its price increases, *ceteris paribus*. (3)

leakage: Income not spent directly on domestic output but instead diverted from the circular flow, e.g., saving, imports, taxes. (9)(18)

liability: An obligation to make future payment; debt. (12)

liquidity trap: The portion of the money demand curve that is horizontal; people are willing to hold unlimited amounts of money at some (low) interest rate. (15)

M1 money supply: Currency held by the public, plus balances in transactions accounts. (13)(14)

M2 money supply: M1 plus balances in most savings accounts and money market mutual funds. (13)(14)

macroeconomics: The study of aggregate economic behavior, of the economy as a whole. (1)(8)

managed exchange rates: A system in which governments intervene in foreign-exchange markets to limit but not eliminate exchange-rate fluctuations; "dirty floats." (21)

marginal propensity to consume (MPC): The fraction of each additional (marginal) dollar of disposable income spent on consumption; the change in consumption divided by the change in disposable income. (9)(10)(11)

marginal propensity to import (MPM): The fraction of each additional (marginal) dollar of disposable income spent on imports. (18)

marginal propensity to save (MPS): The fraction of each additional (marginal) dollar of disposable income not spent on consumption; $1 - $ MPC. (9)(18)

marginal tax rate: The tax rate imposed on the last (marginal) dollar of income. (16)

market demand: The total quantities of a good or service people are willing and able to buy at alternative prices in a given time period; the sum of individual demands. (3)

market economy: An economy that relies on markets for basic decisions about WHAT to produce, HOW to produce it, and FOR WHOM to produce. (22)

market failure: An imperfection in the market mechanism that prevents optimal outcomes. (1)(4)

market mechanism: The use of market prices and sales to signal desired outputs (or resource allocations). (1)(3)(4)(22)

market power: The ability to alter the market price of a good or service. (4)

market shortage: The amount by which the quantity demanded exceeds the quantity supplied at a given price; excess demand. (3)(21)(22)

market supply: The total quantities of a good that sellers are willing and able to sell at alternative prices in a given time period, *ceteris paribus*. (3)

market surplus: The amount by which the quantity supplied exceeds the quantity demanded at a given price; excess supply. (3)

microeconomics: The study of individual behavior in the economy, of the components of the larger economy. (1)

mixed economy: An economy that uses both market signals and government directives to allocate goods and resources. (1)

monetary policy: The use of money and credit controls to influence macroeconomic outcomes. (8)(14)(15)(19)

money: Anything generally accepted as a medium of exchange. (13)

money illusion: The use of nominal dollars rather than real dollars to gauge changes in one's income or wealth. (7)

money multiplier: The number of deposit (loan) dollars that the banking system can create from $1 of excess reserves; equal to $1 \div$ required reserve ratio. (13)(14)

money supply (M1): Currency held by the public, plus balances in transactions accounts. (13)(14)(15)

money supply (M2): M1 plus balances in most savings accounts and money market funds. (13)(14)(15)

monopoly: A firm that produces the entire market supply of a particular good or service. (2)(4)

multiplier: The multiple by which an initial change in aggregate spending will alter total expenditure after an infinite number of spending cycles; $1/(1 - $ MPC). (10)(11)(18)(19)

national debt: Accumulated debt of the federal government. (12)

national income (NI): Total income earned by current factors of production: NDP less depreciation and indirect business taxes. (5)

national-income accounting: The measurement of aggregate economic activity, particularly national income and its components. (5)

natural monopoly: An industry in which one firm can achieve economies of scale over the entire range of market supply. (4)

natural rate of unemployment: Long-term rate of unemployment determined by structural forces in labor and product markets. (6)(15)(19)

net domestic product (NDP): GDP less depreciation. (5)

net exports: The value of exports minus the value of imports: $(X - IM)$. (2)(5)(18)

net investment: Gross investment less depreciation. (5)(17)

nominal GDP: The value of final output produced in a given period, measured in the prices of that period (current prices). (5)(7)

nominal income: The amount of money income received in a given time period, measured in current dollars. (7)

Okun's Law: 1 percent more unemployment is estimated to equal 2 percent less output. (6)

open market operations: Federal Reserve purchases and sales of government bonds for the purpose of altering bank reserves. (14)

opportunity cost: The most desired goods or services that are forgone in order to obtain something else. (1)(3)(4)(12)(20)

optimal mix of output: The most desirable combination of output attainable with existing resources, technology, and social values. (4)(12)

per capita GDP: The dollar value of GDP divided by total population; average GDP. (2)

personal income (PI): Income received by households before payment of personal taxes. (5)

Phillips curve: An historical (inverse) relationship between the rate of unemployment and the rate of inflation; commonly expresses a trade-off between the two. (16)

portfolio decision. The choice of how (where) to hold idle funds. (14)(15)

precautionary demand for money: Money held for unexpected market transactions or for emergencies. (15)

price ceiling: Upper limit imposed on the price of a good. (3)

price elasticity of demand: The percentage change in quantity demanded divided by the percentage change in price. (22)

price stability: The absence of significant changes in the average price level; officially defined as a rate of inflation of less than 3 percent. (7)

private good: A good or service whose consumption by one person excludes consumption by others. (4)

product market: Any place where finished goods and services (products) are bought and sold. (3)

production possibilities: The alternative combinations of final goods and services that could be produced in a given time period with all available resources and technology. (1)(5)(6)(17)(20)(22)

productivity: Output per unit of input, e.g., output per labor-hour. (2)(17)(18)(22)

profit: The difference between total revenue and total cost. (22)

progressive tax: A tax system in which tax rates rise as incomes rise. (4)

public choice: Theory of public-sector behavior emphasizing rational self-interest of decision makers and voters. (4)

public good: A good or service whose consumption by one person does not exclude consumption by others. (4)

quota: A limit on the quantity of a good that may be imported in a given time period. (20)

rational expectations: Hypothesis that people's spending decisions are based on all available information, including the anticipated effects of government intervention. (19)

real GDP: The value of final output produced in a given period, adjusted for changing prices. (5)(7)(8)(17)

real income: Income in constant dollars; nominal income adjusted for inflation. (7)

real interest rate: The nominal interest rate minus the anticipated inflation rate. (7)(15)

recession: A decline in total output (real GDP) for two or more consecutive quarters. (8)

recessionary gap: The amount by which aggregate spending at full employment falls short of full-employment output. (9)(10)

refinancing: The issuance of new debt in payment of debt issued earlier. (12)

regressive tax: A tax system in which tax rates fall as incomes rise. (4)

relative price: The price of one good in comparison with the price of other goods. (7)

required reserves: The minimum amount of reserves a bank is required to hold; equal to required reserve ratio times transactions deposits. (13)(14)

reserve ratio: The ratio of a bank's reserves to its total transactions deposits. (13)

saving: That part of disposable income not spent on current consumption; disposable income less consumption. (5)(9)(16)

Say's Law: Supply creates its own demand. (8)

scarcity: The fact that available resources are insufficient to satisfy all desired uses thereof. (1)

seasonal unemployment: Unemployment due to seasonal changes in employment or labor supply. (6)

shift in demand: A change in the quantity demanded at any (every) given price. (3)

skills gap: Gap between skills required for emerging jobs and the skills of workers. (6)

socialism: An economy in which all nonlabor means of production are owned by the state, which exercises control over resource allocation. (22)

speculative demand for money: Money held for speculative purposes, for later financial opportunities. (15)

stagflation: The simultaneous occurrence of substantial unemployment and inflation. (16)(19)

structural deficit: Federal revenues at full employment minus expenditures at full employment under prevailing fiscal policy. (12)(19)

structural unemployment: Unemployment caused by a mismatch between the skills (or location) of job seekers and the requirements (or location) of available jobs. (6)(16)

substitute goods: Goods that substitute for each other; when the price of good *x* rises, the demand for good *y* increases, *ceteris paribus*. (3)

supply: The ability and willingness to sell (produce) specific quantities of a good at alternative prices in a given time period, *ceteris paribus*. (3)

supply-side policy: The use of tax incentives, (de)regulation, and other mechanisms to increase the ability and willingness to produce goods and services. (8)(19)

suppressed inflation: Inflationary imbalances reflected in nonprice forms (e.g., market shortages and rationing) when prices aren't permitted to rise. (22)

tariff: A tax (duty) imposed on imported goods. (20)

tax elasticity of supply: The percentage change in quantity supplied divided by the percentage change in tax rates. (16)

tax rebate: A lump-sum refund of taxes paid. (16)

terms of trade: The rate at which goods are exchanged; the amount of good *A* given up for good *B* in trade. (20)

trade deficit: The amount by which the value of imports exceeds the value of exports in a given time period (negative net exports). (18)(20)(21)

trade surplus: The amount by which the value of exports exceeds the value of imports in a given time period (positive net exports). (18)(20)

transactions account: A bank account that permits direct payment to a third party, for example, with a check. (13)

transactions demand for money: Money held for the purpose of making everyday market purchases. (15)

transfer payments: Payments to individuals for which no current goods or services are exchanged, like Social Security, welfare, unemployment benefits. (4)(16)

Treasury bonds: Promissory notes (IOUs) issued by the U.S. Treasury. (12)

underemployment: People seeking full-time paid employment who work only part time or are employed at jobs below their capability. (6)

unemployment: The inability of labor-force participants to find jobs. (4)(6)

unemployment rate: The proportion of the labor force that is unemployed. (6)

user charge: Fee paid for the use of a public-sector good or service. (4)

value added: The increase in the market value of a product that takes place at each stage of the production process. (5)

velocity of money (V): The number of times per year, on average, that a dollar is used to purchase final goods and services; $PO \div M$. (19)

voluntary restraint agreement (VRA): An agreement to reduce the volume of trade in a specific good; a "voluntary" quota. (20)

yield: The rate of return on a bond; the annual interest payment divided by the bond's price. (14)

Note: Page numbers followed by *n* indicate footnotes. **Boldface** indicates glossary terms defined in the text.

Problems for Chapter 3

Name: _____

1. According to Figure 3.4, what quantity of typing would be demanded at a price of $2.00 per page at Clearview College if
   (a) Lisa dropped out of school? _____
   (b) Tom's demand doubled? _____

2. According to Figure 3.5, what would happen to the quantity of typing supplied at $3.00 per page if Bob decided he didn't want to type any more? _____

3. Given the following data, identify the amount of shortage or surplus that would exist at a price of
   (a) $5.00 _____
   (b) $3.00 _____
   (c) $1.00 _____

A. Price	$5.00	$4.00	$3.00	$2.00	$1.00		$5.00	$4.00	$3.00	$2.00	$1.00
B. Quantity demanded						C. Quantity supplied					
Al	1	2	3	4	5	Alice	3	3	3	3	3
Betsy	0	1	1	1	2	Butch	7	5	4	4	2
Casey	2	2	3	3	4	Connie	6	4	3	3	1
Daisy	1	3	4	4	6	Dutch	6	5	4	3	0
Eddie	1	2	2	3	5	Ellen	4	2	2	2	1
Market total	—	—	—	—	—	Market total	—	—	—	—	—

4. Graph the official and equilibrium prices for the U2 rock concert (see NEWS, page 57).

PRICE (per ticket)

QUANTITY (tickets per show)

5. In Figure 3.8, when a price ceiling is imposed, by how much does
   (a) the quantity of housing demanded increase? _____
   (b) the quantity of housing supplied decrease? _____
   (c) How large is the resulting shortage? _____

6. In the WORLD VIEW on page 60, menu prices are continuously adjusted. Graph the initial and final (adjusted) prices for the following situations. Be sure to label axes and graph completely.

(a) Customers are ordering too little haddock

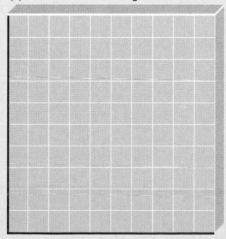

(b) The kitchen is running out of beef ribs

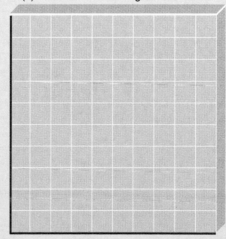

7. On the accompanying graph, reproduce the Clearview typing services market, as illustrated in Figure 3.6.
   (*a*) What is the equilibrium price?   _____

   Now suppose that course requirements stiffen and that students demand four times as many pages at every price. Illustrate the new demand curve on the graph.
   (*b*) What is the new equilibrium price?   _____
   (*c*) What is the new equilibrium quantity?   _____

   If the computer lab then decided to limit the availability of computers for word processing, the supply of typing at every price would decline by 50 percent. Illustrate this change in supply on the graph.

   After these demand and supply shifts,
   (*d*) what is the final equilibrium price?   _____
   (*e*) what quantity is produced and sold at that price?   _____

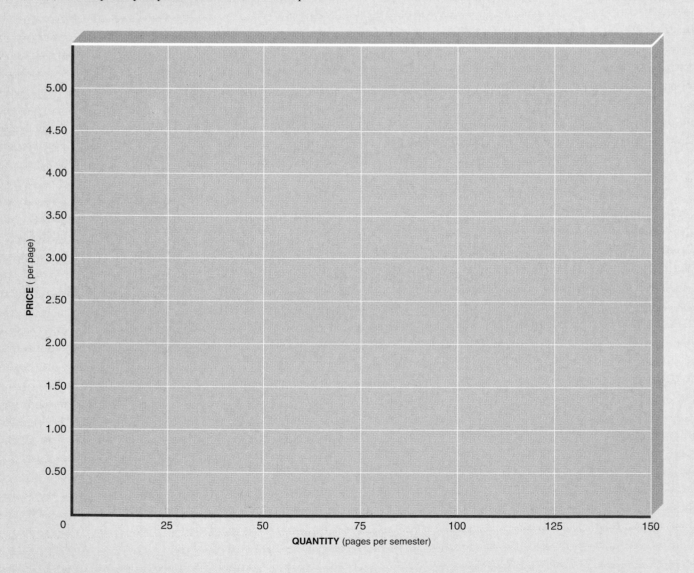

Problems for Chapter 4

Name: _____

1. In Figure 4.2, by how much is the market
   (a) overproducing private goods?   _____
   (b) underproducing public goods?   _____

2. Assume that the product depicted on the graph below generates external costs of $5 per unit.
   (a) Draw the social demand curve.
   (b) What is the optimal output?   _____

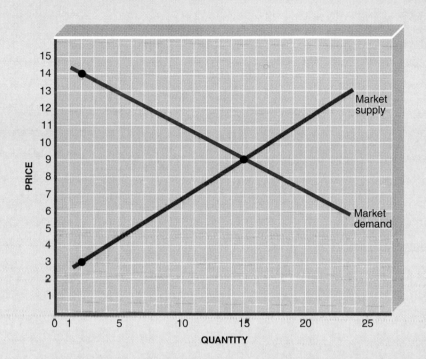

3. (a) Assuming a 10 percent sales tax is levied on all consumption, complete the following table:

Income	Consumption	Sales Tax	Percent of Income Paid in Taxes
$10,000	$10,000	_____	_____
20,000	19,000	_____	_____
40,000	36,000	_____	_____
80,000	68,000	_____	_____

   (b) Is the sales tax progressive or regressive?   _____

4. If a new home can be constructed for $75,000, what is the opportunity cost of federal defense spending, measured in terms of private housing? (Assume a defense budget of $270 billion per year.)   _____

5. Suppose the following data represent the prices that each of three consumers is willing to pay for a good:

Quantity	Consumer A	Consumer B	Consumer C
1	$50	$40	$30
2	30	20	20
3	20	15	10

(a) Construct the market demand curve for this good on the graph below.

(b) If this good were priced in the market at $40, how many units would be demanded? _____

(c) Now suppose that this is a public good, in the sense that all consumers receive satisfaction from the good even if only one person buys it. Under these conditions, what is the social value of the

   (i) first unit? _____

  (ii) second unit? _____

  (iii) third unit? _____

(d) Using the social values computed above, draw a "social demand curve" on the graph below.

(e) Based on the social demand curve, how many units of this good are demanded by society at a price of $40? _____

(f) What is the evidence of market failure in this case? _____

_____

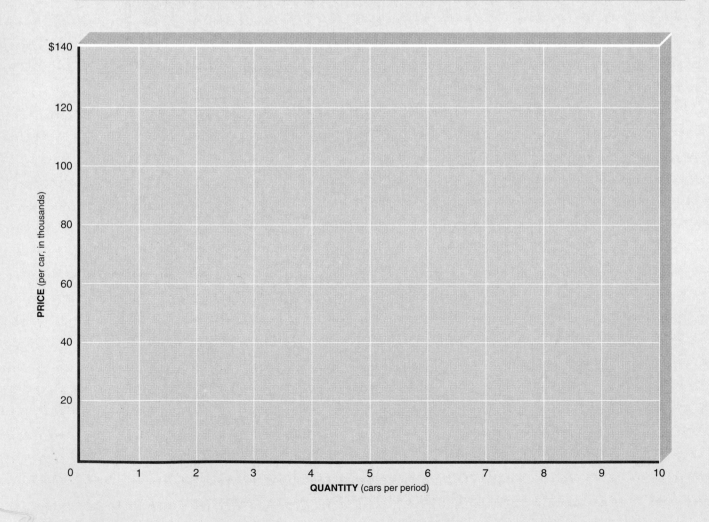

Problems for Chapter 5

1. Suppose that furniture production encompasses the following stages:

   Stage 1: Trees sold to lumber company $1000

   Stage 2: Lumber sold to furniture company $1700

   Stage 3: Furniture company sells furniture to retail store $3200

   Stage 4: Furniture store sells furniture to consumer $5995

   (*a*) What is the value added at each stage?   Stage 1: _____

                                                               Stage 2: _____

                                                               Stage 3: _____

                                                               Stage 4: _____

   (*b*) How much does this output contribute to GDP?   _____

   (*c*) How would answer (*b*) change if the lumber were imported from Canada?   _____

2. If real GDP increases by 5 percent next year and the price level goes up by 3 percent, what will happen to nominal GDP?   _____

3. What was real per capita GDP in 1933, measured in 1990 prices? (Use the data in Table 5.4 to compute your answer.)   _____

4. (*a*) Calculate national income from the following figures:

Consumption	$200 billion
Depreciation	20 billion
Retained earnings	12 billion
Gross investment	30 billion
Imports	40 billion
Social Security taxes	25 billion
Exports	50 billion
Indirect business taxes	15 billion
Government purchases	60 billion
Personal income taxes	40 billion

                                                                                     NI: _____

   (*b*) If there were 80 million people in this country, what would the GDP per capita be?   _____

   (*c*) If all prices were to double overnight, what would happen to the values of real and nominal GDP per capita?   Real GDP: _____

                                                                    Nominal GDP: _____

5. (*a*) Compute real GDP for 1995 using average prices of 1985 as the base year. (On the inside front cover and the first page of this book you'll find data for GDP and the GDP "price deflator" used to measure inflation.)

   (*b*) By how much did real GDP increase between 1985 and 1995?   _____

   (*c*) By how much did nominal GDP increase between 1985 and 1995?   _____

6. Suppose all the dollar values in Problem 4 were in 1990 dollars. Use the Consumer Price Index shown on the last page of this book to convert the numbers to 1998 dollars. What is the value of national income in 1998 dollars? (You'll be converting the figures from their nominal to their real values, with 1998 as the base year.)   _____

7. On the accompanying graph, illustrate (*A*) nominal per capita GDP and (*B*) real per capita GDP
   for each year. (The necessary data appear on the inside front cover and the first page of this book.)
   (*a*) By what percent did nominal per capita GDP increase in the 1980s?   _____
   (*b*) By what percent did real per capita GDP increase in the 1980s?   _____
   (*c*) In how many years did nominal per capita GDP decline?   _____
   (*d*) In how many years did real per capita GDP decline?   _____
   (*e*) What explains the divergence between nominal and real growth rates? _____

   _____

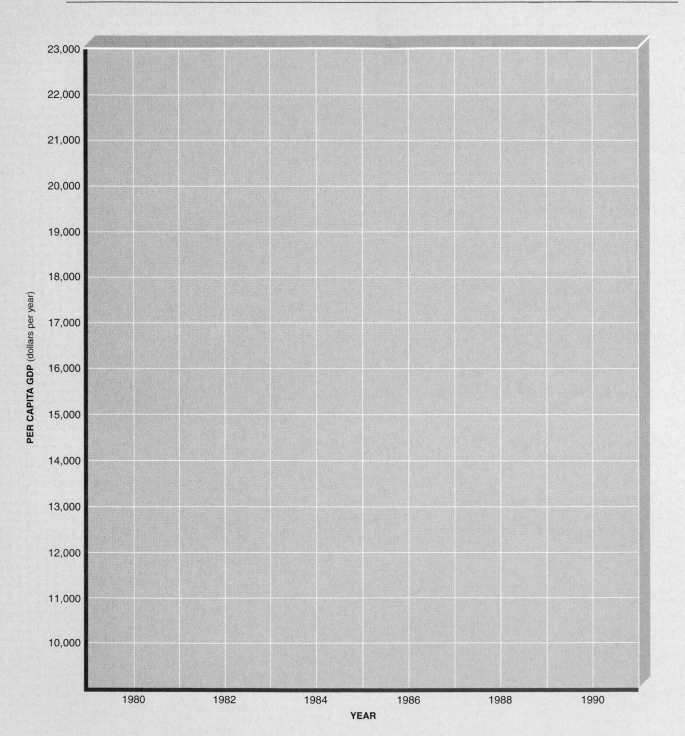

Problems for Chapter 6

Name: _____

1. According to Figure 6.1, what percent of the labor force was
   (*a*) employed?   _____
   (*b*) unemployed?   _____
   What percent of the *population* was employed?   _____

2. Between 1980 and 1990, by how much did the labor-force participation rate of
   (*a*) men fall?   _____
   (*b*) women rise?   _____

3. According to Okun's Law (updated), how much output was lost in 1992 when the nation's unemployment rate increased from 7.0 percent to 7.4 percent?   _____

4. Suppose the following data describe a nation's population:

	Year 1	Year 2
Population	200 million	203 million
Labor force	120 million	125 million
Unemployment rate	6 percent	6 percent

   (*a*) How many people are unemployed in each year?   Year 1: _____
                                                            Year 2: _____
   (*b*) How many people are employed in each year?   Year 1: _____
                                                            Year 2: _____
   (*c*) Compute the employment rate (i.e., number employed ÷ *population*) in each year.   Year 1: _____
                                                            Year 2: _____
   (*d*) How can the employment rate rise when the *un*employment rate is constant?

5. On the accompanying graph, illustrate both the unemployment rate (see inside back cover for data) and the percentage change in real GDP (output) for each year (see the first page of this book for data).
   (*a*) In how many years was "full employment" achieved? (Use current benchmark.) _____
   (*b*) Unemployment and growth rates tend to move in opposite directions. Which appears to change direction first? _____
   (*c*) Does the unemployment rate ever increase even when output is expanding? _____

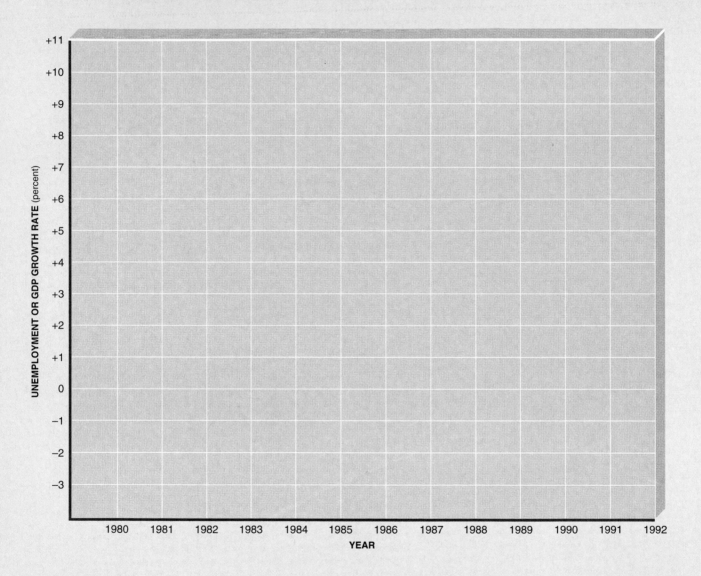

Problems for Chapter 7

Name: _____

1. If tuition keep increasing at the same rate as in 1998 (see NEWS, page 125), what will it cost to attend a private 4-year college 5 years from now? _____

2. Suppose you'll have an annual nominal income of $40,000 for each of the next 3 years, and the inflation rate is 5 percent per year.
   (a) Find the real value of your $40,000 salary for each of the next 3 years.

   Year 1: _____
   Year 2: _____
   Year 3: _____

   (b) Suppose you have a COLA of 5 percent per year in your contract, which raises your $40,000 salary by 5 percent for each of the next 3 years. Given the 5 percent inflation rate for each of those 3 years, what is the real value of your salary for each year?

   Year 1: _____
   Year 2: _____
   Year 3: _____

3. In the WORLD VIEW on page 139, what is the real rate of interest in Brazil? _____

4. Assuming that the following table describes a typical consumer's complete budget, compute the item weights for each product.

Item	Quantity	Unit Price	Item Weight:
Coffee	20 pounds	$ 3	_____
Tuition	1 year	4000	_____
Pizza	100 pizzas	8	_____
VCR rental	75 days	15	_____
Vacation	2 weeks	300	_____
		Total:	_____

5. Suppose the prices listed in the table for Problem 4 changed from one year to the next, as shown below. Use the rest of the table to compute the average inflation rate.

Item	Unit Price Last Year	This Year	Percent Change	Item Weight	Inflation Impact
Coffee	$ 3	$ 4	_____	_____	_____
Tuition	4000	7000	_____	_____	_____
Pizza	8	10	_____	_____	_____
VCR rental	15	10	_____	_____	_____
Vacation	300	500	_____	_____	_____
				Average Inflation:	_____

6. Use the item weights in Figure 7.2 to determine the percentage change in the CPI that would result from a
   (a) 10 percent increase in recreation prices _____
   (b) 6 percent decrease in transportation costs _____
   (c) doubling of clothing prices _____
   (Review Table 7.4 for assistance.)

7. Use the GDP deflator data on the last page of the book to compute real GDP in 1970 at 1998 prices. _____

8. According to Table 7.3, what happened during the period shown to the
   (a) nominal price of gold _____
   (b) real price of gold _____

9. On the accompanying graph, illustrate for each year (*A*) the nominal interest rate (use the "prime" rate of interest) and (*B*) the real interest rate (adjusted for same-year CPI inflation). (The required data appear on the last page of the book.)
   (*a*) In what year was the official goal of price stability met? _____
   (*b*) In that year, what was the
      (*i*) nominal interest rate? _____
      (*ii*) real interest rate? _____
   (*c*) What was the range of rates during this period for
      (*i*) nominal interest rates? _____
      (*ii*) real interest rates? _____
   (*d*) On a year-to-year basis which varies more, nominal or real interest rates? _____

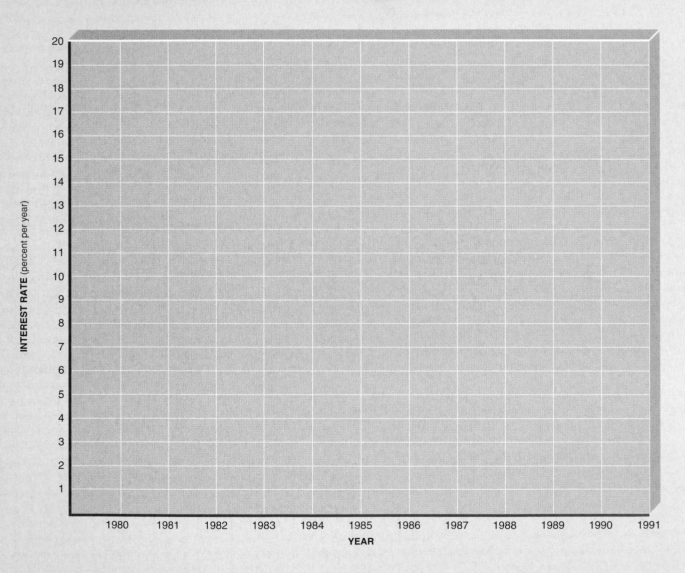

Problems for Chapter 8

Name: _____

1. Suppose you have $500 in savings when the price level index is at 100.
   (a) If inflation pushes the price level up by 20 percent, what will be the real value of your savings? _____
   (b) What would happen to the real value of your savings if the price level instead *declined* by 10 percent? _____

2. Use the following information to draw aggregate demand and aggregate supply curves on the graph below. Both curves are assumed to be straight lines.

Average Price	Real Output Demanded (per year)	Real Output Supplied (per year)
$1000	0	$1000
100	$900	100

   (a) At what price level does equilibrium occur? _____
   (b) What curve would have shifted if a new equilibrium were to occur at an output level of 700 and a price level of 700? _____
   (c) What curve would have shifted if a new equilibrium were to occur at an output level of 700 and a price level of 500? _____
   (d) What curve would have shifted if a new equilibrium were to occur at an output level of 700 and a price level of 300? _____
   (e) Compared to the initial equilibrium (a), how have price levels or output changed in
      (b) output: _____ price level: _____
      (c) output: _____ price level: _____
      (d) output: _____ price level: _____

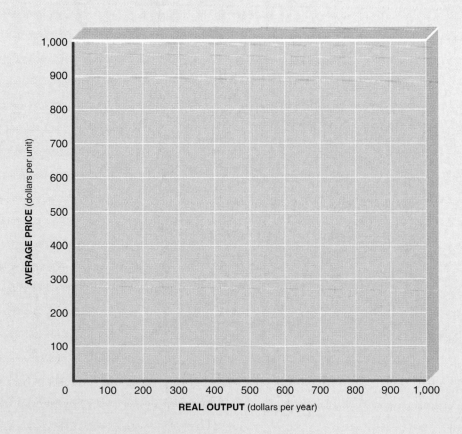

3. Illustrate these events with AS or AD shifts:

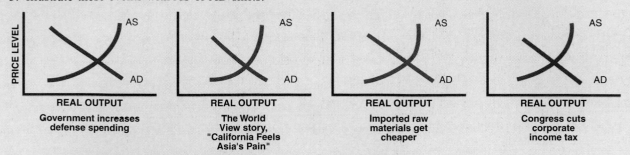

Government increases defense spending	**The World View story, "California Feels Asia's Pain"**	**Imported raw materials get cheaper**	**Congress cuts corporate income tax**

4. Assume that the accompanying graph depicts aggregate supply and demand conditions in an economy. Full employment occurs when $6 trillion of real output is produced.
   (*a*) What is the equilibrium rate of output?   _____
   (*b*) How far short of full employment is the equilibrium rate of output?   _____
   (*c*) Illustrate a shift of aggregate demand that would change the equilibrium rate of output to $6
         trillion. Label the new curve AD₂.
   (*d*) What is the price level at the new equilibrium?   _____
   (*e*) Illustrate a shift of aggregate supply (AS₂) that would, when combined with AD₁, move equi-
         librium output to $6 trillion.
   (*f*) What is the price level at this new equilibrium?   _____

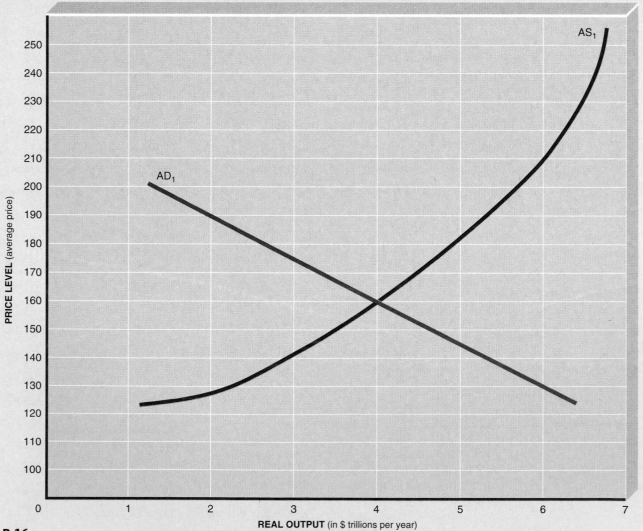

Problems for Chapter 9

Name: _____

1. According to the NEWS feature on page 178, what was the marginal propensity to consume in 1998?

2. Suppose the economy includes only consumers and business (no government or international trade) and that consumer saving is the only source of leakage (so $Y = Y_D$). In this private-sector economy, spending behavior is represented by

$$C = \$450 + 0.5Y \qquad I = \$300$$

(a) Use this information to complete the following table:

Income	C	+	I	=	Desired Spending
$500	_____		_____		_____
1000	_____		_____		_____
1500	_____		_____		_____
2000	_____		_____		_____
2500	_____		_____		_____

(b) What is the value of equilibrium output? _____

(c) If full employment output is $2500, what kind of gap exists? _____

(d) How large is the gap in (c)? _____

3. What happens to equilibrium in Figure 9.12 if
   (a) exports double? _____
   (b) government spending increases by $100 billion? _____
   (c) the marginal propensity to consume increases from 0.75 to 0.80? _____

4. On the accompanying graph, draw the consumption function $C = \$150 + 0.8Y_D$.
   (a) At what level of income do households begin to save? _____
      Designate that point on the graph with the letter A.
   (b) What happens to consumption if income increases by $200 beyond the break-even level of point A? Designate this new level of consumption with point B. _____
   (c) Illustrate the impact on consumption of the change in consumer confidence described in NEWS on page 176.

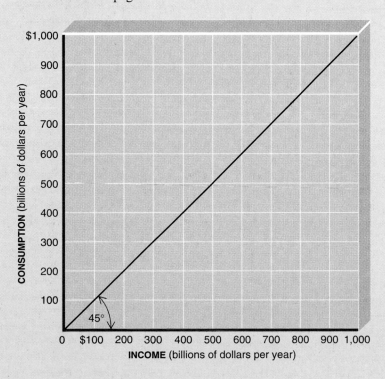

5. Illustrate on the following two graphs what was happening to aggregate demand in Japan according to the WORLD VIEW on page 180.

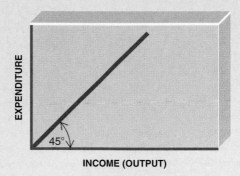

INCOME (OUTPUT)

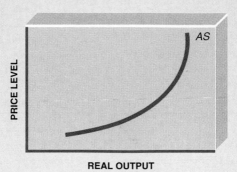

REAL OUTPUT

6. On the accompanying graph, illustrate the desired aggregate expenditures of an economy whose participants have the following spending plans:

$$C = \$10 + 0.8Y \qquad I = \$20 \qquad G = \$30 \qquad X - IM = \$10$$

(a) What is the value of equilibrium output?   _____

(b) How much are consumers saving at equilibrium?   _____

(c) How much nonconsumer spending is being injected?   _____

(d) Assuming that the full-employment level of output is $300, what kind of gap exists and how large is it? Identify the gap on the graph. _____

(e) How much are consumers saving at full employment?   _____

(f) How much (nonconsumer) spending is being injected?   _____

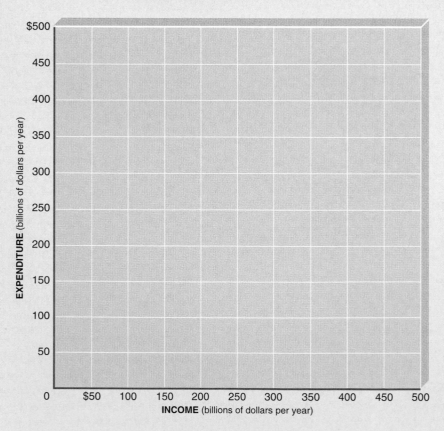

Problems for Chapter 10

1. If the consumption function is $C = \$200 + 0.9Y_D$,
   (a) what does the saving function look like?   _____
   What is the rate of desired saving when disposable income equals
   (b) $500?   _____
   (c) $1000?   _____
   (d) $2000?   _____

2. What is the value of the multiplier when the marginal propensity to consume is
   (a) 0.10   _____
   (b) 0.25   _____

3. Suppose that autonomous investment increases by $100 billion in a closed and private economy
   (no government or foreign trade). Assume further that households have a marginal propensity to
   consume of 90 percent.
   (a) Compute four rounds of multiplier effects:

	Changes in This Cycle's Spending	Cumulative Change in Spending
First cycle	_____	_____
Second cycle	_____	_____
Third cycle	_____	_____
Fourth cycle	_____	_____

   (b) What will be the final cumulative impact on spending?   _____
   (c) Compare your results with those in Table 10.1. With a higher marginal propensity to consume,
       does the cumulative change in expenditure become larger or smaller?   _____

4. Illustrate in the graph the impact of a sudden decline in consumer confidence that reduces autonomous consumption by $50 billion. Assume MPC = 0.8.
   (a) What is the new equilibrium level of real output? (Don't forget the multiplier.)   _____
   (b) How large is the real GDP gap?   _____
   (c) What has happened to average prices?   _____

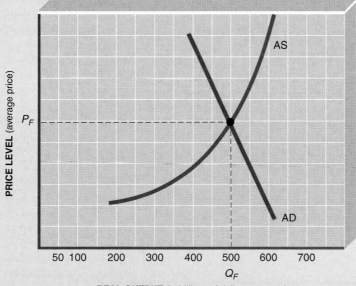

5. The accompanying graph depicts a macro equilibrium. Answer the questions based on the information in the graph.
   (*a*) What is the equilibrium rate of GDP?   _____
   (*b*) If full-employment real GDP is $1200, what problem does this economy have?   _____
   (*c*) How large is the real GDP gap?   _____
   (*d*) If the multiplier were equal to 4, how much additional investment would be needed to increase
        aggregate demand by the amount of the initial GDP gap?   _____
   (*e*) Illustrate the changes in autonomous investment and induced consumption that occur in (*d*).
   (*f*) What happens to prices when aggregate demand increases by the amount of the initial GDP
        gap?   _____
   (*g*) Is full employment restored by the AD shift?   _____

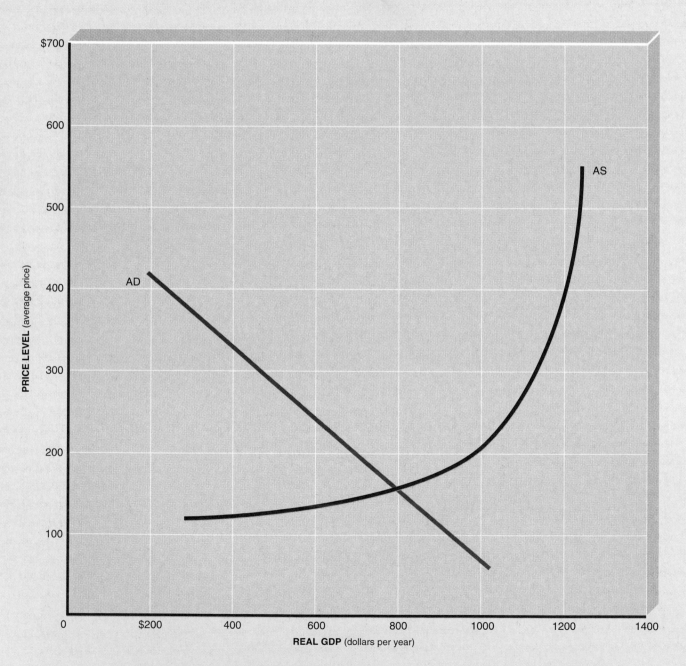

Problems for Chapter 11

1. Suppose the consumption function is

$$C = \$400 \text{ billion} + 0.8Y$$

   and the government wants to stimulate the economy. By how much will aggregate demand at current prices increase with each of the following options?
   (a) A $50 billion increase in government purchases _____
   (b) A $50 billion tax cut _____
   (c) A $50 billion increase in income transfers _____

2. Suppose the government decides to increase taxes by $20 billion in order to increase Social Security benefits by the same amount. How will this combined tax-transfer policy affect aggregate demand at current prices? _____

3. On the accompanying graph, identify and label
   (a) macro equilibrium
   (b) the real GDP gap
   (c) the AD excess or shortfall
   (d) the new equilibrium that would occur with appropriate fiscal policy

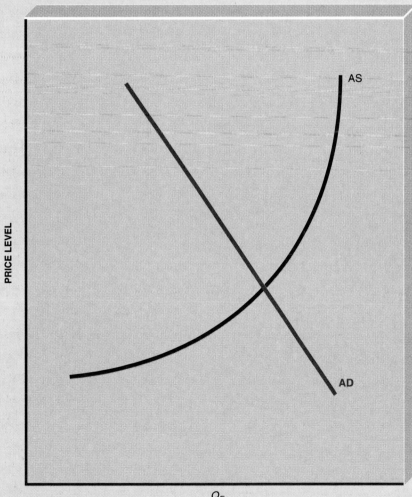

4. By how much would the child tax credit (see NEWS, page 215) alter
   (*a*) initial consumer spending (no multiplier effects)? _____
   (*b*) cumulative consumption (including multiplier effects)? _____
   Assume the MPC equals 0.8.

5. How much of an increase in AD was desired when Japan initiated its fiscal stimulus package?
   (See WORLD VIEW, page 214.) Suppose that half the stimulus package was tax cuts and the rest
   spending increases. Assume MPC = 0.80. _____

6. Use the following data to complete the graph and to answer the following questions:

Price level	10	20	30	40	50	60	70	80	90	100
Real GDP supplied	$500	600	680	750	820	880	910	940	960	970
Real GDP demanded	$960	920	880	840	800	760	720	680	640	600

   (*a*) If full employment occurs at a real output rate of $880, how large is the real GDP gap? _____
   (*b*) How large is the AD shortfall? _____
   (*c*) What will happen to prices if AD increases enough to restore full employment? _____
   (*d*) Assuming MPC = 0.75, how will macro equilibrium change if the government purchases increase by $20? Illustrate your answer on the graph. _____

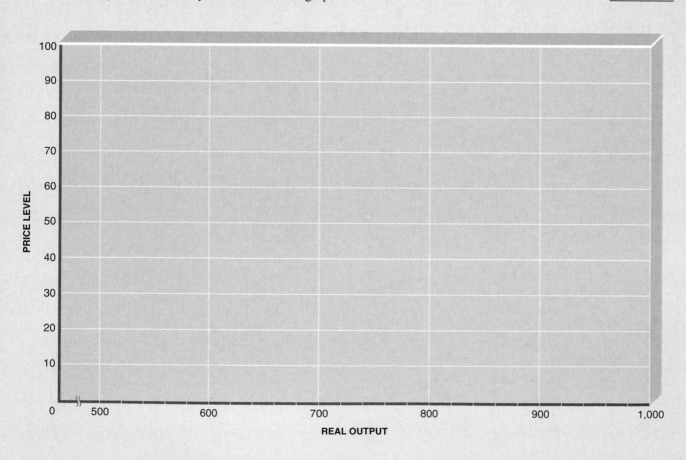

Problems for Chapter 12

Name: _____

1. What would happen to the budget deficit if the
   (a) unemployment rate jumped from 6 percent to 8 percent?   _____
   (b) inflation rate increased by 2 percentage points?   _____
   (See Table 12.2 for clues.)

2. Use Table 12.3 to determine whether and by how much discretionary fiscal policy was stimulative or restrictive in each of the following years:
   (a) 1992–1993   _____
   (b) 1994–1995   _____
   (c) 1996–1997   _____

3. Suppose a government has no debt and a balanced budget. Suddenly it decides to spend $10 billion while raising only $8 billion worth of taxes.
   (a) What will be the government's deficit?   _____
   (b) If the government decides to finance the deficit by issuing bonds, what amount of bonds will it issue?   _____
   (c) At a 10 percent rate of interest, what debt-servicing requirement will the government incur on the newly issued bonds?   _____
   (d) Add the interest payment to the government's $10 billion expenditures for the next year, and assume that taxes remain at $8 billion. In the second year, compute the
      (i) deficit   _____
      (ii) amount of new debt (bonds) issued   _____
      (iii) debt-service requirement.   _____
   (e) Repeat these calculations for the third, fourth, and fifth years, assuming that the government taxes at a rate of $8 billion each year and has noninterest expenditures of $10 billion annually.

	Year 3	Year 4	Year 5
Deficit	_____	_____	_____
New debt	_____	_____	_____
Debt service	_____	_____	_____

   (f) What is the ratio of interest payments, relative to the deficit, with each passing year?   _____

Year 2	Year 3	Year 4	Year 5
_____	_____	_____	_____

   (g) What will happen to the ratio of government debt to government expenditure with each passing year?   _____

4. Use the accompanying graph to illustrate *changes* in the structural and total deficits for the years 1991–1995 (data in Table 12.3). Why do the two measures move in different directions?

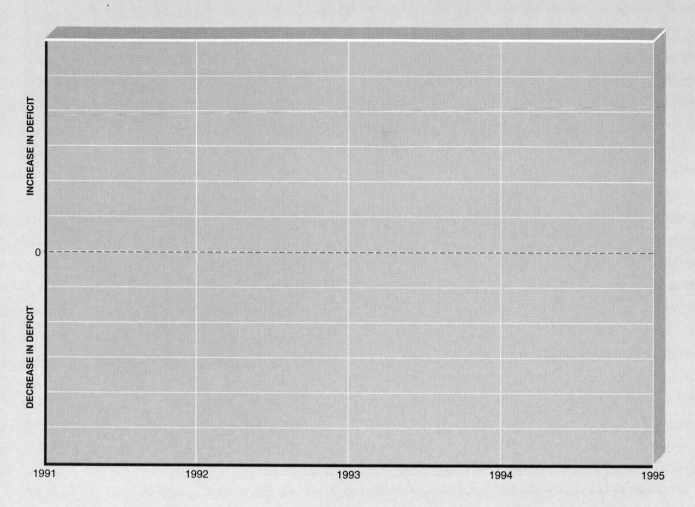

Problems for Chapter 13

1. Suppose a bank's balance sheet looks as follows:

Assets		Liabilities	
Reserves	$500	Deposits	$3,600

and banks are required to hold reserves equal to 10 percent of deposits.
 (a) How much excess reserves does the bank hold?   _____
 (b) How much more can this bank lend?   _____

2. Suppose a bank's balance sheet looks like this:

Assets		Liabilities	
Reserves		Deposits	$500
Excess	$ 60		
Required	$ 40		
Loans	$400		
Total	$500	Total	$500

What is the required reserve ratio?   _____

3. What is the value of the money multiplier when the required reserve ratio is
 (a) 20 percent?   _____
 (b) 4 percent?   _____

4. In December 1994, a man in Ohio decided to deposit all of the 8 *million* pennies he'd been saving for nearly 65 years. (His deposit weighed over 48,000 pounds!) With a reserve requirement of 5 percent, what will be the cumulative change for the banking system in
 (a) transactions deposits?   _____
 (b) total reserves?   _____
 (c) lending capacity?   _____

5. (a) When the reserve requirement changes, which of the following will change for the bank that receives the initial deposit (Bank *A*) (check those items that will change)?

transactions deposits	_____
total reserves	_____
required reserves	_____
excess reserves	_____
lending capacity	_____

 (b) When the reserve requirement changes, which of the following will experience a cumulative change in the total banking system (check all that apply)?

transactions deposits	_____
total reserves	_____
required reserves	_____
excess reserves	_____
lending capacity	_____

6. Suppose that a lottery winner deposits $10 million in cash into her transactions account at the Bank of America (B of A). Assume a reserve requirement of 25 percent and no excess reserves in the banking system prior to this deposit.

   (a) Use step 1 in the T accounts to show how her deposit affects the balance sheet at B of A. _____

   (b) Has the money supply been changed by her deposit? _____

   (c) Use step 2 below to show the changes at B of A after B of A fully uses its new lending capacity. _____

   (d) Has the money supply been changed in step 2? _____

   (e) In step 3 the new borrower(s) writes a check for the amount of the loan. That check is deposited at another bank, and B of A pays the other bank when the check clears. What does the B of A balance sheet look like now? _____

   (f) After the entire banking system uses the lending capacity of the initial ($10 million) deposit, by how much will the following have changed?

   total reserves _____

   total deposits _____

   total loans _____

   cash held by public _____

   the money supply _____

Step 1: Winnings Deposited
Bank of America

Assets (in millions)		Liabilities (in millions)	
Reserves:		Deposits	____
Required	____		
Excess	____		
Subtotal	____		
Loans	____		
Total assets	____	Total liabilities	____

Step 2: Loans Made
Bank of America

Assets (in millions)		Liabilities (in millions)	
Reserves:		Deposits	____
Required	____		
Excess	____		
Subtotal	____		
Loans	____		
Total assets	____	Total liabilities	____

Step 3: Check Clears
Bank of America

Assets (in millions)		Liabilities (in millions)	
Reserves:		Deposits	____
Required	____		
Excess	____		
Subtotal	____		
Loans	____		
Total assets	____	Total liabilities	____

Problems for Chapter 14

Name: _____

1. Assume that the following data describe the condition of the banking system:

   Total reserves: $200 billion
   Transactions deposits: $800 billion
   Cash held by public: $100 billion
   Reserve requirement: 0.20

   (a) How large is the money supply (M1)?   _____
   (b) How large are *required* reserves?   _____
   (c) How large are *excess* reserves?   _____
   (d) By how much could the banks increase their lending activity?   _____

2. In Problem 1, suppose the Fed wanted to stop further lending activity. To do this, what reserve requirement should the Fed impose?   _____

3. What happened to the money multiplier when the Fed changed the reserve requirement in 1992?
   (See NEWS, page 276.)

   _____

4. Assume the banking system contains

   Total reserves: $60 billion
   Transactions deposits: $600 billion
   Cash held by public: $100 billion
   Reserve requirement: 0.10

   (a) Are the banks fully utilizing their lending capacity?   _____
   (b) What would happen to the money supply *initially* if the public deposited another $50 billion
       of cash in transactions accounts?   _____
   (c) What would the lending capacity of the banking system be after such a portfolio switch?   _____
   (d) How large would the money supply be if the banks fully utilized their lending capacity?   _____
   (e) What three steps could the Fed take to offset that potential growth in M1? _____
                                                                              _____
                                                                              _____

5. Assume that a $1000 bond issued in 1999 pays $100 in interest each year. What is the current
   yield on the bond if it can be purchased for

   (a) $1200?   _____
   (b) $1000?   _____
   (c) $800?   _____
   (d) $600?   _____

6. Suppose a banking system with the following balance sheet has no excess reserves. Assume that banks will make loans in the full amount of any excess reserves that they acquire and will immediately be able to eliminate loans from their portfolio to cover inadequate reserves.

Assets (in billions)		Liabilities (in billions)	
Total reserves	$ 30	Transactions accounts	$300
Securities	90		
Loans	180		
Total	$300	Total	$300

(a) What is the reserve requirement?

(b) Suppose the reserve requirement is changed to 5 percent. Reconstruct the balance sheet of the total banking system after all banks have fully utilized their lending capacity.

Assets (in billions)		Liabilities (in billions)	
Total reserves	_____	Transactions accounts	_____
Securities	_____		
Loans	_____		
Total	_____	Total	_____

(c) By how much has the money supply changed as a result of the lower reserve requirement (step b)?

(d) Suppose the Fed now buys $10 billion of securities directly from the banks. What will the banks' books look like after this purchase?

Assets (in billions)		Liabilities (in billions)	
Total reserves	_____	Transactions accounts	_____
Securities	_____		
Loans	_____		
Total	_____	Total	_____

(e) How much excess reserves do the banks have now?

(f) By how much can the money supply now increase?

Problems for Chapter 15

Name: _____

1. Suppose homeowners owe $800 billion in mortgage loans.
   (a) If the mortgage interest rate is 9 percent, approximately how much are homeowners paying in annual mortgage interest? _____
   (b) If the interest rate drops to 8 percent, by how much will annual interest payments drop? _____
   (c) What are homeowners likely to do with their interest rate "savings"? _____

2. Suppose that an economy is characterized by
   $M = \$4000$ billion
   $V = 2$
   $P = 100$
   (a) What is the real value of output (Q)? _____

   Now assume that the Fed increases the money supply by 10 percent and velocity remains unchanged.
   (b) If the price level remains constant, what will happen to real output? _____
   (c) If, instead, real output is fixed at the natural level of unemployment, what will happen when M increases? _____
   (d) By how much would V have to fall to offset the increase in M? _____

3. If the nominal rate of interest is 8 percent and the real rate of interest is 3 percent, what rate of inflation is anticipated? _____

4. Suppose the Fed decided to purchase $10 billion worth of government securities in the open market. What impact would this action have on the economy? Specifically, answer the following questions using graphs where appropriate.
   (a) How will M1 be affected initially? _____
   (b) How will the banking system's lending capacity be affected if the reserve requirement is 25 percent? _____
   (c) How will banks induce investors to utilize this expanded lending capacity? _____
   (d) How will aggregate demand be affected if investors borrow and spend all the newly available credit? _____
   (e) Under what circumstances would the Fed be pursuing such an open market policy? _____
   (f) How could those same objectives be achieved through changes in the discount rate or reserve requirement?

   _____
   _____

5. How much fiscal restraint would have been equivalent to the 1995 monetary restraint that increased short-term interest rates from 3 percent to 6 percent. (*Hint:* Consult Greenspan's rule of thumb.) _____

6. The following data describe market conditions:

Money supply (in billions)	$100	$200	$300	$400	$500	$600	$700
Interest rate	8.0	7.5	7.0	6.5	6.0	5.5	5.5
Rate of investment (in billions)	$12	$12	$15	$16	$16.5	$16.5	$16.5

    (*a*) At what rate of interest does the liquidity trap emerge?   _____

    (*b*) At what rate of interest does investment demand become totally inelastic?   _____

7. Use the accompanying graphs to show what happens in the economy when *M* increases from $300 billion to $400 billion.

    (*a*) By how much does *PQ* change if *V* is constant?   _____

    (*b*) If aggregate supply were fixed (vertical) at the initial output level, what would happen to the price level?   _____

    (*c*) What is the value of *V*?   _____

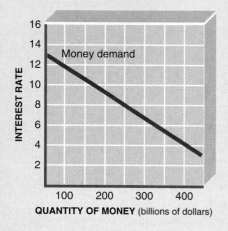

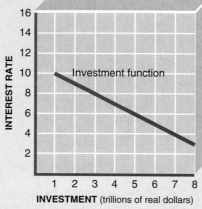

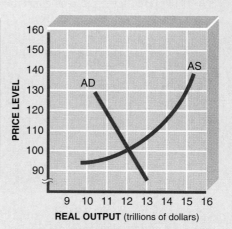

Problems for Chapter 16

1. The Economy Tomorrow section provides estimates of time spent in traffic delays. If the average worker produces $15 of output per hour, what is the opportunity cost of
   (*a*) current traffic delays? $_____
   (*b*) estimated delays in 10 years? $_____

2. Suppose taxpayers are required to pay a base tax of $50 plus 30 percent on any income over $100, as in the initial tax system *B* in Table 16.1. Suppose further that the taxing authority wishes to raise by $20 the taxes of people with incomes of $200.
   (*a*) If marginal tax rates are to remain unchanged, what will the new base tax have to be? $_____
   (*b*) If the base tax of $50 is to remain unchanged, what will the marginal tax rate have to be?   _____%

3. Suppose households supply 230 million hours of labor per year and have a tax elasticity of supply of 0.20. If the tax rate is increased by 10 percent, by how many hours will the supply of labor decline?   _____

4. According to Figure 16.5, what inflation rate would occur if the unemployment rate fell to 4 percent, with
   (*a*) PC_1?   _____
   (*b*) PC_2?   _____

5. On the following graph, plot the unemployment and inflation rates for the years 1989–1995. Is there any evidence of a Phillips curve trade-off?   _____

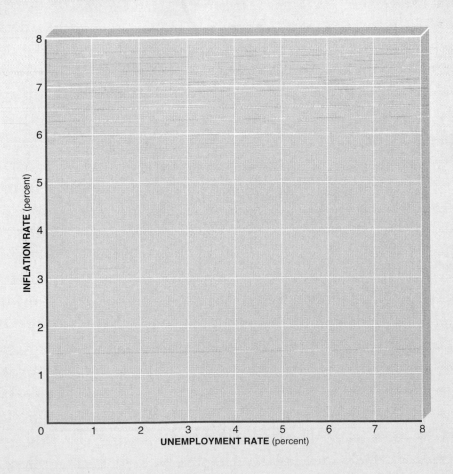

6. Suppose an economy is characterized by the AS/AD curves in the accompanying graph. A decision is then made to increase infrastructure spending by $20 billion a year.
   (a) Illustrate the impact of the increased spending on aggregate demand on the graph (ignore multiplier effects).
   (b) If AS is unaffected, what is the new equlibrium rate of outout?
   (c) What is the new equilibrium price level?
   (d) Now assume that the infrastructure investments increase aggregate supply by $30 billion a year (from the initial equilibrium). Illustrate this effect on the graph.
   (e) After all demand and supply adjustments occur, what is the final equilibrium
      (i) rate of output?
      (ii) price level?

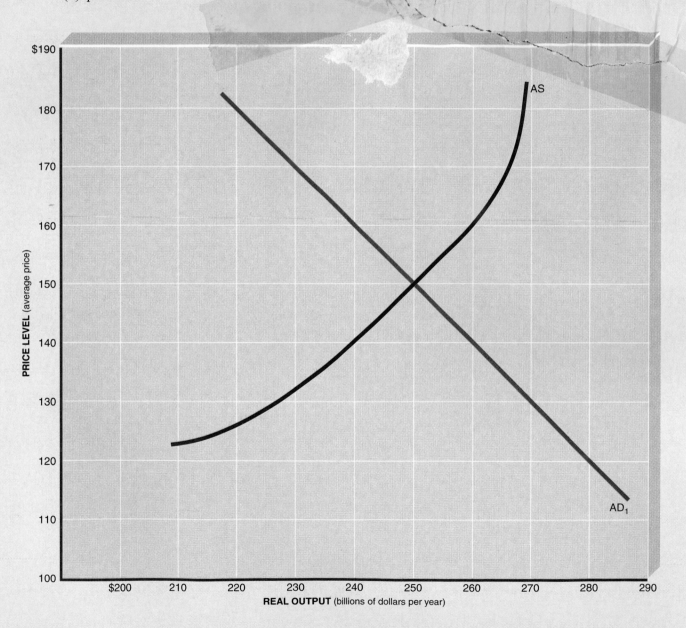

Problems for Chapter 17

Name: _____

1. If real GDP is growing at 3 percent a year, how long will it take for
   (a) real GDP to double?   _____
   (b) real GDP per capita to double if the population is increasing each year by
       (i) 0 percent?   _____
       (ii) 1 percent?   _____
       (iii) 2 percent?   _____

2. Suppose that every additional 5 percentage points in the investment rate ($I \div GDP$) boost economic growth by 1 percentage point. Assume also that all investment must be financed with consumer saving. The economy is now assumed to be fully employed at

GDP:	$6 trillion
Consumption:	5 trillion
Saving:	1 trillion
Investment:	1 trillion

   If the goal is to raise the growth rate by 1 percent,
   (a) by how much must investment increase?   _____
   (b) by how much must consumption decline for this to occur?   _____

3. Suppose that the labor force expands by 1 percent each year solely as a result of immigration. How will average GDP per worker be affected in 10 years if immigrants are always
   (a) half as productive as native-born workers?   _____
   (b) as productive as native-born workers?   _____
   (c) twice as productive as native-born workers?   _____

4. If the labor force increases by 1 percent each year and productivity increases by 2 percent, how fast will output grow?   _____

5. According to the WORLD VIEW on page 341, by how much did GDP increase in the 1980s (the entire decade, not the annual average) in
   (a) Korea?   _____
   (b) the United States?   _____
   (c) Ethiopia?   _____

6. On the accompanying graph, illustrate the investment rate for each year and plot the annual growth
   rate of GDP. Then answer the following questions.

   (a) What was the range for the annual investment rate?   highest _____

                                                                                         lowest _____

   (b) What was the range of annual growth rates?   highest _____

                                                                                         lowest _____

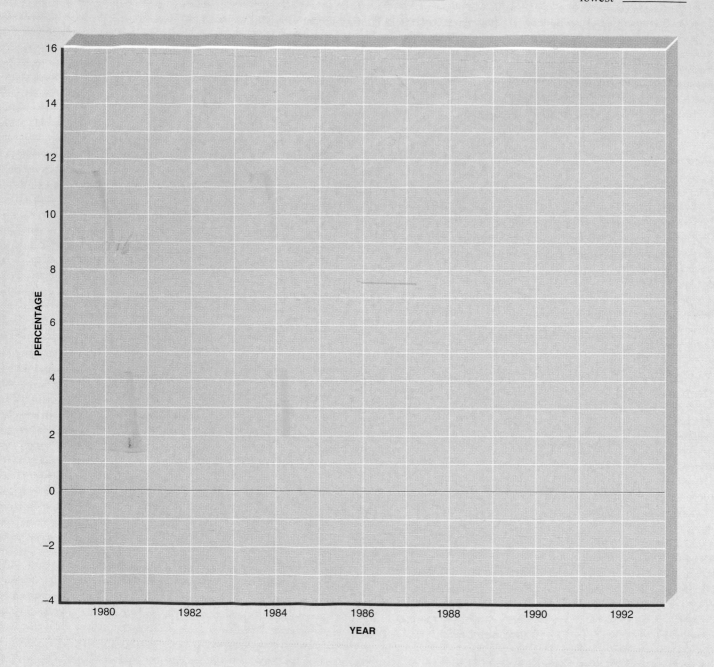

1. Using the data from the inside front cover and the first page of this book, compute the
   (*a*) import/GDP ratio in 1998.   _____
   (*b*) export/GDP ratio in 1998.   _____

2. (*a*) If the marginal propensity to save in a closed (no-trade) economy is 0.05, what is the value of
       the multiplier?   _____
   (*b*) If this same economy opens up to trade and exhibits a marginal propensity to import of 0.10,
       what does the value of the multiplier become?   _____

3. Suppose that the expenditure patterns of a country are as follows:

$$C = \$60 \text{ million per year} + 0.8Y$$

$$I = \$100 \text{ billion per year}$$

$$G = 0 \text{ (no taxes either)}$$

$$\text{Exports} = \text{imports} = \$10 \text{ billion per year}$$

   (*a*) What is the value of equilibrium GDP?   _____
   (*b*) As a result of higher oil prices, this country must now spend an additional $10 billion per year
       on imported oil. Assuming that prices of other goods do not change, what impact will the
       higher oil prices have on equilibrium GDP? _____

4. Recompute the answer to Problem 3 by assuming that the marginal propensity to import equals 0.1
   (and thus that the MPC for domestic goods is 0.7). _____

5. Using the data from the inside front cover and the first page of this text, compute the 1990–1998
   percentage growth for
   (*a*) consumption.   _____
   (*b*) investment.   _____
   (*c*) government spending.   _____
   (*d*) exports.   _____
   What was the fastest-growing component of aggregate demand? _____
   How did this component affect U.S. job growth? _____

6. (*a*) Using the data from the inside front cover of this book, plot on the graph below the annual percentage change in
  (*i*) nominal GDP
  (*ii*) nominal imports
 (*b*) Is faster import growth associated with faster or slower GDP growth? _____
  Why? _____

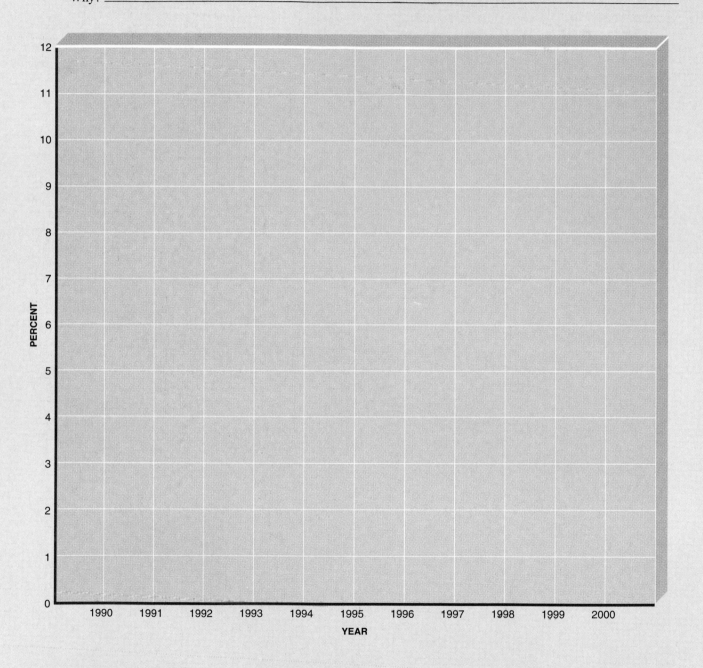

Problems for Chapter 19

Name: _____

1. If the Congressional Budget Office makes its average error this year, by how much will it underestimate next year's budget deficit? (See NEWS, page 383.) _____

2. If the unemployment rate stays 2 percentage points above full employment for an entire year,
   (a) how many jobs will be lost? _____
   (b) If the average worker produces $40,000 of output, how much output will be lost? _____

3. According to the WORLD VIEW on page 378,
   (a) which country had the greatest macro misery in the 1990s? (Compute the "misery in the index" from Chapter 16.) _____
   (b) who had the fastest growth? _____

4. Complete the following chart by summarizing the policy prescriptions of various economic theories:

Policy Approach	Policy Prescription for	
	Recession	Inflation
Fiscal	_____	_____
Classical	_____	_____
Keynesian	_____	_____
Monetarist	_____	_____
Monetary	_____	_____
Keynesian	_____	_____
Monetarist	_____	_____
Supply-Side	_____	_____

5. The following table displays Congressional Budget Office forecasts of federal budget deficits for the following year. Graph these forecasts on the graph below, along with *actual* deficits for those same years (see Table 12.3 for data).

Year:	1988	1989	1990	1991	1992	1993	1994	1995	1996
Deficit forecast (in billions of dollars)	109	135	102	254	279	327	253	162	189

(*a*) In how many years did CBO underestimate the deficit? _____

(*b*) Why was the forecast so wrong in 1990?

_____

_____

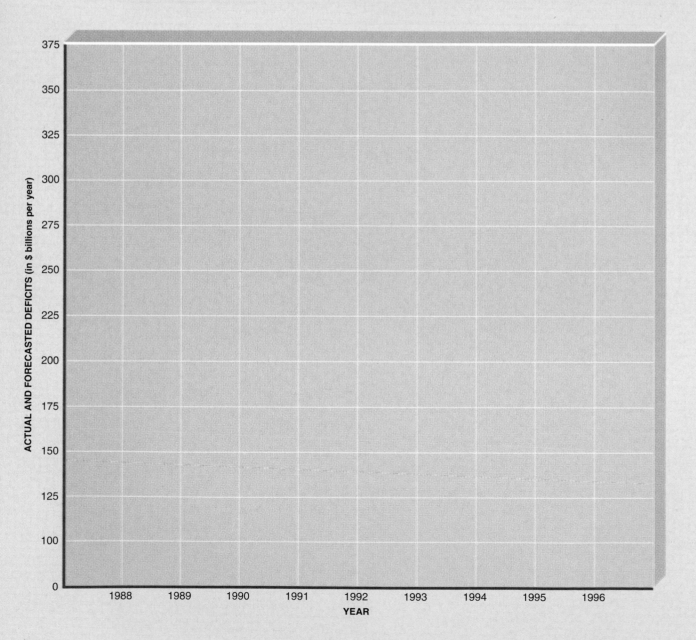

Problems for Chapter 20

Name: _____

1. Suppose the following table reflects the domestic supply and demand for compact disks (CDs):

Price ($)	16	14	12	10	8	6	4	2
Quantity supplied	8	7	6	5	4	3	2	1
Quantity demanded	2	4	6	8	10	12	14	16

(a) Graph these market conditions and identify the equilibrium price and sales.   price/sales   _____

(b) Now suppose that foreigners enter the market, offering to sell an unlimited supply of CDs for $6 apiece. Illustrate and identify

   (i) the market price.   _____

   (ii) domestic consumption.   _____

   (iii) domestic production.   _____

(c) If a tariff of $2 per CD is imposed, what will happen to

   (i) the market price?   _____

   (ii) domestic consumption?   _____

   (iii) domestic production?   _____

2. Alpha and Beta, two tiny islands off the east coast of Tricoli, produce pearls and pineapples. The following production possibilities schedules describe their potential output in tons per year:

Alpha		Beta	
Pearls	Pineapples	Pearls	Pineapples
0	30	0	20
2	25	10	16
4	20	20	12
6	15	30	8
8	10	40	4
10	5	45	2
12	0	50	0

(a) Graph the production possibilities confronting each island.

(b) What is the opportunity cost of pineapples on each island (before trade)?   _____

(c) Which island has a comparative advantage in pearl production?   _____

(d) Graph the consumption possibilities of each island with free trade.

3. Suppose the two islands in Problem 2 agree that the terms of trade will be 1 for 1 and exchange 10 pearls for 10 pineapples.

(a) If Alpha produced 6 pearls and 15 pineapples while Beta produced 30 pearls and 8 pineapples before they decided to trade, how much would each be producing after trade? Assume that the two countries specialize just enough to maintain their consumption of the item they export, and make sure each island follows its comparative advantage.

(b) How much would each island be consuming after specializing and trading?   _____

(c) How much would the combined production of pineapples increase for the two islands due to trade? How much would the combined production of pearls increase? _____

(d) How could both countries produce and consume even more?

_____

(e) Assume the two islands are able to trade as much as they want with the rest of the world, with the terms of trade at 1 pineapple for 1 pearl. Draw the ultimate consumption possibilities curve for each island.

Problems for Chapter 21

Name: _____

1. If a euro is worth $1.25, what is the euro price of a dollar? _____

2. If a pound of U.S. pork cost 40 rupiah in Indonesia before the Asian crisis, how much did it cost during the crisis? _____

3. The following schedules summarize the supply and demand for trifflings, the national currency of Tricoli:

Triffling price (U.S. dollars per triffling)	0	$4	$8	$12	$16	$20	$24
Quantity demanded (per year)	40	38	36	34	32	30	28
Quantity supplied (per year)	1	11	21	31	41	51	61

Use the above schedules for the following.
(a) Graph the supply and demand curves.
(b) Determine the equilibrium exchange rate. _____
(c) Determine the size of the excess supply or excess demand that would exist if the Tricolian government fixed the exchange rate $22 = 1 triffling. _____
(d) How might this imbalance be remedied?

_____

4. For each of the following possible events, indicate whether the demand or supply curve for dollars would shift, the direction of the shift, the determinant of the change, the inflow or outflow effect on the balance of payments (and the specific account that would be affected), and the resulting movement of the equilibrium exchange rate for the value of the dollar.

(a) American cars become suddenly more popular abroad. _____

(b) Inflation rates in the United States accelerate. _____

(c) The United States falls into a depression. _____

(d) Interest rates in the United States drop. _____

(e) The United States suddenly experiences rapid increases in productivity. _____

(f) Anticipating a return to the gold standard, Americans suddenly rush to buy gold from the two

big producers, South Africa and the Soviet Union. _____

(g) War is declared in the Middle East. _____

(h) The stock markets in the United States suddenly collapse. _____

Problems for Chapter 22

Name: _____

The following schedule depicts the daily supply of and demand for TV sets on a small island:

Price	$200	$150	$100	$50
Quantity demanded	0	5	10	15
Quantity supplied	20	15	10	5

Graph the supply and demand curves.

(a) If the government sets the price of TV sets at $50, how will the quantity demanded compare to the quantity supplied? What kind of behavior would you expect from the buyers? From the suppliers?

_____

(b) How might the government intervene with taxes or subsidies to eliminate such behavior?

_____

(c) If the government requires the suppliers to provide 20 TV sets per day, and the suppliers comply, what will be the market price of a set?

_____

(d) If the government requires everyone who receives a set to pay no less than $150 for it, will there be a surplus or a shortage of sets, and how much will quantity demanded differ from the 20 sets being provided by the suppliers? What will happen to inventories of TV sets?

_____

(e) Because of inventory problems, the government drops its minimum price of $150 and decides to institute the full tax or sudsidy necessary to provide 20 TV sets per day. Would the government have to subsidize or tax? How much would the tax or subsidy be, per set?

_____

(f) Because of all the problems surrounding TV sets, a new government is elected, and it decides to let the market make all the decisions about TV sets. How many sets will be sold each day, and at what price will they be sold?

_____